BRISTOL

A WORSHIPFUL TOWN AND FAMOUS CITY

BRISTOL

A Worshipful Town and Famous City

AN ARCHAEOLOGICAL ASSESSMENT

Nigel Baker, Jonathan Brett and Robert Jones

OXBOW | books
Oxford & Philadelphia

Published in the United Kingdom in 2018 by
OXBOW BOOKS
The Old Music Hall, 106–108 Cowley Road, Oxford, OX4 1JE

and in the United States by
OXBOW BOOKS
1950 Lawrence Road, Havertown, PA 19083

© Historic England. Historic England thanks Oxbow Books for publishing this volume on their behalf.

Hardback Edition: ISBN 978-1-78570-877-0
Digital Edition: ISBN 978-1-78570-878-7 (epub)

A CIP record for this book is available from the British Library

Library of Congress Control Number: 2017962133

Typeset in India by Lapiz Digital Services, Chennai

For a complete list of Oxbow titles, please contact:

UNITED KINGDOM
Oxbow Books
Telephone (01865) 241249, Fax (01865) 794449
Email: oxbow@oxbowbooks.com
www.oxbowbooks.com

UNITED STATES OF AMERICA
Oxbow Books
Telephone (800) 791-9354, Fax (610) 853-9146
Email: queries@casemateacademic.com
www.casemateacademic.com/oxbow

Oxbow Books is part of the Casemate Group

This volume has been funded by Historic England (formerly English Heritage)

Historic England

Front cover: Broad Quay c 1785 (BRSMG K514; see also fig 3.6)
Back cover: 14th century face spouted 'puzzle' jug of green-glazed Redcliffe ware, found in Redcliff Street in 1982 (BRSMG Q3052)

Contents

Foreword

'For asmoche as it is righte convenient and according to euery Bourgeis of the Towne of Bristowe, ... for to know and vnderstande the begynnyng and first foundacion of the saide worshipfull Toune.'

Robert Ricart (1479), *The Maire of Bristowe is Kalendar* [The Mayor of Bristol's Calendar]

The words 'English historic city' conjure up images of places like Canterbury, York or Winchester – settlements established in the Roman period (or even before) which later became major cathedral cities, and are now important tourist destinations. Bristol is a historic city in a very different mould. It was not founded until the Late Saxon period. Its prosperity rested primarily on maritime trade rather than on any role as a centre of royal or religious power, and its present-day cathedral was actually a monastic church until after the Reformation. It is a culturally vibrant city today, but it is not perceived as a major focus of heritage tourism (contrasting in this, as in much else, with Bath, only 15 miles or so away).

A combination of rebuilding in the 19th century, destructive bombing in the Second World War and the impact of post-war reconstruction and town planning mean that Bristol's archaeological and architectural heritage is perhaps less well-recognised than that of many other historic towns and cities in England. The lack of substantial Roman archaeological remains – the mosaics, monumental masonry structures and abundant artefacts which so attracted the attention of early antiquarians in other places – may also have resulted in archaeology impinging less on the civic consciousness of Bristol than it has done elsewhere.

Any such lack of recognition belies the extent, interest and value of the city's archaeology. From its origins some time before the 11th century, Bristol became the second or third largest city in England by the 14th century, ranking only below London and, sometimes, York. From the late 15th century onwards, it was a starting point for explorations of the 'New World'. The city became heavily involved in the transatlantic trade in sugar and slaves. Manufacture of brassware and glass for export, as part of the 'triangular trade' between Britain, Africa and the Americas, also became important.

This rich history has left an equally rich archaeological heritage, which has been the object of investigation and recording as far back as the work of William Worcestre in the 15th century. In the 18th century, there was a significant amount of antiquarian observation and historical research here. The 19th century was a time of much demolition and new construction in Bristol, which stimulated both detailed recording of historic buildings and archaeological observation. This work continued into the early 20th century. Large-scale reconstruction after the Second World War prompted renewed efforts to record Bristol's endangered archaeological heritage. Initially, work was ad hoc and on a small scale, but in the 1950s and 1960s a range of excavations were carried out, some funded by the Ministry of Works. In 1968, the City Council's first archaeological officer, Mike Ponsford, was appointed, leading to a campaign of 'rescue' excavations in the city centre. The 1970s and 1980s saw large excavations carried out on deep and well-preserved waterfront sites, with important results. The publication of Planning Policy Guidance Note 16 (PPG 16) on Archaeology and Planning in 1990 resulted in further increases in development-led archaeological work, with a wider geographical spread and some very major excavations undertaken, such as those at Broadmead between 2005 and 2008. Paralleling this has been a renewed expansion of 'buildings archaeology', with even quite modern structures being recorded if they are of interest. Alongside large-scale investigations required as part of the planning process, there has also been a solid and continuing tradition of voluntary archaeological work in Bristol. This has made important contributions on particular topics, such as industrial archaeology.

In summary, Bristol has the benefit of over two centuries of quite intensive archaeological study. This work has not, though, had as great an impact, especially beyond the city, as it might have done or should have done. The city centre is topographically complex, and – as mentioned above – Bristol is not always thought of as a 'historic city' in the way that some other places in England are. A number of excavations, including very important ones on the waterfront in the 1970s and 1980s, have never been fully published. When reports have been published, they may be in local periodicals with sometimes limited circulations. Much information resides in archaeological 'grey literature', the problems of access to which are well-known (although in Bristol these have been ameliorated to some extent by the City Council's innovative 'Know Your Place' website: https://maps.bristol.gov.uk/knowyourplace/).

For a variety of reasons, then, the high importance, value and interest of Bristol's archaeological heritage is less well-known nationally and internationally than that of many other English medieval cities of comparable rank. This is notwithstanding the prompt publication, to a high standard, of a number of important recent excavations.

A significant contributory factor to this under-recognition has been lack, until now, of any single publication which provides a synthesis and overview of the archaeology of Bristol: something which makes the wealth of evidence and interpretation readily accessible, whether to the professional archaeologist working in the city, to the interested local resident or to the wider scholarly community.

This, in essence, is the gap which the present volume seeks to fill. The work has its origins in the 'urban archaeological strategies' programme which was launched by English Heritage (now Historic England) in 1992. Between 1995 and 1997, English Heritage funded the creation of an Urban Archaeological Database (UAD) for Bristol – a detailed and comprehensive database and mapping of past archaeological investigations, and of the monuments, deposits and structures recorded in them, in historic central Bristol. This is now maintained by the City Council as part of the Bristol Historic Environment Record.

The UAD provided the basis for the account of Bristol's archaeology which is presented here. The volume has had a lengthy gestation. A first draft was completed in 2002. A second draft, completed in 2005, was being revised when progress was, most sadly, overtaken by the unexpected and untimely death of Jon Brett, the principal author. Work resumed in 2010, when Dr Nigel Baker was engaged by Bristol City Council to revise and update the earlier draft. Dr Baker and Bob Jones, who served as Bristol City Archaeologist from 1992 to 2016, between them brought the work to completion.

This volume speaks for itself, and does not need to be summarised here. Its importance lies in the fact that, for the first time, there is a single, detailed and comprehensive account of the archaeology of historic Bristol as whole. The archaeology of the city is described, assessed and set in its wider geographical and historical context. A wide range of maps, plans, photographs and illustrations accompanies the text, helping to make the development of the city's topography and architecture clear. A full and detailed bibliography enables the reader to follow up the detail of the evidence and how it has been interpreted.

Bristol today is a thriving modern city. It is proud of its past, but certainly not stifled by it. Indeed, an understanding of the historical evolution and topography of Bristol has been drawn on in a new division of the city centre into distinct quarters, reflected in street signage and maps and aimed at making the centre more 'legible' to residents and visitors alike. This is just one of many ways in which archaeology can be used to help shape the identity and character of today's places; it has been done to very good effect in Bristol.

Writing in his *Kalendar* in 1479, Robert Ricart, who was town clerk of Bristol, stressed how important it was that Bristolians should know about the origins and history of their city (Toulmin-Smith 1872, 8). That remains as true today as it was in Ricart's time, and this volume will stand as a very significant contribution to that aim. Of course, it is by no means the end of the story. Development is proceeding apace in Bristol, presenting new challenges for the archaeological heritage, but also offering new opportunities to learn more about the city's past. The volume serves both to highlight what has been learned from previous archaeological endeavour, and to underscore the importance of continuing this work in the future. Most importantly, this publication will also undoubtedly put Bristol far more firmly on the national (and international) archaeological map than it has been hitherto.

The archaeology of Bristol is extremely rich and diverse. This volume does ample justice to it, and it will undoubtedly raise awareness and appreciation of Bristol's heritage very greatly, both locally and further afield. It is an achievement of which the city can be justifiably very proud.

Roger M Thomas
Historic England
June 2017

List of contributors

Nigel Baker is a freelance archaeologist specialising in historic towns, and has previously published books on Worcester and Gloucester, and Shrewsbury. He worked for Herefordshire Council for eight years and is an Honorary Research Fellow of the School of Geography and Earth Sciences, University of Birmingham.

Jonathan Brett was the Historic Environment Record Officer for Bristol City Council until his untimely death in 2007. He was the principal author of the first two drafts of this volume. He had a first degree in History from the University of Warwick and a Masters degree in Geographical Information Systems and Environment at Manchester Metropolitan University.

Robert Jones was the City Archaeologist for Bristol City Council from 1992 until his retirement in 2016. Prior to this he was a Senior Field Officer with Bristol Museum Field Archaeology Unit. He is a Fellow of the Society of Antiquaries and member of the Chartered Institute for Archaeologists.

Andrew Farrant, Geologist and Karst Geomorphologist, British Geological Survey

Francis Greenacre, former curator of Fine Art, Bristol City Museum

Allan Insole, former Assistant Curator of Geology, Bristol City Museum; former Museums Officer, Isle of Wight County Council; Visiting Lecturer, Dept of Earth Sciences, University of Bristol

Professor Roger Leech, Visiting Professor in Archaeology, University of Southampton

James Rackham, Honorary Research Fellow, Department of Archaeology, University of Nottingham

Vanessa Straker, former Historic England Regional Science Advisor for the South West

Roger M Thomas, formerly Head of Urban Archaeology, Historic England

List of illustrations

List of tables

Jon Brett (photograph R Philpott, National Museums Liverpool)

Acknowledgements

This volume is the culmination of a long process, and many people and organisations have contributed to it. The starting point was the Bristol Urban Archaeological Database (UAD), created by John Bryant and Jonathan (Jon) Brett, formerly of Bristol and Region Archaeological Services (BaRAS).

Jon later became Bristol City Council's Historic Environment Record (HER) Officer. In that role, he was the principal author of the early drafts of this volume, until his work was so sadly cut short by his untimely death in 2007. Jon had a formidable intellect, and this volume owes much to his seemingly limitless knowledge of the history and archaeology of his adopted city. He was a kind and gentle man, an entertaining companion, who is much missed by friends and colleagues.

The project to produce this volume, and the UAD before it, were funded by Historic England (formerly English Heritage). Bristol City Council is extremely grateful for this support, without which the work would not have happened. A considerable debt of gratitude is also owed to Roger M Thomas of Historic England, who oversaw the project throughout its long life. His wise guidance, and his patience in the face of innumerable delays, have been greatly appreciated. Others at Historic England have also played major roles. Vanessa Straker, formerly Regional Science Adviser for the South-West, contributed substantially to the text dealing with the early environment of the city, provided an important overview of some of the excavated environmental evidence, and advised on the palaeo-environmental content of the volume generally. Robin Taylor and then Sarah Enticknap of Historic England's Publishing team provided valuable assistance over publication requirements, especially in relation to mapping and images. On the administrative side, Kath Buxton and Tim Cromack have been especially important in ensuring the smooth running of the financial arrangements, and in providing continuity throughout the long life of the project. Liz Nichols copy-edited the text for Historic England, and it is greatly improved as a result.

Nigel Baker was originally contracted to work on the volume while employed by Herefordshire Archaeology and would particularly like to thank Keith Ray and latterly Tim Hoverd of Herefordshire Council for administering this arrangement.

Many colleagues within Bristol City Council have also given invaluable assistance. Pete Insole, now Principal Historic Environment Officer, drafted many of the maps with great skill and care, despite an already heavy workload. He also gave much useful advice on detailed matters of content and interpretation, and (from 2016 onwards) managed the project for the Council. David Martyn, Senior Conservation Officer, engaged in especially informative discussions on Bristol Castle, and also took many of the photographs reproduced in the volume. John Bryant, formerly of BaRAS, gave freely of his time and extensive knowledge of the city, while Ann Linge, also formerly of BaRAS, was of major assistance in locating images in the BaRAS archive.

Much help was given by staff at Bristol City Museum and Art Gallery, especially Gail Boyle and Kate Iles who facilitated use of the Braikenridge images and advised the authors throughout the project. Kate Iles also freely gave her valuable time in locating and making available excavation images from the museum's archives. Jack Fuller, a volunteer with the museum, found and scanned many archive images with much skill.

Francis Greenacre, formerly curator of Fine Art at the Museum and Art Gallery, contributed significantly on the paintings, drawings and prints, some of which are reproduced in this volume. He also co-wrote the piece on Bristol's important photographic collections.

At Bristol Archives Julian Warren generously shared his extensive knowledge with us, while David Emeney spent many hours finding and copying images from the Record Office and Library collections. David also, with Trevor Coombs of Bristol City Museum and Art Gallery, sourced and delivered the high-quality images of the Braikenridge Collection. The hugely important collections of the city's Central Reference Library have been a major resource for this book, and Dawn Dyer and Jane Bradley of the Library generously shared their considerable knowledge of them.

Mette Bundgaard, Clare Litt, Julie Gardiner, Isobel Nettleton and Katie Allen of Oxbow Books have given much advice throughout the production of the book and many thanks are due to them.

Many other individuals and organisations have given great assistance with successive drafts of the volume.

Professor Derek Keene (University of London) made detailed comments on an early draft, drawing on his great expertise in the development of European medieval towns. The present structure of the work owes a great deal to his wise advice. Brian Ayers (University of East Anglia) refereed the final draft. His expertise in urban archaeology was invaluable for identifying alternative solutions to some complex issues of interpretation, especially of the early medieval town.

Andrew Farrant (British Geological Survey), kindly contributed a commentary on Bristol's complex geology at an early stage. Allan Insole (Department of Earth Sciences, University of Bristol), did extensive further work on this topic and kindly agreed to revise the earlier draft.

Professor Roger Leech (University of Southampton) provided text on houses and households at an early stage, prefiguring his volume on *The Town House in Medieval and Early Modern Bristol* (Leech 2014). We are also extremely grateful to him for allowing us to see his book ahead of publication, and for many discussions on the development of the town house; the results of many of these appear in this volume. James Rackham (currently Honorary Research Fellow at the University of Nottingham) contributed a section on urban diet at an early stage. We are grateful for the valuable contribution that he made based on the evidence available at that time, which is now much augmented by later (post-2005) results.

Neil Holbrook (Cotswold Archaeology) kindly commented on an early draft of Chapter 4 and suggested several improvements and new lines of enquiry in the section dealing with the Roman period. Simon Cox, also of Cotswold Archaeology, gave much useful advice, based on his long involvement with the city's archaeology.

Many organisations and individuals have generously given their permission to reproduce images, and supplied copies of them. We are most grateful to the following:

Martin Watts (Cotswold Archaeology) for several images from Cotswold Archaeology publications; Gary Brown (Pre-Construct Archaeology), for images from the Cabot Circus excavations; Vicki Ridgeway and Cate Davies arranged the collation and sending of these; Keith Wilkinson (ARCA, University of Winchester), for images from his report *Distribution and Significance of Urban Waterlogged Deposits in Bristol*, (Wilkinson *et al* 2013); Ben Ford and Charles Rousseau (Oxford Archaeology), for images from the Finzels Reach excavation, and also for allowing us to see the report ahead of publication; Richard Gregory (Oxford Archaeology North) for use of a photograph of the Powell & Ricketts glassworks excavation of 2007;

Matt Leivers (Wessex Archaeology) for an image from the 2007 excavation of the Great Western Steamship Company's engine works; Andy King (Wessex Archaeology) and Dr Alasdair Brooks (editor of *Post-Medieval Archaeology*) for permission to reproduce the plan of the excavation of the Royal Fort, originally published in *Post-Medieval Archaeology*, vol 48.

Bruce Williams, formerly manager of BaRAS, for use of the reconstruction of Spicer's Almshouse, taken from the report on his 1975 excavations at 94–102 Temple Street. He also, as editor of *Bristol and Avon Archaeology*, gave consent for the reproduction of images from that publication; Jan Broadway, David Smith and William Evans of the Bristol and Gloucestershire Archaeological Society for the use of images from the society's *Transactions* and generally for their support and encouragement throughout; Reg Jackson and Eric Boore, formerly archaeologists with BaRAS, for images from their publications; Mike Ponsford, formerly Curator of Field Archaeology for the City Museum for material from his unpublished MLitt thesis on Bristol Castle, as well as images from his interim report on his 1973 excavations of Greyfriars. Thanks are also due to him and to the Council for British Archaeology for permission to reproduce the elevation drawing of the Norman arcade in St Bartholomew's Hospital. The authors are also especially indebted to him for sharing his extensive knowledge of Bristol's archaeology in discussions over many years. Michael Richardson, of the Special Collections Library of Bristol University, was particularly helpful in locating and making available some of the more obscure reference material.

Sharon Gerber (Royal Archaeological Institute) and Alana Farrell and the staff of the Society of Antiquaries Library for the image of R W Paul's 1912 plan of St Augustine's Abbey; staff of the British Geological Survey for an extract from the current geological map of the Bristol area and of an image from one of their publications; Chloe McCulloch for the use of images from *The Builder*. Staff of the Bodleian Library have been of great assistance throughout in enabling access to the 18th-century James Stewart drawings, agreeing to the reproduction of several of them, and providing high-quality versions of these.

The publication of this volume would not have been possible without the help and generosity of all of these people and institutions. We offer our sincere and heartfelt thanks to all; and if we have inadvertently omitted to mention anyone, we thank them equally, and also apologise for our oversight. Any errors that remain are, of course, our sole responsibility, but we hope that the volume as a whole will be felt a worthy tribute to everyone who helped to make it possible.

Picture credits

Summary

Bristol is a major city and port in the south-west of England. In medieval times, it became the third largest city in the kingdom, surpassed only by London and York. Bristol was founded in the late Saxon period, very probably by 1000 AD, and grew rapidly in the 12th and 13th centuries. Initially, seaborne trading links with Ireland and France were particularly significant; later, from the 16th century onwards, the city became a focus for trade with Iberia, Africa and the New World. This led to the growth of new industries such as brass manufacture, glass production and sugar refining, producing items for export and processing imported raw materials. Bristol also derived wealth from the slave trade between Africa and the New World.

The city has a long history of antiquarian and archaeological investigation, much of it stimulated by demolition and new construction in the urban area from the 18th century onwards. This volume provides, for the first time, a comprehensive overview of the historical development of Bristol, based on archaeological and architectural evidence.

Part 1 of the volume describes the geological and topographical context of Bristol, presents a geoarchaeological deposit model and discusses the evidence for the environment prior to the foundation of the city. The history of archaeological work in Bristol is discussed in detail, as is the pictorial record (which provides information about many important buildings that have since been demolished) and the cartographic evidence for the city. In Part 2, a series of period-based chapters considers the historical background and archaeological evidence for Bristol's development. Chapters cover the period before the foundation of the city (the prehistoric, Roman and post-Roman eras), the establishment and growth of Bristol between about 950 and 1200 AD; the medieval city (1200 to 1540 AD); the early modern period (1540 to 1700 AD); and the period from 1700 to 1900 AD, when Bristol was particularly important for its role in transatlantic trade. Each chapter discusses the major civic, military and religious monuments of the time, and the complex topographical evolution of the city as it expanded from its original Late Saxon nucleus. Part 3 assesses the significance of Bristol's archaeology, and identifies and discusses a range of research themes that might be pursued here in the future.

Résumé

Bristol est une cité et un port importants du sud-ouest de l'Angleterre. Au moyen-âge, elle est devenue la troisième plus grande ville du Royaume, seules Londres et York la surpassaient. Bristol fut fondée vers la fin de la période saxonne, très probablement avant 1000 ap. J.-C., et s'est agrandie rapidement au 12ème et au 13ème siècles. A l'origine, les liens commerciaux maritimes avec l'Irlande et la France furent particulièrement importants; plus tard, à partir du 16ème siècle, la cité devint un centre pour le commerce avec la Péninsule Ibérique, l'Afrique et le Nouveau Monde. Ceci entrainala croissance de nouvelles industries telles que la fabrication de laiton, la production de verre et le raffinage de sucre; produisant des marchandises pour l'exportation et transformant des matières premières importées. Bristol s'est également enrichie grâce au commerce des esclaves entre l'Afrique et le Nouveau Monde.

La ville a une longue histoire d'investigations par des amateurs d'antiquités et des archéologues, en grande partie stimulées par les démolitions et les constructions dans la zone urbaine à partir du 18ème siècle. Ce volume offre pour la première fois, une vue d'ensemble détaillée du développement historique de Bristol qui repose sur des témoignages archéologiques et architecturaux.

La partie 1 du volume décrit le contexte géologique et topographique de Bristol, présente un modèle des dépôts géo-archéologiques et discute des témoignages relatifs à l'environnement avant la fondation de la ville. L'histoire des travaux archéologiques à Bristol est discutée en détail, tout comme le sont les preuves picturales (qui nous apportent des renseignements sur de nombreux bâtiments importants qui ont depuis été démolis) et les témoignages cartographiques de la ville. Dans la partie 2, une série de chapitres organisés par périodes examine l'arrière fond historique et les témoignages archéologiques du développement de Bristol. Ces chapitres couvrent la période précédant la fondation de la ville (les ères préhistorique, romaine et post-romaine), l'établissement et la croissance de Bristol entre environ 950 et 1200 ap. J.-C.; la cité médiévale (1200 à 1540 ap. J.-C.); le début de la période moderne (1540 à 1700 ap. J.-C); et la période de 1700 à 1900 ap. J.-C., quand Bristol était particulièrement importante à cause de son rôle dans le commerce transatlantique. Chaque chapitre discute des principaux monuments civiques, militaires et religieux de la période, et l'évolution topographique complexe de la cité au fur et à mesure qu'elle s'agrandissait à partir de son noyau originel de la fin de la période saxonne. La partie 3 évalue la portée de l'archéologie de Bristol, identifie et examine une gamme de thèmes de recherches susceptibles d'être développés ici dans l'avenir.

Zusammenfassung

Bristol ist eine bedeutende Hafenstadt im Südwesten Englands. Während des Mittelalters entwickelte es sich zur drittgrößten Stadt des Königreichs, hinter London und York. Die Gründung Bristols erfolgte in spätsächsischer Zeit; die Stadt existierte wahrscheinlich schon um 1000 n. Chr. Während des 12. und 13. Jahrhunderts durchlief die Stadt ein rasantes Wachstum. Zu Beginn waren vor allem die Seehandelsverbindungen mit Frankreich und Irland von besonderer Bedeutung; später, vom 16. Jahrhundert an, wurde die Stadt zum Angelpunkt für den Handel mit der Iberischen Halbinsel, Afrika und der Neuen Welt. Dies begünstigte das Wachstum neuer Gewerbezweige, wie z. B. der Messing-und Glasherstellung sowie der Zuckerraffination, der Produktion von Waren für den Export und der Weiterverarbeitung importierter Rohmaterialien. Bristol profitierte auch vom Sklavenhandel zwischen Afrika und der Neuen Welt.

Die Stadt hat eine lange Tradition antiquarischer und archäologischer Untersuchungen, von denen der größte Teil durch Abrissarbeiten und Neubauten seit dem 18. Jahrhundert im Stadtbereich bedingt wurde. Dieser Band bietet nun zum ersten Mal einen umfassenden, auf archäologischen und architektonischen Fakten basierenden Überblick zur historischen Entwicklung Bristols.

In Teil 1 des Bandes wird das geologische und topografische Umfeld Bristols beschrieben, ein geoarchäologisches Schichtenmodell vorgestellt und die Hinweise für die Rekonstruktion der Umwelt vor der Stadtgründung diskutiert. Die Geschichte der archäologischen Arbeiten in Bristol wird detailliert besprochen, ebenso auch die Bildquellen (dieseliefern Informationen zu zahlreichen wichtigen Bauten, die mittlerweile abgerissen worden sind) und das Kartenmaterial für die Stadt. In Teil 2 werden in einer Reihe von periodenbasierten Kapiteln der historische Hintergrund und die archäologischen Belege für die Entwicklung von Bristol betrachtet. In jeweils eigenen Kapiteln werden die Zeit vor Gründung der Stadt (die vorgeschichtlichen, römischen und nachrömischen Perioden), die Gründung und das Wachstum Bristols zwischen etwa 950 und 1250 n. Chr., die mittelalterliche Stadt (1200 bis 1540), die frühe Neuzeit (1540 bis 1700), sowie die Periode zwischen 1700 und 1900, als Bristol wegen seiner Rolle im Transatlantikhandel von besonderer Bedeutung war, nachgezeichnet. Die einzelnen Kapitel behandeln die zivilen, militärischen und religiösen Monumente der jeweiligen Periode, undes wird die komplexe topografische Evolution der Stadt und ihrer Ausdehnung von ihrem ursprünglichen, spätsächsischen Kern nachvollzogen. Teil 3 widmet sich der Beurteilung der Bedeutung von Bristols archäologischen Quellen sowieder Diskussion der Bandbreite von Forschungsthemen, die hier in Zukunft durchgeführt werden könnten.

Übersetzung: Jörn Schuster
(ARCHÆOLOGICALsmallFINDS)

Glossary of terms

AMS – Accelerator Mass Spectrometry. A method of radiocarbon dating using samples that can be as small as 1–2 milligrams.

BHER – Bristol Historic Environment Record. The record of all information about historic Bristol. It contains thousands of entries and includes records of archaeological excavations and finds as well as historic monuments and landscapes. The record is maintained by Bristol City Council and is publicly accessible online via Know Your Place (www.bristol.gov.uk/knowyourplace).

LiDAR – Light Detection and Ranging. Provides highly detailed and accurate models of the ground surface using a pulsed laser beam fired from a plane.

OSL – Optically Stimulated Luminescence. A late Quaternary dating technique used to date the last time quartz sediment was exposed to light.

PART 1: A BACKGROUND TO THE ARCHAEOLOGICAL STUDY OF THE CITY

Introduction

Location and setting

Bristol is the largest city in the south-west of England and is one of the eight core cities in England. Close to the river Severn and to Wales, the city's historic centre stands on a finger of land (at grid reference ST 590 730) between the river Avon and its tributary, the river Frome, with hills rising steeply on its north side and the floodplain of the rivers on the south. Its landscape is distinctive with the valleys of the Avon and Frome in particular having an historic and continuing influence upon the city's topography. The Avon Gorge especially is world-renowned and is nationally important for its rare flora and fauna as well as being probably the most impressive entry to a modern city (Fig 0.1).

Bristol is a unitary local authority with more than 430,000 inhabitants and has a broad-based economy, ranging from manufacturing companies to cultural production. It is an important national location for banking and insurance services but also has a significant proportion of public sector employment. It is home to two major universities, the University of Bristol and the University of the West of England, both of which are experiencing significant increases in student numbers, with over 50,000 students attending both universities. Both make significant contributions to the fields of historical and archaeological research. The city is a major node in the modern road and rail network but in the past the Avon formed Bristol's major highway, winding westward for approximately 13km through the Avon gorge to the Severn estuary. From there its ships reached Europe and the Atlantic. The archaeology of Bristol strongly reflects this maritime history and the wealth and influence that its commerce generated.

The Urban Strategies Programme and the origins of the project

The publication of Archaeology and Planning in 1990, a government planning policy guidance note usually known as PPG16, changed the conduct of English archaeology (Department of the Environment 1990). The document emphasised the role of local authorities in the curation of archaeology, recommending inclusion of policies for archaeology in local development plans, and indicating a practical means of archaeological management through the exercise of their development control and other functions. As a result the need became clear for strategies tailored to the specific local circumstances of the larger towns and cities where development pressure is often greatest. To develop these strategies English Heritage launched its Urban Archaeological Strategies programme in 1992 with the publication of *Managing the Urban Archaeological Resource* (English Heritage 1992). Smaller urban settlements would be subject to a rapid survey (the Extensive Urban Survey) covering, in the Bristol administrative area, places later absorbed into the urban conurbation: Bedminster, and Clifton and Hotwells. These documents have now been largely superseded as a result of a more inclusive approach to the production of Conservation Area Character Appraisals. For the larger urban settlements, including central Bristol, a more intensive approach was envisaged, with three main stages. The first

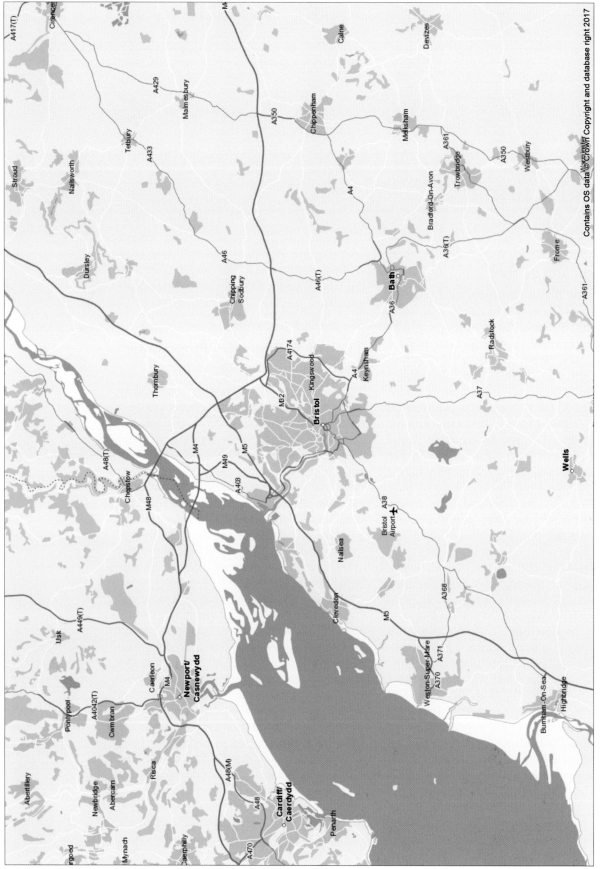

Figure 0.1 Plan of the Bristol region

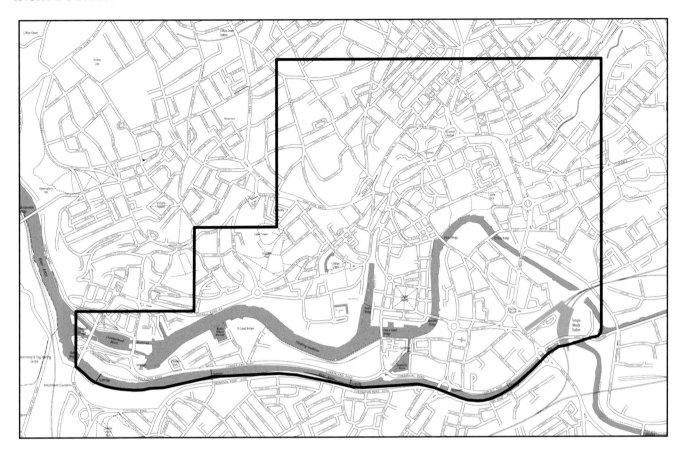

stage, the creation of Urban Archaeological Databases of the available archaeological information, would be followed in the second stage by an assessment of that information. The third stage would be the formulation of management strategies for use by curatorial archaeologists (English Heritage 1992, 8–9); these strategies, based on the judgements made during the assessment, would then be incorporated into local policy. Subsequently, PPG16 was replaced by Planning Policy Statement (PPS) 5 and then in 2012 by the National Planning Policy Framework (NPPF).

The Bristol Urban Archaeology Database

The first step towards an archaeological strategy for Bristol was the compilation of the Bristol Urban Archaeology Database (UAD), which began in early 1996. Two researchers worked full time for 64 weeks, focusing on an area of roughly 5 square kilometres in the centre of the city which extended from the New Cut in the south to Kingsdown and St Paul's in the north, and Old Market in the

east to Brandon Hill in the west. This area covered the Saxon *burh* and the subsequent medieval and early modern expansion. A finger extended west to Cumberland Basin to bring the whole of the Floating Harbour, the most important post-medieval monument in the city, within the study area (Fig 0.2).

The approach developed for the Cirencester UAD (Darvill and Gerrard 1994, 7–13) and adopted for the other urban database projects, was also followed in Bristol. This distinguishes between archaeological recognition events, the excavation, survey, photograph or other record which holds information about the archaeological resource, and monuments, the monastery, factory or other cultural artefact, which are an interpretation and distillation of the relevant recognition events.

The first task of the Bristol project was to compile a comprehensive list of archaeological events from published and unpublished sources (*see* Appendix 1). Other historic and visual sources were then searched selectively, including historic maps, the Braikenridge collection of early 19th-century watercolours held by the Bristol Museum and Art Gallery,

Figure 0.2 Plan of the UAD and UAA study area

photographs published by the Reece Winstone archive, and historic documents, to extract the archaeological information they contained (Brett and Bryant 1997). The second element of the project was the identification of monuments within the landscape. Geographical Information Systems (GIS) software was used to map, where possible, the spatial extent of the events, features and monuments which were identified during the data gathering.

The Bristol Urban Archaeological Assessment

Today the urban conurbation of Bristol covers many square kilometres. Most of this area has been developed since the end of the 19th century but in the medieval period the core of the settlement was focused on a small area at the confluence of the river Avon and the Frome. The study area defined for the Bristol UAD and this assessment (Fig 0.2) encloses this historic core but also seeks to examine the subsequent post-medieval expansion. Consequently the defences built to the north of the city during the civil wars of the 1640s (parts of which have the status of Scheduled Ancient Monuments), the whole of the Floating Harbour (on which much of the economic life of the settlement depended) to the west, and part of the early industrial area of St Philip's Marsh to the east have all been included. Bedminster to the south and Clifton and Hotwells to the north-west have, however, been omitted since they were the subject of separate studies in the Extensive Urban Survey programme.

The first draft of the Assessment was produced in 2002 and submitted to English Heritage for review (Brett *et al* 2002). Following detailed comment, it was decided to produce a second draft, involving significant rewriting, especially of the medieval section of the document. A second draft was then submitted in 2005 (Brett *et al* 2005). Detailed comments and criticisms were made by Professor Derek Keene in 2006, following which a start was made on a significant redraft of the document by the principal author. However, following the untimely death of the author in 2007, the project was put on hold since there were no resources within Bristol City Council to continue at that time.

In 2008, initial discussions were held with English Heritage to re-start the project and Dr Nigel Baker, formerly of Herefordshire Archaeology, was approached to undertake the rewriting of the existing draft. Following an initial project proposal, a detailed Project Design was agreed in 2010. This set out a detailed methodology for a major redrafting of the earlier work, commencing with the production of a sample chapter (chapter 6 of this volume), to explore and solve any problems that might have arisen with the new structure for the volume that was being proposed. A subsequent Project Design was agreed in early 2012 to complete the remainder of the volume.

Approach

The structure of the Bristol Urban Archaeological Assessment was devised at the outset through dialogue with English Heritage. It aimed to retain a common structure with similar assessments carried out elsewhere while allowing for the particular local circumstances of Bristol. Earlier drafts were biased towards the assessment of the archaeological potential and importance of defined geographical units within the city. While the importance of the component geographical elements is still recognised (see below), the chronological narrative is now concerned with the exploration of the city's development on a thematic basis. The study considers the archaeological research carried out in the city up to the year 2014 with the aim of presenting an overview of our current understanding of the evolution of the city. This will form the basis for the development of the management strategy discussed above. The focus is on the core of Bristol, but the impossibility of dividing an urban settlement from its hinterland and, particularly in the case of Bristol, its overseas connections means that in places the text does range more widely.

Document structure

The assessment is divided into three parts, each divided into a number of chapters. The first part puts the study of the archaeology of the city into an overall context. Chapter 1 starts with a summary history of Bristol from the first manifestations of human activity up to 1900. In chapter 2 there is a brief summary of the geology of the city and the changes to its topography and geomorphology, illustrated by the results of a study into the distribution and significance of waterlogged deposits in the city, commissioned in 2012 by English Heritage (Wilkinson *et al* 2013b). Chapter 3 looks at the history of archaeological study in Bristol, from the *Itinerary* of William Worcestre in the 15th century through the works of antiquarians in the 18th and 19th centuries and finally to the establishment of archaeology as an integral part of local planning policy and strategy. This chapter goes on to look at the remarkable range of visual and cartographic sources available to the archaeologist, much of which is now available on line.

Part 2 sets out the development of Bristol from the prehistoric period until the cut-off date of 1900. This is arranged in five chapters dealing with each chronological period and explores the changes in Bristol's urban landscape and assesses the quality of the archaeological resource. The chronological divisions were chosen to reflect the major phases of Bristol's development as follows:

Bristol before AD 950
Evidence for prehistoric, Roman and Early to Middle Saxon occupation in central Bristol (if not in the surrounding landscape) is very limited although the possibilities afforded by detailed analysis of deeper deposits by geoarchaeological prospection are examined. The hypothesis that has been put forward for an early foundation for Bristol, perhaps as early as the 8th century, is briefly examined, while all of the data for the period before AD 950, the earliest date for the founding of the town, is dealt within a single section.

Bristol c 950–c 1200
This chapter discusses the evolution of the town from the earliest date for its foundation which can be demonstrated archaeologically up to the end of the 12th century. This was the period which saw the Late Saxon town plan become formalised, the town become a major port, weathering both the Norman Conquest and 12th-century civil wars, and undergoing initial suburban development before the expansion of the high Middle Ages.

Bristol c 1200–c 1540
The chapter explores the period of Bristol's emergence as a major European port between the 13th and 16th centuries. The period saw the diversion of the river Frome to increase the capacity of the docks, enabling further suburban development, and culminated with the religious controversy preceding the Reformation.

Bristol c 1540–c 1700
The chapter discusses the radical changes in landholding and topography which followed from the disappearance of the monasteries at the beginning of the period. During the 17th century Bristol merchants became involved in a lucrative trade with the new colonies along the eastern seaboard of America and in the Caribbean, stimulating the emergence of new industries in the city at the end of the 17th century.

Bristol c 1700–c 1900
The final period to be discussed saw both Bristol's peak as an economic power and its gradual decline to regional city in the era of the Second Industrial Revolution.

For the purposes of illustrating the physical growth of the city over a 1000-year period, and to emphasise the distinctive development pattern of the city during this period, a number of geographical areas have been defined. They have distinctive attributes that separate them from other areas in the immediate vicinity, by reason of their topography, their development pattern or the particular historic circumstances that resulted in their development (Fig 0.3).

Old City: the extent of the original settlement within the inner circuit of the town walls and the area of the royal castle and its associated land in and beyond Castle Park.

Old Market: the boundaries of the area known as Old Market are defined by the roads to the north and south of Old Market Street, Redcross Street and Unity Street. It also includes the main street, West Street and the back lanes.

Broadmead: the suburb to the north of the castle, its boundaries are defined by Penn Street to the east, the course of the river Frome on the south and west sides and Horsefair on the north.

Redcliffe and Temple: the 12th-century suburbs of Redcliffe and Temple on the south side of the Avon, bounded by the river Avon and the New Cut.

Lewin's Mead: the area of a rock outcrop to the north of the Frome on which the majority of the religious houses were sited, stretching from Park Street to St James Barton.

College Green: including the precinct of St Augustine's Abbey, Canon's Marsh and Brandon Hill.

The Marsh: the area between the circuit of the inner town walls north of Baldwin Street

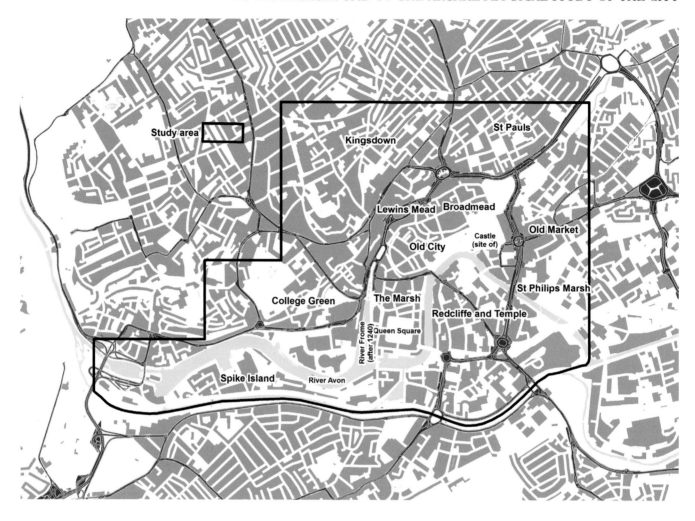

Figure 0.3 Plan of the geographical areas of the UAA

and the land to the south of Queen Square. The northern half of this area was starting to be settled from the 12th century and was enclosed by a wall from the middle of the 13th century. The southern half remained as marsh, although frequently used for recreation until the laying out of Queen Square from 1700.

Kingsdown: including St Michael's Hill and the suburb of Kingsdown created in the 18th century.

St Paul's: the 18th-century suburb created to the north-east of the medieval core of the city. Its boundaries are formed by Redcross Street and Stokes Croft on its south and west sides.

St Philip's Marsh: a triangle of land which became an industrial suburb from the late 17th and more particularly 18th century. It is defined by the river Avon on the south-west and Unity Street on the north.

Spike Island: the finger of land between the river Avon and the New Cut used for

shipbuilding and timber yards in the post-medieval period, defined following the creation of the New Cut in 1809.

Part 3 is concerned with an overarching assessment of the detailed archaeological and historical information contained in the preceding chapters and reviews its significance both in terms of continuing questions regarding Bristol's historical development as well as the city's place in the national scene. It sets out a research agenda by period as well as on a multi-period, city-wide basis, in anticipation of a future strategy for research and conservation that might be addressed in future programmes of archaeological and historical enquiry. This work thus follows on from the regional research framework produced for the South West, both the Resource Assessment and Research Agenda (Webster (ed) 2008) and the subsequent Research Strategy (Grove and Croft 2012).

Chapter 1: The history and archaeology of Bristol: a summary

Bristol as an urban settlement has a history spanning at least a thousand years. From a relatively small site of around 8ha on a rocky elevation above the rivers Avon and Frome, it rapidly expanded, especially in the 12th and 13th centuries and then dramatically in the 18th and 19th centuries to become the city that most of us would recognise by around 1900.

Over the past century in particular there has been an enormous expenditure of time, effort and resources in archaeological enquiry in Bristol. With the extraordinary expansion of archaeological work from the 1970s onwards, under the general term 'rescue archaeology', and the recognition, signified by the appointment by the City Council of a full-time archaeological officer in 1968, that Bristol's heritage was indeed special, there have been unparalleled efforts to record that heritage, often in unpromising circumstances. Nevertheless, there are still major gaps in understanding, either because of lack of opportunity, research objectives too influenced by personal interests, or even through the lack of any overall research frameworks. One of the major problems in summarising the current position in terms of our overall understanding of the history of the town is the absence of analysis and publication, except in the most summary form, of many of the major excavations undertaken in the last 30 years. Some notable campaigns of archaeological investigation have been published in recent years and the results of some of these have been summarised in the following chapters. However, full publication of certain excavation programmes will be crucial for the development of future research agendas, either because they displayed a remarkably complete temporal sequence, or because they shed light on particular aspects of the town's development and contemporary life, or because they produced well-preserved stratigraphic sequences and artefacts.

Pre-medieval settlement

The evidence for earlier, pre-medieval settlement in central Bristol has been largely ignored, with a few exceptions, despite the abundant evidence for prehistoric and Roman exploitation of its hinterland. The discovery of worked flint and bronze artefacts, as well as Romano-British ceramics hint that such settlement is there to be found. The only site so far identified is a small Roman settlement on the high ground to the north of the city centre, discovered in the 1970s (Jackson 2000). A deposit model for the central area (Wilkinson *et al* 2013b) has allowed new questions to be formulated regarding the potential for pre-medieval settlement in the central Bristol area. It appears highly likely that the alluvial floodplain upon which much of the modern centre of Bristol stands formed as a result of relative sea level rise in the late Mesolithic and was permeated by meandering palaeochannels, similar to those which characterised the former landscapes of the Severn Estuary. There were also now vanished valleys of former tributaries of the major rivers – the valley of the Woodwell stream, now followed by Jacob's Wells Road, is one example. The recognition of organic strata, particularly from geoarchaeological prospection, has raised the possibility, albeit relatively slight, for the recovery of evidence for human settlement from the late Mesolithic, although the recovery of such evidence will be beyond the reach of traditional archaeological investigation. Such evidence will only be recoverable through programmes of targeted geoarchaeological investigation. However, it is certainly the case, as has been demonstrated, that pollen analysis of these strata can yield important information man's impact upon the wider landscape, as has been shown at Deanery Road in the north-west of the study area where there was evidence for localised forest clearance in the early Neolithic, with later evidence for short-lived exploitation of the marsh in the Bronze Age (Wilkinson 2006).

The Late Saxon and Norman town and early expansion

By the middle of the 11th century, Bristol was clearly a place of importance: its mention in the *Anglo-Saxon Chronicle* in 1051 as the place from which the ships of Harold and Leofwine departed, then in 1063 as the supply base for an expedition against the Welsh and finally in 1068 when it repulsed a raid by the sons of Harold (Whitelock 1961), shows that by the middle of the 11th century it had been established as a thriving and important settlement. The Late Saxon settlement area, on its sandstone ridge, but with a probably contemporary defended bridgehead on the south side of the Avon, had, by the middle of the 12th century, been enlarged by extra-mural settlement, at Broadmead, in Redcliffe and Temple, in the Marsh to the south and probably to the north as well. There may also have been pre-Conquest settlement outside the original core, in Billeswick and on the north bank of the Frome, later to be subsumed within the expansion of the built-up area across the Frome in the 13th century.

It has generally been accepted, often uncritically, that Bristol's foundation as a port and town can be placed around AD 1000. Yet the town seems to emerge fully developed on to the historical scene by this date, prompting speculation that it had earlier origins, possibly as an outlier to the Mercian kingdom of Offa and his successors. The place of St Peter's church, situated centrally on the peninsula that formed the focus of Bristol's earliest

settlement, is critical and it has been argued (Manco 2009) that it was an early minster church, possibly founded by Offa, perhaps associated with a defended trading settlement predating the Late Saxon town. While this theory is attractive and is worthy of further consideration, it is not currently supported by any archaeological evidence. It has been speculated by Leech (2014, ch 2) that Bristol may have been one of a number of *burhs* founded in the reign of Edward the Elder (899–925) as part of his strategic defence of the south coast and the Severn prior to the Viking raids of 914.

The current archaeological and historical evidence supports the foundation of the town by the late 10th century, probably through royal initiative and its earliest landholders were drawn from the aristocracy. While the earliest documentary evidence for Bristol is of 1051, the establishment of a mint at Bristol, certainly by the reign of Cnut (1016–35) and possibly in the reign of Aethelred II (979–1016), as attested by coin evidence, the earliest of 1009–16 struck by the moneyer Ælfwerd, would indicate that an urban settlement had been established by this time (Grinsell, nd, 174). It occupied a well-defended site surrounded on three sides by the river Avon and its tributary the river Frome. Its situation some 13km from the Severn provided a safe and sheltered harbour, despite the large tidal range, which, throughout the medieval period, was to prove a significant asset in allowing the rapid transport of shipping down the Avon to the Bristol Channel as well as upstream to safe anchorage in the Frome.

Based on the results of excavation, the Late Saxon settlement extended at least as far as the eastern limits of the later castle and included on the west the still surviving grid pattern of streets around the Carfax, the crossing formed by High Street, Broad Street, Corn Street and Wine Street. Michael Ponsford's reinterpretation of the Late Saxon topography of the town, on the basis of excavations at Mary-le-Port Street and on the site of Bristol Castle (Ponsford nd(a), Ponsford 1979), that the Late Saxon town extended from Mary-le-Port Street east as far as the outer ditch of the castle, only extending west after the Norman Conquest, needs to be tested with carefully-planned excavation and research. However, as it stands, the limited archaeological evidence so far recovered suggests that the traditional interpretation of the layout of the Late Saxon town is more likely to be correct, with a planned street layout from the earliest years of the town's foundation (or re-foundation by *c* 1000) extending from the western end of Corn Street at least as far as the eastern end of Mary-le-Port Street. Late Saxon occupation within what became the castle precinct may have been part of an extra-mural settlement or may even have been included within the original planned and defended area (Fig 1.1).

Little work has been carried out on the presumed defences of the early town. Rahtz (Watts and Rahtz 1985, 186) was uncertain whether a double ditch found at the eastern end of Mary-le-Port Street, containing pottery of the late 10th or early 11th century in its upper fills, was part of the original defensive earthwork but the apparent discontinuity of the street pattern at this point might be an indication of this. The medieval name for the north–south street at this point, Defence Street, in use by 1391 (Leech 1997b, 22), could well suggest a defensive line at this point, although not necessarily the ditch excavated by Rahtz, with the street being an early intra-mural lane of the Late Saxon town, along with Bell Lane, Leonard Lane, Tower Lane and possibly Worship Street (Leech 1997b, 22). It has been suggested that the earthen rampart found in the north-eastern corner of the castle bailey might have originally formed part of the town's Late Saxon defensive circuit, based upon a re-evaluation of the dating evidence that came from this excavation (Leech 1997b, 22). An earth bank found during excavation to the west of Small Street in 1990 (BHER 313) may have been part of an intra-mural rampart but this feature was undated. It is generally stated that the earliest stone defences were constructed in the 12th century (eg Ponsford nd(a), 150). It is uncertain whether these stand on an earlier Late Saxon defensive circuit, but it seems likely to have been the case.

Figure 1.1 Bristol c *1100*

The density of the churches within the historic core is an indicator of the early foundation of the town: the three churches at the Carfax, Christ Church, St Ewen's and All Saints might all have pre-Conquest origins: they were all certainly in existence by the mid-12th century, while the church of St Mary-le-Port, excavated by Philip Rahtz in 1962–3, could well have a pre-Conquest origin – certainly the excavated evidence from the adjacent Mary-le-Port street would suggest that it was laid out in this period. St Werburgh's, first mentioned in a charter of 1148–83, could have a pre-Conquest origin and the other churches of the urban core were known to be in existence by the 12th century. St Peter's Church has already been put forward as the possible site of an early minster (see above). Whether or not this can be proved, it is certainly documented as early as 1107 and was considered as the earliest of the Bristol churches in a grant of the church to Tewkesbury Abbey by Simon, Bishop of Worcester (1125–50).

The site of the earliest bridge crossing is also in some doubt. The present Bristol Bridge, an 18th-century structure with later additions, replaced an ornate arched bridge constructed in the 13th century. While it has been suggested that an earlier bridge was located upstream (Ponsford 1985), it is more likely that the present bridge is on the site of the original bridge that gave Bristol ('the place of the bridge') its name.

For the areas immediately surrounding the historic town, the archaeological evidence is uneven. Relatively little archaeological work has been attempted in the Old Market suburb and yet it would seem likely that this area, located alongside an early historic route from the east, would have been settled from an early date, possibly not long after the foundation of the town. The suburb is today characterised by a classic wide market street with burgage plots stretching from the main street to the back lanes behind. This pattern of urban development had probably been established by the mid-12th century. However, it is possible, although yet to be proven, that this development was preceded by a Late Saxon extra-mural settlement, defined by the now-lost Ellbroad Street and Carey's Lane adjacent to the possible Late Saxon defences, later to become the eastern ditch of the castle at the west end of Old Market.

In Redcliffe, by contrast, there has been considerable archaeological work carried out in the last 30 years, much of it concentrated upon the medieval waterfront. Recent research has suggested that an area around the approach to Bristol Bridge, known as Arthur's Fee in the medieval period, may have been settled in the Late Saxon period, perhaps to provide a secure bridgehead (Leech 2009). This enclave at the junction of Redcliff, St Thomas and Temple Streets may have been furnished with a surrounding defensive ditch. Such a defended bridgehead, with perhaps its own distinctive character and economic base, may be seen in London with the relationship between the City of London on the north bank and Southwark on the south as well as in other English and European towns (Vince 1990, 153). The excavation on the site of the former Courage Brewery immediately to the east of Bristol Bridge has tended to support this theory, with the discovery of a large ditch, possibly a boundary or defensive ditch of Arthur's Fee and tentatively dated to the 11th century although probably earlier than later in the century (Teague and Brady 2017b).

To the south of Arthur's Fee, which may have existed from the earliest foundation of Bristol on the north bank of the river, the suburb of Redcliffe and Temple was laid out in the early part of the 12th century, the eastern part of the suburb having been granted to the Templars by Robert of Gloucester. Timbers from the Dundas Wharf excavation in 1982–3, dendrochronologically dated to the 1120s (Nicholson and Hillam 1987; Good 1991) and dating evidence from substantial roadside ditches flanking Temple Street (Teague and Brady 2017b) support the fact that both Redcliff Street and Temple Street were being laid out at this time. Tenements were being set out along Temple Street from the second half of the century, probably at around the same time that similar development was taking place along Redcliff Street. By the end of the century, it would appear that the basic framework of tenements, connecting lanes and north–south drainage ditches ('law ditches') had been set out – these were to survive largely intact until major redevelopments of the 19th and 20th centuries.

To the south of the early walled town, in the area known as the Marsh, south of Baldwin

Street, there is little sign of occupation before the 12th century. Marsh Street is documented from 1164–70 and there is excavated evidence for settlement in the area from around this period. Presumably the tenements that lined Marsh Street were laid out at this time while there is evidence for 12th-century occupation in the Welsh Back area (Blockley 1996, 12–13). A series of long plots were in existence across the Marsh by the mid-13th century, possibly of much earlier origin, calling into question the route of the river Frome prior to its diversion to its present course *c* 1240 (for a discussion on the route of the Frome see Chapters 2 and 5).

Little is known of the area north of the inner town wall and south of the Frome, although, like the Marsh to the south, it is likely that this area had seen settlement in some form by the 12th century. North of the Frome, the Priory of St James had been founded by 1129. To the south of this, Broadmead (*novum burgum de prato*) had been founded by Robert of Gloucester on a grid pattern in the first half of the 12th century, and was being developed after 1150. Excavations here produced evidence for substantial timber structures and a possible crossing of the Frome (Ridgeway and Watts 2013). An industrial area was set out in the 12th century on the north-east angle of a bend of the river Frome: evidence for copper and iron working was recovered together with possible evidence for dyeing (Jackson 2010a). The suburb of Billeswick is less understood although its early origin seems likely, and may date from at least as early as the middle of the 11th century, based on the dating of the 'Harrowing of Hell' relief found in the south transept of the Cathedral. The recovery of possible pre-Conquest burials from the excavation at St Augustine-the-Less in 1983 (Boore 1985, 25) could suggest an early church foundation here, predating the foundation of St Augustine's Abbey in *c* 1140 by Robert Fitzharding. At St Bartholomew's Hospital some evidence was recovered for Late Saxon riverside settlement and the bridge crossing over the Frome at this point has been thought to be pre-Conquest in date (Price with Ponsford 1998, 27).

The construction of the castle, imposed on what had already been an occupied area from the Late Saxon period, took place probably only shortly after the Norman Conquest, although there is considerable uncertainty surrounding its original form. Probably by *c* 1080, it had been replaced by a motte and bailey castle. Again there are differences of opinion on the form of this structure, particularly of the extent of the bailey. However, in the early 12th century, the motte was replaced by a stone keep constructed by Robert of Gloucester, possibly before *c* 1120 (Good 1996, 28).

The medieval town: expansion and consolidation

In the years following the civil war between Stephen and Matilda, Bristol prospered as a mercantile centre so that from the middle of the 13th century it expanded its walled area to both the north and south. As has been seen, this expansion had almost certainly been preceded by a gradual expansion in settlement outside the original walled area. In the case of Redcliffe and Temple this extension of the walled circuit had been preceded by over a century of planned urban growth. A similar situation may have existed to the north and south of the original walled town, in the Nelson Street and Marsh Street/Queen Charlotte Street areas.

The castle, throughout this period, was the subject of continual renewal and rebuilding: a new hall was built in 1239–42. From 1250 there were significant improvements to buildings within the wards, including a new kitchen and pantry and in the 1280s St Martin's Chapel in the outer ward was rebuilt. Several sections of the curtain wall were rebuilt in the late 13th century and in the 14th century a further vaulted chamber was added on the north side of the Great Hall.

The areas that had already seen urban growth, in the Marsh, to the north of the inner town wall and in Redcliffe and Temple, were now formally enclosed by town walls, generally around the middle of the 13th century. The wall enclosing Redcliffe and Temple has been investigated extensively from the 1980s onwards and its terminal tower, Tower Harratz, was fully exposed during development in the 1990s (Jackson 1994a). The southern extension, the Marsh Wall, has been exposed on a number of occasions. In 1979, for example, a possible Water gate was recorded during development works near the south-west corner of the Marsh Wall, near to the point where it turns east along the north side of King Street (Price 1991). More recently in 2006, a substantial stretch of the wall was exposed along Broad Quay (Adam 2008a). The northern extension to the walled circuit has not yet been subject to modern investigation, the only records being those of early plans and drawings. There is, however, strong documentary evidence for the nature of the settlement that was now enclosed by the new northern town wall circuit, with documents referring to tenements and shops along Christmas Street, for example.

North and west of the Frome, the foundation from around the 1230s of a number of religious houses on land that had probably been only sparsely occupied previously but was owned by prospective patrons radically changed the landscape of this part of the medieval town. A religious enclave was created defined by the high ground to the north and west and by the river to the south and east. These foundations followed the 12th-century foundations of St James's Priory (1129), St Augustine's Abbey (c 1140) and the small nunnery of St Mary Magdalen (c 1173).

Other endowments followed: numbers of almshouses and hospitals were founded throughout the town, only a few of which have been investigated archaeologically, such as Spicer's Almshouse in Temple Street (Williams 1988).

Probably one of the most important changes that was to take place to the medieval topography of Bristol was the diversion of the river Frome to its present course in the 1240s, resulting in a major expansion of the town's port facilities. While the physical attributes of the new port have yet to receive detailed archaeological study, it is nevertheless an important indicator of the town's need to compete in an increasingly competitive trading environment. The port undoubtedly played a major part in the life and customs of the town and its people. It was an important part of the urban landscape for many of its citizens. The masts of ships could be seen as glimpses at the end of narrow streets or over the tops of neighbouring buildings. The sounds and smells of the harbour must have been all-pervasive and the everyday economy of the town and its people was intricately interwoven with that of the port.

It has been suggested that nationally, the percentage of the urban population increased from around 10 per cent in 1100 to between 15 and 20 per cent in 1300 (Dyer 1994, xv; Britnell 1993; Bailey 1998). In general terms, therefore, the expansion of Bristol's built-up area and of its economic base can be set in the context of a national upturn in economic activity and urbanisation. The particular effects of this increased economic activity upon the structure, environment and hinterland of the town as well as on the lifestyle of its inhabitants are gradually being seen through the material record (Fig 1.2).

By 1300, Bristol had reached the zenith of its expansion and was not to further extend its urban limits significantly until the 17th century. It was a major exporter of wool cloth and an importer of wine from Bordeaux and the Iberian peninsula. It was importing large quantities of woad for use in its flourishing dyeworks, initially from Picardy and later from Toulouse. Its importance as a major urban centre was emphasised by being granted county borough status in 1373, the first provincial town to be granted such a distinction. The town exhibited all the trappings of civil and religious functions. The business of government was carried out in the Guildhall in Broad Street and the Tolzey, a court where the market dues were also collected or enforced, was established at the junction of Corn Street and Broad Street by 1330. At the heart of the medieval town was the High Cross, which figures prominently in Ricart's 15th-century depiction of the town (Fig 3.20) and is said to have been erected on the occasion of the town's acquisition of county status in 1373, although it may have replaced an earlier structure on the same site.

The emergence of Bristol as a major exporter of finished wool cloth, especially from the mid-14th century, is well documented in works of historical synthesis and is attested in the material record by the survival of dye waste products in excavated waterlogged contexts adjacent to the Redcliffe waterfront (Jones and Watson 1987). There have been other discoveries of dye waste in the Redcliffe area and the recognition of a possible dyer's workshop in Redcliff Street (Alexander 2015), including a stone-lined pit with preserved remains of madder at the base, together with a number of hearths, possibly associated with dyeing, reinforced the impression of an area of the town where dyeing was particularly focused.

Figure 1.2 Bristol c *1300*

Evidence for other industrial processes has been found elsewhere in the town: in Broadmead, there was evidence, from hammerscale, smithing slag and smithing hearth bottoms, for the carrying out of smithing activities, possibly farriery, given the location of the site in relation to the castle immediately to the south (Boyer 2013, 379). Shipbuilding was being carried out around Narrow Quay, although the evidence is confined largely to observations of development in less than ideal circumstances. Tanning was also being carried out in the Redcliffe and Broadmead areas in the medieval period, with reused barrel bases being found on the site of the former Courage Brewery and elsewhere.

The sites of particular industries are hinted at by street names, such as *Knyfesmithstrete* and *Vicus Fullonum* (Tucker Street, the street of the fullers) and the zoning of industries has been detected in other towns, such as Norwich and London where riverside industries can be deduced through the documentary and archaeological record (Ayers 1991; Egan 1991). In Bristol certain industries, such as dyeing and tanning, were similarly sited alongside the river frontages, partly through the need for a convenient water supply and partly because of the convenience of the river as a receptacle for industrial waste. Other examples of zoning have yet to be found, although they are likely to exist either though the symbiotic relationship of trades to each other, such as horners and tanners, or through the suitability of location – at the edge of the town to allow expansion and for cheapness of land, or on the main streets. Thus the Broadmead suburb, especially the land between the river Frome and the castle moat (the 'Weare') appears to have been a focus for the more noxious industries, possibly due its location peripheral to the medieval core, together with the fact that it was prone to periodic flooding, at least until the end of the 14th century. The Redcliffe and Temple suburb was the centre of the cloth-finishing industry and the Weavers' Hall was sited there, but the geography of the various processes which comprised this major activity is still not fully understood. The large open space in the south-east quarter of Temple, the location of the tenter racks for drying woollen cloth, is readily apparent from cartographic sources. The discovery of what may be a dyers' workshop on the east side of Redcliff Street is also a major discovery, and while it is known that Thomas Blanket set up several looms at his property in Tucker Street in the 14th century, the form of the weaving sheds has yet to be the subject of archaeological investigation.

There is frequent archaeological evidence for metalworking, in the form of smithing slags, crucible fragments and occasionally furnace structures, but as yet there has been no overall study of the distribution of metalworking trades. The investigation, at No 2 Redcliff Street, of a furnace for the casting of copper alloy objects, dating from the early 15th century to the late 17th century, is possibly the best example of a small metalworking workshop being set up at the rear of the one of the Redcliff Street properties (Alexander 2015). It might be expected that blacksmiths would have been located at the main entry and exit points of the town, as has been suggested at early medieval Winchester (Barlow *et al* 1976, 434). It is possible that the iron working evidence found in excavation at the southern end of Redcliff Street in 1982 (R H Jones 1983), close to Redcliff Gate, might suggest a smithing workshop serving the passing trade in and out of Redcliff Gate, but without further analysis of the residues this must remain highly conjectural. A similar activity is suggested from the evidence from Broadmead, as outlined above.

Victualing industries, such as bakeries, fishmongers and general food shops were probably placed to serve the passing trade and for this reason were likely to be found most frequently on the busiest streets. Thus *Cokerewe* is found at the north end of High Street, near the Carfax and at the heart of the medieval town by 1370 (Leech 2014, 122).

The general question of the provisioning of the city and the interdependence of Bristol and its hinterland require detailed study over a wide geographic area. Generalised conclusions can be drawn from the evidence available, such as the increasing importance of stockfish from the late medieval period and the increasingly sophisticated demands of the

urban market, but the evidence is meagre and widely dispersed. Bristol was a major importer of fish, both from local waters and from further afield, having in particular established close trading connections with the Irish fisheries. From the late 15th century onwards, Bristol mariners played an important role in developing more distant fishing grounds, in Icelandic waters and as far as Newfoundland (Starkey 2000, 96–7). Much of the fish was probably bought direct from the harbour and yet we know little of its ultimate destination and whether there was any difference between rich and poor in the types of fish consumed. The apparent contrast between the food remains excavated from the castle with those excavated from other sites in the town needs to be fully explored. The existing evidence is undoubtedly skewed and there is a considerable gap between the evidence for foodstuffs retrieved from excavation and the reality of what was actually being consumed in the medieval town. For example, birds are poorly represented in the total assemblages of dietary remains. Yet in 14th-century London one could buy a large range of birds for consumption from the cookshops there, while other wild birds may have formed an important part of the medieval diet. The excavation at Cabot Circus, Broadmead, retrieved samples of hake, herring, whiting and salmon, all fish that may well have come from the Irish fishing grounds, although salmon may also have come from local fishing grounds in the Severn. Freshwater eels were probably caught locally from fishing grounds in the Avon and Severn (Batchelor *et al* 2013, 383).

Of the citizens of Bristol themselves, their health and well-being, their beliefs and their attitudes to life and death, relatively little is still known. Only two large cemetery sites have been excavated; that of St Augustine-the-Less still requires full analysis, while the results of the work at St James's Priory are more illuminating for the health of the occupants of a major religious house than truly representative of the town as a whole. Little is known, also, of the various minorities who undoubtedly lived in the medieval town. One group, in particular, has hardly been studied, namely the Jews who occupied a small area immediately to the west of the castle. Some of the artefacts from the excavation at Peter Street are thought to be of Jewish origin, although the findings from this site await detailed study. The Jewish burial ground lay to the north-west of the medieval town, on the site known as 'Jews Acre' and now occupied by Queen Elizabeth Hospital School. Close to this site is another contemporary Jewish site, interpreted initially as a *mikveh*, a place associated with purification, and more recently as a *bet tohorah*, a place dedicated to washing the dead before burial (Hillaby and Sermon 2004). This has undergone a preliminary survey (Emanuel and Ponsford 1994), but further fieldwork is required to establish its date, form and function and even its authenticity as a truly medieval Jewish monument.

The early modern town: Reformation, Civil War and renewal (Fig 1.3)

Millerd's plan of the city, published in 1673 (Fig 3.22), depicts Bristol as essentially that which had been in existence throughout much of the medieval period. However, while the extent of the built-up area that he depicts would have been familiar to the citizen of the medieval town, major changes in landholding had occurred following the Reformation and the breaking up of the religious institutions that had been such a familiar part of late medieval life. The monasteries that had fringed the outskirts of the medieval town received new lay owners, although there does not seem to be much evidence for an immediate explosion in new building in these areas. Rather, existing buildings were converted for private use, such as the construction of a mansion on the site of St James's Priory by Henry Brayne (Jackson 2006b). At the Dominican Friary in Broadmead, the new owner, William Chester, simply converted the friary into a private residence, surrounded by gardens and orchards. The friary church had been removed, probably fairly soon after the Reformation, as was the Chapter House. The two ranges of the Lesser Cloister, however,

Figure 1.3 Bristol in the late 17th century

were reused and let to the cutlers and bakers guilds (these buildings still survive today), while the tanners guild reused the west range of the Great Cloister (Davenport 2013e, 371). The physical evidence for the effects of the removal of chantries, rood screens and other manifestations of the old religious order has yet to be examined although there may well be evidence surviving within existing churches. The effect of the removal of other symbols of the old religious order, preaching crosses, wayside shrines and other monuments upon the customs and environment of the townspeople remains to be studied in detail.

Initially the period from c 1500 seems to have been one of stagnation and decline, with the cloth industry in particular suffering a decline from which it never recovered. The city's population probably remained more or less static throughout the 16th century, at around 10,000. There is even some evidence of a partial contraction in the built-up area, especially in Redcliffe and Temple where evidence has been found for the demolition of buildings and the reversion of plots to open space for gardening or simply for the disposal of household and industrial waste.

However, the conditions were being created, in the period c 1540 to c 1650, for a major expansion to the urban area and a major shift in its economic base. A significant increase in the urban population, perhaps even doubling in size between 1600 and 1700, created a need to break out beyond the confines of the medieval walled area. Even at the beginning of this period, second residences were becoming established in the more salubrious surroundings on the hills overlooking the valley in which the medieval town was situated. By the late 17th century they were common and were known to contemporaries as lodges, garden houses or summer houses. Often these houses were the antecedents, some by more than a century, of more concerted suburban expansion in the 18th and 19th centuries. They have been the subject of considerable recent study by Dr Roger Leech as part of his study of Bristol houses (Leech 2014, chapter 9). Also during this period, the most prominent merchants were building new mansions, often owing more to rural than urban architectural traditions. One such was Sir John Yonge's Great House, built on the site of the Carmelite Friary. The merchant Robert Aldworth had a house built

south of St Peter's Church. This building later housed the mint and latterly became part of St Peter's Hospital.

The onset of the Civil War in 1642 found Bristol's medieval defences largely intact, but utterly inadequate to cope with the new realities of 17th-century warfare. Therefore a new defensive line was rapidly constructed to the north of the city, extending from the Water Fort at the foot of Brandon Hill and with commanding views of the Avon, to a new fort on the summit of Brandon Hill and thence north-east to a fort at Windmill Hill. From here the line ran through Kingsdown and down to the Frome. It then probably linked with the existing defences around Old Market, reaching the Avon opposite Tower Harratz. There is some evidence that the medieval Portwall was refaced at this period although it has also been suggested that outer works had been constructed to the south of Redcliffe Hill (Russell 2003). It is probable that the defences had been constructed in haste: it was described by the Royalist engineer, Bernard de Gomme, as being 'of meane strength' (Firth 1925). In 1644, the Windmill Hill fort was rebuilt as the Royal Fort under the supervision of de Gomme. Excavation of the site of the Royal Fort in 2009 revealed the eastern ditch, parts of two bastions and a long building interpreted as a barrack block, together with a possible gunpowder magazine (King 2014).

With the more stable political and economic situation following the Civil War, conditions were more suitable for physical expansion than at any time since the 13th century. New housing was laid out along the newly created King Street to the south of the southern town wall. In 1656, the castle was demolished and became a prime development site with new houses constructed within the former precinct area. Surprisingly, given all the archaeological work within the castle, relatively little attention has been given to the archaeological study of this fine group of late 17th-century buildings which survived relatively intact until 1940. Another symbol of the new prosperity within the city following the Restoration was the widespread rebuilding or conversion of older medieval properties on the same site, although there are complex questions of changes in social customs to be considered, especially in relation to the abandonment of the medieval open hall. Rebuilding of earlier medieval properties was widespread, especially within the medieval core of the town, where the wealthiest merchants rebuilt their properties in opulent style. Ornately carved timbers frequently adorned the exteriors of the wealthiest dwellings while within major changes in the use of space were taking place, with the increasing importance of private over public space (Leech 2014, chapter 8).

During this period the first signs of the major changes that were to affect Bristol's trading and manufacturing base may be detected. The loss of Bordeaux in 1453 and the Gascon market must have been a major blow, although Bristol seems to have largely regained its trading position by the end of the century. However, Bristol was facing increasing competition and there is growing evidence for the diversification of trade from its over-reliance on Gascon markets. The cloth industry, the prominent manufacturing industry throughout much of the medieval period was in decline. The Redcliffe and Temple suburbs were particularly affected and during the 16th and 17th centuries suffered considerably by comparison with parishes to the north of the Avon. There is some evidence in the material record for an increase in trading links with the Iberian peninsula, with greater exploitation of the Atlantic trade from the early 17th century onwards. The quantities of Venetian glass, Iberian and Italian pottery found in assemblages from the 16th century, although small relative to the total, corroborate the documentary evidence for a diversification in Bristol's trade at this time. It is likely that much of these more exotic wares found their way to other destinations, such as Acton Court via the port of Bristol.

The changes in trading links also found expression in the major shift in Bristol's manufacturing base, particularly from the mid-17th century onwards. Sugar from the Caribbean allowed the establishment of sugar refining premises throughout the city, while the import of tobacco gave rise to the lucrative clay pipe industry. Other industries, while not directly dependent upon the rapid growth in the trade with North America, nevertheless owed much to the increase in prosperity in the second half of the 17th century. The glass industry flourished from the end of the 17th century, as a comparison between Millerd's maps of 1673 and *c* 1715 makes clear (Figs 3.22

and 3.23), although the precise physical form of this industry has yet to be studied for this early period of its development. The brass manufacturing industry was also becoming established at this time, benefiting in part from the need for commodities to exchange in the notorious triangular trade between England, West Africa and the New World.

The emergence of the modern city (Fig 1.4)

The wealth produced by these newly emerging industries was to receive physical expression in the creation of elegant new squares and streets and in the construction of new public and private buildings. Queen Square was laid out from 1700, with very specific requirements regarding the type of building to be constructed there and strict limitations upon the type of activities to be conducted. The construction of other squares followed, St James Square in 1707, Brunswick Square by 1742 and Portland Square between 1788 and 1790. All of these developments were on land previously undeveloped to any degree and formed part of the major expansion in the built-up area that was taking place from the end of the 17th century. At the same time, medieval monuments, such as the town gates and some of the churches were being rebuilt. New suburbs were being created, some, like Clifton, expanding from earlier medieval nuclei, others, like Kingsdown, built upon previously agricultural land, although in many cases there had been early colonisation by the urban elite in building lodges, garden or summer houses away from the dense urban core. Park Street was created in 1761 and development continued through the 1780s until the end of the boom in speculative development in 1793.

At the same time as the building of fashionable squares and terraces, areas of less exalted artisan housing were being created, presumably in part to serve the employees of the newly emerging industries. Notable among these was the development from the first quarter of the 18th century of the areas north and south of the river Frome. Nathaniel Wade developed a new suburb north of Old Market from *c* 1710 onwards, comprising houses of two-room deep plan. Slightly later, the Penn family were developing the area to the east of the former Dominican Friary: some of these buildings have been

Figure 1.4 Bristol c 1800

archaeologically investigated and the housing showed a contrasting quality, from reasonably sized properties within the former friary precinct to much humbler dwellings to the east (Davenport, 2013f, 388–9). Even close to the medieval core, there were areas of working class housing being created. Immediately to the west of the Cathedral, for example, new streets and housing were being created in the former Bishop's Park with the laying out of College Street and Lower Lamb Street with associated terraces of housing in the late 18th and early 19th centuries (Holt and Leech 2011).

New civic buildings were being constructed: a new Council House was built on the site of the Tolzey in 1704, itself to be replaced in 1824. A major new commercial centre was created with the construction between 1741 and 1743 of the Exchange to a design by John Wood the Elder, while banking facilities were being established during the 18th century to cater for the increase in national and international trade. The first bank was opened in Broad Street in 1750.

The 19th century has generally been seen as a period of significant decline for Bristol, in the face of competition from Liverpool and Glasgow, yet paradoxically it is the period when the city saw the greatest expansion of its developed area since the 13th century (Fig 1.5). New industries were being established, often in areas previously underdeveloped, such as St Judes and St Philips, lying north and south of Old Market, and in the areas to the east of the Dominican Friary. New housing estates were created to cater for the influx of large numbers of workers and their families from neighbouring counties and from Wales and Ireland. In Bedminster, immediately to the south of the city, it has been suggested that the population increased dramatically from 3,000 at the start of the 19th century to 78,000 in 1884 (Bantock and Members of the Malago Society 1997, 7). Despite the apparent overall relative decline, manufacturing industry prospered, although few of the emerging industries have received detailed archaeological

Figure 1.5 Bristol c *1900*

study. New industrial landscapes were being created, a product of the mercantile economy that continued to underpin the prosperity of the 18th- and 19th-century city.

Within the historic core of the city major changes were taking place to facilitate increased traffic caused by the increasing population and improving road communications to and from the city. In 1768, the medieval bridge across the Avon was taken down and replaced by a new stone bridge of three arches. Road improvements included the creation of Bath Street on the south side of the Avon in 1785 to improve access to the new bridge from the south via Temple Street. On the opposite side of the river Bridge Street was created in the 1760s, while a new crossing of the Frome, a bascule bridge constructed in 1714, limited access to the Quay Head to all but the smaller vessels. In 1770 Clare Street was created linking the old city with this bridge. A number of medieval properties were removed to facilitate this.

In the 19th century, major road construction saw the creation of Perry Road and the removal of the narrow Steep Street, in an area of extreme poverty and squalor. In the middle of the 19th century, the construction of Victoria Street cut diagonally through the planned street layout of the medieval suburb of Redcliffe and Temple, severing the line of the medieval Temple Street.

The construction of the Floating Harbour between 1804 and 1809, after decades of discussion about ways to arrest the slow but inexorable decline of the port in the face of competition, radically altered the physical topography of the city. It appears also to have acted as a spur to increased industrial growth, and especially the expansion of port-related activities. At Spike Island, an island created as a result of the construction of the New Cut and Floating Harbour, new docks and shipbuilding facilities were created, notably the dry dock where the SS Great Britain was built. The early creation of a rail network from the late 1820s onwards assisted in the expansion of manufacturing enterprises, especially in east Bristol. In 1837 Henry Stothert took over a former brick manufacturing site in Avon Street in St Philips and set up the Avonside Ironworks, building locomotives which were exported worldwide.

In 1835 the new Council set up by the Municipal Corporations Act had authority over an area six times larger than its predecessor (755 acres (306ha) to 4,461 acres (1,805ha)). By the end of the 19th century, Bristol had further increased its area by two and a half times between 1880 and 1900, with the passing of the Bristol Corporation Act of 1897, and its population had increased by half as much again (Large 1999). New suburbs were being created or massively extended, often engulfing or destroying considerably older rural or semi-urban settlements. With further boundary extensions in the 20th century, bringing in rural hamlets such as Stoke Bishop and Shirehampton, the pattern of modern Bristol was being set, to be radically changed following the widespread destruction of the city centre during the Blitz and post-war remodelling.

Chapter 2: The setting of Bristol: its geology and topography; a deposit model

by Allan N Insole with additions by Robert Jones

Geology

Introduction (Fig 2.1)

Bristol is a geologically complex area. In fact it has the greatest diversity of underlying geology of any British city. Unfortunately very little of the bedrock geology is visible, being hidden by buildings. Bedrock is generally only seen when excavations are made during the construction of new buildings.

The topography of Bristol is very strongly influenced by the character of the local geology. The underlying rock controls the nature of the soil and thus the character of the vegetation and what can be grown in parks and gardens.

Beneath central Bristol, the solid geology (consolidated rocks) consists of rocks representing the Carboniferous to early Jurassic periods. However, the rock sequence is discontinuous with several gaps which represent periods of uplift and erosion (Fig 2.2). Extensive Quaternary deposits of fluvial alluvium underlie much of the central area, forming the river terraces of the Avon and its tributary the Frome, below the soft Triassic Redcliffe sandstone upon which the historic core of Bristol was founded.

The visual character of the older buildings and walls reflect the geology. Usually, the local bedrock provided the building materials for vernacular structures. In areas where there was no suitable building stone available, bricks made from local clays replaced stone. Indeed, it is possible, with a little geological knowledge, to crudely map the varied underlying geology of the city from the extant 19th- and early 20th-century buildings. Building stones, such as the Bath and Portland limestones, were only imported for the construction of prestigious buildings.

The underlying geology around the city also influenced the economy of the city. The development of the local brass industry was due to the local supplies of zinc ore and coal, the availability of water power in the Avon valley and the importation of copper from Cornwall through the Port of Bristol. The famous Bristol glass manufacture again relied on local coal and probably initially sand derived from the so-called 'caves' at Redcliffe, although later the industry relied on sand imported into Bristol from the Isle of Wight.

Carboniferous

1. Upper Cromhall Sandstone

The Upper Cromhall Sandstone consists of quartz sandstones and calcareous sandstones with some limestones and dark grey shales. The unit is organised into sequences which range from limestone through mudstone, siltstone to sandstone. These cycles represent repeated changes in environment from open shallow shelf sea to deltaic conditions and thus several changes in relative sea-level.

2. Quartzitic Sandstone Group (= 'Millstone Grit', Brandon Hill Stone and Brandon Hill Grit)

Rocks of the Quartzitic Sandstone Group are very poorly exposed but occur beneath the fairly steep slopes of Brandon Hill and St Michael's Hill. This geological unit consists of extremely hard, pale grey sandstones, which are pebbly

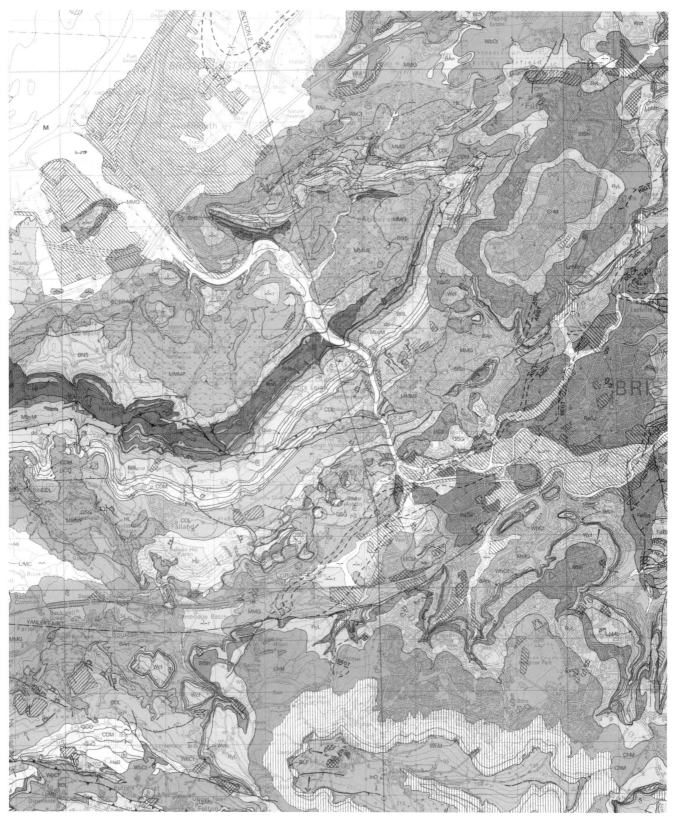

Figure 2.1 The geology of the Bristol area (CP17/017 British Geological Survey © NERC 2004. All rights reserved) (see Fig 2.2 for a cross-section and simplified key)

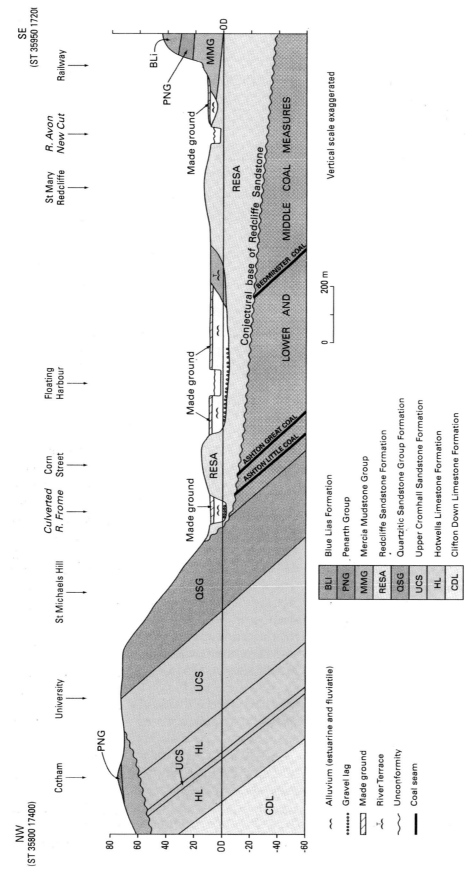

Figure 2.2 Geological cross-section from Cotham to Totterdown, including artificial and Quaternary deposits (CP17/017 British Geological Survey © NERC 2002. All rights reserved)

in places. There are some grey mudstones, seatearths (mudstones containing fossil roots) and carbonaceous (coaly) horizons. This rock unit was deposited in an inland non-marine basin which was rarely penetrated by shallow marine incursions.

3. Coal Measures

The Quartzitic Sandstone Formation passes upwards into the considerably softer strata of the Lower Coal Measures. The approximate boundary of the two being along the base of the main slope north of the city centre with the Coal Measures underlying the low ground extending to the south and east.

The Coal Measures comprise mudstones, thin sandstones and coal seams. This rock unit is unexposed but borehole evidence shows that a lower group of coal seams occur along a line through Canon's Marsh and Broadmead. There is no evidence that these coal seams were mined in this area in the past. This is probably due to the fact that they do not outcrop at surface but are covered by Triassic strata (see below) and more recent Quaternary deposits. There is also evidence to suggest that the seams have been oxidised, and therefore uneconomic to extract.

Higher up in the Coal Measures, the Bedminster Great Coal seam occurs along a line running from beneath the south-east corner of Queen Square via Temple Bridge to Old Market. This seam was worked at depth through Southville, Redcliffe and Temple Meads. All the collieries in this part of Bristol closed before 1926.

Variscan Orogeny

At the end of the Carboniferous major earth movements (the Variscan Orogeny or mountain building episode) occurred. These involved north–south compression and resulted in the folding and fracturing of the Carboniferous strata. This phase of crustal deformation was followed by a period of erosion.

Triassic

Erosion of the Carboniferous rocks produced a topography not dissimilar to that of today with high ground in Failand Ridge, Clifton and Durdham Downs region and low ground in the city centre area. Triassic non-marine sediments were deposited on this irregular erosion surface.

1. Dolomitic Conglomerate

The erosion surface is directly overlain by a rock unit called the Dolomitic Conglomerate. Where it is seen in the Avon Gorge, it can be seen to be 'banked up' against what were originally the steep slopes of the underlying Carboniferous rocks. The Dolomitic Conglomerate consists of a mass of angular to rounded sandstone and limestone pebbles and boulders in a buff to red sandy marl or fine-grained sandstone matrix. The pebbles were derived from the underlying Carboniferous rocks. The Dolomitic Conglomerate represents 'fossil' scree deposits. The climate was arid but with occasional flash floods.

The Dolomitic Conglomerate has been mapped as infilling a 'palaeovalley' cut in the Carboniferous strata. This stretches from Whiteladies Road through Triangle West to Berkeley Square, in the lower part of Jacob's Wells Road, and on the Hotwells slopes above Dowry Square. Away from the steep Carboniferous slopes, the Dolomitic Conglomerate passes laterally into the Redcliffe Sandstone which occupies much of the central Bristol area.

2. Redcliffe Sandstone Formation

The Redcliffe Sandstone Formation is a distinctive dark red ferruginous, fine- to medium-grained sandstone that underlies much of the city centre (Fig 2.2). This rock unit was deposited in an elongate depression extending from Stapleton in the east to Bedminster in the south-west. In central Bristol, the rock consists of red calcareous and ferruginous sandstone up to 40 metres in thickness. Bristol Castle was built on a promontory of this sandstone, but the best exposures are found in the riverside cliffs at Redcliffe Parade and in the New Cut along Coronation Road, Southville.

3. Mercia Mudstone

The Redcliffe Sandstone passes laterally into red mudstones of the Mercia Mudstone group (formerly called the 'Keuper Marl'). As with the Dolomitic Conglomerate and Redcliffe Sandstone, these mudstones rest on an irregular Carboniferous surface, as for example across much of Redland, Cotham, Tyndalls Park and Kingsdown.

The Mercia Mudstone comprises mudstone mainly red in colour but with green mottles and bands. The unit is up to 55 metres thick. It was deposited in a shallow non-marine basin which experienced wet and dry seasons.

4. Blue Anchor Formation

The Mercia Mudstone passes upwards into a greenish-grey mudstone, the Blue Anchor Formation (formerly called 'Tea Green Marl') which is about 4 metres in thickness. This mudstone was deposited in the same basin as the Mercia Mudstone but the climate was wetter so that a shallow lake was almost permanently present.

5. Westbury and Lilstock Formations

The Westbury and Lilstock Formations were formerly united in the Rhaetic but are now recognised as two separate units, which form the high ground in Cotham, north-west of the city centre.

The Westbury Formation consists of dark grey or black mudstone with thin, dark grey limestone bands. The fossils in the limestones indicate a shallow marine environment while the mudstones were deposited in a lagoonal environment. Thus, relative sea-level was generally rising at this time.

The Lilstock Formation (= White Lias) comprises hard, white, flaggy, fine-grained limestones. The famous Cotham or Landscape Marble is a thin, pale limestone with a curious irregularly ridged hummocky upper surface, which occurs in the lower part of the Lilstock Formation (Cotham Member). This limestone has a basal convex upward layer. When cut and polished the rock shows a landscape of dark grey 'hedges' and 'trees' with a pale grey mud in the hollows between them (the 'sky'). This distinctive horizon was formed by the growth of algal mats in a tidal flat environment. This stone was widely used as a decorative stone by the Victorians.

Jurassic

1. Blue Lias Formation

The youngest solid rock unit in central Bristol is the Blue Lias, although its outcrop lies just outside the study area. This comprises alternations of blue grey mudstones and limestones, each individual bed generally averaging about 150mm in thickness. It is found capping the hill crest in the vicinity of Cotham High School. This rock unit was deposited in a fully marine environment.

While younger Mesozoic rocks (Jurassic and Cretaceous) were undoubtedly laid down in the area, they were subsequently completely eroded.

Quaternary

Over the last two million years or so the climate of Britain has varied tremendously with periods of temperate climate interrupted by repeated advances and retreats of glaciers and ice sheets. Collectively these periods have become known as the Ice Ages. We are currently in the most recent of the temperate phases. The actions of the ice sheets and associated climatic changes have been instrumental in forming the British landscape we see today. There is some evidence to indicate that an ice sheet moved into the Bristol area during one of the early glaciations, but Quaternary deposits are notoriously difficult to date.

Geomorphology: a deposit model

Recent modelling of the stratigraphic sequence from the solid geology to the modern ground level, as part of an English Heritage-funded project to look at urban waterlogged deposits, has characterised the strata making up much of the central area of Bristol (Wilkinson *et al* 2013b). The study grouped the stratigraphy into a number of categories in order to separate archaeological strata from post-medieval made ground, to identify waterlogged and non-waterlogged deposits and to separate different intertidal/alluvial facies (see below).

Much of the landscape evolution of the central Bristol area can be related to the stripping off of the Mesozoic cover over the last 1–2 million years, to reveal the old Triassic landscape beneath. This revealed much of the underlying folded Carboniferous landscape. It is probable that the pre-Triassic topography was in many ways similar to that seen today, with high ground along the Clifton Carboniferous Limestone ridge to the north-west and low ground excavated in the softer Coal Measures through the centre of the city. This former topography has now been partially exhumed and subsequently modified by recent erosion following uplift during the Tertiary.

The topography of central Bristol exhibits the huge changes wrought by man, especially over the last 1,000 years. The historic core is dominated by the valleys of the Avon and

Table 1 Categories used in the classification of data (reproduced from Wilkinson et al 2013b, table 2)

Unit	Description	Category
Made Ground	Strata not of archaeological interest, includes deposits where archaeological interest cannot be determined (eg boreholes)	Made Ground
Archaeological Strata 1	Medieval/post-medieval deposits without identified organic preservation	Made Ground
Archaeological Strata 2	Medieval/post-medieval deposits with identified organic preservation (waterlogged)	Made Ground
Proto-urban deposits	Deposits at the top of the Wentlooge Formation, including disturbed ('trampled') alluvium with marsh conditions. Identified in some archaeological works and included in the database where identified	Wentlooge Formation/Made Ground
Alluvium 1	Wentlooge Formation deposits encountered below made ground	Wentlooge Formation
Archaeological Strata 3	Strata containing evidence of human activity outcropping below Alluvium 1	Made Ground
Peat	Peat	Wentlooge Formation
Alluvium 2	Wentlooge Formation deposits encountered below Peat	Wentlooge Formation
Alluvium 3	Alluvial sand strata (probably point bar deposits) encountered below Alluvium 1 in ARCA borehole records (mainly in the Redcliffe area)	Wentlooge Formation
Pleistocene gravels	Avon Formation – fluvial strata emplaced by the River Severn during the Pleistocene (mainly channel gravels)	Avon Formation
Mercia Mudstone	Sand, silts and conglomerates deposited in (mainly) alluvial fan environments in the Triassic (252.2–201 my BP)	Mercia Mudstone Group

Frome, which merge in central Bristol. Both rivers have been greatly modified over the years by man. The excavation of a new channel for the river Frome in the 1240s represents an immense engineering operation, all the more notable given its early date, and has influenced subsequent development, especially of the port, since then. Equally remarkable was the excavation of the New Cut between 1804 and 1809 to divert the tidal river Avon south and east of the city centre, part of the development of the non-tidal Floating Harbour. Both the Avon and the upper Frome valleys were probably developed about 30 million years ago when the area was a low-lying flat plain. Erosion then stripped off the cover rocks to reveal the harder Carboniferous rocks beneath. At some point a tributary of the Avon eroded the soft Triassic sandstone north-eastwards through what is now Broadmead to capture the upper Frome. Meanwhile the Avon stayed on course and began to cut down into the Carboniferous Limestone ridge to create the Avon Gorge.

The glacial and warm climatic oscillations during the Quaternary had a marked effect on the geomorphology of the area. There were four major periods of glaciation but it appears that the Bristol area was probably not glaciated, although at least once the margin of an ice sheet came very close.

With every ice advance, the area experienced periglacial conditions when rock and soil were subject to intense freezing and thawing cycles. In the warmer phases the climate was as warm or even warmer than today. In one temperate phase, hippopotamuses lived in the rivers of southern Britain.

During transition from a temperate to a cold phase, sea-level fell as considerable volumes of water were frozen in glaciers and ice caps. This resulted in the erosional downcutting of the river channels and the deposition of gravels in the middle and upper reaches of rivers. Fluvial erosion continued and was enhanced by episodic high-energy river discharge in a periglacial environment, the rivers being supplied seasonally by ground-ice and snow-patch melt (Bates and Wenban-Smith 2005). This caused flooding and high rates of coarse-grained sediment transport. As a consequence, the rivers consisted of a network of small channels separated by small and often temporary gravel islands known overall as braided channels. The channels repeatedly migrated sideways forming gravel sheets. During the succeeding temperate period, sea level rose, river discharge fell and silt and clay infilled the river channels.

At the beginning of the next cold phase, sea level dropped again causing erosion in the river floodplains. Borehole evidence shows that the Avon eventually cut its channel to a depth of 10.65m below present sea level in the Cumberland Basin. This led to the formation of paired river gravel terraces in the valleys. Three such terraces have been identified in the Bristol area but only a fragment of one, the so-called Floodplain (No 1) Terrace occurs within the study area, near Redcliffe Way. The age of this terrace is unknown. If any other terrace deposits were originally laid down in central Bristol, they may have been subsequently eroded away or destroyed by construction work.

The Avon Formation

The recent deposit model has suggested that this terrace may be one of the later of a series of Pleistocene fluvial terraces of the Avon valley, forming part of the Avon Formation (Wilkinson *et al* 2013b).

Deposits of the Avon Formation are found beneath strata of the Wentlooge Formation within the central urban area, with the surface elevation of the stratum varying between −3 and +8m OD (Fig 2.3).

Wilkinson *et al* (2013b) have suggested that river terraces might be found to the north-east of Castle Park and to the north-west around the St Georges Road and Deanery Road area, with a younger river terrace to be found elsewhere. The modelled thickness of the Avon Formation suggests few patterns although thicker deposits are found from the central and southern part of Redcliffe to Queen Square and Canon's Marsh, perhaps suggesting the main axis of the late Pleistocene river Avon (Wilkinson *et al* 2013b, 26–7) (Fig 2.4).

This is reinforced by the assumption that the younger terrace found in boreholes dates to the end of the last glacial period and that subsequent variations to its surface are the result of Holocene processes. Thus the lowest elevations of the terrace, in the southern part of Redcliffe might indicate a pre- or early Holocene course of the river Avon, while a similar depression around the western end of Baldwin Street in the Marsh Street/Broad Quay area might indicate an early Holocene confluence between the Avon and the Frome.

The Wentlooge Formation

At the end of the last glacial period about 12,000 years ago, sea level began to rise. As a result, the deep trench formed by the Avon was gradually infilled by the deposition of silt and clay. This process continues today, but it is now infilling the artificial New Cut. The silt and clay comprise intertidal strata of the Severn Estuary, known as the Wentlooge Formation (Allen and Rae 1987), dating from the beginning of the Holocene until the commencement of construction of sea defences or the formation of natural barriers to saltmarsh in the Roman period. In central Bristol the process of accretion of the Wentlooge Formation only terminated with the establishment of the first settlement and the construction of barriers and river defences, generally assumed to be in the late 10th century (but see Chapter 4 below). Strata of the Wentlooge Formation underlie all areas in the floodplains of the Avon and Frome rivers, ie outside the area of the early medieval historic core which lies on Triassic Redcliffe sandstone and below the high ground in the north-west of the study area which is formed of deposits of the Quartzitic Sandstone Formation (Fig 2.5).

A *terminus post quem* for the beginning of intertidal deposition of strata forming the Wentlooge Formation is provided by two AMS ^{14}C dates, one from a palaeosol which produced wood charcoal at the base of the Wentlooge Formation at 32–36 Victoria Street, Redcliffe (BHER 4389), of *c* 5200 cal BC (*c* 7.2ky BP) (Beta 245646, 6280±40 BP). The second comes from an alder tree stump found at Canon's Marsh during archaeological monitoring of the construction of a new underground car park in 1998 (BHER 3371). Here the date obtained was *c* 4840–4460 cal BC (*c* 5.5ky BP).

The Wentlooge Formation sequence has, for the purposes of modelling the stratigraphic data, been subdivided into sub-units Alluvium 3, Alluvium 2, Peat, Archaeological Strata 3, Alluvium 1 and proto-urban deposits (*see* Table 1 above). Alluvium 3 was only encountered in Redcliffe and consists of well-sorted, laminated and thinly bedded medium sands to gravels. This stratum probably formed on a large point bar, on the inner edge of a meander which was still forming as late as 1450 cal BC (based on an AMS ^{14}C date from 32–36 Victoria Street (Wk 25623, 3208±31 BP). Alluvium 2 is only defined as a stratum that underlies peat deposits and thus is not strictly separate from Alluvium 1 which overlies the

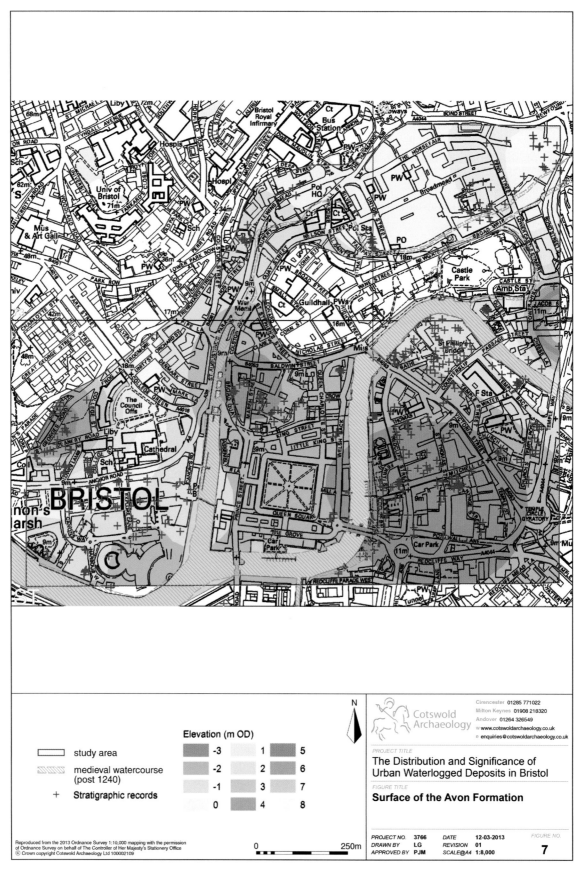

Figure 2.3 Surface of the Avon Formation (reproduced from Wilkinson et al *2013b, fig 7)*

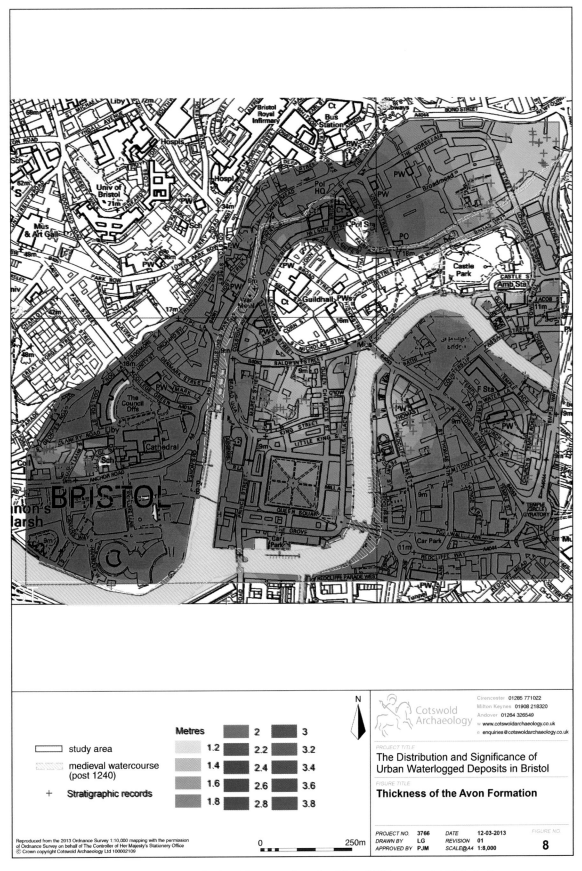

Figure 2.4 Thickness of the Avon Formation (reproduced from Wilkinson et al 2013b, fig 8)

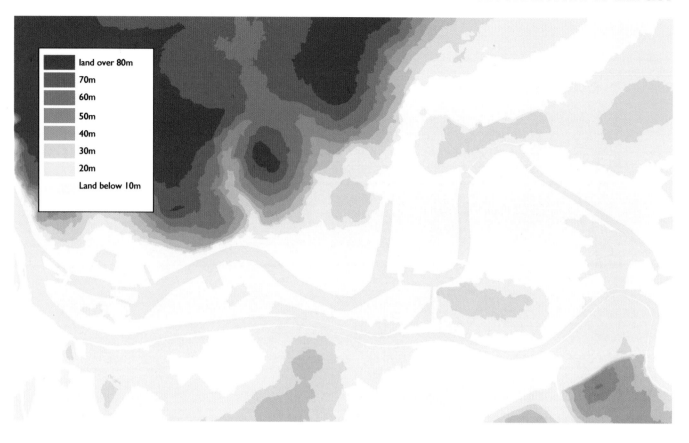

land over 80m
70m
60m
50m
40m
30m
20m
Land below 10m

Figure 2.5 Contour plan using LiDAR data for central Bristol

peat. However, it was noted that Alluvium 2 appeared in geoarchaeological boreholes to be better bedded and had not been subjected to the same degree of post-depositional modification (Wilkinson *et al* 2013b, 31). Organic strata, collectively termed as 'peat' for the purposes of the deposit model, have been found in several places within the central core. These have been dated in several locations: from the Deanery Road area west of the Cathedral (BHER 3822) where dates of *c* 4000–3200 cal BC (*c* 6–5.2ky BP) have been obtained, based on AMS ¹⁴C dates from two organic samples (Wk 10946, 4594±63 BP and Wk 10947 5174±61 BP) (Wilkinson *et al* 2002; Wilkinson 2006); from Broadmead dates ranging from *c* 4300–2600 cal BC (6.3–4.6ky BP) were obtained from seven AMS ¹⁴C samples from bulk organic samples (Wilkinson *et al* 2013b, 28; Wilkinson 2013, 333). The development of the organic strata and the associated development of intertidal and freshwater marsh indicates a constriction of the estuary and its tributaries and a slow-down in the rate of relative sea level rise. Studies of these strata from Canon's Marsh and from the Deanery Road and Broadmead sites suggest that the organic strata formed

initially during the late Mesolithic in the lower lying valley areas in saltmarsh environments and then during the Neolithic on the valley sides in freshwater backswamp environments (Wilkinson *et al* 2013b, 32).

The uppermost level of the Wentlooge Formation ('Alluvium 1') must have formed after 3200–2600 cal BC but before the early medieval settlement of Bristol, at least in the river valleys. The upper level of the Wentlooge Formation as it meets the overlying 'Made Ground' corresponds broadly with the modern topography with the higher levels of this stratum found on the valley sides and the lowest being adjacent to the present course of the Avon and to the east of Broadmead, the latter possibly reflecting a former course of the river Frome. The thickness of the Wentlooge Formation may indicate the location of earlier watercourses. It is at its thinnest on the valley sides, in the St Georges Road/Deanery Road area to the west, in the Lewins Mead and Fairfax Street areas, the latter presumably indicating their locations adjacent to the Frome channel. However, similar thin Wentlooge strata are found south of Queen Square and in the southern part of Redcliffe. Thick deposits of Wentlooge strata are found in Canon's Marsh and at the Baldwin Street/Marsh Street junction, as well as in the area north of Lewins Mead and east of Broadmead (Fig 2.6). These may indicate the former position of the river Frome with a pre-medieval course running into Canon's Marsh and meeting the Avon somewhere south of the present Pero's Bridge. Similarly the deeper Wentlooge Formation deposits to the east of Broadmead may suggest a former course of the Frome in that area, as suggested above.

In two geoarchaeological boreholes used in the deposit modelling project there was evidence for human activity within the Wentlooge Formation. At 32–36 Victoria Street (BHER 4389) a palaeosol producing wood charcoal of late Mesolithic date has already been mentioned. From Broadmead, tile fragments were found at 7.54m below ground level (+1.95m OD), possibly of Romano-British date. It is possible that there is other evidence for human occupation in the pre-medieval period but commercial geotechnical boreholes are generally not refined enough to extract such data while archaeological excavation cannot penetrate into these deeply buried strata. Indirect evidence for human activity during the Neolithic has come from microbiological and sedimentological evidence which suggests human manipulation of the surrounding vegetation and clearance of the woodland to create clearance for cultivation.

Archaeological strata

An important component of the deposit model project was to identify and model waterlogged sequences with archaeological potential (defined as 'Archaeological Strata 2' in the deposit model – see Table 1 above). Such deposits will generally be associated with the period following the settlement of Bristol from the late 10th century, although the potential for earlier pre-medieval settlement evidence has already been identified, particularly from microbiological and sedimentological analyses (see above). The identification of waterlogged deposits is dependent on the quality of the data, usually from programmes of archaeological investigation. Identification of such material is usually impossible from commercial geotechnical work, while in geoarchaeological prospection the separation of waterlogged deposits of medieval date will depend upon the retrieval of associated datable materials. In general it appeared that the greatest thicknesses of waterlogged archaeological deposits occurred, not unexpectedly, in the waterfront areas of Redcliffe, around Bristol Bridge and on the east side of Temple Back, with reasonably thick deposits on the north bank of the river Frome and on the Welsh Back frontage. The relatively shallow thickness of waterlogged deposits from the centre of Redcliffe might be explained by the fact that the upper level of the underlying Wentlooge Formation is relatively high in the area ($>c$ 6.5m OD). The apparent absence of waterlogged archaeological deposits from the area between Marsh Street and Queen Charlotte Street between the inner town wall and the Marsh Wall might be explained by the fact that the only data were from commercial boreholes, which, as discussed above, are unlikely to allow the identification of such deposits. There is a similar lack of reliable data from the area between the inner town wall and the later town wall on the south bank of the river Frome, in the Nelson Street area (Fig 2.7).

Bristol's pre-urban environment

The complex geology and topography of the city and what is known about the former courses of the rivers Avon and Frome have already been described. This is central to any understanding of development of landscape and vegetation and to the identification of areas of potential for recovery of data from excavation. For the pre-urban period (ie before c 1000 AD), the archaeological record relies on the survival of buried soils (former land surfaces), sediment sequences such as peats and alluvial silts from the river floodplains and the plant and animal remains preserved within them. The evidence from early maps and documents is also vital and has been cited widely elsewhere in this volume.

Much of the area covered in this volume lies within the floodplains of the rivers Avon and Frome. The high ground upon which the first settlement of Bristol was founded lies on an outcrop of Redcliffe Sandstone of the Triassic. The river floodplains, as we have seen, comprise thick (up to 7.5m in the centre of Bristol) strata which make up the Wentlooge Formation dating from the beginning of the Holocene (or at least from c 5200 cal BC in

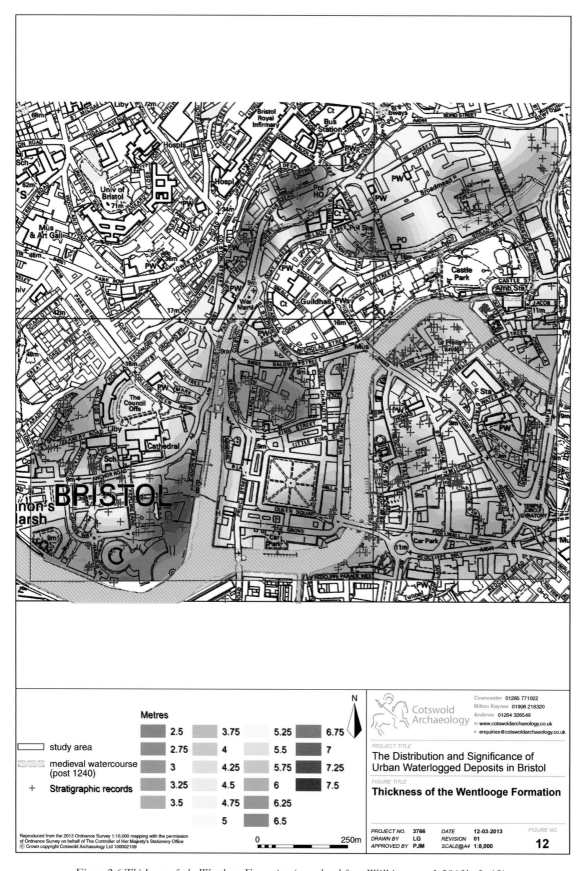

Figure 2.6 Thickness of the Wentlooge Formation (reproduced from Wilkinson et al 2013b, fig 12)

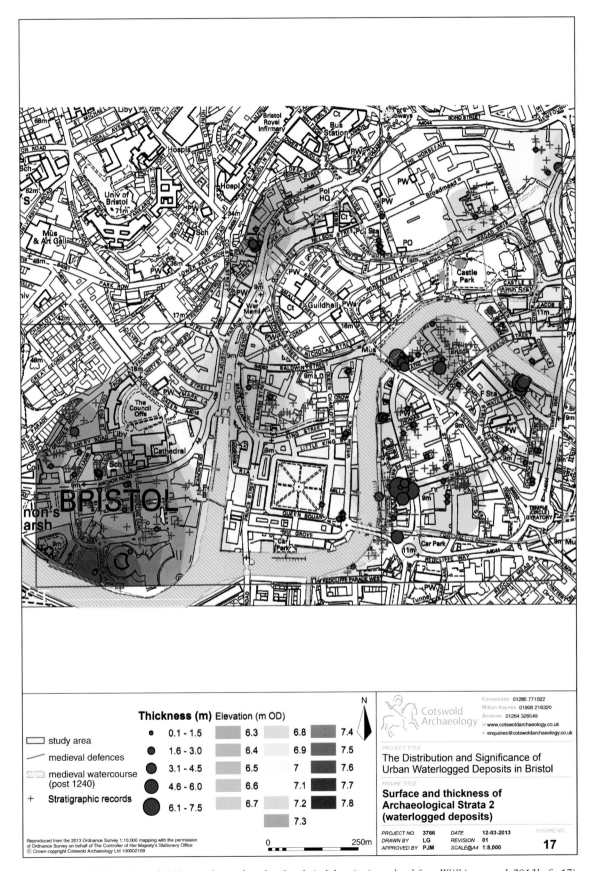

Figure 2.7 Modelled surface and thickness of waterlogged archaeological deposits (reproduced from Wilkinson et al 2013b, fig 17)

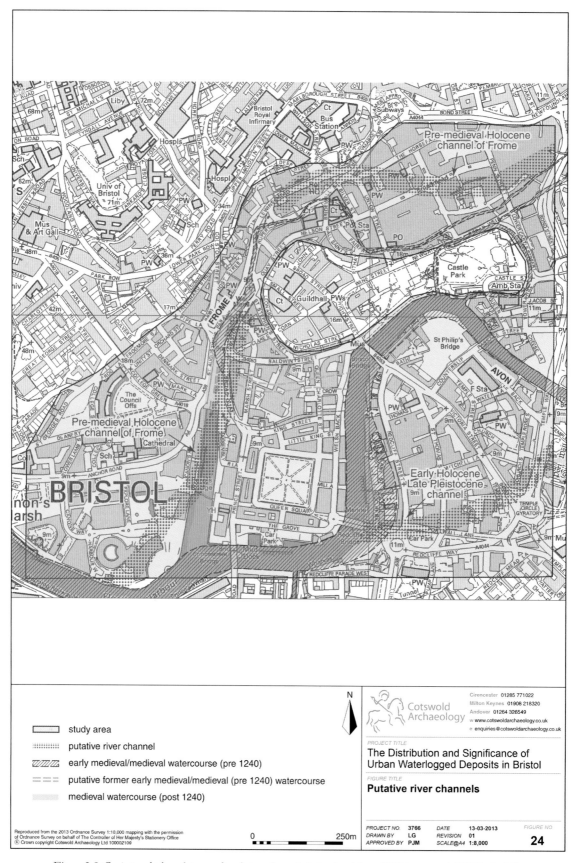

Figure 2.8 Conjectured plan of pre-medieval river channels (reproduced from Wilkinson et al 2013b, fig 24)

Bristol) until the commencement of settlement in the Late Saxon period.

On the basis of the deposit modelling undertaken so far, tentative hypotheses can be put forward regarding the changing courses of the two major rivers, the Avon and Frome. It may be suggested, on the basis of the occurrence of point bar deposits in the Redcliffe area, that the present course of the river Avon as it flows in a meander around the north side of Redcliffe is the result of continual deposition of such deposits from the late Pleistocene which was still continuing in the middle Bronze Age. The late Pleistocene course of the Avon might thus be predicted to have run in the southern part of the Redcliffe peninsula. Likewise the pre-medieval course of the river Frome may be suggested from the modelling of the surface elevation and the thickness of the Avon Formation. The thickness of the Wentlooge Formation might be another indicator, with the Frome running in a NNE–SSW course to meet the Avon below Canon's Marsh (for a hypothetical plan showing the pre-medieval course of the rivers Avon and Frome see Fig 2.8).

The analysis of organic strata has suggested that in the lower lying valley areas, saltmarsh environments were developing in the late Mesolithic while during the Neolithic peats were being formed in freshwater alder carr higher on the valley sides. Human activity associated with these deposits has not been found, apart from proxy indicators of woodland clearance. The likelihood of finding direct evidence for human activity, given the considerable depths at which these deposits occur, must be considered to be low, although any evidence for such activity would be of the highest significance and as indicators of the prevailing palaeoenvironment they are of great value. Nevertheless sheltered marshes with easy access to adjacent woodland resources would have provided abundant food and raw materials for Mesolithic hunter-gatherer communities. The area would have provided habitats for wild game birds, waterfowl, red deer, aurochs, wild boar and much more as well having varied sources of plant food. The reports of artefacts including Bronze Age metalwork confirm the use of the area by later prehistoric farming communities. Their field systems remain on the Downs and in the grounds of Ashton Court, but they could also have extended much closer to the city centre but have since been destroyed (*see* Chapter 4).

Chapter 3: The history of archaeology in Bristol: archaeologists and visual sources

The archaeologists

Ardent antiquaries naturally specialise; but apart from definite study members engaged in the every-day business of life could often spare time for enquiry into matters of historic changes in their own district, or for the arrest of specimens in case of unexpected discovery, which should be systematically and permanently recorded (Pritchard 1903, 139).

Introduction

John Pritchard's vision of the archaeological community in Bristol fully engaged in rescue archaeology was not realised in his lifetime but the idea is grounded in reality. Bristol has a remarkable tradition of active research which stretches over six centuries, a good deal of which is still used in research into the city's past. Before the late 19th century much of this body of work took the form of annals but, as Jonathan Barry (1996, 55) has made clear, it was nonetheless situated firmly within Bristol's wider cultural life and cannot properly be understood without awareness of this context.

Seen and touched by me: William Worcestre's Itinerary

The first to investigate Bristol's historic fabric in any depth was William Worcestre. Worcestre was born in Bristol in 1415, in the parish of St James (*ODNB*), and was educated at Great Hart Hall, Oxford, from 1432. By 1438 he had become secretary to the Norfolk landowner Sir John Falstolf and lived for some of the year at the knight's residence at Caister. Worcestre was despatched to London and elsewhere on Falstolf's business and much of what we know of him comes from correspondence, some amongst the letters of the Paston family

to whom Falstolf was related (*see* Davies 1971–6). When Falstolf died in November 1459 Worcestre became his executor and was involved in a series of lawsuits arising from disputes over the settlement of the estate (Richmond 1996). As a consequence of the ultimate settlement of Falstolf's estate Worcestre gained property in London and at Pockthorpe near Norwich, and it is assumed that until his death in the early 1480s his main home was in Norfolk.

Worcestre wrote several volumes on historical and other subjects during his career (McFarlane 1957) but the itinerary is perhaps the most unusual of his works. Elements of the itinerary were published by Nasmith (1778), Dallaway (1834) and by Harvey (1969). The full text of the survey of Bristol was translated for the first time by Frances Neale (Neale 2000). The manuscript describes the topography of Bristol, recording the dimensions of most of its major monuments and streets (Corpus Christi College MS 210) and was written, mainly in Latin, during a visit Worcestre made to Bristol between late August and late September 1480 (Neale 2000, vii). Worcestre gives his measurements in yards or gressus – his own paces, walking heel-to-toe, which have been calculated at 21–2 inches long (Harvey 1969) – and he may have counted them using his finger joints, writing in his totals later (Neale 2000, viii). The survey usually contains the most precise, and often the only, contemporary description of a medieval monument, and frequently contains other valuable incidental detail. Worcestre also talked to local people to gather information, notably to the porter of Bristol Castle who provided him with his information on the castle keep (Neale 2000, 222–3). As a result Worcestre's survey is one of the few places where something of the perceptions which medieval Bristolians themselves had of their town can be found.

The dignity of being the Second City: antiquarians of the 18th and 19th century

Others soon followed Worcestre in describing Bristol, notably John Leland in the 1540s (Toulmin-Smith 1906–10) and William Camden in the 1570s but these are far less intensive surveys and both men lacked Worcestre's familiarity with the town. Camden's *Britannia* is, however, significant in dismissing as mythical the foundation of the town by Brennus and Belinus *c* 369 BC, refuting any pre-Saxon date, and arguing that not until the reign of Henry I was a castle built. This denial of the antiquity of the city was not, however, accepted by the majority of those writing its histories who, then and later, sought an urban pedigree to match its contemporary significance. There was also more focused recording; the heraldic symbols, monuments and inscriptions of Bristol's churches were recorded in the third quarter of the 17th century, for example (Bristol Archives AC/36074(88)). However, only in the late 18th century did research begin to examine the development of the city in detail. Histories of Gloucestershire, by Samuel Rudder, and Somerset, by the Revd John Collinson, both had long chapters on the parishes in and surrounding Bristol (Rudder 1779; Collinson 1791) but the most substantial work to deal exclusively with the city was William Barrett's 1789 *The History and Antiquities of the City of Bristol*, a book long notorious among students of Bristol for its errors. Barrett was born in Wiltshire in the late 1720s, was apprenticed to a Bristol barber-surgeon in 1744 (Gray 1981, 70–1) and chose to practise and to live in Bristol when it was completed in 1751. He qualified as a surgeon in 1755 and was appointed as doctor to St Peter's Hospital in the same year (Bettey 2003, 2; 7). After a successful medical career he retired to Wraxall, and died in October 1789 in his early 60s. Barrett embarked on research for his history in the 1750s and in August 1760, 'having great materials for such a work by me & continually adding to my store', obtained access to the City records from the Mayor as he was 'in great want of some records out of the Chamber which wou'd throw new lights

upon some obscure parts of the history' (ibid). It seems, from the comments Barrett made in his preface, that a large part of his research had been completed when intention to publish was advertised in the early 1770s (Barrett 1789, v), but the book did not finally appear until the middle of 1789. Like most other historians of Bristol, Barrett was keen to establish that the city's origins were of an antiquity suitable for a city 'exalted,' as his dedication put it, 'to the dignity of being the Second City in the kingdom'. As Barry pointed out, Barrett was the heir to two traditions of historical writing about Bristol. The first was the writing of annals, reflected in the devotion of the final part of the book to a chronology of the city, while the second was a tradition of scholarly research. Barrett had access to a considerable body of work, much unpublished, which had been compiled over several decades (Barry 1996, 56–9). He blended antiquarianism and history, making observations in and around the city. Barrett visited the hillforts of the Avon Gorge, and noted possible Roman structural remains during the construction of the Floating Dock at Sea Mills. He reported other Roman material, 'a curious Roman urn with two handles, tiles, bricks and broken potsherds,' found at Clifton Down (Barrett 1789, 10) and collected Roman coins found in the local area, using these observations to emphasise Bristol's continuity with urban Rome and identifying the city with *Caer Brito*.

The *History and Antiquities* is now widely discredited because of his reliance in the description of medieval Bristol on documents allegedly written by a contemporary monk, Thomas Rowley, but in reality fabricated by Thomas Chatterton. These forgeries, poems and accounts of events and monuments, were produced on scraps cut from medieval documents in the muniment room of St Mary Redcliffe. Chatterton tried unsuccessfully to interest the metropolitan literary establishment in publishing the Rowley documents. The documents provoked debate on their authenticity but most authorities noticed their falsity, most famously Horace Walpole who wrote to Chatterton in 1769 that he would 'never print those extracts as genuine' (Taylor 1971, 376). Chatterton moved from Bristol to London early in 1770 to make his living as a writer but after meeting some success (Suarez 1993–4) took his own life that August. The controversy over the Rowley material survived its creator. Members of Dr Johnson's Literary Club were discussing the documents in April 1771 and Johnson himself intervened to dismiss them in 1776. A rather polarised debate on the place of the poems in the development of English poetry continued until a monograph by Edmond Malone in 1782 authoritatively demonstrated their fraudulence (Rogers 1999).

This extraordinary affair has usually been considered from Chatterton's perspective rather than that of Barrett. Given the dispute over the Rowley material, Barrett's apparently unquestioning acceptance of it is difficult to explain. Indeed, so slight was the justification for trust, that some have charged Barrett with collusion. The answer may simply be misplaced trust. Chatterton claimed he was a welcome visitor to Barrett and that the barber-surgeon was 'not below asking my Advice in any matters of Antiquity' (Taylor 1971, 339). As for Barrett 'no one surely' he wrote 'ever had such good fortune as myself in procuring manuscripts and ancient deeds to help me in investigating the history and antiquities of this city' (*Gentleman's Magazine*, 56, 544, quoted in *ODNB*). Consequently he made the Rowley manuscripts so much a part of the history that, in the words of one of Chatterton's Victorian biographers, 'neither he nor anyone else could separate the golden threads from the worthless tissue, without destroying the whole' (Wilson 1869, 120). He could hardly have been unaware of the disputes over the veracity of the texts even if he was not following the debates of London literary society because London literary society came to him. When Johnson and Boswell visited Bristol in April 1776 they went to view some of the manuscripts. The pair found the documents 'were executed very artificially; but from a careful inspection of them, and a consideration of the circumstances with which they were attended, we were quite satisfied of the imposture' (Boswell 1980, 752). Barrett could scarcely have been ignorant of this verdict but he still did not reconsider. Chatterton's own explanation, stated frankly in his poem 'Happiness', was simple – Barrett was a fool (Taylor 1971, 407). Barrett's culpability remains open to debate but he had far more to lose, indeed did lose, than to gain from accepting the truth of Rowley. The kindest verdict is, perhaps, that he lacked the critical skills necessary for his self-imposed task, yet, despite Chatterton, his

work, as Cronne observed, contains 'important material whose authenticity has been established by research' (Cronne 1946, 3).

Barrett's work overlapped with that of Samuel Seyer (1757–1831), an Oxford graduate, master of Royal Fort School and ultimately the curate of Horfield and rector of Filton, north of Bristol. Seyer published a number of works on ecclesiastical subjects and a collection of charters and Letters Patent relating to Bristol (Seyer 1812) but his major work was a two-volume history of Bristol which was published in the early 1820s (Seyer 1821–3). This built directly on Barrett's work and Seyer makes clear in the preface to his work that he 'was in the constant habit of conversation' with Barrett 'and sometimes saw what he wrote, before it was printed.' Seyer, like Barrett, received help from other researchers and 'few days passed without hearing or seeing something … worthy of observation; a gothic window never before noticed, a fragment of the town-wall, the house where Cromwell was lodged, and the like' (Seyer 1821–3, v–vi). Seyer also made use of several major documentary collections, including the Berkeley papers, though unlike Barrett he failed to gain access to the City's records. His request was refused apparently because of a fear that the legal basis of some of Bristol's privileges might be called into question, as had happened in Newcastle-upon-Tyne (Bettey 2003, 16–17). His work contains useful descriptions of several monuments and finds in the early 19th century but its treatment of the historical period reflects the annalist tradition of Bristol historiography.

Many Relics To Watch: the establishment of the local societies

During the 19th century there was a noticeable shift in the character of work in Bristol towards detailed record in its own right, and this was initially most evident in the examination of historic buildings. This had roots in a number of places but one source was an interest on the part of the architectural profession. Certainly the best-known architect recording Bristol buildings was E W Godwin, who was born in the city in 1833. Godwin began his career as an architect in Bristol and at the age of eighteen he was part of a trio which had made and published surveys on four Bristol churches (Burder, Hine and Godwin 1851). He founded his own architectural practice three years later. Godwin's interest in Bristol's historic buildings continued well into the following decade and he made surveys of surviving elements of several ecclesiastical buildings as well as a brief description of the extant historic buildings in the city centre (Godwin 1863; 1867). George Pryce, the City Librarian, was also working on Bristol's historic buildings. Pryce visited several buildings in the 1850s, recording the surviving medieval roof of No 41 High Street, The Nails in Corn Street, St Mary Redcliffe and a number of wall paintings in the Old Deanery at College Green (Anon 1859). He published works on these investigations and others on the history and historians of Bristol (Pryce 1850). The national societies paid attention to Bristol, with both the British Archaeological Association and the Archaeological Institute making regular visits. The vehicle for much of the subsequent work which took place was, however, the local societies. The largest of these was, and is still, the Bristol and Gloucestershire Archaeological Society. The impetus for the society was a paper on the antiquities of the area written by John Taylor at the time of the British Archaeological Association visit in 1874. This paper was displayed in the Bristol City Library for those who were interested to sign. A public meeting was subsequently held, a committee established to consider forming a society, and Dr John Beddoe FRS, a future President of the Anthropological Institute, elected to its chair, 'thus giving a guarantee to Science that the new Society meant neither diletanteism [sic], nor picnics, nor any combination of the two' (Anon 1876, 11). Beddoe was to produce a number of reports over the next three decades on human skeletal material discovered in the city (see for example Beddoe 1878–9; 1904–6; 1906). The inaugural public meeting was held in April 1876 at Bristol's Museum and on 3 May the Society's Council met for the first time. There were more than 400 founding members and membership was nearly 550 by 1913 while it currently stands at over 800. Almost all of those actively studying the archaeology and history of the city in the late 19th century were members. The other local archaeological society particularly notable for the fieldwork activities of its members was the Clifton Antiquarian Club. According to his own account, the Club was the inspiration of Alfred E Hudd who proposed that 'a small society of persons interested in archaeological subjects was wanted in Bristol.'

A preliminary meeting, to which carefully selected prospective members were invited, was held at Hudd's home at Pembroke Road, Clifton on 6 December 1883, and the club was formally constituted with a membership fixed at forty at a meeting at Bristol Museum on 23 January 1884 (Bristol Archives 10523(2)). There was a strong overlap with the Bristol and Gloucestershire Archaeological Society and more than half of those listed as members at the January meeting were already members of the older society. Membership continued to be exclusive and the mechanism for accepting new members was not established until the departure of some of the founding members in November 1884. It was decided that the committee would vet a list of candidates, those selected would be submitted to the members at the annual meeting and 'those who obtained the most votes should then be separately balloted for' (Bristol Archives 10523(1–4) Minute Book 1). Unsurprisingly, the club seems to have developed a waiting list for membership and in October 1886 John Pritchard and Dr John Beddoe were both among a group of seven associate members who 'should have the privileges of members (except voting) + should become members of the club on vacancies arising'. A journal, circulated to the Royal Archaeological Institute and the Society of Antiquaries amongst many others, was printed annually and the club had an active programme of excursions. In 1885 there was a proposal, unanimously supported, to create a 'working' or fieldwork section within the society, although it is not clear how much active support this subsequently received (ibid). However, the society did undertake a campaign of excavation at the Roman town at Caerwent (Martin and Ashby 1901). Members also pursued a proposal to place commemorative plaques on historic buildings with the City Council. The restriction on membership seems ultimately to have caused an extreme version of the problem suffered by most groups, the reliance on a few individuals for all of the organisational and administrative tasks. In the case of the Clifton Antiquarian Club the secretary, Alfred Hudd, seems to have carried most of this burden for the twenty years of the club's existence. By the end of the first decade of the 20th century this had apparently become a chore and a decision was taken to wind the club up in January 1912 (BTM 17

January 1912). More recently in 2006, the club reformed and is now holding meetings, undertaking research projects and publishing its proceedings biennially.

The late 19th century was a remarkable period for Bristol's archaeology. This was a period in which the fabric of the city was being renewed, and historic buildings removed, but there were also many active observers of this work which revealed important evidence about the city. The creation of Royal Edward Dock at Avonmouth yielded a Bronze Age rapier and other material as well as geomorphological observations (Brett 1996), while the redevelopment of parts of the city centre produced significant evidence for the medieval and early modern town. The list of names associated with archaeological recording in these years is long – W R Barker, W V Gough, Alfred E Hudd, W W Hughes, J F Nicholls, T S Pope, C S Taylor, John Taylor, Robert Hall Warren to name only some of the most prominent – and almost all were members of Bristol's professional middle classes. The man responsible for much of this work was John Emanuel Pritchard, a local auctioneer. Joining the Bristol and Gloucestershire Archaeological Society in 1886, he served as President for two terms between 1918 and 1920, as well as being Chairman of Council between 1920 and 1924. When he was elected to the fellowship of the Society of Antiquaries of London in 1898, his candidature was supported by Sir John Evans and Sir Charles Read (Thomas 1986, 10). Pritchard was involved in most of the organised fieldwork carried out in the city in the late 19th and early 20th century, co-directing, for example, the excavation of sections of the Roman Road at Durdham which confirmed that the monument was indeed a Roman road (Trice-Martin 1900). He had an interest in a wide variety of subjects and published, amongst other things, on Bristol coins and tokens, clay tobacco pipes and the maps and plans of the city. His most significant contribution was however the conduct of a campaign of observation of development across the city over three decades. Throughout the year he visited buildings due for demolition and construction sites, reporting what he found in an annual article published in the local journals. The photographs and illustrations which accompany these reports often give valuable additional information about the form, construction and internal decoration before they disappeared – for example the staircase and other internal fittings of The Lamb Inn in West Street, Old Market (Pritchard 1906b, 268). The most extensive fieldwork which Pritchard undertook was at the site of a new factory developed for J S Fry & Sons in the block between All Saints' Lane, Pithay and Tower Lane. This recorded a long section of the Norman town wall as well as other medieval features and finds. Pritchard reported his work at Pithay in the *Transactions of the Bristol and Gloucestershire Archaeological Society* and it was also publicised in a long article in the *Bristol Times and Mirror* (Pritchard 1926b; BTM 2 February 1926). Perhaps the most striking thing about Pritchard's record of Bristol is its lack of period bias. Material from prehistory to the 19th century was within his field of vision. Pritchard was also concerned with best practice. His archaeological training appears to have come mainly from extensive reading and his professional and personal experience. Yet he seems to have been open to new techniques and was in communication with the geologist Professor Thomas McKenny Hughes, who recorded the archaeology exposed by development in Cambridge, and seems to have gained an understanding of the concept of stratification from Hughes (Thomas 1986; McKenny Hughes 1892). He was also concerned to conserve the fabric of the city through active campaigning and his energetic defence of the Dutch House managed to avert the threat of demolition between 1906 and 1908 (Thomas 1986, 16–17). The First World War caused something of a break in archaeological activity in Bristol. Although Pritchard continued to monitor sites through the war and into the 1920s, it seems to have been with less energy and his active fieldwork had come to an end by the late 1920s. He died in December 1940 (Fig 3.1).

The Spirit of Adventure is Abroad: archaeology in the inter-war and post-war years

The 1920s and 1930s saw a diminution of archaeological effort as the generation active around the beginning of the 20th century retired or died but fieldwork continued, carried out by individuals and organisations. The University of Bristol Spelaeological Society, formed in 1919, was the most notable

Figure 3.1 Distribution of fieldwork by John Pritchard

of these. The society, as the name suggests, focuses its interests on the exploration of Kaarst cave systems (mainly outside Bristol) but also carried out several excavations on prehistoric and Roman sites in the city during the 1920s and 1930s. However, most of the work taking place, of whatever genesis, was in the suburban areas. It was the aspirations of town planning in the mid-1930s, particularly the proposal for an 11-acre civic centre and a new inner circuit road (Hasegawa 1992), which inspired something of a resurgence of interest in the city centre. The Council for the Preservation of Ancient Bristol was founded in late 1936 with members from the Bristol Kyrle Society, the Bristol Society of Architects, the Bristol and Gloucestershire Archaeological Society and several Councillors of Bristol City Council amongst others. Its aim was to produce a schedule of Bristol's archaeological monuments and historic buildings and this was published in the following year (BEP 10

December 1936; Anon 1937). The events of the Second World War and the reconstruction which followed it were the major catalysts for change in the urban form of Bristol. Bomb damage to the centre of Bristol was severe – of the shops on Castle Street, many of 17th-century or earlier date, 95 per cent were damaged or destroyed (Hasegawa 1992, 27) (Fig 3.2). Numerous other historic buildings elsewhere in the city were damaged or destroyed, the best-known casualties being No 1 High Street, known as the Dutch House, and many of the other buildings on High Street, St Augustine-the-Less, St Mary-le-Port, St Nicholas, St Peter and Temple Church (Fig 3.3).

An album of photographs of war damage to the city during the blitz of 1940–1 was made by the photographer Jim Facey, who was chief photographer and picture editor for the *Bristol Evening Post* from 1932 to 1945. His album was donated to the Bristol Archives by his son David and the majority of photographs

can be viewed online, via the Know Your Place website.

Some limited archaeological survey of bombed historic buildings – Spicer's Hall (BHER 901) for example – was carried out by officers of the Ministry of Works before demolition but most, notably No 1 High Street, were removed without record.

The obvious need to replace building stock destroyed by bombing encouraged discussion of the shape of post-war cities within government, professional associations and amongst the general public, generating an expectation of major change (Hasegawa 1999). Active consideration of reconstruction had begun by 1941 and Bristol was one of seven cities visited by the Advisory Panel on Redevelopment of City Centres before the end of 1943. Bristol's city engineer, Marston Webb, held extensive consultations and concluded that although some proposals were radical, 'the spirit of adventure is abroad in connection with post war developments and Bristol would not wish to be behind in this direction' (Hasegawa 1992, 79). A reconstruction plan was submitted to the City Council in March 1944 and was approved in July 1945 (ibid, 67–89). The most controversial aspect of the new plan was the proposal to move the main shopping centre to a new site in Broadmead. This was unpopular with many traders. The local archaeological societies seem to have made comments to the Replanning Advisory Committee, the group established from Bristol's civic groups to advise on the reconstruction. Those by the Council for the Preservation of Ancient Bristol (CPAB) were made as early as January 1942. CPAB argued for the retention of the historic buildings which had survived and that any development scheme should make reference to the past of the area (Anon 1942, 245).

In the event almost all of the many historic buildings of Broadmead and the Castle Street area were removed, but the archaeological

Figure 3.2 Photograph of Castle Street and Lower Castle Street in the 1940s (Bristol Archives 44819/3/248)

Figure 3.3 No 1 High Street (the Dutch House) after bomb damage in 1940 (Bristol Archives Facey Collection ref 41969/1/67)

co-ordinated and the excavation method consisted 'of simply uncovering structures', although Dr Dina Portway-Dobson provided occasional advice (Letter to G Boyle, 8 September 1999). Professional involvement seems to have been limited to a survey of Ridley's Almshouses by B St John O'Neill of the Ministry of Public Buildings and Works in *c* 1950 (BHER 920; St John O'Neill 1951), prompted by the demolition of this Scheduled Ancient Monument. Until recently, our knowledge of the archaeology of the sites of most of the rest of the Broadmead development has rested on the activities of two amateurs, Keith Marochan and Keith Reid, who visited many building sites in the area between 1955 and 1958. The extent of the record they produced is unclear and their primary interest appears to have been post-medieval ceramics. It is unlikely that the pair undertook any formal excavation in Broadmead, although they are reported to have excavated a clay tobacco pipe kiln in Whitson Street (BHER 159) and they monitored redevelopment of the site of Burton's Almshouses in Long Row in 1958 (BHER 3079), publishing the results in the *Transactions of the Bristol and Gloucestershire Archaeological Society* (Marochan and Reed 1959).

Radical redevelopment continued into the 1960s and generated a considerable campaign of opposition to the perceived wholesale destruction of historic fabric (Priest and Cobb 1980). Archaeological excavation took place in response to development proposals in the 1950s and 1960s, either through the City of Bristol Museum or under the auspices of the Ministry of Works, including several directed by Philip Rahtz. His excavations in the Mary-le-Port Street area were in the heart of the Saxon town and predated the campaigns in Winchester and York which shaped the understanding of urban development in Britain. Rahtz felt, with hindsight, that the work he undertook was not of a sufficiently high quality given the importance of the site (Watts and Rahtz 1985, 15). A pioneering attempt to think strategically about the archaeological resource in the Bristol region was made in the 1960s by the Bristol Archaeological Research Group (BARG) with the publication of a two-volume *Survey and Policy* document (Grinsell 1964; 1965). This reviewed what was known about the local archaeology and considered priorities for research. Little progress was made because

work carried out was minimal given the scale of demolition. Excavations, supported by the Ancient Bristol Exploration Fund through public subscription with help in kind from the Bristol Corporation, were carried out on the site of the keep and the south curtain wall by Kenneth Marshall (BHER 416) and G L Gettins (BHER 417), by Norman Quinnell and George Boon (BHER 418) on the town wall above Fairfax Street, by George Boon at Mary-le-Port Street (BHER 419) and by B A M Nelson at the corner of Tower Street and Castle Street (BHER 415; Marshall 1951). Quinnell and Nelson were both recent graduates without substantial excavation experience and Quinnell was employed by Ordnance Survey on the re-survey of the city centre and had to confine his involvement to lunchtimes and evenings. The programme of excavation does not seem to have been

of the lack of a structure to enable research opportunities to be taken.

The rise of professional archaeology

A milestone was therefore reached in 1968 when the City Council appointed Michael Ponsford as Field Archaeologist, based in the City Museum. Ponsford was faced with a development boom which was removing archaeological material at a tremendous rate. He responded to this with a campaign of excavation and observation in the area of Castle Street, the site of the proposed development of a civic centre, which took the elucidation of Bristol Castle as its primary research aim (Ponsford 1979). From a minimal base of staff and funding Ponsford gradually built a full-time team of field archaeologists which was responsible for a substantial rise in the level of archaeological work in Bristol. A limited research framework for the city centre was put forward in a number of short articles (Ponsford nd(a); Ponsford 1985) and the research agenda prioritised the origins and topographic development. Many large excavations were carried out during the 1970s and 1980s, facilitated by the government-funded Manpower Services Commission, with a major concentration of excavation on riverfront sites in the Redcliffe area where stratification was both deep and well preserved. All of these excavation campaigns were, however, marred by a failure to publish more than, for the most part, short interim statements on the results of the research. Resources were largely focused on the excavations, and funding of post-excavation processing and analysis often had to be found from existing funds. A substantial backlog of sites developed in consequence and several major excavations remain unpublished. A further shortcoming was the lack of a formal process of review of the research agenda in the light of changing knowledge to build on the original statement produced by BARG.

In 1975 the Historic Towns Trust published their Historic Towns Atlas volume for Bristol. This took the form of an extended historical summary by leading scholars of the day (Margaret Lobel, the series editor, setting Bristol in its regional context and writing about the post-medieval centuries, Eleanora Carus-Wilson writing the medieval chapters) accompanying a series of maps compiled by W H Johns showing the principal features

of the historic topography. The text is brief, but authoritative, and remains an important source; the topographical development of Bristol is emphasised, though the maps are treated as illustrative of the text rather than as a source for analysis. The maps themselves, the largest of which were printed in colour at 1:2500 scale, were based mainly on Ashmead's 1828 map, which captured a good deal of historic topographical detail that was lost by the time more accurate Ordnance Survey mapping became available later in the century. Further historic detail was captured from earlier cartographic sources, from William Smith's 1568 bird's-eye-view onwards (*see* Fig 3.21), and the sources used to guide the map's reconstructions (of, for example, the castle, city walls and dissolved monastic houses) were enumerated in a series of appendices. Thus properly referenced and lavishly produced, the maps represented a major advance on anything that had gone before; they have, however, been overtaken by forty years of archaeological research and arguably always suffered by presenting an essentially static picture of 'Old Bristol' which is very much at odds with the historical reality of major episodes of rapid, intensive and transformative urban growth.

In Bristol, as elsewhere in England, the major departure of the late 20th century was publication of PPG 16 (Department of the Environment 1990). This stimulated a reorganisation of archaeological provision within Bristol City Council. A proposal to disband the Museum field unit was withdrawn after major public opposition and the unit was reconstituted as Bristol and Region Archaeological Services on a self-funding basis which required it to compete for archaeological work in the market. At the same time the post of City Archaeologist was created in the city's planning department, bringing archaeological concerns much more to the heart of strategic policy as well as development control. The regime instituted by PPG 16 has, overall, been beneficial to archaeology in Bristol. Archaeological work before 1990 tended to focus on certain areas of the city or specific monuments, notably the Castle Park area, the Cathedral and latterly Redcliffe, while other areas saw little or no investigation. By making it a material consideration for the planning process PPG 16 changed archaeology from a request to a requirement. The number of archaeological investigations carried out in Bristol has increased significantly and the temporal and geographical distribution has widened, though it clearly responds to cycles in the wider economy, as has been seen in the aftermath of the economic downturn after 2008. Before 1990 almost all excavation and evaluation took place within the area defined by the inner circuit road, but subsequently there has been increasing investigation of the outer parts of the study area. The emphasis on preservation *in situ* where the archaeology is of national importance also opened the opportunity of seeking the redesign of development schemes to avoid compromise of the resource. Buildings archaeology has become increasingly a routine part of development control work in Bristol, with PPG 16 being applied even to relatively modern structures where they are of interest. The most profound change to derive from the guidance was the transformation of professional archaeology to a commercial environment. The replacement of PPG 16 by Planning Policy Statement (PPS) 5 in 2010 and then by the much briefer National Planning Policy Framework (NPPF) in 2012 (DCLG 2012) has not changed the main thrust of the PPG and has ensured that the main elements regarding the protection of heritage assets have been retained (Fig 3.4).

While Bristol provides sufficient work to employ significantly more professional archaeologists than ever before, the economic

downturn after 2008 has meant that resources are becoming ever more stretched. In addition, while more financial support is now directed towards archaeology from the private sector, fieldwork opportunities and funding remain tied to development rather than research priorities. Amateur groups have also felt gradually excluded from fieldwork. In some areas of Bristol's archaeology this is less noticeable. Investigation of Bristol's industry, for example, has been one of the more actively pursued areas of work on the city's past and benefits from the active support of many interested volunteers often with specialist knowledge. Commendably, some archaeological units have attempted to involve the members of local archaeological societies in its developer-funded excavations where possible, though the tight timescales and safety concerns of modern construction make this difficult. Some new archaeological groups have been formed, dedicated to the undertaking of fieldwork in specific areas, notably the Sea Mills Archaeological Research Team (SMART), which has been working in the Roman town of Sea Mills, advised by archaeologists from Bristol and South Gloucestershire and Bristol University and the Brislington Community Archaeology Project (BCAP), which has carried out fieldwork projects in the Brislington area of South Bristol. The launch of the website Know Your Place in 2011 by Bristol City Council (www.bristol.gov.uk/knowyourplace),

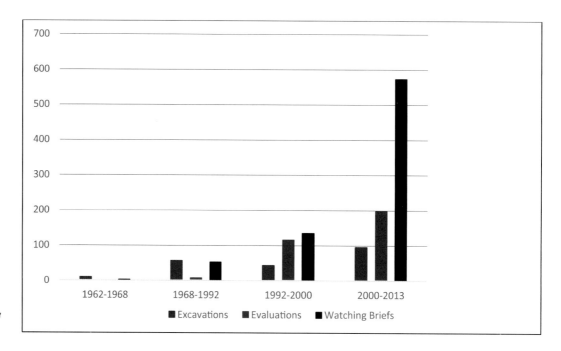

Figure 3.4 Chart showing the rise in the volume of excavations, evaluations and watching briefs between 1962 and 2013

the initial aim of which was to make available to the public historic maps for the Bristol area, has, through a Public Contributions facility, allowed members of the public to add data to the Bristol Historic Environment Record. The public is thereby directly involved in the process of data collection and dissemination.

The challenge for the future is therefore to maintain the wider public interest in archaeology through the promotion of active research, at all levels from primary school teaching onwards, so that the engagement of ordinary Bristolians with the history of their city – so much a characteristic part of past research – is not lost. While the pioneering endeavours of John Pritchard in the late 19th and early 20th century might be more difficult to achieve in the historic heart of the city, with strict regulations regarding health and safety and development timescales, there are still many areas of work that are open to the non-professional, such as research into documentary, pictorial and cartographic sources as well as observations of smaller-scale development projects such as the works of public utilities.

The visual representation of the city

Introduction

Bristol has an exceptionally good record of its changing form compiled by painters, cartographers and, latterly, photographers and film-makers. Images are not simple empirical records and these visual media have had a considerable influence on each other; it has been argued, for example, that a revival of cartography in Britain in the 18th and early 19th centuries defined the frame within which a 're-visioning' of the British landscape took place, in disciplines from landscape painting to travel writing and gardening (Daniels 1993, 61). Three forms of visual record commonly used to inform archaeological research in Bristol, painting, photography and cartography are discussed in the following pages.

Paintings, drawings and prints
by Francis Greenacre
Introduction

There may be no other British town with a more complete visual record of its later medieval appearance than Bristol. It is George

Weare Braikenridge's collection of over fourteen hundred watercolours and drawings, mostly by artists resident in Bristol in the 1820s, that is the foundation for this claim. Remarkably, the quantity is matched both by the aesthetic quality and by the accuracy and detail of many of the drawings. The collection not only dramatically illustrates much of the history of Bristol but is also of relevance to any European urban study.

There are of course many visual records of Bristol dating from before and after Braikenridge's time but, important as they may be, parallels will be found in the records of other towns for much of this material. There are striking exceptions, however: the mid-18th-century drawings by James Stewart in the Bodleian Library and Samuel Hieronymus Grimm's drawings of around 1790 in the British Library. And in the 20th century, the taking, collecting, copying and, above all, the publishing of photographs of Bristol by the indefatigable Reece Winstone was on a pioneering scale and has led to the preservation of much material that might otherwise have been lost.

The 18th century

The originality of Bristol's outstanding 17th-century map-maker, James Millerd (*see below*), is well demonstrated by his engraved 90° panorama of 'The City of Bristol' seen from the south and showing the Avon at high tide, crossed by a single bridge as densely packed with houses as old London Bridge itself. It was published in 1673 and not until the 1730s were comparable panoramas produced by the professional topographers, Samuel and Nathaniel Buck. Their 'The North West Prospect of the City of Bristol' looks across from Brandon Hill, showing two dense lines of ships' masts breaking the roof lines, one along the Avon at Welsh Back and one below, along the Frome on Broad Quay (Fig 3.5). Published in 1734, it prefigures the excited words of the poet Alexander Pope, who wrote in 1739 that there are

> in the middle of the street, as far as you can see, hundreds of ships, their masts as thick as they can stand by one another, which is the oddest & most surprising sight imaginable (quoted in Bettey 1986, 68).

It was perhaps while sketching this view that one of the Buck brothers met James Stewart, a writing master and accountant.

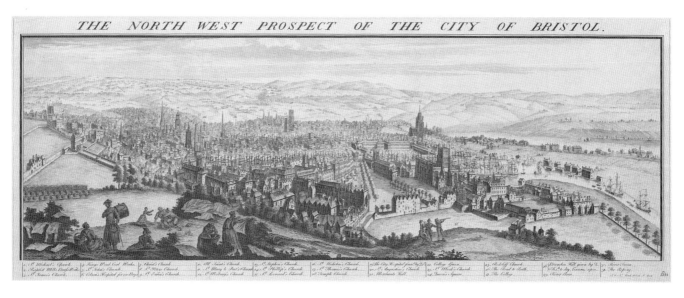

THE NORTH WEST PROSPECT OF THE CITY OF BRISTOL.

Figure 3.5 The North-West Prospect of the City of Bristol, Nathaniel Buck 1734 (BRSMG M5288)

It was a meeting that inspired Stewart 'to take original drawings of the inside and outside of every public building in the city' (Bodley MSS Gough 'Somerset 2' fol xiv), and to begin his *History of the Famous City and Port of Bristol*. Nothing was to be published, but his surviving drawings (Bodley MSS Gough 'Somerset 8' fol xiv; *see also* Eustace 1982, 92), although of modest quality, constitute the earliest group of Bristol views after the impressive vignettes surrounding Millerd's map. Stewart's drawings include several unique views, particularly of early modern houses near St Michael's Hill and Washington's Breach. There are important drawings of the city gates as well as intriguingly incidental views from upper windows.

James Stewart died in 1755 and so, too, did William Halfpenny. Halfpenny was the author of several architectural pattern books and also of *Perspective Made Easy* (Eustace 1982, 91), published in 1731. This includes views of the Drawbridge, of the Hotwells, which was soon to be copied on to a Bristol delftware plate dated 1741–2 (BRSMG N7461), and of Queen Square, an important engraving recently used in the restoration of the forecourts of Queen Square houses. His surviving drawing of Redland Chapel (British Library K Top CXXIV Supp Cat fol 37); illustrated in Eustace 1982, 91) is one of the most enchanting images of the outskirts of Georgian Bristol and his view of John Padmore's complex Great Crane (BRSMG Mb3450, illustrated in Elkin 1995, 12) of 1747 remains one of the principal documents of Bristol's industrial history (Greenacre 2005) (*see* Chapter 8, Fig 8.42).

By far the most familiar image of 18th-century Bristol is the oil painting of Broad Quay (Fig 3.6). It has been endlessly and misleadingly reproduced. Previously dated to around 1735 and often attributed to Peter Monamy, it must now be dated on the evidence of the costume to around 1785 and it can be more convincingly attributed to Philip Vandyke, an artist born in Holland but who was resident in Bristol from 1785 and who, until now, was known only as an obscure portrait painter. Very much better known is Samuel Scott, 1701–92, the Englishman's Canaletto. His small oil of College Green with the High Cross and the Cathedral (illustrated in Liversidge and Farrington 1993, cat 47) was once in the collection of Horace Walpole at Strawberry Hill and it may well have been commissioned by that pioneer of Gothick taste. It is based on an engraving published in 1743 after a drawing by Robert West (BRSMG M698), a sharp reminder of the importance of 18th-century topographical prints as visual records (Fig 3.7).

For the second half of the 18th century it is engravings, perhaps largely sold to the summer visitors to the Hotwells, that provide the most detailed record of the changing appearance of the Avon Gorge and of the spa itself. Finest and most influential were Nicholas Pocock's views on the Avon from St Mary Redcliffe to the Bristol Channel (Greenacre 1982, 46–7). This sequence of eight prints celebrates the most beautiful approach to an inland harbour in the world and the knowledge, experience and sensitivity of the Bristol-born artist and

Figure 3.6 Broad Quay c 1785 (BRSMG K514)

former ship's captain is evident in every one of them (Fig 3.8).

Pocock was to produce sets of varying numbers for over 35 years and he, himself, always added the detailed and delicate colour washes over the etched outline. The earliest are dated 1781 and from 1786 shading in aquatint was added to the engraved plates, presumably to facilitate the adding of watercolour. Sometime after 1809, when the construction of the Floating Harbour was completed, and long after his move to London, Pocock added two more views, one showing the new Prince Street bridge and the other, Cumberland Basin, in order to bring the series up to date.

Perhaps encouraged by Pocock's views on the Avon, a striking number of major British artists were to visit Bristol towards the end of the 18th century, but, as with Samuel Scott, their works are usually of more interest to the art historian than the archaeologist. J M W Turner came in 1791 at the age of sixteen during his summer vacation from the Royal Academy Schools (Wilton 1979, watercolour cat nos 15, 16, 18–21; Tate Gallery *Bristol and Malmesbury Sketchbook*). It was from vertiginous viewpoints in the Avon Gorge that Turner first selected and manipulated his compositions to dramatic effect, foreshadowing his mature work. Thomas Girtin came in 1797 and John Sell Cotman stayed in 1800 at the age of eighteen, en route, like so many other visiting artists, to the picturesque delights of the Wye Valley. Cotman's finest early watercolour depicts St Mary Redcliffe's noble tower enveloped in a grimy haze with the nearby glasshouse and shot tower silhouetted against a dawn sky (BM 1859.528.117 (*c* 1802), illustrated in Wilton and Lyles 1993, pl 42). The muddy banks of the Avon look like slag heaps. It is one of the most powerful images of early industrial England and well reflects the artist's brooding personality.

Of the visiting artists, it is Samuel Hieronymus Grimm (1733–94; *see* Clay 1941) who most nearly anticipates the Braikenridge collection. Born near Berne in Switzerland, Grimm came to England in 1768. Here, one of his most important patrons was the cleric and antiquarian Dr Richard Kaye, for whom

Figure 3.7 The High Cross and the Cathedral c 1750, Samuel Scott (BRSMG K4177)

he did many hundreds of pen and ink wash drawings of a great variety of subjects and places throughout England. In the summer of both 1788 and 1789 Dr Kaye and Mr Grimm stayed in Clifton.

It was perhaps while the doctor took the Hotwell waters that the artist made many sketching expeditions in and around Bristol. Grimm's drawings are often of unexpected and unfamiliar subjects: a Norwayman being unloaded at Hungroad on the Avon (BM Add MS 15546/160); elegant visitors to the Hotwells riding double horses (two to a horse) on the Downs (BRSMG Ma3701); a vast wooden tub full of live turtles newly arrived from the West Indies (BM Add MS 15540/169). More conventional descriptions of Bristol buildings also abound and there is an early interest in hillforts and the remains of Civil War fortifications, but it is the records of customs and curiosities that so unusually enliven the collections (BRSMG Ma3700–3732; BM Kaye Collection Add MS 15540, 15541, 15546, 15547) (Fig 3.9).

The Braikenridge Collection

George Weare Braikenridge (Fig 3.10) was born in 1775 in Hanover County, Virginia, where his father was a merchant and planter (Stoddard 1981; 1983). By 1785 he had been sent to school in Bristol. His mother, a Virginian, and his two sisters came to England in 1793 but all died within weeks of being wrecked in the Bristol Channel, when their ship, under an incompetent master, struck Scarweather Sands. In 1816 or 1817 Braikenridge moved from his Queen Square house to the family home of Winash House, Brislington, two miles east of Bristol. In 1820, at the age of 46, he retired as the senior partner of the leading West India firm of Braikenridge and Honnywill, Dry Salters. In the same year he first employed Hugh O'Neill, much as Dr Kaye had employed S H Grimm 30 years before. Braikenridge had, of course, been collecting for some years but the collection, as we now know it, was thus begun in earnest. Today, it consists of the topographical prints and drawings of Bristol in the Bristol Museum and Art Gallery, the supporting printed and manuscript material once in 36 portfolios and now in the Bristol Reference Library, College Green, and the prints and drawings of Somerset, also once in folio volumes but recently dispersed within the collections of the Somerset Archaeological Society at Taunton Castle. There was once much more: early illuminated manuscripts of superb quality; a very fine library; historical portraits; champlevé enamels and medieval boxwood and ivory carvings and sculpture; metalwork and furniture, often of great interest. Most of this collection was to be auctioned in 1908 and nothing now remains of Broomwell House, Brislington which Braikenridge had purchased in 1823 (the remains of the house were recorded during archaeological works prior to development in 2003–4 (BHER 21806) Longman 2008–9, 83–90). Parts, only, of the remarkable Gothick library survive at Claremont Villa, Clevedon, which Braikenridge had built as a summer residence.

From 1820 to 1824, the last four years of his life, Hugh O'Neill worked almost exclusively for Braikenridge. He produced over four hundred drawings mostly in pencil and grey wash for his employer, who still bemoaned 'his indolent and irregular habits, in which he allowed himself great indulgence'

Figure 3.8 View of the Avon and the Bristol Channel by Nicholas Pocock, 1786 (BRSMG K4169)

Figure 3.9 Detail of A View of the Windmill Camp by S H Grimm, 12 September 1789 (BRSMG Ma3701). It shows Clifton Down Camp and what is now the site of Brunel's Suspension Bridge from the south. The ruins in the middle ground may be the remains of a hermitage recorded by William Worcestre

Figure 3.10 George Weare Braikenridge by N C Branwhite, c 1832 (BRSMG K2817)

(quoted in Greenacre 1973, 255–6). O'Neill, however, was the son of an architect and he himself did several architectural designs including the earliest practical proposals for the Clifton Suspension Bridge, dated 1822 (BRSMG Mb630). He had been a drawing master at Oxford and in Edinburgh before moving to Bath in 1813. His natural and practised facility in the drawing of architecture and his own personal interest in antiquities perfectly matched those of his employer and set exceptional standards for the collection as a whole.

Braikenridge was a careful, even fastidious, man but there is little evidence of much method behind the collection. The Bristol prints and drawings were initially collected to extra-illustrate William Barrett's *History and Antiquities of the City of Bristol* published in 1789 just as the Somerset illustrations were originally bound up with John Collinson's *History and Antiquities of the County of Somerset* published in Bath in 1791. However, the selection of subjects for the drawings appears relatively haphazard with little pre-planning. Although O'Neill died with a list of over thirty items which his patron wanted him to draw, it seems that his own initiative and the

personal interests of subsequent artists were equally important (Stoddard 1983, 67). It is possible, for example, that O'Neill's often unique records of Bristol Castle remains were specifically commissioned by Braikenridge but the enthusiasm with which O'Neill records newly discovered gothic arches or ancient windows and screens revealed by building work or demolition suggests a joint enterprise. Both sought to document the present as well as the past. Braikenridge's own catalogue entry for O'Neill's drawing of a dilapidated Narrow Quay building (Braikenridge Collection, BRSMG M2518, *see* Chapter 7, Fig 7.16) that had once been a colonnaded corn market is a good example of this concern for the continuity of history. Braikenridge notes down the history of the building and adds, first that it was now 'nick-named the Riggers Exchange from the circumstance of the Riggers assembling there to gossip from all parts of the Quay' and secondly that the father of E H Baily (the Bristol sculptor who was later to model Nelson's statue above Trafalgar Square) had worked in this building carving 'some of the finest Ships figure heads of their time' (Braikenridge Collection, Catalogue Vol II: B47).

This contemporary element is stronger still in the work of Thomas Rowbotham (Fig 3.11) who, between 1825 and 1829 did 250 watercolours for Braikenridge and who, in effect, succeeded O'Neill (Greenacre 1973, 261–2). Like O'Neill, Rowbotham came to Bristol from Bath where he had worked as a teacher of marine painting, cottage figures and landscape. His watercolours cover almost every area and aspect of the city but reveal a special enthusiasm for the harbour and its shipping and especially for the sleek new steam packet-boats. The studies for these finished watercolours were made in pencil on the spot and many have survived in a Bristol private collection (*see also* Greenacre and Stoddard 1991, 52; cat nos 8, 12, 13). They confirm the care and accuracy of detail behind the watercolours which were worked up at home and enlivened with invented but convincing effects of light and weather.[1]

Rowbotham was the principal artist for another separate collection made by G W Braikenridge. In 1830 a visitor to Broomwell House recorded that for 'his own village, Brislington, he has a large collection of drawings made at great expense: so as to preserve a complete impression of what Brislington now is, the favourite retreat of Bristol merchants when got up in the world' (Stoddard 1981, 3). Rowbotham's Brislington watercolours are almost all in sepia wash and together form a unique record of a village close to a major city then much settled with elegant country houses and villas but yet to be suburbanised.

Braikenridge's collecting of Bristol drawings was greatly reduced after 1829 but Rowbotham's work for him culminated with three remarkable pen, ink and grey wash panoramas. The views from Totterdown and from Kingsdown are both 180° but the twelve-sheet panorama from the foot of Clifton Observatory covers 360° (BRSMG Mb497–500; Mb503–4).

Rowbotham would be almost forgotten today were it not for his work for Braikenridge and this is truer of other artists represented in the collection. John Manning, for example, perhaps the weakest of the artists, was wisely used mainly for ecclesiastical items, particularly stained glass windows and heraldic shields (Stoddard 1983, 224–5). On the other hand, amongst the 40 watercolours by Edward Cashin are works which rival the fine townscapes by the Dutch 17th-century master Jan van der Heyden, who certainly inspired him (Greenacre 1973, 269–75). And yet we know only that Cashin was a shy young Irishman. His works in the collection are dated between 1823 and 1826 and show an exceptional advance in quality in that short period. But after Braikenridge, Cashin vanishes (Fig 3.12).

There are drawings by 38 artists in the Braikenridge Collection. Some are by local amateurs such as George Cumberland, Revd John Eagles and Revd John Eden. Others are by major artists of the Bristol School such as Samuel Jackson (Greenacre and Stoddard 1986) and James Johnson (Greenacre 1973, 165–80). Both were landscape painters and many of their Bristol views are essentially landscapes concerned with the broader scenery about Bristol rather than detailed topographical records. However, their work, also, can sometimes provide vital information for the archaeologist, historian or urban planner. Jackson's view of St Paul's Church, Portland Square, for example, has provided a

Figure 3.11 Thomas Rowbotham by N C Branwhite (BRSMG K5429)

rare impression of the variety of colours on Bristol's rendered façades derived from locally quarried ochres (Greenacre and Stoddard 1986, illustration 11) (Fig 3.13).

James Johnson's superb watercolours of St Mary Redcliffe drawn in 1828 are amongst the most beautiful of all architectural interiors and one may yet provide vital information for the replacement of the funeral pennants on the monument to Admiral Sir William Penn (Braikenridge Collection, BRSMG M1949–M1954) (Fig 3.14).

Braikenridge also owned a remarkable sequence of larger watercolours by Samuel Jackson of views on the Avon which were never intended to be part of the topographical collection itself (Greenacre and Stoddard 1986, pls 2, 16, 24, 37). Similarly he owned 16 oils and watercolours by Francis Danby, the leading artist of the Bristol School (Greenacre 1988, 137 n 3). All are of rural or semi-rural scenes in or near Bristol. Those depicting the former snuff mills and weirs on the Frome at Stapleton may have been conceived as summer idylls of quiet and seclusion. They are now also significant records of industrial history (ibid, cat nos 12, 16). It is possible that all the works by Danby were acquired together soon after the artist's precipitous flight from Bristol early in 1824 and they may reflect Braikenridge's omnivorous approach to collecting local views rather than an appreciation of their special aesthetic quality.

The 19th century

Although a prodigy, William James Müller, born in 1812, was too young to enjoy G W Braikenridge's patronage, but his early work certainly reflects the influence and interests of that remarkable collector. In 1832 Müller did many striking drawings of medieval Bristol, both interiors and street scenes.

One in particular, of Bull Paunch Lane, foreshadows many Victorian depictions of urban scenes by appearing to turn an appalling slum of dilapidated medieval houses into a picturesque shambles (illustrated in Greenacre and Stoddard 1991, 64; cat no16) (Fig 3.15).

Müller's early biographer records that John Skinner Prout and Müller often sketched

Figure 3.13 St Paul's Church, Portland Square, by Samuel Jackson, 1825 (Braikenridge Collection, BRSMG M2869)

together at this time and that the artists were sometimes pelted with stones (Solly 1875, 14). In an area of such extreme poverty it is hardly surprising that their presence was offensive. Both Prout and Müller probably had publications in mind and Prout did produce *Picturesque Antiquities of Bristol*, consisting of 29 lithographs published in six parts in 1834 and 1835. It was dedicated to Braikenridge and included several lithographs after drawings by other artists in Braikenridge's collection.

Nothing came of Müller's plans however, until long after his early death in 1845. In 1883 20 of his drawings, all probably dating from 1832, were photographically reproduced under the title *Bits of Old Bristol*.

Müller's greatest contribution to the visual history of Bristol rests with his record of the Bristol riots of October 1831. For nearly two days the city was effectively in the hands of a mob, fuelled by 300 cases of fine wines liberated from the Mansion House cellars.

*Figure 3.14 Transept of
St Mary Redcliffe, looking
south, by James Johnson,
1828 (Braikenridge
Collection, BRSMG
M1952)*

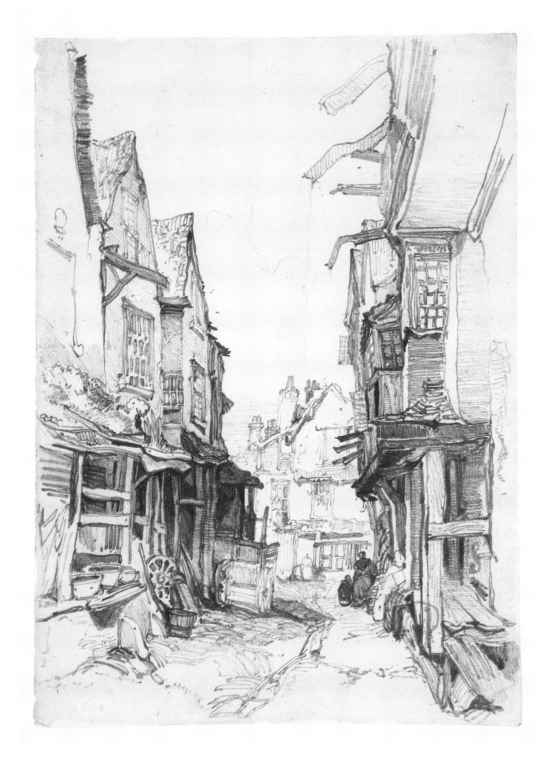

*Figure 3.15 Bull Paunch
Lane, Old Market
(now Lawford Street) by
William Müller, c 1832
(BRSMG M3134)*

Prisons, toll-houses, the Bishop's Palace and the Cathedral's superb library of 3,000 volumes, the Mansion House, the Custom House, and much of Queen Square were all destroyed. Müller, aged 19, witnessed nearly all of this destruction as it happened. His response was extraordinarily accomplished and his watercolours and oil sketches form one of the most comprehensive of all visual records of a national disaster before the advent of the camera (*see* Greenacre and Stoddard 1991, 19–21, 70–82) (Fig 3.16).

In the later 19th century there were many able artists working in Bristol but they largely eschewed the urban scene for rural and coastal views in Devon, Cornwall and in Wales. The period's local records are perhaps best characterised by the work of the prolific Parkmans, Ernest and Alfred, whose pedestrian watercolours were often based on earlier prints and watercolours and even on photographs (eg BRSMG M4004–M4039 and others).

One of the most regularly consulted collections of topographical drawings of Bristol scenes are the 2,500 pen and ink studies by Samuel Loxton in Bristol's Reference Library. Loxton was trained as an architectural draughtsman and surveyor and his drawings of buildings are impressively reliable. Drawn for the *Bristol Evening Post* and *Bristol Observer* largely in the early 1900s, they are in black line only in order to ensure clarity of reproduction in the newspapers. They are somewhat monotonous in style and the functional technique entirely disguises Loxton's admiration for the etchings of James McNeil Whistler, whose work he collected. However, despite necessary economies of detail, it is for the detail that the drawings can sometimes be most useful and items such as railings as street furniture are included with rare accuracy. Loxton was often recording new buildings such as schools and libraries at a time when civic pride and social responsibility combined effectively. His studies,

however bland in manner, reflect their time and are proud and diligent (Loxton 1992).

In comparison with the visual records of other towns, the aerial panorama of Bristol by Lavars and Co stands out (Fig 8.115). This colour lithograph is breathtaking in its detail and its accuracy and will reward hours of examination. It was an act of homage, published in 1887 as a celebration of Queen Victoria's jubilee. The view looks down on Bristol as if from a balloon. In the foreground, the shadow of clouds moves over Bedminster and its colliery and in the far distance a rain storm crosses the Severn. Much modern aerial photography still looks plodding and restricted beside it.

Photography
by *Francis Greenacre and Jonathan Brett*
Photography of Bristol began almost with the invention of the medium in 1839. The pioneer William Fox Talbot, who lived at Lacock Abbey in Wiltshire, took a photograph of the city centre in 1840, and three years later captured the SS *Great Britain*. His photograph, taken in 1843 or 1844, shows the vessel moored by the Canon's Marsh Gas Works where she languished, trapped in the Floating Harbour for some 18 months after her launching, until, at great risk, she was finally squeezed through the Cumberland Basin locks late at night on an unusually high tide (Elkin 1995, 17).

The most distinguished early photographer resident in Bristol was Hugh Owen, a well-connected accountant who was chief cashier at the Great Western Railway. A friend of Fox Talbot and one of the founders of London's Photographic Club, Owen began to take photographs in about 1847, and used mainly the calotype method during his brief photographic career (Winstone 1970, 38–9). An impressive album containing his photographs and those of others is in the Bristol Archives (Bristol Archives 20849(34)). The underlying concern of these early photographs was artistic. Landscape and figure groups are self-consciously composed and street scenes emphasise the picturesque effects of cobbled streets and gabled roofs. Their subject matter was seldom novel. However, one through St John's Gateway to Broad Street and Christ Church, a view that had been repeatedly recorded by earlier artists, is also a masterpiece of early photography with strong and effective contrasts of light and shade and an immaculate composition (Belsey 1996, 21).

From the 1850s photography began to be used more and more for record purposes. In Britain photographers were employed on the national census; 51 worked on the 1851 census but by 1861 there were fifty times the number (Haworth-Booth 1997, 73). The application of photography to the record of historic buildings was not long in appearing. The French Historical Monuments Commission began a programme of recording of historic structures in 1851, while in Britain the Society for Photographing Ancient London set about producing a similar record for the capital in 1867. In Bristol the Bristol and West of England Amateur Photographic Association had been founded in 1866. Its membership grew rapidly and a survey section was formed under the direction of Alfred E Hudd, secretary of the Clifton Antiquarian Club, and William Moline. In 1915 over four hundred photographs in a 'Survey and Record' were presented to Bristol Art Gallery (Winstone 1967, 69) (Fig 3.17).

Most date from the first ten years of the century and the range is remarkably similar to that found in the Braikenridge Collection 75 or so years earlier, but with a very much stronger and narrower interest in the past rather than the present. Church interiors and the fine fireplaces and staircases of early modern

houses are characteristic. Two photographs, for example, show the superb late 13th-century sculptures removed from the north porch of St Mary Redcliffe during the Victorian restoration (BRSMG M3525; M3527). They are piled three deep but are in very much better condition than we find them today after being repeatedly moved. As photographic technology was disseminated more widely and the production of prints became easier, so the volume of photographs of the city increased. Eventually photography became a routine method of record; in 1906, for example, Bristol Municipal Charities commissioned a survey of its properties and sites (Bristol Archives 33041/BMC/12(1)), and these 94 photographs

Figure 3.17 Photograph of 1904 showing the Hatchet Inn, Frogmore Street, by S H R Ghey, Bristol and West of England Amateur Photographic Association (BRSMG M3673)

have been published in an exemplary manner (Costello and Burley 1997). Many of these are now available to view on Bristol City Council's Know Your Place website (Fig 3.18).

Of the many photographers to record the changing city, three are worth particular mention for the value of their work to archaeological understanding. Fred Little (1875–1953) was a professional photographer, a native Bristolian with premises in Narrow Wine Street and later Castle Mill Street. He took many views of landmarks and events in the city and amongst these were several photographs of historic buildings (many demolished soon after) and sometimes a record of the demolition itself; he took a series of views of the demolition of the gate at the top of St John's Steep in 1911 for example (Moorcroft and Campbell-Sharp 1998, 98–102) (see Fig 6.28).

Overshadowing every publication of photographs of Bristol is the extraordinary achievement of Reece Winstone, the son of a Bedminster hosier. Winstone was a professional photographer who recorded both events and monuments in the city over a long career and interested himself in the conservation of the historic environment, becoming chairman of the Bristol Civic Society. He created a picture library of 48,000 photographs collected by purchase and by gift; he had borrowed and duplicated them and copied many from various public collections. The collection is maintained and the publications continued by his son, John Winstone. Over 60 years he also took many thousands of photographs himself and those are the core of his collection. In 1957 he published his first book of photographs *Bristol As It Was, 1939–1914* preceding and encouraging the current fashion by several decades. In 1988 came his 37th, as idiosyncratic as his first, with its cover proudly telling us that he had now published 6,705 photographs. Like Braikenridge, much of the lasting value of his collection relies upon the enthusiasm he brought to recording the present.

Less well known is Philip Street (d 1974), the grandson of the architect George Edmund Street, who recorded the city between the 1930s and the mid-1950s. Architecture would seem to have been his main interest but his work concentrated on the historic environment as a whole, making a study of the site of the Langton Mansion on Welsh Back for example. He appears to have treated photography as an incidental means of record, although the many photographs he took were of a high quality, and in 1964 Street presented several albums of his photographs to Bristol Museum (Neg 9104–9106; Winstone 1979, 22–4).

Another set of important photographs are those of the Hartley Collection, a series of mostly full-plate glass negatives taken by commercial photographers Veale and Co during the 1930s and 1940s and abandoned by them when they moved from their premises in Victoria Street in the 1960s. They were recovered by Ian Hartley who sold the collection to Bristol Industrial Museum in 2003. They typically show places of work, such as the interior of the former George's Brewery in Redcliffe. They are being made available via the Know Your Place website (Fig 3.19).

Other important collections that can be viewed on the Know Your Place website are the images from the Port of Bristol Authority Privileges Book. These images were created in the 1920s as a survey of all the industries around the Floating Harbour that were discharging waste into the harbour or had structures that projected over the water. As such these images are an invaluable record of the harbour immediately prior to the major changes that occurred just before and more especially during and immediately after the Second World War. The Vaughan Collection, early 20th-century postcards collected by Roy Vaughan, are also being added as are the photographs of John Trelawney-Ross, a gifted photographer who worked for Bristol City Council and took thousands of photographs of the city during the 1970s and 1980s, a period when many of Bristol's finest buildings were in a parlous state.

Perhaps the most important innovation of the 20th century as far as the archaeological record is concerned was air photography and several low-level oblique views of the city centre taken in the 1930s survive. Much of the post-Second World War air photography has been commissioned by government agencies, both national and local, and generally comprises overlapping vertical images at scales of 1:12000 or 1:13000, the countrywide coverage taken by the RAF in 1946 being the best-known example. Its primary use is in the identification of relict landscapes or features

Figure 3.18 East side of St Thomas Street, 1906 (Bristol Archives, Bristol Municipal Charities Collection, ref 33041/ BMC/1/1/b/46)

Figure 3.19 Interior of George's Brewery, Bath Street (Hartley Collection, ref 258019)

in the open spaces in and around the city but the RAF series in particular also holds useful information for the city centre before the wave of post-war redevelopment. An almost complete set of the 1946 RAF aerial photographs can now be accessed via the Know Your Place website.

Anthologies of terrestrial photographs of Bristol are now legion but the quality of reproduction has usually been abysmal. Even local museum curators have published Bristol photographs from their own and other public collections with sound scholarship but with little or no reference to their sources and with undue reliance on copy photographs. Sheer quantity and ease of duplication have encouraged us to regard photographs simply as illustrations, not as original works of art or as unique historical documents. At Bristol's Industrial Museum an examination of the only surviving original prints (from collodian negatives) of the earliest sequence of photographs of Bristol, views of the harbour taken in 1854, has led to the identification of both the photographer (the photographer is William Thomas, an important Welsh amateur) and the date (BRSMG 2/1960, Neg 7659–7762; illustrated in Elkin 1995, 13–15). Later copies of these four photographs have been published many times, unattributed, misdated and still fuzzier than the inevitably faded originals.

Substantial collections of both original and copy-photographs are now being made by local societies. The respective publications of the Malago Society and the Brislington Conservation and Amenity Society of photographs of Bedminster and Brislington are impressive compilations (Bantock *et al* 1997; Chard *et al* 1995). The vitality of such societies is some compensation for the dwindling number of specialist staff in Bristol's museums, libraries and record offices. And it is the specialist interest of authors that has drawn attention to previously untapped sources. Paul Elkin's substantial *Images of Maritime Bristol* brings the museum's York and Keen collections to a wider public and for the first time takes advantage of the Port of Bristol Authority Collection referred to above (Elkin 1995). David Eveleigh, formerly curator of social history, has demonstrated the particular importance of photographs as source material for his own discipline and also drawn attention,

for the first time, to the Fry Collection in the Bristol Archives (Bristol Archives 38538; Eveleigh 1996, 1998).

The majority of photographs of Bristol are once again taken by amateurs and, of course, in greater numbers than ever. From an archaeological perspective the most important departure, however, is the substantial body of specifically archaeological photographs of excavation or historic buildings which have resulted from the increasing number of archaeological investigations since the Second World War. Like the compositions of the pioneers of photography, these have developed their own conventions and should perhaps in consequence be approached with as much critical attention to their meanings and the circumstances of their creation as would be invested in an understanding of more obviously art historical sources (Dorrell 1989).

Maps of Bristol
by *Jonathan Brett*
Introduction

The earliest known depiction of Bristol's topography is an illustration in Ricart's *Kalendar*, a chronicle of the town written in 1479 by the town clerk, Robert Ricart, at the request of the mayor (Toulmin-Smith 1872). This perspective view shows what Ricart apparently perceived as the hub of the town, the high cross, town gates and the cross pattern of streets. Yet in concentrating on the administrative and commercial, the extensive suburbs outside the walls are ignored, and this exclusion warns that, like any other historical document, the map must be interpreted in its historical context (Fig 3.20).

Traditionally maps have been assumed to be a neutral, if idiosyncratic, reflection of a place and been treated accordingly (Lobel 1968). While the accuracy (or otherwise) of a map is one important consideration, the purpose behind the cartography has been the subject of most recent studies; the map may be an expression (and sometimes a source) of national identity and hence international rivalry, a means of forging a civic identity, or of emphasising an influence in the townscape (Harley 1988; Schmidt 1997; Hills 1996). In a city so closely associated with exploration it would be naive to assume Bristol's cartography is free of the layers of meaning to be found in the maps of other towns. The view in Ricart's

Kalendar illustrates, and is an illustration of, Bristol's civic self-consciousness in a period when such urban self-consciousness was to the fore in English towns (Rigby 1988).

The most comprehensive source of information on maps of Bristol is the catalogue produced by John Pritchard in 1926 (Pritchard 1926a). Lack of space does not allow any

Figure 3.21 Smith's map of Bristol of 1568 (Bristol Archives PicBox/6/Map/11a)

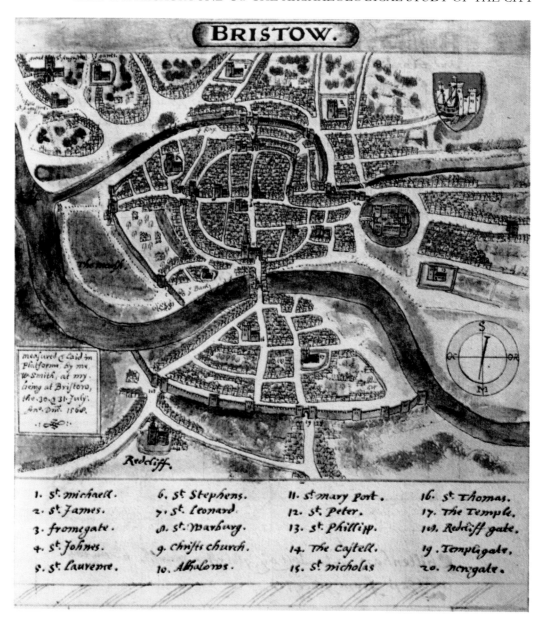

revision of Pritchard's work, and discussion of the many useful plans which record only parts of the city is similarly excluded;[2] instead the city-wide maps usually consulted in the course of archaeological research are briefly reviewed.

Early modern maps
Cartographic recording of Bristol began in detail, as is the case in most other towns, in the 16th century. The earliest example is the map by William Smith now in the British Museum (Sloane MSS 2596, fol 77) (Fig 3.21).

Smith (*c* 1550–1618) was born in Cheshire and became a citizen of London and member of the Society of Haberdashers in 1575.

Between 1578 and 1584 he lived in Nürnberg, working as an innkeeper. He wrote numerous manuscripts on heraldry and topography, including descriptive accounts of London and Nürnberg (*ODNB*). His hand-coloured map of Bristol surveyed, according to the map itself on 30–31 July 1568, forms part of a larger manuscript, 'The Particuler Description of England, with Portratures of certaine of the Chiefest Cities and Townes.' A perspective view, it gives a good impression of the town, particularly the pattern of the streets around the Carfax and picks out the parish churches but is otherwise stylised. The maps of Bristol which followed, notably that by Höfnagle published in 1581 in Braun and Hogenberg's *Civitates orbis terrarum* (illustrated in Millea 2003, 2–3), are all similar in character and draw their inspiration from one another. The 1610 map by John Speed is in the same mould. It was one of a series of maps of English towns contained in his *The Theatre of the Empire of Great Britaine* and corrected some features of the earlier works but, like much of the early modern map-making, gives little more than an impression of the place.

Far more reliable surveys of Bristol were produced in the later 17th century. Pritchard notes the existence of a survey of the town by Philip Stainred or Stainread, produced in 1653 at the request of the Corporation of Bristol and since lost. The results of the survey pleased those who commissioned it and Stainred was asked to 'amplyfy the map' (Pritchard 1926a, 333). The most significant 17th-century maps of the city are, however, those of the series produced by James Millerd towards the end of the century when the city was beginning a period of economic prosperity which lasted well into the 18th century. Millerd's life has been little researched and his career is therefore obscure. He was born probably *c* 1635, pursued a career as a mercer and married Rachel Lewis in St Nicholas Church in February 1662/3 (McGrath 1955, 118; Hollis and Ralph 1952, 9). By 1696 the couple had a daughter, Rachel, and were living on Bristol Bridge in the parish of St Thomas (Ralph and Williams 1968, 14). Millerd was active in the life of the city, being a guardian of the poor for the ward of St Thomas as well as serving as coroner (Butcher 1932, 45–6, 172), and Latimer records that he stood in the election for civic chamberlain in 1698 but was defeated (Latimer 1900, 361–2).

Between 1670 and *c* 1732 Millerd published several editions of a detailed perspective view of the city, increasing in artistic accomplishment and complexity between the first in 1670[3] and that of 1673 (Fig 3.22), which (with its emphasis on Bristol's maritime aspect) was presented to the Corporation and the Society of Merchant Venturers. In response the Merchant Venturers presented the mercer with plate engraved with the Society's arms as 'a token of our retaliation of respect to him' (McGrath 1952, 116). The map was republished with important revisions in 1684 and in the early 18th century, the sudden appearance of the cones of glass furnaces in particular reflecting the development of the city as an industrial centre (Fig 3.23). A further edition was produced in the mid-1730s recording, amongst other changes in the urban landscape, the re-erection of the High Cross at the centre of College Green. Millerd's motivation for producing the maps is unknown but they seem to be a product of civic pride; the churches are immediately identifiable, the major private houses are marked and there are vignettes of civic buildings (particularly sites of commerce) in the borders. The 1673 map in particular has been found to be generally reliable in its depiction of the city. However, we do not know the process by which the maps were produced. It seems unlikely that Millerd himself had the skills of a land surveyor and it is reasonable therefore to infer that, if measurements were made on the ground, he employed a surveyor to make them. Millerd's map of Chepstow, made in 1686, is similar in its style to the 1670 Bristol map and the title suggests a surveyor may have been employed (Shoesmith 1991, fig 4). The earliest version of the Bristol map, however, has the appearance of a sketch, though whether a plane table or other drafting aid was used is one of the questions only further detailed research may answer.[4]

The first two-dimensional plan of Bristol was produced by the surveyor John Rocque in the 1740s. Rocque, who was to make surveys of several European cities, was of Huguenot descent and had mainly produced surveys of houses and their gardens before coming to Bristol. The Bristol map was his first town survey (Varley 1948, 85). The map was published in 1742 in four large sheets and, no doubt with an eye to enhancing sales, was dedicated to the mayor 'the Recorder & Aldermen, the Sheriffs & Common-Council-men' of the city. Its record of garden layouts, apparently reliable,[5] is potentially one of its most valuable features. A second major survey was made by Benjamin Donne, the librarian of the City Library in King Street, who supplemented his income by running a mathematical school. His map of the city was published in 1769 and the Corporation demonstrated its appeal to civic pride by awarding Donne 20 guineas. Editions of his plan were published until 1791 (Pritchard 1926, 341–2).

The 19th century
By the 19th century the land surveying profession was well established and surveyors

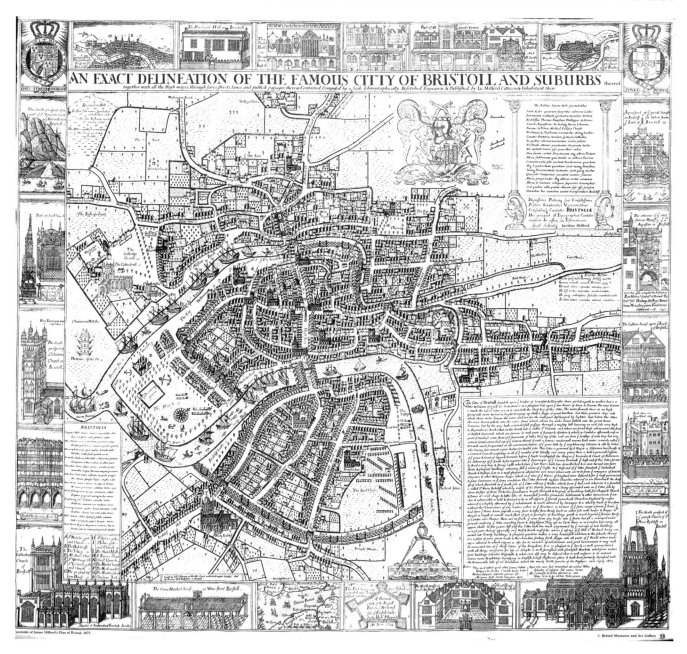

Figure 3.22 James Millerd's plan of Bristol of 1673 (BRSMG Mb6690)

based in Bristol served the requirements for survey in the surrounding countryside. One of these, John Plumley, began a survey of the city in 1813 but on his death it was taken over and completed in 1828 by George Ashmead who later became the Corporation's surveyor (Pritchard 1926, 346–7). The map, the most detailed survey of the city then made, was published on six sheets at a scale of 1in to 200ft (approximately 1:2400). It shows the locations of major buildings and street numbers of the remainder and records the city not long before it was significantly altered by a wave

of redevelopment. The survey, particularly useful for the locations of early 19th-century industrial sites, was not superseded until the Ordnance Survey 1st Edition map produced in the early 1880s and it is no coincidence that the last edition of the Plumley and Ashmead map was published in 1882.

Large-scale maps of the city became common in directories and guides published during the century but towards the end of the century the most detailed map of Bristol ever produced was created by the Ordnance Survey. In the 1880s Bristol was chosen as one of the

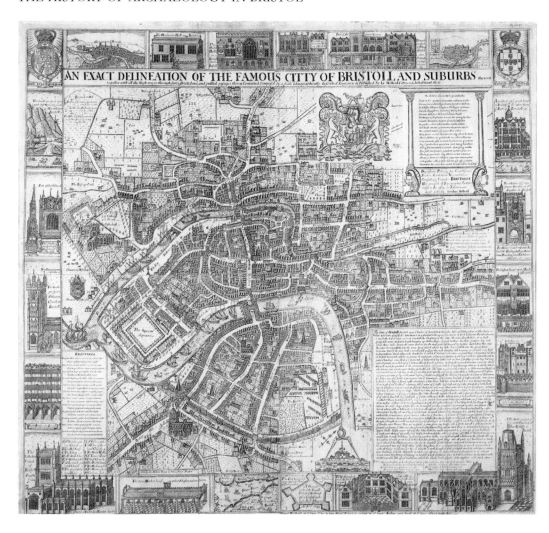

Figure 3.23 James Millerd's plan of Bristol of c 1715 (BRSMG M4173)

nine cities which would act as centres from which the completion of the cadastral survey of England and Wales would be completed. As part of this project a detailed survey of Bristol began in the early 1880s. This survey was published at a scale of 1:500, covered the whole extent of the city at that time, and is unprecedented in the level of detail it recorded. Forty-two sheets cover the study area and are set within a county grid. The majority of the work of the Ordnance Survey at the time was measured using a chain by a surveyor assisted by a chain-man, and there is no indication that the Bristol survey was an exception. The survey was conducted by the creation of a sufficiently dense network of triangulation points and detail was then measured off the main chaining lines. Surveyors were instructed to establish the position of all offsets further than 80 links from the main line by triangulation; the direction of those under 80 links were

estimated. Only where it was unavoidable, normally in 'crooked alleys and courts', was a theodolite traverse made. The measurements were recorded in a field book which was then handed on by the field survey team for plotting, when their involvement ended unless a line was found to require remeasuring (Harley 1980, 168–71).[6] The maps were reproduced using the new photozincographic process by which a printing plate could be produced directly from a photographic print of the map sheet. In 1865 all of Ordnance Survey's surveyors were urged by their director Sir Henry James to familiarise themselves 'with the local history, and (by personal inspections) with the objects of antiquarian interest in the districts which they are surveying in order that all such objects may be properly represented on the plans' (Harley 1980, 174), and by the 1880s the recording of antiquities had become standard practice. The 1st edition survey records the position of the major archaeological monuments in the city and, in the case of the town walls, traced their line. This mapping was usually drawn from informed locals and therefore accurate but could sometimes be very misleading; in Bristol, for example, the site of a Benedictine priory is marked at St Philip and Jacob's Church.

The 1880s survey was used well into the 20th century until made redundant by the retriangulation of the country in the late 1930s and the subsequent resurvey. In urban areas the new survey was at a scale of 1:1250 which has remained the largest survey scale commonly available. The advent of widespread digital mapping and GIS technology has made it easier to manipulate maps and tailor them for specific purposes. Archaeology is benefiting from the ease with which it is now possible to integrate historic data with cartographic information and the new paths for research which have opened up as a result.

Artists and the landscape today

Many artists and photographers continue to be inspired and fascinated by the landscape of their city. The river Avon and the Severn figured in a recent sequence of photographs inspired by the First World War and public art is increasingly being incorporated into new development, in some cases as an interpretation of archaeological monuments or features, to enhance a sense of place or to challenge assumptions. The most notable Bristol-born artist of world renown concerned with the landscape is Richard Long. A sculptor and land artist, Long has created work across the world. In 1998 he walked the Community Forest Path, a 45-mile walking route encircling Bristol. The works Long produced following the walk are colour photographs with a superimposed text,[7] images evocative of their time and, potentially, as inspiring to their contemporaries as were Nicholas Pocock's etched views along the Avon from Bristol to the Channel two hundred years ago. The works of Long, and of the other artists now working in Bristol's public realm, are another re-visioning of the landscape – but the art is now inscribed into

the landscape itself, ultimately to become part of the archaeological record.

Notes

1   Of O'Neill's on-the-spot studies for his Braikenridge drawings, 172 also survive (BRSMG Mb2968/1–172). Braikenridge himself mistakenly claimed that these drawings, sold after O'Neill's death for the benefit of his creditors, were 'memoranda' made by the artist after the drawings in Braikenridge's Collection (Bristol Reference Library, Braikenridge Collection Vol XXVI, 113). The studies were purchased by John Skelton and formed the basis of his Skelton's etchings of the antiquities of Bristol from original sketches by the late Hugh O'Neill published in Oxford in 1825. Several of the studies are of subjects not to be found in the Braikenridge Collection

2   For example, the surveys of Temple by J Blackamore *c* 1786 (BRSMG M1671), the Port of Bristol by W White and the property-related surveys contained in the Corporation Plan Books and the Dean and Chapter Plan Books in Bristol Archives. De Wilstar produced a number of surveys of areas of the city outside the UAD study area.

3   The first edition is reproduced with a short discussion by Pritchard (1909). It is signed 'I. M.' and is generally attributed to Millerd. Lobel (1968, 55) notes the influence of Speed's map on Millerd's.

4   The influence of Millerd's maps on local cartography is not clear but the map of Bath published by Guidot in 1731 is very reminiscent in form and style to Millerd's work.

5   The only tests of the Rocque map in this regard have been at Southwell Street (BHER 404) where horticultural features very like those it depicts were recorded and at Queen Square (BHER 3369), where the map was successfully used within a GIS to position evaluation trenches across the line of early gravel paths.

6   The original survey notebooks were among the material stored at Southampton which was destroyed during the Second World War.

7   *Home Land Walk/A Continuous Walk Of 45 Miles In 16 Hours Around Bristol Or The Community Forest Path/A Walk Encircling My Birthplace And The Birthplace Of Four Generations Of My Family/* Richard Long 1998

PART 2: THE DEVELOPMENT OF BRISTOL

Chapter 4: The period to *c* AD 950

There has been a human presence in the landscape immediately surrounding Bristol since the Palaeolithic. Yet in spite of the diversity of the archaeological record, surprisingly little is known about the settlement of the area before the late Iron Age. The majority of evidence for activity in the Bristol area before AD 950 has been gathered outside the present, city-centre, study area. This is partly because the built-up nature of central Bristol means that in many locations the evidence has either been removed or has not been accessible. Work has tended to focus on the excavation of major monuments (hillforts, for example) rather than wider investigation, and these consequently form islands of knowledge in a landscape which otherwise remains obscure. In this chapter the environs of modern Bristol are explored first, before looking in greater detail at the area of the historic city centre.

The Bristol region in the prehistoric and Roman periods

The Palaeolithic

A large number of Lower Palaeolithic artefacts have been found along the Bristol Avon, at St Anne's to the east of the city centre and in much greater numbers, indeed in probably the largest concentration in the south-west region, on either side of the river at Shirehampton and Abbots Leigh to the north-west (Lacaille 1954; Roe 1974; Wessex Archaeology 1994). The Avon river system is of Middle Pleistocene date and there are two places in Bristol where the associated sediments contain artefacts. Eight handaxes have come from the Greensand

on the south side of the river in St Anne's and a wider range of finds, with evidence of Levallois and flake technologies, have been recovered from the gravel terraces at Shirehampton, though none are well dated (Wymer 1999, 184–7; Bates and Wenban-Smith 2005). It should also be noted that mammal remains are preserved in the Shirehampton terraces (Bates and Wenban-Smith 2005; Rutter 1829, 315), and in 1842 faunal material apparently of Pleistocene date was recovered from a 'fissure' at Durdham Down, raising the possibility that the Carboniferous Limestone in the city may also have the potential for Lower Palaeolithic material (Wilson 1885–8). Almost no Upper Palaeolithic material has been recovered from Bristol.

The Neolithic

Despite the well-known Neolithic sites in the region, for example the trackways in the Somerset Levels, the timber and stone circles at Stanton Drew and Priddy or the Cotswold-Severn chambered tombs, evidence for the Neolithic in the Bristol area is currently very limited. The most significant monument is a chambered tomb at Stoke Bishop (Grinsell 1979; Smith 1989) but the distribution of stone axes does suggest that the river Severn and the Bristol Channel had a major cultural and economic influence on the area (Darvill 1989, 37). The palaeoenvironmental work so far undertaken points to extensive wooded areas, but with increasing clearance on both the upland and fen edges, as well as some cereal cultivation (Smith 1989, 35–6; Gardiner *et al* 2002, 30). The identification of ash deposits in an area that had become probably marginal land on the northern fringes of the river Avon suggested localised forest clearance in the immediately adjacent upland areas (Wilkinson *et al* 2002; Wilkinson 2006).

The Bronze Age

Evidence for the Bronze Age, on the other hand, is more extensive. Metal finds, including some manufactured in Ireland, have been recovered at several locations along the river Avon and hoards were found at Coombe Dingle and Kingsweston. Barrows are known or suggested in a number of places. In the 1990s a settlement site was excavated at Savages Wood, Bradley Stoke, to the north of Bristol as well as a group of sites by Lawrence Weston Road on the North Avon Levels (Tratman 1925; Anon 1875; Bingham nd; Erskine 1994–5). These were spreads of stone and burnt material within the alluvium and have been radiocarbon dated to 890–530 BC. Working surfaces of some kind, the sites seem to have been seasonally occupied implying, according to Locock, that local communities settled on the upland pursued a multifaceted economic strategy (Locock *et al* 1998; Locock 2001). Broadly, the Bristol area appears to conform to what is known of much of southern England: land was worked from small farmsteads, like Savages Wood and probably also near Ashton Court, west of the Avon. Lynchets containing Bronze Age pottery, very similar to that from Savages Wood, were also identified (Cross 1993, 23).

The Iron Age

Settlement was widely distributed in the Bristol region during the Iron Age. Past archaeological research was focused on the hillforts at Kings Weston Hill and the group around the Avon Gorge (Rahtz 1956–5; Rahtz 1958–9; Haldane 1975). More recent work, notably in the Severn estuary, has started to produce a more rounded picture, pointing to the exploitation of the wetland and intertidal zones. A domestic settlement site excavated at Hallen on the Avon Levels in 1992–3 suggests use of the wetland grazing as part of a system of transhumance – a pattern which the intertidal sites at Goldcliff indicate may have been common around the Severn estuary (Gardiner *et al* 2002; Bell *et al* 1999).

Activity in the immediate vicinity of the hillforts has also been elucidated recently by excavations at Henbury School, about 6km north-west of Bristol city centre (BHER 21855). These uncovered part of a cemetery, first recognised in 1982: 24 crouched inhumations, thought to date from the mid- to late Iron Age were found, although dating evidence was sparse. Slightly later than the burials, dating to the very end of the Iron Age, was a large rectilinear enclosure, *c* 85m by 50m, defined by a series of ditches. Lacking internal features its interpretation is problematic, though it may have enclosed a series of houses or other structures, evidence of which had not survived, or it may simply have been a large corral for livestock (Russell 1983; Evans *et al* 2006). About 4km south of the city centre, excavations in 1997 at Inns Court on the site of a 15th-century manor house revealed part of a substantial Roman building of later 3rd-century date with evidence of the occupation of the site from the late Iron Age onwards (Jackson 1999a; Jackson 2007a). Hitherto unsuspected evidence for late Iron Age and Roman settlement was also found in Bedminster during excavations by Avon Archaeological Unit in 2005 and 2006 (Young and Young 2014–15).

In 2008–9 a programme of excavation in the grounds of St Bede's School in Lawrence Weston, about 7km north-west of Bristol city centre, found a sequence of late Iron Age and early Roman roundhouses, replaced by a large enclosure ditch. There appears to have been little activity on the site after the 1st century AD, until a complex series of field boundary ditches were laid out in the late 3rd century (Clarke 2010).

The Roman period

By AD 47, Roman control had been established in much of southern England and the Fosse Way is commonly taken to mark the western boundary zone of Roman occupation at this time. The South West was used as a base for the conquest of Wales, begun in AD 53–4 and completed by the late 60s, after which military campaigning shifted to the north of England. Roman rule was meanwhile consolidated in the conquered southern territories and several military bases became civilian centres. The fort at Cirencester was replaced by the *civitas* capital, Corinium Dobunnorum, *c* AD 100, and a 1st-century naval base at Sea Mills, just inland from the mouth of the Bristol Avon, became a civilian port in the early second century (Holbrook 1994). Towns developed at Bath, Camerton and probably at Keynsham, all linked by a network of roads (La Trobe-Bateman 1997c, 13–14). Rural settlements, including several villa sites, have been identified across the region and a sophisticated economy with significant external trade developed; dock structures are known on the Welsh side of the Severn at Caerleon and Barland's Farm, Magor, while the possible development of a port at Clevedon in the 3rd to 4th century has been suggested (Boon 1978; Nayling and McGrail 2004; La Trobe-Bateman 1997b, 6).

The evidence available for Roman occupation in the Bristol area is much more extensive than that for the earlier periods, though the location of most archaeological excavation has been determined by development pressures rather than research objectives. The nature of the evolving relationship between the native and Roman culture locally remains to be investigated but it seems that the transition to Roman rule in the Bristol area was characterised by a large measure of continuity. At Henbury School, the farming community established in the Iron Age continued through until the end of the 4th century AD (Evans *et al* 2006). The settlement lay close to the suspected route of a Roman road from Sea Mills to the *colonia* at Gloucester. The road was fully excavated in 2006 (BHER 24528) and was found running on a north-east to south-west alignment, constructed with a gently graded camber, without drainage ditches, sometime during the 2nd century AD (Young 2011). There is fragmentary evidence for other Roman roads in the Bristol area, notably at Durdham Down (Trice-Martin 1900) and Lawrence Weston (Boore 1995b) and Henbury, and the network can be conjecturally reconstructed in its broad outline (Russell and Williams 1984).

The major Roman settlement in the Bristol area was the port town of Abonae at Sea Mills which has long been a focus of archaeological interest. Elements of the town were observed during construction of the Severn Beach railway in the late 19th century, the Portway for road traffic in the 1930s and the Hadrian Close housing estate immediately after the Second World War (Ellis 1893–6; Trice-Martin 1923; Portway-Dobson 1939; Boon 1945). More recently (2008), extensive evaluation work at Hadrian Close has demonstrated that this area lay at the heart of the Roman town, with well-preserved Roman deposits in all areas of the site, some very close to the modern ground surface (BHER 24589). The pottery assemblage appears to display a preponderance of early Roman (1st to early 2nd century) wares, as has other recent work in the area (Foundations Archaeology 2010). The few large developments that have offered the opportunity for area excavation suggest that Abonae was a fairly typical small town, though major questions about its spatial organisation remain unanswered (Bennett 1985; Ellis 1987).

Overall, archaeological work together with other evidence suggests an extensively farmed rural landscape, utilising the wetlands, with village-scale settlements and a number of small towns (Williams 1983; R H Jones 1996; Jackson 2007). The Roman economy was complex and there is good evidence for regional and international trade. Settlement continued into the 5th century at Abonae and possibly also at Redfield in east Bristol where samples of human bone from interments were dated to 340–640 cal AD at a 95.4% confidence (Wk-11396).

Post-Roman

The history of the area after the Roman withdrawal is obscure but it may have fallen within the political control of the Hwicce, a group subject to the overlordship of the kingdom of Mercia. The Wansdyke, an earth bank and ditch running between Maes Knoll and Bath, was constructed after the end of the Roman Empire to mark, Costen suggests, a territorial boundary between the 'Old Welsh of Somerset to the south and the new English groups to the north' (Costen 1992, 71). Place-name evidence suggests widespread post-Roman settlement across the region and evidence from Somerset indicates the development of sizeable estates; there may have been an estate centre at Bedminster to the south of the city centre for example (ibid, 80–110). An estate centre existed at Westbury-on-Trym by the early 9th century and quite possibly before (Orme and Cannon 2010). Christianity may have arrived in the region by the early 7th century and a monastic site was established at Westbury in the 960s (Taylor 1897–9, Orme and Cannon 2010).

Archaeological evidence for post-Roman occupation of the Bristol area is slight, and consists mainly of chance finds or surviving fragmentary monuments, particularly cross fragments and the surviving elements of some churches (Rahtz nd, 79). Archaeological excavation has been very limited although the results have been interesting. Excavation at Cadbury-Congresbury found that the hillfort had been re-occupied in the 6th century and the largest monument in the area, the Wansdyke, has recently been the subject of a campaign of investigation (Alcock 1995, 13–43; Barrett *et al* 2000; Young 1994–5, 68). Within Bristol, observation of pipe-laying at Kings Weston Hill in 1966 identified inhumations believed to form part of an early Christian cemetery, while excavation at Westbury College in 1968 found evidence for timber buildings and part of a cemetery associated with the monastic site (Godman 1972; Ponsford 1981). However, even when the archaeological record is supplemented with the available historical evidence, our knowledge of the area in this period is quite poor.

Evidence for prehistoric and Roman settlement in historic Bristol (Figs 4.1 and 4.2)

Within the city centre no archaeological excavation has yet recorded any features of pre-Roman date. The majority of the evidence for the Roman and pre-Roman periods has come largely by way of chance finds of objects, often made during deep excavation or dredging in the 19th and early 20th centuries, and recovered without record of their original context. Indirect evidence for human activity in both the Mesolithic and Neolithic periods, in the form of management of the surrounding vegetation, is suggested by the detailed analyses of strata retrieved during geoarchaeological prospection (Wilkinson *et al* 2013b).

Several excavations in the city centre have produced assemblages of residual flint artefacts, some large – like those recovered on the south side of Upper Maudlin Street (BHER 316; 432; 3399) and at Union Street (BHER 3590). The former ranges in date from the Neolithic to the Early Bronze Age but also includes a single blade of likely Mesolithic date (Jackson 2000a, 44–5, 75–7). However, the only indication of prehistoric activity so far known from a primary, *in situ*, context are three undated worked flint flakes found in clay overlying the bedrock at Southwell Street (Brett 1994, 13); little can be inferred from these objects (BHER 404).

A larger assemblage of material is available for the Bronze Age although as yet it consists exclusively of stray finds. A bronze axe was found in the river Avon when a new lock was excavated at Cumberland Basin 'about 20 feet below the river bank' (BHER 3282), and during widening of Bristol Bridge *c* 1874, several axes of Early and Middle Bronze Age date were found on the southern bank of the river Avon, together with part of a sword blade (BHER 50). The finds were dispersed without record and whether the finds formed part of a hoard or were associated with other features or finds is likely to remain unknown (Pritchard 1904, 329–30). An axe and spearhead were also found during construction at the Co-operative Wholesale building at Narrow Quay in 1932 but again the context of the finds was not recorded (BHER 3235: Tratman 1946, 174).

Reported evidence for the Iron Age within the city has come primarily from the observation of deep excavations for the construction of a new factory at Pithay in 1900 by John Pritchard (BHER 3153). A small group of animal remains was recovered from 'a depth of fully 12 ft. beneath the cellar level …' of the post-medieval buildings on the site, and included two bone needles (7½ and 5½ inches long), sawn antler and horn and a whetstone. On the basis of an opinion from Professor William Boyd Dawkins, Pritchard interpreted these finds and further material from Fairfax Street in 1903 as being of Iron Age date (Pritchard 1900, 269–70). Two bone needles and a fragment of antler came from a depth of 'over 20 feet below the sloping bank of the Frome, in the blue alluvial deposit' while a slate whetstone was recovered 'at considerable depth in the bank, further down the stream' (BHER 188; Pritchard 1904, 331). In 1906 Pritchard again recorded what he took to be Iron Age material in the Pithay district (BHER 3125). Most significantly, animal remains and pottery sherds came from depths of between 30 and 40 feet (Pritchard 1907a, 151–3).

Another discovery, made in 1848, may also belong to this period. In that year excavation of a deep sewer in Quay Street, close to the town wall, exposed a log-boat (BHER 411). The only known account reports that: 'at a considerable depth from the surface, [the workmen] discovered a canoe, fourteen feet long, and four feet wide, shaped from a single trunk of timber, the wood being comparatively

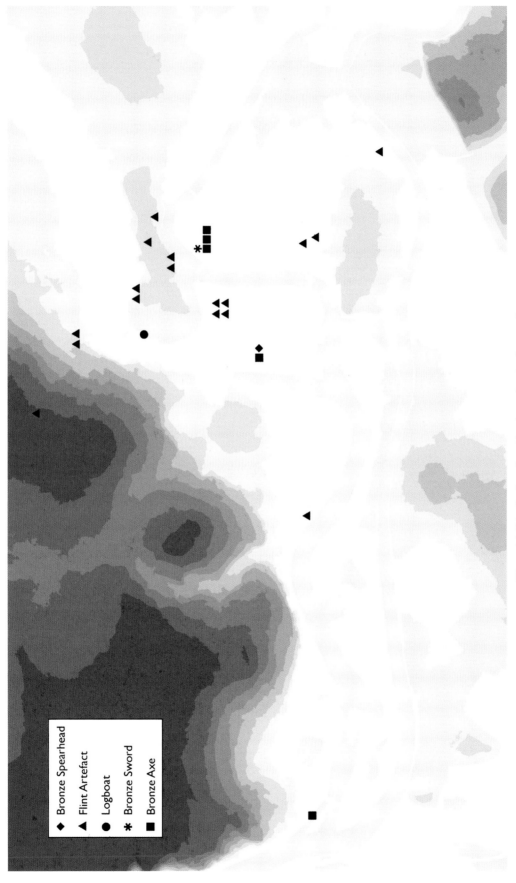

Figure 4.1 Distribution of prehistoric artefacts in the central area

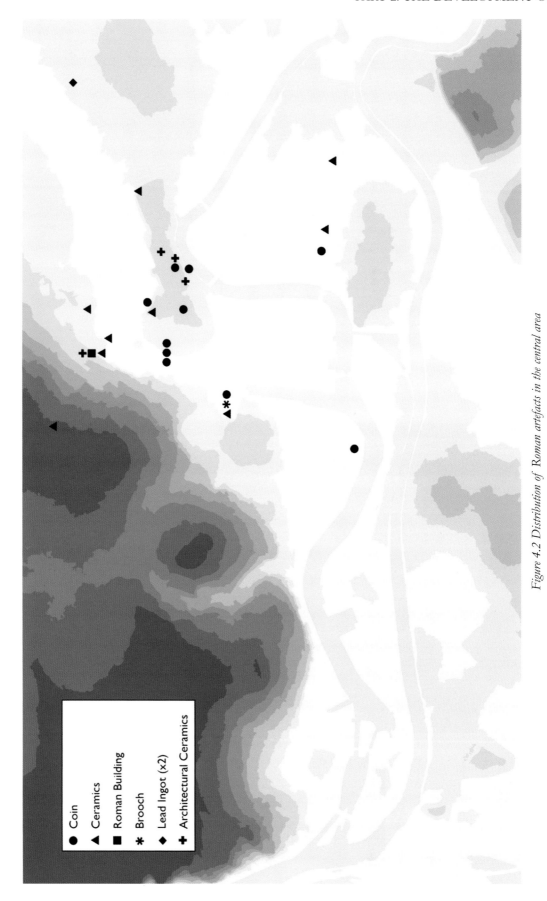

Figure 4.2 Distribution of Roman artefacts in the central area

sound. Unfortunately this relic of antiquity had to be sawn through, as it was found impossible, without great risk of injury to the workmen, to remove it entire' (*Bristol Mercury and Western Counties Advertiser*, 23 December 1848). The lack of a more detailed description makes it very difficult to interpret and date the find.

Romano-British material is distributed widely across the city centre but the bulk of it consists of coin finds and residual (out-of-context) pottery. The context of most coin finds is unknown but Samuel Seyer reported that four were found on the southern side of Bell Lane while laying the foundations for a house in 1808 (BHER 277), while a late 3rd- or early 4th-century coin of Maximianus was found in alluvial clay '11 feet below the roadway' at the junction of All Saints' Street and All Saints' Avenue in July 1900 (BHER 3283; Seyer 1821, 208; Pritchard 1900, 265). More substantial was the discovery, during commercial excavation, of two lead ingots in Wade Street in 1865 – lying in the former channel of the river Frome according to a contemporary account (BHER 2518; Anon 1866). Marks on their surfaces establish that the ingots were cast in the same mould as two ingots found near Wells in 1956, possibly linking the Bristol area to the Mendip lead industry (Elkington 1976), while isotope analysis suggests the lead was mined in the Bristol/Frome/Weston-super-Mare area (G Boyle pers comm). In 1910 groundworks for the construction of the Hippodrome Theatre on the west side of St Augustine's Parade exposed a feature variously described as a 'pebble track' or 'cobbled causeway', which was observed, though not recorded, by Alfred Selley, a local collector, running in the direction of St Augustine's Parade and was associated with Roman pottery, coins and an 'undoubted' brooch (BHER 220; Davies 1927, 42; Tratman 1961–2, 164).

The strongest evidence for settlement in the Roman period has come from excavations close to Upper Maudlin Street in the 1970s when clear evidence of a settlement of at least two phases was recorded. A late 3rd- to 4th-century building with stone foundations, as well as part of an associated yard surface and a small iron-working furnace, were excavated at the northern end of the Moravian chapel in 1973 (BHER 316) while in 1976, at its southern end, a further wall, also of stone with

post pads suggesting a timber superstructure, was uncovered. Slots in the subsoil within this building were interpreted as the possible remains of a floor. In both excavations the wall fragments were found to overlie earlier ditches (BHER 432: Jackson 2000a, 45–9).

No definite evidence for the period between the end of Roman occupation and the Late Saxon period has yet been recorded in the historic city centre.

The origins of Saxon Bristol

As the following chapter will describe, Bristol appears quite suddenly in the historical and archaeological record, with coinage from the second decade of the 11th century implying that it was already a defended trading-place that took its name from the bridge across the Avon, and documentary references from 1051 onwards making it clear that *Brycgstow*, as it was known, was associated with shipping and with the Irish connection. While there is no definitive evidence for the place's origins prior to the early 11th century, a number of inferences may nevertheless be drawn from features of the town recorded in later years.

Bristol lay at the western end of the royal manor of Barton Regis. Amongst the churches of the medieval town, one, St Peter's, stands out as having the characteristics of an old minster (or mother-church): it was well-endowed with land, drawing revenues from half of the manor of Barton, and had rights over a daughter chapel at Mangotsfield. A bishop of Worcester noted, in the early 12th century, that St Peter's was locally recognised as the senior church in Bristol (Boucher 1909). This however, raises further questions: when, and by whom, was the church founded, and why on that particular site?

The close association of a pre-Conquest fortified site and a major bridge, as seen at Bristol, was not just a characteristic of the 10th century but may also, it has been argued, have been found in the 8th, particularly in the kingdom of Mercia as a consequence of the defensive strategies of Offa and his predecessor Aethelbald. It has been suggested by Jean Manco that Bristol may owe its origins to an Offan fortification occupying the same footprint as the later Saxon defended town. St Peter's, likewise, could have been founded by Offa, either as an isolated minster church on the edge of the royal estate, or directly associated with a fortification or, conceivably, with a fortified settlement and its market. In connection with the latter, it has been noted that the church immediately west of St Peter's, St Mary-le-Port, was alternatively named St Mary in Foro (in the market place) (Manco 2009). The view that Bristol may have been founded as a town – rather than as a military fortification with a royal minster attached to it – complete with a planned street system, as early as the late 890s, has been supported by Jeremy Haslam (2011, 216–17). It has also been postulated by Leech (2014, 13) that Bristol may have formed part of the strategic defensive network to counter the threat of Viking raids in the early 10th century. Attractive as these hypotheses are, archaeology has yet to provide corroborative evidence.

The site of Saxon Bristol

The site of Saxon Bristol – the core of the medieval city – has long been recognised as providing an almost uniquely perfect combination of access for trade and protection for defence. It is an east–west ridge at the junction of the River Frome with the Avon, the former flowing around a broad flat-topped sandstone headland overlooking the confluence. The much narrower ridge extending to the north-east is squeezed between the Avon to the south and the Frome to the north, and it was at this point that St Peter's church was built. As the following chapter will describe, excavated evidence now shows that, by the time of the Norman Conquest, occupation extended across the headland and along the ridge, further than St Peter's, to the outer limits of the later castle (Chapter 5, below).

One aspect of the natural topography of central Bristol that remains unclear is the exact position of the Frome and its confluence prior to its well-documented diversion in the 1240s to its present more southerly position. The curving western edge of the natural headland that was followed by the medieval defences was clearly shaped by an early channel of the Frome cutting into the natural sandstone – but was this the channel that was still open, until its diversion, in the medieval period? Another possible channel has recently been identified further south, south of Baldwin Street, from the analysis of LiDAR data showing as an area of slightly depressed ground (*see also* Chapter 2). However, historical evidence has been used to suggest that, up until its diversion, the Frome channel ran on a line still further south, approximately represented by King Street. This, as the following chapter will explore, is the line most consistent with the internal topography of the medieval built-up area. The initial results of the deposit model (*see* Chapter 2) also suggest a more complex model than that provided by earlier historic sources.

Chapter 5: 'Almost the richest city of all in the country': Bristol, *c* 950–*c* 1200

The Late Saxon town (Figs 5.1 and 5.2)

The difficult question of Bristol's origins was briefly explored in the preceding chapter (*see* pp 79–80). The paucity of surviving documentation continues to be a problem almost up to the Norman Conquest, historical sources not mentioning *Brycgstow* until 1051 when the *Anglo-Saxon Chronicle* records the flight of Earl Harold and his brother Leofwine from the town by ship to Ireland (Whitelock 1961, 120), incidentally disclosing that Bristol's role as an Irish Sea port was already established. In the face of a lack of other evidence, the date by which Bristol had been founded has been inferred from coin finds in Scandinavia and elsewhere. The earliest coin was struck between 1009 and 1016, in the reign of Æthelred II, by a moneyer named Ælfwerd (Grinsell nd, 174; Lobel and Carus-Wilson 1975). From the laws governing the issue of coinage in this period we can however also infer that Bristol was already a defended place. To this may be added the place-name itself, as discussed earlier, signifying the importance of the bridge over the Avon as a feature of primary importance to the town. Otherwise, apart from deductions drawn from later documentary evidence, including Domesday Book, and from the urban topography recorded in later centuries, knowledge of the existence and form of pre-Conquest Bristol is derived entirely from archaeological research.

The archaeological evidence

The physical evidence for the pre-Conquest occupation of the headland in the Avon–Frome confluence – the historic core of Bristol – has come from a handful of excavations since the Second World War. Limited excavation at Cheese Market to the north-east of St Mary-le-Port in the 1950s (BHER 419) had already observed pottery similar to Saxon ceramics from East Anglia (Marshall 1951) before major excavations were conducted by the late Philip Rahtz around St Mary-le-Port in 1962–3 (BHER 358). These produced the earliest and the largest assemblage of likely pre- and early post-Conquest material so far excavated in Bristol. At the east end of Mary-le-Port Street a double ditch at least 1.5 metres across and orientated north–south was discovered. Within the fill were sherds dated to the later 10th or early 11th century, and the excavator suggested that the cut itself may have dated to the first (aceramic) period of Late Saxon occupation (Watts and Rahtz 1985, 147) (Fig 5.3).

Another ditch was recorded at the west end of the site, this time running east to west, with stakeholes on its northern bank marking the line of a fence. Only animal bone and charcoal were recovered from its fill and it, too, was ascribed to this earliest phase. Excavation by St Mary-le-Port Church recorded evidence for a Late Saxon street, worn into the underlying ground by the passage of wheeled vehicles and pedestrians, and post-dating both of the early ditches. A cross-section of the deposits making up the street surfaces was obtained and a coin of Harold (1066) was recovered from the latest of these, indicating an early post-Conquest date for

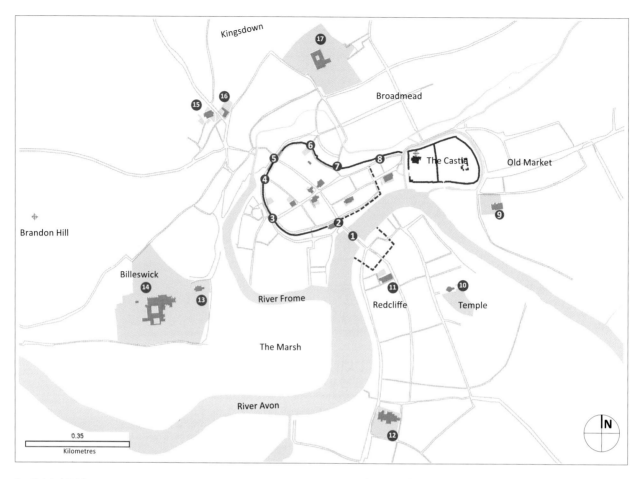

1   Bristol Bridge

2   St Nicholas' Gate

3   St Leonard's Gate

4   St Giles or King Edward's Gate

5   St John's Gate

6   Blind Gate or St John's Arch

7   Pithay Gate

8   Aldgate or Old Gate

9   Church of SS Philip and Jacob

10   Knights Templar Church

11   Church of St Thomas the Martyr

12   Church of St Mary Redcliffe

13   Church of St Augustine-the-Less

14   Abbey of St Augustine

15   Church of St Michael-on-the-Mount Without

16   Nunnery of St Mary Magdalen

17   Priory of St James

[shaded] Churches

[shaded] Cemeteries and ecclesiastical precincts

━━━ Town walls and defences/
━ ━ conjectured alignment

Figure 5.1 Bristol c *1200*

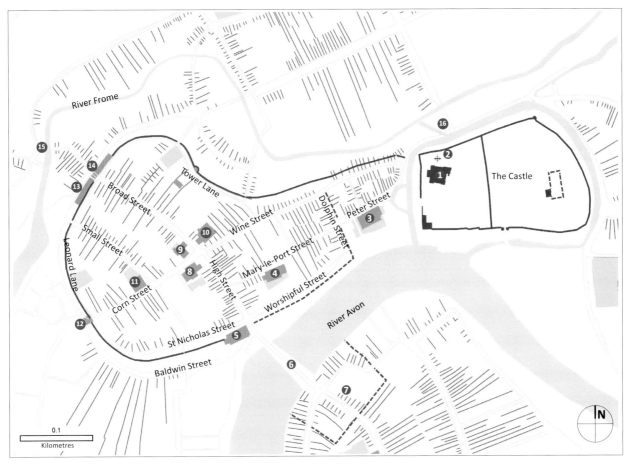

1 Castle Keep	9 Church of St Ewen
2 Chapel of St Martin's	10 Christ Church
3 Church of St Peter	11 Church of St Werburgh
4 Church of St Mary-le-Port	12 Church of St Leonard
5 Church of St Nicholas	13 Church of St Lawrence
6 Bristol Bridge	14 Church of St John the Baptist
7 Arthur's Fee	15 Frome Bridge
8 Church of All Saints	16 Castle Mill

 Churches

           Cemeteries and ecclesiastical precincts

           Town walls and defences/
           conjectured alignment

Figure 5.2 Historic core of Bristol c *1200*

*Figure 5.3 Mary-le-Port
plan of excavation areas
(reproduced from Watts
and Rahtz 1985, fig 23)*

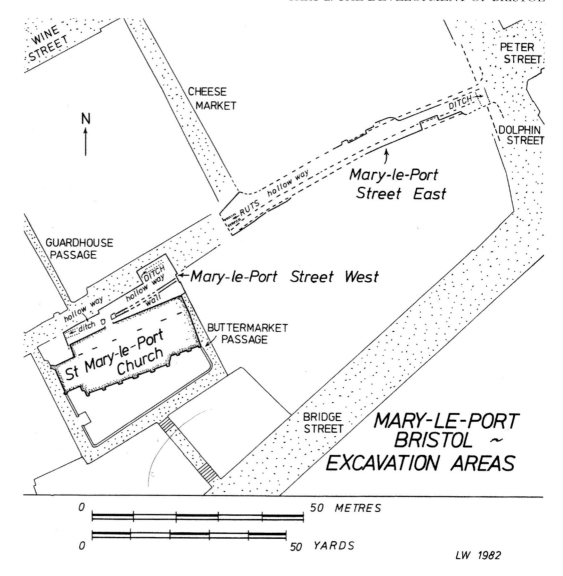

its deposition and, by inference, a probable pre-Conquest date for the rest. By the north-east corner of the church, on the south side of the hollow way, elements of a timber building of at least two phases, and dating to the 11th or 12th centuries, were recorded. The first phase was represented by a row of large postholes. The evidence for the second was again postholes and cuts for possible timber sills. Something of the internal arrangement of space could be identified, with a threshold on the line of the Saxon street, and heat scorched stones, one with iron slag fused to it, interpreted as the remains of a hearth. Fragments of daub

suggested the likely form of the building's superstructure (ibid, 78–80). Iron slag and crucible fragments were among the finds. These, with the evidence of a possible hearth, led the excavator to believe that iron working had taken place within the building.

West of St Mary-le-Port, Late Saxon and Norman evidence came from excavations at the site of the Crown Courts in Small Street where two small trenches were dug in 1990 (BHER 313). In one, immediately behind Small Street, 11th-century postholes and a cess pit were recorded; in the second, against Leonard Lane, a possible earthen bank was found that may have been a precursor to the medieval town wall (Williams 1992, 54: *see below*). Late Saxon pits were also recorded at Fitzharding House, Tower Lane in 1979–80 (BHER 320) beneath the remains of a Norman building (Fig 5.4). A large Late Saxon cess pit was excavated on an adjacent site at Newmarket Avenue in 1990 (BHER 472; G L Good pers comm).

On the ridge to the east of the headland, excavations on the north side of Peter Street in 1970 (BHER 409) and 1975 (BHER 319) recorded part of a possible Late Saxon boundary and postholes which may have been from two timber structures of similar date (Boore 1982, 8). Further east along the ridge, substantial evidence for Late Saxon occupation came from a series of excavations and watching briefs carried out on the site of Bristol Castle from the late 1940s to the early 1970s (Fig 5.10).

The earliest deposit was a layer of clay, found in three discrete places (BHER 488, 448; 3287), interpreted as a former land surface. From it, on the Middle Terrace site, a single sherd of pottery of the same late 10th- or early 11th-century fabric as was found in the fill of the double ditch at Mary-le-Port Street was recovered. The Middle Terrace site produced other evidence for Late Saxon occupation including the remains of what was interpreted as the fire-pit of a metalworking furnace. Dating to *c* 1000–70, the structure consisted of a pit with a semi-circle of stakeholes, perhaps part of a clay superstructure, around its northern edge. Areas of ashy material filled the pit while the surrounding soil showed signs of heat scorching and a perforated stone at the southern end was believed by the excavator to be the base of a forge-stone. Other pre-Conquest deposits also produced iron smithing slag (Ponsford 1979, 499–500). Evidence for other structures, in the form of several postholes and possible beam slots, was recorded during the excavation of these three areas but no complete building plans could be defined with any confidence (ibid, 241–2) (Fig 5.5).

The defences (Fig 5.2)

Saxon Bristol was clearly a defended settlement but almost nothing is known about its defences. So, while archaeological evidence clearly shows

that both the headland and the ridge to the east were occupied in the pre-Conquest period, there is minimal excavated evidence at present to show how or where this settlement was defended.

Given that the headland was occupied, it is highly likely that the later, Norman, wall that encircled it followed a course that had been determined by earlier, pre-Conquest, defences. The possible bank found by excavation close to Leonard Lane may belong to these, but no finds were recovered from

Figure 5.4 Overhead view of the Tower Lane excavation 1979

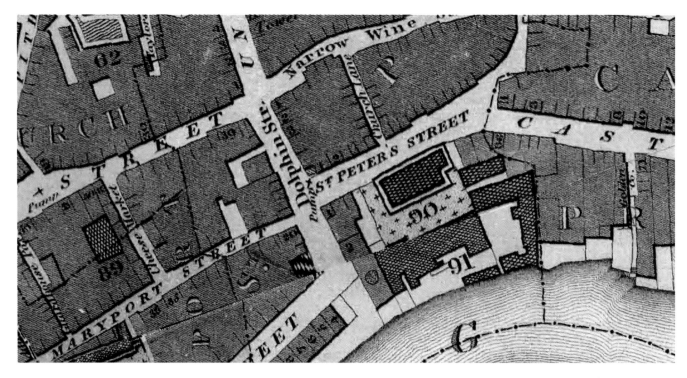

it to confirm its date and too small an area was sampled to establish its character beyond doubt (BHER 313).

But the ridge too was almost certainly defended, possibly along the slopes overlooking the rivers to the north and south, more certainly by barriers erected across the ridge, compartmentalising it and offering obstacles to any hostile force approaching on dry land from the east. Philip Rahtz was uncertain whether the double ditch he excavated at the junction of Dolphin

Street and Mary-le-Port Street (*see above*) was a property boundary or part of a larger defensive circuit enclosing the settlement, though Mary-le-Port Street appeared to terminate at it in its earliest phase (Watts and Rahtz 1985, 186). That there was such a ditch or other barrier across the ridge at this point is predictable from the later topography, Dolphin Street forming a clear fault-line in the town plan, neither Mary-le-Port Street nor Wine Street continuing across it without an abrupt change of alignment and width (Fig 5.6).

Attention has also been directed to the earlier name of Dolphin Street: Defence Street, which was in use by 1391 (Leech 1997b, 22). A similar discontinuity is apparent in the city streets 90 metres further east, where Narrow Wine Street and Peter Street similarly came to an abrupt end. This undoubtedly reflects the presence of the former castle perimeter, but it is quite possible that there was a pre-Conquest cross-ridge barrier in the same position, possibly an even more substantial one than the ditches under Dolphin Street. The best archaeological analogue for such a feature remains Lydford in Devon, where the planned Late Saxon peninsula-end settlement was primarily protected by a substantial rampart and ditch thrown across the neck of the peninsula (Addyman 1966). Similar features are apparent on the peninsula site of Saxon Shrewsbury, one cross-ridge feature having been dated to the early 11th century; another, outer, defence across the peninsula neck, remains unexcavated beneath the later medieval defences (Baker 2010).

Excavation in the north-east corner of the castle bailey found evidence of an earth rampart and a timber gatehouse, possibly the castle's first east gate, both dated by the excavator to the late 11th century (*see below*). It has however been suggested that the imprecision of the dating evidence could allow for these structures being pre-Conquest, belonging to pre-castle town defences, the excavator also commenting on the similarity of the Bristol gatehouse to the excavated pre-Conquest gatehouse at South Cadbury hillfort (Leech 1997b, 22). In short, the eastern ditch of the medieval castle, cutting across the ridge from Avon to Frome (and surviving to this day, culverted) may represent a third, outermost, cross-ridge defensive feature of the pre-Conquest period.

Bristol Bridge

Although it has been suggested that Bristol Bridge has been moved southwards from an original site below Dolphin Street (Ponsford 1985, 112–13), the more widely-shared view is that it has always been on its present site, at the foot of High Street, where the slope up onto the headland is far more gentle than the steep gradient up onto the ridge further east.

Across the Avon, Redcliff Hill and the marsh to its north were probably rural in character, and administratively distinct from Bristol, being part of the manor of Bedminster in the county of Somerset. The possible exception is the very northern tip of Redcliffe where, Dr Roger Leech has suggested, the southern abutment of Bristol Bridge may have been enclosed by a defended bridgehead. This was the area known by the late 13th century as Arthur's Fee or Stakepenny, which appears to have had an identity that was distinct from its surroundings. It was an approximately rectangular area around 120m across and 80m deep, the boundaries on its north-eastern and south-western sides later becoming major property boundaries known as Law Ditches (Jackson 2006a; Leech 2009) (Fig 5.2).

Recent excavations offer support for this hypothesis in that a substantial ditch at least 7m wide in its primary phase, recut to a maximum width of 15.5m, contained a buttercup seed and a hazelnut shell which produced calibrated radiocarbon dates of 1021–1155 (NZA 30143) and 991–1152 (NZA 30153) respectively. While not conclusive, this is consistent with an early, pre-Conquest, date for the laying out of the defended bridgehead (Teague and Brady 2017a, 28) (Fig 5.7).

The first port of Bristol and its trading connections

The location of the wharves of pre-Conquest Bristol, two centuries before the diversion of the river Frome in the 13th century, is uncertain. Welsh Back is the most obvious site, but there is also the possibility that at

Figure 5.7 Finzels Reach excavation 2007 showing possible Late Saxon ditch, looking north-west (reproduced from Ford et al 2017, fig 2.3)

least part of the northern bank of the Frome below Baldwin Street was used as wharfage before its diversion. The early harbour need not necessarily have had built stone or timber wharves. There is a long tradition on the Severn and its estuary, particularly on the North Somerset coast, of the use of informal landing places, tidal creeks for example, while from other evidence it is clear that ships were often unloaded by horse and cart via a simple plank (Green 1996; Trinder 2005). The place name *Rakhyth*, the modern Rackhay to the west of Queen Charlotte Street, may suggest a former landing place of this type. It may be that we should be expecting no more than a hard-standing, though perhaps with associated jetties of the kind which have been found on the Late Saxon waterfront at New Fresh Wharf in London (Steedman *et al* 1992, 21–39).

The secret of the success of Bristol as a port serving the Severn Estuary, the Irish Sea and, later, the Atlantic, is hinted at as early as the mid-12th century by the *Gesta Stephani*. It interrupts its narrative of the civil war of the 1130s–40s to provide the earliest written description of Bristol, emphasising its situation between the two rivers and noting the tidal range which 'drives back the current of the rivers to produce a wide and deep expanse of water' capable of accommodating a thousand ships (Potter 1955, 47–8). Until vessels outgrew the Avon channel in the 19th century, it was this twice-daily tidal surge that helped propel shipping to and from Bristol and the sea, giving it a huge natural advantage over Gloucester, historically its only potential rival as a Severn Estuary port, but one which was separated from the sea by a much longer, more dangerous and convoluted passage between shifting sandbanks.

In addition to the *Anglo-Saxon Chronicle*'s record of the flight of Earl Harold and his brother to Ireland in 1051, in 1063 the town was reported to be supplying ships to a punitive expedition by Harold against the Welsh and it is known to have traded with Scandinavia and Ireland from early in its history (Whitelock 1961, 120, 136). Although the nature of this commerce is unknown, a trade in slaves is generally acknowledged as one of the sources of the town's wealth – foreshadowing the greater involvement in the exploitation of human misery in the later 17th and 18th centuries. Slaves, usually either the young, prisoners of war, or those who had fallen into debt, formed a large stratum of Late Saxon society and the people traded through Bristol were apparently transported to Ireland for further shipment to Normandy or Iberia (Pelteret 1981). Clerical opposition to the slave trade was led by Wulfstan, Bishop of Worcester, in whose diocese the town lay, who undertook active preaching against the trade in the town in the years after the Norman Conquest (Darlington 1928, 43).

The internal topography of the early town (Fig 5.2)

The traditional understanding of the early topography of Bristol, widely accepted before the Second World War, developed from the work of antiquarians and amateur archaeologists and is stated concisely in Stephenson's examination of the origins of English towns. Here, the town is argued to be a pre-Conquest *burh*, located at the western end of the rock outcrop or headland defined by the Frome and the Avon, the Norman castle created on its east side in the 1080s (Stephenson 1933, 202–4).

This orthodox interpretation of the topography has been challenged by Michael Ponsford, using the results of the excavations at Mary-le-Port Street and his own investigations on the site of Bristol Castle to argue that the earliest nucleus of the Late Saxon town, or *burh*, in fact lay on the ridge: from Mary-le-Port Street and St Peter's church extending east as far as the outer ditch of the castle, represented by Lower Castle Street. Occupation, according to this view, gradually spread to the west to incorporate the area which became the Norman walled town; effectively, the town was re-sited after 1066 (Ponsford 1979, 25–7; Ponsford nd(a), 145–6; Aston 1982, 127). This radical hypothesis has however been questioned by Roger Leech (1997b, 18–24), who disputed the need to abandon the traditional view of the early growth of Bristol, citing, in particular, the presence of pre-Conquest pottery across the Norman town on the headland, the pre-Conquest parallels for its distinctive planned street system, and the density of early churches there.

An alternative perspective is that these divergent views of Bristol's early growth need not be as mutually exclusive as they first appear. In the preceding chapter the probability of the origin of St Peter's church as an early, perhaps 8th-century, minster church on the royal estate was briefly discussed. Such a church, with its cemetery, would almost certainly have stood apart from its secular surroundings in some kind of ditched enclosure. The partitioning of the Bristol ridge has also been referred to, and the origin of the topographical discontinuities either side of St Peter's church, at each end of Peter Street, may perhaps be found in a former minster enclosure. Little is known of the pre-Conquest occupation to its east, destroyed by the Norman castle, but there is every chance that here was another fundamental component of the earliest settlement, possibly a site of high status positioned on a tactically advantageous site adjoining what appears to have been Bristol's senior church. The list of English towns whose Norman castles took over establishments that are known to have been of existing administrative importance or already defended is growing. Stamford, Stafford and Shrewsbury are in the latter category; Wallingford is in the former, its castle replacing a probable Anglo-Saxon royal hall where the housecarls (mercenary troops of the royal household) once dwelt (Drage 1987, 119; Cuttler *et al* 2009; Baker 2010, 106; Christie *et al* 2013, 148–9). If there was ever a royal hall in Bristol (and none is documented), it is most likely to have been on the site of the castle.

But, for the first planned urban settlement, catering for a density of population, it is surely, as Leech suggests, to the heart of the Norman town that we should turn. Its fundamental distinguishing characteristic is exactly what was emphasised by Robert Ricart in his bird's-eye-view of 1479, the earliest image we have of medieval Bristol: the cruciform street plan contained within encircling walls with the High Cross at the centre (Fig 3.20).

The principal (upright, north–south) arm of the cross is formed by Broad Street and High Street, the horizontal (west–east) arm by Corn Street and Wine Street. Small Street runs exactly parallel to Broad Street; Mary-le-Port Street ran parallel to Wine Street. Both Small Street and Mary-le-Port Street look as if they were planned as rear service lanes behind the main street plots, though both had developed plots of their own by the time records are

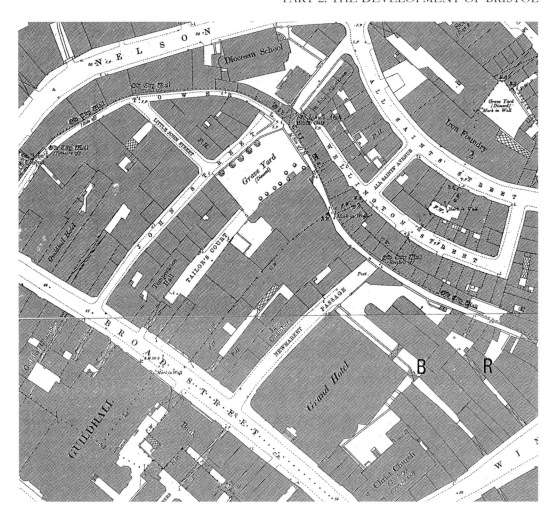

available; Mary-le-Port Street, as we have seen, was of Saxon date, built up before the Conquest. Archaeological evidence supporting a pre-Conquest date for the street plan was also found by an excavation in 1990 on Small Street where Late Saxon features were found respecting the alignment of the street (BHER 313; J Bryant pers comm).

The characteristics of the street plan – the cruciform arrangement of the main streets, secondary (or at least narrower, perhaps less important) streets running exactly parallel to the main streets – strongly suggest a deliberately planned, designed, origin. The details of this landscape hint at a slightly more complex process. Roger Leech has drawn attention to the slight curve in the plans of some of the Broad Street plots, and has suggested that these might betray an agricultural origin, house-plots or burgages having been formed by simply enclosing pre-existing agricultural strips, citing also the later property name 'halffurlonge' in the south-west quarter.(Fig 5.8).

As he also noted, this feature is absent from the smaller, much more densely packed plots in the south-east quarter around St Mary-le-Port (Leech 1997b, 24; Leech 2014, 15). Without detailed analysis (and field measurement of surviving plot frontages would be unlikely to be productive), it appears as if Broad Street and the northern and western quarters were subject to different developmental processes from the south-east quarter.

Whether the basic framework of the cruciform arrangement of the main streets originated in a single act of planning is uncertain – and therefore so too is the degree of probability that the cruciform plan was deliberately engineered for its Christian symbolism. High Street and Broad Street form what could be considered the more ancient or primary through-route over the headland, linking Bristol Bridge to the Frome Bridge. Wine Street too can be seen as a primary route bringing traffic onto the headland from the ridge. Corn Street, its western continuation, appears to have had a more local significance: from the 13th century it took traffic towards the Quay on the Frome, though there is no evidence that this area was developed before the Norman Conquest.

There is nothing inherently closely datable in this urban landscape of streets and plots: the rectilinear arrangement of streets can certainly be paralleled in Middle and Late Saxon contexts, particularly the 9th-century Wessex *burhs* of King Alfred (Biddle and Hill 1971), but such simple design elements can be found in later contexts too. This also applies to the provision of streets immediately within the defences encircling the headland, clockwise: Lawrence Lane (later Bell Lane), Tower Lane, St Nicholas Street and St Leonard's Lane; and, as Dr Leech has suggested, possibly Dolphin (Defence) Street and Worshipful Street (later replaced by Bridge Street) on the adjoining ridge. While such 'wall streets' allowing access to defended urban perimeters are a feature of Late Saxon planning, they too can also be found in post-Conquest contexts, like Wall Street and Gaol Lane in 12th-century Hereford.

It is, as has been suggested, the concentration of church foundations on the headland, and their distribution, that are the clearest indications of the pre-Conquest origins of the built-up area. The churches will be considered in more detail below but their relevance to the development of the town needs some discussion here. The central Carfax was dominated by a cluster of three churches: St Ewen's on the north-west corner, Christ Church on the north-east and All Saints on or near the south-west corner. The parallels with the central Carfax at Gloucester are quite striking, the churches clustered there being St Michael's, All Saints' and the chapel of St Martin. St Michael's and All Saints' are most likely to have been pre-Conquest foundations, established on their central corner sites at an early stage of the development of the built-up area (Baker and Holt 2004). St Ewen's in Bristol however may have been an early post-Conquest foundation, mirroring the churches of St Owen/Audoen in Hereford and Gloucester.

It has been suggested that the central churches in Bristol were founded contemporaneously, they and their parishes amounting to carefully-planned ecclesiastical provision, a separate parish to each quarter (Morris 1989, 210) (*see* Fig 6.46). The wards of Bristol, secular administrative units principally concerned with the maintenance of the defences, were also based on the quarters and took their names from their respective parish churches – St Mary-le-Port, Christ Church, All Saints and St Ewen's. However, it is equally possible that the churches were founded separately over a period of time and acquired their parishes later, the simplicity of the town plan determining the logic of both the parishes and the wards.

The number of churches sited on the defended perimeter is another singular feature of early Bristol which has for many years been thought of as a likely pre-Conquest characteristic (Lobel and Carus-Wilson 1975, 5). Four churches (St Nicholas, St Leonard, St John and St Lawrence) were placed over the town's main gates with a fifth, St Giles, over the smaller St Giles' Gate at the bottom of Small Street. In fact St John's, at the end of Broad Street, was a foundation of *c* 1192 (*see below*) and St Nicholas' may have been an early post-Conquest foundation, the dedication being most popular at the turn of the 11th and 12th centuries, found in association with a new suburb in Worcester and with a new transpontine suburb and its bridge at Gloucester (Baker and Holt 2004).

In addition to the churches around the Carfax and on the gates, early Bristol had two more parish churches. St Mary-le-Port has been shown by excavation to have had probable pre-Conquest origins (p 92); St Werburgh's on the corner of Corn Street and Small Street was in place by 1148–83 and has a dedication that could equally well belong to the 10th century or to the late 11th (*see below* p 108).

It is also the case that *all* the churches on the headland closely mimic the orientation of the nearest streets or the defences, none within the walls being truly east–west (in contrast, for instance, to the post-Conquest St Stephen's just outside the early town wall). This too may be taken as an indication of a pre-Conquest or at least pre-12th-century date for most or many of the churches of the intramural core (Morris 1989, 208–9).

Outside the defences

Within the Avon–Frome confluence, pre-Conquest occupation appears to have been restricted to the headland and the ridge before the 12th century. There is no sign of occupation outside the southern defences until the development of the Marsh Street suburb, first referred to in 1164–70. However, the ground south of Baldwin Street, (which ran around the outside of the southern defences) was, certainly later, divided into a series of very long, large, irregular plots (Fig 5.16). These are well documented from the mid-13th century on, and nowhere in the documentary evidence is there any hint that they had been extended over the old, pre-diversion, channel of the Frome. This led Roger Leech to conclude that, contrary to the long-held belief that, before its diversion in the 1240s, the old Frome channel lay below Baldwin Street, it had in fact run much further south, just beyond this plot series, on the line of what was later to become King Street (Leech 1997b, 27). The long Baldwin Street plots in fact bear a strong resemblance to the antennae-like plot-systems found widely on the fringes of pre-Conquest towns – for example in York, Gloucester and Shrewsbury – where access to floodplains and external watercourses was carefully apportioned, arguably for the grazing and watering of livestock on a large scale, commensurate with the needs of urban market places (Baker *et al* 1993). The Marsh suburb at Bristol appears to have evolved within and been partly shaped by this extramural plot pattern, whose central portion survived the Middle Ages while its western side was fragmented by the development of Marsh Street and its eastern side by the development of plots (again in the 12th century) facing Welsh Back.

North of the River Frome, the pre-Conquest history of Lewins Mead is largely unknown, although there may have been pre-Conquest settlement at Billeswick to the south-west. The validity of the traditional assumption that this settlement was located between St Augustine's Parade and College Green cannot, however, be firmly established without archaeological excavation. It has been argued that Late Saxon pottery from the river bank at St Bartholomew's Hospital suggests that the river crossing over the Frome is of early date and it is known from documentary evidence that a bridge had been built there by 1111 (Smith 1964, 89). The bank of the river in this area was probably shady wooded marsh, around a probable creek in the area of Narrow Lewins Mead; a possible fence recorded during the excavation at St Bartholomew's may have been intended to control grazing animals (Price with Ponsford 1998, 27). Our knowledge of the early

exploitation of the land on the river cliff above Lewins Mead is still minimal. Much of the ground above the river is likely to have been in agricultural use but excavation has also produced indications of iron working and other activity by the 12th century, suggesting widely spread but low-intensity activity, including some manufacturing. There is as yet, however, no archaeological evidence for domestic occupation of the area between the Late Saxon period and the foundation of the priory of St James, the first of the post-Conquest extramural monastic sites.

The Church

While the density of church foundations within the Avon–Frome confluence is particularly characteristic of the Late Saxon period, the great majority of individual churches went unrecorded until the 12th century and cannot, without archaeological evidence, be proven to be of pre-Conquest origin. These are discussed below in the context of Norman Bristol; this section deals only with those that have more definite evidence of a pre-Conquest origin.

One of the most interesting results of Rahtz's work at St Mary-le-Port was the discovery of features interpreted as a possible Late Saxon or very early post-Conquest church. A foundation of earth-bonded stone was found at the western edge of the standing church tower while another lay parallel to and south of the later line of the north wall of the church. While these features appeared to present a coherent plan, they were very ephemeral and could not be interpreted as the remains of a church with absolute certainty (Watts and Rahtz 1985, 95–7). Inside its east end was an area of heat scorched soil, thought to have been the result of secular industrial activity, although this may have belonged to an earlier phase. A new church was built in mixed Brandon Hill Grit and Pennant sandstone during the Norman period. This structure was very fragmentary, comprising only parts of the north wall, chancel and south wall, but enough remained to indicate that it had no aisle; it was itself rebuilt to give a two-cell plan later in the period (ibid, 98–9).

The College Green area west of the Frome may have been the location of a church or chapel by the middle of the 11th century.

This has been inferred from the presence of the Harrowing of Hell relief in the south transept of the Cathedral. The relief was found in 1831 beneath the floor of the chapter house, where it had been reused as a grave slab, and shows Christ descending into the mouth of hell, from the apocryphal gospel of Nicodemus (Fig 5.9).

While a range of arguments can be advanced for provenance and date (Oakes 2000, 64–72), by consensus the stone is dated to the mid-11th century; the influence of the Winchester School on the style of carving has recently been noted. It is likely that the fragment came originally from an architectural context, possibly from the main entrance of a church (Muñoz de Miguel 1997; Smith 1976). There is a tradition of a chapel dedicated to St Jordan, reputedly one of the followers of St Augustine, in College Green (Seyer 1821, 225). Certainly, a chapel was reported to stand there by William Camden in the 16th century and what may be this structure is also shown in a later 17th-century drawing by Willem Schellinks (reproduced in Hulton 1959). The date and function of this structure are, however, currently unproven.

Other possible archaeological evidence of a pre-Conquest church in the College Green area consists of six adult inhumations excavated at the south-east corner of the church of St Augustine-the-Less in 1983–4 (BHER 1686). Two of the inhumations were contained by cist graves while another was within a head-niche, and all were on a different alignment to the subsequent building on the site (Boore 1985, 25). Samples from three were radiocarbon dated in the early 1990s and calibrated in 2004, producing dates of 1020–1250 cal AD (BM-2599), 1240–1400 cal AD (BM-2600) and 970–1190 cal AD (BM-2601) at a 95.4% confidence (Ambers *et al* 1991, 58).

The early Norman town (Figs 5.1, 5.2, 5.15, 5.16, 5.17, 5.19)

The historical framework

The town appears in the historical record more often after the Norman invasion of 1066. Bristol submitted to the new monarch in 1067 and retained its status as one of two major mints in the area as well as, by inference, its political status (Stewart 1992, 63). Norman

control of much of England remained weak after the Conquest and was subject to a number of challenges. In 1068 two of Harold's sons who had fled into exile in Ireland launched an unsuccessful raid on Bristol using ships supplied by the king of Leinster, Diarmit mac MáelnamBó, while another raid in the South West during the following year also failed to provoke the intended rising (Hudson 1994, 146).

Bristol, one of four boroughs in Gloucestershire, is not well served by Domesday Book, though there are nevertheless signs of a well-established urban community there by 1086. Bristol mostly appears as part of

Figure 5.9 Harrowing of Hell relief, Bristol Cathedral (photograph D Martyn)

the large rural manor of Barton. As well as the land, ploughs and personnel of the rural manor and its constituents, it records that the whole manor, including Bristol, rendered the substantial sum of 110 marks of silver (*c* £73) annually to the crown, with a further 33 marks of silver and one of gold to Geoffrey de Mowbray, Bishop of Coutances, a supporter of William during and after the Conquest who was responsible for the successful defence of Somerset in 1069, and may have been the port reeve of Bristol (Williams 1995, 21; Moore 1982, 163b). The Domesday surveyors were told this by the burgesses: a casual reference to the presence, in 1086, of tenants holding land by the distinctively urban custom of burgess tenure, with its implications of inheritability of property and right of representation in the urban community. The same entry for Barton also records that the Church of Bristol held land assessed at three hides' extent in the constituent manor of Mangotsfield (DB Gloucestershire fol 163).

The Domesday entries for other rural manors add more information about early Bristol. Attached to Worcester Cathedral's manor of Westbury-on-Trym were two houses, in Bristol, rendering 16 pence annually (DB Gloucestershire fol 164v). Across the Avon in Somerset, the Bishop of Winchester's manor of Bishopsworth included ten houses in Bristol (and two in Bath) (DB Somerset fol 88). The phenomenon of urban plots attached to rural manors is a familiar feature of Domesday-period boroughs, representing the presence of the rural landholding or thegnly class in urban affairs. However, apart from the very substantial total annual render recorded for the manor of Barton (143 marks/*c* £95), implying a flourishing, remunerative urban place, Domesday Book contains no information on total numbers of households – no indication of population; though it is likely, from the analogy of other contemporary, less valuable, boroughs to have numbered in the low thousands.

In 1093 the lordship of Bristol was acquired by Robert FitzHamon and subsequently passed to Robert, the Earl of Gloucester. The town became, with Gloucester, one of Robert's twin centres of power and was drawn deeply into the civil war which arose over the succession to the throne after the death of Henry I Stephen of Blois was crowned in preference to Matilda, Henry's designated heir, who launched

a challenge for the throne in 1139. The earl was one of her main backers and, with support from Robert Fitzharding, he established a base for her at Bristol. Contemporary accounts show that Stephen besieged the town, though it has been suggested that his presence was in fact a reconnaissance (Potter 1955, 43–4; Sharp 1982, xix–xx).

Sporadic fighting continued, resulting in Stephen's capture in battle at Lincoln in February 1141 and his imprisonment in the castle at Bristol. He was released at the end of the year in exchange for Robert of Gloucester who had been taken prisoner during attacks on Winchester. With Robert's death at the end of 1147 Matilda abandoned the campaign and left England early the following year, but her son Henry continued the struggle until he was forced to flee temporarily in 1149, sailing from Bristol to Normandy (Warren 1973, 37–8). The political situation settled into a stalemate which was resolved at Winchester in 1153 when Henry was accepted as Stephen's heir. Henry's accession to the throne in October 1154 was significant for Bristol as the town began to reap the rewards of its consistent support for his cause.

Bristol remained a source of Angevin power and thus a significant political entity. As well as gaining access to the Angevin empire, the privileges of the burgesses of the town were confirmed in charters issued by Henry in 1155 and were reaffirmed ten years later (Harding 1930, 2–5). Another charter in 1174 granted Bristol's merchants immunity from tolls on the British mainland and in France (Watt 1986, 152–3).

Robert of Gloucester's son William inherited the earldom and lands on both sides of the Severn estuary – but not, apparently, his father's political weight (Crouch 2000, 236–7). The involvement of relatives in rebellions against Henry II in the mid-1170s led to him being forced to surrender his estates and Bristol Castle to the Crown. William never recovered his estates. On his death in 1183 they passed to his heiress Isabel, who married the king's younger son John. Figures for the revenues of the earldom at this time indicate that Bristol accounted for between 19 per cent and 26 per cent of its total income (Painter 1943, 166). With the death of Henry and the accession of Richard I in 1189, the royal connections of the town were weakened, though Richard's successor John was a frequent visitor to his castle at Bristol throughout his reign, usually spending at least two nights there each year (Duffus Hardy 1835).

When the king of Leinster, Diarmit Mac Murchada, was forced out of Ireland in 1166, it was to Bristol that he looked for sanctuary. Entertained as the guest of Robert Fitzharding, he travelled to Aquitaine to gain the help of Henry II and then seems to have used Bristol as a base from which to negotiate with Norman lords in Wales for their military support in the recapture of his kingdom. When the adventure failed, prompting the conquest of Ireland by Henry II in 1171, Dublin was granted by charter to Bristol (Otway-Ruthven 1968, 50). It has been argued that the grant implies Dublin should be settled as though it were depopulated, and the tradition of Oxmanstown on the north bank of the Liffey may support some expropriation (Connolly and Martin 1992, xv). Few Bristol merchants are, however, recorded in the Dublin merchant roll between 1190 and 1222, even though they possessed the same rights as in Bristol (Connolly and Martin 1992, 1–48). A more widely accepted interpretation is that Bristol was being held up as the model for Dublin to follow (Watt 1986, 152–3).

The castle (Figs 5.2, 5.10, 5.11, 5.12, 5.13)

Little is known of the earliest history of Bristol Castle. It may have been built by Geoffrey de Mowbray, Bishop of Coutances, in the immediate aftermath of the Conquest, though it is not referred to until 1088 when, under Geoffrey, it became the headquarters of the rebellion against William Rufus. Other than that Symeon of Durham could describe it at this time as a *castrum fortissimum*, nothing is known from historical sources of its early physical form (Lobel and Carus-Wilson 1975, 3).

As discussed earlier, there is also some ambiguity, as well as many major unknowns, in the archaeological record. The ambiguity arises from the excavations in the north-east corner of the castle bailey and the possibility, suggested subsequently, that a number of the features dated by the excavator to the 11th century and attributed to the first phase of the Norman castle could have been of slightly earlier date and belonged to pre-Conquest public defences. Disregarding, for the moment, this possibility, the evidence suggests that

the earliest castle took the form of a simple enclosure or ringwork, and that this was rapidly superseded by the earthworks of a motte and bailey castle.

The Late Saxon features at Middle Terrace were sealed beneath an earth bank on which the curtain wall of the Norman castle had been built. The remains of the wall had been seriously denuded by stone quarrying but it was nevertheless possible to establish that it had been 1.3m thick and constructed of Pennant sandstone with fragments of lias limestone and Old Red sandstone. To the south (BHER 448) further parts of this wall were found together with a metalled surface divided by the slot for a timber sill with a single posthole in the centre. This evidence, coupled with square structures found on either side of the metalling, was interpreted as an early defended gate (Ponsford 1979, 294–6). Landscaping work close to New Gate in the north-west corner of the castle exposed one small fragment of a Pennant sandstone wall and part of the foundation of another. On the basis of the similarities in their materials and construction, these were taken to be further parts of the curtain wall. Both the walls and the gate structure were ascribed to the same period, *c* 1070–*c* 1080, and were thought by the excavator to be evidence of a Norman stone-walled ringwork castle (ibid, 89–90; 102). It was also inferred that the defensive ditch around this ringwork probably followed the line of the later castle ditch.

The ringwork thus identified was succeeded, probably *c* 1080, by a motte and bailey castle, elements of which have been recorded at intervals over the years (Ponsford 1979, 102). A section of the motte ditch was uncovered in 1948 during excavation on the site of the keep (BHER 414), while Ponsford recorded other sections of the ditch in a trench at Cock and Bottle Lane, close to New Gate (BHER 452) and on the southern side of Castle Park, some 65m to the south-east of St Peter's Church (BHER 458; Marshall 1951, 16). Excavations in 1989 on the site of the keep (BHER 459) found more of the motte ditch and also part of the bailey ditch, which ran north from the motte ditch and widened out by some 2m on its west side (Good 1996, 27). One enigmatic structure recorded in the excavations of 1948 and 1989 was a stone wall, pre-dating the later keep, built across the width of the motte ditch. Constructed mainly of Brandon Hill Grit and

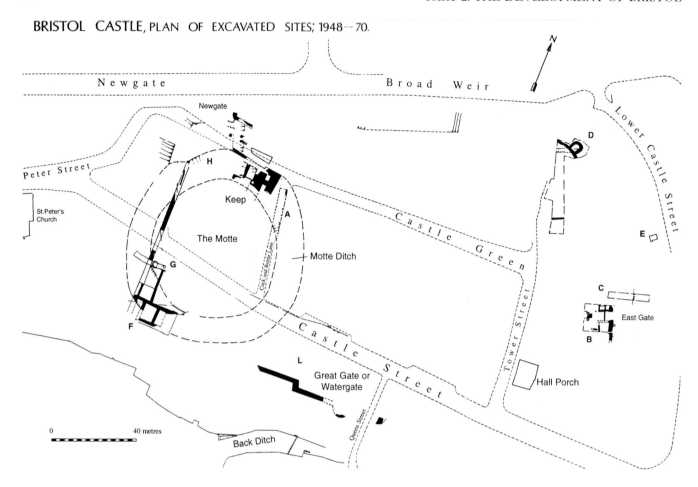

BRISTOL CASTLE, PLAN OF EXCAVATED SITES, 1948–70.

Figure 5.10 Plan of Bristol Castle excavated sites 1948–70 (reproduced from Ponsford 1979, fig 6)

1.4m thick, the wall followed the profile of the ditch and survived almost to its lip. Its function is unclear, although it may have been part of the bailey curtain wall (Marshall 1951, 40; M W Ponsford quoted in Good 1996) (Fig 5.11).

The motte and bailey phase of the castle also suffers from some significant problems of interpretation. Enough of the motte ditch has been seen to establish that the motte was ellipsoidal in plan with a north–south diameter of about 60m. However, only a small part of the bailey ditch has been recorded and its line in this period remains open to dispute. Mike Ponsford believed the bailey was very similar in extent to the later medieval castle, but Roger Leech has proposed a very different, much smaller, bailey based on a distinctive curving property boundary mapped on the north side of Castle Street, and the existence of a tower, allegedly on the same line, photographed in the late 1920s (*see* Leech 1997b, fig 1; Pritchard 1929, 232; pl II). The bailey ditch would, according to this model, have curved from the motte ditch southwards towards the river cliff. The suggestion is ingenious but at least

partly flawed, in that the tower in fact appears to have stood elsewhere (Davis's Court, nearly 60m to the north-west), and the suggested smaller bailey would indeed have been small, extending less than *c* 50m east of the motte. Nevertheless, the hypothesis cannot be entirely dismissed. Small inner baileys within much larger outer baileys were a feature of the Norman royal castles built in Chester and Shrewsbury, and it is not impossible that Bristol too had an inner bailey. Later in the 12th century (1147–65) a charter of William of Gloucester confirms the donation of houses and a yard within the castle to Margam Abbey but neither the position nor the function of these is clear from the document (Patterson 1973, 116). The uncertainty merely underlines the very limited extent of excavations in and knowledge of the castle and the extent to which it was reorganised in the course of the 12th century.

In the early 12th century the Earl of Gloucester constructed a stone keep on the site of the motte, which was levelled and the motte ditch infilled.

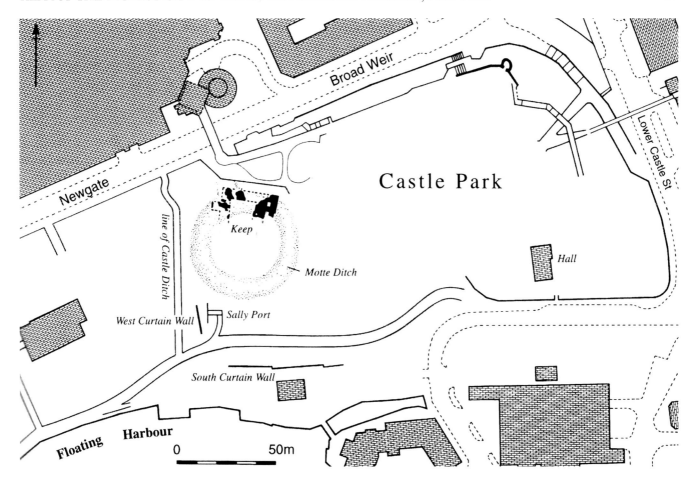

The pottery assemblage recovered during the 1989 excavation did not give a clear date for the infilling but the absence of Ham Green wares was taken as a possible indication that it may have occurred before *c* 1120 (Good 1996, 28). The north-east corner of the keep was first uncovered by groundworks for the construction of the Llewellin and James copper works in Castle Green in the 1870s, and again in 1948 (Swayne 1879–80, 329; Marshall 1951, 40). The 1989 excavation recorded the entire width of the northern part of the keep, and found that it had been heavily quarried for building stone in the mid-17th century. However, the north-east corner was well preserved and within this area of stonework, which measured approximately 12m by 10m, were the well and two large stone-lined shafts, both measuring roughly 3m by 2m. Other discrete areas of walling belonging to the northern part of the keep including part of its west face survived, and close by the base of a garderobe was identified (Figs 5.12, 5.13).

The first of a series of strategic water-management projects in Bristol's history was undertaken, perhaps at this time but possibly earlier, to construct a leat off the river Frome. This connected with the castle moat under the present Broadweir and provided water for the Castle Mill. The watercourse still exists and rejoins the course of the Frome at River Street, becoming an open channel of water further east at Wellington Road.

The town defences (Fig 5.2)

The inner circuit of town walls, following (it has been suggested, above) the earlier, pre-Conquest defences around the curving line of the river cliff from High Street to Pithay, and at least the major gates on the axial roads, were in position by the later 12th century (Patterson 1973, 41–2). Excavations in 1975 on Peter Street discovered densely cut pits of 12th-century date, thought by the excavator to be associated with the quarrying of sand for the construction of the town wall (Boore 1982, 8). There is also historical evidence that

Figure 5.11 Plan of the Castle Keep excavation 1989 and parts of the south and west curtain walls revealed in 1992–3 (reproduced from Good 1996, fig 3)

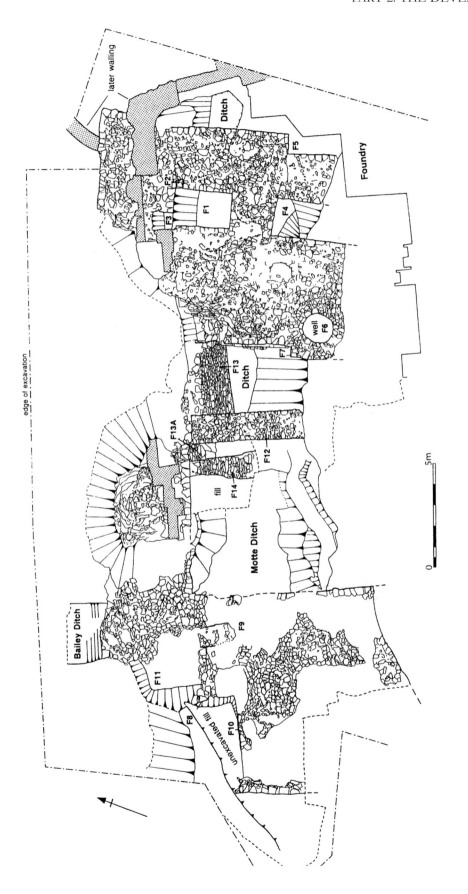

Figure 5.12 Detailed plan of 1989 excavation showing the motte and bailey ditches and the Keep (reproduced from Good 1996, fig 4)

Figure 5.13 Photograph of 1989 excavation of Castle Keep from the east

Baldwin Street, running around the outside of the wall on the southern side of the town, was in existence by this time (Maclean 1883, 22). The walls, built mainly of Brandon Hill Grit, have been observed on several occasions, though often in circumstances which did not allow for detailed recording.

The town wall has been recorded several times in St Nicholas' Church. Work by the City Engineers to the crypt in 1971 found it hidden behind substantial 18th-century walls: it was over 2.4m thick and bonded in red sandy mortar (BHER 40; Fowler 1972a, 53). It was seen again during works below the tower in 1972 (BHER 64) and at the west end of the crypt in 1984 (BHER 83); there, a rebuilt section of the wall was found to be set on traces of an earlier, possibly Norman, wall (Youngs *et al* 1985, 162; J Bryant pers comm).

On the south side of the town it was recorded on the site of Nos 41–3 Baldwin Street in 1957 (BHER 484). The upper part of the wall had been rebuilt relatively recently; the lower part was constructed mainly of Brandon Hill Grit. Two large arched recesses at the centre of the exposed section were tentatively interpreted as drainage features (Rahtz 1960, 224–6, 275) (Fig 5.14).

At No 65 Baldwin Street in 1974 a wall standing on the presumed line of the inner circuit wall was found to be of post-medieval date, but excavation immediately in front of it (BHER 523) recorded the stone foundations of the town wall as well as a further stone wall of a similar construction against it (Price 1979b, 21). Further west, the wall was seen in excavations for a sewer in Corn Street in 1833 (BHER 3244): 'Its direction is from underneath the houses, on the eastern side of St Stephen's Street to the same side of Baldwin Street, but beyond the front of the houses now standing in the upper part of it. The thickness of the wall in this place could not be ascertained, as part only of it was uncovered. So much of its eastern side as was visible was plastered and formed one of the walls of a chamber, immediately under the arch on which St Leonard's Gate stood' (*BTM*, 25 May 1833). Nearby in Corn Street the western face was photographed in the basement of No 30 in 1977 (BHER 303).

Around the north side of the circuit, the antiquary Samuel Seyer noted in the early 19th century that on Tower Lane a semi-circular tower was incorporated into a house, and that the inner town wall was revealed 19 yards from the street by the destruction by fire of a house at the eastern end of the northern side of Wine Street and that it continued into the house to the west (BHER 268; Seyer 1821, 266). In Pithay in

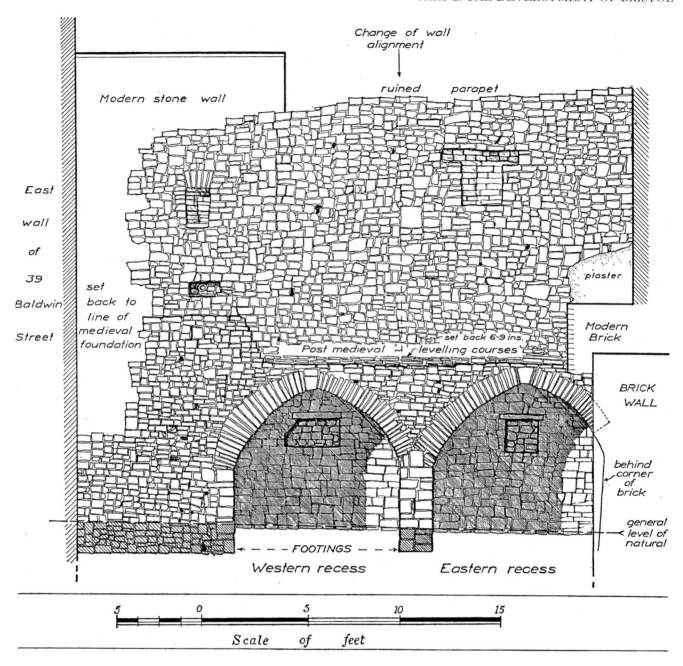

Figure 5.14 Elevation of the town wall recorded in Baldwin Street in 1957 (reproduced from Rahtz 1960, fig 2)

1900 groundworks for the construction of a new factory exposed a section of the town wall between Pithay and St John's Steep; it was photographed by J E Pritchard, who dated it to the Norman period. Pritchard also examined the tower observed by Seyer before this section of the circuit was destroyed (Pritchard 1901, 274–6).

At Peter Street excavation by M W Ponsford in 1970 (BHER 409) recorded part of a substantial wall of Brandon Hill Grit, interpreted as the town wall, against which a building had

been erected. A further length of this wall, 1.6m thick and (including the foundation courses) surviving to a height of 2.10m, was recorded to the north during the adjacent 1975 excavation (BHER 319; Boore 1982, 8).

Urban growth
The Old City (Fig 5.2)

It will be clear from the foregoing that the processes of population growth and urban expansion taking place in the core of *Brycgstow* in the 11th and early 12th centuries are largely invisible: undocumented and, so far, insufficiently explored by excavation. The discovery in excavations on Tower Lane of a wealthy, stone-built first-floor hall built right at the back of one of the Broad Street plots at some time after *c* 1130 (*see* p 115) is very suggestive of an increasingly dense urban environment. What had once been open space, probably garden ground well behind the main street frontage, was now being built over for high-status domestic accommodation accessed off the lane. But, while suggestive, one excavation cannot by itself adequately represent the initial urbanisation of a great city centre. Equally suggestive however is the character of 12th-century tenement planning where it *has* been more accessible to archaeological excavation: in the new, fast-growing suburbs. These will be considered properly shortly, but in this context it is worth noting that, even by the mid-12th century, the majority of houses on the west side of Redcliff Street appear to have been built at right-angles to the frontage, constrained by narrow plots in a street for which there was clearly fierce competition for tenements (Leech 2014, 72). The wealthiest citizens, too, were building outside the walls. The de la Warre family were probably responsible for the construction of a late 12th-century domestic aisled hall, on a site later developed for St Bartholomew's Hospital, at the western end of the Frome Bridge, overlooking the river and, from its nearby slipway, probably part of a commercial establishment (Price with Ponsford 1998).

Outside the defences
While the intensification of settlement in the old core is more easily inferred than demonstrated from the evidence currently available, there is in no doubt that the early to mid-12th century saw Bristol begin a rapid, substantial and sustained process of extramural growth, mostly at the instigation of its manorial lords. There were three such major developments. The *feria*, east of the castle, was part developed by *c* 1165. Across the Frome, Broadmead was being built up between the 1150s and the 1180s: both were urban promotions by Robert, Earl of Gloucester. Across the Avon, Redcliffe was developed by two agencies: Robert Fitzharding in Redcliff

fee, where building was in progress *c* 1123–33, and the Knights Templar in Temple Fee, on land granted to them between 1128 and 1148. All of these new 12th-century suburbs were as regularly planned as the constraints of their sites allowed.

The feria or Old Market (Fig 5.15)
The earliest documentary references to the *feria* and *foro* date from the mid-12th century (Birch 1875, 209–91; Potto Hicks 1934, 172–3; Ross 1959, 111). The suburb was partly developed by *c* 1165 (Leech 2014, 11). The name 'Old Market' was in use by the later 15th century. John Gaywode's will of 1471 records 'Olde Market' and William Worcestre mentions 'le veyle Market' in 1480 (Neale 2000, 110–11).

The most likely origin of the suburb is in the regularisation of marketing activity taking place outside the east gate of the castle, along the main road to London and Gloucester, leading to the distinctive swollen cigar-shape of the street space. The impetus behind the development of the suburb is uncertain. Lobel and Carus-Wilson suggested that its founder was either Robert FitzHamon or Robert, Earl of Gloucester but, without further documentary evidence, the question will remain unresolved (Lobel and Carus-Wilson 1975, 5). The suburb was clearly planned, though some aspects of the local topography may have been inherited from an earlier landscape. Ponsford's discovery of Late Saxon features at Middle Terrace could suggest that Saxon settlement spread as far as the west end of modern Old Market Street where Redcross Street intersected Ellbroad Street and Carey's Lane. These lanes curved around the north-east side of the castle and may be the lane 'which leads to Glebrugge' cited in a charter of April 1292 (Ross 1959, 113). This enigmatic arrangement seems to fit with neither the castle nor Old Market and may therefore reflect the fossilisation of part of an earlier landscape but, with negligible fieldwork undertaken so far, this awaits demonstration.

Old Market Street is an archetypal medieval market street, around 30m across at its widest and about 350m long, with narrow burgages extending back from the street on both sides. Back lanes parallel with the main street, Redcross Street to the

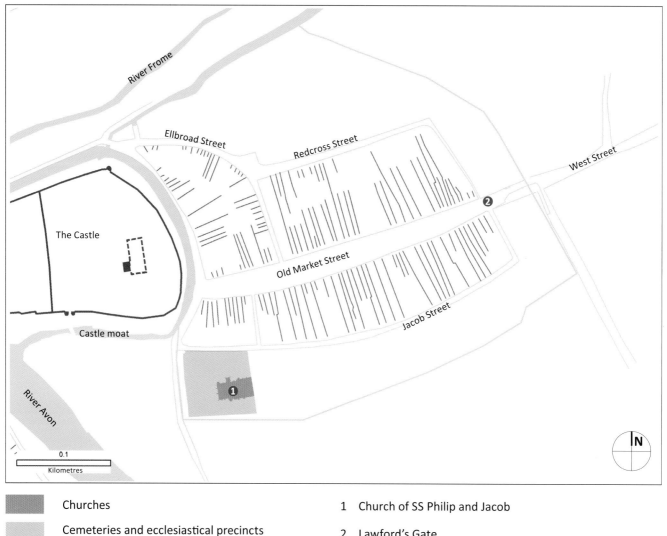

Churches

Cemeteries and ecclesiastical precincts

Town walls and defences/
conjectured alignment

The Great Ditch

1   Church of SS Philip and Jacob

2   Lawford's Gate

Figure 5.15 Old Market c *1200*

north and Jacob Street to the south, define the rear of these plots. The plot widths seem to have varied depending on their location in the street, but generally they were 4.75 to 5.75 metres. The historical evidence suggests their medieval spatial organisation was similar: a house on the street front with gardens and/or industrial activity towards the back lanes, although archaeological excavation is needed to test the accuracy of this impression. In terms of the actual urbanisation process and the type of individuals that lay behind it,

Roger Leech cites a document pre-dating 1166 by which the Earl of Gloucester's chaplain granted to Robert, son of Swein, four properties with rents from a fifth; three were already built up with houses, another with a 'longhouse' (*longam domum*) the only such reference in Bristol to such a rural building type, and a reminder of the close physical and economic proximity of the countryside (Leech 2014, 20). At the west end of the street, by the castle ditch, there was a cross, presumably a market cross (Neale 2000, 112–13).

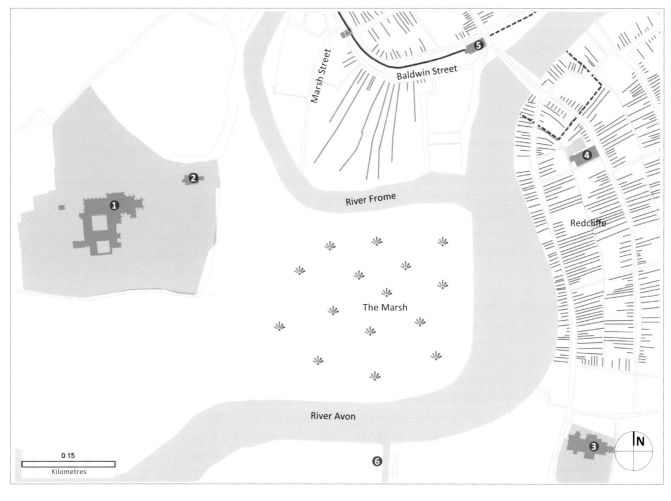

1   Abbey of St Augustine

2   Church of St Augustine-the-Less

3   Church of St Mary Redcliffe

4   Church of St Thomas the Martyr

5   Church of St Nicholas

6   Trin Mill

■ Churches

■ Cemeteries and ecclesiastical precincts

— Town walls and defences/
- - conjectured alignment

The Marsh suburb (Fig 5.16)
There is also evidence for the extension in the 12th century of occupation into the area to the south of Baldwin Street, mostly floodplain in the Avon–Frome confluence probably already divided into large tenements (p 92). At least the northern end of Marsh Street was in use by the 12th century and excavation has found features of 12th-century date on the north side of Baldwin Street, just outside the town wall

(Smith 1964, 92; Price 1979b). Excavations between Welsh Back and Queen Charlotte Street in 1958 (BHER 3051) and 1995 (BHER 1579) recorded features cut into the alluvial clay, including, in the 1995 excavation, postholes and possible gullies dating to the 12th century (Blockley 1996, 12–13). No function was immediately apparent for these features, which had been buried by an artefact-rich clay deposit thought to have derived

Figure 5.16
The Marsh c *1200*

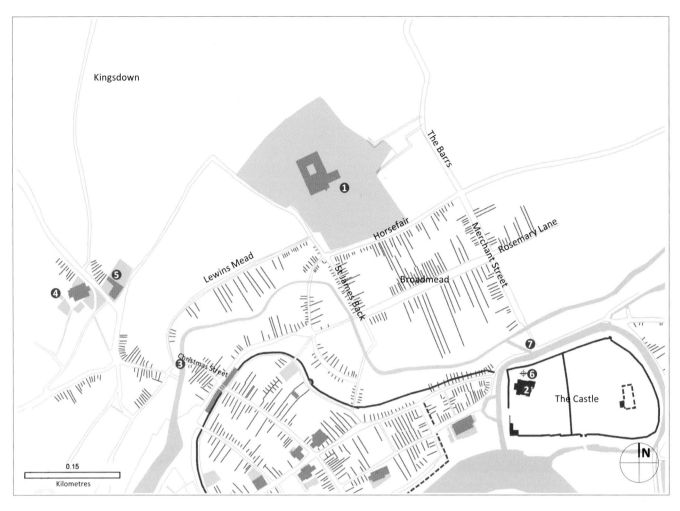

1   Priory of St James
2   Castle Keep
3   Frome Bridge
4   Church of St Michael-on-the Mount Without
5   Nunnery of St Mary Magdalen
6   Chapel of St Martin
7   Castle Mill

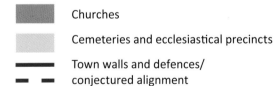

Churches

Cemeteries and ecclesiastical precincts

Town walls and defences/
conjectured alignment

Figure 5.17 North of the Frome c *1200*

from the dumping of rubbish, a conclusion confirmed by further investigation in 2000 (BHER 3581; Townsend 2003).

North of the Frome (Fig 5.17)
The principal planned urban extension north of the Frome was Broadmead, the 'new borough of the meadow' (*novum burgum de prato*), founded by Robert, Earl of Gloucester between the castle and his Priory of St James (founded *c* 1129). It was being developed in the period between *c* 1150 and 1183 when a burgage was granted towards its eastern end (Lobel and Carus-Wilson 1975, 5; Leech 2014, 17). It was strategically placed across the main road north to Gloucester on relatively flat ground at the foot of St Michael's Hill. Broadmead itself was the principal east–west street, wide

Figure 5.18 12th- to early 13th-century oak trough from Cabot Circus excavation

enough to accommodate a market with long, broad plots running off it perpendicularly. Merchant Street/Old King Street, with their much shorter plots, crossed at right-angles, forming a simple grid. Archaeological evidence from this area is scarce, though what has been found suggests that much of the area was marsh right through the 12th century. This picture is, however, with recent investigations, beginning to change.

Excavations for the new Cabot Circus shopping centre (BHER 4279) found evidence for settlement around the upper reaches of the Frome in the later 12th century. Evidence for wooden structures, at least one of which was fairly substantial, was found on the south side of the Frome. The existence of a bridged inlet extending south from the Frome has been suggested following the analysis of a collection of planks and beams of later 12th-century date, and there was evidence of industrial activity including a well-preserved oak trough (Fig 5.18) (Goodburn 2013, 250–1).

Other smaller-scale developments were taking place north of the Frome in the course of the 12th century. Immediately south-west of Broadmead, part of the channel of the Frome was diverted below Lewins Mead to create an industrial complex comprising timber buildings and a circular furnace base on the reclaimed channel, and to lay out St James's Back, perhaps as a quayside (Jackson 2010a). Copper alloy and possibly iron were being worked here, with at least one possible dye-vat base also investigated (BHER 3590). This site, together with the Cabot Circus excavations, does confirm that the more offensive industries are likely to have been sited on undeveloped land immediately outside the town walls.

In Kingsdown a settlement appears to have developed at the foot of St Michael's Hill toward the end of the 12th century when St Michael's Church is known to have been built. Lack of evidence means the form of this settlement is unknown and the only 12th-century evidence so far excavated comes from a site to the north of Southwell House. Mounded features, possibly for cultivation and containing abraded 12th-century and later pottery, were found here, raising the possibility that there may also have been a small farm or other dwelling near the top of St Michael's Hill (Brett 1994) (BHER 404). Little is known about the College Green area beyond the immediate vicinity of the abbey, and both Brandon Hill and Canon's Marsh must be presumed to have remained essentially rural in character. A charter of 1148–83 refers to an orchard at Wardwell, probably Woodwell, by Jacob's Wells Road, for example (Patterson 1973, 41–2).

Redcliffe and Temple (Fig 5.19)
Across the Avon, concerted and co-ordinated action in their respective fees by Robert Fitzharding and the Knights Templar was producing one of the greatest planned urban extensions in early 12th-century England – though even this was created around retained earlier landmarks. In the Temple Fee the building of the Temple Church and its preceptory was followed by the laying out of Temple Street and its plots. Excavations on the Finzels Reach (formerly Courage Brewery) site found substantial roadside ditches flanking the line of Temple Street, together with the slight trace of a south-westerly return following the line of the south side of Arthur's Fee as postulated by Leech (2009) (HER 24838). The evidence suggested that the area was being drained possibly from the 1120s or slightly before, with Temple Street being laid out at this time and the two fees demarcated. The excavators suggested that the ditch which formed the eastern side of the defended bridgehead may have been an important relict feature in the marshy landscape, which was used to define the land given to the Templars in the earlier 12th century. It was from the second half of the century that the first evidence for the regular subdivision of the land into tenements was recognised, defined by ditches and gullies (Teague and Brady 2017a, 38). Excavation at Nos 76–96 Victoria Street (BHER 88) also showed that the definition of property boundaries close to the preceptory had begun by the later 12th century (Ennis *et al* 1997). The Templars continued to invest in their suburb, building dwellings for rent, and by 1185 there were 28 messuages, producing (together with their other property in the area) an annual income of just over £2 9s (Lees 1935, cxxi; 58).

Immediately to the west, Fitzharding's agents developed Redcliff Fee around two further parallel streets, St Thomas Street and Redcliff Street. Approximately mid-way between each of these three north–south streets (Temple Street, St Thomas Street and Redcliff Street) were common boundary watercourses, the Law Ditches, though, as discussed already, at least one of these can be seen to have been of earlier, probably pre-Conquest, origin. Redcliff Street may also, as an approach road to the bridge, have been part of the pre-Conquest landscape. Redcliff Street would, as part of the new suburb, have been particularly attractive commercially in that its west-side plots backed onto the Avon and offered ample opportunities either for private river-frontage or simply access to unlimited water for industrial processes. Temple Fee in contrast was less well placed to foster such commercial development, though it was closely linked to the countryside to its south-east. Cross lanes (east–west) provided connections between the main streets and the two fees. Archaeological evidence from Redcliff Street shows that the plots that survived there in the 19th century had generally retained the same boundaries since first they were first laid out in the 12th. It is possible to identify a degree of regularity in the boundaries of the plots along both Redcliff Street and St Thomas Street based on a standard plot frontage width, most commonly six yards.

Much of the evidence for the settlement of Redcliffe has come from excavation of waterfront sites on the west side of Redcliff Street. Two sites in particular, Dundas Wharf (BHER 344) and Nos 95–7 Redcliff Street (BHER 447), produced 12th-century riverside structures and evidence of a clear sequence of riverside reclamation. Dendrochronological dating from Dundas Wharf showed that development there was underway by the 1130s. At 95–7 Redcliff Street, the east bank of the Avon was identified some 15m to the west of modern Redcliff Street. A wicker fence marked the line of the bank, and timbers found on the eastern, landward, side of this were believed by the excavator to be the remnants of a riverside structure, possibly a landing stage. River silts were deposited on the west side of the fence enabling dumping of material in the late 12th century to reclaim a further 8m of ground, retained in turn by a plank fence (Jones 1986, 7–9). The western end of Tucker Street had also been established and built up by the mid-12th century, some plots

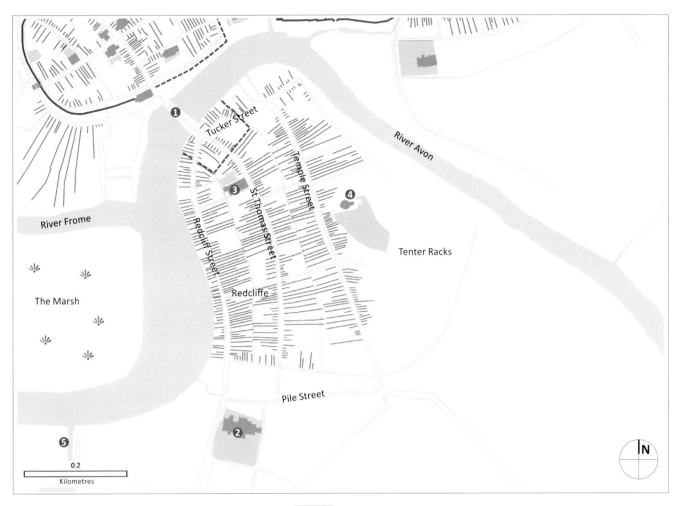

1   Bristol Bridge

2   Church of St Mary Redcliffe

3   Church of St Thomas the Martyr

4   Church of the Knights Templar

5   Trin Mill

   Churches

   Cemeteries and ecclesiastical precincts

   Town walls and defences/ conjectured alignment

   Law Ditches

possibly having access to the river via slipways (Cox 1998d, 6–7; Jackson 2006a). Excavations at 2 Redcliff Street also suggested that the tenements there were being laid out in the early 12th century (Alexander 2015).

To the south and south-west, there is little evidence for settlement of the Redcliffe suburb. Pile Street appears to have formed the southern boundary of the main built-up area of Redcliffe and may have been a principal east–west route. To the west, on the south bank of the river Avon was Trin Mill, at the confluence with the Malago stream (now the entrance to Bathurst Basin), which had

apparently been constructed by 1170–83 on land granted to St Augustine's Abbey between 1154 and 1170 (Walker 1998, 6, 12).

The Church

Parish churches in the core (Fig 5.2)

Relatively little is known of the Late Saxon and early Norman phases of the parish churches; the chronology of their foundation is also largely uncertain, given the limited archaeological and documentary evidence, the latter usually providing an earliest reference rather than an actual foundation date. St Mary-le-Port has already been discussed as a likely Saxon

Figure 5.19 Redcliffe c 1200

foundation. St Peter's, held by tradition to be the oldest church in Bristol, is first mentioned in 1107 when its grant to the abbey at Tewkesbury was confirmed (Johnson and Cronne 1956, 73–4; Taylor 1909, 209; *see* Chapter 4 and p 89). St Werburgh is first mentioned in a charter of 1148–83. It is often taken to be a pre-Conquest church on the basis of its dedication to a Mercian royal saint, and could have been a foundation in the early 10th century (Thacker 1985). Yet Werburga's cult appears to have had a resurgence in the later 11th century as a result of the translation of the saint's remains to Ely in 1095 and the simultaneous writing of her life by Goscelin: consequently the dedication could well be of post-Conquest date (Ridyard 1988, 186n; Butler 1986, 46). St Ewen and Christ Church were believed by Taylor to have been founded before 1147. St Ewen was certainly in existence by 1160 when its priest was Turstin (Birch 1875, 290) and William of Gloucester granted the advowson of All Saints in Corn Street to St Augustine's Abbey in the 1150s (Taylor 1909, 217; Patterson 1973, 43–4). The gate church of St Leonard is mentioned in another of his charters which dates to between 1148 and 1183, while St John, the gate church at the end of Broad Street was founded *c* 1192 and, like St James's Priory was under the control of Tewkesbury abbey (Taylor 1909, 217; Patterson 1973, 41–4). The chapel dedicated to St Martin in the outer ward of the castle may have originated as another of the churches of the Late Saxon town (Leech 1997b, 23).

All Saints, where two bays of the Norman aisle remain, St Ewen and St Mary-le-Port were all built (or rebuilt) during the later Norman period, and this may well be the case with many of the other central churches. In the course of the 12th century a number of external religious institutions acquired properties in Bristol; Tewkesbury Abbey's acquisition of St James, St John and St Peter has already been noted while St Peter's Abbey at Gloucester owned property in and around the town (Hart 1863, 172–4).

East of the castle, the church of SS Philip and Jacob had been founded before the end of the 12th century to serve the newly developed Old Market or *feria*. Originally cruciform in plan, its earliest surviving fabric belongs to the 13th century (Wadley 1886, 148).

Redcliffe (Fig 5.19)
St Mary Redcliffe was in existence by 1158, Taylor suggesting a foundation date of *c* 1150

(Jones 1883, 203; Taylor 1909, 204). The 12th-century church seems to have occupied much the same footprint as the present structure, and the architectural influence of Salisbury Cathedral has been noted by several authorities. Building on this scale implies that its founder, Fitzharding's, ambitions for Redcliffe may have gone so far as to wish to rival Bristol rather than merely extend it. Only the inner north porch together with parts of the nave and south aisle survives from the Norman building (Rodwell 2004). John Britton published a plan and drawings of the structure in the early 19th century (BHER 503; Britton 1813) and other 12th-century architectural fragments have been found on the site in the past.

The dedication of the other 12th-century Redcliffe parish church, St Thomas the Martyr, cannot have been made before 1170, suggesting that it was either founded as part of the planned suburb, or was inserted into it later.

Monastic houses (Figs 5.1, 6.45)
St James's Priory
Founded by Robert of Gloucester in *c* 1129, St James's Priory was the earliest of what was to be a succession of monastic foundations across the Frome. It was a Benedictine house established as a cell of Tewkesbury Abbey (Graham 1907, 74). It has been suggested that a temporary building preceded the building of the priory church (Potto Hicks 1932, 58). The nave of the priory church survives, as does the west end, which retains much of the Norman detailing, particularly its blind arcading and a rose window (Fig 5.20).

Excavation in 1995 (HER 3155) established that the church was around 50m long, confirming the measurements made by William Worcestre in the late 15th century (Neale 2000, 266–7). Because of the relatively limited structural survival, little more can be said of the church in the 12th century beyond the possible existence of a side chapel to the north transept.

The internal layout of the precinct is also poorly understood, although the cloister lay on the north side of the church and the monastic burial ground has been tentatively identified at its east end. The great gate of the priory lay at the south-eastern end of Whitson Street, Rocque's 1742 plan indicating a vehicular arch and adjacent pedestrian arch. Little else of the complex is known although its boundaries may have extended as far north as the line of Marlborough Street.

Figure 5.20 West front of St James's Church (photograph D Martyn)

Figure 5.21 Head niche burial excavated at St James's Priory (reproduced from Jackson 2006b, fig 57)

The human remains recovered during the excavations at the east and west ends of the priory church form the largest and earliest assemblage from the town to have been studied so far. They provide interesting evidence for the health of the urban population and for burial practice, the average age at death of the population being 45 years or older, although a peak also occurred in the range 26–35 years (Fig 5.21). Head-niche burials are known from other excavated contemporary burial sites, while a parallel for four clay-filled burials located on the northern edge of the burial ground, although not dated by finds, can be found in a Late Saxon or Norman burial from Barton-on-Humber (Jackson 2006b).

St Augustine's Abbey
St Augustine's Abbey, an Augustinian monastery, was founded by Robert Fitzharding in *c* 1140. The historical evidence for the foundation of the abbey was reassessed by Dickinson in

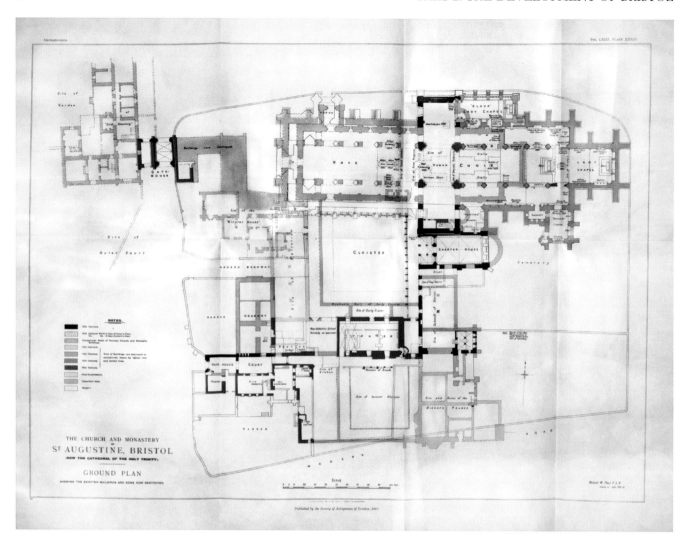

Figure 5.22 Paul's plan of St Augustine's Abbey (reproduced from Paul 1912, pl XXXIV)

1976 and led him to suggest that the first step in the process was the construction of a small church, completed by 1146, on what would later be the site of the church of St Augustine-the-Less. A community of religious drawn from the canons of the abbey of St Victor at Paris was settled there and the monastery may already have acquired abbey status by the time of the move to the adjacent site. That church was dedicated by four bishops *c* 1170 (Dickinson 1976). Excavations in 1983–4 (BHER 1686) confirmed the existence of a church on the site of St Augustine-the-Less in the 12th century, a small building with a two-cell plan (Boore 1985), but it is not clear whether this was initially monastic or parochial; it had certainly acquired parochial status by the later 12th century. In the most recent review of the evidence it has been suggested that

Dickinson's hypothesis cannot be sustained and that a more probable explanation for the events of the early years of St Augustine's is that the church of St Augustine-the-Less was used for the daily worship of the monks until building of the abbey church was completed (Walker 1998, xxii).

The main abbey precinct buildings, as completed by the end of the 12th century, were sited on the edge of a terrace of rock immediately above the marsh; site preparation appears to have involved some levelling and terracing. Roland Paul's review of 1912, though far from definitive, remains the only systematic attempt to phase the surviving buildings, despite some recent reflection on the evidence (Paul 1912; Oakes 2000) (Fig 5.22).

The abbey complex comprised the abbey church with the main cloister to its south.

Figure 5.23 Chapter House of St Augustine's Abbey. Samuel Loxton, early 20th century (Loxton Collection, Bristol Reference Library E347)

The chapter house, situated on the east side of the cloister, is lined on the north and south sides by seating with blind arcading above; lunettes between the arcade and the vaulted roof are decorated in a carved basket-weave pattern (Figs 5.23 and 5.24).

At its west end, the Romanesque arched entrance is flanked by two-light arched windows set within a larger Romanesque arch. The chapter house dimensions recorded by William Worcestre (equivalent to 30m long and 9.6m wide: Neale 2000, 278–9) suggest a building longer than now exists. A small trench was dug outside the building in the 19th century to test whether it might have been one bay longer but no indication of this was found. To make sense of Worcestre's dimensions, Paul suggested that the chapter house may have been built with an apse (Paul 1912, 236). The abbey gateway is now a freestanding structure which has a central, highly decorated Romanesque freestone arch and similar blind arcading (Fig 5.25).

To the south-west of the cloister another, less ornate, Romanesque arch survives beneath Abbey House in College Square. The passage into which it leads, along with a group of four blocked windows, were identified as contemporary structures by Paul when he published a plan and drawings of them, and his 1912 review identified them as part of the abbot's lodgings (BHER 4189; Paul 1899). A stone building excavated in 1992 at the west end of the abbey church was perhaps a guest house for the abbey (BHER 1685) (Bryant 2015). Beyond the claustral buildings it is probable that there were other agricultural buildings supporting the farming of the adjacent abbey lands. The southern precinct wall of St Augustine's was identified in the Harbourside excavations of 2003–4 in the northern part of Canon's Marsh (BHER 4455). The wall seems initially to have bounded a garden; probably contemporary with it was a stone-revetted watercourse (which appears on Rocque's map of 1742) which was probably part of the abbey's water management system dating from the foundation. It was crossed by a narrow stone bridge on the line of a lane skirting the southern side of the precinct (Alexander and Harward 2011).

Perhaps the most uncertain aspect of St Augustine's in this period is the form of the

Figure 5.24 Lunettes above the blind arcade in the Chapter House (photograph D Martyn)

abbey church itself. The Norman building was apparently fully aisled, 61m long by 33m from north to south transept, but its form cannot otherwise be reconstructed with any certainty or in any detail.

St Augustine's increased its properties through endowments from *c* 1150. William, Earl of Gloucester, granted Billeswick and Canon's Marsh to the abbey in the 1150s, while outside Bristol it gained Aylworth from the future Henry II in 1154, Almondsbury and Leigh from Robert Fitzharding, Blacksworth and Kybor in Glamorgan from William of Gloucester and further lands in Wales from other benefactors (Cronne and Davis 1968, 48; Patterson 1973, 38–45).

St Mary Magdalen

After St Augustine's in the 1140s, the next monastic house to be founded north of the Frome was the nunnery of St Mary Magdalen,

in *c* 1173. This was a house of Augustinian nuns established by Eva Fitzharding, the widow of Robert, and endowed with lands in Southmead (Graham 1907, 93). The house was located at the foot of St Michael's Hill on the northern side of its junction with Upper Maudlin Street and is one of the least understood monastic sites in the city. A large building, probably the abbey church, lay along the north side of Upper Maudlin Street. This appears to have survived, at least in part, into the later 19th century when photographs appear to show medieval stonework forming the north wall of the King David Inn (Winstone 1962, pls 165–6). Excavation at the north-east end of the King David residences did identify part of a stone building of uncertain function and other material dating from the first years of the institution, as well as the probable location of a burial ground just to the north of the church (BHER 3617) (Longman 2001). However, the scale of the work was limited and only a little light was cast on the main features of the precinct. Its boundaries and much of the internal layout remain uncertain – it is not clear whether there was a cloister, for example – but the line of Horfield Road and the lower part of St Michael's Hill may reflect part of the precinct perimeter.

Monastic houses in Redcliffe

The Knights Templar founded a preceptory after their acquisition of the eastern part of the marsh. Its role is not certain (although it was apparently one of the larger in England) and there is currently not enough evidence to define its precinct with certainty. However, Templar and Hospitaller preceptories were bounded by an often substantial ditch, so a ditch and a rubble wall observed alongside Water Lane during the laying of services in 1972 could indicate that the lane marks its north side (BHER 98: Gilchrist 1995, 74; Good 1992, 7). The internal layout of the precinct also remains to be established but the main feature was clearly the church, excavated by Andrew Saunders in 1960 (Brown 2008). This was a circular stone building, 18.5m in diameter, making it the same size as the Templar church in the City of London (RCHME 1929, 139). The rotunda was surrounded by an ambulatory 1.8m wide and at the eastern end there was an apsidal chancel approximately 9m long (Fig 5.26). There is evidence for a hall to the north of the church which, although not dated to the 12th century, was believed by its excavator to be attributable to the Templar occupation of the site (Good 1992, 20–1). This arrangement suggests a plan similar to that of preceptories elsewhere, the buildings being arranged informally around a central space.

A hospital dedicated to St John was founded on the west side of Redcliff Hill, in the area of Redcliffe Way roundabout. It had been founded by the mid-1180s and was given a water supply as part of the grant to St Mary Redcliffe. Its form during the 12th century remains unknown (Latimer 1901, 173).

The Jewish community

A Jewish community was established in the area around St Peter's Church between 1159 and 1194, apparently as a branch of Oxford's community (Hillaby and Sermon 2004, 145) and part of the second wave of communities to be established during the 12th-century

Figure 5.25 Abbey gateway from the south (photograph D Martyn)

colonisation. Adler identified the names of 24 adults who belonged to the community in the second half of the 12th century (Adler 1928, 185) and it contributed £22 14s 2d (1 per cent) of the Northampton Donum of 1194, ranking it 13th of the 21 listed in the return (Hillaby 2003, 33). Remarkably little is known about the first decades of the Bristol Jewry (which is discussed at greater length in the following chapter). The primary archaeological evidence was gathered during the excavation at Peter Street in 1975 (BHER 319; Boore 1982, 8–9). However, the post-excavation analysis has not been completed, meaning that the material which the various finds assemblages

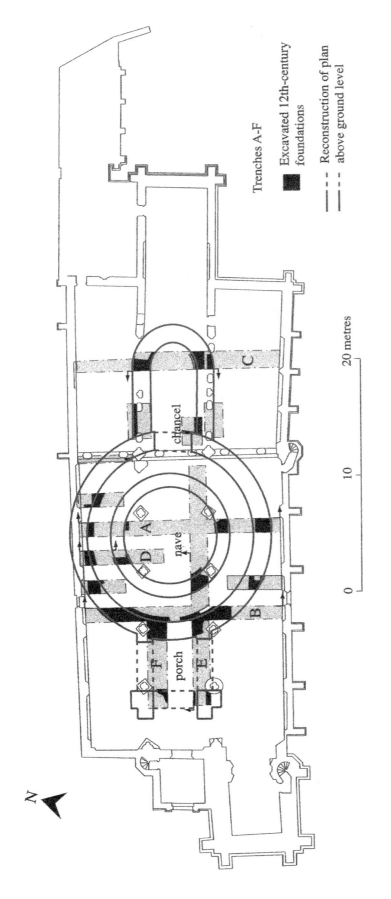

Figure 5.26 Plan of Templar Church (reproduced from Brown 2008, fig 2)

may contain for both the first half century of the Jewry and Saxon and Norman industry is similarly unknown.

Houses and housing

It will be apparent by now that the excavated sample of 12th-century Bristol is small and very unevenly distributed, with a strong bias away from the old core (where there have been few excavations) and towards the suburb of Redcliffe. It is also the case that, as in most English medieval towns, excavated evidence is far more often available for the backs of tenement plots than it is for the street frontages. This has serious implications for understanding the development of housing in the town's earliest centuries. In terms of buildings actually surviving, the bias is entirely, in this period, towards the stone dwellings of the wealthiest citizens.

What is apparent is that the most common forms of tenement planning known in late medieval English towns were already present in Bristol in the 12th century. For example – the narrow-plan tenements (already briefly discussed) excavated in Redcliff Street, contained what appear to have been (or started life as) open halls, distinguished by an open hearth, laid out at right-angles to the frontage. The hall identified at 87 Redcliff Street, of early to mid-12th-century date, lay one room back from the frontage, accessed via a side passage. The Canynges House plot was similarly built-up at right-angles to the frontage, with two phases of 12th-century construction (Leech 2014, chapter 5). The familiar process (known to geographers as the *burgage cycle*) by which long urban plots were built up sequentially from front to back was in Redcliffe already well advanced by the end of the 12th century.

A contrasting form of tenement-planning is also apparent: that in which the hall lay across the width of the plot behind a commercial frontage. This type was first described at Tackley's Inn, Oxford, but appears to be common to the central streets of most of the larger western English medieval towns (Chester, Shrewsbury, Worcester and Hereford, for example), offering a combination of maximum commercial returns from shop rents with a less intensive, higher-status domestic use of space away from the frontage. One example in the old core of Bristol was the

Cyder House (51–2 Broad Street) where a 12th-century first-floor hall occupied the rear of the plot with a passageway running under it to the rear (Fig 5.27).

Similarly at Nos 20–1 Small Street, possibly the town-house of Bath Priory, a partly-aisled hall occupied the full width of the plot, away from the frontage (Leech 2014, 78). An alternative courtyard-based plan-form is known from the intramural edge of the core at Nos 22–8 St Nicholas Street where a later 12th-century open hall was built at right-angles to the frontage, but as part of a broader arrangement set around a courtyard; the form of the frontage buildings is however unknown before the 16th century (ibid, 80) (Fig 5.28).

Fragments of other 12th-century high-status domestic buildings are known from the old core. The early to mid-12th-century stone house excavated at Fitzharding House, Tower Lane in 1979–80 (BHER 320) has already been briefly referred to. It measured about 25m by 9m externally and was built mainly of Brandon Hill Grit with walls up to 1.23m thick with decorative internal quoins of oolitic limestone. It had a smaller room at its west end and a larger principal room to the east, accessible from Tower Lane via a doorway in the gable wall. There was evidence of an internal timber-framed partition towards the east end and fragments of a stone floor. There was also a hearth of pitched stone against the dividing wall at the west end of the main room suggesting that this was not simply an undercroft used solely for storage. A less substantial wall butted against the south-east corner may have belonged either to a courtyard wall or possibly to an external staircase; a narrow outbuilding at the south-west corner (only partly investigated) contained the garderobe or privy (Boore 1984, 11–18; 1980) (Fig 5.29).

Parts of the surviving north-west wall of the Norman House excavated at Newmarket Avenue were recorded (BHER 472) and in a survey in 2000 (BHER 3656) an extant Romanesque architectural moulding has been noted in the wall of No 43 Broad Street (Leech 2000c). Excavation on the north side of Peter Street in 1970 (BHER 409) and 1975 (BHER 319) investigated a cellared building roughly 7 metres square. A cresset lamp was found within the cellar and the excavator suggested that the building may therefore have been one of the Jewish-owned buildings

known from documentary evidence to have been located in the area (Boore 1982, 8; Emanuel 2000).

As noted earlier, just outside the core at the site of St Bartholomew's Hospital, in *c* 1175 to *c* 1180, close to the Frome Bridge (first recorded 1192: Hart 1863, 173), a Norman aisled hall was built on the site of a partially infilled creek (Figs 5.30, 5.31). This, Price inferred from their

role in the foundation of St Bartholomew's Hospital, may have belonged to the de la Warre family who certainly owned property close to Billeswick by the mid-12th century (Patterson 1973, 41–2; Price with Ponsford 1998, 34). The building was apparently domestic in character, and what remains of its fabric suggests a grand building which would have been a landmark for those crossing the Frome. Its orientation

Figure 5.28 Part of 12th-century arcade from Nos 22–8 St Nicholas Street in 1827 by T L Rowbotham (Braikenridge Collection, BRSMG M2487)

Figure 5.29 Reconstruction of 12th-century house excavated at Tower Lane (reproduced from Boore 1984, fig 6)

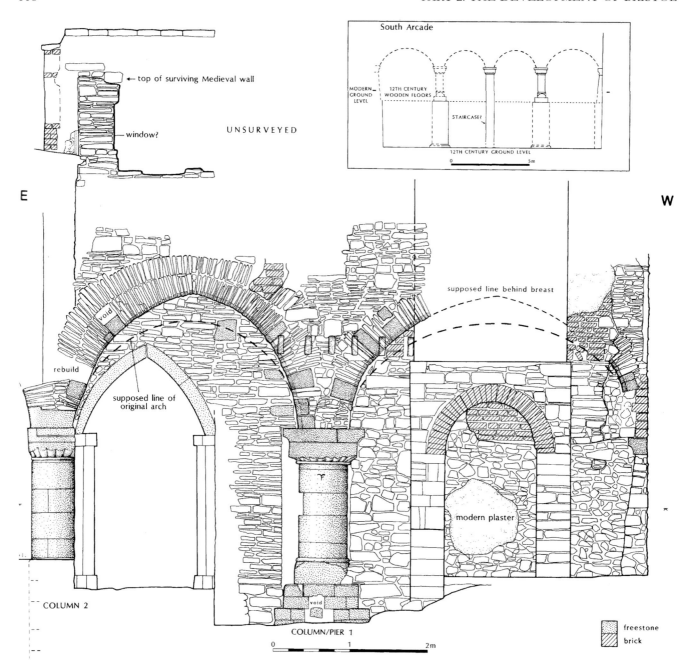

Figure 5.30 Elevation of Norman arcade in St Bartholomew's Hospital (reproduced from Price with Ponsford 1998, fig 17)

to the river, particularly when coupled with the discovery of a nearby slipway, may point to an additional commercial function.

Buildings with dedicated commercial functions are even scarcer in this period than primarily domestic ones. To a large degree this is a reflection of the lack of both excavated evidence and early surviving buildings on street frontages, as a consequence of intensive and frequent rebuilding and the presence of cellarage. Exceptions occur when the cellarage itself is of early date, and there are examples of

12th-century cellars, or undercrofts, from Corn Street. No 32a, on the corner with St Nicholas Street, was known as the 'Peynted Tavern' by 1532, and its semi-basement undercroft was recorded in the 1850s (Fig 6.92). The front part of the cellar had a ribbed vault with a decorative central boss and was accessed off Corn Street by a central arched doorway. Three arched openings to the rear gave access to a much plainer rear room. Across the road at No 35 Corn Street was another 12th-century cellar of similar form, with a smaller, decorated room

Figure 5.31
St Bartholomew's
Hospital: south doorway
to 12th-century hall
and 13th-century arcade
(photograph D Martyn)

to the front and a larger, plainer room behind (Leech 2014, 157). The two-cell form of these cellars, with a decorative front (for customers) and plainer rear (for storage), strongly suggests that they were taverns, accessed off the street and potentially let separately from the house above: the type is widely paralleled in other towns (for example London, Winchester and Winchelsea). Again, these structures are a hint that many of the familiar features of the urban fabric and commercial infrastructure well known in Bristol from the later medieval centuries had been fully developed before the end of the 12th.

The economy: industry, trade and diet
Industry (Fig 6.87)
Even the limited documentary record shows that 12th-century Bristol supported a range of crafts and industries. A charter from the 12th century recording the grant of various properties by William fitzGregory makes reference to a variety of economic functions within the town – a brewhouse, bakehouse, smiths, a furrier and a goldsmith, while the mint was located near the church of St Ewen (Patterson 1973, 164).

Iron working is attested by finds from Middle Terrace and Mary-le-Port Street, and there is evidence of leather working and of weaving from the Mary-le-Port Street sites (Watts and Rahtz 1985, 190). More recently the excavations on the Cabot Circus site near Broadmead (*see* p 105) found evidence of industrial activity in the form of an oak trough, possibly originally used for mixing or slaking lime. Its secondary use was uncertain though a notch had been cut in it, possibly to drain liquid. Possible secondary uses for this artefact include tanning, fulling or the retting of flax or nettles (Goodburn 2013) (*see* Fig 5.18).

A variety of industrial processes was being carried out adjacent to the Frome following the construction of a riverside wall, probably early in the 12th century. Their exact nature is unclear but the presence of hammerscale and some smithing pan suggests that smithing was taking place. The working of copper alloy has been suggested from the presence of half a stone mould, found close to a hearth, for the

Figure 5.32 12th-century musical instrument bridge from Finzels Reach excavation (photograph Oxford Archaeology)

rear of properties on the west side of Temple Street contained evidence for various craft working activities, including hide processing, tanning, leather working and horn working, wool processing, dyeing and smithing (one pit also contained an extremely rare bridge from a four- or five-string musical instrument, made from yew (Allen 2017, 243) (Fig 5.32).

In a property on the east side of the street, 12th-century barrel-lined pits contained lime-rich deposits, one with animal hair, probably relating to tanning or tawing (Brady 2017, 134; Allen 2017, 243; Wilson 2017, 277) (Fig 5.33).

On the eastern frontage there may have been a smithy in the late 12th century, with a hearth, an associated charcoal-rich layer containing hammerscale, tiny smithing spheres and iron shavings; a nearby pit contained dribbles of iron slag. In the garden soils to the rear, large quantities of hammerscale flakes and smithing spheres were discovered, indicating that the smaller smithing debris was being dumped in the back yard.

By the river, remains of dye plants (madder, weld and dyer's greenweed) were recovered from dumps of late 12th-century domestic refuse. Fullers' teasel achenes and receptacular bracts, also from riverside dumping, provide evidence for the use of teasels in cloth finishing (Jones 2017, 272). Pit fills contained further evidence of dyeing waste: madder root fragments, weld seeds and twigs from the coppice stools of dyer's greenweed.

Exactly how the Avon waterfronts were exploited around Redcliffe is not always clear. At this period its channel would have been wider: the riverbank, particularly at the southern end of Redcliff Street, was much closer to the street frontage than it is today (having moved westwards by continual encroachment), and as a result a greater area of the bank and river bed was exposed at low tide than was the case in later centuries prior to the creation of the Floating Harbour. If the interpretation of the Dundas Wharf timbers as the remains of a riverside wall and stairs, and the battered wall at Bridge Parade as a slip, are correct, it would imply that regular access to the river channel was sought in this period and formalised through the creation of riverside structures. But their purpose – whether for wharfage, fishing, or merely securing access to running water for craft production – remains uncertain.

simultaneous casting of six decorated objects, two unfinished lozenge-shaped rivets, other unfinished copper alloy objects and pieces of copper alloy sheet (Jackson 2010a).

Once again, however, the greatest weight of evidence comes from the Redcliffe suburb. At No 2 Redcliff Street there was some evidence for 12th-century industrial activity, with madder (for dyeing) being found in some waterlogged pits together with cobbling waste consisting of leather scraps and shoe fragments (BHER 4456) (Alexander 2015). Further east, in Temple Fee, the Finzels Reach site (BHER 24838) found abundant waste in the upper fills of the ditches either side of Temple Street, including horn cores (probably relating to tanning and horning), leather working waste and smithing debris. Pits to the

Figure 5.33 Late 12th-century barrel-lined pits used for tanning from Finzels Reach excavation (reproduced from Ford et al 2017, fig 2.25)

Trade

From the archaeological and historical evidence Bristol can be seen to have had important trading and political connections with Ireland, particularly with its east coast. Pottery from the Ham Green kilns has been found at sites between Drogheda and Waterford, at Waterford forming 45 per cent of all of the medieval pottery found in the excavations around Peter Street (Sweetman 1984, 182; Hurley and Scully with McCutcheon 1996, 286–7). There are documented links between Matilda's camp and southern Ireland, and Bristol appears during the Norman period to have formed one pole of a political axis with southern Ireland. It is noteworthy that the *Historia Novella* reports that when Stephen's supporters threatened to send their prisoner, the earl of Gloucester, to Boulogne it was countered by the Angevin party that they 'would send the king at once to Ireland if they heard of any wrong done to the earl' (Flanagan 1989, 69–70; Potter 1955, 67–8). Given the established trading routes and the references linking Bristol and Ireland in the *Anglo-Saxon Chronicle* it is quite likely that similar political connections were well established before 1066. It certainly seems accepted that there was a long-established, if small, community of

Bristol merchants in Dublin (Barry 1992). This suggests that some Hiberno-Norse influence should be expected in the material culture of early Bristol, although Watts and Rahtz found no clear evidence for this in the assemblages from Mary-le-Port Street. A sherd of French pottery found at Peter Street in 1975 suggests another maritime link.

Diet

The evidence from recently published excavations is beginning to transform our understanding of changing dietary patterns. Cattle, sheep/goat and pig generally dominate the animal bone assemblages. The range of animal bone from the excavation at Finzels Reach, which produced one of the largest assemblages recovered so far from Bristol, shows that the inhabitants of the site were consumers of both beef and mutton, with cattle being more frequent in the mid-12th to mid-13th century and sheep/goat more numerous in the mid-13th to mid-14th century (Strid 2017, 261). This is in slight contrast to the evidence from the Cabot Circus fieldwork where sheep and sheep/goat were the most numerous taxa throughout (Warman 2013, 279). The excavation at 1–3 Redcliff Street showed that there was a preference for younger ovicaprids during the earliest period (early 12th to mid-13th century), suggesting a preference for lamb over the cheaper mutton, perhaps indicating the higher status of the inhabitants in this period.

The fact that Lent, Fridays and Saturdays, plus Wednesdays in the early medieval period, were religious non-meat days meant that fish and shellfish were a major element of the urban diet during the medieval and post-medieval period (Wilson 1973; Grant 1988a; Grant 1988b). The on-site sieving programmes from Dundas Wharf (BHER 344) and Nos 95–7 Redcliff Street (Canynges House) (BHER 447), which would have retrieved the smaller fish bone, were not followed up with post-excavation analyses through lack of funding. Therefore, until recently, fish have been almost entirely absent from the archaeological record. However this picture is changing as more information is analysed and published. The Cabot Circus fieldwork produced a considerable variety of fish from many sources, principally marine and estuarine species (Armitage 2013, 287). Similarly, recently published results from the excavations at Nos 1–3 Redcliff Street have added significantly to the current picture of fish consumption in this period, with the majority of the fish consumed being estuarine/marine fish species (Armitage 2015, 103–4). Particularly noteworthy was the higher component of conger eel compared with other Bristol sites. Conger eel were considered a highly prized (and presumably expensive) delicacy and their presence in the Redcliff Street assemblage further confirms the fact that the inhabitants were relatively well off in the 12th and 13th centuries. The large assemblage of fish bone from the Finzels Reach excavation has shown that the composition of the assemblage did not vary greatly over the medieval period, with herring and common eel being the most frequent, with cod and flatfish also present (Brady 2017, 130; Nicholson 2017, 264–6).

Charred remains of free-threshing wheat, barley and rye, in addition to waterlogged cereal bran, were recovered from Finzels Reach, Cabot Circus and Nos 1–3 Redcliff Street. While these cereals may have been used for bread making, the charred remains indicate that some material was burnt, possibly as sweepings from domestic buildings or stables. However, most of the processed grain would have been taken to the city's mills for the production of flour. Fruits, both cultivated and wild, such as grape, cherry, plum, walnut, hazelnut, as well as sloes and blackberries have been found on all these sites as well as on the Redcliffe waterfront excavations (Jones 2017, 270–1; Batchelor *et al* 2013, 385–6; Cobain 2015, 118–19; Jones and Watson 1987).

Population

The sites so far excavated have not added much to our knowledge of the inhabitants of early Bristol and the size and composition of the population before 1200 is not known with any certainty. The population was probably drawn by immigration from nearby villages and smaller towns, although the established presence of merchants from the town's trading partners can be assumed, as can that of seamen from communities overseas. Yet Bristol's population remains in relative obscurity as far as the archaeological record is concerned. The skeletal material recovered at St James's Priory does, however, give some information. The status of those buried close to the east end of the church is unknown but the lay people interred alongside the regular clergy within the monastic burial ground were probably of a fairly high social status. A majority of males was observed in head-niche graves at both ends of the priory church, and the modal average age at death for both sexes was 45 years plus. The average height of the males was in the range of 1.71–1.75m. Eight children under 15 years of age were found in head-niche burials, and of these two were five years old or younger (Jackson 2006b).

Chapter 6: 'The Worshipful town': Bristol *c* 1200–*c* 1540

The historical framework

Government

By the beginning of the 13th century a formal structure of local government was in place. At the centre was the mayor, the office first being recorded in 1216, who was supported by a governing Council (Ralph 1973, 6). This comprised 48 members by 1344 and had a range of responsibilities including the sanction of all guild regulations. From 1312 the town was in dispute with Edward II's Constable over tallage in an episode known as the Burgesses Revolt (Fleming 2004, 13–17). Escalation over the next four years saw a series of arrests of townsmen, an attack by them on the castle mill, draining of the castle moat and construction of siege engines, and finally the bombardment of the town from the castle which led the Council to seek terms with the Crown (Fuller 1894–5, 177–87).

Edward III granted county status to Bristol in 1373, and as the first such county borough the town obtained notable independence. It was no longer subject to the judicial oversight of Gloucestershire and Somerset, and where the constable of the castle had been able to impose royal justice the mayor now acted as escheator for the Crown. With the Sheriffs, who became Justices of the Peace, the mayor could hold courts and try felons. Crown rights such as Treasure Trove also passed to the town (Harriss 2005, 282). In the mid-15th century Bristol was granted its own Admiralty Court with the Mayor as its Commissioner (Cronne 1946, 71–3). In 1499 Bristol was granted a further royal charter which placed administration on a similar footing to that of the City of London (ibid, 164). It established a body of six aldermen (including the recorder) and expanded the range of judicial powers enjoyed by the Mayor and Commonalty.

Population

The Black Death reached Bristol in the summer of 1348 and its ships seem to have helped to spread the disease around the country. Evidence for the impact of plague in Bristol is thin but, as in other urban centres, mortality was no doubt high. Boucher points to the list of members of the Council for 1349 in the *Little Red Book* as evidence of the scale of deaths. Fifteen of the names were struck through and he estimated on that basis that between 35 and 40 per cent of the population died (Boucher 1938, 37). But prosperity allowed the town to rebuild and maintain its population and, for the first time, population figures are available – at least for the tax-paying members of the community. In 1377 Bristol had a taxpaying population of 6,345 (Russell 1948, 142–3), only just over one quarter of the figure for London but nevertheless making it the third city of the kingdom after York. The composition of the population would have consisted of significant numbers of immigrants from the surrounding area and Penn identifies the pull factors of Bristol as second only to London (Penn 1985, 261). The diversity of nationality and ethnicity in the medieval population is far from clear. Individual migrants from abroad may be identifiable from surname evidence. John van Ende, haberdasher, leased a property in Broad Street in 1480 for example. The town also had a significant resident Irish population, but unfortunately the entry for the town in the alien subsidy returns for 1440, which recorded the exact size of the community in the kingdom, is badly damaged (Bolton 2000, 8).

The Jewish community

As was the case in other medieval towns, Bristol's Jewish community was consistently persecuted until their expulsion from England in 1290. King John levied a new tax to take one-thirteenth of moveable property from his subjects in 1207. This was accompanied by a tallage of 4,000 marks on England's Jews and in addition demanded that one-tenth of the debts owed to them should be signed over to the Crown. This became as much a tax on the debtors as the Jews because the lands of debtors who had fallen behind in their payments began to be seized by the Crown. In 1210 John called leaders of the various Jewish communities to Bristol where they were imprisoned in the castle and reputedly tortured. All Jews were then arrested and their loans confiscated. A tallage of 60,000 marks, known as the Bristol tallage, was imposed for their release and the redemption of the bonds which required a payment of at least 40 shillings by even the poorest Jews. This led many to leave the country and even more debts passed to the Crown, causing yet more resentment amongst Christians who led attacks on communities around the country. With John's death the situation was eased and royal orders were made to protect Jews in Bristol and other cities (Stacey 2003, 42–4). This was to be only a brief hiatus before overt persecution resumed. In 1266 the Jewry was attacked by followers of Simon de Montfort and the *archa* burnt (Adler 1928, 159), and in 1275 in response to a demand by his mother, Eleanor of Provence, Edward I decreed that the Jewish communities were to be expelled from towns from which she received an income. The Jews at Gloucester were moved to Bristol but most seem to have moved on to other towns relatively quickly (Adler 1928, 164). The Statute of Jewry of 1275 required that all Jews live in towns which, like Bristol, had an *archa*. An attack was led on the Jewry in 1275 by William Giffard and several buildings appear to have been burned. There was some attempt to punish those who took part, and the Crown pursued looters from the incident over the following months (Jenkinson 1929, 123, 202, 221).

National politics

Bristol was drawn into the heart of national politics at intervals and commercial interests seem to have decreed the side taken by the town's elite. In the 13th century Henry III and then Edward I used Bristol to provide logistical support for their military campaigns in Wales (Sharp 1982, xxii), and the town provided 22 ships to Edward III at the siege of Calais in 1347 – only three less than the number sent from London (Rodger 1997, 496). It has been argued that the Hundred Years War created financial and political pressures which, over the long term, made urban elites increasingly important to the exercise of power by the Crown (Liddy 2005). However, relations between Bristol and the Crown were often less than harmonious. When Queen Isabella landed to depose Edward II in early 1325 the king fled to the West Country, having lost control of London. One of his main advisors, the Earl of Winchester, Hugh Despenser, was established in Bristol Castle. When Isabella's force arrived at Bristol in October the burgesses supported the Queen and Despenser was forced to surrender. An assembly of the landed aristocracy gathered there and on 26 October proclaimed Edward and Isabella's son Prince Edward (later Edward III) as keeper of a realm that his father had deserted. The following day the assembly condemned Despenser and sentenced him to death (McKisack 1959, 85–6).

Bristol was once more, briefly, at the centre of events in 1399 when Henry Bolingbroke seized the Crown from Richard II. Bristol Castle was fortified by Richard's forces but the town supported Bolingbroke when he marched his army to the castle on 28 July and the fortress immediately surrendered. Three of Richard's councillors who were present, the Earl of Wiltshire, Sir Henry Green and Sir John Bushey, were arrested and, on the following day, were tried before the Constable of the Castle for treason and executed, an event later dramatised by Shakespeare (*Richard II*, Act III.1).

In the mid-15th century Henry VI imprisoned Bristol's MP Thomas Yonge for proposing in the 1451 session of Parliament that the Duke of York be declared heir apparent to the throne (Griffiths 1991, 95). His action had probably been agreed with the town's mayor and common Council and marked disenchantment with Lancastrian rule in the face of political instability. In June 1453 Bordeaux and Gascony were lost to the French, precipitating mental collapse in the king. As the crisis continued to damage Bristol's economy the town's elite appears to have been drawn increasingly to the Yorkist side (Fleming 2013, 202). Henry VI's queen, Margaret, became ruler as Henry became more ineffective. The Duke of York secured recognition as heir to the throne but was captured and executed by the Lancastrians at the end of December 1460. His son Edward claimed the throne in March 1461 and secured it with victory over the Lancastrian army at Towton (Harriss 2005, 640–4). The new king, Edward IV visited Bristol in September and several charters were issued or confirmed over the next year, including the right to collect the fee farm. This proved to be a persistent source of contention between the town and the Exchequer; discontent was compounded by the king's foreign policy which appears to have been disadvantageous to Bristol's trade. The town supported the Earl of Warwick's alliance with Queen Margaret which saw Edward forced into exile and Henry VI briefly restored to the throne. However, Edward returned in March 1471, defeated Warwick at the battle of Barnet and then Margaret's forces, which had passed through Bristol collecting artillery and men, at Tewkesbury on 4 May. The restored king visited punishment on identified supporters of the Lancastrians among the Bristol elite but did not penalise the town as a whole (Fleming 2013, 215). Bristol does not seem to have played any significant role in the subsequent disputes over the throne.

Trade

Bristol's trading links were already extensive. The marriage of Henry of Anjou (later Henry II) to Eleanor of Aquitaine in the 12th century had brought the Bay of Biscay into Bristol's trading sphere, laying the foundation for a great part of the town's later medieval wealth. A Guild of Merchants had been established by the mid-13th century (Lobel and Carus-

Wilson 1975, 9). Ships travelled regularly between Wales, the South West and Ireland, but also came from further afield. In 1275, for example, a vessel from the Hebrides belonging to Alexander of Argyll was seized and its crew arrested in Bristol on suspicion of piracy (McDonald 1997, 152–3).

Trade with established partners in mainland European and Ireland continued and the range of goods was wide. The dressings of the windows of the gatehouse of Sword Castle, built for the Archbishop of Dublin and Glendalough, Fulk de Sandford, or his brother John between 1256 and 1294, for example, are of Dundry stone (O'Donovan 2003, 269). Bristol was one of the three ports of embarkation for Ireland specified in 1389 (Bolton 2000, 8). Southampton seems to have been the main port for export of wool produced in Gloucestershire and Somerset because the voyage to Flanders was shorter (Simpson 1931), but the volume of exports through Bristol was significant even so. The port was exporting 78 cloths in 1307–8 and was the fourth most commonly used by alien merchants (Childs 1996, 125, 134), though there was a dip in exports in the 1320s. An ordinance issued in May 1326 established Bristol as one of 14 new wool staples. This was a political move by Hugh Despenser the younger, who was Constable of Bristol Castle, to garner support in the South West – but the move proved unpopular elsewhere, and in 1328 the staples were abolished. The 1330s saw volume increase with 21 woolsacks exported in 1331–2 and 122 in the following year, 64 of which were owned by alien merchants. Bristol merchants thus did not monopolise the export of wool through the port and this enabled a wider range of participation than was the case elsewhere. From the 1330s, in a practice which seems to have begun in Bristol, knights in the region began to involve themselves in the wool trade, probably collaborating with local merchants to shift exports away from the southern ports (Nightingale 2000, 43–7). Gascony provided the vast majority of the wine consumed by the royal household, Church and commoners in England, and Bristol had a virtual monopoly of the trade. For a long period Gascony was too remote from the scene of the fighting for the Hundred Years War to have had much effect on it, but famine in 1347 and the plunder of the countryside by rival armies not long afterwards drastically reduced its wealth. This proved only a temporary setback, however. In the 1370s Gascony took half of England's cloth exports, most shipped through Bristol, and Bristol imported thousands of tuns of wine in return, some of the barrels to be reused as linings for wells and tanning pits.

The first half of the 15th century saw further growth and prosperity for the town, reaching a peak in the 1440s. For example, between 1400 and 1416 over 30 licences were granted to Bristol merchants to trade goods and purchase salmon in Ireland (O'Neill 1987, 38–9), while in the autumn of 1443 six ships left Bordeaux for Bristol carrying 1,614 tuns of wine (Carus-Wilson 1928, 65). Amongst the wealthiest were the Canynges family, with their extensive business interests and large merchant fleet, which William Worcestre says was of ten ships ranging between 50 and 900 tons (Neale 2000, 262–3). Ship-owning was part of the portfolio of many Bristol merchants. Several owned ships outright or held shares in ships, a means of spreading the very significant financial risks. One merchant, having spent £500 on building a vessel was forced to sell a quarter share 'for lak of good' (Scammell 1961, 115). Trade in the Severn Estuary was subject to piracy by neighbouring Welsh lordships, prompting national legislation to counter the problem (Griffiths 1991, 67), but outside British waters the dangers could be even greater. In 1484 during a naval conflict between England and Brittany three ships including the *Trinity*, a large vessel which had previously been involved in trade with North Africa, and the *Mary Grace*, were captured by the Breton privateer Jean de Coetanlem (Davies 1994, 230–9). Much of Bristol's trade was with Gascony, which escaped most of the disruption of the Hundred Years War, and had remained fairly steady. However, the loss of Gascony in 1453 dealt a serious blow. Bristol is thought to have suffered quite significant economic stress in the slump of the 1450s and 1460s. The volume of wool exports and of wine imports declined and the town is believed to have experienced a substantial loss of population (Hatcher 1996, 268). When Henry VII visited the town in the spring of 1486 after his victory at Bosworth he was treated to a series of pageants intermingled with complaints 'that Bristow is fallen into decaye' (Bettey 1985, 4).

The loss prompted a search for new markets. Bristol ships exploited the Atlantic and later the Icelandic fisheries, rapidly gaining a major interest in the importation of stockfish (dried cod) from the mid-15th century (Carus-Wilson 1967, 129). Merchants also looked further afield. Robert Sturmy embarked on an ultimately fatal journey to the Levant in 1457 (Bettey 1998, 7) and wealthy Bristolians financed other voyages of exploration. William Worcestre reports that John Jay set sail on an abortive voyage to 'the island of Brazil' in July 1480 (Neale 2000, 234–5). The following year Thomas Croft made another voyage 'not by cause of marchandise but to thentent to serche & fynde' the island Jay had failed to reach (Pope 1997, 15; Reddaway and Ruddock 1969). Bristol mariners had apparently been aware of a coastline to the west between 45 and 60 degrees of latitude for some decades, and knowledge of their discovery had reached Castile in 1497 (Vigneras 1956, 505), and on discovering this Zuan Caboto, a Venetian better known in the Anglophone world as John Cabot, secured letters patent from Henry VII for a voyage there. He arrived in the town to raise financial backing and ships (Williamson 1962, 47–8) and in 1497 made landfall on the North American mainland, probably in Newfoundland.

Urban growth (Figs 6.1, 6.3, 6.8, 6.23)

The growth of Bristol's economy was such that, even before *c* 1200, the space available on the peninsula between the Avon and the Frome was no longer sufficient and, as we have seen in the previous chapter, new suburbs were added to the east, north-east and south-east: the Old Market, Broadmead and Redcliffe, all of which survive as individual and distinct quarters of the modern city. Old Market had a layout reminiscent of a small medieval street borough; Broadmead was laid out with a simple rectilinear street grid; Redcliffe (which remained part of Somerset until 1373) with a more extensive and sophisticated grid adapted to existing topographical constraints (*see* pp 106–7).

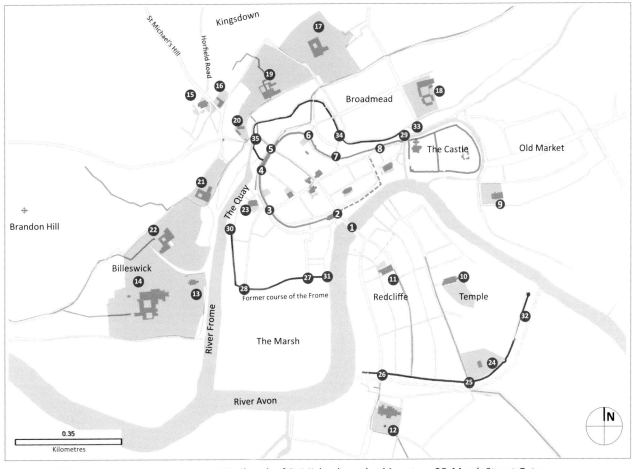

1 Bristol Bridge	15 Church of St Michael-on-the-Mount Without	28 Marsh Street Gate
2 St Nicholas' Gate	16 Nunnery of St Mary Magdalen	29 Newgate
3 St Leonard's Gate	17 Priory of St James	30 Viell's Great Tower
4 St Giles or King Edward's Gate	18 Dominican Friary	31 Marsh Gate
5 St John's Gate	19 Franciscan Friary	32 Water Gate
6 Blind Gate or St John's Arch	20 St Bartholomew's Hospital	33 Castle Mill
7 Pithay Gate	21 Carmelite Friary	34 Aylwards/Nether Pithay Gate
8 Aldgate or Old Gate	22 St Mark's Hospital	35 Frome Gate
9 Church of SS Philip and Jacob	23 Church of St Stephen	
10 Temple Church	24 Austin Friary	
11 Church of St Thomas the Martyr	25 Temple Gate	Churches
12 Church of St Mary Redcliffe	26 Redcliff Gate	Cemeteries and ecclesiastical precincts
13 Church of St Augustine-the-Less	27 Back Street Gate	Post 1200 defences
14 Abbey of St Augustine		Conduits

Figure 6.1 Bristol c *1300*

The early 13th century saw rapid urbanisation continue, with development on the south side of Baldwin Street where new land was made accessible from the old urban core by the diversion of the River Frome in 1240–7 (*see* p 143), and along Lewins Mead, where large parcels of land were given over to the precincts of religious houses and other areas occupied by housing. All of these new suburbs were added as blocks at the edges of the existing built-up area and most were developed on reclaimed wetland. Relatively little reworking of the existing urban topography seems to have taken place. However, the functions and relative importance of these new suburbs to the economy of the town is far from clear, largely because of the lack of detailed historical and archaeological study within most of them.

The Old Market (Fig 5.15)

By 1200 it would appear that Old Market had been established as a market settlement with its typical wide street and back lanes and possibly defended from the outset by a wide ditch. Outside Lawford's Gate, which closed the eastern end of the Old Market, West Street led east to London, and a hundred metres or so beyond the gate was the junction with the road to Gloucester which ran north towards Stapleton. Development was taking place along West Street by the 13th century. A charter of the mid-13th century records a croft of Thomas the cordwainer opposite his house next to the lane to Stapleton (Walker 1998, 345–6). How intensive this early occupation was is uncertain in the absence of fieldwork, but some of the lanes on either side of West Street were clearly established. A charter, of *c* 1274, discusses land outside Lawford's Gate that extended 'from the street in front to the street behind' (Ross 1959, 114). Probably much of the land around the street was agricultural – the documentary evidence and the discovery of the ditch on the south side of West Street (BHER 3577) tend to support this – with discrete buildings. By the 15th century much more development seems to have taken place. The discovery of two 15th-century party walls in the middle of the south side of West Street (BHER 380) implies that a significant part of the street is likely to have been built up.

The market was regulated by the Pie Poudre court which was being held by *c* 1327 thought to be on the site of No 74 Old Market Street, now the Stag and Hounds public house (Ross 1959, 112) (Fig 6.2).

The parish church, SS Philip and Jacob (ie St James), had been built by the late 12th century and stood on the east side of a roughly square churchyard on the south side of Jacob Street, just to the east of the King's orchard. Here it was outside the planned area with the southern side of the churchyard against the county boundary (Harding 1930, 162–3).

Broadmead (Figs 5.17 and 6.3)

The foundation of Broadmead in the 12th century was discussed in the previous chapter (p 104). The name Broadmead was first recorded in *c* 1235–45 in relation to a shop on its south side (Ross 1959, 86). The suburb was clearly planned. A grid of streets was laid out with Broadmead, running north-east from St James's Back, continued eastwards by Irish Mead (later Rosemary Lane), and Horsefair to the north forming the main streets. At the junction of Broadmead and Irish Mead, King Street (*de vico regali*: *see* Ross 1959, 113), later Old King Street, and Marshall Street (later Merchant Street) formed a north-west to south-east axis, dividing the suburb into quadrants. Three of these were divided into regular narrow plots, extending back from tenements on the Broadmead frontages across the entire width of the block. Land parcels on Merchant Street and Old King Street were shallower, extending only *c* 25–30m back from the street to the side boundaries of the Broadmead plots. A property recorded in Old King Street in 1315, for example, measured 17ft (5.2m) wide by 91ft (27.8m) deep (Ross 1959, 122). Gardens are also frequently mentioned in the property records (*see* Veale 1933, 239).

The southern edge of Broadmead was defined by the north bank of the River Frome. Its northern extent was marked by the Barrs ('le Barres'), which were in place in the 1380s (Wadley 1886, 11) with houses standing nearby (ibid, 12). Their form is unknown but, given their position, they were presumably timber gates to prevent grazing animals from straying into the suburb rather than any more substantial barrier, as, for example, at York.

Figure 6.2 Stag and Hounds, No 74 Old Market Street in 1824 by George Delamotte (Braikenridge Collection, BRSMG M2785)

They also apparently marked a social barrier since William Worcestre mentions several times that it was where tenants of his father 'dwell as wanton women' (Neale 2000, 6–7). Whether Worcestre meant that they were prostitutes or was merely following contemporary mores in being censorious of unmarried women not living within an established household is unclear. However, in 1344 Bristol prevented lepers and prostitutes from remaining within the town, suggesting the former interpretation (Karras 1996, 18–20).

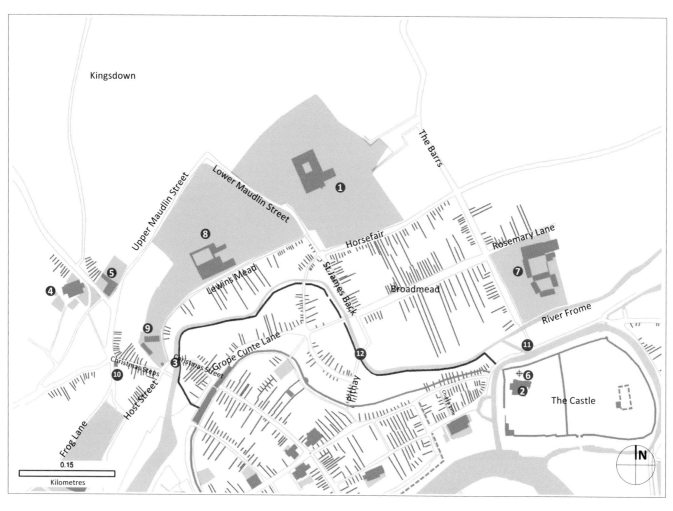

1   Priory of St James

2   Castle Keep

3   Frome Gate and bridge

4   Church of St Michael-on-the Mount Without

5   Nunnery of St Mary Magdalen

6   Chapel of St Martin

7   Dominican Friary

8   Franciscan Friary

9   St Bartholomew's Hospital

10 Foster's Almshouse

11 Castle Mill

12 Aylwards/Nether Pithay Gate

   Pre 1200/post 1200 Churches

   Cemeteries and ecclesiastical precincts

   Post 1200 Town walls and defences

Figure 6.3 North of the Frome c 1300

Archaeological knowledge of the Broadmead suburb is derived almost entirely from modern investigation (Figs 6.4 and 6.5).

Recording during construction of the Broadmead shopping centre in the 1950s was confined to the work of two avocational archaeologists, Keith Marochan and Keith Reed. More recent excavated evidence from the low-lying area around the Frome, south of St James's Back and between the river and the castle moat, indicates that occupation in this area was well established by the mid-12th century. There was evidence for active management of the river with frequent

Figure 6.4 General view of Union Street excavation, 2000 (reproduced from Jackson 2010a, fig 5)

dumping to raise the ground above flood levels and the construction of riverside revetments. Tenements were being laid out before the foundation of the Dominican Friary on the north side of the river, and they would remain broadly the same as those mapped in the 19th century. In the late 13th century, substantial stone buildings adjacent to St James's Back were constructed, one of which was later, in a document of 1549, termed the 'mansion house', illustrating the changing use of space in the growing medieval town (BHER 3590, Jackson 2010a) (Figs 6.6 and 6.7).

Given its peripheral location in relation to the main focus of the medieval town, it is not surprising that there was evidence for industrial production, in particular iron working, in the area. The presence of an industrial complex adjacent to the river at St James's Back has been discussed in the previous chapter (*see* p 105). From the area to the south of the Dominican Friary, between the Frome and the castle moat, there was evidence for smithing, while some of the iron working may have been associated with farriery, possibly related

to the proximity of the castle immediately to the south. There was also some evidence for the processing of hides (Ridgeway and Watts 2013). Documentary evidence for land use in the area suggests that there was a mix of shops and tenements and open space and gardens. Some questions remain unanswered, particularly about the suburb's origins and early chronology. There does not, for example, seem to have been much development in Rosemary Street even as late as the 17th century, though why the expansion of Broadmead finished here is unclear.

Lewins Mead (Figs 5.17 and 6.3)

At the start of the 13th century the Lewins Mead area appears to have been largely agricultural in character with scattered loci of domestic and industrial activity, particularly just beyond the edges of the town. The Frome ran through the middle, separating the town on the south side of the river from the land to the north. The three centuries between 1200 and 1500 saw the area become urbanised, particularly to the south of the river and around St James's Back and Pithay.

Figure 6.5 General view of Cabot Circus (Quakers Friars) excavation, 2005–6 (reproduced from Ridgeway and Watts 2013, fig 1.3)

The land on the south side of the Frome had a character quite distinct from that on the north, consisting of a narrow strip of marsh immediately below the inner circuit town wall. In the 13th century this land was enclosed by a new town wall. The decision to construct it may relate to the diversion of the Frome in the 1240s, but the wall has never been archaeologically excavated and consequently there is no physical evidence for its date. The use of the area between the walls seems to have been varied though little direct archaeological evidence for the nature of the activity here has so far been recovered. The documentary evidence is strong however. Christmas Street was probably a commercial frontage and there are numerous documents amongst the deeds to the properties of St John's parish which refer to tenements and shops along it in the 14th and 15th centuries. There were also dwellings in the other streets in the area. A deed of 1307 records a shop next to the stone house of Adam de Temple in Nelson Street (then Gropecuntelane) (Bristol Archives P/StJB/D/2/15) and, bearing in mind the proximity of the quayside, the medieval name

is eloquent about the presence of another specialised trade and the likely character of the street (Holt and Baker 2001). Dwellings are also recorded around Pithay from the 14th century. The density of development is less clear. There were gardens in this part of Lewins Mead and the churchyard for St Lawrence was located in this area. A deed of July 1330 records two tofts in Nelson Street, one of which ran back to the town wall suggesting buildings were probably sited on the street frontages.

To the north of the Frome, at the beginning of the 13th century only St Mary Magdalen Nunnery at Upper Maudlin Street and St James's Priory had been established but, in the course of the century, monastic houses came to dominate the area (*see* p 187). Between them, however, there was housing. Houses were standing in Frogmore Street by the mid-1230s. The area between St Mark's and the Frome had been developed by the mid-12th century and there is evidence of rebuilding of properties here in the late Middle Ages (BHER 308). Tenements in Host Street (Horssestret) are recorded in a deed of 1337 (BRL, Braikenridge Collection 107), and a hall

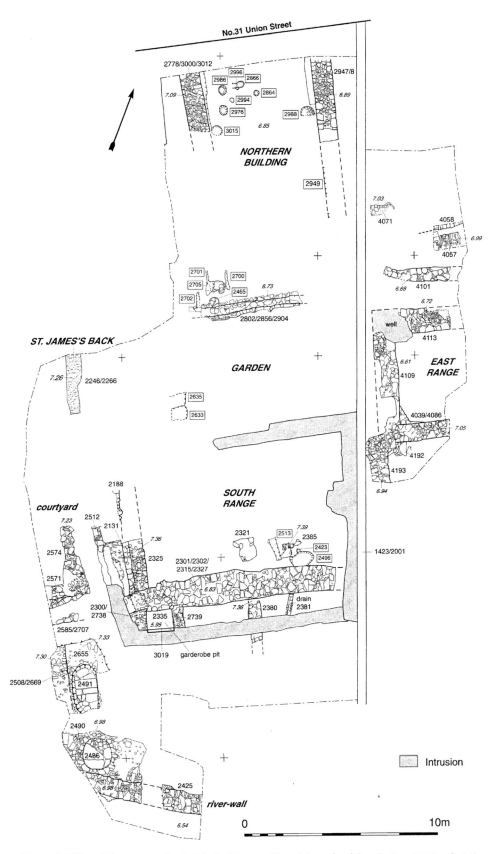

Figure 6.6 Plan of features associated with the 'Mansion House' (reproduced from Jackson 2010a, fig 18)

*Figure 6.7 Elevation
of the west gable wall
of the south range of
the 'Mansion House'
(reproduced from Jackson
2010a, fig 21)*

and five shops stood at the north-west end of the street in September 1434. Christmas Street (Knyfsmythstrete) was also lined with dwellings and a wall of later medieval date is still visible in The Christmas Steps public house (formerly the Three Sugar Loaves) (BHER 370; Bryant and Kear 1982). The street name obviously indicates a grouping of medieval craft specialists here. There were also substantial private houses and one that was excavated in 2000 at St James's Back (BHER 3590) nicely illustrates the changing use of space in the growing medieval town, as the industrial uses that characterised the site when it was on the urban fringe were supplanted by the construction of an imposing dwelling as it became submerged within the built-up area as the Broadmead suburb was developed.

Redcliffe (Fig 6.8)

The Redcliffe district, across the Avon, lay in the county of Somerset, outside the jurisdiction of Bristol until 1373. Additionally, its eastern half lay within the Temple Fee, seen by the Knights Templar and latterly the Hospitallers as a distinct legal entity even after 1373. The suburb was developed from the 1120s, and the framework for settlement established at that date (and in part inherited from an even earlier period) remained in use in the 13th century

(Chapter 5). By the beginning of the century the three principal north–south streets – Redcliff Street, St Thomas Street and Temple Street – were lined with houses, although there is some evidence that St Thomas Street may not have been as extensively developed, at least at the beginning of this period, as the other two streets. In Redcliff Street, by the late 13th century, if not before, property boundaries were becoming fixed, with stone boundary wall foundations defining more permanent plot divisions, as indicated by the excavation at Nos 1–2 Redcliff Street (Alexander 2015) (Figs 6.9 and 6.10).

Excavations at Finzels Reach appeared to suggest that, while the buildings on the Temple Street frontage were being constructed on stone footings from the mid-13th century or earlier, at the rear of the properties adjacent to the south-west side of Temple Street, the plot boundaries consisted, at least until the late 14th century, of well-defined ditches, which served to drain the area and channel water and waste into the Law Ditch at the rear of the properties. The Law Ditch, which was first seen as the substantial ditch that may have formed part of the pre-Conquest boundary of Arthur's Fee (*see* Chapter 5), was successively recut and by the late 13th century had been partially lined with stone, possibly at the initiative of individual

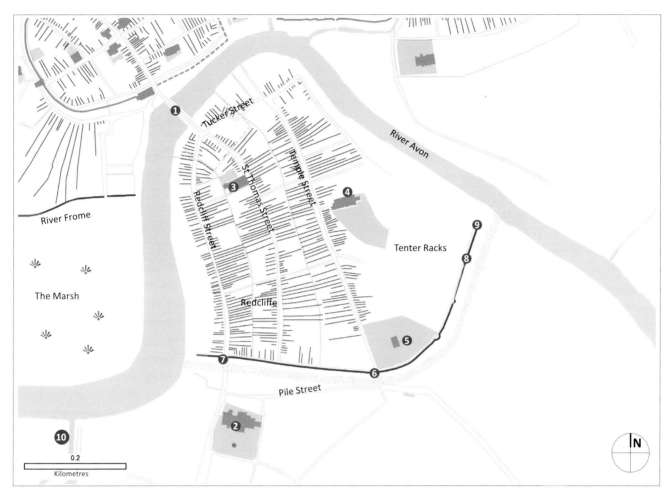

1   Bristol Bridge   6   Temple Gate

2   Church of St Mary Redcliffe   7   Redcliff Gate

3   Church of St Thomas the Martyr   8   Water Gate

4   Temple Church   9   Tower Harratz

5   Austin Friary   10 Trin Mill

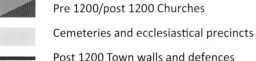   Pre 1200/post 1200 Churches

          Cemeteries and ecclesiastical precincts

   Post 1200 Town walls and defences

          Portwall ditch

          Law Ditches

Figure 6.8 Redcliffe c *1300*

Figure 6.9 Nos 1–2 Redcliff Street. Late 13th- to mid-14th-century stone-founded buildings (reproduced from Alexander 2015, fig 3.9)

property holders (Brady and Teague 2017, 57). Substantial timber-lined wells were found near the rear of the Temple Street properties, one dating to the mid-13th–14th century and the other to the late 14th–15th century. They may well have been wine tuns or possibly beer barrels, one with incised markings and two tap holes and a bung hole, reusing what were readily available commodities once they had outlived their original function (Allen 2017, 244–6) (Figs 6.11, 6.12 and 6.13).

The area of Redcliff Pit around St Mary Redcliffe Church, was also developed but the areas east and west of the church and also Temple Meads, east of Temple Street, seem to have been agricultural land.

This basic framework remained in place, with development during the 13th century and later being at the level of the individual burgage plot. Those which backed on to the river Avon were extended by reclaiming land from the river. The process of reclamation seems to have occurred on the initiative of individual property owners, a wall being built out into the river and the ground behind raised by dumping. Unlike waterfront revetments excavated elsewhere in the United Kingdom, those in Redcliffe were unusual in the extensive use of stone in their construction, and Bristol had some of the earliest stone quays in the country (Good 1991, 34–6) (Figs 6.14, 6.15).

The extent of reclamation varied depending on the location. At the north end of Redcliffe, adjacent to Bristol Bridge, the extent of reclamation was only a few metres during the Middle Ages, probably because of the practical constraint of the bridge. However, on

Figure 6.10 Nos 1–2 Redcliff Street. Plan of period 2a: late 13th to mid-14th centuries (reproduced from Alexander 2015, fig 3.7)

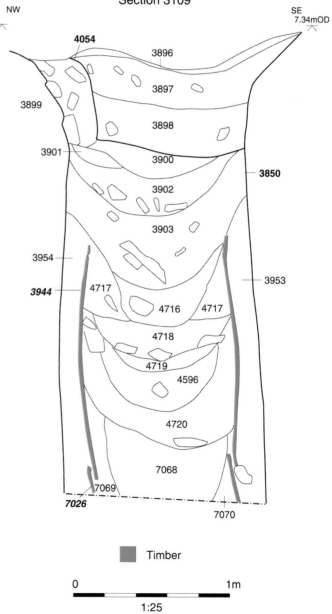

Section 3109

NW

SE
7.34mOD

4054

3896

3897

3899

3898

3901

3900

3902

3850

3903

3954

3944

4717

3953

4716   4717

4718

4719

4596

4720

7068

7069

7026

7070

■ Timber

0   1m

1:25

the southern side it was considerably greater, increasing to a maximum of over 50m at the south end of Redcliff Street. Building into the river allowed proper wharfage to be created. A quay wall allowed vessels to berth at high tide and settle on the mud as the water receded and goods could be unloaded straight on to a dry, level surface; it also created the space to erect warehousing (Fig 6.16).

This reclamation process has been explored on a number of major excavation sites from Bristol Bridge south along Redcliff Street. In 1981 a site on the south-west side of Bristol Bridge was excavated (BHER 341), recording what the excavator interpreted as a series of docks, one of stone and timber which survived to a height of about 2m was provisionally dated to the mid-13th century. A timber revetment at the rear was partly built of ships' timbers (Fig 6.17).

A second dock, 6m square, on its south side was replaced by a larger dock in the late 13th century. All three docks appeared to have gone out of use in the 14th century and a substantial realigned quay wall of stone, about 2m across, was built across the former dock entrances which were subsequently filled with refuse (Williams 1982). The excavation at Nos 127–9 Redcliff Street in 1982–3 (BHER 344) found that the slipway which separated two of the 12th-century properties had remained in use into the 13th century. When new quay walls

were built to the west of the 12th-century line, the slipway was extended. In the 14th and 15th centuries the buildings and the slipway were again extended westwards to the river (Good 1991) (Fig 6.18).

Figure 6.12 Late 14th- to 15th-century barrel-lined well from Finzels Reach excavation (reproduced from Ford et al 2017, fig 3.32)

(opposite) Figure 6.11 13th-century barrel-lined well from Finzels Reach excavation (reproduced from Ford et al 2017, fig 3.6)

Figure 6.13 Detail of above showing incised markings (reproduced from Ford et al 2017, fig 6.61)

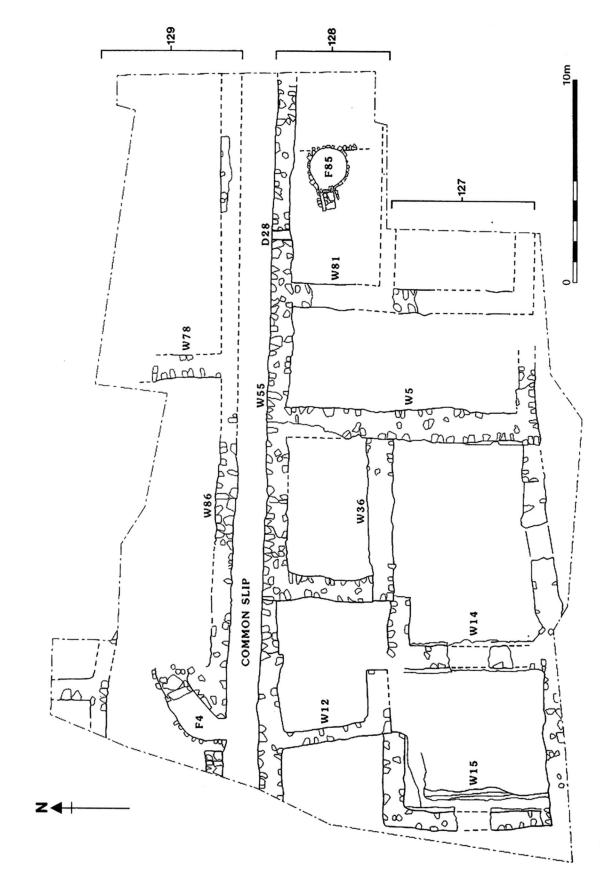

Figure 6.14 Nos 127–9, Redcliff Street. Plan of medieval tenements and riveryard extensions in the 14th and 15th centuries (reproduced from Good 1991, fig 11)

At the southern end of the street, fieldwork at Nos 98–103 and 95–7 Redcliff Street also recorded successive quay walls and the extension of riverside tenements. Excavation at Nos 98–103 (BHER 3629) identified 13th- and 14th-century features and deposits within the seven tenement plots covered by the site, and on the site of No 103 one wall was interpreted as a 13th-century riverfront wall. The evidence for 14th-century activity within the site was limited. An existing slipway between two tenements on the southern side of the site went out of use and a relieving arch was built blocking it, an indication of the redevelopment and extension of the plot. A surviving fragment of a 14th- or 15th-century wall forming the boundary between Nos 100 and 101 Redcliff Street was also recorded (Lowe 2001), but little further evidence of 15th-century activity was encountered

(Insole 2001a). On the site to the south, 95–7 Redcliff Street, excavation in 1983–5 (BHER 447) found more extensive evidence of later medieval reclamation. During the late 12th or early 13th century the original building on the street frontage was demolished and another built over it; at the same time the waterfront was extended 8m westwards by dumping layers of stone, clay and organic refuse behind a post and plank structure. During the 13th century a stone quay wall with a slipway was built 14m west of the 12th-century river bank (Fig 6.19).

The 14th century saw the movement of the river front 17m further west where a substantial stone river wall was built. Immediately to the south of the wall was a gully, possibly used as a dock, while to the east was another wall which was thought likely to have supported a jetty. Later in the century this wall was extended

Figure 6.15 Stone waterfront revetment wall at Nos 127–9 Redcliff Street

Figure 6.16 Excavation at Nos 127–9 Redcliff Street 1983 from the south

Figure 6.17 Nos 143–7 Redcliff Street. 13th-century timber revetment, reusing ships' timbers

southwards, blocking the dock. Another dock or gully at least 6m wide was formed to the north of the first by mounding soil to form a bank. The 13th-century river wall and slipway were sealed beneath approximately 2m of dumped material on which a series of buildings which fronted on to a courtyard were constructed. The function of these is uncertain, though they may have been warehouses, possibly with domestic accommodation above. In the 15th century the later dock was filled in and a courtyard created over the area (Fig 6.20). Part of a standing medieval arcade within the north wall of No 95, part of William Canynges' house, was also recorded (Jones 1986; *see* pp 220–222) (Fig 6.21). The arcade still survives, complete with ogee-headed piscina (Fig 6.22).

Development in the Marsh (Fig 6.23)

Construction of the new Frome channel in the 1240s (explored further below) remade

Figure 6.18 Nos 127–9 Redcliff Street. Medieval slipway looking towards the river

the topography of this part of Bristol, in effect extending southwards the peninsula between the two rivers. The new channel was at least 300m long, defining a new boundary between the town and the precinct of St Augustine's Abbey and the suburb of Billeswick. The main quay for international shipping was re-sited here and the original Frome channel was infilled to create new space for suburban development. There is still little understanding of the scale of this engineering operation: whether it consisted of deepening an already existing tidal creek (Elkin 1991, 32), or the excavation of a

completely new channel through the Marsh. Nevertheless, from this period onwards, if not before, until the creation of the Floating Harbour in the 19th century, the Quay and Welsh Back became the twin foci of the port of Bristol. The Tallage Roll of 1313 indicates that the area was taken into the administrative quarters of All Saints and St Ewen (Fuller 1894–5) and the parochial structure was also reorganised. The eastern part of the area became part of the parish of St Nicholas, a strip in the centre of St Leonard's, while a new parish of St Stephen was created for the western part, the parish church being built by the early 1290s (Dawson 1981, 18) (*see* Fig 6.46).

The pre-13th-century course of the Frome, passing through the Marsh to the south of Baldwin Street to a confluence with the Avon somewhere at Welsh Back is unknown, but three locations have been put forward. The first is on or just to the south of the line of Baldwin Street and has a long pedigree, having been put forward by Worcestre and later Seyer. The second possibility is at the centre of Welsh Back, drawing on Smith's 1568 cartographic depiction of what appears to be a long ditch, taken to be a relict section of the river. The mid-13th-century name for Marsh Street was Scadpullestrete (probably from the Old English verb *scádan* meaning to separate or divide) and subtle topographic features can also be held to support a course in this area. Dr Roger Leech rejected this because of a lack of mention of 'any feature that may have been an abandoned river course' in property records, arguing instead that King Street was created on the line of the original channel (Leech 1997b, 26–8 and fig 2). This argument receives considerable topographical support from the existence of a series of long, early plots extending south from Baldwin Street to King Street (*see* p 92). Wherever the course of the river was, it is clear that before the Frome diversion the Marsh south of Baldwin Street was exploited, with structures or enclosures formed by timber posts and gullies, and also some dumping (Blockley 1996, 12–13; Townsend 2003).

Inside the area newly enclosed by the Marsh Wall, two main thoroughfares – Marsh Street (Merschestret by 1361) and Queen Charlotte Street (Baste or Back Strete) – ran north–south,

Figure 6.20 Nos 95–7 Redcliff Street. Plan of excavation (reproduced from Jones 1986, fig 2)

parallel to the quays, Back Street with a dog-leg at its northern end. The L-shaped Maiden Tavern Lane connected Baldwin Street to the east side of Marsh Street, while a number of alleys ran between Marsh Street and Broad Quay. There was a group of lanes around St Stephen's Church and the churchyard on its south side, while to the north of the church Fisher Lane led from a rectangular space at

the quay where the fish market was held to St Leonard's Gate.

Development began in the second half of the 13th century. The site later occupied by Richard Spicer's house on Welsh Back was levelled by the re-deposition of alluvial clay prior to the construction of new stone buildings, and a similar process of reclamation is probable elsewhere. This development

*Figure 6.21 Arcade at
No 95 Redcliff Street
immediately following
discovery*

seems to have been concentrated on the quays
and the other street frontages, while the area
between Marsh Street and Queen Charlotte
Street seems to have consisted mainly of
gardens.

The detailed topography of the area
is most clear for the later 15th century,
however, because of William Worcestre's
survey. Worcestre describes Baldwin's Cross, a
stone cross at the junction of Queen Charlotte
Street (formerly Back Street) with Baldwin
Street (Neale 2000, 84–5), and also mentions
the adjacent Baldwin's Cross mill, whose
'thoroughs' were described by Samuel Seyer
(Seyer 1823, 24). 'Le Rakhyth' was a building
measuring 27.8 by 21.5m which Worcestre
places on the west side of Knapp's chapel,
presumably meaning on the opposite side
of Back Street where the later street named
Rackhay is sited (Neale 2000, 126–7). The
place-name element *hythe*, meaning 'landing-
place on a river', may suggest the presence of
a former quay or wharf, as suggested earlier
(Chapter 5, p 88) (Gelling 1993, 76). At the
north end of Welsh Back there was a conduit
head 9 feet long (2.75m) (Neale 2000, 34–5,

104–5), while near the Marsh Gate, at the
south end, was the crane and Worcestre also
mentions heaps of wood and other goods
close by (Fig 6.24).

To the south of the Marsh Wall, the Marsh,
an area of about 11.8ha bounded by the Avon
and the newly diverted Frome, remained an
unenclosed space subject to periodic flooding
and was certainly meadow in the early 15th
century (Bristol Archives P/StJB/D/2/102
& 103). The major landmark was a timber
post called 'Gybtayllour', possibly a crane, at
the junction of St Augustine's Reach with the
Avon (Neale 2000, 158–9; 276–7).

The College Green area (Fig 6.23)
At the beginning of the 13th century,
development in the College Green area was
concentrated around the Green itself. St
Augustine's Abbey lay on its south side and St
Augustine-the-Less, then a two-cell building,
at the south-east corner, while the streets
to the north-east were occupied by housing.
Development beyond the immediate vicinity of
College Green was limited to single buildings
or groups of buildings. The 1313 Tallage Roll

Figure 6.22 Current view of eastern half of arcade of Canynges House, 95 Redcliff Street (photograph R Jones)

mentions nine 'schoppa' in 'Wodewelle Strete' (modern Jacob's Wells Road) (Fuller 1894–5, 236) and William Worcestre notes a house called 'lymotes' at the edge of the county boundary, 'towards the hamlet of Rownham' (Neale 2000, 32–3). Throughout the Middle Ages the majority of the land in the area was agricultural.

Kingsdown (Fig 6.3)

The area saw new development in the 15th century. On Park Row, around 200m south-west of St Michael's Church, a house and garden was leased to John Barret in the early 1460s (Leech 2000e, 109) and ribbon development was gradually creeping up St Michael's Hill. Four tenements, a cottage and a garden, part of the endowment of the Chapel of the Three Kings of Cologne made by John Foster (Manchee 1831, vol 1, 82), stood on the site of Nos 31–41 St Michael's Hill by the 1480s, for example (Leech 2000e, 11). The north-eastern wing of the Old Rectory may date from this period and houses and shops are recorded around both the church and St Mary Magdalen Nunnery (Bettey 1997, 4). St Michael's Church was also substantially rebuilt in the 15th century (*see* p 179). Despite this development the character stayed essentially rural. The slopes of Kingsdown were used for meadow, pasture and occasionally arable. Closes or small fields extended right across the area to Stokes Croft where the land, like 'Priouresorchard' in the area of Marlborough Hill Place (Latimer 1897–9, 113–14; Harding 1930, 158–9), mainly belonged to the Priory of St James.

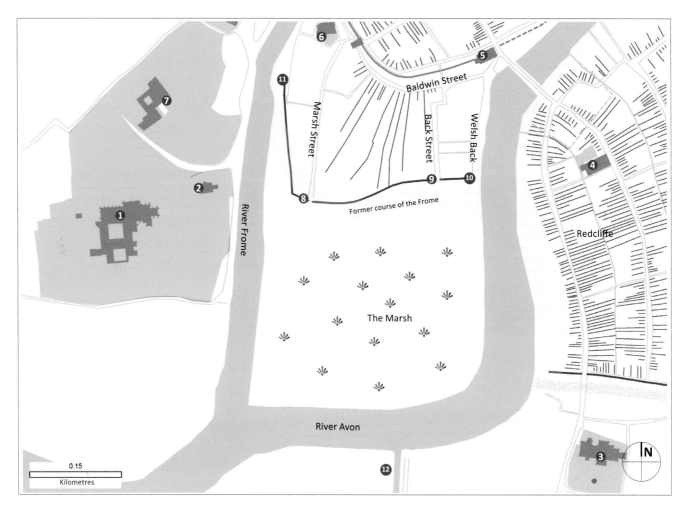

1   Abbey of St Augustine

2   Church of St Augustine-the-Less

3   Church of St Mary Redcliffe

4   Church of St Thomas the Martyr

5   Church of St Nicholas

6   Church of St Stephen

7   St Mark's Hospital

8   Marsh Street Gate

9   Back Street Gate

10 Marsh Gate

11 Viell's Great Tower

12 Trin Mill

   Pre 1200/post 1200 Churches

   Cemeteries and ecclesiastical precincts

   Post 1200 Town walls and defences

Figure 6.23 The Marsh c 1300

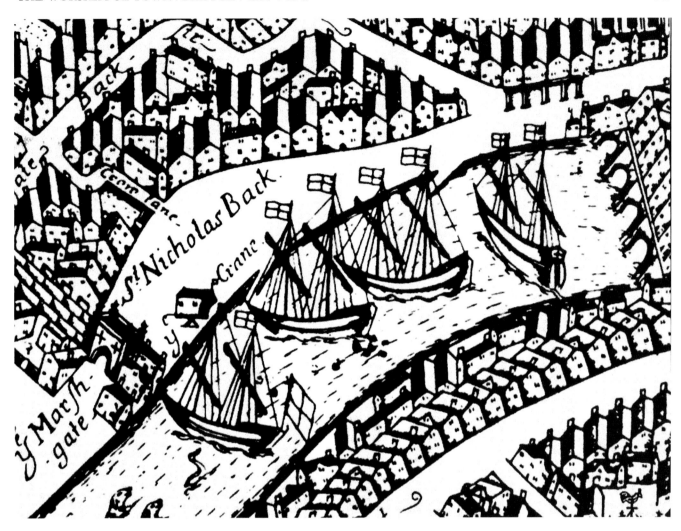

Public works: the castle, defences and public buildings (Fig 6.1)

The port

With Bristol's economy flourishing, the capacity of the port was expanded, an initiative that helped secure the prosperity of the town for several centuries. The decision must have been taken in the late 1230s and the main feature of the scheme was a diversion of the river Frome from its original course into a new channel. Agreement was reached with the Abbot of St Augustine's in March 1240 enabling the creation of St Augustine's Reach flowing north–south through the former marsh by 1247 (Walker 1998, 375–6). The heart of the port shifted to the new quayhead just to the south of St Giles gate, the available

wharfage increased and deeper berths were probably also created.

Bristol Bridge

The buoyant economic environment of the early 13th century and the later consolidation and development of the administration and liberties of the town engendered much new public building. In 1247 Bristol Bridge was rebuilt in stone. The superstructure was of Pennant sandstone (Price 1979a) and William Worcestre reports that it was 75 yards long and 5 yards wide (Neale 2000, 2–3). It was supported on three piers. The central pair of arches, as recorded by a drawing (Fig 6.25) of *c* 1760 were higher and wider than the arches at the northern and southern ends and each pier had a cutwater at either end. Houses lined both sides of the central carriageway of the bridge by the later 14th century (Veale 1938, 117–18) and, while their form is not clear, they appear to have comprised a shop at ground-floor level with tenements above. Some of the buildings were cellared and Worcestre records five 'very strong' stone arched cellars on each side of the bridge and four cellars at either end of the bridge (Neale 2000, 12–13).

Bristol Castle

The excavated sample of the castle, which occupied the eastern end of the Avon–Frome peninsula, is extremely limited in relation to the size of its overall footprint, consisting mainly of small, discrete investigations almost none of which has been published (Fig 5.10). Attempting to divine a coherent picture of the monument is therefore very difficult and any interpretation, given the present state of our knowledge, remains entirely provisional. In the following account, a summary of the documentary evidence is given first, followed by the archaeological evidence.

The castle was under royal control at the beginning of the 13th century and was administratively separate from the town, a distinction which was maintained by its specific exclusion from the County Borough of 1373. Relations between the town and the Constable of the Castle were not always easy but the Burgesses Revolt was by far the most extreme example of their collapse. During the revolt the moat was drained and the castle mill was attacked and, despite the end of the crisis, Hugh Despenser the younger was still having a palisade 'between the castle ditch and the gate towards the town' repaired in the early 1320s (Fuller 1894–5, 184).

Accounts detailing Crown expenditure in the 13th century list extensive new building, repair and maintenance. These works included a new hall built between 1239 and 1242 and a gate-tower between 1244 and 1250 (Colvin 1963, 579). Over four years from 1250 nearly £550 was expended on improvements to buildings within the wards, including a new kitchen and pantry near the hall (Colvin

Figure 6.25 Bristol Bridge c 1760, shortly before its demolition (Seyer MS, Bristol Reference Library, Braikenridge Coll III.i.389)

1963, 579). The windows of St Martin's Chapel in the outer ward were also enlarged at this time and in the early 1280s the chapel and some adjoining chambers were rebuilt (Colvin 1963, 579–80). William Worcestre, writing in 1480, records that although it was dedicated to St Martin the chapel was then in the service (*deuocione*) of St John the Baptist. A monk from St James's Priory was meant to be present daily, but Worcestre comments that a service was only performed on Sunday, Wednesday and Friday (Neale 2000, 240–1). The bridge leading towards St Philip's Church had to be rebuilt, along with sections of the curtain wall nearby (Colvin 1963, 580). Work was done to a door in a wall in the middle of the castle in 1294–5 (Sharp 1982, 36) and in February–March 1295 two lengths of curtain wall were rebuilt (Sharp 1982, 37). One, by the long stable, had apparently collapsed onto the building. The Constable's accounts for 1302–3 also mention the great chamber beyond the gate towards St Philip's, the granary and the long chamber – which were presumably all later 13th-century buildings (Sharp 1982, 58).

From the 14th century few new buildings were constructed. Effort was concentrated on repairs and maintenance, although occupation continued within the wards (Ponsford 1979, 88). The northern vault of the Great Hall was however added to the building. 15th-century works were similarly directed to repair. In 1402–3 preparation for a visit by the king included reconstruction of the drawbridge outside the water gate. Four decades later repairs were carried out to the keep, the king's and queen's chambers, the prince's chamber, the kitchen and the three chapels – one in the outer ward, one in the inner ward, and the third in the keep. However, dilapidation of the castle was clearly becoming difficult to prevent and by the time Worcestre visited in 1480 several buildings were in a poor state of repair. The Constable's lodgings were in ruins and the roof and floors had been stripped out of one of the chapels (Neale 2000, 240–41).

The castle: archaeological evidence
The Norman motte and bailey castle had been rebuilt in stone in the early 12th century and the keep built over the infilled motte ditch.

By the opening of the 13th century, the curtain walls and extramural moat enclosed the keep, inner and outer wards (*see* Chapter 5). The first of Mike Ponsford's excavations in 1968 was at the northern end of Cock and Bottle Lane, on the line of the motte ditch (BHER 452; Site A in Ponsford 1979). After the ditch had been filled in in the 12th century several structures were built over it. Three deep post pits each approximately one metre across were found on the east side of the site: these had contained square timbers, occasionally renewed, and were interpreted as part of a building thought to have been abandoned before 1300. In the same year (1968), an excavation near Lower Castle Street (BHER 448; Site B) found a short section of a medieval wall 1.3m wide, interpreted by the excavator as a part of the east curtain wall. Adjacent were the structures interpreted by the excavator as the east gate of the castle, though this now seems questionable, given the lack of a connection with the street pattern outside, particularly if the Old Market suburb is considered to have been, in origin, a typical medieval street market developed along the approach road to the castle. Recent exploration of the culverted castle moat also suggests the presence of a bridge of medieval or possibly of early modern date on the line of Castle Street, where the main east gate might be expected (Fig 6.26). The presence of a gate at the east end of Castle Street might appear to be logical although the date of construction of the gate has been questioned. The 'Nether Gate' is mentioned as such in the 1373 perambulation of the county boundary (Harding 1930, 162–3), while William Worcestre places the gate into the castle from the east either at the western end of Jacob Street or possibly opposite the south-west corner of St Philip's Churchyard (Neale 2000,105).

An adjacent building with a mortar floor and a small oven or furnace which Ponsford tentatively suggested might have been related to the kitchens of the nearby King's Hall could as easily have been a bakehouse or brewhouse.

The curtain wall at the north-eastern corner of the outer ward was rebuilt in the 13th century after it began to lean outwards, and a D-plan tower built against its outside

Figure 6.26 Underside of the bridge spanning the moat under Castle Street (photograph Nigel Baker)

face – partly, the excavator suggested, to act as a buttress. No direct dating evidence for the tower was recovered, but on the basis of its form it was considered to be of 13th-century date (Ponsford 1979, 93–5).

To the south lay the Great Hall, possibly the new hall of 1239–42. Relatively little is currently known about its overall form. However, a tentative reconstruction has been put forward by Ponsford (1979, fig 44) (Fig 6.27), although this raises considerable questions of interpretation, particularly with regard to the account by William Worcestre of the form of the hall.

The surviving Vaulted Chambers, probably part of its porch, consists of two adjoining rectangular chambers with quadripartite ribbed vaults; the southern porch has been dated to the mid-13th century on architectural evidence. The structure appears to have been described by William Worcestre in the early 1480s who noted it as being 10 yards long, 'with an arched vault above

the entrance of the great hall' (Neale 2000, 238–9). The kitchens were on its south side (Neale 2000, 240–1).

In 1970 a site towards the south-west corner of the castle (BHER 458; Site F) was investigated. The excavation principally focused on one room of a larger building founded on the fill of the motte ditch. In its earliest phase (from *c* 1225) the room had been used as a smithy; finds of domestic refuse, including animal, fish and game bones, led the excavator to conclude that the room was later used as a kitchen, and finally a buttery. The identity of the building is uncertain, though it may have been part of the Constable's quarters, which Worcestre described as being to the south of the keep (Neale 2000, 240–1). Further south, in the south-west corner, was another building, built up against the west curtain wall, whose identity was even less certain. The excavator felt that this may have been a gate at the inner end of a barbican, though this explanation is not fully

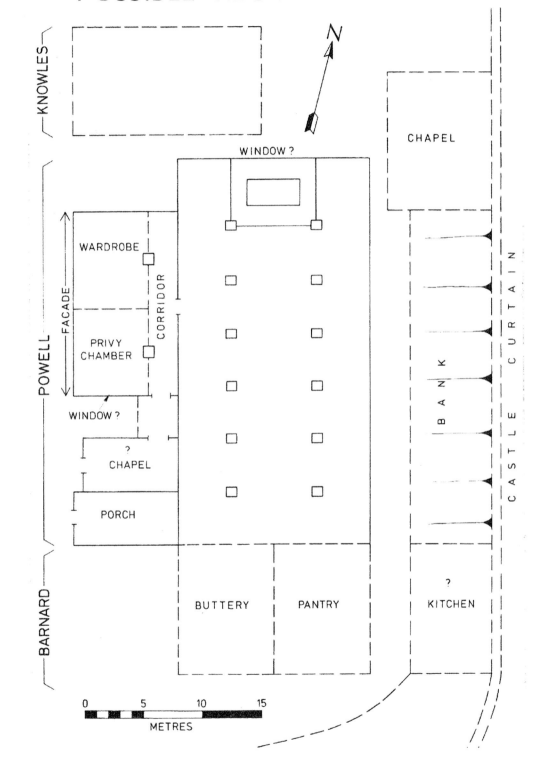

Figure 6.27 Reconstructed plan of the Great Hall, Bristol Castle (reproduced from Ponsford 1979, fig 44)

consistent with the evidence, specifically two walls crossing the presumed entrance passage (Ponsford 1979, 116–17, 162, 330–6, 462–3). A barbican is in fact known to have been built in front of the west gate in the early 1220s, documents relating to properties between the castle and St Peter referring to both the barbican and ditch (Leech 1989, 236, 239–40). The documented barbican is however most likely to have been located slightly further north in an area traditionally ascribed to it by Bristol's antiquaries. Immediately to the north of the excavated area the upper opening to a tunnel, or sally port was found (BHER 475; Site G). This was cut westwards under the western curtain wall and through the natural sandstone to the Avon, probably in the 13th century, although there was no direct dating evidence.

The city defences (Fig 6.1)

One of the very few contemporary images we have of the medieval defences clearly expresses their importance to Bristol's civic identity. The Bristol of Ricart's *Kalendar* is old Bristol, 'standing on a hill between four gates', the Christian symbolism very evident, the circular enclosure of the walls framing the cruciform arrangement of the central streets (Toulmin Smith 1872, 16) (*see* Fig 3.20).

But this late 15th-century view was highly stylised as, even two centuries earlier, Bristol's defences were far more extensive and complex, new suburban growth having been enclosed, in stages, by new town walls. Bristol in fact came closer than any English town to reproducing the successive concentric defences widely evident among the great cities of continental Europe. By the mid-13th century, when the medieval defences had achieved their maximum extent, Bristol and its suburbs were enclosed by approximately three kilometres of masonry wall, pierced by 15 named gates and many additional posterns and water gates. If the walls of Bristol Castle are included in the equation the figure rises to around 3.7km. The outer wall followed the south bank of the Frome above the quay head and enclosed the narrow area between the river and the original town wall; it cannot at present be dated but may have been built at the same time as the Frome was diverted – by which time housing was spreading beyond

the old wall. The Marsh Wall, built before 1313 (Fuller 1894–5, 226), stood across the Marsh to the south of the old urban core. The Portwall ran through the middle of Redcliffe and was built between 1232 and 1240 and has been shown by excavation to survive over long stretches of its course (*see* pp 164–171). The Old Market too was protected or at least demarcated by an earthwork circuit and was gated at its east end.

The function of these walls and other barriers is debatable. A solely defensive purpose is questionable, and the relative emphasis placed on defensibility, the control of traffic for economic purposes, and making a statement of civic pride and identity probably varied from stretch to stretch, and from period to period. Civic identity was certainly a factor long after any military necessity had ceased – as the rebuilding of the Redcliff and Temple gates in the 1730s amply demonstrates (Creighton and Higham 2005, 235). There was also an inbuilt tension between the need for the free movement of traded goods, and the needs of defence, such that (as in many other English towns) the quays occupied substantial gaps in the defences. For just this reason the Marsh Wall could never have been wholly effective as a military defence of the suburb developing south of Baldwin Street, though it may have been wholly effective in making a statement of the importance and power of the town to mariners arriving at its quays. A partial answer to the question of the function of Bristol's walls may lie in the idea of deterrence. While local tactical considerations may have taken second place to the needs of trade, this may not have been immediately obvious to attacking forces and, *in extremis*, local deficiencies may have been felt to be addressable with temporary timber works, as was the case in 15th-century Shrewsbury (Baker 2010).

The inner ('Norman') town wall

Although by the later Middle Ages the built-up area had practically submerged the original town wall circuit, it, and its gates in particular, retained their symbolic importance – as Ricart's *Kalendar* shows (*see above*) – and the gates were improved and rebuilt on many occasions. St John's Arch or

Blind Gate had a segmental two-centred arch, suggesting a post-Norman (re)construction. The gate survived as late as 1911 when it was demolished (Fig 6.28). The fabric of the only surviving gate, St John's, dates to the 14th century (Fig 6.29).

An 18th-century drawing of St Nicholas Gate shows it with a four-centred arch, suggesting it was at least partly rebuilt in the late Middle Ages (Jones 1991, pl 5), and James Stewart's 1746 drawing of St Giles' Gate records an ogee-headed arch (Fig 6.30).

The most extensive rebuilding is likely to have been at St Leonard's Gate at the south-west end of Corn Street which became the main entrance to the town after the diversion of the Frome. The later medieval gate is known to have been a three-sided structure extending over St Stephen's Street. The church is recorded by Barrett as being of just two bays, with a 65ft tower above the arch leading into Corn Street (Barrett 1789, 506). With the creation of the outer wall, Oldgate near the end of Church Lane, also known as Aldgate or 'Bloudeyate', became redundant.

The outer wall
Probably in the 13th century, the strip of land north of the old town wall on the south side of the Frome was enclosed by a new wall. It has not been excavated and consequently there is no physical evidence for its date; nor is much known about its construction. It is mainly known from post-medieval plans and topographic drawings and from William Worcestre's description of some of its major components.

The first gate was the Frome Gate; there is no evidence for the wall further south, the 13th-century quay and quay head occupying a gap in the outer defences. The Frome Gate stood on the Frome Bridge, a two-arched structure with a central cutwater on each side, carrying Christmas Street over the river. A section of the bridge was recorded during road widening in 1970 (BHER 125; Moorhouse 1971, 152; Neale 2000, 82–3). The bridge was gated at each end; at the north-west end a freestone cross was set over the bridge arch (Neale 2000, 6–7, 62–3, 70–3). Worcestre also described Prior's Slip, 30 stone steps leading down to the river, at this end of the bridge (Neale 2000, 72–3, 216–17). The bridge and

slip are also depicted on Millerd's 1673 plan (Fig 6.31).

Beyond Frome Gate the wall ran along the edge of the river. It was recorded there by Seyer about 3m from the river 'in the Cooper's yard adjoining to the dwelling-house of Bridewell' at which point it was 8ft (2.5m) thick and then 'in the last state of dilapidation' (Seyer 1821, 271; Bristol Archives 04479(1) Corporation Plan Book A fols 24–25). There were five interval towers. Worcestre describes a square tower at the end of Christmas Street (Neale 2000, 216–17), and there were two round or semi-circular towers to the north-east. 'Monken Bridge', later Bridewell Bridge, crossed the Frome around 60m south-west of St James's Churchyard and there was another semi-circular tower 48m to the east of Bridewell which was described by Seyer and recorded in several drawings of the area made in the 1820s (Seyer 1821, 270–1) (Fig 6.32).

Aylward's Gate, later known as Nether Pithay Gate, stood at the foot of Pithay with a bridge carrying the road over the Frome to St James's Back. The bridge is recorded as early as 1285 (Veale 1931, 164) although the gate is not mentioned until the late 14th century.

New Gate was erected close to the castle sometime prior to 1313 (Fuller 1894–5, 265). Worcestre records it as 9 yards long by 4 yards wide (Neale 2000, 250–1) and notes that there was a large cellar beneath (ibid, 12–13). The medieval gate appears to have had round towers on at least the eastern side and was of two storeys, with a room above the gate (Fig 6.33). At first-floor level on the north-east facing elevation there was a cross-window at the north-western side with a trefoil-headed window under a gable top towards the centre of the elevation (Fig 6.34).

Part of a wall and circular tower found close to the north-west corner of the castle (BHER 476; Site H) were interpreted as a part of New Gate; the walls were approximately 2.2m thick. Further evidence probably relating to the gate, including a wall with a gated arch, was found in watching-briefs in 1971 (BHER 127, 134, 135).

The Burgesses' Wall
In addition to the conventional defences of the town and its suburbs, and the castle, Bristol was for a short time in the early 14th century

Figure 6.28 St John's Arch during demolition in 1911 (photograph Fred Little, Bristol Reference Library 2377 L/956 StJ)

Figure 6.29 St John's Church and Gate from the south (photograph D Martyn)

distinguished by what can only be described as an internal siege-work, a short-lived defensive structure dating from the Burgesses Revolt when the town was, temporarily, at war with its castle (*see* p 123). In 1975 an excavation north of Peter Street found small surviving sections of a substantial 13th-century wall of Pennant sandstone and red sandstone with

The South View of Sr Giles Gate ——————————————— J.S. delin. June 10th, 1746.

Figure 6.30 St Giles Gate from the south by James Stewart, 1746 (Bodleian Library, Western MS, Gough Somerset 2, fol 42)

an associated bank. This was interpreted as the 'Burgesses' Wall', constructed during the Burgesses Revolt of the early 14th century. In the second half of the 14th century the wall was demolished and Church Lane established on its line (BHER 319).

The Old Market (Fig 5.15)

A large ditch (*magno fossato*) enclosed the Old Market during the Middle Ages and is described in the perambulation of the 1373 county boundary (Harding 1930, 160–3). The ditch followed a line north-east from the King's Orchard along the south side of the churchyard of SS Philip and Jacob (following modern Unity Street) to Midland Road, turned to run past Lawford's Gate (Veale 1938, 184), then passed north-west to the river Frome. The ditch may have been located several times,

at Lawford Street in 1986 (BHER 381), by Wellington Road in 1998 (BHER 3335) and most recently in 2017 at Unity Street (P Insole pers comm). At the east end of Old Market Street, just beyond the point where the back lanes curved round to meet it, the highway narrowed to pass beneath Lawford's Gate. This gate, 'Laffordesyate', was in existence by the late 12th or early 13th century and the accounts of the Constable of Bristol Castle begin to record a keeper of the gate among the castle garrison in 1293 (Walker 1998, 372–3; Sharp 1982, xxxv). The original form of the gate is unknown but it appears to have been rebuilt in the later Middle Ages; the only known illustration (by James Stewart in 1745) shows a single late medieval arch, which Rocque's map indicates was around 2.75m wide (Fig 6.35).

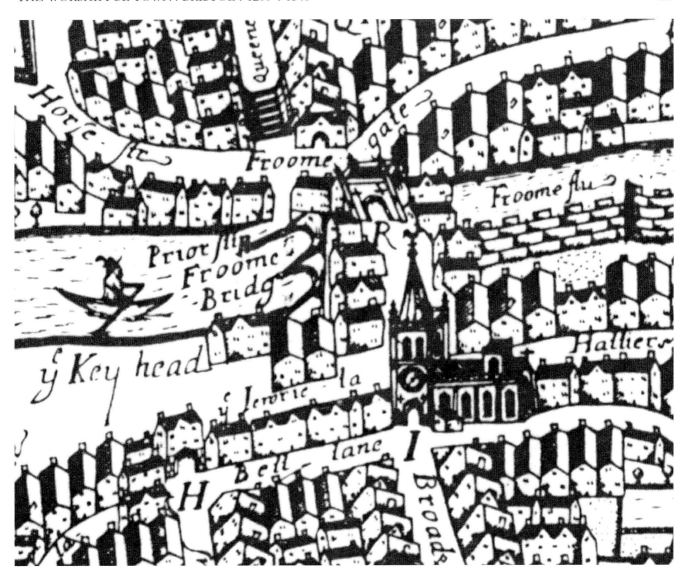

The primary function of Lawford's Gate was presumably to control access to the market. Whether the ditch enclosing the suburb was associated with any form of defensive palisade or bank has still to be established, as has the dating of both ditch and gate.

The Marsh Wall (Fig 6.23)
The Marsh Wall had been constructed by 1313 (Fuller 1894–5, 226) and enclosed an area of 7.5ha between Baldwin Street and what later became the line of King Street, leaving the Marsh to the south as open ground. The wall followed a sinuous path westward from the Marsh Gate by the Avon to a tower at the south end of Broad Quay, and then turned north along Broad Quay to Viell's Great

Tower, 30 yards in circumference according to Worcestre, which stood near the junction of Baldwin Street and Clare Street (Neale 2000, 214–15). It is probable that the Great Tower was a terminal tower. The wall has traditionally been held to have continued northwards from the Great Tower to meet the Norman town wall near St Giles' Gate. The only supporting evidence for this is the reported discovery of a section of wall during the construction of Clare Street in *c* 1771 (BHER 246; Seyer 1823, 51). As that wall was reported to be 5½ ft wide (1.68m, rather than the usual 2.5m) its identification as part of a town wall must be questionable and, as discussed earlier, it is probable that the quay was open and unenclosed.

Figure 6.31 Extract from Millerd's map of 1673, showing Frome Gate and Prior's Slip (BRSMG Mb6690)

Figure 6.32 Bastion near Bridewell in 1820 by Hugh O'Neill (Braikenridge Collection, BRSMG M2447)

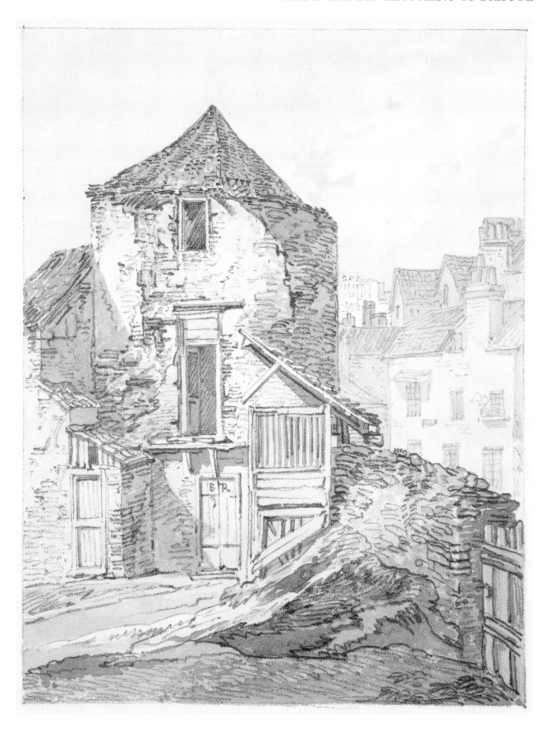

Where excavated, the Marsh Wall was around 2.5m wide and built primarily of Brandon Hill Grit bonded in a red sandy mortar. Despite one reported observation of supporting timber piles, its foundations seem to have consisted of mixed rubble deposits laid directly on the alluvial clay. There may have been a ditch in front of the King Street section of the wall but there is as yet no firm evidence for this, though if Leech's hypothesis regarding the pre-diversion course of the Frome is correct (*see* p 92 and 144), its old channel may have been reused as an extramural ditch.

The wall running south along Broad Quay has been seen at a number of locations. In 1970 a length of its east face was exposed and reported to be founded on timber piles 4–5m

Figure 6.33 East end of New Gate during demolition in 1821 by Hugh O'Neill (Braikenridge Collection, BRSMG M2718)

below the level of the pavement (BHER 405; Price 1991, 24). Two years later a small excavation in the cellars of Nos 1–2 Broad Quay found a wall – tentatively interpreted as the Marsh Wall – at least 4.25m thick, but incorporating a reused 14th-century window (BHER 3234; Fowler 1973a, 53). In 1979 the construction of an extension to Bristol and West House exposed a previously unknown gate. The subsequent rescue excavation showed that it consisted of two parallel arched tunnels, divided by a narrow Pennant sandstone wall, with a surface of Pennant flagstones partially surviving between them.

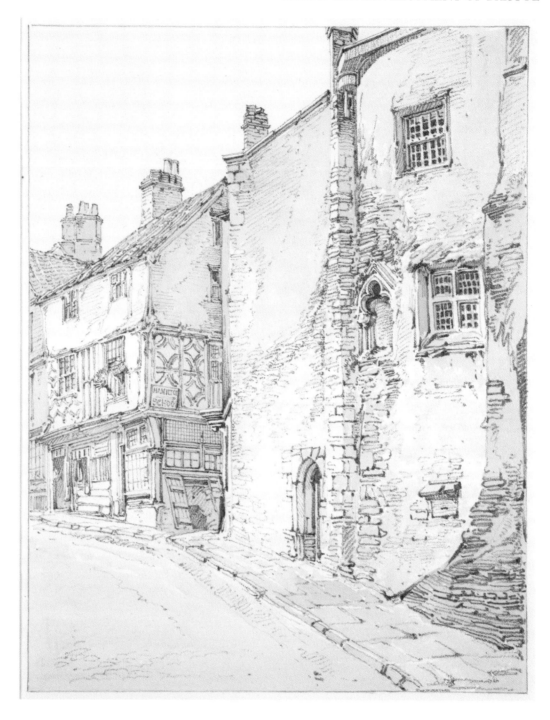

The gate was interpreted as part of a water gate and the few sherds of associated pottery were of 12th- to 13th-century date, suggesting that the gate was contemporary with the construction of the wall (Price 1991). More recently, in 2006, a site between Marsh Street and Broad Quay was excavated and another section of the Marsh Wall identified (HER 4342) (Fig 6.36). At that point it was at least 1.8m wide, with angled buttresses on the inner face. Pottery indicated a construction date in the late 13th century. An adjacent medieval wall surviving over 7.5m high may have flanked a stone slipway leading to the Frome (Adam 2008a).

Further gates stood at the ends of Marsh Street and Back Street and were, with the intervening bastions, noted by Worcestre (Neale 2000, 204–5); the last remnants of the Back Street Gate were also reported

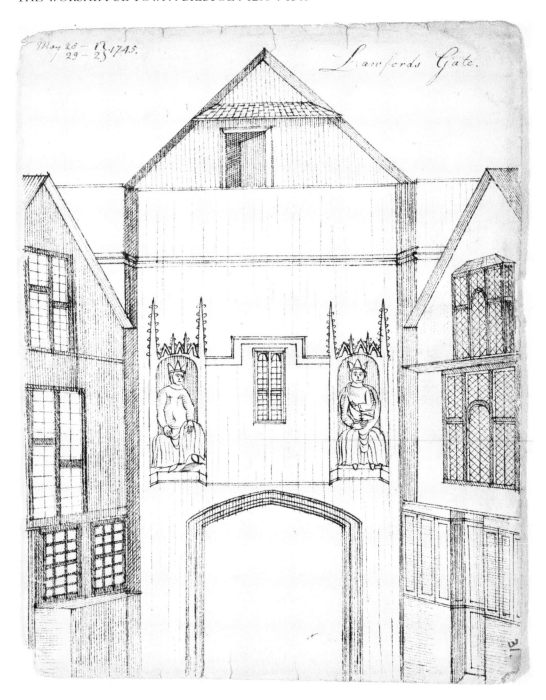

May 28 – 17 1745.
29 – 29

Lawfords Gate.

Figure 6.35 Lawfords Gate, as depicted by James Stewart in 1745 (Bodleian Library, Western MS, Gough Somerset 8, fol 31)

by Seyer in 1819 (BHER 248; Seyer 1823, 49–50). One bastion was excavated at the rear of St Nicholas's Almshouses on King Street (BHER 441) (Barton 1964). It was semi-circular, built of Pennant sandstone and Brandon Hill Grit and founded on a large irregularly-shaped platform built on the alluvial clay. Inside were a sand layer interpreted as a working surface, and a stone-lined tank in which mortar appeared to have been stored (Fig 6.37).

A 14-metre section of the Marsh Wall was excavated in 1995 on the site of Merchant Venturers House. It was constructed of Brandon Hill Grit with some Pennant sandstone, again 2.5m wide, and founded on a mixed deposit of Brandon Hill Grit, sand and gravel, and clay, laid directly on clay without supporting piles (BHER 2456; Burchill 1995b).

The Marsh Gate at the south end of Welsh Back was reported by Worcestre to be two yards wide and, unlike the gates of the Norman

Figure 6.36 Part of the Marsh Wall adjacent to Broad Quay as exposed in 2006

town wall, there was no accommodation above (Neale 2000, 214–15).

The Portwall (Fig 6.8)

The first of many murage grants was made to Bristol in 1232 allowing money to be raised from tolls for the construction of new defences for the town and its suburbs. The men of Redcliffe and the tenants of the Knights Templar were given the responsibility for walling their suburb, the work financed by the tolls collected from the gates leading into it; the Redcliffe portion of the work was finished by 1240 (Lobel and Carus-Wilson 1975, 7). The rationale guiding the line of the wall is uncertain, although mercantile security must have been a factor. St Mary Redcliffe was left outside the defences, overlooking them from its hill top site, suggesting perhaps that the planning of the defences was dominated by

military imperatives – achieving the shortest length of wall between bends of the river, or more likely utilising the fact that the wall sat at the lowest point in an area known as Redcliff Pit, allowing the creation of a water-filled ditch. The Portwall ran from Freshford Lane eastwards across Redcliff Street, St Thomas Street and Temple Street and then turned north-east through Temple Meads to end at the circular terminal tower, Tower Harratz, close to the Avon (Fig 6.38).

The Portwall and its extramural ditch have been investigated on many occasions, beginning with work by W J Pountney at the western end in 1915–16 (BHER 321; Pountney 1920, xxxi). He observed commercial excavation of the Portwall ditch in the Redcliffe Way area and noted that it had been filled in the first half of the 18th century. In 1965 a section was excavated across the width of the ditch

opposite the south end of St Thomas Street, but did not reach the bottom (BHER 408; Hebditch 1968); in 1982 a second section was excavated across the ditch some 60m west of Hebditch's trench; again, it did not reach the bottom but demonstrated that it was 15m wide and more than 5m deep (BHER 312; Iles 1983, 52).

There was a series of interval towers along the Portwall; these were described by William Worcestre (and located by him relatively accurately), and some have been excavated (Neale 2000, 212–13; Williams 1981a, 11–13; Williams 1981b, 35–46, BHER 342; Williams and Cox 2000; BHER 509; Good 1993). The most extensive investigation has been of the eastern half of the Portwall at Temple Quay where almost the entire length of the wall between the Floating Harbour and Temple Gate has been traced. In 1983 a 70m stretch of

wall with a semi-circular tower at the southern end was excavated (Fig 6.39). This was bonded in a different mortar to the main body of the wall, implying it had been built first, and had later begun to lean into the Portwall ditch (BHER 312; Iles 1984, 59).

Tower Harratz, the terminal tower at the north-east end of the wall, was located and excavated in 1994. The tower was circular, built of Pennant sandstone, and measured 13m in diameter at foundation level. It had been constructed around a core of clay, 5.4m across, with six clay spines (each roughly 1.6m wide) apparently formed by cutting of the alluvial clay, radiating from the centre (BHER 463; Jackson 1994a) (*see* Fig 6.38). Subsequent re-interpretation of the excavated evidence to the south of Tower Harratz has suggested that there were 22 'casemates' or bays giving access to arrow loops at 5.75-metre intervals (Cox

Figure 6.37 Bastion on the Marsh Wall in King Street, excavated in 1960

Figure 6.38 Tower Harratz, excavated in 1994

2000) (Fig 6.40); the clay 'spines' of Tower Harratz may have defined similar bays.

The wall itself was constructed of Pennant sandstone, just over 2m thick and founded directly on the alluvial clay. William Worcestre mentions a walk two yards wide, apparently on the top of the wall (Neale 2000, 92–3). On the inside of the wall an intra-mural lane, Portwall Lane, was created and, leaving a narrow berm, a ditch 15m wide and 5m deep, was dug in front of the wall. No convincing evidence has been found for a rampart. However, excavation on the eastern stretch of the Portwall in 1999, suggested that a 'causeway' of redeposited clay had been laid prior to the deposition of a series of cobbled surfaces making up the intra-mural lane (BHER 3519; Insole 2000c). Deeds dating to the reign of Henry III (1216–72) record properties extending to this 'new foss'.

It has been a traditional assertion that during construction of Bristol Bridge the Avon was diverted into the Portwall Ditch (Barrett 1789, 76). Hebditch was sceptical of this, noting the

disparity of width, and hence capacity, between the ditch and the river (Hebditch 1968, 135). The traditional belief also neglects the tidal character of the Avon, which would make construction in the tidal window a much more straightforward proposition.

There were gates at the end of Temple Street and Redcliff Street. Very little is known about the medieval form of Temple Gate beyond Worcestre's statement that it was 9 yards long by 3 yards wide and had a square tower (Neale 2000, 10–11, 212–13). Redcliff Gate was, by c 1350, a double gate, the two gates standing on either side of the Portwall Ditch, six yards wide, the inner gate 19.2m from the outer (Bickley 1900, 1–2; Neale 2000, 98–9, 212–13), but again little more is known for certain about its form. A previously unknown water gate was also found in 2000, 60m south of Tower Harratz. When this was excavated it was found to have flanking casemates with arrow loops. In the early to mid-14th century the gate and arrow loops were blocked, and then the ground level was

*Figure 6.39 Bastion on
the Portwall, excavated
in 1983*

raised, the lane along the inside of the Portwall created and successively resurfaced. There was some evidence that the gate had been partially demolished in the 15th century (BHER 462, 3643; Cox 2000) (Fig 6.41).

In general this part of the Portwall exhibited a sophistication of design that was absent from Bristol's other defences, and it might well have reflected the military authority and experience of the Templars, whose land

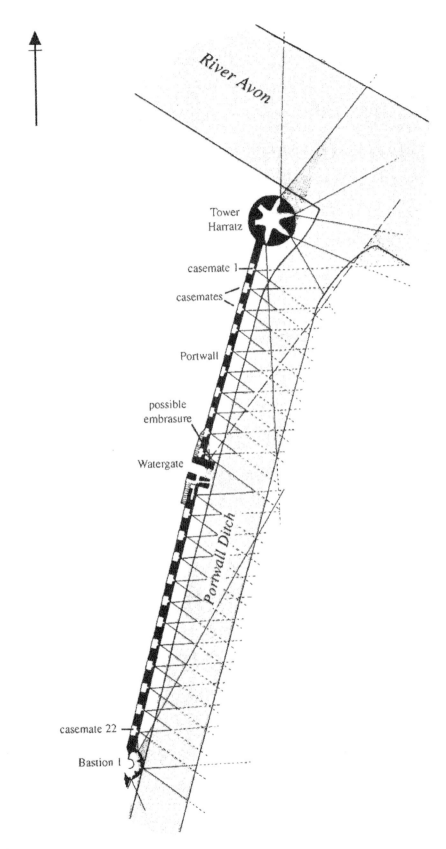

Figure 6.40 An interpretation of the Portwall at the northern end, based on excavated evidence (reproduced from Cox 2000, fig 51)

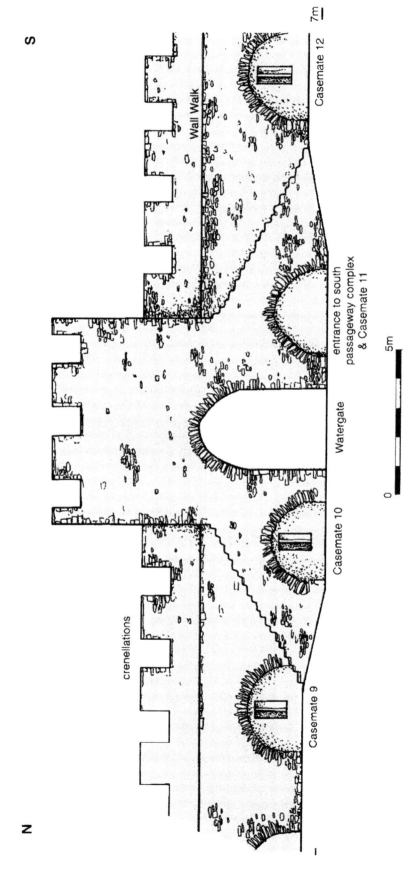

Figure 6.41 Conjectured reconstruction of the west face of the Water gate (reproduced from Cox 2000, fig 52)

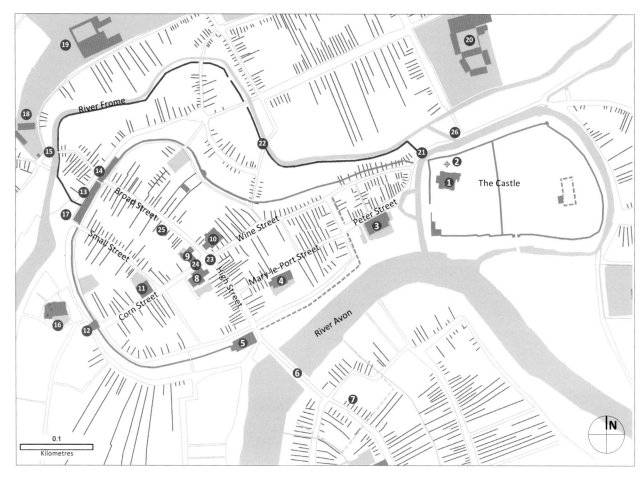

1 Castle Keep	12 Church of St Leonard
2 Chapel of St Martin	13 Church of St Lawrence
3 Church of St Peter	14 Church of St John the Baptist
4 Church of St Mary-le-Port	15 Frome Gate and Bridge
5 Church of St Nicholas	16 Church of St Stephen
6 Bristol Bridge	17 Church of St Giles
7 Arthur's Fee	18 St Bartholomew's Hospital
8 Church of All Saints	19 Franciscan Friary
9 Church of St Ewen	20 Dominican Friary
10 Christ Church	21 New Gate
11 Church of St Werburgh	22 Nether Pithay Gate and Pithay Bridge
	23 High Cross
	24 Tolzey
	25 Guildhall
	26 Castle Mill

Pre 1200/post 1200 Churches

Cemeteries and ecclesiastical precincts

Post 1200 Town walls and defences

Figure 6.42 Historic core of Bristol c 1300

Figure 6.43 The Guildhall in c *1813 by M H Holmes (Braikenridge Collection, BRSMG M2436)*

it crossed (Creighton and Higham 2005, 173, 212).

Public buildings (Fig 6.42)
The business of local government, in the hands of the Mayor and governing Council, was conducted in the Guildhall, a two-storey building on the south-west side of Broad Street (Fig 6.43).

Worcestre gives the Broad Street frontage as 21m (Neale 2000, 120–1) and this matches the dimensions of the building in the 18th century, when it also extended 35m back from the street. The internal arrangements during the Middle Ages are not clear but the chapel of St George was accommodated within the building. Worcestre states that St George's was nearly 11m long and around 6.5m wide, and also mentions the association of a fraternity of merchants and mariners with it (Neale 2000, 278–9; 210–11).

The consequences of the Mayor's judicial decisions were often experienced in two nearby buildings. The pillory stood near the centre of Wine Street, close to the junction with Pithay, 80m to the east of the High Cross. It was described by Worcestre as a circular ashlar limestone building with cells and iron bars on the windows and on the roof there was a timber structure (*instrumentum de arboribus opere carpentarij constructum*), presumably stocks (Neale 2000, 66–7). Newgate Prison stood on the north side of Wine Street and, although fabric from the medieval building was still extant in the early 19th century (*see* for example Braikenridge Collection, BRSMG Mb13, Fig 6.34 above), very little is known of its form.

The Tolzey (tolselde), the court where market dues were collected or enforced, occupied the plot at the corner of Corn Street and Broad Street and was in existence by 1330 (Sharp 1982, 48). The medieval form of the building is not clear as the building was rebuilt in 1550. However, Worcestre records a street frontage of 5 yards and also a flat lead roof, presumably leaning out over Corn Street to create a covered area, as was the case with the post-medieval building. The rooms above, he said, were used for Council meetings (Neale 2000, 12–13) (*see* Fig 7.27).

The heart of the medieval town was its central crossroads or Carfax, at which stood the High Cross (Fig 6.44). This appears prominently in the highly stylised bird's-eye view of Ricart's *Kalendar*, where it is shown as an open structure on a two-stage plinth surmounted by an elaborate, crocketed spire with a cruciform finial. According to local tradition the High Cross was erected in 1373 to celebrate the confirmation of county status, although it may have replaced an earlier cross on the same site (Barrett 1789, 473). However, the earliest surviving written record of the cross is in the early 15th century and the structure itself was probably of that date (Bickley 1900 vol 2, 182; Liversidge 1978, 10–11).

Guild buildings

The role of confraternities like the Fraternity of the Assumption in the life of the town was clearly important and several were established in the centre, but very little is currently known about the halls in which they met. The Fraternity of St John the Baptist was founded in October 1399 and had its hall on the northern side of Tailors' Court from 1438. Rebuilding in the 18th century removed the majority of the medieval fabric and almost nothing can therefore be said about the form of the hall (Leech 2000c). The Guild of Kalendars had a house above the north aisle of All Saints' Church. The guild was an association of secular clergy and laity with the purpose of meeting on the first day of the month to celebrate mass and intercede on behalf of the living and for the souls of the dead. The Bristol Kalendars were one of only a handful of similar guilds in the country, the others being at Exeter and Winchester, and its origins are obscure although it was apparently in existence by the early 13th century (Neale 2000, 210–11; Orme 1978, 35). The house at All Saints' seems to have been built in the 14th century, though little is yet certain about its form. The guild was wealthy enough to maintain a prior and three chantry priests, and in the mid-15th century created a public theological library there. The initiative seems to have come from the Bishop of Worcester with the aim of creating a centre of religious orthodoxy to counter the influence of Lollardy, and the library was open for private study for four hours each weekday (Orme 1978, 40–3). Work on the south side of Cart Lane (HER 1688) recorded a wall of squared stone blocks at the southern edge of the site. This, given the quality of the construction, was thought possibly to have been the north wall of the Weavers' guild hall, known to have been located in this area, though the identification is probable rather than definite (G L Good, pers comm).

The Church and religion (Figs 6.45, 6.46)

The parish churches and chapels of the urban core

The religious geography of this part of the city had largely been established by the 13th century and most of the existing churches, and their parishes, survived through the Middle Ages. That all of the parish churches underwent major alterations and rebuilding through the Middle Ages is evident from the surviving fabric, archaeological evidence,

Figure 6.44 Bristol High
Cross, at Stourhead, where
it was relocated in 1766
(photograph D Martyn)

19th-century drawings and photographs and the late medieval churchwardens' accounts and chantry commissioners' surveys of the 1540s. But the lack of modern surveys of most of the surviving structures means that the understanding of their chronological development is limited.

One of the best understood of all the central-area churches is St Mary-le-Port, as a consequence of the extensive excavations by Philip Rahtz in 1962–3 (BHER 358, BHER 3173). The existing two-cell church was considerably extended during the 13th century. The west wall was retained but a north aisle

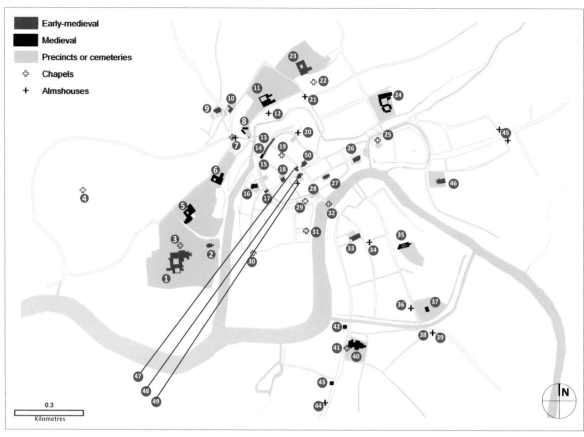

1 Abbey of St Augustine	18 Church of St Werburgh	35 Temple Church
2 Church of St Augustine-the-Less	19 Chapel of St George	36 Spicer's Almshouse
3 Chapel of St Jordan	20 St John's Almshouse	37 Austin Friars
4 Chapel of St Brandon	21 Chester's Almshouse	38 Friary of the Friars of the Sack
5 Hospital of St Mark	22 Chapel in St James Churchyard	39 Magdalen or Redcliff Almshouse
6 Carmelite Friary	23 Priory of St James	40 Church of St Mary Redcliffe
7 Chapel of the Three Kings of Cologne and Foster's Almshouse	24 Dominican Friary	41 Chapel of the Holy Spirit
8 Hospital of St Bartholomew	25 Chapel of St Martin	42 Hospital of St John the Baptist
9 Church of St Michael-on-the-Mount Without	26 Church of St Peter	43 Hospital of St Mary Magdalen
10 Nunnery of St Mary Magdalen	27 Church of St Mary-le-Port	44 William Canynges Almshouse
11 Franciscan Friary	28 Church of St Nicholas	45 Barstaple's Almshouse
12 Spencer's Almshouse	29 Chapel of St John	46 Church of SS Philip and Jacob
13 Church of St John the Baptist	30 Chapel of St Clement	47 Church of St Ewen
14 Church of St Lawrence	31 Chapel of St John the Evangelist	48 All Saints Almshouse
15 Church of St Giles	32 Chapel of the Assumption	49 Church of All Saints
16 Church of St Stephen	33 Church of St Thomas the Martyr	50 Christ Church
17 Church of St Leonard	34 Burton's Almshouse	

Figure 6.45 Distribution of churches, chapels, hospitals, almshouses and monastic sites

1	St John's	
2	Christ Church	
3	St Peter's	
4	St Mary-le-Port	
5	All Saints	
6	St Ewen's	
7	St Werburgh's	
8	St Lawrence	
9	St Stephen's	

10	St Leonard's
11	St Nicholas'
12	St Augustine's
13	St Michael's
14	St James'
15	SS Philip and Jacob's
16	Temple
17	St Thomas
18	St Mary Redclffe's

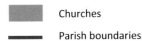 Churches

▬ Parish boundaries

Figure 6.46 Plan of medieval parishes

was added to the nave; transepts were built and the chancel was extended. There may also have been a tower above the new crossing. There was no surviving evidence for a south aisle and the excavator inferred its presence on the basis of a likely symmetry of plan. In the later

15th century a tower was added to the west end and the north aisle was enlarged. A new chancel was also built at this time and a stucco screen base was found at its west end. If the south aisle existed, it must have been severely truncated when the south wall was rebuilt. In

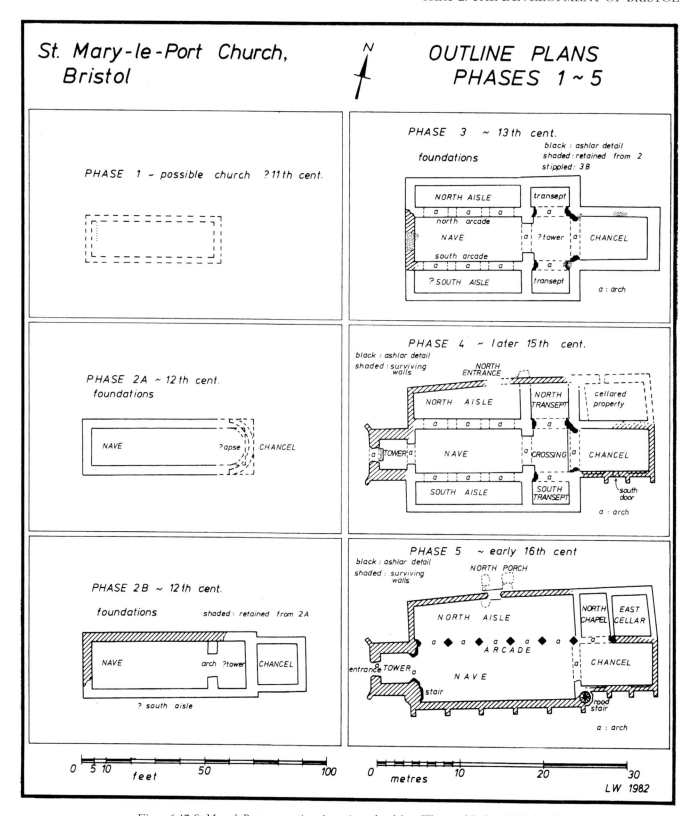

Figure 6.47 St Mary-le-Port construction phases (reproduced from Watts and Rahtz 1985, fig 48)

the early 16th century a new arcade was built between the north aisle and the nave (Fig 6.47) (Watts and Rahtz 1985).

The other churches present a far less complete picture of periodic extensions and alterations. At St Nicholas', for example, the crowde, or lower church, was extended in four phases between the 13th and the 15th centuries; the north aisle was built between *c* 1250 and 1375 while the south dated from about 1400 (Egan 1989, 27; Ponsford *et al* 1989a, 248). St John's crypt dates to the 14th century and the roof of the chancel to the 15th century. Monitoring of conservation work to the crowde of St John the Baptist in 1998 (BHER 3368) recorded several of the late medieval chest tombs inside the church and identified red and green paint on several, suggesting the character of their decoration (Pilkington 1999). At All Saints' the 12th-century west end of the nave was retained, but the churchwardens' accounts record several alterations and repairs in the 15th century, including the reconstruction of a Chapel of Our Lady on the north side of the church in *c* 1450 by Richard Haddon (Burgess 1995, 9). The eastern end of the nave is of 15th-century date and fragments of a 15th-century wall painting survive within the church. The Guild of Kalendars was responsible for a series of projects in the 14th and 15th centuries, building above the north aisle, while the Glebe House, built into the south aisle, appears to date to the second half of the 15th century (*see above*; Orme 1978, 38). At St Ewen's in October 1399 the burgesses John Thorp and John Sherp gained the agreement of the Crown to establish a chapel dedicated to St John the Baptist. This apparently occupied the whole south aisle and the fraternity's book includes an inventory of 1401–2 recording the ornaments of the altar of the chapel, which comprised hangings, vestments of green, gold and ruby and an altar frontal depicting the life of St John (Fox 1880, 13).

It is not clear when some of the churches acquired churchyards. St Lawrence's acquired a plot on the southern bank of the Frome, between the town walls. St John's interred its parishioners in St James's Churchyard until it was granted a garden at the north-east end of Tailor's Court in 1390 (Bristol Archives P/StJB/D/2/75); the use of the plot as a churchyard was confirmed by the Bishop of Worcester in 1409. The grant included a right of access through the gate of a tenement on Broad Street but this right was disputed by the Fraternity of St John, whose hall the funeral processions had to pass, and the dispute was not finally resolved until 1499.

There were also some new foundations. St Giles' Church at the north end of Small Street was in existence by *c* 1285, but by *c* 1350 it had been subdivided into properties rented out by the Corporation (Leech 1997, 118–19). The Chapel of the Assumption was built in the middle of Bristol Bridge in the 14th century. A chapel at ease to St Nicholas's Church, it was endowed with the gifts of several members of the Fraternity of the Assumption of Our Lady including the burgess Elias Spelly (Maclean 1883–4, 239–40; Neale 2002, 142–3). In addition to providing priests to perform masses on Saturdays and distributing alms to the poor, the revenues were to be used to fund the maintenance of the bridge (Maclean 1883–4, 239–40). The best description of the structure comes from William Worcestre who noted that it was 25 yards long and 7 wide with a square four-stage stone bell tower (Neale 2000, 2–3, 142–3, 150–1). The fenestration comprised four large windows on each side and a 'high' window above the main altar. One or more of the windows contained stained glass depicting the founders from the Fraternity of the Assumption and their wives (Neale 2000, 142–3). In addition to the crypt, Worcestre mentions the chapel, a hall with offices, an upper room and highest room. There was also a smaller chapel with an altar to the east of the main altar, three yards long (Neale 2000, 166–7). Beneath the building there was a large crypt which, Worcestre notes, accommodated the councillors and officers of the town and was used for public meetings (Neale 2000, 12–13).

Parish churches and chapels outside the urban core

Ecclesiastical provision in the areas outside the urban core offers a mixture of continuity and change: old church foundations were maintained and extended, but there were new foundations too, both parochial and non-parochial.

Some parochial reorganisation took place as a consequence of the diversion of the

The Old Merchants Hall, from an Engraving of 1673
being Part of the Old Chapel of St Clement

HO'Neill. 1821
From Mr H. Smith's Sketch

Figure 6.48 Old Merchants Hall from an engraving of 1673, showing part of St Clement's Chapel by Hugh O'Neill, 1821 (Braikenridge Collection, BRSMG M2498)

Frome: St Stephen's was founded and its parish probably created out of the existing parishes of St Augustine-the-Less and St Nicholas. St Giles went out of use by the middle of the 14th century. St Stephen's Church was substantially rebuilt in the 15th century. The former mayor John Shipward funded the construction of the tower in 1453

and the south porch was built at the beginning of the 1480s (Nicholls and Taylor 1881, vol 2, 190; Neale 2000, 132–3).

Other religious buildings were developed or rebuilt in the Marsh suburb in the 15th century. On Welsh Back a chantry chapel dedicated to St John the Evangelist was founded by the former Mayor of Bristol, Thomas Knapp or

Knape, who died in 1404. Worcestre records the building as 13 yards long and 6 yards wide but its form and internal layout are otherwise unknown (Neale 2000, 196–7). Under the terms of Knapp's will two priests were to be maintained in perpetuity to perform a daily service and to pray for the souls of Knapp and his wife (Wadley 1886, 68–9). At its dissolution in 1548 there was no plate, but the ornaments were valued at 26s 5d and the property endowments brought in £21 15s annually (Maclean 1883–4, 238–9). St Clement's Chapel was founded in 1493 just to the east of the Marsh Street Gate, outside the Marsh Wall, on a site leased by the Corporation to John Drewe for the Guild of Mariners to found a chantry chapel dedicated to the patron saint of mariners (Warren 1907, 187–90; Manchee 1831, vol 1, 237) (Fig 6.48).

It was a rectangular two-storey structure; the main entrance was a four-centred arched opening in the centre of the south wall and the fenestration seems to have consisted of lancet windows. The internal dimensions were recorded as 67ft 6in from east to west by 23ft north to south but how the internal spaces were organised is not known. It was managed by proctors appointed by the guild and served by one priest (Pritchard 1907b, 226–7).

The Old Market was served by the parish church of SS Philip and Jacob. It had been built by the late 12th century and stood on the east side of a roughly square churchyard on the south side of Jacob Street, within the Old Market perimeter ditch but outside its series of planned burgages (Harding 1930, 162–3). Originally cruciform in plan, little fabric from the Norman church has been identified, other than a font with a square scalloped base. The earliest datable components of the building are the nave, chancel and lower tower (formerly the south transept) which are of the early 13th century. The church underwent major alteration in the mid-15th century when the present north chancel aisle and upper tower were built. Windows of the 15th century survive in the south chancel and east chancel aisle walls and the church had a chapel dedicated to St Nicholas by 1473 (Wadley 1886, 148).

On the hillside above Lewins Mead, St Michael's Church was substantially rebuilt in the 15th century. A drawing of the church in 1746–7 by James Stewart shows that the chancel, south aisle and a two-storey south porch were all of later medieval date (Fig 6.49). The present tower was described by Worcestre in 1480 as newly built (Neale 2000, 230–1). The dimensions he recorded show that it was 26 yards long, about the same length as Paty's 18th-century replacement, but substantially narrower at 10 yards wide (Neale 2000, 230–1).

The Chapel of St Brandon on Brandon Hill had been established by the end of the 12th century and belonged to St James's Priory (Neale 2000, 226–7). Very little is known about the form of the building. There was a resident anchorite, with whom Worcestre discussed the height of the hill, though he did not describe the chapel (Neale 2000, 182–5). In the early 1540s the chapel was, according to John Leland, 'now defacyd'. Digging of the foundations of Cabot Tower at the summit of Brandon Hill towards the end of the 19th century disturbed a floor of beaten earth bounded by a wall of massive stones set in very hard mortar (BHER 2457). These were probably part of the Civil War defences (*see* Chapter 7), but beneath was a 'well-made' grave lined with masonry and orientated east–west. Two more skeletons were found nearby and fragments of green-glazed tile were also recovered (Anon 1897–9, 336–7; Fryer 1897). The most likely explanation of these discoveries is that they were part of the site of the chapel.

On College Green, the 12th-century church of St Augustine-the-Less continued in use with minor alterations until the 14th century (Boore 1985, 25–7). It was then substantially rebuilt and expanded, with a new aisled nave and western tower giving an increase of over 260 per cent in the floor area from 165 to 432 square metres. In 1480 William Worcestre recorded the new nave as 24 yards long and 6 yards wide with the north and south aisles each 4 yards wide (Neale 2000, 152–3). Initially the old chancel was retained but this too was rebuilt at the end of the 15th century, and when Worcestre saw the church it had clearly not been completed (Neale 2000, 152–3).

The ecclesiastical landscape in Redcliffe: parish churches, chapels and preaching crosses

The three parish churches of the Redcliffe suburb – St Thomas's, the Temple Church and St Mary Redcliffe – have seen radically different levels of archaeological/architectural

The South East Prospect of S.ᵗ MICHAELS in Bristol...................... J.S. delin. Jan 10 1746-7

Figure 6.49 Drawing of south-east prospect of St Michael's Church by James Stewart, 1746–7 (Bodleian Library, Western MS, Gough Somerset 8, fol 50)

investigation, and the level of understanding of each building varies accordingly. The volume of material published on St Mary's in particular is substantial, but interpretation of the evolution of the medieval church has been complicated by the Victorian restoration and, despite recent research (Smith 1995; Monckton 1997, 1999) it was possible for one author to conclude that that the church 'has received limited study since the contributions of Barrett and Britton in the 18th and 19th centuries respectively' (Monckton 1999, 42). Further more detailed study of the surviving fabric has been undertaken by Dr Warwick Rodwell as part of the compilation of a comprehensive Conservation Plan for the church (Rodwell 2004).

Although the 14th-century tower remains, little is known of the medieval form of the church of St Thomas, because of rebuilding in

the 18th century and a lack of archaeological investigation. However, a drawing of the interior by Stewart in 1749 does give some insights. The nave had at least four bays, with aisle arcades on either side. The three westernmost bays of the nave were vaulted, but the fourth bay was raised as a lantern (also shown by Millerd in 1673), and there are indications that there may have been short transepts to the north and south. The choir probably occupied the fifth bay, with a sixth containing the chancel. Most of the architectural features are late medieval in date suggesting that the original church had undergone substantial rebuilding. There is documentary evidence for chapels within the church dedicated to the Virgin Mary and St Nicholas by the late 14th century and one to St John the Baptist in the first half of the 15th century (Wadley 1886, 5, 18, 134).

The churchyard does not seem to have been established until the late 13th century when Thomas de Berkeley granted two messuages on the north side to be used as a cemetery (Walker 1998, 263).

The origins of the Temple Church lie in the gradual modification of the circular Templar church to parochial use after the suppression of the order in 1312. The Templar church seems to have been used for worship by the local community from a time not long after the Hospitallers acquired the site, and in 1331 John Fraunceys the Younger founded a chantry in the church. It was made a vicarage in 1342. The apsidal chancel was extended and a chapel built on its north side in the late 13th or early 14th century; another chapel was added to the south side of the chancel in the early 14th century. The circular church was apparently demolished in the 1390s to allow the construction of a new and greatly enlarged aisled nave. A tower was built at the south-west corner from 1441. Before it was completed it began to lean westwards, and when the upper stage was added, *c* 1460, it was at a different angle to the lower part (Fig 6.50).

In the 15th century a section of the south chapel in the chancel was rebuilt and buttresses were added to the exterior (Taylor 2000; Brown 2008). The main chapel within the church was the Chapel of St Katherine, established by the Weavers' Guild; some of the medieval glass, removed in the 19th century, was published by Hudd (1904–8). There were other chapels within the church, including ones dedicated to St James and the Holy Trinity by the 1390s and SS Andrew and Nicholas by 1479 (Wadley 1886, 35, 54, 163). A freestanding chapel of St Mary the Virgin stood outside the entrance to the church by the late 14th century, although nothing is known of its form (Wadley 1886, 55). The churchyard was on the south side of the church and it is known that half an acre of land adjacent to the existing churchyard was taken over from the Knights Hospitallers in 1348–9 to bury victims of plague (Boucher 1938, 35). By 1391 there was also a cross in the churchyard (Wadley 1886, 30).

The form of St Mary Redcliffe in the 13th century is largely unknown but elements of the later phases of building do survive. The tower was added in the late 13th century and in the early 14th the south nave aisle, south porch and the south transept were built. The hexagonal outer north porch was built *c* 1320–5 and housed the chapel of the Blessed Virgin Mary (as distinct from the Lady Chapel) (Cannon 2004b; Neale 2000, 242–3) (Fig 6.51).

The spire collapsed into the nave in *c* 1445 (Smith 1995, 77–9). Traditionally, the need for reconstruction of the nave has been attributed to the damage caused, and William Canynges the Elder and his grandson William Canynges the Younger have been thought to be responsible. Monckton has challenged this interpretation, arguing that other spire collapses did not generally cause a level of damage necessitating the entire reconstruction of the nave, questioning the role of the Canynges family as patrons of the reconstruction and re-dating the building works to the 14th century (Monckton 1997, 137, 58–60). The reconstruction of the north transept and north nave aisle thus emerges as part of the same planned phase of rebuilding which saw the construction of the south nave aisle and south transept. Several chapels are recorded inside the church in the 15th century, including a chapel dedicated to St Nicholas, a chapel of St Blaise and another of St Stephen (Wadley 1886, 68, 105, 139, 157).

In the churchyard, a chapel of the Holy Spirit was erected to the south-west of the church in *c* 1250 (Smith 1995, 36). This appears initially to have had a two-cell plan with the entrance, protected by a porch, on the north side. Documentary evidence suggests that during the medieval period the chapel included an annexe for lepers, tended by religious from the hospital of St John the Baptist. On the south side of the churchyard there was also a stone preaching cross. There were two other medieval stone crosses in the area, the Stallage cross at the north end of Temple Street and a stone cross near Trin Mills (Walker 1998, 314; 376).

Monastic houses
St Augustine's Abbey (Fig 5.22)
Despite an erratic administrative and financial history, St Augustine's Abbey saw continued building and rebuilding between 1200 and its dissolution in 1539. Gifts and other acquisition of property in the region had placed St Augustine's Abbey amongst the wealthiest Augustinian houses in the country by the end of the medieval period and enabled extensive rebuilding (Walker 2000); some

Figure 6.50 Temple Church from the south-east (photograph D Martyn)

chronological markers for programmes of construction or repairs are given in Abbot Newland's roll (Jeayes 1889–90).

The abbey church and the great gate were on the north side of the precinct, by College Green. The cloister was on the south side of the church with a lower cloister below it; the outer court, now College Square, was to the west.

Relatively little work seems to have been undertaken on the church during the 13th century. The Elder Lady Chapel was built between 1218 and 1222 on the east side of the north transept during the rule of Abbot David (1216–34). The abbot sought the services of a stonemason 'L' to undertake the work, probably Adam Lock the master mason at Wells Cathedral, although Thurlby proposes that an assistant may in fact have been the chapel's designer (Hill 1944; Rome 2000, 88; Thurlby 1997, 37). The interior was polychromatic and

was influenced by both the Elder Lady Chapel and Glastonbury and Wells. The vault of the chapel, however, seems to have been built between 1270 and 1298, possibly replacing a wooden vault (Thurlby 1997, 33–5). The rood-altar was in place by the 1240s (Paul 1912, 239) and the bells may have been recast in the late 13th century. A bell-casting pit was found in 1992 containing many fragments of bell mould. There is also a surviving bell of *c* 1300 in the central tower (Bryant 2015). Paul also suggested that the night stairs may have been repositioned against the west wall of the vestry for a time (Paul 1912, 239).

A small stone building, interpreted as a workshop, possibly for stone carving, was also excavated in 1992 at the south-west corner of the church and seems to have been in use between the later 13th century and the early 14th (BHER 1685) (Boore 1992). Its dating

is imprecise, so it is not clear whether it was associated with general repairs, the replacement of the vault of the Elder Lady Chapel – which seems most likely – or the early 14th-century building campaign of Abbot Edmund Knowle (1306–32).

A visitation by the Bishop of Worcester in 1278 uncovered maladministration by the abbot and misbehaviour on the part of the canons (Graham 1907, 76). While the situation had improved by the mid-1280s the abbey's finances were still insecure and Edward I increased its income and instructed the Constable of Bristol Castle to eliminate the abbey's debts (Bettey 1996, 11; Graham 1907, 76).

Alterations to the abbey were far more extensive in the 14th century. The choir was reconstructed and three chapels were added: the Lady Chapel at the east end and the Newton and Berkeley Chapels, with the adjacent sacristy, on the south choir aisle (Warren 1904–8a). Sir Nikolaus Pevsner hailed the European significance of this architecture, arguing for its creation between *c* 1298 and 1322 by a single designer. While Pevsner's estimation of St Augustine's significance has not been challenged, his interpretation is less widely shared. Even in the 1860s E W Godwin believed that Abbot Knowle's rebuilding of the choir 'did not extend much beyond the remodelling of the eastern part of the choir, with its two aisles and Lady Chapel', attributing the Berkeley chapel and the Newton Chapel to Abbot Snow (1332–41) (Godwin 1863, 54). More recently Morris identified an 'additive process of design' of three phases between *c* 1298 and *c* 1340. The first had stylistic similarities to work at Exeter Cathedral while the following phases drew their inspiration from Wells, and Morris extended his argument to identify three possible designers, Nicholas de Derneford, who is known from a petition of 1316 to have worked at Bristol, Thomas of Witney and William Joy (Morris 1997). Cannon pointed again to the observation made by several authors that the eastern arm of the abbey church has the character of 'a single, light-filled hall'. St Augustine's, he suggests, 'may be the largest hall church of its date in Europe, and the most monumental in scale ever constructed in England' (Cannon 2004a, 27). He identifies the Berkeleys as key patrons, noting the architectural features characteristic of buildings associated with the family – for example the stellate wall recesses and the military motifs. The stained glass of the Lady Chapel windows, for example, seems to have been a figurative scheme with depictions of saints in the upper tier, including St Mary the Virgin, St Stephen and possibly St Edmund,

and figures of knights and, perhaps, abbots below. The whole was framed by heraldic decoration (Brown 1997, 110). Again, stylistic similarities with Wells, and also with Christ Church Cathedral, Dublin, have been noted in the stone carving (Stalley 1990). Knowle also rebuilt the King's Hall, which Paul tentatively identified as the Deanery and the King's Chamber and 'reparid And kevered the Freytoure wt othir goode dedis' (Paul 1912, 244; Jeayes 1889–90, 128).

In the second half of the 14th century the fortunes of the abbey declined. The precise effect of the Black Death and subsequent visitations of plague on the number of religious is unknown, but there were 25 canons in the 1340s and after 1348 never more than 20 (Bettey 1996, 18); in 1363 Abbot Coke (1353–65) obtained leave to ordain canons at 22 years of age (Graham 1907, 77). The abbey once more lapsed into financial instability in the 1360s and in 1366 Edward III placed it under the supervision of Maurice de Berkeley and three other commissioners (Graham 1907, 77). None of this seems to have halted new building, however. To the south of the church a substantial two-storey range, containing the *cellarium* with accommodation above was added to the west side of the cloister in the later 14th century (Boore 1992). A large stone barn was built on the west side of the outer court. Evidence for the barn was recovered during excavation in 2001 (Insole 2003). It appeared to have stone bases which would have supported the roof (Fig 6.52).

Other substantial, buttressed stone structures, probably also associated with the management of the abbey grange, were built in Canon's Marsh in the late 13th or early 14th century. The function of these is uncertain, because of the fragmentary nature of the remains. However, excavation by Cotswold Archaeology in 2007 uncovered the remains of buildings on the southern edge of the Abbey precinct, close to the southern precinct wall. There was also evidence for the management of the system of water-filled channels that ran through and round the Marsh, feeding the fishponds that lay to the west of the precinct (BHER 4455) (Alexander and Harward 2011).

Much of St Augustine's 15th-century building work was focused on the abbey's estates. Within the abbey itself Abbot Hunt (1472–81) had the roof of the choir re-leaded (Jeayes 1889–90, 130). More substantial change began when Abbot Newland (1481–1515) instituted a major project, continued by his successor Abbot Elyot (1515–26), to rebuild and enlarge the nave of the church. This was incomplete at the Dissolution, the new walls having risen only to the level of the windows. Other work was completed however. The building later known as Minster House was created between the west end of the new nave and the abbey gate (Fig 6.53).

This was a two-storey structure, essentially a modification and reuse of existing structures, notably the possible Norman guest house (excavated in 1992), with some new work which included a first-floor hall (Bryant 2015).

On the south side of the cloister, the refectory was rebuilt, with further construction to its south-west (BHER 146; Wilson and Hurst 1961, 312–13). The upper floors of the abbey gate were also substantially remodelled in the late 15th century and there is evidence that at least the statuary on the front of the rebuilt gatehouse and the lunettes and vaults above the gate were painted. The building later known as the Old Deanery was also built on the west side of the gate.

The abbey water supply is believed to have come from a feather off the Gaunt's Pipe, close to the junction of York Place and St George's Road, which then ran south-east to a conduit head in College Square (Lobel and Carus-Wilson 1975, 9). The location of the conduit head is possibly shown by Millerd in 1673 as a small building slightly to the east of centre in the square (Fig 6.54).

A later conduit house was constructed in the cloisters following the Dissolution (*see* Chapter 7, p 270). The water was then presumably carried north-east to supply the abbey refectory. The service buildings seem to have been located to the south and south-west of the cloister and William Worcestre mentions granaries, bakehouses and brewhouses accessible via the abbey gate and there was a dovecote to the east of the lower cloister (Neale 2000, 52–3; Boore 1979). The abbey operated a grammar school in the late Middle Ages, and the vicar of St Augustine-the-Less was paid to teach there in 1491 (Graham 1907, 78). Evidence for

Figure 6.52 Excavation of a medieval barn in Lower College Square in 2001

manufacturing within the precinct is currently limited to the bell-casting and the possible stone-carving workshop excavated in 1992 but there is certain to have been more taking place over the lifespan of the abbey.

The abbey's use of the lands surrounding the conventual buildings is broadly clear. The abbot's park lay to the north-west, between the conventual buildings and St George's Road. College Green was the abbey cemetery, also used by St Mark's Hospital which stood on its north-east side. The Green was covered with gravestones and tombs but the extent of the area used for inhumation has not been defined. The land between the abbey church and St Augustine-the-Less was certainly used for burial (Pritchard 1929, 241) and later building encroached on the edges of the cemetery. As well as St Jordan's chapel, a stone pulpit was sited in College Green by the late Middle Ages. The resolution of the dispute between the abbey and St Mark's over the Green in the mid-13th century also gives some insight into the use of the space. St Mark's renounced any claim over the Green in return for rights of access. Grazing of animals by either abbey or hospital was curtailed, with the priest of St Augustine-the-Less responsible for driving off or impounding any beasts, although the abbey retained the right to herbage (Ross 1959, 35–9).

Canon's Marsh was the abbey grange. At the beginning of the 13th century the

Marsh extended much further east, bounded on two sides by the Avon opposite Redcliffe and Trin Mills. The northern boundary was the harbour in the Frome (*portus Frome*). Abbot William Bradstone conveyed this eastern part of the Marsh to the town in 1240 to enable the diversion of the Frome into a new north–south channel (Walker 1998, 375–6). The precise boundaries, and hence size of this land transfer, remain unclear but it must have been at least 10ha. The inference from the relatively low purchase price of 9 marks is that the Marsh was not of great economic value to the abbey. The retained part of

Canon's Marsh was being utilised for a hay meadow by the 15th century, and probably much earlier (Beachcroft and Sabin 1938, 28, 112–13).

Other monastic houses (Figs 6.1, 6.3 and 6.45)
The foundation of monastic houses and hospitals, begun in the previous century, continued and reached a peak in the 13th and, by the end of the century, most of the major monastic orders had houses in Bristol. A striking phenomenon was the clustering of monastic foundations along the north bank of the river Frome, evolving into a distinct enclave wrapped around the western and northern sides of the medieval town, with limited secular occupation between and around the precincts. This distinctive concentration of ecclesiastical institutions was rooted in the availability of land in the hands of patrons on the growing edge of the contemporary built-up area, and in the topographical constraints offered by the natural relief, watercourses and approach-roads.

The process had begun in the early 12th century with the foundation of St Augustine's Abbey in the south-west and the Priory of St James in the north, the former by Robert Fitzharding, the latter by Robert, Earl of Gloucester, followed by the Nunnery of St Mary Magdalen, between the two, by the wife of Robert Fitzharding (*see* Chapter 5). In the course of the 13th century these houses were joined by St Bartholomew's Hospital outside the Frome Gate (probably around 1232–4), St Mark's (later Gaunt's) Hospital (after 1230) across College Green from St Augustine's, the Franciscan Friary (*c* 1230) above Lewins Mead, the Dominican Friary (1227/8) east of Broadmead, and the Carmelite Friary (1256) above Host Street (Lobel and Carus-Wilson 1975, 7–8). All of the larger sites, and some of the smaller, followed the conventional arrangement of church, cloister and ancillary buildings, but several – most clearly St Bartholomew's – were constrained by their sites and adopted more *ad hoc* arrangements (Price with Ponsford 1998). Almost all of the houses appear to have had chequered episodes in their administrative and financial history and some, most notably the Friars of the Sack (founded outside the Temple Gate *c* 1266, abolished 1274), were

but short-lived. The largest houses were, on the other hand, assiduous in protecting their interests against each other and against the Mayor and Commonalty, and also succeeded in developing a healthy income. The archaeological evidence from those precincts which have seen more than a minimal level of archaeological investigation, points to

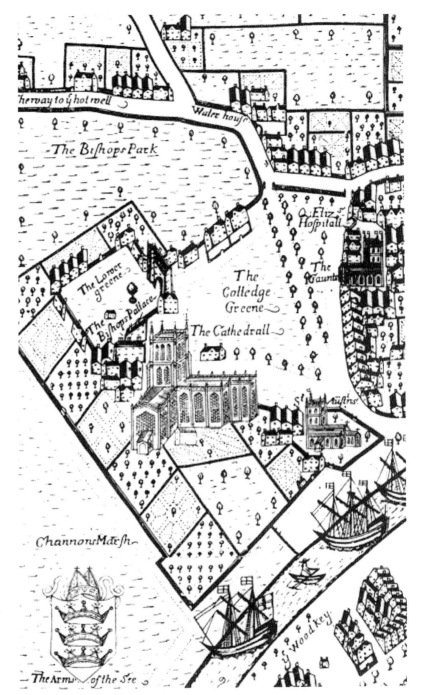

Figure 6.54 Extract from Millerd's map of 1673 showing the Cathedral and possible conduit head in College Square (BRSMG Mb6690)

at least one major later medieval rebuilding campaign affecting each. However, while some excavations have been fully published others await detailed analysis and publication, and without these results it is impossible to draw out the nuances of the evolution of the monastic sites from the relatively coarse phasing of the interim reports.

In the discussion that follows, the institutions comprising this monastic enclave are described first, commencing with those that had been founded in the previous century.

The Priory of St James

The development of the priory is relatively well documented, and the precinct, its buildings and its cemeteries have been the subject of considerable archaeological investigation.

Throughout the later medieval period the Priory of St James prospered by carefully protecting its own rights against other Bristol monasteries and establishing new sources of income, including, from 1310, the right to levy 3d on each hogshead of wine coming into the port in the week leading up to the feast of St James (Graham 1907, 74). The nave of the church served as the parish church for the Broadmead area and, following the usual practice, maintenance of the nave was the responsibility of the parish. However, in *c* 1374 the parishioners funded the construction of a bell tower (later recorded by William Worcestre: Neale 2000, 134–5), while refusing to replace the roof of the nave, instead reaching agreement for the priory to take on the responsibility. The surviving nave and the tower were surveyed in the later 1840s or very early 1850s and interpreted by E W Godwin and James Hine as being of late 14th-century date (BHER 3580; Burder *et al* 1851, 1–3). The south aisle was also extended, encroaching onto the edge of the parish churchyard. Excavation in 1995 to the east of Cannon Street (BHER 3155) found that the truncation of the remains of the choir had removed any evidence of the later medieval phases of that part of the church. However, an east–west wall was found to have been inserted at the east end in the 14th century, blocking off the south transept. The excavator suggested that this may have been associated with the construction of the new tower and the separation of parochial and monastic functions. In 1789 William Barrett described surviving parts of the east end of

the church as consisting of: 'a square room with niches in the wall round it, in length 24 yards, and of breadth in the clear 8 yards … It appears to have been vaulted with freestone, of which the side walls were built very strong' (Barrett 1789, 382; Jackson 2006b).

The west side of the cloister walk, on the north side of the church, was also rebuilt in the 14th century and two bays from this rebuilding survive in the rear wall of Church House (Bryant 1993, 28–33) (Fig 6.55).

Three chapels were recorded inside the church in the 13th and 14th centuries: one dedicated to St Thomas (Wadley 1886, 37, 95, 129), another to St Anne (Neale 2000, 278–9), and the chapel of the Blessed Virgin Mary (Wadley 1886, 62; Neale 2000, 266–7, 278–9). The latter may have been the largely freestanding structure just to the south-east of the tower recorded on a plan of 1744 (Bristol Archives P/St.J/V/38/3).

During the 15th century the roof of the nave was replaced and in 1497–8 a new reredos built: this was 'to aryse in height w^t iij storyes of pryncypall ymages And secundearyes to fulfill after the height' (Nicholls and Taylor 1881, 31). In 1504–5 a screen was erected in the chancel (Nicholls and Taylor 1881, 32).

The parochial churchyard to the south of the church was 11,900 square metres in area. It was enclosed by a wall, with access via gates and a stile at the north-east and south-west corners. By the late 15th century a freestone chapel 10ft square stood on its the western side (Neale 2000, 194–5, 210–11). Robert Hall Warren suggested that a medieval tiled pavement discovered in 1894 when the White Lion Inn was demolished was part of this chapel (Warren 1893–6). The churchwardens derived income from the churchyard, making several leases of small market pitches within it in the 15th century, and even one within the church (Jackson 2006b). Elements of later medieval buildings constructed on the edge of the cemetery were excavated at the west end of the church in 1993–4 (BHER 3156). Excavation in Haymarket in 1954 (BHER 3078) recorded around 40 inhumations in the eastern half of the churchyard. These were arranged in parallel rows and relatively few had evidence for coffin furniture, leading the excavator to believe that most individuals had been buried in shrouds (Mason 1957). In the same area in September 1997 (BHER 3277) at least 12 more inhumations were found cut into rock. Five were articulated (four male and one female adults) while the other individuals were represented by disarticulated bone (including one child). All had been buried in shrouds. One of the skeletons was radiocarbon dated and produced a date of AD 1290–1440 at a two-sigma calibration (540 ± 40BP Wk 6139).

The monastic cemetery at the east end of the church was considerably smaller, and around 1300 square metres of it was excavated in 1995 (Fig 6.56). Here the ratio of males to females was three to one, and just 11 per cent of inhumations were aged 16 years or under at death (Jackson 2006b). A clear socioeconomic difference between the parochial and monastic burial grounds emerges from the excavated evidence. There was a far greater proportion of burials in coffins in the monastic cemetery than in the parochial cemetery, where shroud burial seems to have been more usual (Mason 1957; Burchill 1997). The relative levels of osteoarthritis and DISH in the skeletal material also suggests that the monastic population interred there was wealthier than the general population.

The priory gardens and orchards lay to the north of the claustral buildings; to the east lay St James Barton, where the priory's barns were located (Neale 2000, 98–101). Early modern documents record several barns, including 'the Great Barn called ye Priory Barn' and a dovecote (Jackson 2006b; Latimer 1897–9). A copy of a drawing of 1630 (Bristol Archives PicBox/4/bch/22) of the ruinous priory shows the remains of buildings between the church and St James Barton, though their function is unclear Fig 6.57).

The Nunnery of St Mary Magdalen
St Mary Magdalen's, at the junction of Upper Maudlin Street with St Michael's Hill, was a small house and not particularly wealthy. Its endowments were limited, and in 1347 its rights in the manor of Rowerdecote were sold to St Mark's Hospital, presumably to raise money (Ross 1959, 206–7). Despite occasional donations – Roger Cantok endowed a perpetual chantry in the church, for example (Veale 1938, 189–90) – the house had an annual income of only £20 at its dissolution (Bettey 1990, 7).

There is little evidence for its physical form. William Worcestre records the overall length of the church as the equivalent of 14.5m and its width as the nave and three aisles, with four arches (*constat ex navi et tribus alis. ac .4. arches*) but says little more (Neale 2000, 228–9). How far the poverty of the house constrained new building or alterations is unclear, though the only excavation to have taken place within the precinct did record at least one substantial building campaign, on the north-eastern side of the site in the 15th century. The excavator suggested it may have represented either the

reconstruction of the south-west corner of the cloister or a new adjacent building (BHER 3591; Longman 2001).

St Bartholomew's Hospital
John de la Warre founded St Bartholomew's Hospital between 1232 and 1234 on a site at the western end of Frome Bridge, adjacent to the Franciscan Friary, another foundation of the same family. The hospital was for both men and women and was run by a master with brethren and sisters; de la Warre also established two chaplains to pray for the souls of his family. At least by the late 15th century the hospital followed a monastic rule, but which one is unknown.

The house was relatively poor. Its initial endowment was small and the new hospital was largely accommodated in an existing building, a 12th-century domestic hall and its undercroft, to which a new porch was added and internal alterations made (Fig 6.58).

A new building of indeterminate function was built to its north, on the site of an earlier slipway, before demolition in the late 13th to early 14th century. At that time the site was expanded by the addition of ranges to the south-west and north-east, the latter possibly containing dormitory accommodation, a kitchen and refectory. An inventory of 1303 records the buildings of the hospital as the hall, kitchen, bakehouse, pantry, larder, cellar, granary and guest house – which correlate well with the buildings excavated on the site; the chapel and infirmary lay at the southern end of the site in the former domestic hall. At the north-east end of the precinct were the garden and the hospital's burial ground.

The structural failure of the Norman hall during the 14th century led to a major phase of rebuilding. Subsidence towards the Frome prompted remedial works to provide support, and the floor of the undercroft was raised. In the second half of the 14th century it was finally demolished and the undercroft infilled. Rebuilt off the original walls to roughly the same footprint, the replacement building – a lighter, two-storey structure, possibly with a clerestory above the south arcade – became the hospital church and infirmary. Inside the building, 30 burials from this and the subsequent phase were excavated. The majority of the skeletons were over 45 years of age at death, with a handful of

Figure 6.56 Overview of the St James's Priory excavation of 1995

children, and the group was equally divided between males and females. There was also evidence of disease amongst the skeletal material, the majority of the adults exhibiting osteoarthritis.

The hospital experienced administrative difficulties in the 14th and 15th centuries and its running was taken on by a prioress and the sisters in the middle of the 14th century. A master was reinstated after an inquiry in 1387 but the finances of the institution remained shaky. Through the 15th and early 16th centuries only relatively minor physical alterations were made and the hospital was closed in 1532 (BHER 3286; Price with Ponsford 1998).

St Mark's Hospital

St Mark's, or the Gaunts Hospital, stood on the east side of College Green. Its origin may lie with an almonry built by Maurice de Gaunt in the first two decades of the 13th century to provide a daily meal for one hundred by agreement with St Augustine's Abbey (Ross 1959, xii). However, it is his nephew Robert de Gournay, who in 1230–2

confirmed the endowment of an almonry (*elemosinarie de Billeswyk*), who was formally acknowledged as the founder (Graham 1907, 114; Ross 1959, 266). The charters of the early 1230s were for the maintenance of a master and brethren who were to feed 27 poor people each day. There was a gradual transition from daily distribution of food towards resident almoners in the late 13th to early 14th century, but it is not clear what effect, if any, this had on the accommodation within the site. The house was Augustinian and the Bishop of Worcester specified that the habit was to follow the style of the house at Lechlade with a badge consisting of a red shield with a white cross and three white geese (Ross 1959, 8).

The precinct was defined by College Green, probably Frogmore Street, by Mark Lane and extended north-east to Pipe Lane, where in 1850 George Pryce recorded a niche for a statue with the remains of a winged lion carved in stone near it on the wall of the house on the corner, also recorded by Samuel Jackson in 1824 (Fig 6.59) (BHER 284; Pryce 1850, 55–6; Winstone 1957, pl 28).

ST JAMES' CHURCH & PRIORY, 1630.

The available evidence for the form of the hospital was mainly collected in the 19th century. When the Lord Mayor's Chapel, the former hospital church on the south-western side of the site, was restored between 1888 and 1889 the works were monitored by W R Barker. He identified six medieval building phases. The main walls of the nave were dated to the original construction in *c* 1230; the south aisle was dated to *c* 1285, the south porch and organ tower were built *c* 1487 and the chancel walls *c* 1500. The south aisle chapel was dated to *c* 1500–10 and the Poyntz Chapel to between 1510 and 1520 (BHER 544) (Barker 1892) (Fig 6.60). Groundworks for the construction of the adjacent Merchant Venturers' School exposed evidence of a destroyed north transept, including a tile pavement. On the west side of the transept arch was the remaining half of a piscina and on the east side a massive door jamb. Together with a fragment of medieval stonework found 55ft 6in (16.98m) from the north wall of the nave, which was interpreted by Archdeacon Norris as 'a portion of a pier with adjoining window sill' (Barker 1892, 43), this was taken as confirmation that the cloister lay to the north of the church.

In 1824 a group of very early 16th-century wall paintings depicting the Nativity, the Trinity and a 'Noli Me Tangere', was discovered when a house on the north side of the Lord Mayor's Chapel was redecorated (FFBJ, 28 February 1824). These paintings had decorated a closet with hagioscopes built within the north wall of the chapel. One of the hagioscopes gave a view of the high altar, and probably of other altars in the nave. A Netherlands influence on the style of the paintings has been noted, and the pigments subjected to detailed chemical analysis, revealing the use of rarely used compounds (Howard 2003, 161; 175; Gill and Howard 1997) (Fig 6.61).

The Master's House stood close to the east end of the hospital church. A photograph of 1930 (Winstone 1979, pl 100) and a series of drawings of the Master's House made in the months after it was destroyed in February 1941 together record a 13th-century window at first-floor level and an ogee window and Perpendicular door, suggesting that the building was constructed in the 13th century and altered in the late Middle Ages.

The orchard and gardens were located to the north-east against Frogmore Street (Neale 2000, 52–3). A dispute with St Augustine's Abbey (resolved in 1251) over the hospital's use of College Green for burial suggests that St Mark's did not have a cemetery within the precinct.

The Franciscan Friary (Figs 6.62 and 6.63)
The precise date at which the Franciscan Friary in Lewins Mead was founded is unknown, but

the order may have established a temporary base within the town by 1230 (Weare 1893, 15). Certainly the friars were present in Bristol by 1234 when they were granted wood for fuel by Henry III and had relocated, almost certainly to the Lewins Mead site, by the 1250s (Graham 1907, 110). The walled precinct occupied a block of land between Lewins Mead and Upper Maudlin Street and covered an area of around 27,000 square metres by the end of the 15th century.

Excavation by M W Ponsford in 1973 (BHER 317) identified two main phases of building: the initial construction of the friary in the 13th century and its subsequent expansion in the later 14th. From the first, the church and the main conventual buildings were sited on flat ground (first prepared by dumping around a metre of sandstone and clay) on the northern side of Lewins Mead, running back towards a cliff

created by the Frome. The western half of the choir and a small part of the nave of the friary church, and the south-east corner of the cloister including the chapter house, were recorded; the spatial organisation of much of the remainder of the friary during this early phase is largely conjectural. The church was a simple rectangular building with the nave separated from the choir by a dividing wall. The church was 11m wide with a series of at least six stone cells, each 4m square, on its southern side. A range of buildings, including the chapter house, was found to the north of the chancel. A burial found immediately to the west of the chapter house was taken as an indication that, during this earliest phase, there had been no cloister walk.

The discovery in the excavations on the hillside below Upper Maudlin Street of mid-13th-century features that were probably derived from cultivation suggests that, as was

Figure 6.58
St Bartholomew's Hospital: 13th-century arcade in south porch (photograph R Jones)

Figure 6.59 Building on Pipe Lane showing a carved winged lion in 1824 by Samuel Jackson (Braikenridge Collection, BRSMG M2547)

the case in later centuries, the gardens and orchards were sited there.

The archaeological and documentary evidence for the 14th- and 15th-century friary is more complete, though not all the excavations have been fully published. The 1973 excavation found that from the late 14th century the friary was expanded; the church was rebuilt and substantially enlarged to the south, the original nave becoming the north

aisle. An extension was added to the east end of the chapter house and a cloister walk, thought to be rectangular in plan (measuring 25m east–west by 17m north–south), was created. At the east end of the new nave significant numbers of inhumations were found (Ponsford nd (b)).

In 1892 a building containing medieval fabric was identified at the north-east corner of the precinct. Surveyed by T S Pope (BTM,

Figure 6.60 The tower and sacristy (Poyntz chapel) of St Mark's Hospital from the south-east in 1825 by Samuel Jackson (Braikenridge Collection, BRSMG M2591)

22 April 1892; BHER 3559), its dimensions suggested that it was the same building that had been recorded in a more complete state in the late 1850s by E W Godwin and Robert Hall Warren, which Godwin believed incorporated the friary dormitory roof (BHER 3557). Parts of the walls, including a buttress at first-floor level, were of medieval date and at the rear there was an 'outer hall or lobby' which gave access from the ground floor to the land on the higher level' by a flight of steps (Weare 1893, 33–4). Internally it appeared originally to have comprised a hall at both ground and first-floor level. The building was also drawn by Samuel Loxton in the early 20th century (Fig 6.64), and parts of two Gothic round trefoil windows were extant in the west-facing elevation until *c* 1921.

Figure 6.61 The Trinity, Nativity and Noli Me Tangere wall paintings, Lord Mayor's Chapel (photograph D Martyn)

A stone building, interpreted as the lodge of the warden or the guest house, was built on the hill above the cloister in the 14th century. This was a ground-floor hall, approximately, 8.5m long by 5.5m wide, orientated approximately east–west on a terrace cut into the rock. An open hearth with a moulded freestone surround and over 400 reused glazed floor tiles set on edge was built into the west wall replacing an earlier fireplace. Also during the 14th century what appeared to be an extension 'of an inferior build' was added to the east end of the building, increasing its overall length to 22m (BHER 444; Ponsford *et al* 1989b, 42–4).

In its late 15th-century form the church nave had large four-bay aisles on either side. William Worcestre visited the friary twice (in 1478 and 1480), but recorded different dimensions on each occasion for the overall width of the nave (24.7m and 29.5m) and for the length of the nave and choir (51m and 63m) (Neale 2000, 174–5, 226–7). The alterations to the church in the later 15th century were referred to in the course of a dispute when, in the late 1470s, William Spencer drew attention to his contribution to the 'newe makinge of the Quere and body of the Churche' and 'Repaireng of al the Remenaunte of the howsinge and Bildings of the saide Frerys' (Veale 1953, 68). An inventory made at the friary's dissolution records the candlesticks and vestments in the choir and vestry but gives few further clues about the decoration of the church. Worcestre also mentions a bell tower (*campanilis turris*) 4 yards square but is not explicit about where it was or whether it was a freestanding structure (Neale 2000, 174–5).

The friary burial ground was between the west end of the church and the adjacent precinct of St Bartholomew's Hospital and inhumations have been reported on many occasions. Burials were disturbed during rebuilding of a warehouse in 1851 and a further discovery was made of bones and the remains of oak coffins in drainage works a few years later (BTM, 22 April 1892). More human remains were found on the same site in *c* 1877 along with 'an underground passage' (BTM, 22 April 1892); further human remains and oak coffins were found in 1894 (BHER 153) and it was observed by G E Weare that they were found close to the edge of the path which originally led from Lewins Mead to the Greyfriars – presumably the lane called Blackfriars (Pritchard 1895, 175). In 1970 a trench dug for a gas pipe cut through five inhumations, oriented east–west (BHER 23).

Evidence for water management within the friary has been found on several occasions. Fresh water came to the cloister via the Greyfriars Conduit, later known as the All Saints Conduit, which collected water from a spring on the northern side of Upper Maudlin Street. Discovered on the south side of Upper Maudlin Street in 1970, the conduit was almost 2m high and had three branches with slightly pointed vaults. A complete 13th-century freestone doorway was also recorded (Fowler 1972a, 53) (BHER 21). Other substantial underground chambers were found within the precinct in the 19th century and during the 1973 excavation but whether these features carried fresh water or were for drainage is unclear.

The Carmelite Friary
The Carmelite Friary was founded in 1256 (Lobel and Carus-Wilson 1975, 8). With very little archaeological evidence available – the only controlled excavation, which was carried out in 2007, remains unpublished (BHER 4369; Heaton 2008) – interpretation of the

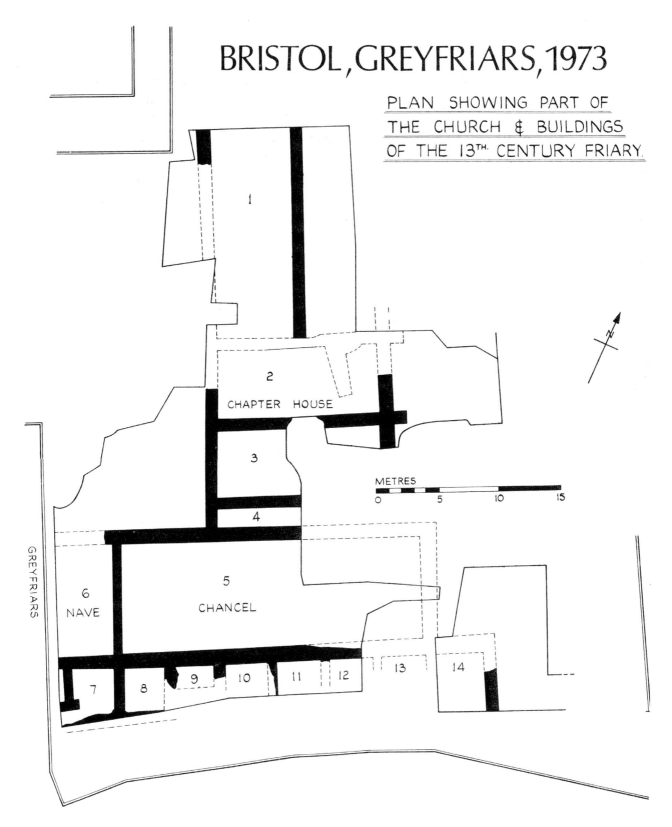

Figure 6.62 Plan of the Franciscan Friary (reproduced from Ponsford nd(b), fig II)

*Figure 6.63 Overview of
the Greyfriars excavation
in 1973*

physical form of the friary is highly conjectural. The walled precinct was a rectangular plot on the north side of St Augustine's Place (now Colston Street) covering around 7,500 square metres, probably defined by Pipe Lane, Host Street and the now lost Steep Street. It is unclear whether Trenchard Street existed as a back lane for the precinct, but the discovery of a substantial group of human remains in 1932 (*see* pp 200–201) indicates that, at the least, widening of the street has encroached on it.

The church and burial ground appear, from substantial medieval walls observed by Pritchard in 1904 and the many burials discovered since the late 18th century, to have been at the south-western end of the site (Pritchard 1906a). The orientation of the church has not been firmly established: William Worcestre seems to suggest that the west end of the church was close to Trenchard Street but his description is opaque (Neale 2000, 187–8). However, while fragmentary, the walls recorded by Pritchard suggest an east–west orientation parallel with Pipe Lane (Fig 6.65).

Evidence for the form of the church is equally limited. Worcestre gives two slightly different sets of measurements for the nave, (equivalent to) 24m and nearly 29m long by 13.4m or 14.5m wide, with a choir measuring 24m long (Neale 2000, 50–1, 278–9). Bishop Ingworth, one of the Crown commissioners at the Dissolution, mentioned 'a chapell and an yle off the Church' as well as (with a view to salvage) 'dyverse gutteres, spowtes and condytes lede, the rest all tylle and slate' (Weare 1893, 74). The chapel may have been that dedicated to St George, known to have stood in the church by 1412, although there was also a chapel dedicated to St Mary by 1393 (Wadley 1886, 89, 51). The tower of the church was just under 2.7m wide and with the spire, Worcestre says, was 200ft high, though he also remarks that the tower wall was only just over 2ft thick (Neale 2000, 100–1). There were three large traceried windows at first-floor level on the Colston Street frontage (BRSMG M2531; BRSMG M2532; Winstone 1983, pl 86), but if this was an element of the church which had survived *in situ* or had simply been reused is likely to remain unknown. (Fig 6.66)

Whether a tiled floor found in Trenchard Street in 1932 and a late medieval window

observed in 1989 formed part of the church or some other building is unclear. However, the 2007 excavation revealed evidence for buildings near to the corner of Pipe Lane and Trenchard Street, one of which was found to form the foundation for the façade of the now-demolished No 2 Trenchard Street (Heaton 2008).

Worcestre recorded the cloister as 21.4m square (Neale 2000, 50–1). Evidence for its position within the precinct is minimal and the

Dissolution-period inventory is of no further help (Weare 1893, 76–8). The north-eastern end of the precinct presumably consisted of ancillary buildings and the orchard and gardens mentioned in the grant of the site to the Corporation in 1541 (Latham 1947, 91).

One other architectural feature of the church may have survived dissolution in the 1530s. In 1542 Thomas White bequeathed a screen from the building to Bristol Cathedral, where it was erected as a choir screen.

Figure 6.64 Drawing of a medieval building, probably part of the Franciscan Friary (Samuel Loxton, early 20th century. Bristol Reference Library D230)

*Figure 6.65 Plan of
discoveries at the Carmelite
Friary (reproduced from
Pritchard 1906a)*

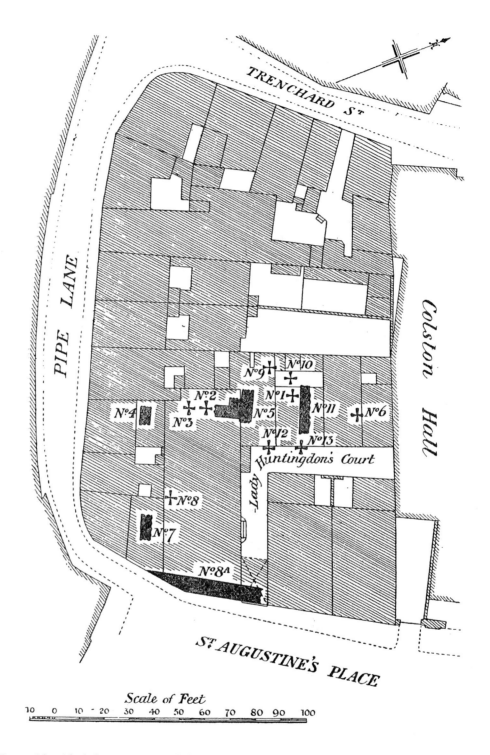

Warren identified the remnants of this as the heavily restored late medieval screen now set in the fourth bay of the south choir aisle (Warren 1904–8b; Warren 1904).

With the exception of the fragmentary structural remains, including those found in the unpublished 2007 excavation, almost all the archaeological evidence for the Carmelite

Friary comes from the discovery of burials (Fig 6.65 above). In April 1788 workmen digging at the corner of Pipe Lane discovered 'a great quantity of human bones and some entire skeletons' amounting, it was thought, to between 30 and 40 individuals; no fragments of coffins or coffin nails were found (BHER 3666; *Gentleman's Magazine* 1788, 455). In 1904

John Pritchard, observing the groundworks for a new gas company office, recorded several sections of probable medieval walls and a number of burials (BHER 46; Pritchard 1906a). More human remains were found by Pritchard in 1913–14 (BHER 233; Pritchard 1920, 133–8; Beddoe 1906) and in November 1932 several more skeletons and a pavement of medieval floor tiles were found during excavation in Trenchard Street (Nabb 1987, 40). In 1989 a window of late medieval date was found in the front wall of No 2 Trenchard Street (BHER 622) (Fig 7.38). More disarticulated human remains were discovered inside No 2 Trenchard Street in 1999 (BHER 3464; Burchill 1999b). Twelve articulated skeletons were found in the 2007 excavation (BHER 4369), all from the area close to the junction of Pipe Lane and Trenchard Street (Heaton 2008).

The friary obtained its water supply from the St John's conduit which ran along Pipe Lane and Host Street. Worcestre also mentions a statue of St Mary in a shrine in the precinct

Figure 6.66 Lady Huntingdon's Chapel, showing three traceried windows in 1823 by Hugh O'Neill (Braikenridge Collection, BRSMG M2532)

Figure 6.67 Reconstruction of the Dominican Friary and its surrounding area (after Ridgeway and Watts 2013, fig 6.12. Reconstruction drawn by Jake Lunt)

wall near the corner of Host Street and Steep Street (Neale 2000, 18–19).

The Dominican Friary (Fig 6.67)

The Dominican Friary, or Blackfriars, was founded in 1227–8 by Maurice de Gaunt in the south-east quarter of the planned Broadmead suburb. The altar and burial ground were dedicated by the Bishop of Worcester in 1230, though in the face of some protest from the Priory of St James (Graham 1907, 74); Henry III licensed the extension of the burial ground two years later (Graham 1907, 109). The precinct was said to have been enclosed by a wall and lay between Merchant Street on the west, Rosemary Street on the north and the River Frome to the south (Neale 2000, 160–1). On the east side was the Great Orchard, its western boundary lying between Philadelphia Street and Penn Street (Bryant and Leech 2000).

A reconstruction of the internal layout of the precinct can be attempted from the surviving buildings, from William Worcestre's measurements and from recent archaeological discoveries (Fig 6.68).

The church lay to the north of the cloisters and, from Worcestre's measurements, was 54.6m long with a choir 24m wide and a nave 18m wide (Neale 2000, 162–3). Archaeological evidence for the church was found in the course of recent excavations for drainage trenches. Burials and tiled floors were found, together with evidence for a passage passing between the nave and the choir (a 'walking place'); the choir probably had flanking aisles, which would explain the width recorded by William Worcestre (Ridgeway and Watts 2013). Documentary evidence adds a few further details. In 1389 Simon Halleway requested burial in front of the image of the Blessed Mary (Wadley 1886, 23) and the inventory

Figure 6.68 Reconstructed ground plan of the Dominican Friary (reproduced from Ridgeway and Watts 2013, fig 6.6)

Figure 6.69 Cutlers Hall (photograph D Martyn)

made at the Dissolution in 1538 records a pair of organs, together with an extensive collection of vestments in the sacristy (Weare 1893, 84–6).

To the south of the church lay the Great Cloister and, beyond it, the Lesser Cloister. Worcestre measured the former, at 21.4m on each side, presumably representing the cloister walk (Neale 2000, 50–1). The claustral ranges were built on a different orientation to both the surrounding streets and the watercourses constraining the site to the south. This divergence was not obviously a consequence of liturgical requirements, but the factors influencing it remain unknown. The orientation of the west side of the Lesser Cloister may have responded to the alignment of Merchant Street and its associated properties, which were already in place.

One claustral building survives in the Great Cloister (Fig 6.69). This is the south range, known as Cutlers Hall, possibly the friary refectory, although both Leighton (1933) and Watts and Davenport (2013) suggest that it may have been the dorter. It is constructed in Pennant sandstone (like all the claustral ranges) that may be contemporaneous with the foundation of the friary in the late 1220s. The surviving arch-braced collar roof may be late 13th or early 14th century, though the building's south external elevation is entirely Victorian. However, a recent study of the roof (Watts and Davenport 2013, 359–60) has suggested that the roof in its present state may be the result of 15th-century and subsequent repairs and alterations, culminating in the addition of tie beams in 1845 (Fig 6.70).

Figure 6.70 Roof of Cutlers Hall (photograph R Jones)

Excavated evidence suggests that the east claustral range was occupied by the chapter house; the west range incorporated the building later known as Tanners Hall. In 1933 building work on the City Motors Ltd garage exposed the remnants of a damaged blind traceried window, which was surveyed, photographed and a reconstruction drawing produced

(BHER 3407; Winstone 1979) (Fig 7.41). The discovery prompted a survey of the remains of the friary by Wilfred Leighton, which included sections through the south range of the Great Cloister and the south range of the Lesser Cloister (BHER 928; Leighton 1933). In 1936 a second window was discovered just to the east of the first, this one having contained glass, unlike the first (BHER 3424; *BEP*, 9 December 1936). Leighton argued that the western of the two windows discovered in the 1930s was at the north end of the western claustral range (*see* Leighton 1933, fig 4). The subsequent discovery of the second suggests it was more likely that both were within the south wall of the nave, but this remains to be established.

To the south was the Lesser Cloister, of which Bakers Hall was the south range (Fig 6.71). This may originally have been the infirmary and contains a ground-floor passage,

Figure 6.71 Bakers Hall (photograph D Martyn)

probably part of the cloister walk, and a first-floor hall of which the late 13th- or early 14th-century roof of a two-stage arch-braced collar truss design, also survives (Fig 6.72).

A blocked doorway at the western end of the south wall and the observed truncation of the roof timbers indicate that the hall was truncated at its western end, probably before the Dissolution. Excavated evidence suggests that the Lesser Cloister was entirely enclosed by a now-demolished west range, and that its buildings were not constructed in a single phase. What were probably the side walls of this range were also found during the excavation of 2005–8. However, the excavation in this area was limited and little can be said of its form or function (Ridgeway and Watts 2013).

The main cemetery for the friary probably lay to the east of the principal friary buildings,

in the area later occupied by the Quakers' burial ground. However, there were also burials elsewhere in the precinct, including inside the friary church, as previously noted. Discoveries of human remains have also been made in the north-west corner of the precinct, at the west end of the church. In 1814 workmen discovered three stone coffins between Rosemary Street and Merchant Street containing the skeletons of two men and one woman (BHER 2525; Pryce 1850, 87). Probably in the 1920s inhumations, in two groups of three, were found on either side of the street named Quakers Friars, off the southern side of Rosemary Street: one under the highway, one under a building opposite (BHER 4232; Leighton 1933, 166; fig 4). The friary's obit book, as recorded by Worcestre, notes that there was a cross in the burial ground erected by William Curteys (Neale 2000, 164–5).

The southern side of the friary was probably defined by a river wall, and there may also have been a landing place since Worcestre specifically mentions the friary when discussing the navigability of the Frome (Neale 2000, 174–7). A document of 1614 also mentions a former dovecote east of the lower cloister (Bryant and Leech 2000). In 1232 the friars obtained the right to a conduit from a spring at Pennywell, later agreeing with Bristol the replacement of this supply, apparently with a feather off the Key Pipe (Leighton 1933, 152–3).

Almshouses in the Lewins Mead area (Fig 6.45)
The monasteries were not the only institutional buildings in the Lewins Mead area, a number of almshouses being founded there within a few years of one another at the end of the 15th century. The earliest was founded on a site opposite the church of the Franciscan Friary on the southern side of Lewins Mead

Figure 6.72 Roof of Bakers Hall (photograph R Jones)

by William Spencer in *c* 1474, out of the estate of William Canynges according to William Worcestre (Lobel and Carus-Wilson 1975, 26; Neale 2000, 224–5). Spencer claimed he built the almshouse and found 'diverse pore folkes therein to pray for the welfare of oure Souveraigne lorde the Kyng Our Souveraigne lady the quene and all theire noble issue and for the helthe of his oune soule' (Veale 1953, 68).

The main evidence for the form of the building comes from two 1821 drawings by Hugh O'Neill which show a narrow, single-storey range divided into a number of individual dwellings, end-on to the street standing on the eastern side of a courtyard (BRSMG M2867; BRSMG M2868) (Fig 6.73).

John Foster founded an almshouse in 1483 at the north-west end of Christmas Steps

Figure 6.73 Spencer's Almshouse, Lewins Mead, looking north, 1821 by Hugh O'Neill (Braikenridge Collection, BRSMG M2867)

to provide residential accommodation for a number of poor people. The form of the original building is not clear, but it is likely to have been similar to the subsequent building, with ranges on the northern and eastern sides of a central courtyard. Foster's will of 1492 suggests that the residential accommodation consisted of 13 rooms (Manchee 1831, vol 1, 80). The almshouse chapel was near the western end of the north range. This had the unusual dedication to the Three Kings of Cologne, that is, the Magi, strongly suggesting some connection with Cologne Cathedral. The chapel was an integral part of the foundation and Foster, under the terms of his will, established a chantry for a priest to sing daily in the chapel. The almshouse escaped dissolution in 1547 because of this relationship, the commissioners concluding that it was 'w[ith] out the Compasse of the Statute, & the king ma[jesty] not entited therunto by fforce of the same' (Maclean 1883–4, 248–9) (Fig 6.74).

The almshouse for St John's parish, on the south-east side of St John's Steep, is reputed to have been founded at the end of the 15th century (possibly in 1491). The form of the medieval building is unknown but it had fallen into a 'ruinous' state by 1721 (Manchee 1831, vol 2, 3).

Hospitals and almshouses in the Old Market area (Fig 6.45)
On either side of Lawford's Gate, just within the perimeter of the Old Market, were the Trinity Hospital sites. The southern almshouse was founded by John Barstaple (d 1411) in the early 15th century and confirmed by a grant of Henry V in February 1417 (Manchee 1831, vol 1, 499–500); the northern almshouse was founded by Barstaple's widow. The almshouse was administered by the Fraternity of the Holy Trinity and St George and William Worcestre, writing in 1480, noted that it was for 13 poor men. The history of the site was reviewed by Leighton (Leighton 1913) and while the original form of the hospital is undefined, some information can be drawn from the documentary and visual record. The hospital had a chapel and Worcestre mentions that John Barstaple had appointed Nicholas Barstaple as the first 'master of the priests of the chapel' (Neale 2000, 82–3). An inventory of 1653 suggests the pulpit and some of the seating then in the chapel may have been medieval and

at least part of the late medieval two-storey west range of the hospital was drawn by Hugh O'Neill in 1822 (Leighton 1913, 283; BRSMG M2764) (Fig 6.75).

Outside Lawford's Gate was the Hospital of St Lawrence, a leper hospital founded by John, Earl of Mortain who, as king, confirmed the foundation in 1208. Very little is known about the hospital and Price has pointed out that the foundation date is quite late in comparison with the establishment of leprosaria elsewhere in England (Price with Ponsford 1998, 198–9). According to William Worcestre the hospital stood approximately 640m from the gate (Neale 2000, 108–9): the exact position has not been established, although a plot on the east side of the junction of Lawrence Hill and Barton Road seems the most likely location. Worcestre gives some basic information on the layout, mentioning 'the church, and the house and hospital attached to the said church', but its form is otherwise unknown (Neale 2000, 109). Edward IV gave responsibility for the hospital to the Dean and Chapter of Westbury College in 1465.

Religious houses in Redcliffe (Fig 6.45)
Redcliffe and Temple were populated with several religious institutions, mainly sited along the major roads into the area. At the beginning of the 13th century St John's Hospital and the Knights Templar preceptory were already established.

St John's Hospital
The development of St John's Hospital is poorly understood. William Worcestre indicates that it had a church and cloister and his measurements suggest that both were of a relatively modest size (Neale 2000, 248–9). In Redrock Garden to the west of the church a hermitage was created by quarrying into the cliff face at its south end in 1347 (Nicholls and Taylor 1881, vol 2, 119) (Fig 6.76).

The hospital also took over responsibility for the Chapel of the Holy Spirit in the churchyard of St Mary Redcliffe in the 13th century. It was at the centre of some controversy at the beginning of the 15th century because of allegations of Lollardy amongst the regular clergy and mismanagement by the then prior, John Seyntpoull. A commission was appointed in 1404 to investigate the charges and in 1411 the goods and estates of the hospital were

*Figure 6.74 Foster's
Almshouse (photograph
D Martyn)*

Figure 6.75 Part of the medieval west range of Trinity Hospital (south) in 1822 by Hugh O'Neill (Braikenridge Collection, BRSMG M2764)

sequestered by the Crown. By 1442 there was apparently only one brother in residence (Hudson 1988, 122n; Scott Holmes 1914, lx–lxi, 80, 83–4).

The Templar preceptory
At the beginning of the 13th century Bristol's Templar preceptory 'was plainly the fiscal centre of a wide circumference of outlying lands, in Gloucestershire, Somerset, and Dorset, in Devonshire and in Cornwall' (Lees 1935, cxxxii). Little is known about the development of the site during the 13th century but it clearly underwent a drop in status within the order. By the time the Templars were suppressed in 1312, administration of the

Figure 6.76 Entrance to Hermitage in Redrock Garden, part of St John's Hospital (photograph D Martyn)

order's lands in Somerset had been moved to Temple Combe. The preceptory was granted to the Knights of the Hospital of St John of Jerusalem at the Templars' suppression but it is not evident that any members of the order established themselves on the site. A quarter of a century later it was listed only as one of their estates and the circular church was still standing (Larking 1857, 184).

In 1971 excavation to the north of Temple Church, within the Knights Templar precinct, identified the construction of a new hall in the Hospitaller phase (Good 1992, 5–6) (Fig 6.77).

After the suppression of the order in the early 14th century the Templar buildings continued in use for a period. The hall building was demolished in the 14th century to be replaced by a larger stone structure, the southern half of which was subject to internal alterations later in the medieval period. A garden, bounded on its eastern side by a

shallow ditch, was established on the east side of the site at around the same time.

A vicarage for Temple Church was also built towards Temple Street in the 14th century. This was an L-shaped stone building with a tiled floor and internal wooden partitions dividing the ground-floor rooms. Excavation in the vicarage garden, between the vicarage and the 14th-century stone building, showed that it was used in the following century for casting copper alloy and a number of outbuildings were probably associated with this manufacturing (BHER 314; Good 1992). Temple Fee still belonged to the Hospitallers at the time of the Dissolution (Latham 1947, 94).

The Augustinian Friary
A number of new institutions were also established in the Redcliffe area in the 14th century. A house of Augustinian Friars was

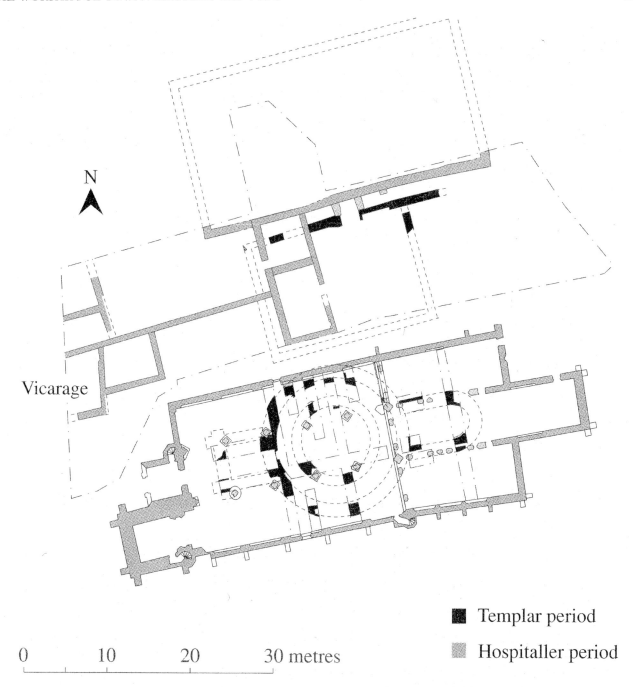

■ Templar period

▨ Hospitaller period

0   10   20   30 metres

founded by Simon de Montacute *c* 1313, and four years later it was given an adjacent plot by William de Montacute (Graham 1907, 110). The precinct was situated on the east side of Temple Street, on the north side of the junction with Portwall Lane and the church was under construction in 1329 (Leech 2001). In 1344 a further four acres were added to the site by Thomas of Berkeley (Graham 1907, 110). Worcestre's description shows that the friary

consisted of a church and cloister. He gives the overall length of the nave of the church as 60 yards and its width as 9 yards; the bell tower was five yards wide and the cloister 30 yards long (Neale 2000, 162–3). The inventory made at its dissolution does not add greatly to the understanding of the arrangement of buildings within the site (Weare 1893, 80–2). However, Leech suggests that some of the conventual buildings may have survived until the mid-19th

Figure 6.77 Plan of 1971 excavation, with earlier 1960 excavation (reproduced from Brown 2008, fig 1)

century and been recorded in a plan of 1847 (Leech 2001; Bristol Archives 3359(1) t).

The Friars of the Sack
This lay just outside Temple Gate. It had been established by 1266 and the church was mentioned in a deed of 1322, confirming its existence at that date (Graham 1907, 111). The friary did not, however, survive to the 15th century. The order was suppressed in 1274 and most of the buildings may not have survived long after this date.

Almshouses in Redcliffe and Temple (Fig 6.45)
There were several medieval almshouses in Redcliffe and Temple but very little is known about them. Two were on the west side of Redcliff Hill. Close to St Mary Redcliffe was the Hospital of St Mary Magdalen, a leper hospital for women. It was in existence by *c* 1226 when a grant was made by the Prebendary of Bedminster, Gilbert de Lacy, allowing the inmates a chantry and a chaplain (Warren 1907, 205–6). William Worcestre mentions a cross and chapel but little else is currently known about the institution (Neale 2000, 94–7). Further south was the Redcliff Poor House or William Canynges's Almshouse. This is reputed to have been founded in the early 1440s by William Canynges, who bequeathed 20s to each of his 'poor almsmen dwelling on Redcliffe Hill' at his death (Manchee 1831, vol 2, 56; Williams 1950, 75). Rocque's 1742 plan shows the building parallel to, but a little set back from the road. Canynges also endowed a college of chaplains on the south side of Redcliffe churchyard and Worcestre describes this building as around 20 yards long with four freestone windows lighting the four priests' rooms (Neale 2000, 74–5).

The Redcliff Hospital (as depicted on Millerd's 1673 map) on the south side of Temple Gate is thought to have been the almshouse founded by Roger Magdalens of Nunney (Lobel and Carus-Wilson 1975, 26). The building was aligned parallel to the street and was approximately 23m north-west to south-east and 5.5m wide. The building survived the Reformation and in 1831 there were 14 residents (Sampson 1909, 87–8).

Only one, or possibly two, medieval almshouses in this area have been recorded archaeologically. The first is Burton's Almshouse, on the north side of Long Row ('la Langerewe'). The almshouse is traditionally held to have been founded in 1292 by Simon Burton. Marochan and Reed's fieldwork (BHER 3079) appears to support a high medieval date, although their discoveries have never been reviewed. If they are correct, the medieval establishment consisted of two ranges of buildings with a courtyard at the rear (Marochan and Reed 1959) (Fig 6.78).

The second was found by excavation in 1975 at Nos 94–102 Temple Street (BHER 443). There, a 13th-century stone-founded building had possibly been constructed on a raised platform. In the following century two buildings were erected, the longer parallel to the street, the other at right-angles at its northern end. These were believed by the excavator to have been the almshouse founded by John Spicer, with the smaller range occupied by a chapel (Williams 1988, 123–4) (Fig 6.79).

The Jewish community
By the 15th century, tradition placed the original location of the Jewish quarter in Bristol at St Giles (Neale 2000, 26–7). Historians have accepted this, taking it to imply a re-location to Wine Street, under the protection of the nearby castle. However, later property records contain no evidence of the medieval Jewry in the St Giles area and the tradition remains to be confirmed (Hillaby and Sermon 2004, 132; Leech 1997c, 118). The area between Dolphin Street and the castle, on the other hand, can be positively identified as the site of the Jewry, at least by the later 13th century. The accounts of the Constable of Bristol Castle record the rental of houses in Wine Street ('Winchestrete') which belonged to Cresse le Prest, son of Isaac the Jew, and Benedict of Winchester, and also of a tenement outside the castle formerly of Moses of Kent (Sharp 1982, 39–40, 49–50). Little is known of the spatial organisation of this area – apart from the location of the synagogue on the north side of Wine Street. How densely Jewish families were settled there, and where other features were sited, notably the community's *mikveh*, are unknown. The Peter Street excavation suggests that occupation of the area immediately after the expulsion in 1290 may have been limited. The construction of the substantial wall, whether in the Burgesses' Revolt or for some other reason, and establishment of new tenement plots in the later 14th century, imply a discontinuity of occupation in this part of the town.

Figure 6.78 North-west face of Burton's Almshouse in 1824 by Edward Cashin (Braikenridge Collection, BRSMG M2088)

On the north-west side of Brandon Hill, a plot was rented from St Augustine's Abbey by the Jewish community, and provided a cemetery sometime after 1172, when these were allowed in the provinces (Hughes 1997). This was on the site now occupied by Queen Elizabeth's Hospital School, traditionally called 'Jews Acre', and tombstones with Hebrew inscriptions were discovered when the school was erected in 1843 (Pryce 1861, 23).

In 1987, during investigation of the conduit system which ran down Jacob's Wells Road, a subterranean structure was discovered just to the north of the junction with Constitution Hill, and this was recorded between 1987

Figure 6.79 Reconstruction of part of Spicer's Almshouse, Nos 94–102 Temple Street (reproduced from Williams 1988, fig 10)

and 1989 (BHER 282). Apparently consisting of a single chamber cut into the hillside, the stone lintel over its entrance bore a barely legible inscription which appeared to be in Hebrew. This immediately suggested that the monument was associated with Bristol's medieval Jewish community and it was interpreted as a *mikveh*, a bath for ritual purification (Emanuel and Ponsford 1994). Subsequent removal of overburden in front of the chamber by the owner revealed what appears to be a second, lower, chamber of unknown size. It has been suggested that at least one of the letters of the inscription is the Hebrew character *chet* and this is confirmation of a Jewish association (Hillaby and Sermon 2004, 128–9). Yet, given its condition, the interpretation of the inscription is (and is likely to remain) uncertain, leaving the character of

the entire monument in dispute. An alternative reading of the inscription, together with the distance from the Jewry, and the proximity of the cemetery led Hillaby and Sermon (2004) to suggest that the monument was instead a *bet tohorah*, for the preparation of corpses before interment (Fig 6.80).

However, the Jewish connection with this monument has been doubted by some, including James Russell, who has suggested that, at least by 1235–45, any Jewish connection with the monument must have ceased, if indeed it had any connection at all, when the rights to the spring were acquired by St Mark's Hospital (Russell 1999).

After expulsion of the Jews from England in 1290 the cemetery was rented out and the accounts of the Constables of Bristol Castle record the rent for the site in the subsequent

decade (Veale 1933, 74; Hillaby and Sermon 2004, 140).

Houses and housing

The available evidence for the forms of housing to be found in Bristol prior to the late medieval period is, as we have seen in the previous chapter (*see* p 115), extremely limited – a combination of lack of excavated sites in the central core and the frequent inaccessibility of street frontages to urban excavators. This picture begins to change from the 14th century as buildings begin to survive to the present day (over 100 houses survive from before *c* 1700 and over 360 have been recorded), or survived long enough to be recorded by the city's artists and antiquarians (Leech 2014, chapter 1). Historical evidence survives too, in particular probate inventories,

from the early 15th century on, listing portable goods and furniture on the death of their owner, listed room-by-room and therefore an invaluable source for the layout of houses and – with caution – the use to which different rooms were put. And, with the survival of contemporary rentals, comes intriguing evidence of the polarisation of wealth in the city in terms of the housing available to the rich and to those of less prosperous means, if not to the very poorest in society who remain, as ever, virtually invisible.

The characteristic house-type of the wealthiest citizens was the hall-house – distinguished by an open hall, the principal room, open from the floor to the underside of the roof and internally arranged with a high end (better heated, more secluded, more architecturally distinguished) and a low end (more accessible, less comfortable,

Figure 6.80 Conjectured bet tohorah, *No 33 Jacob's Wells Road*

decoratively plainer). But within this house-type enormous variation is evident in terms of architectural distinction, the size of the building, the space available on the plot and how the hall was fitted around or took precedence over its urban surroundings and the ever-present imperatives of commerce.

Perhaps the best single exemplar of the housing of the medieval urban elite is Spicer's Hall on Welsh Back, built for Richard Spicer (d 1377), thrice mayor between 1354 and 1373, one of Bristol wealthiest merchants. Spicer's Hall (which was gutted by fire during a bombing raid in the Second World War) occupied a plot wide enough for the hall to be built parallel to the street, set back behind the commercial frontage. It was accessed via a passage from the street, through a door whose fine contemporary Gothic detailing advertised the sophistication of the house behind.

Figure 6.81 Spicer's Hall, looking north in 1826. Note the inserted first floor, with arches in the north and west walls extending below and the top of a window in the east wall, by T L Rowbotham (Braikenridge Collection, BRSMG M2244)

The passage led, first, into the hall, from which it was separated by a screen; beyond the hall it led into a rear courtyard. At the far (north) end of the hall, under its fine open timber roof, was the high end, lit from the courtyard by a tall oriel window; the hall was probably heated by a central hearth set in the floor rather than a wall fireplace (Fig 6.81).

At the opposite end, on the other side of the passage, was a two-storey block with a stone-vaulted ground floor and a private chamber above. Next to it, on the frontage, was a three-storey block containing further living accommodation serving the hall, communication between the two being via a gallery over the entrance passage. There were more buildings at the back of the plot close to Baldwin Street (Leech 2014, 90–1).

On the street frontage north of the entrance passage were two further buildings (7a and 7b Welsh Back) built for Richard Spicer, but for renting out rather than his own household's use. They appear in a later rental as 'shop-houses', in which the principal accommodation was a room over a ground-floor shop, without an open hall. Each was of three storeys and was owned separately from the remainder of the Spicer's Hall plot by the mid-15th century; Spicer appears to have had other, similar, investment properties fringing his plot to the north on Baldwin Street and to the west on Back Street (Leech 2014, 119).

More modest hall houses than Spicer's Hall, their planning adapted to smaller and more restricted plots, are known across the city from archaeological and historical sources. In Redcliff Street the excavated plots Nos 70 and 72 contained structures, including an open hall on No 72, built at right-angles to the street down a narrow (17–18ft wide) plot (Fig 6.82) (R H Jones 1983; Leech 2014, fig 5.1); the hall was approached and no doubt lit from a passage to one side.

Similarly at No 144, a hall lay at the back of the plot, at right-angles to the street, served by a passage. Early 19th-century watercolours reveal similar hall ranges running back from the frontage behind Nos 12 and 13 Baldwin Street (Leech 2014, figs 5.4, 5.5). Halls of 14th- or 15th-century date have also been recorded on Christmas Street at Nos 1 and 2 (Leech 2014, fig 5.6) and 24 (ibid, fig 5.7 and chapter 5).

How were such buildings lived in? Towards the end of this period, probate inventories begin to survive and show how the houses of at least the better-off townspeople may have been furnished. The probate inventory of Giles George, who lived in or near Broad Street or Small Street, survives from 1496. Her house had two ground-floor rooms, the hall and the kitchen: the hall was clearly the main living room as the iron goods for the hearth are listed, together with furniture (tables, stools, chairs, a banker and cushions), lighting (a five-light candelabra) and decoration (cloth hangings). This sounds like the back, living quarters, of a house whose frontage, probably with storeys over a shop, was already in separate ownership and therefore left out of the inventory (Leech 2014, 91).

The very smallest urban open halls, often only of a single bay width, are not as evident in Bristol as they are in some other towns, Coventry for example. This may be a question simply of survival and the availability of the evidence – in the sense that such buildings are the least likely to have survived the subsequent centuries of dynamic economic growth – but there are indications, as Roger Leech has recently noted from the documentary evidence that such buildings may in reality have been uncommon. Rentals, surviving from the early 15th century, make a clear distinction between 'hall houses' – properties distinguished by the presence of an open hall – and 'shop-houses', where a shop was present without an open hall and the principal domestic room was placed on the first floor, over the shop. It is also clear that hall houses were almost invariably let for more substantial rents than shop houses. Shop-houses usually had only the shop on the ground floor, implying very restricted single-cell footprints, although potentially multi-storeyed (Leech 2014, 70). Such buildings could also be unheated – surprising, given modern notions of comfort – although cooked food was readily available from nearby cookshops and warmth was obtainable in taverns.

Shop-houses were common across the city, and a surviving contract from 1472 shows how they might have been built. The contract was between the client, Alison Chestre, and a carpenter, Stephen Morgan, for a new house on the High Street. It was to have a shop, a hall above with an oriel window (presumably projecting from the frontage), a chamber above the hall and another chamber above

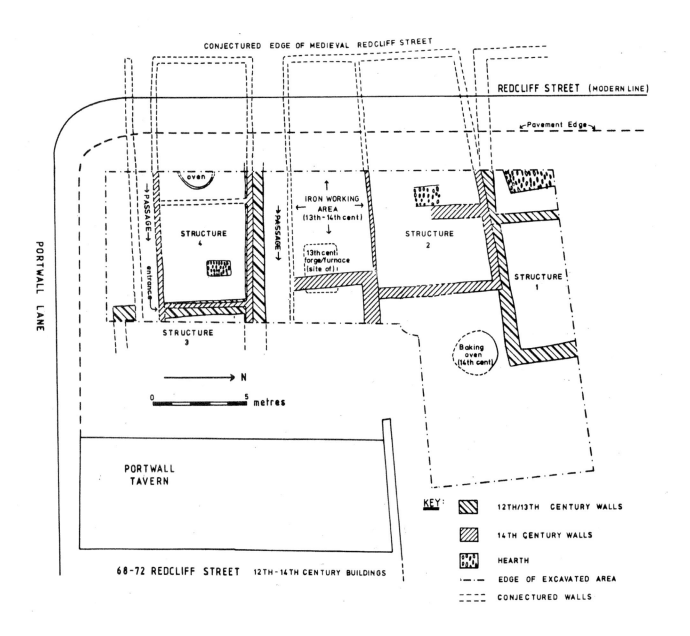

Figure 6.82 Plan of excavation at Nos 68–72 Redcliff Street (reproduced from Jones 1983, fig 2)

that. In short, this was a four-storey (unless there was a pre-existing or pre-contracted cellar) shop-house, built on a single-cell footprint in one of the city's principal streets. Very similar buildings can be identified in the surrounding streets with the central Carfax in particular dominated by an even simpler form, the shop and solar, two-storey, one-up-one-down buildings. And, although, according to contemporary rentals, shop-houses without open halls generally tended to be the cheaper properties, there was nevertheless a wide social spectrum of people living thus 'over the shop' (Leech 2014, chapter 6).

From the very end of the Middle Ages, in the late 15th century, there are indications that wealthy Bristolians were beginning to adopt a different lifestyle, one in which the hall no longer combined the functions of a semi-public or ceremonial space with that of the principal living room. The latter was increasingly a more private space, either a single room (later called the parlour) or, for the wealthiest, a suite. The best single exemplar of the trend is Canynges House (95–7 Redcliff Street), the property of William Canynges (d 1474), a wealthy merchant and five times Mayor of Bristol.

Figure 6.83 William Canynges Hall, Nos 95–7 Redcliff Street, in 1821 by Hugh O'Neill (Braikenridge Collection, BRSMG M2048)

There was the usual commercial frontage, behind which was the great hall (Jones 1986; Leech 2014, fig 5.37–8), accessed by a passage running between the shops (Figs 6.83, 6.84). The hall, together with its fine arch-braced roof, survived until it was demolished for road widening in 1937.

Beyond the hall was probably a parlour, initially at least a room of some pretension containing a fine tiled floor (Fig 6.85). This

was removed in 1913 and is now housed in the British Museum. Beyond this lay a courtyard closed off by a range built across the plot. Beyond that, and a second inner courtyard, was a new range, described by William Worcestre as 'a fair tower' but occupying the full width of the Avon waterfront. It was built of stone, with four great windows overlooking the river (Fig 6.86).

As Dr Roger Leech has pointed out, not only did this building provide the last word in private quarters, far away from the street and even the hall, it emulated palatial mercantile houses in other great cities, notably London and Bruges. It may even have accommodated Edward IV on his visit to Bristol in 1461 (Leech 2014, 95). Although William Canynges probably rebuilt the old great hall too during his ownership of the property, the social centre-of-gravity of the establishment had nevertheless shifted – the hall was not yet a mere entrance lobby (as in the modern

*Figure 6.85 Tile floor
from Canynges House, now
in the British Museum
(Bristol Reference Library.
Braikenridge Collection,
vol XXIV part 1,
pp 770–1)*

usage of the word), but it was on the way to becoming one.

Industry, economy and trade (Fig 6.87)

Bristol was a major manufacturing and processing centre for the region throughout the Middle Ages. A pottery-manufacturing centre, its ceramic wares are found widely in Europe. Its trading links were clearly wide: connections with Ireland established in the early years of the town remained important; so too did the trade with France, particularly the importation of wine. These trading links can to be traced to some extent through the distribution of imported ceramics but the volume of such wares found during excavation is generally quite low, suggesting onward shipment. Documentary evidence points to the presence of some highly specialised trades, for example bell-casting, which relied on serving a wide catchment. The ancillary industries of the medieval port, most notably shipbuilding, are archaeologically entirely unknown, though major vessels were being built. William Worcestre records a rope house alongside the Avon and the use of the Frome frontage near Marsh Gate for shipbuilding (Neale 2000, 23). There are other documentary references to masthouses and storehouses in Marsh Street, with trades associated with shipbuilding being located there. Analysis of the occupational structure of the town before the 15th century is difficult because the records of admissions to craft guilds have not survived, but Penn's study of the distribution of craft-related surnames from the 1313 tallage suggests that Redcliffe was an important industrial quarter (Penn 1989, 69). The archaeological evidence for medieval industry is far from uniformly distributed, reflecting the still uneven spatial distribution of excavation. The majority has come from Redcliffe, tending to confirm the picture presented by the historical evidence of an area dominated by the cloth industry.

Figure 6.86 North wall of 'Canynges Tower' in Redcliff Backs (photograph D Martyn)

Industry, economy and trade in Redcliffe

Successive excavation sites from both sides of Bristol Bridge south along Redcliff Street have produced well-preserved evidence of processes associated with the medieval cloth industry.

Just east of the bridge, an excavation on the western half of the Courage's Brewery site (BHER 3770) found, inland from a 13th- or 14th-century quay wall, a series of contemporary hearths. These were circular structures with a stokehole on one side and were interpreted as probable vat bases, associated with the dyeing industry. Sampling of the fills of a ditch and other deposits identified teasels and dye plants, but also straw and hay implying the stalling of animals nearby. Part of a domestic building roofed with green-glazed ceramic tiles was also found, but the majority of the site appeared to have remained open ground used for industrial purposes (Jackson 2006a). More

recent excavation of the Brewery site (Finzels Reach) in 2007 showed that the plots, laid out in the second quarter of the 12th century, were at first characterised by timber-framed buildings on the frontages with industrial activities (smithing and tanning) behind. The medieval waterfront was originally defined by a wattle revetment, replaced in the mid-13th century by a wall. The construction of buildings on stone footings in the mid-13th century was broadly contemporary with the intensification of activity along Temple Street. The textile industry – represented by excavated ovens, hearths and wells and abundant remains of the dye plants madder, weld and dyer's greenweed – came to dominate the site and supersede earlier trades, seemingly being carried out on an almost industrial scale after *c* 1200 (Teague and Brady 2107b, 133) (Fig 6.88). There was also evidence from this site for the use of teasel heads for cloth fulling (Jones 2017, 272).

Figure 6.87 Distribution of medieval industries from archaeological and documentary sources

Key
Cutlers Location of medieval industries known from documentary sources

Dyers Location of medieval industries known from excavated evidence

Tanners / Whittawers
Metal Workers
Castle Mill
Iron and Copper Workers
Soap Makers
Cutlers
Mercers
Grocers
Goldsmiths
Cookshops
Cordwainers
Butchers
Fish Market
Mill
Iron Workers
Coopers
Turners
Hoopers
Shipbuilding
Weavers
Tenter Racks
Tanners
Dyers
Fullers
Dyers
Copper Workers
Dyers
Smiths
Dyers
Mill

0.5
Kilometres

Figure 6.88 Finzels Reach. Late 14th- to 15th-century hearth (reproduced from Ford et al 2017, fig 3.28)

A site to the south-west of Bristol Bridge (BHER 341) found a series of medieval docks; next to one of these in the late 13th century stood a dyer's or a soapmaker's workshop; this stood until the quay was redeveloped in the 14th century (Williams 1982).

Excavations at No 2 Redcliff Street in 2007–8 (BHER 4456) found extensive evidence of industrial activity, with pits containing tanning or dyeing waste from the 12th and 13th centuries associated with substantial timber buildings. Later in the 13th or 14th century these buildings were rebuilt on stone foundations and tenement boundaries established that persisted into the 19th century. A number of stone-lined hearths were built, possibly associated with

dyeing. A well-preserved stone-lined cistern containing quantities of madder was found, reinforcing the perception that there was a medieval dyeworks in operation (Figs 6.89 and 6.90).

In the mid-14th to early 15th century a copper working furnace was built, probably for the production of cauldrons/posnets. Further furnaces were constructed in the period between the early 15th and late 17th centuries (*see* Chapter 7) (Alexander 2015).

The excavation at Dundas Wharf in 1982–3 (BHER 344) found, in the tenement on the south side of a slipway, two circular hearths, 1.5m in diameter with a stokehole on the western side. The function of these could not be determined from internal evidence but they were interpreted as

Figure 6.89 Nos 1–2 Redcliff Street: stone-lined cistern containing madder residues (reproduced from Alexander 2015, fig 3.13)

possible dye vat bases. A dump of dye plants was found behind one of the river walls indicating that dyeing was taking place in the vicinity but it was not possible to link this to the hearths (Good 1991). However, documentary sources suggest that dyers occupied part of the site in the second half of the 15th century (*see below*). At Nos 95–7 Redcliff Street, the excavation in 1983–5 (BHER 447) found a 13th-century quay wall with a slipway. On its south side, a large stone building several storeys high was erected: six ovens, on average 1.5m in diameter, inside it suggested that it had an industrial rather than a domestic use. The ovens were again interpreted as the bases of dyeing vats (Jones 1986).

At Nos 83–7 Redcliff Street, at the south end of the street, excavation took place on the frontage in 1980 (BHER 342) and at the rear in 1999 (BHER 3501). The sequence began with construction of a stone slipway in the 13th century; in the 14th century, a new building was constructed on the street frontage while small-scale dumping was taking place at the rear, followed by a more substantial reclamation episode to raise levels. In the mid-14th century a series of tenements was built on Redcliff Street while the newly levelled area remained a utilitarian space with waste being dumped over the riverbank. Sampling of these deposits identified domestic rubbish and also dyeing waste. In the late 14th century a new timber-framed building was constructed on Redcliff Street. This was clearly industrial in character and a loom-base, hearth and associated system of drains were recorded inside, leading the excavator to interpret the building as a dyer's workshop. The interior of this building was reordered in the 15th century and a large loom was inserted into a principal room on the street frontage. A hearth, interpreted as a bakehouse and oven, was found above the slipway at the rear of the building (Williams and Cox 2000).

To the south of Redcliffe Way relatively little fieldwork has taken place. On the west side of Redcliff Hill in 1970 several pits were excavated, one of 14th- to 15th-century date producing burnt clay, ash and pottery wasters which led to the identification of Redcliffe ware (BHER 421; Moorhouse 1971, 152).

*Figure 6.90 Nos 1–2
Redcliff Street: mid-14th-
century circular stone-built
hearth (reproduced from
Alexander 2015, fig 3.14)*

The spatial organisation of industry in Redcliffe: a summary

Excavation suggests that there was a quite definite spatial organisation of industry within the Redcliffe suburb and, within the dominant cloth industry, further zoning of its constituent processes and activities. 'Zoning' at the level of the street or district is apparent in the concentration of dyeing along the western side of the suburb, along both sides of Redcliff Street, with ready access to water, and the corresponding clustering of tenter racks for drying woollen cloth in the open space of Temple Meads to the east. This was not, however, an exclusive geography – other trades were intermingled, quantities of leather offcuts found at Nos 95–7 and 145–7 Redcliff Street, pointing to the existence of leather working on or near both sites. The street name Tucker Street (*vicus fullonum*), east of Bristol Bridge, points to the activities of fullers in that area, reinforced in the archaeological record by the presence of fullers' teasel heads in deposits from the Finzels Reach excavation. At the level of the individual plot too, there was functional segregation: industrial dye-vats and their furnaces, tanks and water-channels in the rear of the plots, with storage and wholesaling space integrated with the wealthy dwellings on the street frontages. And again, the cloth industry did not monopolise these spaces: the waterfronts could be and probably were multi-functional, even to the extent of accommodating William Canynge's new private apartments in the 15th century.

The limited evidence so far collected suggests that there was a different range of industry away from the river. Iron working, bell-casting and the casting of copper alloy objects have been identified close to Portwall Lane, the latter also identified in the northern part of Redcliffe. The 1313 Tallage Roll lists two crockers (potters) in the Redcliffe quarter (Fuller 1894–5, 251). Pottery wasters found on the west side of Redcliff Hill suggest the presence of pottery production in the locality, typically perhaps in an extramural or peripheral location, though the precise position of the kilns remains unknown.

Industry and trade in and around the urban core

Archaeological evidence for medieval industry and trade in the old urban core is less evident, and has been archaeologically recorded on a much more limited scale than in the Redcliffe suburb, although this may be a reflection more of the lack of archaeological opportunity. The urban core generally is most likely to have been the most viable area for manufacturers of the highest value goods (workers in precious metals, for example, a goldsmith is recorded at No 30 High Street (later the Angel) in 1463 (Leech 1997c, 78), but there is likely to have been a marked economic and social differential between the main street frontages and the minor lanes and plot backlands. This appears to be borne out by the excavated evidence that more workaday manufacturing may have been taking place on backland sites. The excavations on the southern side of Tower Lane, for example, recorded horn working and possibly metalworking in the immediate vicinity (BHER 320; 472; Boore, 1984). Leech (2014, 144) has noted the apparent congregation of specific trades in defined parts of the town. Cordwainers were to be found in Mary-le-Port Street and butchers and fishmongers in the Shambles, while the presence of a red-light district might be suggested by the explicit street name, *Gropecuntelane* (now Nelson Street), a name documented in several other medieval towns (Holt and Baker 2001). The river Frome frontage near Marsh Gate was used for shipbuilding, with storehouses and masthouses running back from the quayside.

Just beyond the walls in the Broadmead suburb there is evidence of industrial production more characteristic of the medieval urban fringe, perhaps not surprisingly, given its somewhat peripheral location and its location adjacent to the river: iron working in particular has been found, with evidence for smithing and possibly farriery, perhaps related to the proximity of the castle immediately to the south; lime pits also suggest the presence of tanners or possibly whittawers (Davenport 2013d, 366–7). On the north side of Broadmead, lay the Barres, as previously noted (*see* pp 128–129) possibly the haunt of prostitutes.

As Leech (2014, 15) has pointed out, the four principal streets of the town were laid out to accommodate street markets, while specialised markets existed in other areas: for example, the butchers market in the Shambles (Worshipful Street) and the fish market on the Quay. Cook shops were to be found in High Street, the upper end of the street being known as 'Cokerewe' by 1370 (Leech 1997c, 80–2). Five of the buildings at the north end of High Street were occupied by cooks in 1470, with occasional nuisances being caused by this trade since in that year it was regulated that 'no Coke caste no stynkyng' water in the high' Street' (Bickley 1900, 132–3).

Leech (2014, 145–6) has introduced the concept of *selds*, known in London and Chester and probably equating to large street stalls. These were located on the more central streets, with a number recorded on High Street and at the northern end of Welsh Back, with buildings behind. They appear to be early in date, from the early 13th century at least with only one recorded after the first half of the 14th century. Shops would have been distributed throughout the medieval town, often recorded in medieval deeds, such as a row of shops along Christmas Street recorded in the deeds to the properties of St John's parish in the 14th and 15th centuries. The shops would have been open to the street behind unglazed windows with removable shutters and frequently identified by eye-catching signs and ornamentation (Leech 2014, 147).

The cellars in the medieval town were particularly noted by William Worcestre in 1480, counting a total of 142 cellars in all (Neale 2000, 41–65). Many have been recorded by Roger Leech and others and may have been used for a variety of functions. Many would have been for storage, particularly for wine, given the importance of the trade in Bristol, such as that below the Green Lattice, No 41 High Street, which was let to Richard Haddon, the owner of Haddon's Tavern on the opposite side of the street (Leech 2014, 150). As Leech has pointed out (ibid, 152), the word 'cellar' to Worcestre and other inhabitants of the late medieval town could mean both underground

Figure 6.91 Nos 21–4 High Street. View of quadripartite vault (photograph R Jones)

vaults and above-ground structures, used as 'storehouses'. The excavated buildings at Dundas Wharf, extensions to Nos 127 and 128 Redcliff Street and constructed on land reclaimed from the river (*see* p 139), may have been constructed as storehouses between the 14th and 15th centuries. From 1452 until at least 1496 No 127 Redcliff Street was inhabited by dyers, as was No 128, and the buildings excavated on the waterfront could have been used for the storage of dyed wool cloth, as well as the tools of the dyeing trade (Leech 2014, 153; Good 1991, 39). Another use for the cellars would have been as taverns, with a clear architectural division between the more ornate part where wine or beer was sold or consumed and the plainer rear part, presumably used for storage. At Nos 21–4 High Street, known as 'The George' by 1532 and occupied by a vintner by 1556,

the vaults, which still survive, consist of a quadripartite, four-bay vault, with chamfered ribs, clustered side columns and three-quarter round columns in the corners. To the rear is a plain vaulted chamber, probably used for storage (Fig 6.91).

At No 35 Corn Street, archaeological survey during conversion works in 1995 recorded the decorative vault which lay on the Corn Street frontage, with a less ornate vault to the rear (BHER 372). At No 32 Corn Street, vaults wrongly thought to be part of the crypt of St Leonard's church, can now been seen to be another cellar with a commercial function as a tavern at least by 1532, when it was known as the 'peynted taverne' (Leech 2014, 157) (Figs 6.92 and 6.93).

Bristol ended the 15th century, as a town that was densely occupied, ringed, on its northern and western sides, by religious houses, many

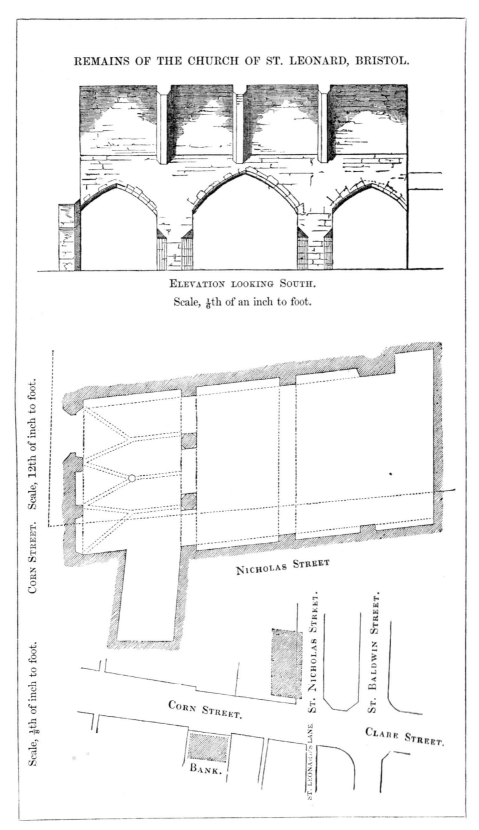

Figure 6.92 Drawing of vaults under No 32 Corn Street (reproduced from Bindon 1853)

Figure 6.93 Vaults under No 32 Corn Street in 1827 by T L Rowbotham (Braikenridge Collection, BRSMG M2294)

with large precincts. Its core was encircled by concentric rings of town walls built, certainly in their second phase, more as an investment in, and a statement of, civic pride and identity, rather than for any defensive function (Coulson 1995). The urban core was not to see major expansion until the later 17th century, so that Smith's 1568 map depicts essentially the town as it had been formed by the major infrastructure works and foundations of the 13th century. The town was not static however, with properties being subdivided to take advantage of the commercial potential of the space. Ancient churches were being rebuilt in the late medieval period and Bristol's merchants were beginning to explore new trade routes, an initiative that was to underpin much of Bristol's subsequent development pattern.

Chapter 7: 'A City and Emporium': Bristol, *c* 1540–*c* 1700

Introduction and historical framework

By 1500 Bristol had long possessed the characteristics of a major city. It was home to probably 10,000 people – native Bristolians, migrants from its extensive hinterland and people from overseas – and provided a commercial and administrative centre for the surrounding counties. This domination of the region was not, however, recognised in its official status and it was only in 1542 that Bristol was formally granted the status of a city. At the same time a new diocese was created with the former church of St Augustine's Abbey as its cathedral.

The four decades between 1520 and 1560 seem to have been a time of economic dislocation as they were in many English towns. The cloth industry, a significant source of the city's medieval wealth, suffered particularly badly, experiencing a decline from which it never really recovered.

While the population of Bristol is thought to have remained at around 10,000 throughout the 16th century, it probably doubled between 1600 and 1700. Like all pre-industrial cities the increase in population required the number of new arrivals to exceed local mortality rates and the broad perspective which has emerged from historical study of migration is that a combination of factors normally lay behind this movement. It has been suggested that many of the people moving westward to the new colonies as indentured servants had probably been forced off the land by enclosure but betterment may have been a greater

motivation as the wealth of the city increased on the back of the Atlantic trade.

National politics

While the city's ruling elite addressed itself primarily to issues of trade and local administration, the intrusion of national political issues into the running of the city could not be avoided. Like all English early modern urban centres Bristol had only indirect influence at national level and this was exerted through patronage relationships. National issues often found expression in conflicts over local powers, and an unusual polemical battle from the pulpits in the 1530s over reform of the Church is one example of this. In March 1533 local clergy invited Hugh Latimer, a supporter of Henry VIII's divorce from Katherine of Aragon, to deliver a sermon. Latimer preached what were subsequently condemned as 'diverse schismatic and erroneous opinions' in support of reform, and when the Mayor invited him to deliver the Lenten services that Easter the local clergy organised sermons in support of the status quo by the friar William Hubberdine and Edward Powell, prebendary of Bedminster. An attempt by the Corporation to arrange a sermon by a supporter of Latimer was blocked by the diocese of Bath and Wells and the controversy thereby became linked with the ability of the Corporation to exercise its powers (Skeeters 1993, 43). The affair ended that summer with a successful petition by the Mayor and Aldermen to Thomas Cromwell for action against Hubberdine, who spent two years in the Tower. Cromwell himself (the city allying itself to a rising star) was invited to become Bristol's Town Recorder.

Broadly, the city maintained good relations with the Crown until the civil wars of the 1640s, despite the disruptions to trade caused by foreign policy and the establishment of monopolies by courtiers at the expense of Bristol merchants. The issue of ship money which arose during the years of Charles I's personal rule did not prove particularly divisive, partly because of the Corporation's decision to meet part of the cost of the assessments from its own resources, £200 of the demanded £1,200 in 1635 and £150 of £800 in the following year (Sharpe 1992, 637). Bristol also sent a draft of 200 men required for the Second Bishop's War in the spring of 1640 (Fissell 1994, 208).

When Charles I raised his standard at Nottingham in August 1642 Bristol tried, like many other places, to take a neutral position but as a strategic port (used, for example, to move troops to Ireland in the 1590s) it could not evade the conflict (McGurk 1997, 165–88). Parliament installed a garrison in December 1642 and a defensive circuit of roughly 4.5km was created which reused the medieval walls but also involved the construction of a new line of defences around the north half of the city, from the foot of Brandon Hill through Kingsdown to Stokes Croft. The mouth of the Avon was defended by requisitioned merchantmen stationed in Kingroad (McGrath 1955, 150).

Royalist forces, with headquarters at Oxford and considerable strength in the West Country, set out to clear the Severn valley of Parliamentary troops and Bristol was assaulted and captured after a brief siege in July 1643. The defences were strengthened over the following year by the Royalist engineer Sir Bernard de Gomme and, among the ports captured that year, Bristol was crucial to the Royalist importation of arms and supplies from France, Holland and Spain (Lynch 1998).

In 1645 the New Model Army launched a campaign to gain control of the West Country, and the recapture of Bristol was one of its major objectives. The Bristol Channel was blockaded by Parliamentary ships and when the fort at Portishead was captured on 28 August they moved up the Severn toward the mouth of the Avon. Their artillery opened fire on 4 September and the army launched its main attack on the east side of the defences on 10 September against Lawford's Gate and Prior's Hill Fort, breaching the line at Lawford's Gate and leaving the Royalist governor Prince Rupert no option but to surrender the city (Gentles 1992, 72–6). With, as one chronicler put it, 'the face of God now shining upon Bristol' a new military governor was installed and the Corporation was purged of royalist sympathisers (Sprigge 1854, 132). That the city was retaken, despite the efforts of de Gomme, was probably due as much to an inability (in common with the earlier Parliamentarian commander) to man such a long defensive line adequately as to any inherent physical or design weakness.

Subsequent fighting did not greatly affect the city, although there was some unrest amongst the garrison troops in 1647 and the civil wars undoubtedly had a negative effect on trade (Firth 1992, 162). Individual experiences give a vivid sense of the disruption of war; the misfortunes of the merchant Richard Locke at the hands of both armies included the requisition of his ships, plunder and burning of his house in Bedminster, and imprisonment (McGrath 1955, 150–5). Some property damage was caused directly by the fighting and Royalist troops fired buildings in the settlements surrounding Bristol as the Parliamentarian forces approached. The greatest destruction was probably in Bedminster (Bates-Harbin 1912, 202), but when compared with the towns of northern and midland England, where many dwellings and churches were gutted, the area escaped relatively lightly (Porter 1994, 75–89). The sieges which preceded the assaults were short and there was no attempt to subject Bristol either to intense bombardment or to mining which related to a more general inhibition in the use of siege-trains because of, Parker suggests, the danger they faced in moving around the country (Parker 1996, 26).

The expansion of the naval fleet begun by the Commonwealth government and continued after the Restoration meant an increase in shipbuilding which could not be accommodated in the naval dockyards and was therefore dispersed to other ports, Bristol among them. Civilian vessels were also drawn into naval service to fill out the fleet; during the Second Dutch War of 1664–7 a number of merchantmen, including some Bristol ships, were hired to act as men-of-war (Fox 1998, 15). The fleet also demanded manpower and, with its large population of seamen, the city was an obvious source, though recruitment was difficult because of the poor rates of pay (Capp 1989, 287). Impressment was hindered by a lack of holding facilities for its victims and the city authorities were required to organise levies, supplying 500 sailors to the Royal Navy in 1664, and 950 in 1678 (Davies 1991, 74).

Bristol celebrated the accession of Charles II and the new king visited the city in the early autumn of 1663 (Hutton 1991, 210). However, the Restoration inaugurated an extended dispute between the Corporation and the Crown over the membership of the City Council. The Corporation was slow to grant restitution to royalist supporters, and royal confirmation of the charters of the city was delayed until those who had been excluded from power after 1645 were restored (ibid, 168). Even after this issue had been resolved, disputes between the Crown and the Corporation continued, with the King insisting on the appointment of a Loyalist as town clerk in 1676. The reaction to the Popish Plot and the Exclusion Crisis of the early 1680s included both the revocation of borough charters and measures against dissent. Bristol's charters were replaced, not without controversy, by a new charter in 1684 which gave the Crown considerable control over appointments (Latham 1947, 29–56). As a result so many burgesses were dismissed that the value of corporate offices was reduced and it became impossible to fill vacancies. Administration was effectively paralysed; no ordinances were passed while the charter was in force and the city descended into debt.

Bristol was generally held to be one of the most disaffected cities in the realm by the time of the Duke of Monmouth's rising in 1685, and as the most significant urban centre in the South West, Monmouth's forces settled on it as their primary objective. In the event the rising gained little support from Bristolians, although the Bristol lawyer Nathaniel Wade was an important adviser to the Duke. Wade dissuaded him from making an attack on the south side of the city because of the strength of the defences there. Instead, while making a feint at Bristol, the army marched to Pensford intending to launch a surprise attack on the city from the east and thereby increasing the chances of success. Foiled by the weather and the rapid approach of the royal army, Monmouth's troops withdrew into Wiltshire, then to Somerset and final defeat at Sedgemoor (Clifton 1984, 180–5). In October 1688, just before James II escaped to France, the 1684 charter was withdrawn and the previous situation reinstated. Bristol was occupied in the name of William of Orange by Shrewsbury's troops but the action was unnecessary as the city's attitude to the Glorious Revolution seems to have been supportive.

Trade

Bristol entered the 16th century with a number of established trading relationships, ranging from the Baltic to North Africa and notably with Ireland, which continued to form a substantial proportion of the city's commerce (40 per cent in the later 16th century). In the second quarter of the 16th century, John Smythe, for example, exported cloth, wheat and lead from the mines at Mendip and brought in raw materials and luxuries, iron and oil (sold for soap-making and use in wool working) from Spain and wine from Gascony, while in 1667 another Bristol ship, *The Mayflower*, carried a similar cargo to Livorno (Vanes 1974, 3–11). When the Crown granted exclusive rights to trade with Iberia to the Spanish Company in 1577, 76 of the members were Bristol merchants and by the time those rights were renewed in 1605 the number stood at 97 (McGrath 1952, 2–3, 20–3). Bristol maintained its commerce with the Mediterranean world throughout the 17th century, trading with Cadiz, Livorno and Venice though its volume was reduced. Bristol ships either sailed direct to the Mediterranean or used a triangular route, sailing to Ireland or to Newfoundland to fish directly or more commonly to buy fish from local fishers, and returning to Bristol with a cargo of consumer goods (Pagano de Divitiis 1997, 110–11).

However, the period between 1500 and 1700 has long been seen as important in the foundation of Bristol's remarkable 18th-century prosperity as it was in these two centuries that the city's commerce shifted its focus from Gascony, the dominant trading partner of the late Middle Ages, first to Iberia and then, because of war with Spain in the 1580s and the mid-1620s, to the Atlantic.

Perhaps the most important aspect of Bristol's history in the 17th century was its emergence as a major Atlantic port from the 1630s. The port was not much involved in the various 16th-century expeditions. Its merchants did, though, trade with the Spanish and Portuguese Atlantic islands until the war of 1585, exporting woollens, other textiles and some luxury products in return for commodities, sugar, wine and woad, previously acquired in either Iberia itself or in other Mediterranean countries (Scammell 1986, 298–9). When war terminated this commerce some Bristol ships took instead to privateering, with varying degrees of success (Andrews 1959, 59–71).

However, it was when the English colonies in the Caribbean and on the American mainland had been firmly established in the mid-17th century that Bristol really became engaged in the Atlantic trade. The colonies were at first a mixture of tobacco plantations and smaller farms producing other commodities, notably cotton, and were worked mainly by indentured servants: some transported as punishment but many others using the agreement of indenture as a means of reaching a better life in the New World. Many of those who sailed from Bristol came from the towns and villages of its hinterland but other travelled from as far afield as East Anglia (Hargreaves-Mawdsley 1954). Of the emigrants to Pennsylvania the majority, outside London, came from the West Country, specifically from Bristol, and most of the men were artisans (Dunn 1986; Vann 1986, 160–1). From the 1640s the West Indies' planters changed their production to sugar to take advantage of a rise in prices caused by the Thirty Years War. Barbados led the way with considerable Dutch financial and technological help and initially New Amsterdam merchants transported raw Barbadian sugar to the duty-free ports of Rotterdam and Amsterdam (Matson 1998, 75).

The switch to sugar led to the adoption of a labour force of African slaves and the English slave trade developed in response. It was controlled by the Company of Royal Adventurers into Africa with Bristol merchants only becoming directly involved to any great extent after the monopoly was ended in 1698 (Beckles 1998, 227–9). An idea of the scale and diversity of Bristol's trade towards the end of the 17th century is given by the records of the Society of Merchant Venturers: in the year beginning in September 1685, for example, 2,602 hogsheads of sugar were imported from Jamaica, 7,050 hogsheads of Virginia tobacco, and 231 bags of cotton wool from Barbados.

Goods also arrived in those twelve months from places as far afield as Gallipoli, Riga and Newfoundland while animal products but also linen and fish arrived from Irish ports (McGrath 1955, 288–93).

Urban growth

General trends (Fig 7.1)

As already noted (p 233), in the first half of the 16th century the cloth trades in Bristol – a staple industry of the medieval town – went into terminal decline and the urban population remained more or less static at about 10,000 throughout the century. There is very little evidence of an increase in the built-up area at this time – in fact the reverse is true, with archaeological evidence beginning to point to a contraction at the margins of the settlement in those districts where the cloth trades had been particularly important, notably Redcliffe and Temple. The contraction appears to have taken place in the early or middle part of the century and lasted into at least the early 17th century. For example, at the southern edge of the suburb, on the corner of St Thomas Street and Portwall Lane, excavation (BHER 451) of a late medieval building which had been used for metal casting found that it had been demolished in the mid-16th century and the plot used for gardening and for the disposal of tanning waste; it was built on by a new stone building in the 17th century (Good 1989, 23–4). Similarly, excavation on the street frontage of Nos 30–8 St Thomas Street (BHER 3553) found that buildings had been demolished in the early to mid-16th century. The site remained open for many years, a first garden soil developing over the rubble around the end of the century, and a second, distinct garden soil, probably derived from domestic waste, developing across the site even in the later 17th (Jackson 2004). Similar evidence for the establishment of open spaces and gardens is found at the excavations at Nos 55–60 St Thomas Street (BHER 4273), reinforcing the impression of increasing open space in the area from the 15th century onwards (Davenport et al 2011). The fortunes of the Redcliffe suburb revived substantially in the course of the 17th century, with evidence from excavation and pictorial sources for the renovation or renewal of a good deal of the building stock.

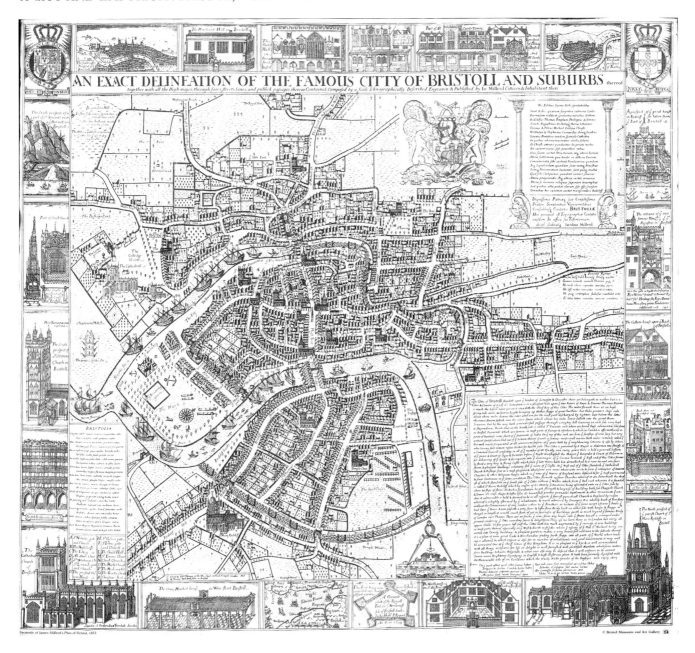

Fascimile of James Millerd's Plan of Bristol, 1673

© Bristol Museums and Art Gallery

Central Bristol, the castle and the Old Market

The basic medieval topography of the historic core of Bristol remained essentially unchanged through the 16th and the early 17th centuries, despite a rapid turnover in the ownership of property in the mid-16th century as a consequence of the Dissolution of the monasteries and the redistribution of their property holdings. Most topographical change in these centuries in the central areas took place at the level of the individual plot, but even here change was muted, confined to the gradual evolution of the housing stock as changes in use and design, evident since the 15th century, continued (*see* p 217). Bristol also escaped the kind of disastrous fire which destroyed many other early modern towns, largely because of the use of stone in party walls but also thanks in some measure to the efforts of the Corporation which, in an ordinance of 1594, ordered that inhabitants who boiled 'tallow, oils, pitch or such like in their houses, henceforth should provide themselves with out-houses in their gardens, or in other convenient places' to avoid the

Figure 7.1 James Millerd's plan of Bristol of 1673 (BRSMG Mb6690)

danger of fire (quoted in Hall 1957, 127n). By far the most dramatic physical change in central Bristol in this period took place in the late 1650s, following the demolition of the castle and in the context of an improving economy.

The castle, having been outside the jurisdiction of the city since its inception, had been formally incorporated into the city in 1629 and was bought by the Corporation the following year. Following a long period of decline it was refortified in the Civil War and then its demolition, ordered by Parliament, took place in 1655–6. Redevelopment began soon after, with Millerd describing the former precinct as having 'faire streets & pleasant dwellings' (Fig 7.2).

Plots mainly around 6m wide were let along the existing roads within the castle and leased for construction of new houses, limited to three storeys (Ponsford 1979, 58). Generally the buildings were timber-framed with stone party walls, and had gables facing the street frontage. The ground floor on the main commercial streets almost invariably held a shop and there was domestic accommodation

above. An element of uncertainty remains as to the degree to which existing roads within the castle were reused, or new ones laid out at this time. Nevertheless, the 600-year life of the castle had been conclusively ended and a new urban character established over the area that would remain until it was itself ended by further conflict 300 years later.

The redevelopment of the castle also had implications for the Old Market further east, Castle Street and Old Market Street having effectively been turned into a single commercial thoroughfare. Renewal took place within the pre-existing medieval framework of streets and plots, the housing along both Old Market Street and West Street being rebuilt from the mid-17th-century, the visual character of the area changing with it. The new dwellings consisted of gabled buildings of two or three storeys with stone party walls and internal timber framing in many cases. Some at least (No 41 Old Market Street for example) followed a local pattern in having a single room, front and rear, with a central staircase. West Street, as one of the main routes

Figure 7.2 Extract from Millerd's map of 1673, showing the Castle precinct and Old Market (BRSMG Mb6690)

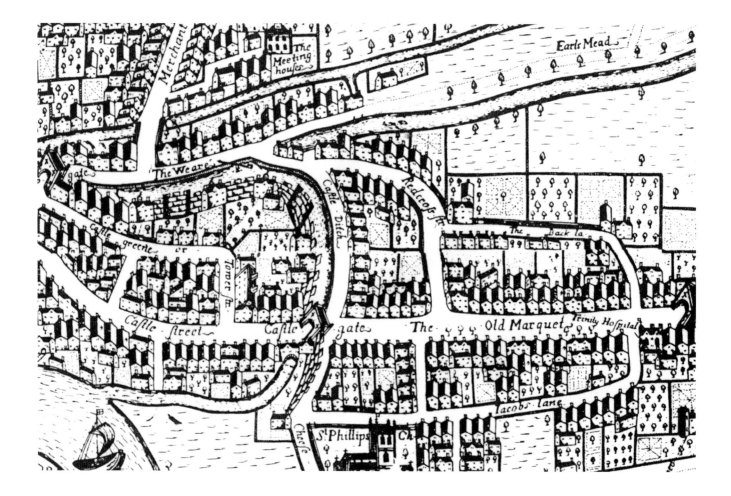

into and out of Bristol, had a number of large inns positioned along it, such as the Lamb Inn, built in 1651 (Fig 7.3).

Away from the main thoroughfares, land lying towards the river and in St Philip's Marsh seems to have remained agricultural: the Mayor's Audit for 1556–7 records the rentals of several gardens on the north side of Old Market in the area of Redcross Street as well as two tenements, 'a Garden and a Stewe to kepe lampernes', while by 1627–8 the tenements, garden and stew were

in the tenure of a Mrs Langley (Livock 1966, 12, 54, 91, 153). There are similar references in other documents and Jacob Elton, father of the MP Sir Abraham Elton, is reported to have been a market gardener in St Philip's Marsh in the 17th century (Latimer 1893, 162).

Lewins Mead and Broadmead (Fig 7.4)
In Lewins Mead and Broadmead the principal physical impact of the 16th century arose from the suppression, between 1538 and 1540, of

Figure 7.3 Lamb Inn, West Street in 1828 by T L Rowbotham (Braikenridge Collection, BRSMG M2783)

Figure 7.4 Extract from Millerd's map of 1673, showing Lewins Mead and the area north of the river Frome (BRSMG Mb6690)

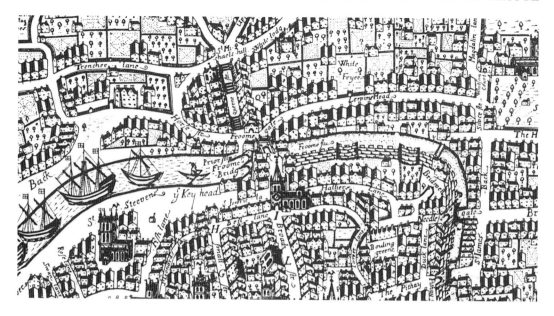

the monastic houses that would have given these districts such a distinctive character in the Middle Ages, and their gradual (or not so gradual) demolition. There was no change in the street pattern established in the medieval period, nor was there much change in the extent of the built-up area, except in one particular respect, discussed below in relation to the hillside overlooking these quarters (pp 241–8).

Lewins Mead comprised a mixture of shops and tenements in the mid-16th century. A renewal of domestic housing seems to have been occurring here, as elsewhere, in the 17th century, changing the visual character of the area. New gabled buildings were put up in the streets around St James's Churchyard, in Lewins Mead, Host Street, Christmas Steps, and College Green as well as Pithay and St James's Back. The houses were commonly two- or three-storey gabled structures, examples of which survive at Nos 68 and 70 Colston Street (Fig 7.5), and some had extensive decorative plasterwork (Fig 7.6).

The density of dwellings on the west bank of the Frome was apparently not as great as in the area of Pithay: buildings fronted on to the street but had gardens behind; a sale document of 1608 for example refers to several tenements in Host Street with 'backside garden and well' (Ralph 1979, 116). Frog Lane and Frogmore Street seem to have comprised mainly two-storey houses or cottages fronting on to the lane with garden plots between and

behind. A few of these 17th-century houses survive here, the most well-known being the Hatchet on the north side of Frogmore Street (Fig 7.7), constructed between 1661 and 1675 (Leech 2014, 169).

Some of this housing was clearly built in blocks, presumably as speculative development, like a group of four, apparently identical, gabled buildings on the north side of Host Street, for example (Winstone 1972, pl 31). Other buildings conceal early modern fabric behind apparently later facades. Inspection of the rear of No 7 Frog Lane in 1998 (BHER 3325), for example, revealed that it is a modest gabled building of two storeys plus attic which was refronted in the 19th century.

The western half of Broadmead remained built up within its basically medieval framework while the eastern half continued as orchards and gardens into the 18th century: Rosemary Street (Rosemary Lane) still ended at a gate leading into a field according to Millerd's 1673 map (Livock 1966, 12) (Fig 7.8). Chester's Almshouse had been built by 1537 on St James's Back but almost nothing is known of this institution.

Although the areal extent of development seems to have remained largely unchanged, the 17th century saw extensive renewal of the housing stock. On the main thoroughfares, where information is most readily available, this new building consisted largely of gabled houses of two or more commonly three

Figure 7.5 Nos 68 and 70 Colston Street (photograph D Martyn)

storeys, often with a shop occupying the ground floor. New building took place in Broadmead, Horsefair, Merchant and Old King Street and the streets on the south side of the quarter, Broad Weir and Castle Mill Street. Some, like Nos 10–13 Broadmead, were clearly built as a group, presumably as a speculative development. There is some indication of a detached kitchen at No 19 Broadmead, and it is likely that other properties had them. In Rosemary Street a terrace of four houses, Nos 18–24, survived until removed for the redevelopment of Broadmead (though No 24 was gutted during an air raid in June 1941). These were two-storey cross-gabled structures, though the ground floor was apparently residential, and the smaller scale of the building here may reflect less intense commercial demand in a peripheral street (Fig 7.9 and Winstone 1964, pl 55).

St Michael's Hill and Kingsdown (Fig 7.10)

St Michael's Hill, overlooking Lewins Mead and Broadmead, entered the 16th century mostly laid out as closes and orchards, with settlement gathered around St Michael's Church at the foot of the hill (Leech 2000e). Much of the land was owned by the Dean and Chapter of Bristol Cathedral, granted to it by the Crown as part of the endowment of the diocese in 1542. By the 17th century the south- and east-facing slopes had begun to be divided into walled gardens owned by the city's wealthy elite, many of the gardens containing a small 'garden house', also known as 'lodges' (*see also* p 245). These 'second residences' were used principally for recreation but some at least probably also had an economic function. For example, the house 'att the hill' belonging to George Lane

stood close to the junction of Queen's Road and University Road; an inventory made at its owner's death in 1631 recorded not only furnishings but also '3 hiues for bees', 'a dozen and half of milk pans' and agricultural tools, suggesting that food production was a significant aspect of the activity within the building (McGrath 1955, 76–8).

The level of development began to increase in the first half of the 17th century – Nos 23–9 St Michael's Hill for example were probably built *c* 1637 (Leech 2000e, 75; Leech 2014, 181) – but remained diffuse and domestic in character (Fig 7.11).

The Commonwealth saw the beginning of a process of development that continued

Figure 7.7 The Hatchet, Frogmore Street (photograph D Martyn)

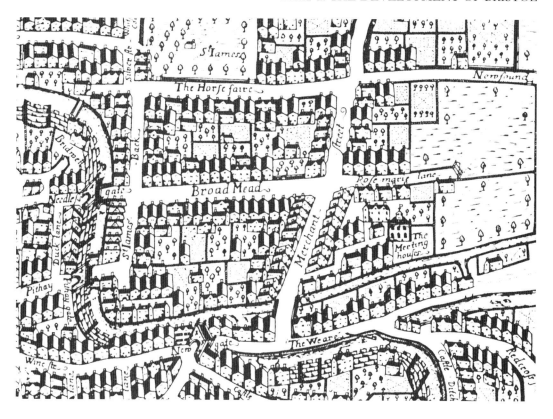

the parish by 1662. The fragmentary 17th-century wall noted at Upper Church Lane in 1992 was probably part of the garden house, later known as Rupert House, built by the merchant Richard Stubbs (Insole and Leech 1998). Houses were built within the Royal Fort from the late 1650s and the remaining parts were apparently converted into dwellings (Bettey 1997, 7; King 2014).

Larger residences were built too, like the surviving three-storey rubble-stone house at the top of St Michael's Hill, Oldbury House, of the 1680s (Fig 7.12).

Charitable building followed the residential when Edward Colston chose the eastern side of St Michael's Hill as the site for his new almshouse at the end of the 17th century (Fig 7.13).

Despite the new building, the hill did not entirely lose its rural character and a windmill standing on the north side of Cotham Road from at least the early 1670s made a highly visible agricultural landmark.

The hillside between Park Row and Frogmore Street was also the site of several garden houses or summer houses from the early 17th century, many of which still

throughout the 18th century, probably spurred by the confiscation and sale of the Dean and Chapter lands. By the middle of the 17th century the number of garden houses had increased, with at least 19 in

Figure 7.10 Extract from Jean Rocque's plan of 1750, showing St Michael's Hill and Kingsdown (BRSMG M707)

survived at the end of the 19th century. No 7 Stoney Hill, for example, was built by Thomas Wells *c* 1664 although there had been a lodge there since 1631 (R Leech pers comm; Leech 2014, 244; Jones 1946, 182–3). Another, a cross-gabled house of two storeys with attics, stood on the south side of Upper Wells Street until 1961 (Winstone 1986, pl 124). The house excavated at Deep Street in 1989 (BHER 444) was also a garden house and is thus unique in being the only example of this type of monument to have been excavated (Ponsford *et al* 1989b). No 10 Lower Park Row was built by 1634 for the merchant George White (Fig 7.14). It still survives and was surveyed in 1978–9 by staff of Bristol Museum in advance of its anticipated demolition (BHER 377) (Bryant and Winstone 1983). It is a house of three

storeys plus attic with a number of mid-17th century features, panelling, panelled doors and fine fireplaces. One in the basement with a bread oven survived until the 1970s. Leech (2014, 244) suggests that given the substantial proportions of the property, White may have used the building as his principal residence rather than as a lodge.

This pattern of suburban development is almost unique to Bristol. While garden houses or lodges can be identified in London (Schofield 2011, 70), they lie within heavily developed areas and have therefore suffered major attrition. On St Michael's Hill, by contrast, some are still extant, many survived into the 20th century and were recorded, and the sites of others are known to survive with relatively little disturbance to their associated deposits. Together they represent an unusual

*Figure 7.11 Nos 23–9
St Michael's Hill
(photograph R Jones)*

*Figure 7.12 Oldbury
House, St Michael's Hill
(photograph D Martyn)*

Figure 7.13 Colston's Almshouse, St Michael's Hill (photograph D Martyn)

Figure 7.14 No 10 Lower Park Row (photograph R Jones)

and significant resource for the investigation of the culture of the mercantile elite of the 17th century.

Development in the Marsh: King Street

Although much of the Marsh remained open space – put to a variety of public and recreational uses – in the 16th century, and was clearly a significant resource for the city, buildings and industrial uses were beginning to encroach upon it (Fig 7.15).

The historical evidence indicates that the area was grazed throughout the 16th and 17th centuries, the Corporation receiving payments for this from the city's butchers. That the Marsh was the site of riotous assemblies in 1549 and 1561 suggests that even then it may also have been a traditional place of assembly. *Adam's Chronicle* reports that in 1572 a structure was erected 'for practice shooting with guns with bullets' (Fox 1910), which may be the 'gonne house' referred to in the Mayor's Audit in 1628 (Livock 1966, 97), while the trained bands used the Marsh for drill in the 1630s (Fox 1910, 113, 203–4; McGrath 1981, 9). The clearest example of the overlap between military and recreation use is the staging there of the entertainment for Queen Elizabeth I during her visit to the city in 1574. A route was laid into the Marsh and a platform was erected there for the royal party to view a large mock battle at Trin Mills, apparently lasting for three days and 'verie costlie and chargeable (especially in gonnepowder)' (Bettey 1985, 7, 9).

The 17th century saw the consolidation of recreational activity there. A bequest was made in 1610 for repairing of the Marsh and the interest of £4 per annum was used to pay two labourers to maintain it (Latimer 1900, 42). A bowling green was also created in the corner in 1622, but was removed to make way for a battery of four guns during the Civil War (Roy 1975, 261). The green was reinstated in 1656, the replacement being surrounded by a low stone wall and given a lodge on one side for the bowlers to use (Hughes *et al* 1996, 10; Exwood and Lehmann 1993, 102). A more common use of the area was perhaps for walking, several visitors to the city in the 17th century commenting on the walks through the Marsh by the elms of the ropewalks.

Some domestic and other buildings were also sited there. The Mayor's Audit of 1557 records a rope house at the southern end of Welsh Back, against the Marsh wall which had 'an essmente in the highe wey to seyne Ropes a dore and a entry into a stable in the mershe with an esmente in the towne wall' (Livock 1966, 4). Another rope house is mentioned near St Clement's chapel at the end of Marsh Street, suggesting that the tree-covered avenues shown by Millerd in 1673 had been established by the mid-16th century (ibid, 14).

Excavation at Broad Quay House (BHER 442) (Good 1987b) implies that the western edge of the Marsh was probably the site of earth-cut shipbuilding docks in the 16th century. St Clement's Dock is the only one of these to have been excavated so far and the archaeological evidence indicates that it went out of use not long after the last ship built there, the *Minion*, was launched in 1581 (*see* p 264). A series of ordinances was made between the mid-1650s and the 1670s to end both shipbuilding and the storage of timber in the Marsh; hauliers were also subject to heavy fines for offences of dumping there (Hughes *et al* 1996, 11–12). By the end of the 17th century Narrow Quay in particular was in demand for building land: the docks were infilled and housing or other buildings erected on the site. Aldersky Lane and Currant Lane were laid out over the site of Aldworth's dock in the early 1670s and a colonnaded corn market (Fig 7.16) was built slightly later at the south-west corner of Currant Lane.

Millerd's 1673 map (*see* Fig 7.15) shows another group of buildings, including what appears to be a substantial dwelling, facing on to the line of the western ropewalk in the area of Assembly Rooms Lane. A process of infilling and building may explain the rather patchy nature of development along Narrow Quay depicted by Millerd, with the open space perhaps indicating sites where docks had been infilled but not built over.

The King Street scheme was the first step in the organised development of the Marsh, begun during the Commonwealth; No 33 King Street was the first of a number of substantial new dwellings built there for wealthy clients. Thomas Wickham signed the lease on a large plot in 1650, agreeing to build six houses within ten

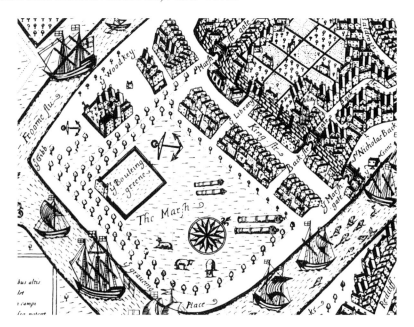

Figure 7.15 Extract from Millerd's map of 1673, showing the Marsh (BRSMG Mb6690)

Figure 7.16 The Corn Market, Narrow Quay, c 1840 (Bristol Reference Library, ref 382/L93.11 Nar)

years. By 1658 No 33 (Fig 7.17), a gabled house of three storeys, attics and basement with an attached warehouse, was complete and several chimneys had been built into the city wall to its north. There is a chimney-piece on the ground floor and the first-floor room overlooking the street has a plasterwork ceiling and decoration (Leech 1997a; Leech 2014, fig 8.45).

Figure 7.17 33 King Street (photograph R Jones)

Also built in the 17th century, Nos 36 and 37 King Street had similar interior decoration, a staircase with splat balusters and a chimney-piece (Pritchard 1906a, 130). St Nicholas's Almshouse was built on a plot donated by the Corporation in 1652. The two-storey gabled building contained sixteen rooms and additional revenue was raised by the letting of the cellars at an annual rent of £10 (Manchee 1831, vol 2, 200).

In the heart of the area, away from the waterfront, the dwellings were less elaborate. Queen Charlotte Street (Back Street) was lined with tenements and shops, several of which had gardens. In 1608 five tenements in Queen Charlotte Street together with two stables and a pigsty which had been converted into a dwelling, and two void grounds in the west corner of the Rackhay, were bought by Robert Byrriatt of Marshfield (Ralph 1979, 116). According to Millerd's map the area west of Queen Charlotte Street was laid out as a mixture of gardens and orchards and one part of a garden close to Rackhay had become a second extension burial ground for St Nicholas's by 1673 (Leech 1997c, 5–7).

College Green (Fig 7.18)

The changes of property ownership which followed the Dissolution at the end of the 1530s liberated plots for housing development. At least three substantial gabled houses were built on the west side of College Green, including Southey House (No 11 College Green) (Fig 7.19), and it would appear that the ribbon of dwellings fronting on to Limekiln Lane (modern St Georges Road; *the way to ye Hotwell* on Millerd's 1673 map) which is recorded by an early 18th-century plan probably originated in the later 17th century; certainly a group of buildings is recorded by Millerd's 1673 map on the north side of St George's Road, at the junction with Brandon Steep (Bristol Archives Corporation Plan Book A fol 39e). On the site of the demolished abbey nave, houses, possibly prebendal houses, were built in the 17th century; a watercolour by Hugh O'Neill in the Braikenridge Collection shows a house of two storeys with attics on the south aisle of the nave and another of three storeys, possibly with a pentice roof, at the east end of the south nave aisle (Fig 7.20).

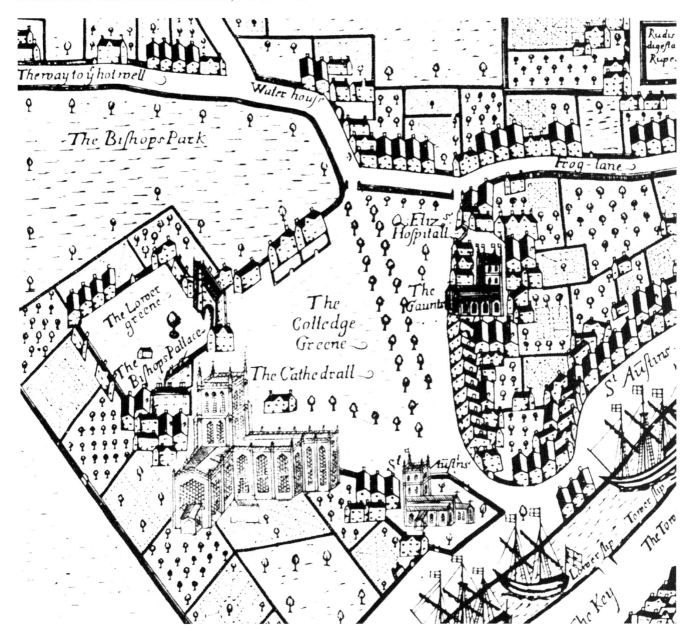

Figure 7.18 Extract from Millerd's map of 1673, showing the College Green area (BRSMG Mb6690)

Excavation to the south of the outer precinct of St Augustine's Abbey (BHER 4455), which had produced important information about the early layout of the area between the outer precinct and the Marsh to the south, showed that the basic arrangement of channels and access to and from the Marsh survived into the post-Dissolution period. There was also evidence for the flood defence of the Marsh, with a bank, probably originally over 4m wide, constructed by the mid-17th century (Alexander and Harward 2011).

Public works: the castle, defences and public buildings

Bristol Castle (Figs 7.2, 7.21)

The decline of Bristol Castle, already evident in 1480 from William Worcestre's account of buildings in disrepair, robbed, or in ruins (p 151), continued in the 16th century. When John Leland visited in the early 1540s he could only note 'the ruines of it' (Toulmin-Smith 1910, 88). The site was formally incorporated into the city by Letters Patent in 1629 and the Corporation purchased it in 1630 (Latham 1947, 144–9). The charter confirming the purchase states that the precincts of the castle included a mansion house occupied by Francis Brewster, 43 tenements, three gardens, a woodyard, and the 'Inner Greene' (Latham 1947, 150–62). Brewster's mansion house was apparently on the east side of Tower Street and had incorporated the entrance porch and antechamber of the Great Hall (Braikenridge Collection, BRSMG M2731–M2733). The Corporation used the castle as the base for the trained bands and in 1631 an armoury was built. A 'hansome Artillery House' in the castle yard recorded in 1634 may be the same building (Ponsford 1979, 49).

With the outbreak of the Civil War, the castle became the base for the Parliamentarian governor, Nathaniel Fiennes. How extensively it was refortified is currently uncertain, but a 'Halfe moone below the Castle' – likely to be the mound recorded by Millerd's plan in the Kings Orchard – probably formed part of this work. In 1643 the Royalist forces captured a total of 33 cannon sited at different locations in the castle (Roy 1975, 262–3). The Royalist engineer Bernard de Gomme described the castle as large, old and weak (Firth 1925, 185) and it was probably de Gomme who was responsible for the mid-17th-century works recorded by a number of archaeological investigations. For example, evidence for the re-cutting of the castle ditch has been identified at New Gate (BHER 24) and on the east side of the castle between Tower Street and Lower Castle Street – together with fragmentary walls of mid-17th-century structures close to the ditch, which may have had a defensive function (BHER 3287; Ponsford 1979, 307–1). The tower at the north-east corner was also partly rebuilt (BHER 488). On the west side of the castle, Ponsford's Site G, part of the curtain wall was refaced in the 17th century (BHER 475; Ponsford 1979, 355).

After the Civil War, Parliament ordered the demolition of the castle. This took place in 1655–6 and excavations in a number of locations have found traces of the work. Ponsford identified the infilling of the ditch and the sally port and the demolition of the north-east corner tower (BHER 3287, BHER 475, BHER 488; Ponsford 1979, 304–11, 353–67). The keep was also plundered for building stone, excavations in 1948 and 1989 finding that the west wall had been almost completely removed by means of intersecting quarry pits with some pillars of masonry left between (BHER 414: Marshall 1951, 16; BHER 459: Good 1996, 25–6). The structures Ponsford interpreted as the east gate of the castle were also demolished at the same time (Ponsford 1979, 301–2).

However, some elements of the castle survived for a period. Millerd's 1673 map shows that New Gate and the East Gate at the end of Castle Street still stood, together with the north and east curtain walls and two mural towers, and the northern and eastern moats. Although the castle appears in 1673 to have been fully redeveloped and built up, it was only the western perimeter, closest to the city's commercial core, that had already entirely vanished.

Excavation has also encountered the new housing of the later 17th century. At Ponsford's site G (BHER 475) a 17th-century cellar was found, together with two stone rubble buildings of similar date at Site D. One of these, interpreted as a house built by the Powell family, was a substantial stone building 6.9m wide with a Pennant sandstone flagstone floor (Ponsford 1979, 354, 96–7).

The city defences

Bristol's medieval defences, having achieved their maximum extent in the mid-13th century, were still substantially complete in the mid-16th: this much is evident from William Smith's map of 1568 (*see* Fig 3.21).

The inner circuit had largely disappeared beneath encroaching housing before the end of the Middle Ages though, as Ricart's *Kalendar* shows, the gates still stood and retained their symbolic significance in the 15th century (*see* p 154). Even by the 1580s all the sections of city wall at slightly further remove from the commercial core survived: the Marsh Wall, extending south from the Great Tower on Broad Quay and east to the Avon; the outer wall from the Frome Gate to New Gate along the southern bank of the Frome, and the Portwall and its ditch enclosing the Redcliffe and Temple suburb.

Figure 7.19 Southey House, College Green in 1919 (Loxton Collection, Bristol Reference Library L917)

There is some archaeological evidence for the maintenance of the defences here, investigation on the south side of Portwall Lane in 1965 (BHER 408) identifying a late 16th- or early 17th-century re-cutting of the Portwall ditch (Hebditch 1968, 134).

A century, and a civil war, later, Millerd's maps of 1671 and 1673 show relatively little change to the city's defences apart from the destruction of the castle: the Marsh Wall south of Broad Quay had vanished beneath housing and, just around the corner, the east–west stretch between the Marsh Gates was still extant although beginning to be obscured as King Street was developed in front of it. Otherwise, the outer wall with its mural towers along the Frome was still intact; so too was the Portwall.

At the outbreak of the Civil War in 1642, the medieval defences may have been relatively complete but they had never been modernised and were ill-equipped to withstand bombardment by gunpowder artillery – although the Portwall remained formidable enough to deter the Duke of Monmouth's attack on the south side of Bristol in 1685. The castle, as we have seen (p 151), was in a state of disrepair after a century of neglect by the Crown. To make the city defensible, new defence lines and artillery positions had to be hastily added to the medieval walls, gates and ditches.

And so, in 1642, a new defensive line was rapidly built to protect the north side of Bristol (Fig 7.22). This ran from a Water Fort commanding the Avon at the foot of Brandon Hill, up to a fort on the top of Brandon Hill, north-east to a fort on Windmill Hill (which necessitated the demolition of the windmill), then on to Colston Fort at Montague Place and across the hill, possibly following the line of the back of Kingsdown Parade, to Prior's Hill Fort, located on the 1st edition of the OS near the western junction of Fremantle Road and Kingsdown Parade, but alternatively located by Russell (2003, 25) near the south-west corner of Fremantle Square. The defences then continued downhill to Stokes Croft, which was blocked by a 'Spurreworck

Figure 7.20 Two gabled houses on the south side of the Cathedral nave in 1821 by Hugh O'Neill (Braikenridge Collection, BRSMG M1887)

in the Line & a strong high Traverse, or Fore worck, watching and shutting up the highwaye, with a strong port of timber barres on the East side of it' (Firth 1925,

184). The gate and the position of the adjacent bastion on the south side of Ashley Road may be identifiable on later mapping. However, Russell (2003, 26) has suggested

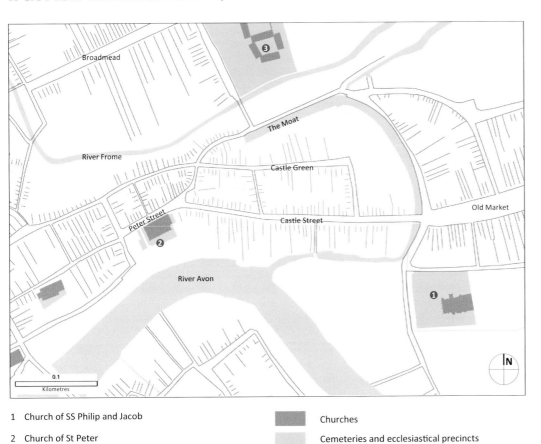

*Figure 7.21 The Castle
precinct in the late
17th century*

1   Church of SS Philip and Jacob

2   Church of St Peter

3   Quakers' Meeting Hall

Churches

Cemeteries and ecclesiastical precincts

that the defences adjacent to Stokes Croft lay to the south, at the junction of Stokes Croft with City Road. He is followed in this by King (2014). The defences then ran to the south-east, through the Portland Square area towards a gun position at Newfoundland Road; the exact line remains, however, unknown.

The nature of the defences is only now beginning to be established by direct archaeological intervention but the Royalist engineer Bernard de Gomme made a brief survey of the whole circuit in which he describes the line across St Michael's Hill as 'of meane strength', at greatest 6ft high and the ditch in front 6ft wide and 5ft deep (Firth 1925,180–203). These new defences adopted some of the principles of *trace Italienne*, the use of bastions along the line with a ditch in front to keep enemy guns at a distance, but, that it was essentially merely strung between individual strongpoints is indicative of the haste with which it was created; indeed it may have merely strengthened or enhanced existing field boundary walls or other features. As far as is known the wall was constructed by drafts of labour using Brandon Hill Grit which was presumably quarried from the external ditch. The historical accounts make no reference to additional features in front of the wall, although these may well have existed. Seyer, for example, noted an angular redoubt in Bullock's Park at the north-western end of Park Street (Seyer 1823, 303). Evaluation trenches (BHER 1129) and a subsequent watching brief (BHER 578) on the north side of Park Row found evidence for a massive ditch orientated north-east to south-west. This was at least 50m long, between 7.5 and 9m wide and, where it was sectioned, 2.2m deep. It was probably part of Essex Fort, just inside the line of the main defences (Fig 7.23) (Bryant, 1994c).

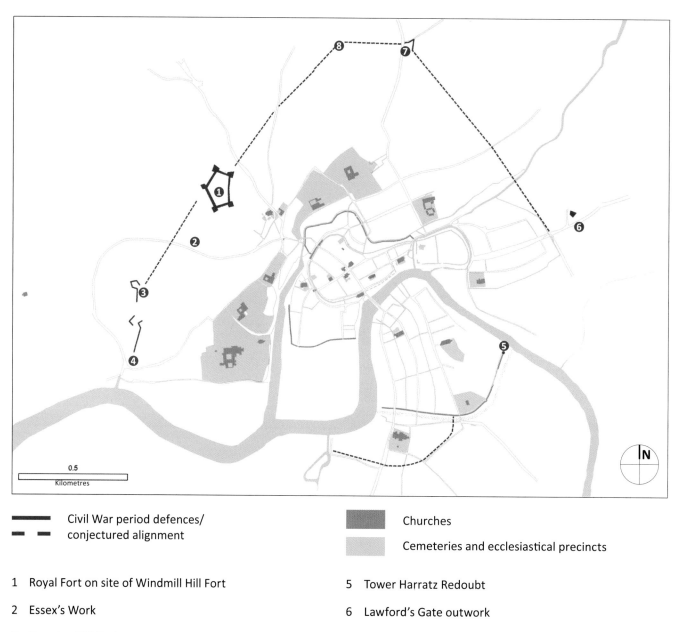

- Civil War period defences/
  conjectured alignment

- Churches

- Cemeteries and ecclesiastical precincts

1   Royal Fort on site of Windmill Hill Fort

2   Essex's Work

3   Brandon Hill Fort

4   The Water Fort

5   Tower Harratz Redoubt

6   Lawford's Gate outwork

7   Stokes Croft Gate

8   Prior's Hill Fort

Figure 7.22 Bristol in the Civil War

Brandon Hill Fort was described by de Gomme as 'some 18 foote square, & as many high; its Graff or mote but shallow & narrow, by reason of the rockynesse of the grownd' (Firth 1925, 184). This fort, and presumably also the Water Fort at the foot of Jacob's Wells Road, was constructed of Brandon Hill Grit. Their precise form has yet to be established but both were gunnery platforms, the Water Fort equipped with two sakers and Brandon Hill Fort with three minions and a 'Rabonett' and both were involved in the skirmishing which preceded the main Royalist assault on 26 July 1643. At the summit of the hill, part of Brandon Hill Fort survives and on the slopes below it the ditches forming part of the line can be traced. However, archaeological evaluation in 2011 found that the upper bastion defensive ditch had been deeply recut in the 1890s. The adjacent standing masonry walls and the earth bank were found to be a folly dating from the later 18th century, although it remains to be seen whether this work reused or sealed an earlier Civil War period construction (BHER 25047; King 2011). In 1897 excavation for the foundation of the Cabot Tower disturbed post-medieval deposits of ash and dark soil containing clay tobacco pipe fragments and lead shot (BHER 2457) and these were close to a part of a structure of 'massive stones' with a floor surface on one side and traces of a passage or another room on the other which may have represented part of the fort (Fryer 1897, 219–20). The earthworks on the hill were surveyed by Bristol City Museum in the late 1980s (BHER 192) and again by James Russell in the 1990s (BHER 3336) as part of a more general examination of the Civil War defences of the city (Russell 2003).

When de Gomme set out to strengthen the line, the Windmill Hill Fort was rebuilt and renamed the Royal Fort, orders for labourers to work on its construction being issued in the summer of 1644 (CSP Dom, 1644–5, 235). In May 1999 geophysical survey, using a range of techniques, was carried out on the site (BHER 3479), identifying part of the inner edge of the ditch surrounding the fort as well as the sites of houses built over the ditch later in the 17th century (Leech 2000e, 20–1). A major excavation took place on the site in 2009 and revealed the eastern ditch, parts of two bastions and a probable barrack block 6m wide and over 26m long (BHER 24786) (Fig 7.24).

At its northern end this building had been dug into the underlying bedrock, possibly to lower its profile and ensure that it was not exposed above the fort ramparts. Contrary to later accounts and depictions, the excavation demonstrated a lack of stone revetment over much of the length of the defences although there was some evidence for masonry revetment at one of the bastions. A stone-lined subterranean chamber, 7.6m wide and 4.3m deep, had packing behind the lining of clay and stone. It is unlikely to have been for water storage since it was found to drain well and has been interpreted as the gunpowder magazine for the fort. Finds from the excavation included lead gun shot, two lead powder flask caps and an iron cannon ball. After the surrender of the city to the Parliamentarian forces in 1645, the Royal Fort continued in use in view of the continuing threat of a Royalist resurgence. It was finally decommissioned and slighted in 1655. Some buildings were stripped for building materials and some stone quarrying was carried out, resuming an activity that had been taking place since the medieval period. Other buildings remained in use. The area became a desirable location for settlement by the wealthy and new buildings were constructed towards the end of the 17th century, incorporating remains of former Royal Fort buildings (King 2014).

A certain amount of the fabric of the fort is still extant, including the gatehouse and a small section of one of its stone bastions to the south of Royal Fort House. These sources, together with property records from the decades after 1660 (including a 1669 diagram of the fort by Philip Stainred) (Fig 7.25) and later cartography, allow the position and form of the fort to be reconstructed (Leech 2000e, 19–20).

In the event, although Prince Rupert considered a direct assault on Brandon Hill Fort, neither fort was directly attacked (Roy 1975, 261; Firth 1925, 185, 195). The breach of the line which allowed the Royalist armies to take the city by storm was made by Colonel Washington's troops in the area of Queen's Road and the fighting proceeded southward toward the historic core.

Old Market was also brought within a new, temporary perimeter, though its precise line has never been discovered. It is known to have passed from Stokes Croft, across the Frome to Lawford's Gate and may then have continued towards the Avon, but whether following the line of the medieval defences or another line, further south, terminating closer to Tower Harratz is not clear. Bryant's observation of a 17th-century wall in 1982, though, may suggest the former (BHER 297). There are references to a gun position at Newfoundland House and a 'platform' at the road to Stapleton (Roy 1975). Old Market escaped heavy fighting during the

Royalist storm of the city in July 1643, but the Parliamentarian army assaulted and captured Lawford's Gate in 1645. Documentary evidence suggests that the gate had been one of the elements reinforced by the Royalists after the capture of the city in 1643; the survey of the ordnance captured in 1643 recorded only one cannon at the gate but Sprigge reports that the New Model Army regiments assaulted a 'double work', capturing 22 cannon and 'many prisoners in the works' (Roy 1975, 261; Sprigge 1854, 125, 116). Russell (2003, 27) infers that the fortifications may have taken the form of an outwork with two concentric lines of ramparts like that identified protecting the east gate at Gloucester and this is supported by the results of a limited excavation well to the east of the medieval defensive line of Old Market (BHER 3923). Here an 'L'-shaped ditch, filled with pre-1660 ceramics and clay pipe, was interpreted as part of defensive outworks constructed during Royalist occupation between 1643 and 1645 (King 2010).

Redcliffe was also affected by the civil wars. The south side of the city was attacked in 1643 by Royalist forces and again in 1645 by the New Model Army, but on neither occasion was there a successful breach of the perimeter. From historical sources it is known that the Parliamentary defenders had mounted cannon along the wall in 1643, three at Tower Harratz, others on Redcliff Gate and Temple Gate, and in the towers along the wall. There was also a cannon on St Mary Redcliffe church and apparently several others in outworks, 'the Hornework at Bedmester gate' or 'the demibastion by Trayne mills' (Roy 1975, 262). On the evidence of the siting of cannon Russell has argued for a line of defences enclosing the southernmost part of Redcliffe which lay outside the protection of the Portwall (Russell 2003, 28–31). This could have consisted of strongpoints linked by entrenchments but there is neither cartographic nor archaeological evidence to confirm the hypothesis.

There is, overall, no clear archaeological understanding of the measures taken to upgrade the medieval defences of Redcliffe. Field investigation in the area has been determined by development pressure and has therefore concentrated on the eastern part of the Portwall. Some evidence of post-medieval re-facing of the wall has been found although the dating is, so far, uncertain. A stair leading to a narrow passageway within the wall, possibly a sally port, recorded in

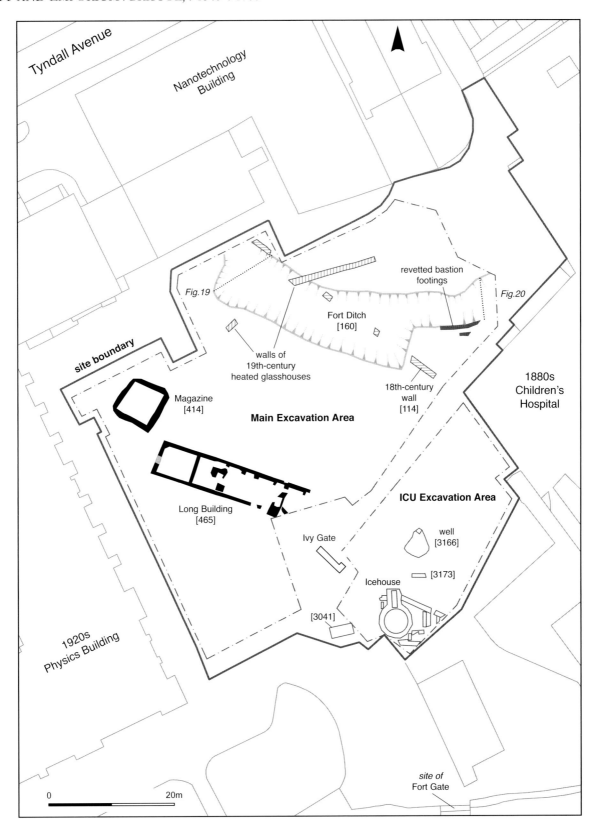

Figure 7.24 Plan of Royal Fort excavation (after King 2014, fig 13)

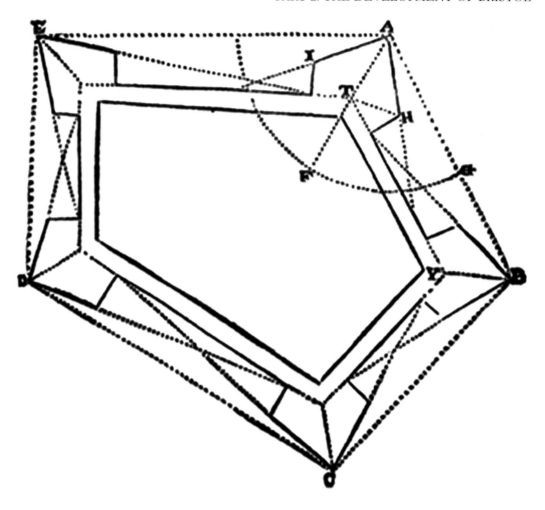

Figure 7.25 The Royal Fort, Bristol: Philip Stainred's geometric plan of the fort (published in Sturmy 1669)

1994 (BHER 463), may have been related to Civil War refortification (Jackson 1994a, 13). Excavation at the Water gate at Temple Quay (BHER 3643) in 2000 found that the gate was subject to major alteration in the early to mid-17th century, when two drain culverts were cut, a new possible musket loop or sally port was created and a new rectangular structure built immediately east of the gate (Cox 2000). To the east of Tower Harratz a small stone building with a complex construction history was excavated in 1997 (BHER 3158) outside the line of the wall: an arched opening in the south wall was interpreted as a musket loop leading the excavator to suggest that it may have originated as a redoubt associated with the Civil War defences (Cox 1997) (Fig 7.26).

The afterlife of the defences

As already noted, the medieval defences – other than the castle – survived the Civil War with little change, though much of the

new defensive line of the 1640s disappeared relatively quickly and the Royal Fort was partially demolished in 1655–6, although substantial elements seem still to have been discernible in the late 19th century.

The Marsh Wall (which had not featured in the fighting) appears to have been the first section of the medieval defences outside the castle to succumb to post-war redevelopment. King Street was created in the early 1660s, probably on the line of the ditch in front of the wall. Buildings were already extant against the wall itself on the north side of the street and plots were being leased by the Corporation to speculative builders by 1663; a typical lease required the building: 'upon the premises in the front part thereof three sufficient messuages or tenements, fitt and convenient for tenants to live therein containing in height three storeys besides the roof within three years next coming' (Ralph 1944, 165). Barton's investigation of

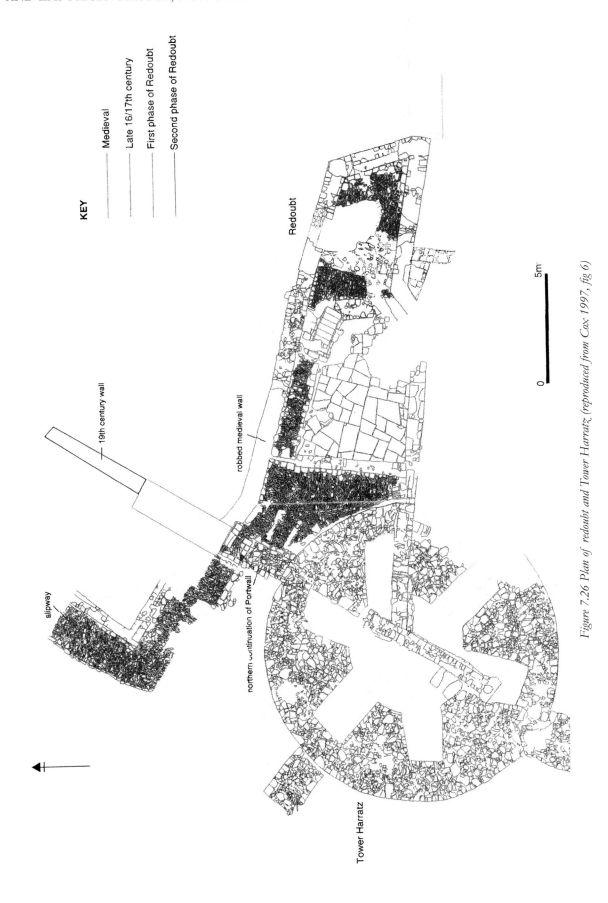

KEY

Medieval

Late 16/17th century

First phase of Redoubt

Second phase of Redoubt

Redoubt

19th century wall

robbed medieval wall

slipway

northern continuation of Portwall

Tower Harratz

5m

0

Figure 7.26 Plan of redoubt and Tower Harratz (reproduced from Cox 1997, fig 6)

a bastion on the Marsh Wall in 1960 (BHER 441) revealed that it was incorporated into a dwelling in the mid-17th century and a flagstone floor laid within it; subsequently it was demolished and sealed beneath the yard of St Nicholas's Almshouses (Barton 1964). In Redcliffe, the Portwall ditch was infilled in the decades around the end of the 17th century (BHER 408, BHER 312; Hebditch 1968, 134).

Public buildings

The public buildings of the city centre were enlarged and improved in the 16th and 17th centuries. The Tolzey was rebuilt in 1550 and in 1617 the height increased to admit five tall windows; by 1657 the Corporation had purchased the adjacent house on the corner with Broad Street to increase the accommodation. It was damaged by fire soon after the Restoration; the repaired structure was a five-bay two-storey building with a portico protecting the area in front of the ground floor, with three nails (bronze pillars used in the course of settling trading deals) sited between the columns. Above the bay leading to the entrance was a statue, probably of Charles II (Fig 7.27).

A second Tolzey, the Merchants' Tolzey, was constructed on the south side of Corn Street *c* 1616 against the north side of All Saints' Church to serve the function of an Exchange. It was removed in *c* 1782, having been supplanted by John Wood's Exchange in 1743 (Fig 7.28).

A market house, described by Millerd as a Corn Market, had been built in the centre of Wine Street by 1673, essentially a pitched roof structure supported by columns along the north and south sides (Fig 7.29).

A new stage was added to the High Cross with effigies of Tudor and Stuart monarchs in 1633–4. The meal market on the south side of Wine Street was built in 1570 and the New Market, on both sides of an alley off the east side of Broad Street was founded in 1598 as a meat market. Nothing is known of these structures archaeologically.

Port facilities at the Quay

The Quay was at the heart of Bristol's maritime commerce and when Samuel Pepys visited a third-rate under construction in the

Marsh in July 1668 he thought the Quay 'a large and noble place'. He also gave a glimpse of the community in Marsh Street, as the 'poor people of the place' rejoiced at the return to her birthplace of his servant Deb (Latham and Matthews 1995, 235–6). Other contemporary visitors note the vitality of the quays and it is known that some of the dockside features were renewed during the 17th century. The crane on Welsh Back, for example, was 'all new made' in 1634 (Fox 1910, 239).

Back Hall continued to be used through the 16th and 17th centuries 'for the keeping and weighing of strangers' goods' and the Corporation was concerned with the condition of the building by the late 1680s when a committee was set up and instructed to inspect the hall. This led to the repair of the 'forepart' of the structure in 1688 (Blockley 1996, 145–6). A tenement at the southern end of Welsh Back (Fig 7.30) was known as the Custom House by 1583 but it is not clear if it actually performed this function. With the next-door tenement, the Rose and Crown, it was granted to the merchants John Gonning the elder and John Gonning the younger and in the 1660s the two properties were formed into a single building which is known to have been used as a Custom House, a structure of three storeys with attics and a rented-out cellar.

Many property documents of the mid-16th century refer to storehouses along the Quay which appear to have consisted of cellars or other storage spaces with a dwelling above or nearby, and this use of the area seems to have continued into the following century (Leech 1997c, 136–41). *Adams's Chronicle* reports that the flood of January 1606/7 inundated the houses of Welsh Back, 'doing much hurt in merchants' cellars to wood, sugars and salt [and] butts of sack did swim in the cellars above ground' (Fox 1910, 183).

Archaeological evidence for actual docks in the Marsh has come from the area of what is now the site of Broad Quay House in Narrow Quay. John Pritchard reported in October 1902 that workmen had found the remains of a boat in the area of Aldersky Lane during 'deep and heavy digging' for construction of a new warehouse for the Co-operative Wholesale Society (BHER 208). This was not the 'shapely

galley of the Romans' Pritchard had hoped for but, he concluded, the remains of a small craft sunk in Aldworth's Dock dating to the 17th century when the dock went out of use (Pritchard 1903, 141); documentary evidence suggests that Aldworth's Dock was built *c* 1625, a date consistent with the archaeology (Latimer 1900, 88; Good 1987b, 33). Evidence for more vessels was recovered in 1956 when deep excavation for an extension to the CWS building probably disturbed the dock once more. These excavations were monitored by F G Webb for the Bristol and Gloucestershire Archaeological Society and parts of at least five vessels associated with 17th-century pottery were observed, the largest having a beam of at least 18 feet. The nature of the work did not, however, allow Webb to make a measured record of the ships before their destruction

(Bristol Archives 39290/FW/LN/20–1; 23) (BHER 453).

In 1978, archaeological excavation before redevelopment of the CWS site by G L Good (BHER 442) recorded the north-east corner of the dock whose stone walls were 1.8m wide. The ribs of a carvel-built vessel, apparently reused to form a working surface, were found close to the north dock wall (Fig 7.31).

When the dock went out of use in the later 17th century much refuse, including butchers' waste, was dumped into it. In a second trench to the north, a large pit, interpreted as the 16th-century St Clement's Dock, was found with a group of stone walls, believed by the excavator to relate to the working of the dock, located on its north side. As was the case with the later Aldworth's Dock, large quantities of refuse had been dumped into the dock,

Figure 7.27 Extract from Millerd's map of 1673, with vignette showing the Tolzey (BRSMG Mb6690)

Figure 7.28 Extract from Millerd's map of 1673, with vignette showing The Merchants' Tolzey and All Saints' Conduit from Corn Street (BRSMG Mb6690)

Figure 7.29 Extract from Millerd's map of 1673, with vignette showing the Corn Market, Wine Street (BRSMG Mb6690)

including leather shoes and textile fragments (Good 1987b). The excavation of St Clement's and Aldworth's docks suggests a possible developmental pattern where earth-cut docks were replaced later by more formal stone docks, but with only two examples excavated from the period, any attempt to understand the industry awaits the recovery of more evidence. The number and positions of other early modern docks is unclear and the question of whether docks were positioned simply in Narrow Quay or along other parts of the waterfront as well is still to be resolved. Aldworth's Dock has produced the largest assemblage of ship timbers so far recovered in Bristol, though the majority were destroyed without study. These vessels are likely to have been roughly contemporary with the infilling of the dock, simply dumped there at the end of their useful lives and it can be anticipated that any surviving parts of Aldworth's dock or infilled early modern docks elsewhere in the Marsh will probably produce equivalent material.

Industrial use of the Marsh in the early part of the 17th century remained focused on shipping. The 1628 Mayor's Audit records a dwelling house and garden in the Marsh, a saw pit 'at the further end of the key', the new house and 'spinninge way' of James Younge and a rope house, and the 'spinninge way to Gibtayler' held by the Society of Merchant Venturers (Livock 1966, 83–4). Shipbuilding continued through most of the 17th century.

The Church

The Reformation was a landmark in Bristol's urban development. Considerable property passed from ecclesiastical to lay ownership in the 1530s and 1540s as a result of government religious policy, and the reorganisation of parts of the physical landscape followed on from this as the new owners reworked the monastic precincts. This was not purely a physical process. In late medieval England the charitable functions of the religious houses and the commemoration of the dead were important elements in the life of the community; chantry and guild chapels, wayside shrines, votive statuary and outdoor preaching crosses were spread throughout Bristol (Duffy 1992, 139). Their significance in the lives of its people can now scarcely be comprehended, but as symbols of the old

Figure 7.30 The Old Custom House, Welsh Back in 1823 by Hugh O'Neill (Braikenridge Collection, BRSMG M2241)

religion their removal was an important part of the Reformation. The process by which they were physically eliminated and reused has seen only limited archaeological study, but is clear in outline. The abbey church of St Augustine became the cathedral of the new diocese. The cloister ranges of St James's Priory were converted into a private mansion, and the same occurred at the Dominican Friary, purchased by William Chester after 1538 (*see* p 275). Something similar seems to have occurred at the Carmelite Friary. At St Bartholomew's Hospital the reuse of the hospital buildings as a school seems to have been achieved with only relatively modest alterations to the fabric, the need to accommodate the remaining almoners until their deaths no doubt inhibiting any more dramatic remodelling of the site. Other religious houses and freestanding chantry chapels like Knape's Chapel, or the Chapel of St John the Evangelist, were either pillaged for building stone or reused for other purposes, the wall paintings whitewashed and forgotten like the 'Noli me Tangere' at St Mark's Hospital or the Old Deanery at College Green (Gill and Howard 1997, 97–8). Stone altars and fittings were often removed to the parish churches though some may simply have been disposed of; the facts regarding the origin of the 'Cristo de Bristol', a figure of Christ belonging to a church in Northern Spain, are lost but tradition holds that it was recovered from the mud of the Avon, where it had presumably been thrown, by the captain of a ship visiting the port and taken to his parish church (Fraser 1935, 153). The parish churches themselves lost their chantry chapels, roods and Easter sepulchres and churchwardens' accounts for several churches

Figure 7.31 Ships' timbers recovered from Narrow Quay in 1978

record the smashing of stone altars, but again the physical process of loss and augmentation, particularly regarding the shifting religious policy of the mid-16th century, has yet to be examined archaeologically (Bettey 1979, 11). Bristol is, however, fortunate in having rich documentary evidence to provide a context for future attempts to understand the effects of the Reformation on its landscape.

The parish churches and chapels of the urban core

While archaeological investigation of the parish churches and chapels of central Bristol has been very limited, only St Mary-le-Port and St Augustine-the-Less having been comprehensively excavated, the 16th and 17th centuries appear to have been characterised by minor structural change, a good deal of which arose as a consequence of the Reformation, and specifically of the suppression of religious fraternities and chantries – the majority of which were accommodated within parish churches. When the chantries were suppressed at the end of the 1540s the stone altars were removed along with other evidence of Roman Catholic religious practice (Skeeters 1993, 81; Maclean 1883–4).

Documentary sources are, at present, more informative on these subjects than the physical evidence. Taking St Ewen's as an example, at the Dissolution the advowson was acquired by Henry Brayne as part of his purchase of the properties of St James's Priory. The Chapel of St John the Baptist was dissolved in 1547 (Maclean 1883–4, 245) and in 1551 the parish rented the chapel site to the Bristol Corporation to allow the reconstruction and enlargement of the Tolzey (Masters and Ralph 1967, xiv). Unusually, for the period, a new two-stage tower was built at St Ewen's in 1637. The Chapel of the Assumption on Bristol Bridge was a freestanding structure and after it was dissolved in 1547 the Corporation bought the building for £40 (Latham 1947, 112–16). It was then rented out as a warehouse and seems to have continued to provide revenue for the city in this way through the 17th century. In 1649 Walter Stephens, draper, was ordered to repair the arch over the highway which was in a dangerous state (Latimer 1900, 224). The Chapel of St John the Evangelist on Welsh Back, belonging to St Nicholas's, was suppressed and seems to have been acquired by the Corporation, which was receiving rent for the site in 1557 (Livock 1966, 55). William

Smith's map indicates that it was still extant in 1568 but it is not mentioned in the Mayor's Audit of 1623 and the cleared site ultimately became an extension cemetery for the parish of St Nicholas. St Clement's Chapel, lying outside the town wall at the end of Marsh Street, seems to have been absorbed into the Merchant Venturers' Hall and Millerd's map suggests that it was still extant in 1673. The chantries in St Stephen's were also suppressed and the single incumbent pensioned off but, in the absence of an analytical survey of the church, the impact of these changes on the fabric are unknown (Maclean 1883–4, 243–4; Skeeters 1993, 155).

Continuing repairs to the fabric of the surviving churches has produced a steady trickle of new information about their evolution and changes to their finishes and furniture. In the early 1920s C F W Dening made a measured survey of the substantial and ornate oak reredos in a classical style installed in 1697 in St Peter's Church (BHER 4096: Dening 1923, 121–3; pl 43); the pews in the church were replaced with box pews the following year (Fig 7.32).

At St Nicholas's, during conservation work in the crypt or lower church in 1983–4, the matrix of a 16th- or late 15th-century brass was uncovered and evidence was seen of a staircase formerly connecting with the medieval upper church (BHER 83, 278 and 3033). At All Saints' Church in 1988 removal of the external render on the south chancel wall revealed a pair of blocked wide semi-circular-headed windows of probably early 17th-century date (BHER 944). In 1998 conservation work in the crypt of St John's found fragments of the wall plaster which had covered the walls of the crypt in the 17th century and several ledger stones set in the floor along with memorial wall tablets, including those to the Donning family and a 'Son of Guildhall', dated to the late 17th century (BHER 3368: Pilkington 1999, 68).

Suburban parish churches and chapels

The impact of the Reformation on the church of SS Philip and Jacob in Old Market is, again, not known in detail. The two chantries of SS Philip and Jacob, founded by John Kemys and by Robert Forthey, were suppressed in the late 1540s but little is known about the effects of liturgical reorganisation on the fabric, although

the stone altars and rood screen were removed as they were in other Bristol churches; a Baroque porch (recorded in a drawing by James Stewart) (Fig 7.33) was added to the church in the 17th century.

St Augustine-the-Less is one of the better-understood Bristol churches as a consequence of its total excavation (BHER 1686) (Fig 8.95). This showed that, in the course of the 17th century, the chancel was rebuilt 1.1m wider, the nave arcades were reorganised and the pier bases reconstructed, while a two-room building, which had probably served as both vicarage and vestry, was added to the south side of the chancel. This survived only as a scar on the new south wall. Burial in brick vaults also began inside the church and a red ochre wash survived on the interior faces of one of these vaults (Boore 1985, 27–8). The 17th century also saw brick burial vaults beginning to be installed in the nave of St Mary-le-Port.

Little seems to be known of the impact of the Reformation on the interior of St Mary Redcliffe, though the churchwardens' accounts for 1550 record payments for repainting of the church, presumably with a view to concealing the medieval decoration (Smith 1995, 111). Little is otherwise known about the works carried out in the years following the Reformation. The two chantries founded by William Canynges were suppressed in 1547. The Chapel of the Holy Spirit, founded in the early 13th century, was also suppressed as a former chantry chapel, with the removal of its altar in 1550. It was later, in 1571, converted into a school, the Queen Elizabeth's Free Grammar and Literature School. The church was repainted in 1550 to remove all traces of 'superstitious images' and the medieval stone altars were removed in 1560. The chancel was levelled in 1566 (Rodwell 2004).

Monastic houses

St Augustine's: abbey and cathedral

When St Augustine's Abbey was surrendered to the Crown in December 1541 Abbot John Newland's rebuilding of the nave was unfinished, the walls standing 'as high as the sills of the windows on the north side and at the west end' (quoted in Bettey 1993, 2). The abbey precinct and nearby lands were soon leased to a William Greensmith of Hampton

Figure 7.32 Nave of
St Peter's Church in 1828
showing box pews and
the high altar by James
Johnson (Braikenridge
Collection, BRSMG
M2670)

Figure 7.33 SS Philip and
Jacob as depicted by James
Stewart 1748 (Bodleian
Library, Western MS,
Gough Somerset 8, fol 7)

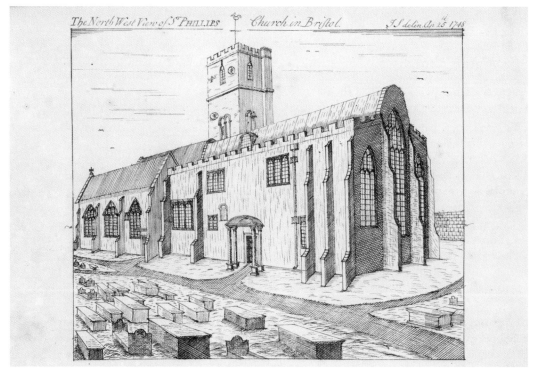

in Middlesex but were recovered when the abbey was chosen as the site for the new diocese of Bristol in 1542 (Bettey 1990, 23).

The diocese was only poorly endowed and was consequently an unpopular appointment from which its incumbents often strove to

Figure 7.34 Entrance to Bishop's Palace in 1821 by Hugh O'Neil (Braikenridge Collection, BRSMG M1909)

escape. Without enough money to complete Newland's design, the half-built walls of the nave were demolished and the transept blocked, forming the west front for the next three hundred years. A building on the south side of the former abbey was converted to use as a palace for the bishop: 19th-century illustrations show it to have been a substantial stone building of apparently late medieval origin; the rear doorway was a four-centred arch, above which was a shield bearing the rebus of Abbot Newland (Fig 7.34).

Several of the other monastic buildings were also retained. The barn on the west side of College Square, for example, appears to have survived until at least the mid-17th century (Bristol Archives DC/E/40/28/2).

The Cathedral, like the parish churches, was affected by the liturgical injunctions issued by successive Tudor monarchs. The Dean and Chapter were instructed by the commissioners in 1561 to remove the 'divers tabernacles for Images as well as in the fronture of the Roodeloft of the Cathl Church of Bristol, as also in the frontures back and ends of the walles wheare the com table standeth' and instead make 'a playne walle wth morter plastr or otherways & some scriptures to be written down in the places' (quoted in Britton 1830, 52). Several of the monuments of medieval religiosity were removed, possibly as a result of the suppression of chantries in the reign of Edward VI. The chapel in the centre of College Green survived long enough for Camden to observe it, but had been removed by the mid-17th century; a windmill was erected on Brandon Hill in 1568 'where before St Brandon's Chapel stode' (Hudd 1894–5, 134). The pulpit in front of the cathedral may also have been a casualty. The politics of religion calmed somewhat during Elizabeth's reign (at least in regard to its effect on the fabric of church buildings) but reappeared in the reign of Charles I in reaction to Archbishop Laud's Arminianism.

The investigation of the site of Minster House in 1992 (BHER 1685) found some changes associated with the dissolution of the abbey: the cellarium was apparently demolished not long after 1539 and a gabled kitchen block, which survived into the 19th century, had been built by the mid-17th century to serve the new domestic function of Minster House (Fig 7.35).

Other, less significant, changes included the rebuilding of one of the larger drains and the construction of a garden wall. Analysis of the faunal remains identified a change in consumption patterns after 1539 with the representation of the bones of sheep or goat outnumbering those of cattle for the first time. The remains of a conduit house, constructed shortly after the Dissolution in the centre of the cloisters, presumably linking with the existing water supply that had been established in the medieval period, was found during evaluation and a watching brief in 2010 (BHER 24898) (Blockley 2010). A possible medieval dovecote (BHER 1457M) discovered during fieldwork at Deanery Road (BHER 3592; BHER 3822; BHER 3823) was demolished some time before the 18th century (Cox et al 2006, 63).

The cathedral church escaped damage both during the fighting and the iconoclasm that followed. The cathedral clergy were, however, ejected from their posts with the abolition of the episcopacy, though some like George Williamson, a prebend and also Vicar of All Saints', were restored in the 1660s (Walker 1714, part II, 4). The abolition also led to the sale of Dean and Chapter lands, and in Bristol, as elsewhere, a Parliamentary survey cataloguing those properties was made in 1649. The Bishop's Palace clearly became a political target. Walker reports that its roof was stripped of its lead and, after the ejection of the bishop, it was used as a malthouse; 'there they Ground, as well as Made, great quantities of Mault for several Years as is well Remembered by many yet living in Bristol' (ibid, 3). Canon's Marsh was acquired by one John Pester during the Commonwealth who brought a case in Chancery against the Dean and Chapter in 1662–3 alleging that when the marsh was restored to the Dean and Chapter they reneged on an agreement to lease the marsh to him (Bristol Archives DC/E/40/8/2). The cathedral itself seems to have had some degree of immunity from the despoliation and members of the Corporation continued to attend services in the cathedral and keep their seats in repair (Lehmberg 1996, 48).

Other monastic houses

The Priory of St James

St James's Priory was dissolved in January 1540, and Latimer suggests that the Commissioners caused the lead to be stripped from the roofs of the church and the Lady Chapel not long afterwards. Certainly Leland's description in the early 1540s indicates that the priory church had rapidly become dilapidated (Latimer 1897–9, 110; Toulmin-Smith 1910, 88). The priory site and its estates were acquired by Henry Brayne in the summer of 1543, and Brayne apparently created a great house out of the claustral ranges while retaining many of the ancillary buildings; an agreement of 1578–9 on the division of the property between the husbands of Brayne's two daughters refers to a brewhouse, bakehouse and a dovecote

Figure 7.35 Minster House and associated buildings in 1821 by John Sanders (Braikenridge Collection, BRSMG M1752)

(Latimer 1897–9, 119, 126). If a drawing of the priory (usually dated to the early 17th century) is reliable (*see* Fig 6.57), the walls of the priory church were still standing in the early 17th century, though the ceramic evidence recovered during excavation suggests a late 16th-century date for the demolition of the east end (BHER 3155).

The western end of the church survived because of its parochial function and it must have been reorganised after the Dissolution. Understanding of these alterations is incomplete, mainly because of the limited extent of investigation of the fabric of the church. The south aisle is known to have been rebuilt in 1689 though the enlargement of the church which has traditionally been supposed was at best minimal (Bryant 1993, 21). Recording in 1993 did, however, identify a series of windows with brick voussoirs which had been inserted into the wall of the south aisle in the late 17th century (BHER 623) (Bryant 1993, 21–3). The porch was also added during the period, possibly indicating that the adoption of the Great Gate as the entrance to the Brayne's mansion prevented the parish from using the doorway in the west front for access (Fig 7.36). Documentary evidence for horticultural activity during the 17th century is consistent with the excavated evidence of cultivation trenches, rubbish pits and cess pits, dug at random across the site, which suggest that it remained undeveloped in this period. Some of these were found to contain waste from bone working, probably for the production of handles for tools (Jackson 2006b). The ceramic assemblages in particular suggest that the households of the properties to the east of the church were of moderately high status with good quality imported and locally produced tablewares being recovered from associated rubbish pits (Fig 7.37).

The Nunnery of St Mary Magdalen

The Nunnery of St Mary Magdalen – the first of Bristol's monastic houses to surrender – was dissolved under the Act of Suppression of 1536. At the time of the surrender of this house it was found that the community numbered one novice and one elderly nun (Page 1907). The nunnery site and most of its property was granted to a London merchant tailor, Henry Brayne (L & P xx (pt 2), 225). The church became a dwelling, probably reusing the

Figure 7.36 South porch of St James's Church (photograph R Jones)

existing buildings (Skeeters 1993, 80). Brayne sold the site to William Gorges of Wraxall in 1554. In 1596 the site was sold again, this time being divided into two parcels, the buildings on the western side and the orchard on the eastern (Longman 2001, 4–5). Excavation in 2000 (BHER 1054M; BHER 3617) recorded the construction of a new building abutting the existing late medieval structure on Upper Maudlin Street; there was also evidence for the rebuilding of the medieval walls in the late 17th or early 18th century (Longman 2001, 14–15).

St Bartholomew's Hospital

The first monastic house had already disappeared from Lewins Mead even before the surrender of St Mary Magdalen. St Bartholomew's Hospital was transferred in January 1531/2 from the de la Warre family to John and Robert Thorne who undertook to establish a school on the site. The agreement specified that the existing almoners were to be allowed to live out their remaining lives there and presumably the buildings which formed their accommodation survived for a period as a result. The reasons for the closure of the hospital are not clear but it has been suggested that it was a financial burden which the de la

Warres were keen to relinquish (BHER 3286; Price with Ponsford 1998, 122–5).

St Mark's Hospital

St Mark's Hospital surrendered on 9 December 1539 and was bought by the Corporation, the chapel of the hospital becoming the Lord Mayor's Chapel, which still survives today. The claustral buildings survived until the late 16th century and the tombs of the 'three founders of the Gaunts' were removed in 1591 (Barker 1892, 77).

In 2011 a small excavation (BHER 25018) at the junction of Pipe Lane and Trenchard Street, within the precinct, showed that Pipe Lane developed from the late 16th century onwards. The earliest activity noted was a large quarry pit, backfilled by the early 16th century. The first building on the site (No 9 Pipe Lane) was constructed around the early 17th century and was subsequently extended in the 18th and 19th centuries. This building survived until demolition in 1937. A painting of 1824, together with a photograph of 1903 and drawing of 1912, show a niche in the north-west corner of the building, together with a carving of a winged lion in the north-west gable (*see* Fig 6.59). The carving is traditionally associated with

*Figure 7.37 Late
17th-century pottery
from rubbish pits east of
St James's Church*

St Mark and it may have been retrieved from the demolished remains of the hospital. It has been suggested that the niche once contained a religious statue of the Virgin and Child, perhaps to denote the northern corner of the precinct of St Mark's Hospital (Mason 2012).

The Franciscan Friary
The Franciscan Friary was leased from the Crown by the Bristol merchant William Chester and was bought by the Corporation in 1541 (Latham 1947, 84–92). A better understanding of the subsequent development of the site awaits the analysis of the evidence collected during the several excavations within the precinct, but the friary appears to have vanished through gradual redevelopment. A two-storey stone building was built inside the cloister while the guest house on the cliff above was demolished and the plot later used for the construction of a lodge. Excavation within the precinct, at the top of the slope, against Upper Maudlin Street, found a late 16th-century wall, built to divide the former precinct into two new properties. Part of a later 17th-century formal garden was also found. The hillside had been terraced to provide a level site. The garden was laid out sometime around 1670, a number of clay tobacco pipe

bowls, including one of red earthenware made in the eastern Mediterranean, providing dating evidence. A low retaining wall was built across the centre and a series of planting beds and gravel paths, some edged with pitched stones, laid out (BHER 3399) (Jackson 2000a, 54–60).

The Carmelite Friary
The end of the Carmelite Friary in St Augustine's Place came on 10 September 1538 and, again, the site was purchased by the Corporation; the buildings were quarried for stone to repair the church of St Thomas in 1543–4 (Skeeters 1993, 81). Excavation in 2007 (BHER 4369) (Heaton 2008) confirms that, following the surrender in 1538, the friary buildings were rapidly demolished. A large pit was found, filled with demolition rubble and artefacts dating from the mid-16th century onwards. Little structural evidence was found although two small sections of wall appeared to date to the 17th century. A building survey of No 2 Trenchard Street (BHER 4368), which formerly occupied the western section of the site, showed that this building contained surviving remnants of buildings of the 16th and 17th centuries, including part of a window that may have been salvaged from an earlier friary building (Fig 7.38) (King 2007a).

Figure 7.38 Remains of a possibly 16th-century window within No 2 Trenchard St (photograph R Jones)

John Yonge acquired the site and its gardens from the city and in 1568 began to build the Great House, perhaps the most impressive of all the Bristol mansions (Gomme *et al* 1979, 77). It consisted of a main block with east and west cross-wings one bay wide enclosing a central courtyard, in the style of a country house. There were large eight-light mullioned windows on all of the main elevations (Winstone 1987, pl 131) (Fig 7.39). Inventories from the 17th century record a great hall, the 'little studdie' and outhouses, a coach house and stables as well as a water cistern to control supply to the main house (Hall 1949, 122–3). The extent to which the Great House was specifically adapted to the needs of an urban merchant, rather than copying country house designs such as Rushton Hall in Northamptonshire or Condover Hall in Shropshire, more appropriate to the rural gentry, is uncertain. It was placed at the foot of a hill below Park Row facing towards the gradient, and what was clearly intended to be the main entrance was away from the Frome along a small back lane (Fig 7.40), an organisation of space suggesting that the rear ground floor may have been used for the storage of goods unloaded at the quay. After the house was completed, Yonge created gardens extending up the hillside to the Red Lodge (built *c* 1590) and the White Lodge. By the mid-17th century, however, the house had ceased to be a domestic dwelling.

The Dominican Friary
The Dominican Friary in Rosemary Street was dissolved on 10 September 1538; the site was bought by William Chester and remained the property of the Chester family into the early 17th century. Part of the friary, probably the church, was quarried for building stone and for stone to rebuild the altars in St Werburgh's (Skeeters 1993, 82–3), but the discovery of two 15th-century traceried windows in the wall of a garage in 1933 and 1936 showed that at least some of the friary fabric was merely absorbed into other buildings (Leighton 1933, 164–6; *Bristol Evening Post*, 9-12-1936) (Fig 7.41).

While excavated evidence also suggested the demolition of at least parts of the church, elsewhere there are clear signs of continuity of use, with William Chester turning the friary into a private residence. Various buildings in the former friary were being leased, by the Bakers Guild from before 1499, by the Cutlers who leased their hall from the Chesters in 1570 and the Tanners who were also probably in their hall (in the former west range of the Great Cloister) at around the same time (Davenport 2013e, 371–2). There was little evidence of redevelopment in the friary precinct in the 16th and 17th centuries, but rather adaptation of existing buildings, with dumps of material, mostly of red clay overlying earlier floors and dated by pottery to the 16th century. The excavated evidence suggests that areas of the site were now given over to casual dumping of domestic waste with some hint of horn working and possibly tanning waste. By the mid-17th century, the land had been acquired by the Hollister family and the first Quaker meetings were held in the Great Orchard of the former friary in 1654 (*see* p 280) (Davenport

2013g, 393). Several of the ancillary buildings also survived for a considerable time, a lease of 1614 referring to a 'little house (sometime being a dove house)' which had been part of the friary, while the gardens and orchards seem to have been retained as recreational space; in his will Chester left to his brother 'the bowlinge alle with the lyttell orcharde and a lyttell hous to sit in the saide orchard' (quoted in Leighton 1933, 158).

Redcliffe
As one of the quarters of the medieval town where religious houses (albeit the houses of the smaller orders), were sited and had property, Redcliffe and Temple experienced considerable change in land ownership during the Reformation. The friaries and hospitals were surrendered over a period of roughly six years, the first being the Austin Friary by Temple Gate which was dissolved on 10 September 1538. The Corporation bought the Knights Hospitaller preceptory at Temple Church in 1544 and also tried to acquire St John's Hospital in Redcliff Pit, surrendered in March of that year. Despite these efforts the site was granted to a Dr George Owen in April 1544, and the buildings were probably demolished soon afterward (Latimer 1901, 176). Excavation immediately to the north of Temple Church in 1971 (BHER 314) found that, after the suppression, only one wing of the Hospitallers' main buildings escaped demolition. This was altered several times: in the late 16th or early 17th century cobbled areas (possibly raised fireplaces) were inserted into it while heavier cobbles were laid to form a paved area outside. In the following century machinery of some kind was placed inside: postholes and mortared stonework at the south-west corner formed what may have been the base for a rotary mill for grinding pigment, an interpretation suggested by the discovery of a dump of ochre soil in an adjoining outbuilding (Good 1992, 12).

A number of medieval institutions survived through the period and there was at least one foundation of a new almshouse during the 17th century. Under the terms of the will of Dr Thomas White, ten tenements were erected on the north side of a garden ground on the north side of Bear Lane. These buildings survived into the 1820s, being described then as 'a range of chambers under one roof' (Manchee 1831, vol 1, 113–14, 119) (Fig 7.42).

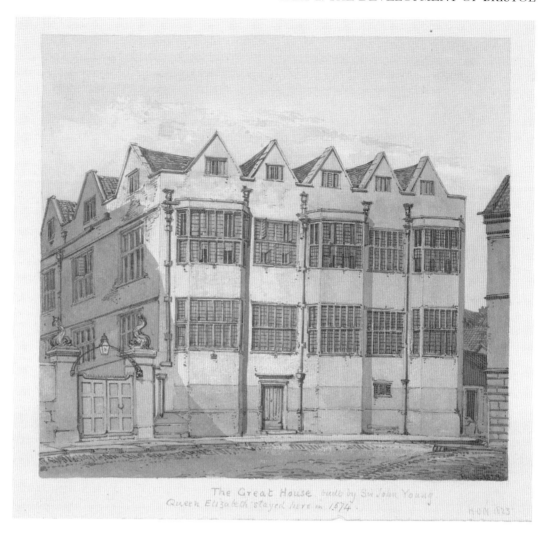

Figure 7.40 Extract from Millerd's map of 1673, with vignette showing the Great House, looking from the north-west (BRSMG Mb6690)

Millerd's map indicates that the ground to the south was enclosed as a garden or yard (Fig 7.43).

In his will in 1679 Alderman Thomas Steevens instructed his executors to found an almshouse in the parish of Temple on the south side of the junction of Temple Street and Cart Lane as well as the one named after him in Old Market Street (*see* p 280). This almshouse had been demolished by 1872 with its inmates

Figure 7.42 Temple Street
frontage of Dr White's
Almshouse in 1821
with Neptune's statue
adjacent by Hugh O'Neill
(Braikenridge Collection,
BRSMG M2126)

transferred to the Old Market almshouse and is depicted in a Braikenridge drawing of 1824 as a two-storey building of five bays (Fig 7.44).

Other hospitals
Old Market had a number of institutional buildings. The late medieval buildings of Trinity Hospital were rebuilt in the 17th century and were described in 1828 as

consisting of two separate structures on either side of Old Market Street; the block on the north side of the street had 24 apartments while the southern had 22 and an annexed chapel (Figs 7.45 and 7.46). The residents each had an apartment with a fireplace 'furnished by themselves', and each building possessed a communal kitchen (Manchee 1831, vol 1, 79). Another almshouse was

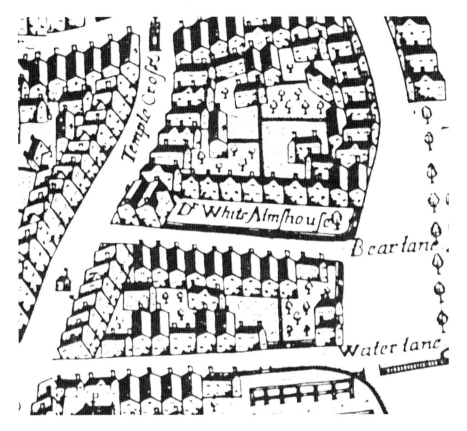

Figure 7.43 Extract from Millerd's map of 1673, showing Dr White's Almshouse (BRSMG Mb6690)

Figure 7.44 Alderman Steevens Almshouse, Temple Street in 1824 by E Cashin (Braikenridge Collection, BRSMG M2144)

Figure 7.45 Trinity
Hospital (north side) in
1824 by George Delamotte
(Braikenridge Collection,
M2761)

founded by Alderman Thomas Steevens who directed in his will of 1679 that his executors purchase 'two several void grounds, one within the parish of St Philip and St Jacob' on which they should build 'an almshouse, fit and convenient for twelve poor men or women'. They found a site on the north side of Old Market Street consisting of a tenement plot which had been divided into three small houses, a stable and garden (ibid, 167–8). The original form of the almshouse is however unclear, since the buildings were reconstructed in 1725.

At the western end of Broadmead, on St James's Back, Chester's Almshouse was founded, possibly by 1537, presumably by William Chester, mayor in 1537 and 1552. It had six inmates in 1803, but otherwise little is known of this institution.

Nonconformism

When the religious control which had been exercised by the Church was removed in the mid-1640s, radical religious groups began to

appear across the country. In Bristol, a surge of nonconformist religion followed the abolition of the episcopate in the 1640s. Broadmead was a quarter inhabited by artisans as well as wealthier merchants in the 17th century and this social profile may have been a factor influencing the founding of a number of nonconformist meetings there during the civil wars and the Commonwealth. A Baptist church was established on the north side of Broadmead, behind Nos 10–13, and this was replaced by a new meeting house, 40ft by 50ft, in 1695.

Quakerism arrived in Bristol in 1654 and the first meetings were held in an orchard at the Dominican Friary, then owned by Dennis Hollister, a wealthy grocer and a former member of the Baptist congregation. The Quakers bought the Hollisters' house and the friars' burial ground in 1670 and a new Meeting House was constructed in 1670–2, depicted on Millerd's maps of the 1670s as a two-storey building with a lantern in the roof (Fig 7.47). Detailed survey of the present Meeting House showed that it had been built over the remains

Figure 7.46 Trinity Hospital (south side) in 1822 by Hugh O'Neill (Braikenridge Collection, M2772)

of east range of the former Lesser Cloister (Davenport 2013a, 343).

In Redcliffe, a tradition of religious dissent established in the Middle Ages continued into the 17th century and beyond. The Society of Friends established a meeting in an alley off the west side of Temple Street in the 1650s and a Presbyterian meeting was founded at Tucker Street in the later part of the century. Presumably these were based in ordinary dwelling houses, but whether any were altered to accommodate religious practice is so far unknown.

Non-conformists continued to meet after the end of the Commonwealth but the passing of the Conventicle Act soon after the Restoration signalled official approval for the repression of dissent. While the act was ignored in some places (in Gloucester it was used only once), in Bristol it inaugurated a period of aggressive victimisation (Hutton 1993, 210). Non-conformists were imprisoned, meetings at Quakers Friars were frequently broken up and the galleries in the meeting house were broken down (Mortimer 1977, xxxi).

Houses and housing

The trend away from the traditional use of the open hall for formal, communal, meals and towards the 'retreat into the parlour', already evident in the 15th century (*see* pp 220–3), continued in the 16th. This can be seen from the probate inventories of a number of wealthy citizens from the years either side of 1500. In each case the house was multi-roomed, with a hall, parlour, buttery, kitchen and two or three chambers. In each case the hall appears to have been an open hall, in that no other rooms are recorded above. In most cases the hall was still the most 'important' room, still clearly invested with the symbolism of the feudal hall, and usually equipped with a folding table, stools or forms, hangings, bankers and cushions, andirons for the fireplace, candlesticks and weapons, presumably hung on the walls. The parlours however had tables, cupboards, bankers, cushions, candlesticks and, in some cases, beds; it is fairly clear that this is where most of the living took place, that these rooms were used for dining, and could be used for sleeping.

It would be wrong however to see this trend as uniform across the entire population of Bristol, and probate inventories also yield glimpses into houses that changed little or not at all in these centuries. For example, in 1618 the house of Edward Morris, merchant, on the corner of Small Street and Corn Street, consisted of a shop with two chambers above it and a loft above them. Behind was a kitchen, an unheated parlour, and an open hall (with no room over it) at the rear. Although the back parlour and the hall were similarly furnished, only the hall was heated. Or, in 1627, the wealthier establishment of Humphrey Clovill, goldsmith, on the Christ Church–Wine Street corner, had no parlour at all, and its hall (probably open) was still the principal room in all senses: it was heated, panelled with wainscot, furnished and decorated with painted cloths and pictures. Such instances of the persisting tastes of elderly or conservative citizens do not however alter the general picture, which was in the direction of more, and more specialised, rooms (Leech 2014, chapter 5).

Such changes can sometimes be followed in an individual, identifiable property. For example, the earliest probate inventory that can be linked to a specific house concerns

No 20 Small Street, home to some of Bristol's wealthiest inhabitants in the 16th and 17th centuries. It was rebuilt in the 1540s by its owner, John Smythe: the open hall was retained and given a new hammer-beam roof, but it was unheated; a new chamber block with a stair tower was added on the frontage. This included a parlour with a chamber over, and formal meals now took place in the parlour. By the 1660s it was the town house of Sir Henry Creswick, of Yorkshire gentry origin, admitted a burgess in 1608, and an inventory survives from 1668. The open hall had been retained: it was still unheated, and the brass candelabra hanging from the roof, the maps, pictures, weapons and armour there point to its having become a purely symbolic or ceremonial space designed, as Dr Leech observes, to emphasise the honour, lineage and legitimacy of its owner. The chamber block built in the 1540s now had three parlours: a 'great parlour' for the reception of visitors, containing a reading desk, musical instruments, pictures, carpets and plenty of furniture; the 'little parlour' and the 'old parlour' were both heated, both near the street, one was barely furnished, the other was a study. But where there had been a chamber above, on the first floor, there was now a dining room, heated, with a table, sideboard and a number of chairs (Leech 2014, 108) (Fig 7.48).

A parallel example of changes characteristic of the post-medieval period in a well-documented house can be found just down the street. John Butcher – draper, alderman, mayor – rebuilt the front of Nos 16–17 Small Street just before 1600 as a three-storey block, two rooms wide, with attics and a cellar; a medieval open hall at the rear was retained (Leech 2014, 102–3, figs 5.48, 5.49). The anatomy of the house is visible in a probate inventory of 1623. The hall was unheated, but had wainscoted benches, a paternoster in wall panels, a map of the world on the wall and a profusion of weapons, a sign perhaps of its owner's aspirations to gentry status. There were three parlours, all wainscoted. The front parlour was unheated with a painted ship in a frame, the 'little parlour' also at the front, was heated, carpeted but sparsely furnished, and the 'backer parlour', while unheated, had a sideboard, cupboard, table and hangings and may have been used for dining. Within

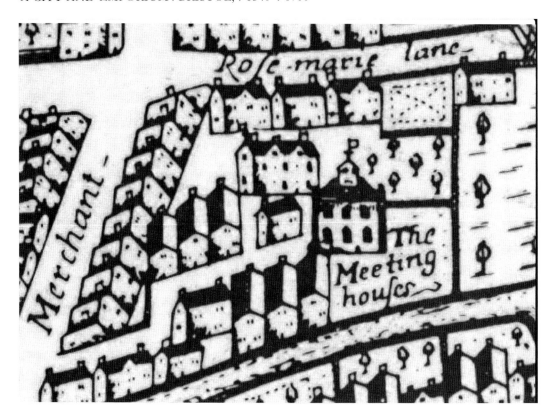

Figure 7.47 Extract from Millerd's map of 1673, showing the Quakers' Meeting House (BRSMG Mb6690)

five years however the open hall had been ceiled over by John Butcher's son Nathaniel. The new room created above the hall was the principal chamber. The 'parlour' was now more comfortable, heated and clearly the main social focus of the house, with embroidered chairs and stools and seating for up to fifteen. But the old hall, despite the alterations, remained furnished much as it had in John Butcher's day, with tables, stools, a great chest, two virginals, pictures, armour and weapons. Here, as in many other Bristol houses, the symbolism of the hall, whether or not it was an open hall, survived, even though its original function had begun to change even in the medieval period. The hall was to remain a cultural artefact of the city's merchant elite even into the 1680s (Leech 2014, 106–9).

There were however other pressures acting upon the medieval open hall, particularly in the more congested central streets. Competition for space in such areas was such that many domestic open halls were reused for commerce or other functions, and there are records of halls converted into tan-houses, a school-room, store-rooms and, particularly in the

High Street, taverns, as at Haddon's Tavern, stretching from High Street to Wine Street, the largest known medieval tavern in the city. Similarly at No 30 High Street was the Bull or the Angel, possibly a tavern by 1472: its 15th-century hall lay adjacent to St Nicholas's Street (Leech 2014, fig 5.55). The process had already begun in the later Middle Ages: as early as 1346 city ordinances were published stipulating that weavers' looms were to be located in plain sight – in shops and halls, not in solars or cellars. An inventory of John Gauge's house of the late 15th century recorded cloths and a press for cloths in his hall. It is also the case that, particularly where a hall lay across the width of the plot, there was a recurrent need for access through it. This was usually via the cross passage at the low end of the hall (as in Spicer's Hall on Welsh Back) and, in course of time, such traffic led to the establishment of permanent rights-of-way. These halls were sometimes known as 'through-houses', the first recorded instance of this description being in 1446 (Leech 2014, 114–15).

Meanwhile, while the open hall evolved from a multi-functional domestic space into

a symbolic space, the 'shop-house' – the simpler, vertically stacked structure, lacking an open hall, based literally and figuratively on the ground-floor shop – went from strength to strength almost without change, and was a dominant feature, certainly of the central streets, throughout the 16th and 17th centuries.

However, whereas the medieval rentals point, in general, to a degree of social distinction between the (more expensive) hall-house properties and the (cheaper) shop-houses, by the mid-16th century 'even those who lived in the smallest shop-houses were generally prosperous citizens' (Leech 2014, 123). This may well be

Figure 7.49 South side of Mary-le-Port Street in 1826 by T L Rowbotham (Braikenridge Collection, BRSMG M2801)

partly due to fierce competition for space on the principal trading frontages. Streets such as Peter Street and Defence (Dolphin) Street were characterised by the 15th century by buildings with single-room footprints and detached kitchens behind. By the mid-16th century these were home to, for example, a goldsmith, a saddler and a soapmaker. Similarly, in the single-room-plan dwellings in front of Christ Church, from the 1530s through the remainder of the period, lived a goldsmith (his probate inventory of 1633 reveals a richly furnished interior) and, for example, a hosier, milliner, tailor, pewterer, surgeon, upholsterer and a grocer. Along Mary-le-Port Street in speculatively-developed heated houses of four storeys with attics built by the landlord of the Swan Inn, lived grocers, tailors and ironmongers (Fig 7.49).

*Figure 7.50 John
Langton's House, Welsh
Back, after a painting
by Robert Harman
1732, by Hugh O'Neill
(Braikenridge Collection,
BRSMG M2265)*

Occasionally, such buildings were chosen or built by the merchant elite. No 12 Welsh Back was built *c* 1623 by the merchant John Langton on a 20ft wide plot (Leech 2014, 126–7) (Fig 7.50). It had an ornately carved staircase and a belvedere on the roof. Above the shop was the principal chamber containing a chimney-piece with the royal arms and a decorated plaster

Figure 7.51 No 1 High Street (also known as the Dutch House), early 20th century (Loxton Collection, Bristol Reference Library D220)

ceiling, a clear equivalent of the 'symbolic hall' found in more expansive dwellings.

The best-known shop-house of all was probably No 1 High Street, built or rebuilt in 1676 and destroyed in 1940 (Leech 2014, 136 and fig 6.32) (Fig 7.51).

Trade and industry

The period between 1500 and 1700 has long been seen as important in the foundation of Bristol's remarkable 18th-century prosperity. In those two centuries the city's commerce shifted its focus from Gascony, the dominant trading partner of the late Middle Ages, first to Iberia and then, because of war with Spain in the 1580s and the mid-1620s, to the Atlantic. These fluctuations in the city's economy and the tremendous social and cultural changes which also took place are clearly expressed in the archaeological record. At the domestic level the variation in the source of Bristol's imports can be followed in the pottery assemblages, with Iberian wares becoming increasingly common in the 16th century; much of the Venetian glass, Iberian and Italian pottery used at Acton Court a few miles to the north of the city was probably imported through Bristol (Vince and Bell 1992). At the broadest level, the wealth generated by the development of Bristol's Atlantic trade is reflected right across the archaeological record. It enabled the wave of housing reconstruction which characterised the later 17th century; it led to the appearance of new industries and it led to the consumption of new luxury commodities. The Atlantic economy began to change the face of Bristol in this period, though change was most often accomplished within frameworks established centuries earlier.

Inherited patterns are strongly evident in the city centre, whose occupational geography changed little through the late medieval and early modern periods. The wine trade continued to be important in the 16th century around High Street where vintners and a number of inns and taverns are recorded. Shoemakers were the dominant trade in Mary-le-Port Street in the 16th century but their presence had diminished by the 18th (Leech 1998b). The occupational structure may have begun to reflect the new products available from the Atlantic trade but the main streets were clearly established as a centre for the retailing of luxury or specialist goods. Heavier industry was located elsewhere in the city, although metalworking was taking place close at hand: dumped industrial waste, in the form of a group of 17th-century crucibles, furnace lining, iron slag and horn fragments, was recovered by excavation from Mary-le-Port Street (Watts and Rahtz 1985, 69, 162, 177–8). As in earlier periods, the Frome was a magnet for water-using trades. In Broad Weir, between the Frome and the 'Weare', some evidence was recovered during excavation for industrial activity, including possibly hide processing and related activities. A large rectangular stone tank, dated to the 16th century by associated

pottery was filled with a high proportion of horn working waste. Documentary sources also indicate the presence of many tanners and whittawers along the Weare during the 17th century (Ridgeway and Watts 2013, 404).

Sugar refining

The first sugar refinery in Bristol was set up by Robert Aldworth in *c* 1607 in premises at his residence, the former St Peter's Hospital, to refine Portuguese product from Madeira (Leech 2014, 176) (Fig 7.52). The development of sugar production in the Caribbean led to the emergence of a sizeable sugar refining trade in the city in the second half of the 17th century, the new industry for the most part located in the poorer or more artisan-dominated areas of the city. Several sugar houses were set up in Lewins Mead. The earliest seem to have been sited in existing buildings: the Great House in St Augustine's Place, for example, became a sugar house in *c* 1654. Water for its three pans was drawn from St John's Conduit (without permission) and cottages were built in the grounds of the house to provide dwellings for the refinery workers (Hall 1949, 141). Inventories record not only the utensils required for sugar making but also the equipment, the vats and coolers, installed in the various rooms (ibid, 156–7); refining continued on the site until 1708. Another sugar house was founded at Whitson Court in 1667 by Thomas Ellis which consisted of a refinery, warehouse and mill; another was built in Lewins Mead in 1684 (Hall 1944, 19; Hall 1965, 121). Sugar houses sprang up in Redcliffe too, the earliest known in Temple Street by the partnership of John Hine and Richard Lane in 1662. Hine had attempted to establish a sugar house the year before but had been forced by complaints from nearby residents about the danger from fire to move into a former brewery by Temple Church (Hall 1957, 127–8). Over the next few years this building was converted into a sugar house and two dwellings were constructed, along with two warehouses on the gardens of the plots (ibid, 132). Refineries were also created at Tucker Street in 1685, in the Great House by Bristol Bridge between 1685 and 1715, and at No 18 Redcliff Street in 1695 (Hall 1965, 120–1). Little is known about the archaeology of these quite expansive, space-hungry premises, although an evaluation in 2006 (BHER 4276) revealed traces of the Rodgers sugar refinery, established in 1684, south of Old Market Street (Hart 2006).

Tobacco pipe manufacture

The lifting of restrictions on the importation of tobacco in 1638 allowed the clay tobacco pipe industry to develop and Bristol became a major centre for pipe manufacture. A Company of Tobacco Pipe Makers was founded in 1652 and the number of makers obtaining their freedom increased rapidly up to 1700 (Jackson and Price 1974, 14–15). Lewins Mead was one of the main sites for the manufacture of tobacco pipes in the city and at least two makers are known to have worked on the site of St Bartholomew's Hospital in the second half of the 17th century, although no definite evidence for the manufacturing process was found by excavation (Price with Ponsford 1998, 160). Nor has archaeological work yet found evidence for 17th-century tobacco pipe kilns anywhere else in this area. The best evidence for the technology

Figure 7.53 Finzels Reach: possible clay pipe kiln (reproduced from Ford et al 2017, fig 4.9)

of production comes from the 19th century when the industry was in decline in Bristol; the archaeological evidence for its early years derives mainly from assemblages of pipes recovered through excavation. However, there is evidence from the excavation at Finzels Reach for 17th-century clay pipe production from a property on Temple Street, with wasters in direct association with an oven which had been inserted into a building behind No 7 Temple Street (Fig 7.53). It is possible that here there was a workshop, situated in an outbuilding behind the main residence, being used by Flower Hunt, an important pipe maker in 17th-century Bristol, whose main residence was in Castle Street (Higgins 2017, 195–6). A group of clay pipe wasters dating to the late 17th century recovered during excavation at St Bartholomew's Hospital (BHER 3286) included two pipes which retained the wire inserted into the stem to form the bore (Price with Ponsford 1998, 160). Most of the work on the early modern pipe-making industry to date has, however, concentrated on the documentary record and finds recovered through observation of highways or building works.

Soap making

Soap manufacture is documented in Bristol from the late 15th century. A noxious process and a fire risk (involving the boiling and rendering of animal fats), it was particularly appropriate for back-plot premises well separated from domestic accommodation (Leech 2014, 175–6). In 1556 soap making was being carried on in a house in Lewins

Mead which backed on to the river Frome. There are also 17th-century documentary references to the industry in other houses along the Frome, both in Lewins Mead and in Hallier's Lane (formerly Gropecuntelane, now Nelson Street), where Simon Hurle leased the building in which he had his soaphouse from the parish of St John from 1671 until the early 18th century (Bristol Archives 11178(3)). The Bristol soap making industry was the victim of local and central government regulation in the early 17th century. In a series of ordinances in 1618 the Corporation tried to insist that soap boilers use only olive oil, but the monopoly established by Charles I for the Company of Soapboilers virtually ended the industry in the city. The Bristol producers – without any great support from the Corporation – came to an agreement with the Company which allowed them to produce 600 tons per year, but an order of 1635 limited their markets to Wales and the Western ports as well as imposing an additional £4 tax. In 1638 another royal order reduced the number of soap houses to four (Latimer 1900, 67, 121–2).

Glass making

Glass making developed rapidly in the late 17th century although the history of these early glassworks is obscure. A furnace was established at Redcliff Wharf possibly by the late 1670s and the St Thomas Street, Redcliff Gate, Red Lane and Temple Backs glasshouses are known to have been in production at the very end of the 17th century, but may have been operating for some years before this. There has so far been little archaeological investigation of 17th-century glassworks in the city – some have been subject to archaeological evaluation – although traces of a hitherto unsuspected 17th-century glasshouse were discovered during the excavation of Sir Abraham Elton's glasshouse on Cheese Lane (*see* pp 385–6) and many of the specifics of the Bristol industry are unknown. The glasshouses seem to have produced mainly bottles but no attempt has yet been made to identify their products or to establish their (possibly worldwide) distribution.

Industry in Redcliffe

Redcliffe and Temple may be the area in which the economic fortunes of early modern Bristol

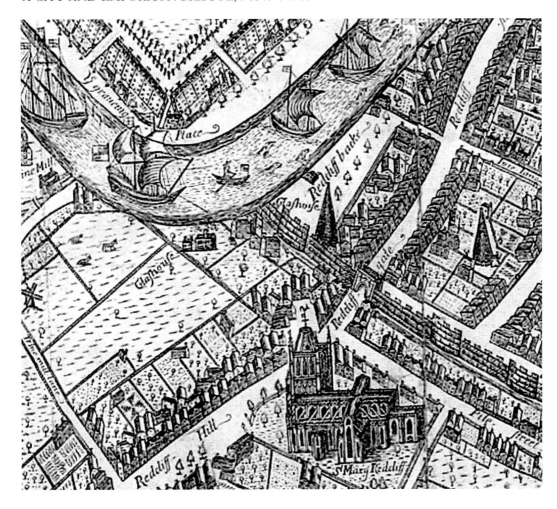

Figure 7.54 Extract from Millerd's map of c *1715, showing detail of Redcliff Wharf glasshouse (BRSMG M4173)*

are most closely reflected at a local level and future archaeological work may provide insights into the decline of the cloth trades as well as the emergence of new industries, sugar refining, glass making and probably clay pipe making (*see above*). The reasons behind the appearance of a number of glass manufacturing sites at the end of the 17th century in particular have not been convincingly established, although that the majority of these glassworks were producing bottles may imply a link with the trade in wine. The preservation of these glassworks is variable but the best opportunity for study of the development of the industry throughout the entire span of its history may be at Redcliff Wharf where the furnaces do not appear to have been disturbed by later development (Figs 7.54 and 7.55).

Archaeological and documentary evidence suggests that there was a considerable diversity in the industries being undertaken in Redcliffe during the 16th and 17th centuries. It was also a period of change: cloth manufacturing, which had been an important industry in the later Middle Ages, declined with the decreasing volume of cloth exports in the early 16th century and there was a large reduction in the number of apprentices entering cloth-related trades in the 1530s and 1540s. Although production continued, the industry continued to dwindle in the 17th century (Sacks 1991, 56–7). Excavation at Nos 85–7 Redcliff Street in 1980 (BHER 342) established that industrial activity, likely to be associated with the cloth industry, which began on the site in the medieval period had continued until the mid- to late 16th century (Ponsford nd (a), 156). In the mid-16th century the medieval loom was removed. Two large rectangular pits filled with iron slag and sand were found but the nature of this industry was not clear. A furnace, possibly a lime kiln, was built in the 17th century but had gone out of use by *c* 1659 (Williams and Cox 2000, 27).

Figure 7.55 Extract from Millerd's map of c 1715, showing early glass cones in the Redcliffe area (BRSMG M4173)

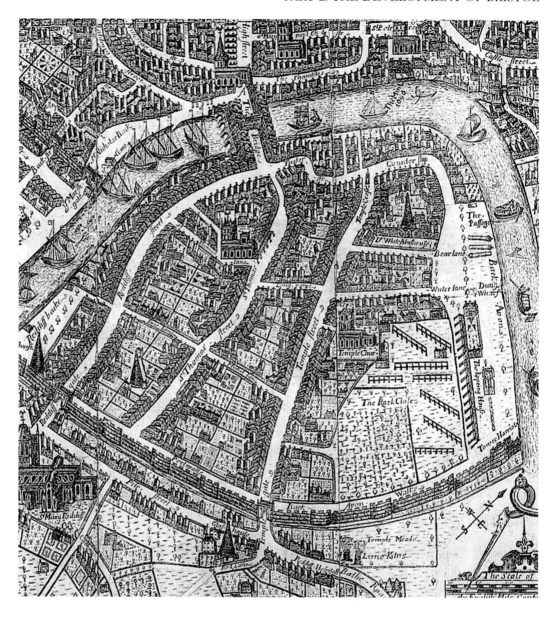

Excavation at No 2 Redcliff Street (BHER 4456) found an assemblage of clay mould fragments. These were probably associated with the manufacture of cauldrons or posnets, candlesticks and chafing dishes. Several furnaces were excavated, one of which was a complex stone-built structure 2m long and 1m wide with a probable stone chimney and one end divided by a central partition wall (Fig 7.56). This structure may have operated as a reverbatory furnace for the melting of copper alloy for the manufacture of large items such as cauldrons. Crucible fragments were found within the fill and contained traces of copper, zinc, lead, antimony and tin, while copper slag

was also found. The mould fragments may date to the period *c* 1400–1580/1600, although a 16th-century date is favoured (McSloy 2015, 63) (Fig 7.57).

Some of the smaller industries have been identified through excavation and documents record the presence of several other trades, but most have received little attention. There is, for example, the possible milling of pigment near Temple Church (*see* p 275) or the pin making identified by excavation in the southern half of Temple Street (BHER 1688). Documentary evidence for the 17th century records trades from soapmakers, bakers, wiredrawers and woodworkers to brewers and distillers, and rope-makers are known to have worked on the Portwall berm. A covered ropewalk, an open-sided building with a pitched roof supported on columns, was created at Temple Back in the second half of the 17th century (Fig 7.58).

Brick making also appeared in the late 17th century. In 1698 Mr Gibbs, who had been landlord of the Saracen's Head six years earlier, was paying rates to the parish of St Mary Redcliffe for a brick kiln in Redcliff Meads, while other kilns are known near Bedminster Causeway and on the east side of the Avon, as shown by Millerd in 1673.

Extractive industries

The early modern period also sees a great increase in the available historical evidence for the exploitation of the resources of the city's hinterland. Both coal and wood were used for fuel, the former from coalfields east of the city and in South Wales, coal beginning to achieve primacy over wood from the late 16th century. In the first decades of the 17th century the Crown was concerned that the mines in the Kingswood royal forest were worked by squatters and that local landlords were usurping its monopoly of coal extraction. Certainly Bristol Corporation claimed early in the reign of James I that one of these landlords had pushed up the price of Kingswood coal (Thirsk 1992, 335; Hatcher 1993, 178–81). Coal was not the only resource which came from the city: lime from Bristol was being bought at Worcester in 1569 while in 1637 the Earl of Cork sought 'ffree stone chymneis, doores, and lightes, readie made at the free stone quarries at Donderry Hill' for a house he was building (Airs 1995, 129, 114). Similarly the early modern rebuilding of St Peter's, Waterford used large quantities of Dundry stone for its architectural stonework (Hurley and Scully 1996, 393–400).

One enigmatic structure is Baber's Tower to the south-east of Jacob Street. Millerd's 1673 map depicts a house with a prospect tower or stair tower (Fig 7.59). Leech (2014, 274) has suggested that this building was a 'mansion house … heretofore used as a lodge' – formerly called 'Enderbie's Castle' and by 1627 known as Baber's Tower. William Baber was an unlicensed gunpowder maker who was investigated in 1634 for bringing quantities of saltpetre into the city at night.

Figure 7.56 Nos 1–2 Redcliff Street: possible reverbatory furnace of early 15th- to late 17th-century date recovered during excavation in 2007–8 (reproduced from Alexander 2015, fig 3.18)

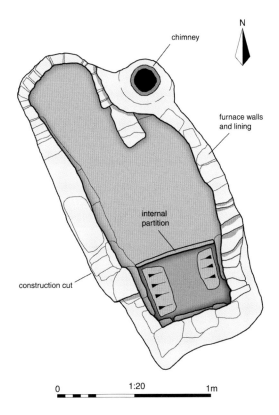

He established a works at Oxford to supply the Royalist forces during the Civil War and returned to the city while it was under Royalist control between 1643 and 1645 to manufacture powder. It has been suggested that the building shown by Millerd was the

0   100mm

*Figure 7.57 Nos 1–2
Redcliff Street: clay mould
fragments (reproduced from
Alexander 2015, fig 4.8)*

site of this works, although there is at present little firm evidence to support this contention (Buchanan 1995–6, 128–34).

Victualling

The supply and distribution of food to early modern Bristol is a question which is only beginning to be tackled, either by archaeologists or historians, although the volume of documentary evidence for the purchase and management of food increases considerably after 1500. Much of the land at the edge of the city was in some form of agricultural or horticultural use: there are many references to gardens and the riverside land along Cheese Lane, below Newfoundland Lane (modern Newfoundland Way), as well as land in Kingsdown which may have been used for grazing. Butchery was concentrated in Worshipful Street as it had been in the Middle Ages and cattle were pastured in the marsh in the time between their arrival

in the city and slaughter. Property records make incidental references to the presence of pigsties, and stews for holding fish in the back yards of tenements (*see* for example No 6 Welsh Back in Leech 1997c, 164). First-hand evidence for imported foodstuffs came from the recovery of a large deposit of grapes, probably representing a spoiled cargo of imported raisins or currants from southern Europe. These had been deposited during the process of dumping waste materials close to Welsh Back as part of the general raising of the ground level to construct Queen Square. The dumps as a whole should therefore date to the late 17th century and may represent a spoiled cargo of fruit that had been unloaded at a nearby quay (Jones 2008–9, 48).

Animal bone assemblages have been recovered from early modern contexts in most of the larger excavations in Bristol, but few have been analysed. The more recent large-scale

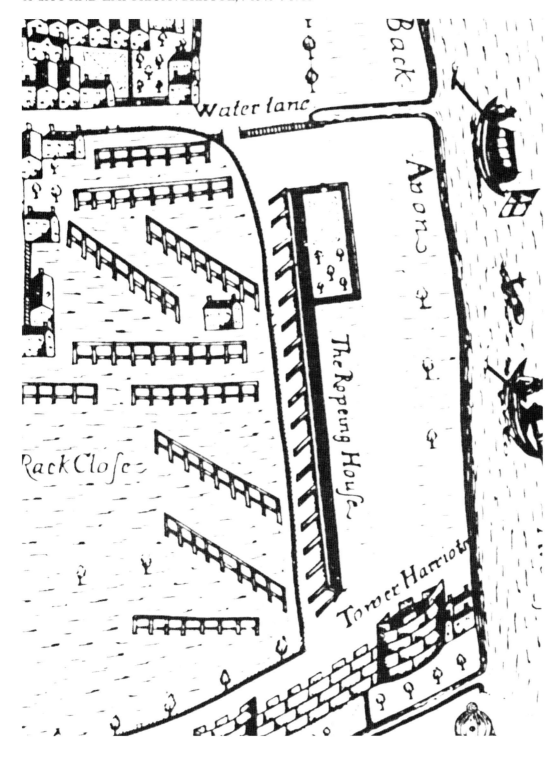

Figure 7.58 Extract from Millerd's map of 1673, showing the Ropewalk on Temple Back (BRSMG Mb6690)

excavations, particularly Cabot Circus (BHER 4279–4281), the former Courage Brewery site (Finzels Reach) (BHER 24838), Union Street (BHER 3590) and Nos 1–2 Redcliff Street (BHER 4456) are beginning to provide important new data as they are fully analysed and published. Apart from these, those which have been analysed were small: at Back Hall (BHER 1579) only 149 bone fragments could definitely be dated to the period and just over 700 at Minster House (BHER 1685), while at Victoria Street (BHER 88) and St James's Priory (BHER 3155) most of the early modern animal remains were in fact waste from bone

working. The data available is not therefore adequate to allow any reliable conclusions to be drawn about consumption, either in relation to social status or geographical location. In general however the food animals represented comprise primarily cow, goat/sheep and pig. Those which have been studied show some interesting features. Most of the animal remains from the excavation at Narrow Quay in 1978–9 (BHER 442) came from a single late 16th-century context that appeared, from the consistent nature of the butchery, to have originated from a single butcher. Comparison with a smaller late 15th-century assemblage, again from a single context, indicated a possible shift to butchery of younger cattle and, by extension, a concentration on prime beef. The butchery of sheep on the other hand showed a wider age range in the later period (Good 1987b, 121–5).

Chapter 8: 'Tis the Merchant that is the true practical Philosopher': Bristol, *c* 1700–*c* 1900

Introduction and historical framework

Bristol ended the 17th century as one of the most important ports of the Atlantic world and, during the 18th, attained perhaps its greatest economic power, with deep involvement in the development of Britain's American and Caribbean colonies and a commercial hinterland extending along the Severn from South Wales to the Midlands. Shipping was the basis of its wealth as it had been in the preceding centuries; coastal and inland trade still contributed substantially to the city's economy, but a large proportion of its wealth now came from the Atlantic (Hussey 2000).

Supplying the demand for luxury goods, and particularly sugar, was easily the most lucrative part of the Atlantic trade for the city (*see* p 353). Average per capita sugar consumption in England and Wales grew from 4lbs per year in 1700 to 24lbs by the end of the century (Shammas 1993, 178–83) and its price consistently fell, increasing the scale and social range of its consumption. Imports had reached 270,000 cwt in 1800 and continued to grow in the 19th century reaching 630,354 cwt by 1855 (Morgan 1996, 58). The transformation of the Caribbean islands from settler colonies, orientated toward subsistence farming, to large-scale coffee, tobacco and especially sugar production required both labour and financial capital on a large scale, requirements supplied by Bristol merchants. Slave ships sailed to West Africa, from Cape Verde to the Bight of Biafra, carrying copper, brass, sometimes tobacco and later iron of considerable value, their captains often being given precise instructions as to the cargoes they were to buy for the second leg of the journey to the Americas. One of the cargoes Captain William Barry carried to West Africa in the 1730s was expected to purchase '240 choice slaves, besides a Quantity of [elephants'] teeth … provided they are large' (quoted in Thomas 1997, 310). Slaves made the transatlantic crossing shackled below decks and prey to disease which caused many deaths before landfall. In the Chesapeake or the Caribbean the slaves were sold into a brutal plantation system, and rice, coffee, molasses or tobacco bought with the proceeds for the return home (Blackburn 1997, 309–68; Walvin 1993, 233–52). In the early 18th century, Bristol was the second slaving port in the country after London, and briefly achieved dominance between 1730 and 1739 before being overtaken by Liverpool (Richardson 1998, 446). Nor was this the only trade in humanity in which Bristol merchants engaged. The port became a centre for the transportation of convicts, a total of 3,339 passing through on their way to Maryland or other destinations, in comparison with 5,239 from London (Ekirch 1987, 70–5).

The Atlantic trade dominated the city's economy. It encouraged the maritime and maritime-related trades, stimulated manufacturing, and the revenue generated was spread into building, consumption and cultural activities. Consequently it also coloured local politics. Bristol merchants were an important Whig grouping in the early 18th century but lost influence when the Bute ministry came to power mid-century. As national relations with the North American colonies deteriorated, the merchants forged links with the Rockingham opposition and at the end of the 1760s Richard Champion condemned the Grafton ministry for seeking 'to oppress a people who are so great a support to our manufactories and commerce' (Guttridge 1934, 2–3). Edmund Burke, known as an opposition figure and an advocate of compromise with the colonies, was invited to stand for election as one of the city's two MPs in 1774 and retained the seat until 1780 when his views on Irish trade reform and the laws on debt fell foul of other mercantile concerns.

The port slipped into decline in the 19th century. The tidal character of the Avon had long posed a problem for shipping. As vessels became ever larger they were in increasing danger of breaking their backs as they settled on the beds of the Avon and Frome. Although the problem was identified in the mid-18th century, nothing was done until the early years of the 19th when a scheme, designed by William Jessop, to maintain a fixed water level in the two rivers was implemented with the creation of the Floating Harbour between 1804 and 1809 (Buchanan 1969; Malpass and King 2009). But the remedy came too late, and the narrow Avon Gorge prevented the largest ships from reaching the port: Brunel's SS *Great Britain* was too large to return to the dock where it was built. Other modes of communication began to gain importance. Canal building in the late 18th century had a direct effect on the city, while the rail links to London, the Midlands and the South West built from the late 1830s rivalled freight movement by ship and allowed a greater degree of passenger movement.

Disruption of production in the French Caribbean colonies by revolution and war from the 1780s had created a period of increased profit for the owners of the West Indies plantations but the early decades of the 19th century saw a depression in sugar prices. The plantations were reliant on credit, the debts incurred through the costs of operation being recouped from profits made with each harvest. With depression the planters could not cover their initial costs, and at emancipation most of the Jamaican and Barbadian plantations had been mortgaged, many to Bristol merchants (Butler 1995, 44). The end of preferential tariffs and, later, competition from European beet sugar caused a collapse in the value of

plantations (Heuman 1999). The British slave trade was abolished in 1807, partly as a result of a long and high-profile local campaign (Dresser 2001, 130–47), and full emancipation was achieved in 1838. The volume and value of goods moving in and out through the port continued to rise but Bristol experienced a decline relative to other British ports – notably Liverpool, a rival from the 18th century. Despite the purchase of the docks by the Corporation in 1848, and the development of the port facilities at Avonmouth from 1877, the port never regained its former importance. The coastal trade, however, remained very significant in the 19th century and it was not until around 1900 that the tonnage of the international trade exceeded that of the coastal (Large 1984, xiii).

Bristol grew immensely between 1700 and 1900. This growth is partly explained by the enlargement of its administrative boundaries in 1835, 1895 and 1897 but much was the result of migration, incomers drawn by the attractions of a major regional centre. The 20,000 inhabitants in 1700 had become 61,000 by the census of 1801, but the period of greatest increase was between 1801 and 1841 when the population doubled to 125,146. The city never equalled the growth rates of Manchester or Birmingham, but by the beginning of the 20th century it was home to over a third of a million people (Meller 1976, 31). Bristol's expanded population required houses. During the 18th century new areas of housing appeared at the edges of the urban area, with a particular surge in the 1780s and early 1790s. New areas of suburban terraced housing were constructed during the 19th century, most rapidly later in the century.

The industry of the city expanded from the late 17th century. There were large pottery and metalworking industries, while the glass industry, which supplied bottles and fine glassware to North America, had a high reputation for its window glass (Schwind 1983).

Despite an attack by the poet Richard Savage in the early 18th century on its 'low'ring Brow' (Tracy 1962, 257–60) the city had an active civic and cultural life; it has been argued that, for the middle classes, membership of a civic culture and its constituent societies was most important (Barry 1993). The Hotwells, on the River Avon below Clifton, emerged as a fashionable spa at the end of the 17th century but reached its greatest popularity in the first decades of the 18th, with a season distinct from that of Bath (Hembry 1990, 246). Political life was largely the preserve of an exclusive group of merchants and councillors, but the city was the arena for more violent political expression, most famously in 1831 when much of Queen Square was burned down during the rioting associated with the passage of the Great Reform Bill. Bristol retained its long tradition of religious non-conformity, and was a notably important centre in the establishment of Methodism. John Wesley first came to Bristol in 1739 and lived in the city for three years preaching in the city churches, Newgate Gaol, and latterly at open-air meetings. The established church, however, remained the dominant religious power in the city through the 18th century and was a strong influence on its cultural life, but by the time of the religious census in 1851 Anglicans numbered only 44 per cent of those attending a Sunday service (Dresser 1996a, 116).

Urban growth

In the course of the late 17th and 18th centuries the economic geography of Bristol was transformed, partly by the operation of market forces and partly by new regulation. The medieval and early modern pattern – in which residential functions co-existed side-by-side with trading and manufacture conducted at a shop/workshop scale, more or less throughout the city – was breaking down. There had, as we have seen, always been differentiation between districts: for example, the concentration of shops in the main streets of the old centre (Leech 2014, chapter 7) and the concentration of textile trades in the waterfront tenements of Redcliffe. However, from the late 17th century the growing scale and specialisation of manufacturing enterprises meant that their premises began to overshadow their residential neighbours and neighbourhoods while accounting for an ever-increasing proportion of the expanding built-up area. While industrialisation did not leave the main streets of the old city centre unaffected, its inherited geography, infrastructure and symbolism ensured its differentiation from the periphery and it became a true central business district, dominated by the public and commercial buildings necessary to transact the business of the Atlantic and regional economies.

The construction of Queen Square in 1699–1700 was a significant turning point in the development of the city, and not only in terms of urban design. From at least 1709, land uses there were strictly controlled by conditions in the leases of the new buildings, guaranteeing that industry would be excluded from it. Similar strict building specifications were also laid down for St James's Square (1705–15) and thus, for some citizens, and some districts, the separation of workplace (with its concomitant hazards and nuisances), from dwelling, was achieved and formalised. But not for all, and it is no coincidence that it was in the old, increasingly grim, unregulated, mixed-use neighbourhoods, Lewins Mead, Broadmead and Redcliffe, that non-Conformism flourished (pp 395–403).

The Old City (Figs 8.1 and 8.2)

The historic core was renewed between *c* 1700 and the 20th century, but the most significant changes to its topography were made during the latter part of the 18th century. Renewal had two main aspects: the removal or rebuilding of many of the major landmarks of the medieval city centre; and the widening of old streets, the insertion of new ones, with new buildings, and the rebuilding or re-fronting of many smaller buildings, particularly in the mid- to late 19th century.

Increasing traffic congestion led to the removal of several of the remaining medieval landmarks in the heart of the city. Condemned by some as 'a ruinous and superstitious Relick, which is at present a public nuisance', the High Cross was taken down from its original position in 1733 to be re-erected at College Green, where it stood until 1762 (Liversidge 1978, 2). After a period of storage in the Cathedral, the stones of the cross were given to Henry Hoare of Stourhead where it was re-erected in 1766 (*see* Figs 3.7 and 6.44).

St Nicholas Gate was demolished with the adjoining church in 1762, St Giles Gate in *c* 1771, while St Leonard's Gate, church and vicarage were demolished and the parish amalgamated with St Nicholas under the terms of an Act of 1766 which enabled various street improvements (6 Geo. III; Leech 1997c, 119). St Peter's Pump (also known at St Peter's

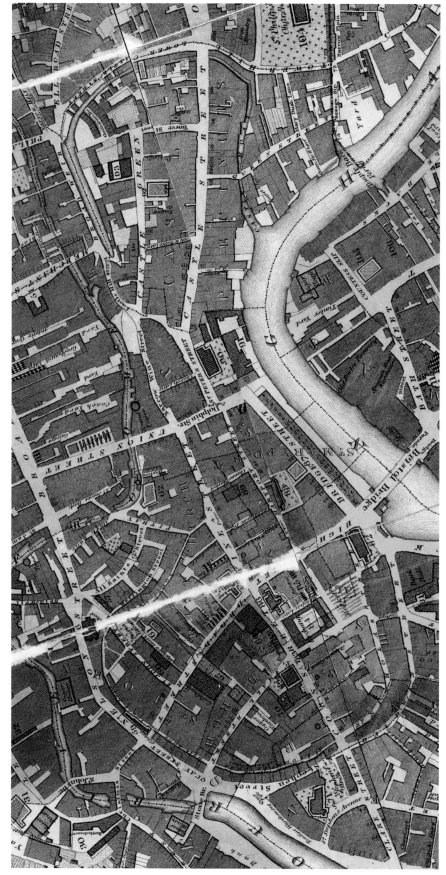

Figure 8.1 Extract from Plumley and Ashmead's map of 1828, showing the historic core (Bristol Archives 04481)

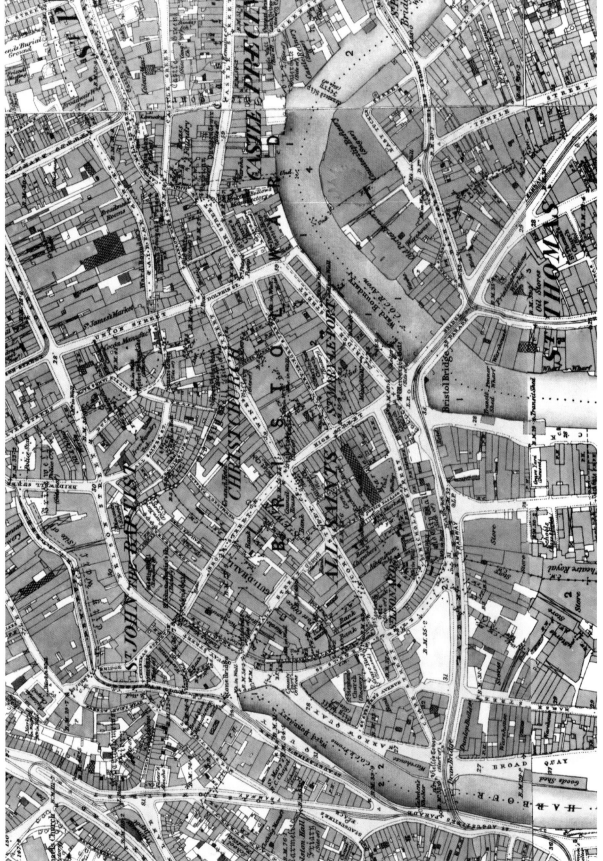

Figure 8.2 Extract from the 1st edition of the Ordnance Survey map of 1884, showing the historic core

Cross), at the west end of Peter Street, was removed and the water supply from the well beneath repositioned to the east side of the junction of Dolphin Street and Peter Street under the terms of the same Act; the Trustees of Bristol Bridge were then approached by Henry Hoare for permission to collect the stones of the superstructure and re-erect them on his Stourhead estate – where the structure still stands (Fig 8.3).

John Street was created between 1742 and 1786 but the last major topographic change of the period did not come until 1878 when the church of St Werburgh, despite a last minute attempt to retain at least the tower (*The Builder*,

Figure 8.3 St Peter's Pump in its present location at Stourhead (photograph D Martyn)

11 March 1876, 250), was demolished for the widening of Small Street.

The narrow width of the medieval Bristol Bridge led to a campaign for its rebuilding. The Corporation invited three architects to contribute designs – that submitted by James Bridges was accepted in 1758 – and obtained an Act of Parliament which allowed the cost of the scheme to be recovered from a variety of taxes and tolls (33 Geo. II; Manson 1997). The new bridge was completed by 1768. Along with the replacement of the bridge, new thoroughfares to link it to Broadmead were planned. Bridge Street, with a row of four-storey houses designed by Thomas Paty, was constructed in a terrace dug across the line of Worshipful Street (Leech 1998b).

The city's merchants pressed for the replacement of the Merchants' Tolzey. Designs were invited for a new Exchange, and Parliamentary approval was obtained for its construction in 1722. Despite tenacious efforts by William Halfpenny to interest the Corporation in several designs, John Wood the elder was chosen as the architect. Wood, was to 'contrive a BUILDING round an AREA, proper for about Six Hundred People to Assemble in, in such Manner, as that it should have the outward Appearance of one Grand Structure' (Wood 1969). Between 1741 and 1743 he created a building with a central trading area, a coffee house and a tavern on the Corn Street frontage and eight four-storey houses or business premises, a single room on each floor, along its east and west sides. Survey of the building (BHER 3374) has found that, despite later campaigns of alteration, the Exchange Tavern is well preserved as are features of the separate houses, notably the kitchens, and in one the chimney-piece, range, cupboard and boiler all survive (Leech 1999a; 2014, 314) (Fig 8.4).

Venues for the social intercourse associated with commerce were numerous around the Exchange. The Elephant Coffee House on the west side of All Saints' Lane had been one of the buildings swept away, but Wood included a coffee house in the north-east corner of his new Exchange building and, when the company of Barber Surgeons was dissolved in the latter part of the 1740s, its hall was also leased out as a coffee house (Wood 1969). Thomas Paty designed another at 56 Corn Street, which was built in 1782 and still survives (Ison 1952, 91–2).

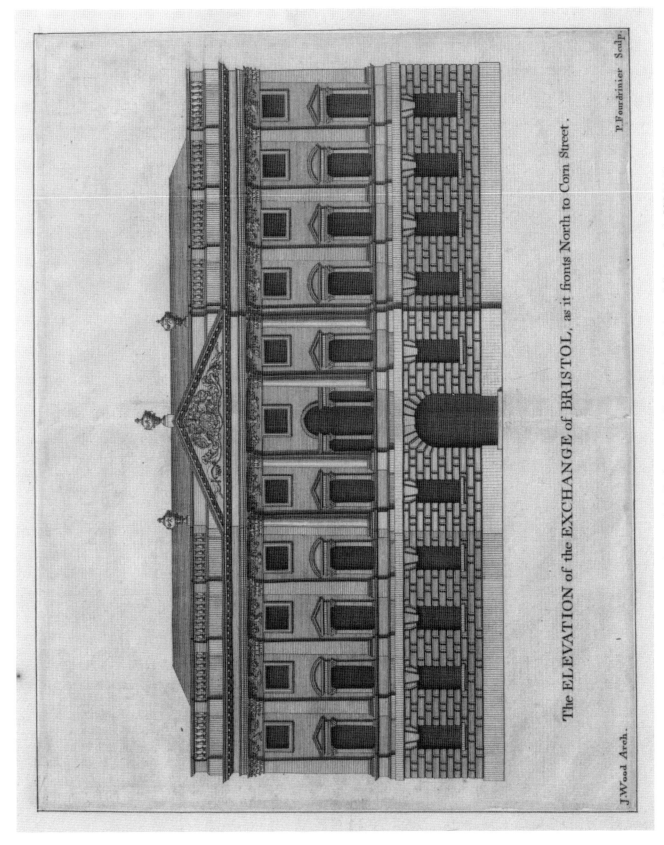

Figure 8.4 Corn Street elevation of the Exchange, 1745 (Bristol Reference Library Collections Braik. XIV.269)

The Tolzey site itself was redeveloped in 1704 when the Council House, an ashlar building occupying the site at the corner of Broad Street and Corn Street, was built. The remaining fabric of St Ewen's Church was incorporated into the building *c* 1790 for office accommodation, three stages of the church tower being used to store the city archives (Fig 8.5).

In 1821 the architect Robert Smirke was employed to rebuild the Council House, the ornate structure now known as the Old Council House which was completed in late 1827. There was a further phase of alteration in 1898–9 when three 17th-century houses in Broad Street were removed to enlarge the building. A new Council chamber was created but the changes left Smirke's building largely intact (BHER 3606) (Leech 2000d).

Figure 8.5 North side of Corn Street in 1824, showing the Council House, shortly before its replacement by Edward Cashin (Braikenridge Collection, BRSMG M2334)

The necessity of credit facilities in internal and international trade meant that banking facilities grew up within the city in the 18th century to serve the needs of the merchant community, and the bank owners tended to be drawn from that community. Bristol's first bank was established in Broad Street in 1750, the partners including Onesiphorus Tyndall and Isaac Elton, and moved to offices at 35 Corn Street in *c* 1791 (Bryant 1995a). What was to become Miles Bank was established in 1752, the partners including Thomas Goldney and Richard Champion (Stembridge 1998, 62–3). Several more were founded around Corn Street in the following decades which, by 1770, had emerged as the centre of banking in the city. Many of the buildings constructed for these institutions still line the street. The West of England and South Wales bank founded in 1834 had its head office in Bristol and the building constructed between 1854 and 1858 at 53–5 Corn Street to house it is still extant. The insurance industry was similarly drawn to Corn Street, and examples of offices built for insurance companies still exist – like the offices for the Liverpool, London and Globe Assurance offices built at 36 Corn Street by W B Gingell between 1865 and 1867. Almost all of the banks and insurance firms advertising in the Bristol directories of the 1890s had offices in Corn Street or Clare Street. The block defined by Broad Street, Corn Street and Small Street was, as well its banking functions, also becoming the legal quarter of the expanding city by the late 18th century, and a replacement building for the Guildhall, where the courts for the City and the Quarter Sessions were held, was constructed in 1843.

A second main aspect to the area was the further development of public facilities for retailing. A market place was created on the south side of The Exchange and Samuel Glascodine designed the arched market entrance off High Street built in 1744–5. The meat and fish markets, and the fruit and vegetable markets, were concentrated in the area on the south side of The Exchange, and the Somersetshire Market House lay on the west side of Exchange Avenue. The organisation of the space of the markets established by the end of the 18th century has remained broadly consistent since then, although the arrangement of structures was formalised by new buildings (Bristol Archives 26163). The

Butchers' Shambles, eight rows of north–south stalls occupying most of the area between the Exchange and St Nicholas Street, were in a state of serious disrepair by the mid-19th century and were replaced in 1849 by the existing Market House. The Market Chambers was constructed on the site of the Somersetshire Market House at around the same time. A new building for the Fish Market was erected on the southern side of St Nicholas Street in 1897, and a cluster of public houses developed around the market, particularly on the south side of St Nicholas Street.

The area between Wine Street and Bridge Street developed as the main shopping area from the 18th century, the traditional pattern of craftspeople combining their dwellings with workshops and shops giving way to pure retailing. High Street, Wine Street, Mary-le-Port Street and Bridge Street were lined by shops by the late 19th century and large retail stores, notably Jones' and Verrier's, occupied the south side of Wine Street (Fig 8.6). Despite these developments, industrial premises, large and small, continued as a feature of, and immediately around the renewed central business district.

Old Market (Fig 8.7)

At the beginning of the 18th century Old Market still retained its medieval street pattern and most of this survived the 20th century, although the creation of Temple Way in the 1960s and subsequent large office developments along its east side destroyed the western end of Old Market Street. Similar in its mix of residential, commercial and industrial uses to the neighbouring area of Broadmead, the otherwise minimal changes to its form which did occur relate to the construction of larger industrial buildings and the improvement of traffic flow. In 1768 Lawford's Gate was removed and the eastern end of Old Market Street widened. In the early 1880s the City Council's Street Improvement Committee created a new road, St Matthias Park, between Redcross Street and Broad Weir, which required the compulsory purchase of the burial ground on the north side of Redcross Street. The western part of the cemetery, unaffected by the road, was then bought by the Sanitary Committee and laid out as a public park, again as a resource for the expanding population, the Lord Mayor opening the newly landscaped space in June 1886.

The Lawford's Gate House of Correction was built by the County of Gloucester in the late 1780s north of West Street. Designed by William Blackburn, the two-storey building had 20 cells on each floor, a petty sessions room designed for weekly courts, and a two-room keeper's house (Whiting 1975, 138–41). It had gone out of use by 1860 but was not demolished until the early 20th century (Fig 8.8).

One of the most significant housing developments in the city was undertaken by Nathaniel Wade in the area of Earlsmead from c 1700–10. Great and Little Ann Streets, Great George Street and Wade Street were all part of this development, which consisted of relatively modest terraced houses one-room deep (Fig 8.9).

These seem to have been developed specifically for artisans and shopkeepers, in

Figure 8.6 Mary-le-Port Street c 1935 (Bristol Reference Library 78/ L93.11 Mar)

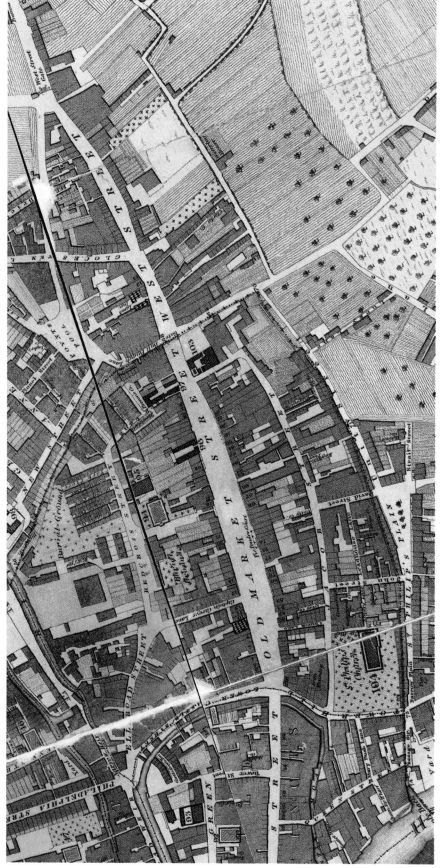

Figure 8.7 Extract from Plumley and Ashmead's map of 1828, showing Old Market (Bristol Archives 04481)

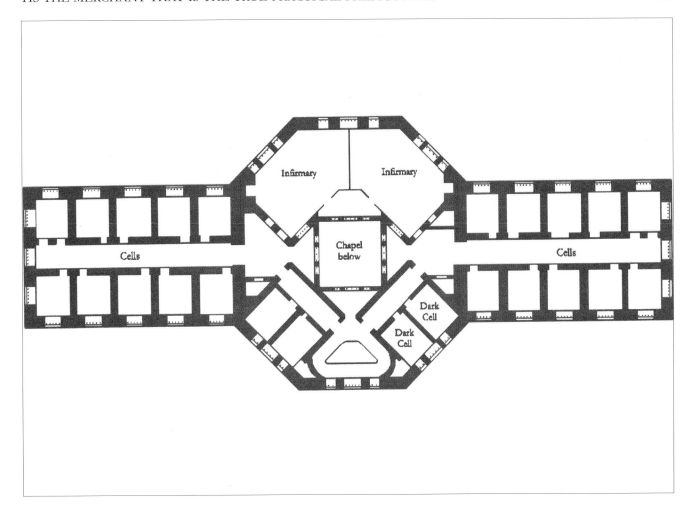

Figure 8.8 The plan of the House of Correction, Lawford's Gate, from a late 18th-century plan by William Blackburn (redrawn by J R Brett)

contrast to most contemporaneous projects in other parts of the city aimed at a wealthier clientele (Leech 1999c; Leech 2014, 344). Excavation adjacent to Wade Street has provided detailed evidence for the development sequence of part of this area together with associated evidence for the material culture of its inhabitants (Avon Archaeology 2014; Corcos *et al* 2017). Most of these buildings were demolished in a slum clearance programme in the 1930s. No 17 Wade Street is one of the surviving examples and Roger Leech has noted a similarity between the plan-form of this building and that of workers' housing in Frome (Leech 1981, 17; *see also* pp 406–8) (Fig 8.10).

College Green (Fig 8.11)
At the beginning of the 18th century College Green and Brandon Hill formed a block of open land on the west side of the city. The Bishop's Park lay between the Cathedral precinct and the western end of St George's Road, with St George's Road itself forming its northern boundary and Anchor Lane the southern. Rocque's map of 1742 shows that there were fishponds at the centre and on its southern edge. In 2008 a site was excavated that had formerly been occupied by 18th- and 19th-century housing, lying within a former valley, identified in this and previous excavations, at the centre of Bishop's Park (BHER 25013: Cox *et al* 2006; Holt and Leech 2011). The physical evidence for the late 18th-century development of Bishop's Park is consistent with the documentary sources which illustrate the spread of new suburban development, commencing in the mid-17th century, initially of houses for single families and their servants. The evidence from the excavation shows the gradual subdivision of these houses to allow for multiple occupation during the 19th and 20th centuries, together with the decline in status, exacerbated by the demolition of some of the properties to allow for the construction of Deanery Road in 1869.

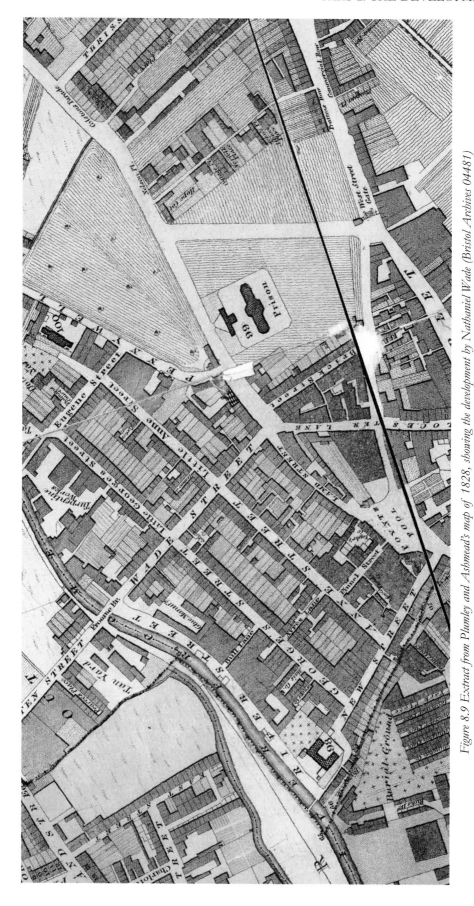

Figure 8.9 Extract from Plumley and Ashmead's map of 1828, showing the development by Nathaniel Wade (Bristol Archives 04481)

Figure 8.10 No 17 Wade Street (photograph R Jones)

To the south of the Cathedral were enclosed gardens or orchards and a ropewalk recorded by Millerd's map of *c* 1715. Part of one of the walls of the ropewalk, probably dating to the late 18th or early 19th century, may have been identified in an excavation in 1997 (BHER 456), while further evidence for the ropewalk and land management in Canon's Marsh was recovered during excavation by Cotswold Archaeology between 2003 and 2008 (Tavener 1997; Alexander and Harward 2011). The land at the centre of Canon's Marsh was enclosed into a single field, Great Ground, used for grazing cattle and surrounded by what seem to have been substantial ditches, features on the scale of the rhines found on the Avon Levels

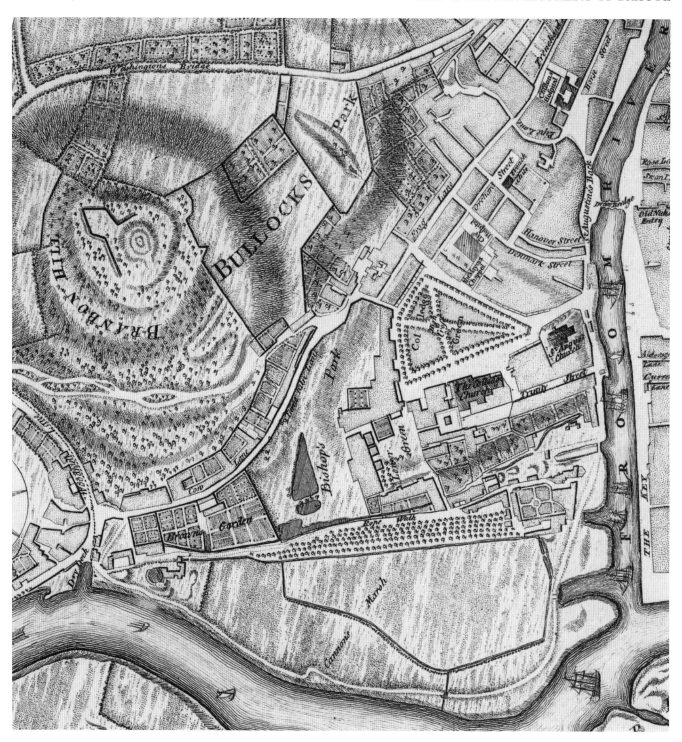

Figure 8.11 Extract from Jean Rocque's plan of 1750, showing College Green and Brandon Hill (BRSMG M707)

(Bristol Archives DC/E/3/4). Between 1742 and 1828 Great Ground was divided into four smaller closes.

It was with the speculative building of the mid-18th century that major changes really began to be made to the topography of the area. Park Street was created in 1761, plots leased out and housing erected along it as far

as the Great George Street junction (Ison 1952, 211–12). The Dean and Chapter obtained Parliamentary approval for the granting of leases for building in the Bishop's Park in 1770 and College Street, Lower Lamb Street (originally Back Street) and Lower College Street had been laid out by the time of Donne's map in 1787. Charlotte Street and the

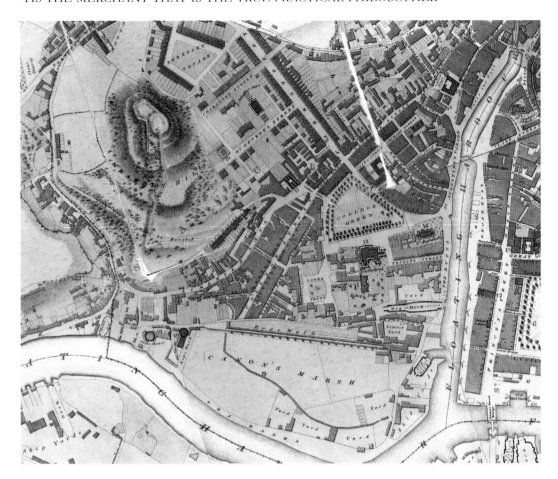

Figure 8.12 Extract from Plumley and Ashmead's map of 1828, showing College Green, Brandon Hill and Park Street (Bristol Archives 04481)

remainder of Park Street were developed in the late 1780s and, as with the lower part of Park Street, the Patys were prominent among the architects. Berkeley Square was a development by James Lockyer with the housing arranged around three sides of a square, the central space turned into a garden shared by the residents and the open side giving views over Canon's Marsh towards Bedminster. The development was incomplete when Lockyer and his partners went bankrupt in 1793 and several of the houses in the square and in Charlotte Street were not finished until the early 19th century (Ison 1952, 214) (Fig 8.12).

Brandon Hill remained a public open space throughout the 18th and 19th centuries and briefly gained a use as an arena for political meetings in the early decades of the 19th century. The City Council created a constabulary to police the hill but adopted a more subtle means of controlling the space from the 1840s, laying out gravel walks and terraces to create a more formal public park (Poole 1996, 87–8). The top of the hill was

laid out as a circular gun emplacement for cannon captured during the Crimean war in August 1857, the boundaries of the space were formalised in the late 19th century and, in 1897, Cabot Tower was built to commemorate the 400th anniversary of the voyage which discovered Newfoundland (Lambert 2000, 15–18; Townsend 2011).

Lewins Mead (Fig 8.13)

The district between the Frome and St Michael's Hill was one of social and economic diversity in the 18th and 19th centuries, although in the 19th the area of the Frome floodplain gained a reputation as one of the poorest parts of the city.

Housing developments and the demands of traffic movement within the city resulted in significant changes to the street pattern in the area between St Augustine's Parade and St James Barton during the 18th and 19th centuries. The first new scheme to be built was Orchard Street, whose houses were constructed between 1717 and the early

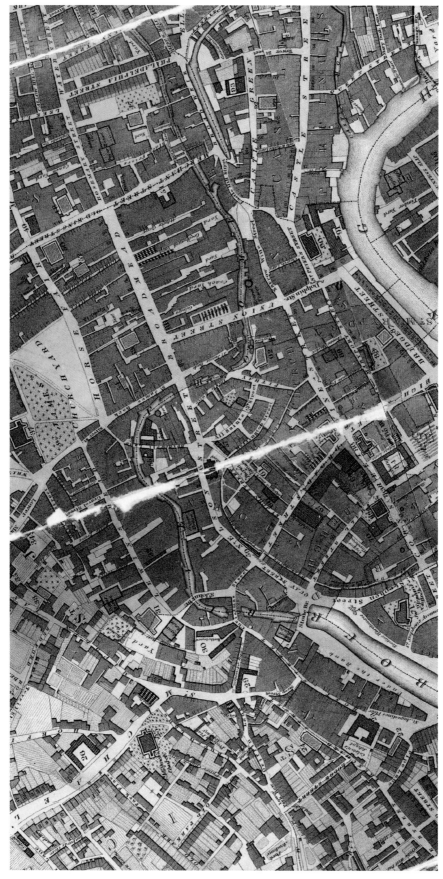

Figure 8.13 Extract from Plumley and Ashmead's map of 1828, showing the Lewins Mead area and the upper reaches of the Frome (Bristol Archives 04481)

1720s on the site of the former garden of the Hospital of St Mark, at that time occupied by the Grammar School (Figs 8.14 and 8.15).

More extensive development took place to the north and east of St James's Church: Cannon Street had been laid out by 1744 and the many streets and courts to the north of it were in existence by 1786 (Jackson 2006b). Housing had already occupied much of Stoney Hill by the 17th century but the gardens between Sir John Yonge's Great House, then owned by Edward Colston, and the Red Lodge were still in existence at the time of Rocque's survey in 1742. Offering a large block of available land, these gardens were developed for housing in the later 18th century: Lodge Street, the houses on both sides designed by Thomas Paty, was created in 1784 and 1–6 Lower Park Row not long after. Other changes were intended as enhancements to mobility within the city and Nelson Street, in effect a slight realignment and widening of the former Hallier's Lane (previously Gropecuntelane), was created in 1792 (Bristol Archives 00228(14)). Whitson Street was driven between Marlborough Street and Lower Maudlin Street across the site of Whitson Court in 1827, and to improve traffic flow Steep Street was removed and Perry Road, opened on the 20 August 1868, and Colston Street created.

Lewins Mead was one of those areas of the city where 17th-century housing survived into the mid-19th, and inquiries into the sanitary condition of the city tended to concentrate on the condition of the housing there, where the state of the dwellings, often in multiple occupation and consequently squalid, was exacerbated by the state of the River Frome (De La Beche 1845). Many houses oversailed the Frome, their drains emptying directly into it: 60 to 70 gouts were counted between Christmas Street and Stone Bridge, a roughly 100m stretch, in 1850 (De La Beche 1845, 21–2; Clark 1850, 61) (Fig 8.16).

Construction of the Floating Harbour between 1804 and 1809 ended the twice-daily tidal flushing of the city rivers, and the insertion of lock gates at Stone Bridge slowed the flow of the Frome to the point of stagnation. The consequences for public health were serious. To address the problem, Mylne's Culvert was constructed to carry the discharge from the Frome from the Stone Bridge, under Broad Quay (where its brick culvert was found

in a watching-brief in 1997, together with its wood shuttering surviving *in situ*: BHER 3275), under the Floating Harbour on the line of Prince Street Bridge, and out into the tidal New Cut. But it failed to solve the problem, and the Council's Frome Committee was told in 1840 that an urgent remedy was necessary (Bristol Archives 0491). It agreed to culvert the Frome on 31 July 1840 and the space created was used to construct Rupert Street, linking Under the Bank to Bridewell Street.

Broadmead (Fig 8.17)

The progress of development in Broadmead is clear, at least in outline, from the cartographic evidence. At the beginning of the 18th century Merchant Street, lined on both its east and west sides by buildings, marked the eastern edge of the built-up area as shown by Millerd in 1673 (*see* Fig 7.8). By 1742 the remainder of the block between Rosemary Lane and Milk Street had been developed, while Water Street led to a lane which crossed the remaining open land to Horseshoes Bridge across the Frome (south of Philadelphia Court). On the east and north sides of the meeting house in Quakers Friars were orchards and gardens (Bristol Archives P/StJ/ChW/6). East of the former Friary, development of Penn Street began in 1743 and of Philadelphia Street in 1763. On the north side, a major expansionary episode commenced soon after 1719, when the land was sold off by Hannah Callowhill, the wife of William Penn. Development of the north side of Water Street started and the street was extended to the east as part of the development of the last remaining quarter of the area (Leech and Bryant 2000; Davenport 2013f, 388). New streets – Callowhill Street, Hanover Street and Clark Street were laid out and largely built up in the 1720s and 1730s. Excavation of this area revealed small three-storey, two-cell houses, with small back yards largely occupied by cess pits, although there were substantial variations in design (*see* p 408). This was completed by the 1770s. Union Street and the bridge across the Frome were begun in 1771 (Latimer 1893, 396).

South of Quakers Friars, on the former Dominican friary precinct, between the Frome and Broadweir, excavation has identified some rearrangement of tenement boundaries during the 18th century, and evidence for the

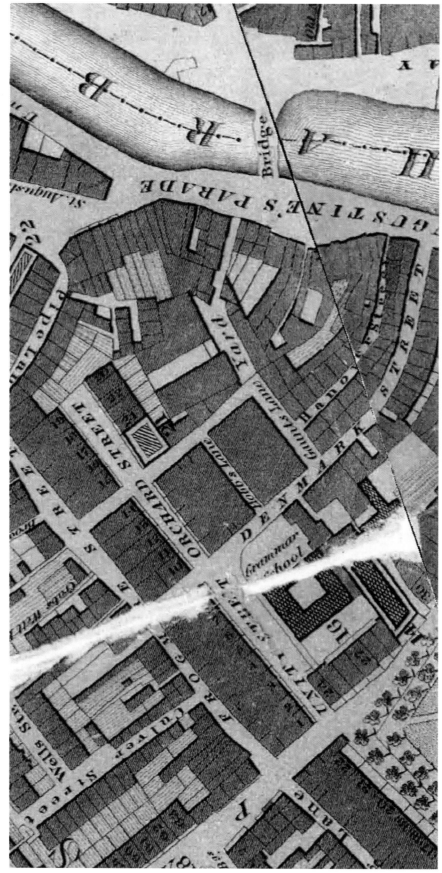

Figure 8.14 Extract from Plumley and Ashmead's map of 1828, showing the Orchard Street area (Bristol Archives 04481)

Figure 8.15 Nos 10–14 Orchard Street 1906 (Bristol Municipal Charities collection, ref 33041/ BMC/12/1/b/12)

tanning industry in the form of five cylindrical stone tanks, lined with reused wooden casks (Figs 8.18 and 8.19).

Following reclamation, some development took place with new bridges built across the Frome and houses erected on vaults over the river (BHER 4279/4281; Davenport 2013b, 347) (Fig 8.20).

Although the basic street pattern had been completed by 1800, some significant changes nonetheless occurred later in the 19th century (Fig 8.21). Lower Union Street had been created by 1878 and earlier, in 1824, Lower Arcade, a new shopping arcade designed by James and Thomas Foster, was built between Horsefair and Broadmead. Another, Upper Arcade, was created the following year, running north from Horsefair to Barton Alley off St James Barton. These Gothic Revival arcades had Ionic columns marking entrances at either end which were reached by steps; the glazed roofs were supported by cast iron pillars and a frieze (Gomme *et al* 1979, 241–2). The lower arcade had 36 single-cell plan shops while the 1880s' Ordnance Survey map indicates 38 in the upper. Another commercial development was St James's Market, opened in 1776 on the east side of Union Street.

The River Frome remained open throughout the 18th century, but by the 1840s there was, as already discussed, growing pressure for the resolution of the problem of increased nuisance from sewage. By 1850 the part of the river which ran through Broadmead had been culverted, allowing the creation of Fairfax Street, while the section at St James's Back was enclosed at the instigation of Fry's *c* 1854 (Leech 1998a).

It is clear from late 18th-century directories that many craftsmen operating small manufacturing businesses inhabited the streets around Broadmead. The range of trades present at the end of the 18th century was broad, from cabinet makers and turners, to bakers, shoe makers and other clothing manufacturers, and it seems likely that the dwellings of craftsmen in the area also comprised workshops and shops. More is known, however, about the larger industrial concerns, and these are discussed below (pp 353–387).

Kingsdown

The documentary and cartographic evidence makes clear that St Michael's Hill was still, at the beginning of the 18th century, mostly open ground, divided into large closes; settlement

*Figure 8.16 Rear of a building on St John's Bridge adjacent to Frome Bridge, showing overhanging privies in 1821 by Hugh O'Neill
(Braikenridge Collection, BRSMG M2894)*

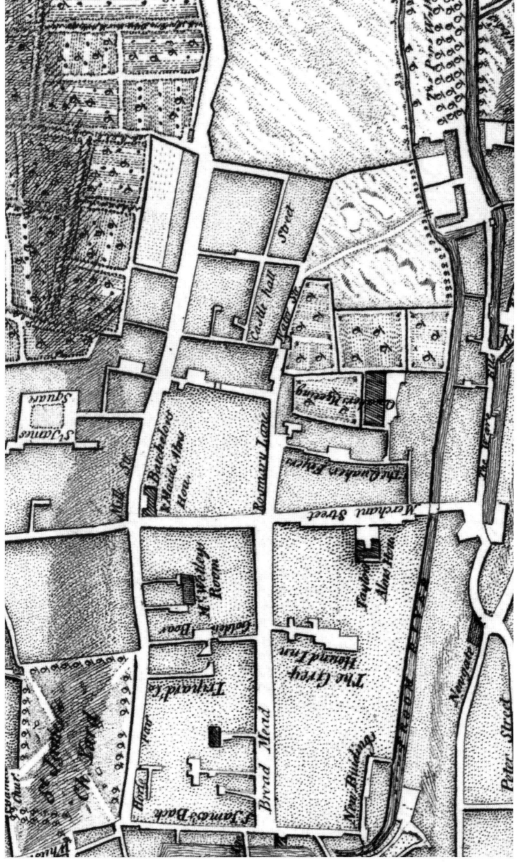

Figure 8.17 Extract from Jean Rocque's plan of 1750, showing the Broadmead area (BRSMG M707)

Figure 8.18 18th-century tanning pits excavated at Cabot Circus (reproduced from Ridgeway and Watts 2013, fig 3.54)

was mainly confined to the lower, southern part of the hill. The lodges and gardens of the Bristol merchants, first built there in the mid-17th century continued to be used, and several more were built. The area of Kingsdown Parade in particular was, at the time of Rocque's map of 1742, occupied by gardens and small buildings (Fig 8.22).

Onesiphorous Tyndall, a councillor of the Corporation, who was involved in the Atlantic trade and part owner of slave ships in the 1720s, had begun to acquire leases on the hill in the early 18th century (Parker 1929, 134; Bettey 1997, 8). His son John acquired the lease for a park owned by the Dean and Chapter. He predeceased his father and Tyndall's second son, also named Onesiphorous, inherited at his death. In 1757 the second son died and the Tyndalls' property passed to his heir Thomas. Thomas Tyndall quickly bought the freehold on the Royal Fort, demolished many of the walls which marked the boundaries of the land parcels and set about creating a park which enclosed some 68 acres. He created a gateway flanked by entrance lodges on Park Row by demolishing existing houses there (including that of the teacher and artist James Stewart), then commissioned a design for the present Royal Fort house from James Bridges. This was built and the park was largely complete by the 1760s (Figs 8.23 and 8.24).

Housing development was underway at the top of St Michael's Hill. Southwell Street had been laid out by the time of Rocque's map, and within a decade construction at

Walker Street was beginning. The houses along these streets were built piecemeal by small speculators: a Monmouthshire watchmaker, Thomas Pierce, erected a handful of houses in Southwell Street in the early 1750s (Bristol Archives 4268 (2–4)). To accommodate the growing number of parishioners, the parish church was substantially rebuilt, to a design by Thomas Paty, between 1774 and 1777 (Figs 8.25 and 8.26).

More housing was built later in the 18th century. The development boom led a consortium to draw up plans in 1792 to develop Tyndall's Park with a square, crescent, circus and several streets. Persuading Thomas Tyndall to sell the park for £40,000, and the Dean and Chapter to allow the development of some of its land on the hill, for which they obtained a 1,000-year lease, Parliamentary approval was gained in 1792 and the excavation of foundation trenches begun. The scheme fell victim to the end of the speculative boom in 1793 and was never built. Control of the park reverted to Tyndall who, faced with an area scarred by trenches and obstructed by the new development of Berkeley Square and the upper part of Park Street, obtained the services of Humphry Repton to landscape the park. Repton visited the site in February 1799 and discovered it 'surrounded by large chasms in the ground' and 'immense heaps of earth & broken rock which had been dug out to form the cellars and foundations'. He produced a Red Book just over two and a half years later containing his proposals for planting the spoil heaps and reducing the sides of the trenches (Daniels 1999, 238).

At the end of the 19th century Kingsdown was primarily a residential area, semi-detached villas having been built in the area of Woodland Road in the 1860s, and much other housing by the 1890s (Gomme *et al* 1979, 273–4).

The area of Park Row and Queen's Road saw the construction of a number of civic buildings with a strong educational theme from the middle of the 19th century. The Bishop's College (1839), later a volunteers' club with a drill hall behind, became the Salisbury Club in 1888. The School of Industry for the Blind was built at the end of the 1830s on the site now occupied by the Wills Memorial Building; this was a translation of the Blind Asylum established at Lower Maudlin Street in 1792. The Fine Art Academy building in Queen's Road was designed by John Henry

Hirst in 1855, with interiors designed by Charles Underwood; it was completed in 1857. A university college was founded as a result of public pressure in the 1870s and housed in buildings on Park Row, and the Corporation built a new museum and library at the junction of Queen's Road and University Road between 1867 and 1871 (Fig 8.27). A new synagogue was designed for Park Row by S C Fripp and built in 1874 (Fig 8.28). The interior was by Hyman Henry Collins of London and is typical of his work. In 1876 the Bristol Grammar School bought land to the north of Queen's Road as its new site and moved from Unity Street to the new buildings in May 1879 (Hill 1951, 103–7). This burst of institutional building was consolidated in the early 20th century with the construction of an Art Gallery, the further expansion of the University College and the translation of the Baptist College from Stokes Croft to a new building at Woodland Road.

Redcliffe and Temple (Fig 8.29)

In 1700 the topographical framework of Redcliffe and Temple was still that which had been established in the 12th century but, in the 18th and 19th centuries, this was substantially modified. Some of the changes were emblematic of the area casting off its medieval form to industrialise. While the Portwall can no longer be recognised above ground, its removal was gradual, with some parts demolished and others (as demonstrated by archaeological investigation) refaced and incorporated into new buildings. The medieval town gates at the ends of Redcliff Street and Temple Street were rebuilt in 1730–1 and 1734 respectively with classical designs, and removed altogether around the end of the century: Redcliff Gate in 1771 and Temple Gate in 1808 (Fig 8.30).

The main area of open ground available for development was the Rack Close and the land beyond the Portwall, either pasture or under cultivation; the berm between the wall and its ditch was used as garden ground at least until the mid-18th century. Development had begun in the southern part of the Rack Close by 1742. Avon Street, Rose Street, Brooks' Court and Tower Street were built and a tree-covered rope walk had been laid out along the west side of the former intramural lane. A string of buildings lay along the north side of Temple Back. In the southern part of Redcliffe, urban

growth took the form of ribbon-development along Redcliff Hill and Guinea Street. In 1718 Captain Edmond Saunders built a substantial house on the south side of Guinea Street, leasing the land adjacent, and by 1725 the street was being described in a lease as 'new-built'; Saunders had been responsible for the construction of 11 new houses in Guinea Street by 1743 (Ison 1952, 156) (Fig 8.31).

Somerset Square, to the south-east of St Mary Redcliffe, was laid out in 1756 and the north and west sides developed by 1770. The south and east sides were built after 1828. The remaining undeveloped parts of the Rack Close and the land between the River Avon

Figure 8.19 Detail of 18th-century tanning pit showing cask base (reproduced from Ridgeway and Watts 2013, fig 3.55)

Figure 8.20 View of bridge over river Frome carrying lane from Broad Weir to Quakers Friars, 1821 by Hugh O'Neill (Braikenridge Collection, BRSMG M2904)

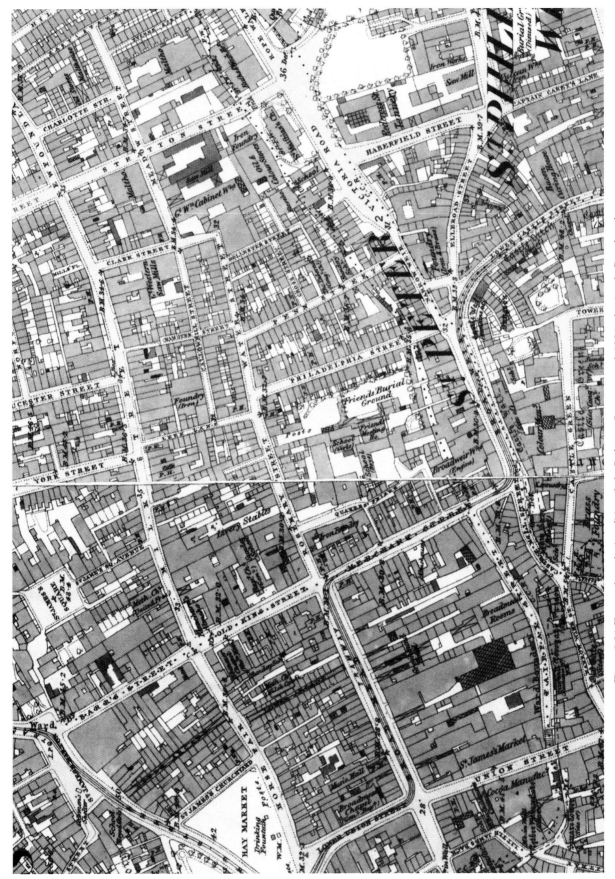

Figure 8.21 Extract from the 1st edition of the Ordnance Survey map of 1884, showing the Broadmead area

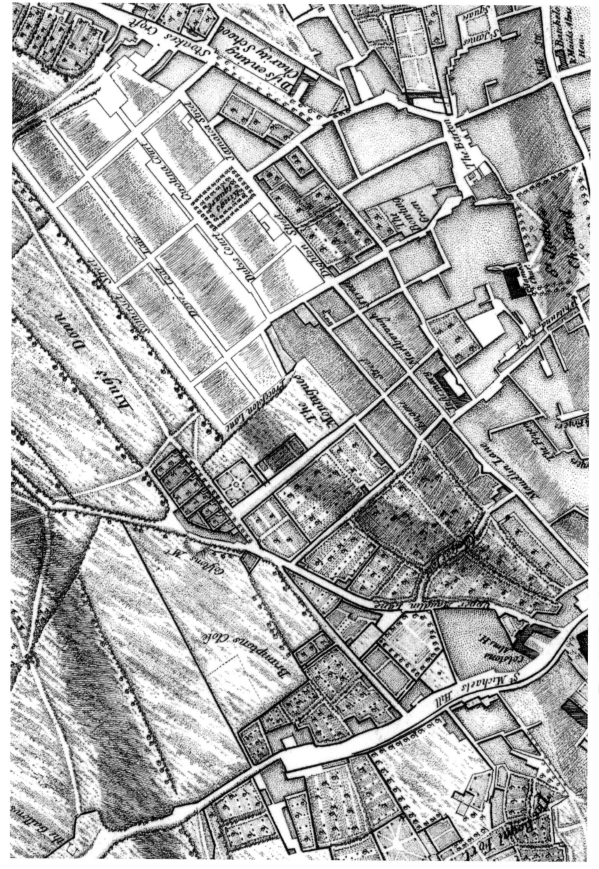

Figure 8.22 Extract from Jean Rocque's plan of 1750, showing Kingsdown and St Michael's Hill (BRSMG M707)

and the New Cut were developed between 1770 and 1828.

In the late 18th century, the ancient topography of the approaches to Bristol Bridge was remodelled. The reconstruction of the Bridge itself in the 1760s left the main route out of the city to the south unaltered, traffic reaching Temple Street via the inconvenient dog-leg route along Tucker Street. In the late 1780s, to improve the situation, the Bridge Trustees decided to create a new road between the bridge and Temple Street. Most of the properties lining Tucker Street were removed to allow construction of Bath Street across its line and new houses, designed by Thomas Paty, were built along it (Bryant 1994a) (Fig 8.32).

Major topographical changes took place to the south of the Redcliffe suburb in the first half of the 19th century. As part of the work to create the Floating Harbour in 1804, the New Cut was excavated to carry the tidal Avon between Redcliffe and Bedminster, effectively forming a new river channel. The scheme also called for 'an Entrance Bason with Locks and Gates … at a Place called Trim Mills … the same to be so constructed as to admit Ships of the largest Burden usually frequenting the Port of Bristol' (quoted in Buchanan 1969, 191). Bathurst Basin, an enlargement of an existing mill pond, provided the second major entrance to the harbour.

The Great Western Railway Company chose a site in the south-east of the suburb for its new terminus (Channon 1985, 25). Most of the land on which the terminus was sited, lying between the New Cut and Pipe Lane, was bought from the Corporation in 1836 after the railway act gained royal assent. The station itself, designed by Brunel, was built between 1839 and 1841 (*see* p 387).

Baldwin Street and the Marsh (Figs 8.33 and 8.34)

At the beginning of the 18th century the topography of the area between Baldwin Street and King Street still retained much of its medieval framework, while the quays bounding it to east and west ensured a continuing maritime influence. The creation of King Street in the mid-17th century (p 248) led to the construction of a number of institutional buildings along its north side, and the early 18th century saw their completion and refurbishment. The Merchant Venturers' Almshouse, begun in 1696, was

Figure 8.23 Royal Fort House (photograph D Martyn)

completed in the first few years of the 18th century (Fig 8.35).

Immediately to the west the Merchant Venturers' Hall, which from the mid-16th century had used the earlier St Clement's Chapel, was the subject of considerable alteration and extension to the north between 1718 and 1722; additional rooms, including a new 'Great Room' were created and the frontage of the building completely rebuilt (McGrath 1975, 111). Between 1738 and 1740 the City Library, founded in 1613 and housed within a lodge of Robert Redwood in King Street, was rebuilt, possibly to a design by James Paty, while the Coopers' Hall, designed by William Halfpenny, was built between 1743 and 1744 as a replacement for the earlier hall which was demolished to make way for the Exchange in Corn Street (Gomme *et al* nd, 34). In 1766 The New Theatre (renamed the Theatre Royal in 1788) opened on the north side of King Street, financed by a consortium of councillors and merchants. James Barker, carpenter of the Drury Lane

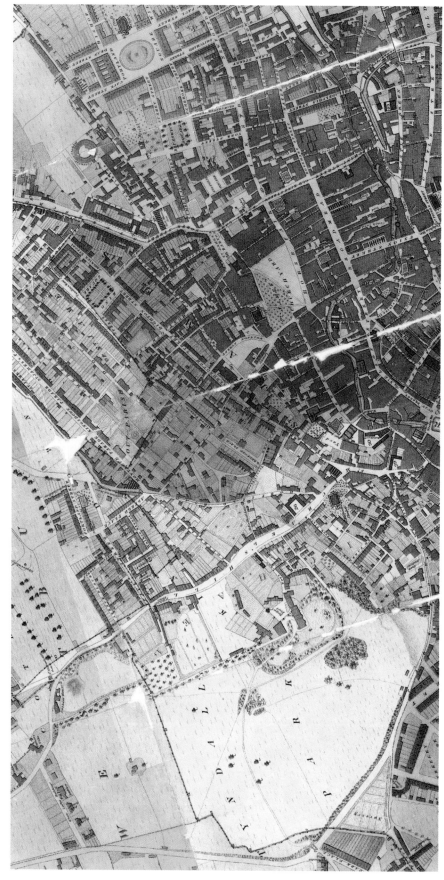

Figure 8.24 Extract from Plumley and Ashmead's map of 1828, showing Tyndall's Park and Kingsdown (Bristol Archives 04481)

Figure 8.25 St Michael's Hill in 1824 (Bristol Reference Library Collections ref Braik. XIII. 155)

Figure 8.26 St Michael-on-the-Mount Church from the south-west (photograph D Martyn)

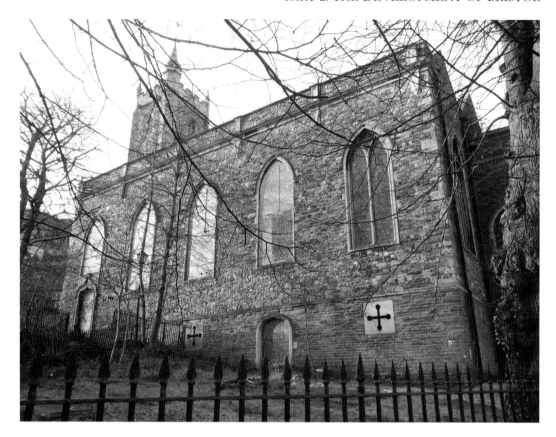

Figure 8.27 The City Museum in the early 20th century (now Browns restaurant) at the junction of Queens Road and University Road (Bristol Reference Library LS.72a)

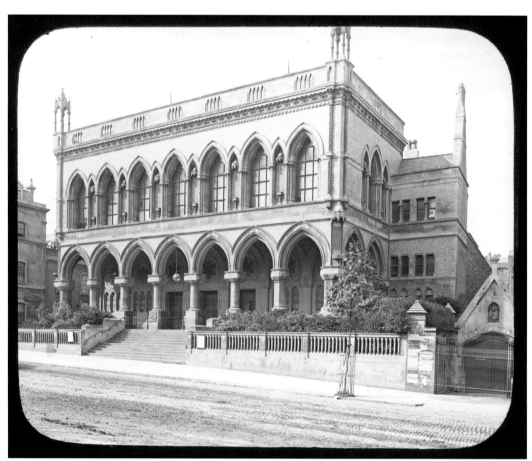

Theatre, produced the plans, the construction was supervised by Thomas Paty and the interior décor was designed by Michael Edkins, better known locally as a ceramic artist (Barker 1974, 8; Priest 2003, 68) (Fig 8.36).

Substantial changes to the topography of the area occurred in the late 18th and 19th centuries, mainly as the result of the creation of a new Frome crossing in 1715 and the long-term decline of the port. A drawbridge was built between Broad Quay and St Augustine's Parade, and to minimise the span of the bridge, piers carried the roadway out from the east side of Broad Quay narrowing the Frome channel and preventing access to the quay head to all but the smaller coastal vessels (Fig 8.37).

In 1738 demolition of the Back Street Gate was ordered to allow better access to Queen Square (*see below*); the gate at the junction of Welsh Back and King Street may have been removed at the same time (Ralph 1981, 10). Another measure to enhance the flow of traffic was the creation of Stone Bridge, a rusticated ashlar structure, only around 6ft wide, built in 1755 a short distance downstream from Frome Bridge (Fig 8.38); the drawbridge was also renewed in the 1750s. In 1770 Clare Street was created to provide a direct route from the heart of the city to the drawbridge and buildings around the north end of Marsh Street were compulsorily purchased under the terms of an Act of Parliament of 1766 and removed, along with Rose Alley and Swan Lane (Leech 1997c, xviii). The churchwardens of St Stephen's applied for permission to demolish a number of

Figure 8.28 The synagogue on Park Row in the early 20th century (Loxton Collection, Bristol Reference Library E532)

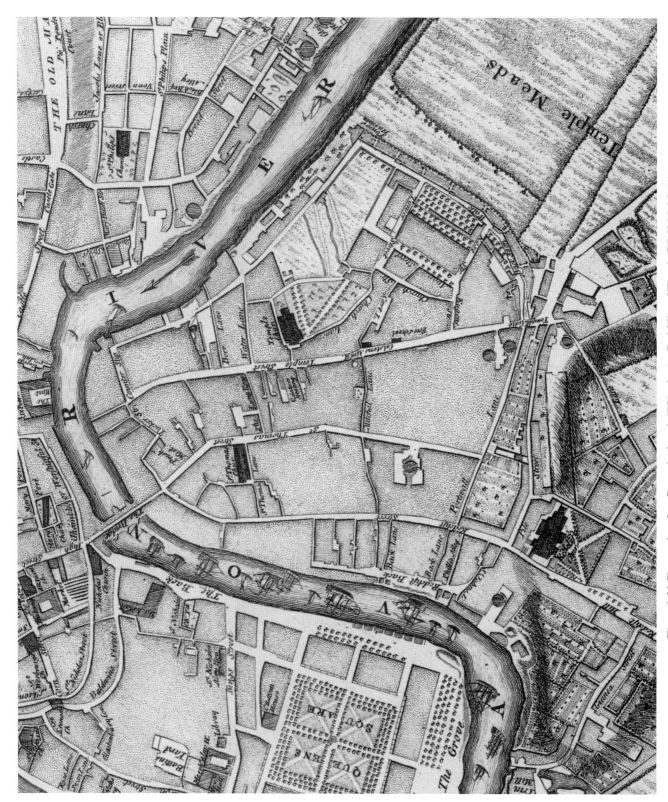

Figure 8.30 Temple Gate in 1751 (Bristol Reference Library Collections ref Braik.III.i.457)

Figure 8.31 No 10 Guinea Street (photograph D Martyn)

an extension of the line of Baldwin Street towards the Drawbridge in 1877, removing Glastonbury Court in the process. The new road opened in March 1881 (*see* Fig 8.39).

Perhaps the most significant change to the local topography came at the end of the 19th century. The frequency of shipping coming to the docks in the heart of the city had been much reduced by both the long-term decline of the port and the opening of the new dock at Avonmouth in 1877, and there was pressure to convert the drawbridge into a fixed bridge. Sir George White, who saw the opportunity for his Bristol Tramways Company to bring more tramlines into the centre of the city, was a champion of the scheme, and debate about it on occasion became heated. One of the arguments thrown at the 'Basculites' who wanted to retain a swing bridge, was that the dockside at the quay head was by then so under-used that 'a goodly portion of it is at present used to stack snow' (*BTM* 11-12-1890). An Act of Parliament was obtained and in 1892 the drawbridge was replaced by a fixed stone bridge (St Augustine's Bridge), and the now redundant portion of the Floating Harbour between Stone Bridge and the drawbridge was culverted. On the newly created space a wooden hall was built to hold an Industrial and Fine Art Exhibition between August 1893 and January 1894, and after this closed the space was turned into a public park, Magpie Park, lined by London plane trees and with a bandstand and the statue of Edmund Burke as major features (Fig 8.39).

Queen Square

During the early 18th century the Marsh was transformed from an open space given over to industry (mostly shipping-related) and leisure into an elite residential area. The first house of what was to become Queen Square was built by a Dr Reade, who acquired a lease of land on which to build in October 1699 and had begun construction by February 1700 (Ison 1952, 140). Over the next three years more than 25 houses were erected, surrounding a central grassed area with no initial layout of formal paths, although the east and west sides reflected the ropewalks which had run through the Marsh.

The ground surface was raised, one Thomas Berry being paid £34 for hauling the soil (topsoil being brought from the close known as Stokes Croft on the north side

buildings in order to widen the 'very narrow and incommodius' streets around the church in 1774, remodelling St Stephen's Lane to create St Stephen's Avenue and removing the western part of the churchyard (*Commons Journal* 34 (1772–4), 515, 659). The dog-leg at the north end of Baldwin Street, of medieval origin, was removed *c* 1795. Traffic congestion became an issue again in the later 19th century, and Parliamentary approval was sought for

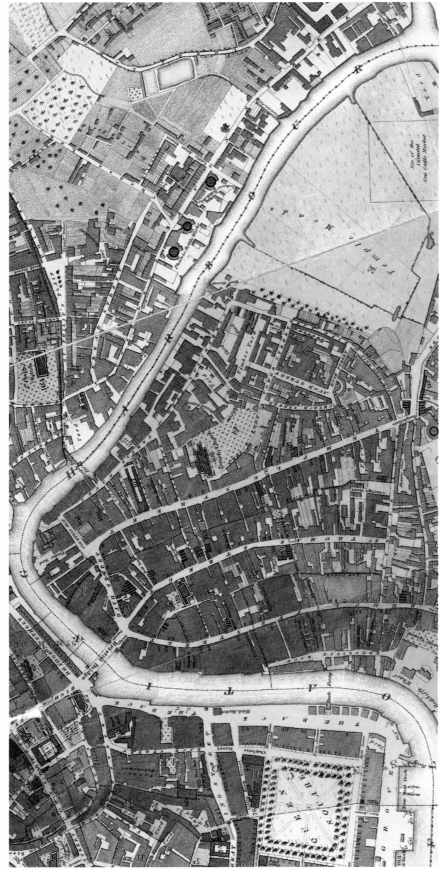

Figure 8.32 Extract from Plumley and Ashmead's map of 1828, showing Redcliffe and Temple (Bristol Archives 04481)

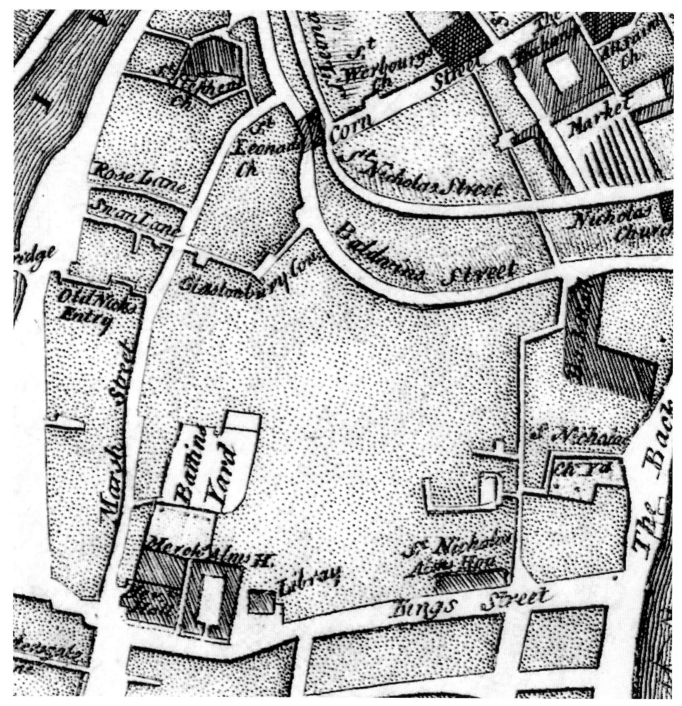

Figure 8.33 Extract from Jean Rocque's plan of 1750, showing Baldwin Street and King Street (BRSMG M707)

of the city), and the roads which had been laid out in front of the houses were paved. An archaeological evaluation in 1998 in the south-west corner of the grassed area found that the square had been raised by dumping more than 2.5m of material, of industrial origin (BHER 3369). Remnants of a loose gravel path, likely to have been part of the original scheme of walks, were also found (Insole 1999b).

By the time Millerd came to revise his map of the city around 1715 there were buildings on all four sides and the centre was railed, with two syncopated rows of trees inside.

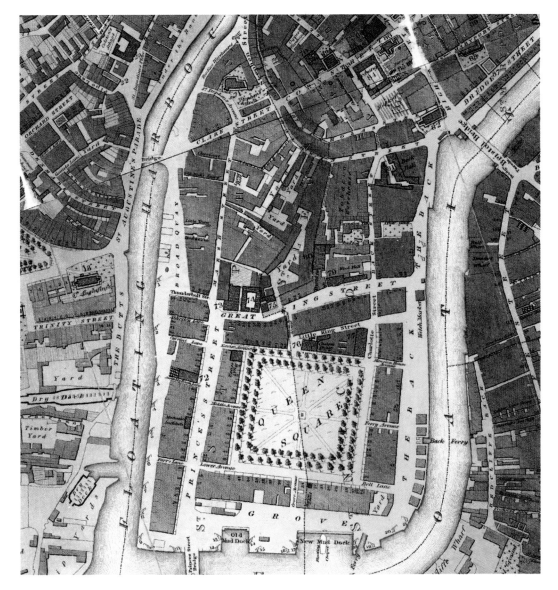

Figure 8.34 Extract from Plumley and Ashmead's map of 1828, showing Baldwin Street, King Street and Queen Square (Bristol Archives 04481)

The Corporation leases specified the design and materials of the houses and the range of activities which could be carried on within them. Tenants who agreed their leases in 1709 were to construct the façades of their buildings of brick, lay a forecourt in front, and were 'to build noe mean sordid building on any of the said Ground to be Receptacles for poor people etc nor to lett any house or building for shopps for Smiths, Workhouses for Chandlers, Publicke Brewhouses, bakehouses or any other Shoppes for Tradesmen' (Bristol Archives 0435(8) fol 254). The last part of the square to be built was the north-west corner, and the buildings there were completed by 1732 (Fig 8.40).

Emphasis was clearly on maintaining the square as an 'agreeable place of habitation, as well as of resort in the weather, for the ladies and gentlemen', The remaining industry was removed, the ropewalks which had run through the area from the mid-17th century were removed after lobbying in 1710 (Barrett 1789, 85; Hughes *et al* 1996, 16). The only commercial building in the square itself was the Custom House, a three-storey building with a full width portico, constructed in 1709 (Fig 8.41). The formal laying-out of walks in the grassed area at the centre of the square was undertaken to provide a setting for the Rysbrack statue of William III, erected in the centre of the square in September 1736;

paths converging on the statue were created on north–south and east–west axes and lined with trees.

The development of Queen Square inspired similar development in Prince Street on its west side, where substantial domestic buildings, like the mansion at No 40 built in 1740–1 and the surviving Nos 66–70 of *c* 1725, were constructed. An Assembly Rooms designed by William Halfpenny was built on the site of four small tenements and opened in January 1756. The lease agreement gave the Corporation up to six days free use of the rooms each year 'for the entertainment or accommodation of any of the Royal Family that may come to this City' (Ison 1952, 109). Narrow Quay, the Grove and Welsh Back, the waterfront areas fringing Queen Square and Prince Street, retained their maritime roles with cranes (including the Great Crane, designed by John Padmore, erected on the west side of Mud Dock *c* 1735) (Fig 8.42),

warehouses and docks along Narrow Quay and the Grove.

Despite the development of Queen Square, the area remained a traditional site for assembly and protest. In 1783 for example seamen gathered in the square to express their grievances to the Society of Merchant Venturers and, at the end of the 18th and the beginning of the 19th century, the Mansion House in the north-east corner of the square was stoned by crowds on a number of occasions as an expression of political opposition to the Corporation (McGrath 1975, 223–4). A large demonstration against Catholic Emancipation was held in February 1829 and in late October 1831 the square was the focus for highly destructive rioting after the defeat of the Reform Bill in the House of Lords (Dresser 1996a, 111; Harrison 1988, 196–200). The Custom House, Mansion House and 27 other houses, mainly on the north and west sides

Figure 8.36 King Street in 1825 showing Theatre Royal, Coopers' Hall and St Nicholas Almshouse to the right, by T L Rowbotham (Braikenridge Collection, BRSMG M2509)

of the square were gutted by fire, the damage initiating a long period of decline (Hughes *et al* 1996, 34) (Fig 8.43).

Rebuilding occurred only slowly and the status of the square declined, the surviving buildings passing into multiple occupation while the walks and railings in the centre fell into disrepair. The fencing was replaced with iron rails in the mid-19th century but the buildings remained in use either as offices or as multiple-occupancy rented accommodation, often for manual workers. By 1896 Queen Square was dominated by offices, the west side only remaining primarily residential.

Queen Square is one of the earliest examples of the renaissance of urban planning following the end of the Commonwealth in 1660 (Borsay 1989, 74–9), but its importance in the urban design history of Bristol did not prevent its further decline, culminating in the insertion through it – *diagonally* – of the Inner Circuit road of 1936. Its political and cultural significance is also difficult to underestimate. It long retained its role as a place of popular assembly and, through its association with the commercial and political activities of the

Corporation, who promoted it and sited the Custom House and Mansion House on its north side, it was sometimes the stage on which the political process was acted out, particularly party-inspired protest against the Corporation in the late 18th century. The annual Corporation procession and the routes for the chairing of members both took in the square, and in 1832 the polling booths for the reformed Parliament were sited there. The 1936 road was removed in 2000 and only then was its decline finally arrested.

St Paul's (Fig 8.44)

At the beginning of the 18th century much of the St Paul's area formed part of the Full Moon and Stokes Croft estates. Newfoundland Road, then known as Newfoundland Lane, and Stokes Croft were established thoroughfares which ran through an agricultural landscape punctuated by occasional residential properties, many built in the 17th century, like Ashley Cottage and the building known as The Whistry, also known as the Pest House, on the south side of Newfoundland Road. This building was constructed in the 17th century and recorded

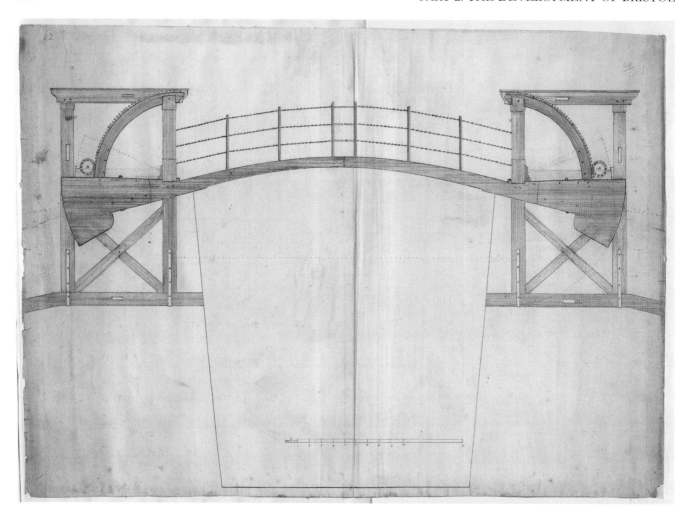

Figure 8.37 The mechanism of the original drawbridge on the site of St Augustine's Bridge (Bristol Archives Corporation Plan Book B fol 62)

by Millerd in 1673. Urban development along North Street and Stokes Croft seems to have begun in the late 17th century, influenced by the buoyancy of the city's economy, and progressed along the street very rapidly. The Full Moon public house dates to 1690 and No 84 Stokes Croft had been built by 1715.

To the south of Stokes Croft a series of increasingly large urban squares was laid out, each pushing development further to the east. St James's Square was the first, being laid out in *c* 1705 with building completed by 1715. Overall it was just over 90m across, with the main access from Milk Street and a narrow footway leading from the north-west corner to St James Barton. Lanes at the north-east and south-west corners led to subsidiary terraces. The houses surrounding the Square were a uniform three storeys in height with brick façades, from which Ison inferred that their construction had been the subject of similar controls to those applied in Queen Square

(Ison 1952, 150). Like Queen Square there was a central rectangular garden defined by a line of trees (Fig 8.45).

King Square was being constructed from 1737, possibly, Ison suggests, a speculation promoted by Giles Greville, with George Tully designing the layout (Ison 1952, 173–4). The houses built were substantial three-storey cellared structures, with brick façades and detached ancillary buildings to the rear.

Development continued on Stokes Croft, the scale of building varying from small dwellings to institutions. At the south end of Stokes Croft the Unitarian Almshouse, which also housed Stokes Croft Endowed School, was founded in 1722 by public subscription (Manchee 1831, vol 1, 202). The building consisted of a central range with two wings, each of three storeys, on the northern and southern sides of the site to create a central courtyard (*see* Fig 8.109). By 1742 buildings lined both sides of Stokes Croft as far as the

Figure 8.38 Stone Bridge, the entrance to Mylne's culvert and the floodgates in 1828 by T L Rowbotham (Braikenridge Collection, BRSMG M2825)

Ashley Road junction and there was an avenue of trees 130m long at the south-western end of the street. Hillgrove Street and Thomas Street were in existence – though only partly developed – on the north-western side, while to the south-east of Stokes Croft, Moon Street formed a back lane for the buildings fronting on Stokes Croft. The eastern end of Wilder Street was developed and the line of the remainder of Wilder Street and Grosvenor Road had been established. A row of three houses stood on the west side of St James Barton, the northern with a large formal garden (90m long and 30m wide) to the rear. This was laid out with geometric planted beds and also seems to have had banqueting houses, similar to those at Clifton Hill House, at the north-east and south-east corners.

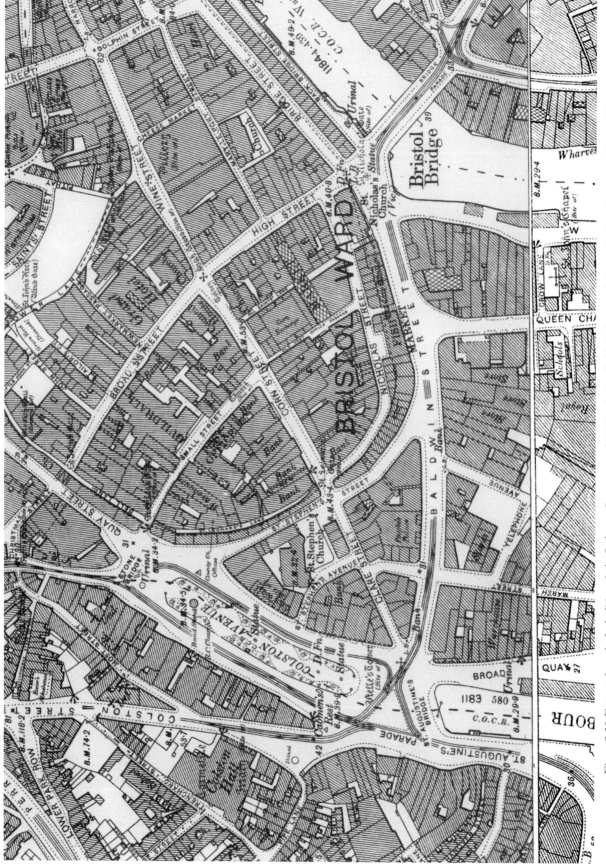

Figure 8.39 Extract from the 2nd edition of the Ordnance Survey map of 1903, showing Baldwin Street and the newly culverted section of the river Frome

Figure 8.40 No 29 Queen Square, constructed by 1720 (photograph R Jones)

East of St James's Square and south to the Frome, however, land-use was still agricultural. Rocque's plan shows an area north of Newfoundland Road divided into closes in which there are several 'swapes' – wells with a bucket attached to a counterweighted arm. These may indicate market gardening in the area, a possibility given some support by fieldwork at Nos 1–13 St Paul's Street (BHER 3642) which found a great depth of garden soil dated to the period *c* 1720–60 (Samuel 2001).

While the majority of the undeveloped area was cultivated or pasture, Rocque also recorded woods in the area between Grosvenor Road and Ashley Road, the north-eastern half with long straight avenues reminiscent of rides. Whether this represents some form of designed recreational landscape or forestry (or perhaps even both) is still to be established. Despite the gradual eastward creep of construction, agriculture or related activity proved persistent, continuing well into the early 19th century. A watercolour by T L Rowbotham in 1826 of land on the north side of Wilder Street records sheep grazing on Meer Furlong (Fig 8.46).

The Circular Stables at the east end of Back Fields, a circular structure 50m in diameter, had been built in 1761, the first riding school in Bristol. It comprised buildings arranged around a central yard with a probable entrance in the north-west part of the building. An archaeological watching brief carried out in 2008 (BHER 4441) revealed evidence for radial walls between the two main outer walls as well as a drain between these walls, suggesting the existence of individual stables. The building subsequently became a circus as early as 1790, when Ben Handy and Thomas Franklin built 'a new riding school and ring for performances'. The wooden amphitheatre, complete with roof, opened on 22 March 1790 with a permanent circus building erected in 1839 (Reynish 2008) (Fig 8.47).

The development of Georgian upper-middle-class dwellings continued throughout the 18th century. Brunswick Square, developed on gardens belonging to Sir Abraham Elton and Joseph Loscombe, was laid out soon after 1766. The design of the Square, 120m from east to west with diagonal cross-paths, was by George Tully, but it is not clear if he was also responsible for the design of the houses.

This Draught of ŷ North Prospect of Queen-Square in ŷ City of Bristol, is Humbly Inscrib'd to ŷ Ingeniou

Wᵐ Halfpenny Delin.

Figure 8.41 North prospect of Queen Square c 1730 (Bristol Reference Library collections ref Braik.XVIII.382)

A VIEW of the GREAT CRAIN and SLIP at the Lower end of Princefs Street

Figure 8.42 The Great Crane, erected 1735 (Bristol Reference Library collections. Braik.IV.159)

muel Workman, Teacher of ỷ Mathematicks in Bristol, by his Humble Servant. W.ᵐ Halfpenny.

Figure 8.43 North side of Queen Square c 1831, showing ruins of the Mansion House and Custom House after the riots of 1831, by Revd John Eden (Braikenridge Collection, BRSMG M2212)

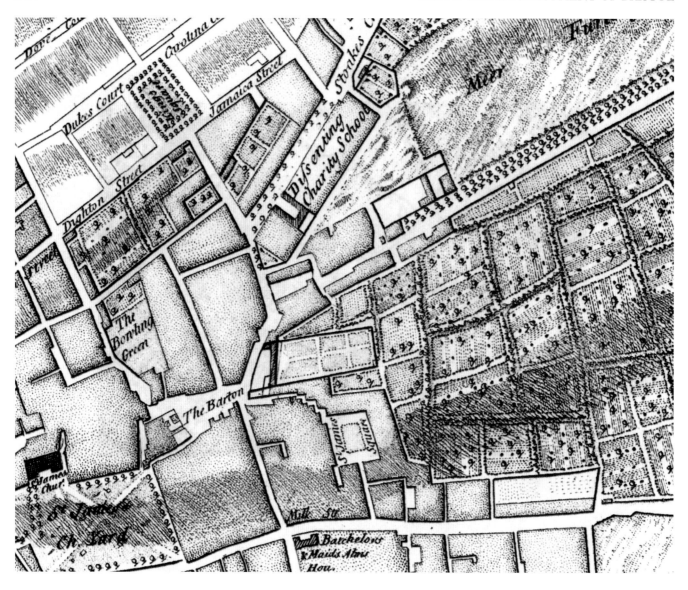

Figure 8.44 Extract from Jean Rocque's plan of 1750, showing St Pauls (BRSMG M707)

The first of these were occupied from 1771 but development of the square was erratic The east side was not completed until the mid-1780s because, according to Ison, 'the supply of new dwellings in this quarter far exceeded all demands' (Ison 1952, 205). By 1773 Cumberland Street had been pushed east–west through the large formal garden at St James Barton and the north–south routes of York Street and Gloucester Street set out. The Brunswick Square Burial Ground was also in existence, although at this time its extent was limited to roughly the area occupied by Surrey Chapel. It had expanded to approximately its modern extent by 1828, although Plumley and Ashmead's 1828 plan of Bristol suggests that an area at the north-east corner was not then

in use for burials. The junction of Ashley Road with Stokes Croft was realigned 20m to the north in the second half of the 18th century. Ashley Place on the north side of Ashley Road was designed by William Paty (Priest 2003, 104) and Priest argues for Paty's involvement in the design of Portland Square (Priest 2003, 112–16).

Portland Square, commonly attributed to the architect Daniel Hague, was laid out during the last of the 18th-century building booms, between 1788 and 1790, and was the largest created in St Paul's. The parish of St Paul was created out of the parish of St James in 1787 to serve the growing population. An initial design for the new parish church by James Allen was replaced by a design by Daniel Hague and work

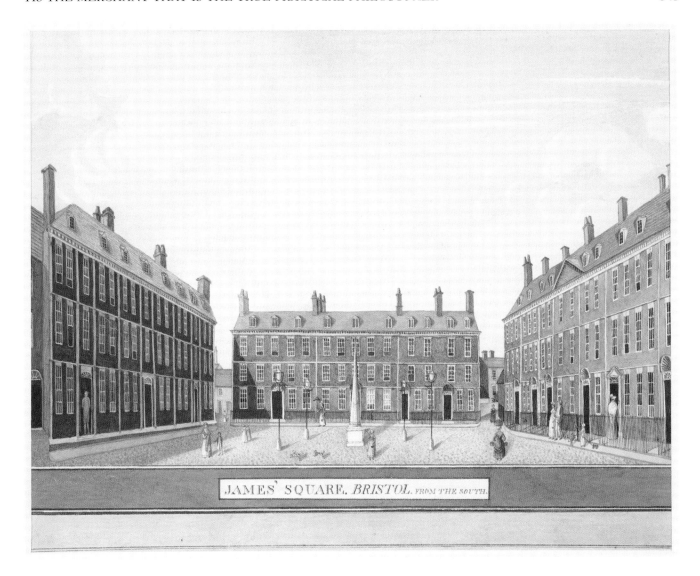

JAMES' SQUARE. *BRISTOL.* FROM THE SOUTH.

began on building the church on the eastern side of the Portland Square in April 1789. It was completed in 1794 and stands close to the Portland Square frontage with its churchyard to the rear (Fig 8.48).

The rest of Portland Square was divided into 34 plots, with back lanes behind the houses in the manner of King Square. These were offered for sale in March 1790 'with common sewers already and ready to be made' (quoted in Ison 1952, 220), but the end of the boom left the buildings unfinished and they were only completed in the early 19th century. By 1801 14 seem to have been occupied; a number were auctioned in October 1811 but construction continued until 1814. Three-storey buildings with extensive cellars, the houses have a thin ashlar

skin to the façades while the other walls are of Pennant rubble. The internal plans were broadly similar in most cases though there are significant variations between properties. In Nos 27 and 28, for example, the stairs are lit by a lantern. There were other differences too: for example, only those houses on the north side of the Square seem to have had coach houses.

Lambert (1997) suggests that the large oval garden at the centre of the Square is likely to have been an integral part of the overall design. The original planting scheme is not clear, but the earliest cartographic record, the Plumley and Ashmead plan of 1828, records a peripheral path around the edge and a circular planting bed at the centre with crescent-shaped beds to the north and south (Fig 8.49).

Figure 8.45 A view of St James's Square, from the south, c 1806 by Dr Thomas Pole (BRSMG K4352)

Figure 8.46 North side
of Wilder Street in 1826
looking south-west –
St Paul's Church tower
on the left, Savage's Sugar
House on the right, by T L
Rowbotham (Braikenridge
Collection, BRSMG
M3442)

An obelisk was erected in the centre in 1810 to commemorate the 50th anniversary of George III's reign and this was replaced in the following year by a Coade Stone statue of the monarch – which was itself pulled down and damaged beyond repair by republicans on the night of the 23 March 1817 (Ison 1952, 223).

By 1828 there were buildings along both sides of Wilder Street and a number of new streets were being created (Fig 8.50).

Bishop Street, Orange Street and Wilson Street to the east of Portland Square, and to the south Pritchard Street and Paul Street had been laid out, though the north sides of Bishop Street and Wilson Street were unbuilt (with the exception of Nos 40–2 Wilson Street). North of Newfoundland Road, the building was domestic, and comprised substantial middle-class houses. Industry was still present. The

ropewalk on the northern side of Wilder Street had gone out of use but another ropewalk, around 200m long, had been established on the southern side of Grosvenor Road. A tannery was located on the west side of Houlton Street.

Agriculture, though diminishing in extent, still dominated the eastern part of St Paul's. The large wooded area shown by Rocque had become a nursery and been divided into smaller plots and the boundaries of these followed the lines established by the chases. It appears from the 1850 sanitary report that the gardens, Stokes Croft or Jeffery's Gardens, were probably also still being used for cultivation, and the same is true of the gardens near Ashley Road (Clark 1850, 88).

Portland Square 'flourished as a fashionable place of residence for about a century' (Ison 1952, 221), but the economic and social character of St Paul's began to change

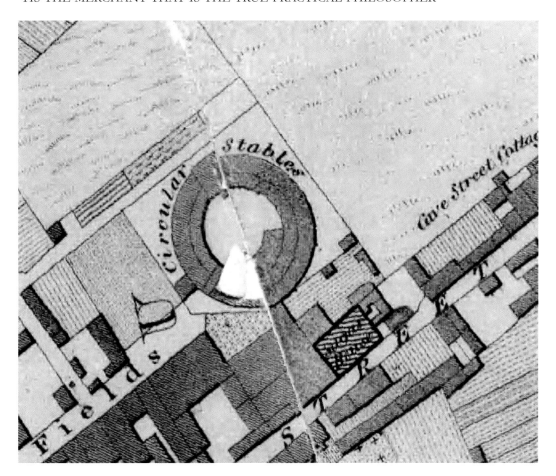

Figure 8.47 Extract from Plumley and Ashmead's map of 1828, showing the Circular Stables (Bristol Archives 04481)

rapidly in the mid-Victorian period. City Road had been created by 1850. The Full Moon estate was sold in lots in 1869 (Bristol Archives 9685 (13)). The nursery was developed early in the following decade and the plot boundaries were fossilised as the streets between City Road and Ashley Road – Brigstocke Road, Drummond Road and Dalrymple Road.

St Philip's Marsh (Fig 8.51)

At the beginning of the 18th century, St Philip's Marsh was mainly agricultural in character, bisected by the Wain Brook which, with its upper reaches lined with withy beds, flowed south-west into the river Avon at Cuckold's Pill. Initial industrialisation was being mapped from the later 17th century, confined to the bank of the Avon, only gradually creeping inland and downriver to the south-east. There were gardens remaining against Cheese Lane in the 1740s for example, and closes known as The Dings in use as 'arable and pasture land' to the east (Bristol Archives 5755 (1)). Between Cuckold's Pill and the Brick Yard Pool was a building named by Rocque as The Sty, probably a piggery.

The street pattern also developed gradually. Broad Plain, Bread Street, Kilkenny Street, Little Avon Street, Anvil Street and Blackboy Alley had been laid out and the plots alongside developed by 1742, although Kilkenny Street had development only on its southern side. The Crown and Anchor public house on the southern side of the junction of Kilkenny Street and Upper Cheese Lane (now New Kingsley Road), one of the oldest buildings in the area, was extant by 1794 (Fig 8.52). Sadly, it was demolished in 2004.

A cemetery for the Jewish community had been established on the site of the brickyard by March 1759 when the yard, together with a house and garden, were advertised for sale (FFBJ 31 March 1759).

By the time of Plumley and Ashmead's survey in 1828 (Fig 8.53), housing was being developed in The Dings. These early houses were often set back from the streets behind their long gardens. The development of

Figure 8.48 St Paul's Church in 1794 (Bristol Reference Library collections ref Braik.XI.ii.11)

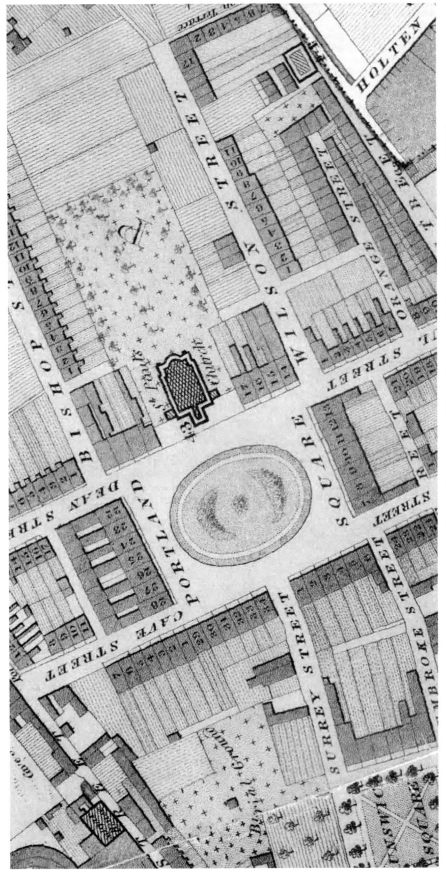

Figure 8.49 Extract from Plumley and Ashmead's map of 1828, showing Portland Square and St Paul's Church (Bristol Archives 04481)

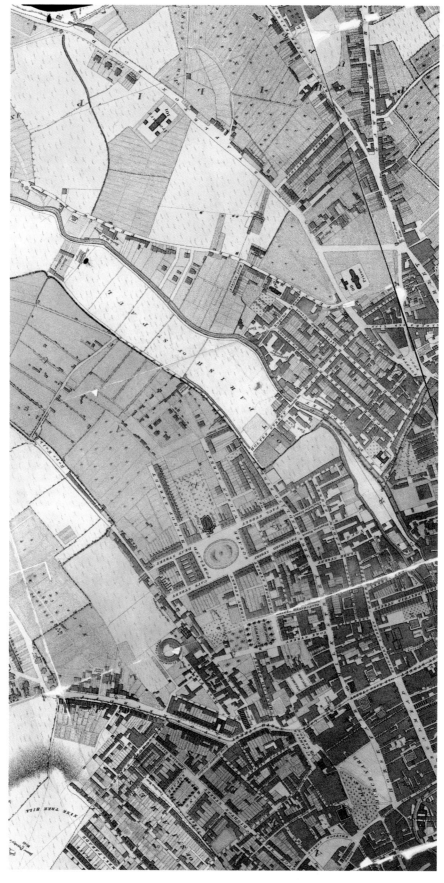

Figure 8.50 Extract from Plumley and Ashmead's map of 1828, showing St Pauls (Bristol Archives 04481)

housing in the area has not been studied in detail but appears to have been piecemeal with speculative builders erecting homes and then leasing them. The 1847 tithe survey for St Philip and Jacob indicates that often all of the houses on one side of a street could belong to a single owner: a Mrs Hamilton owned the north side of Tyler Street, for example, and others owned equally large groups of houses (Bristol Archives EP/A/32/10). Union Road, Waterloo Lane, Oxford Road and Freestone Road had been laid out by 1828, although parts remained undeveloped, and only the north-west corner of the area between Barton Road and Kingsland Road remained as open land. To the east of Kingsland Road the land remained agricultural. Tyler Street and the southern part of Barton Vale had been laid out and developed by 1847, as had some of the land to the east of Kingsland Road, for example William Street (Bristol Archives 28538 (1–7)).

The construction of railways from the 1830s on had a significant effect on the topography of east Bristol but it was the later 19th century that saw the major part of the area built up, a process which was largely complete by 1880 and mixed often noisome industry with domestic dwellings. Further housing was built in the Dings, with a number

of nonconformist chapels and schools to serve the population in Horton Street, Louisa Street and Old Bread Street by the 1890s. A good deal of the existing housing had become slum dwellings by the end of the 19th century and was removed or replaced in the early 20th century: Albert Square, by Barton Road, for example, was demolished in 1936 (Burnett 1986, pl 6). Also, while the railways came to dominate the topography of the area, its communications with the rest of the city were poor; it was not served by tramways and the first road link to St Philip's from the south was not created until the building of the Totterdown Bridge in 1888.

Spike Island and the New Cut (Fig 8.54)

It was the creation of the Floating Harbour between 1804 and 1809, to a design by William Jessop, that radically altered the character of the area. The New Cut, an integral part of Jessop's scheme, was a new channel for the river Avon roughly 3km long between Netham and Rownham, and its excavation turned the land at the northern edge of the parish of Bedminster into an island. This maintained a constant water level in the previously tidal course of the Avon through the city centre. The main entrance lock was at Rownham, giving access to Cumberland Basin and from

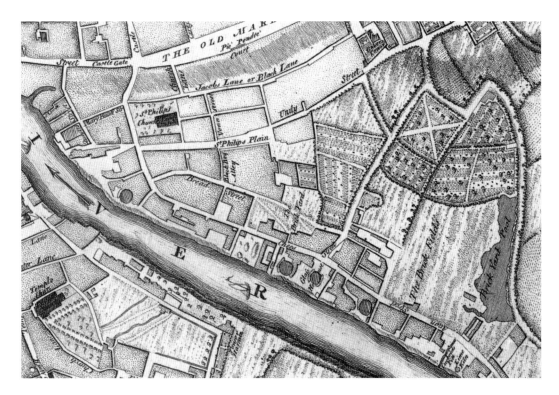

Figure 8.51 Extract from Jean Rocque's plan of 1750, showing St Philip's Marsh (BRSMG M707)

there, through Junction Lock, to the wharves around the city. To allow the discharge of excess water from the harbour Overfall Dam was created near Merchant's Dock. It was also intended that silt dredged from the harbour would be deposited in front of the dam in the expectation that the flow of water would carry it away into the New Cut. Instead the silt merely accumulated and in 1832 Isambard Brunel, when asked to suggest a solution, indicated that a culvert should be provided under the dam to scour out the mud at ebb-tide, converting the Overfall to Underfall in the process (Buchanan and Cossons 1969, 43–4; Malpass and King 2009).

The line of Cumberland Road seems to have been established along the north side of the New Cut fairly soon after its creation but housing was only slowly built along it. By 1828 a row of five or six small villas with large south facing gardens stood to the west of Hanover Place and other dwellings were built along the road in the decades which followed. Perhaps indicating that the area remained peripheral to the city, the New Gaol, designed by H H Seward, was sited at the eastern end of Cumberland Road in 1816. The Governor's House stood at the centre of the prison and the four cell blocks were sited radially around its north side (Fig 8.55).

The gaol was one of the targets for the rioters during the 1831 disturbances, and after breaking in and releasing the prisoners, the buildings were burned down. It was subsequently rebuilt on the same plan. It is apparent from the documentary record that the conditions in the building were spartan, and even after the rebuilding maintenance was neglected. By the early 1840s overcrowding was a problem and inspectors noted that the day rooms were converted into ten extra cells. The water supply came from a well which was contaminated by river water during summer and was later deepened to avoid the problem. The treadmill worked a pump which distributed water around the prison but whether this was drawn from the well or from the river is unclear. However, in the 1840s the prison inspectors complained of river water, which gained ingress to the well in the summer and meant drinking water had to be purchased, corroding and blocking

Figure 8.52 Crown and Anchor Public House in 2001 shortly before demolition

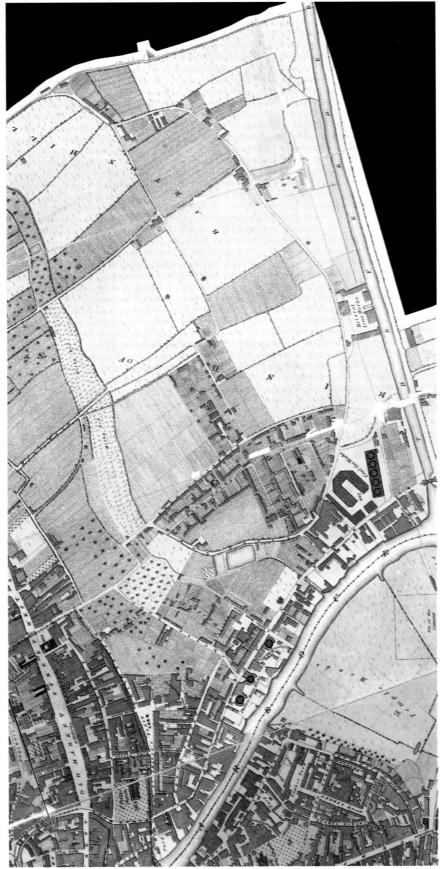

Figure 8.53 Extract from Plumley and Ashmead's map of 1828, showing St Philip's Marsh (Bristol Archives 04481)

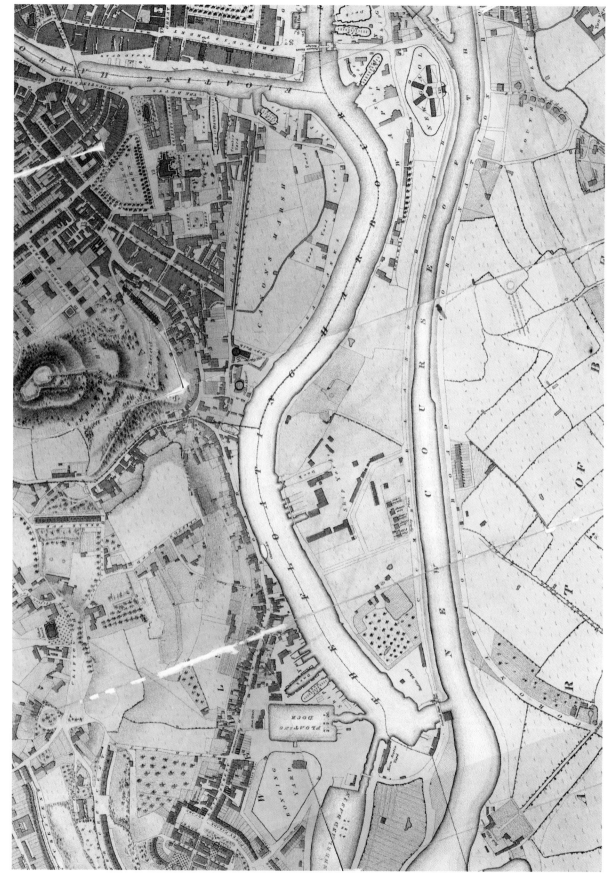

Figure 8.54 Extract from Plumley and Ashmead's map of 1828, showing the New Cut and river Avon, from Cumberland Basin on the west to Wapping on the east (Bristol Archives 04481)

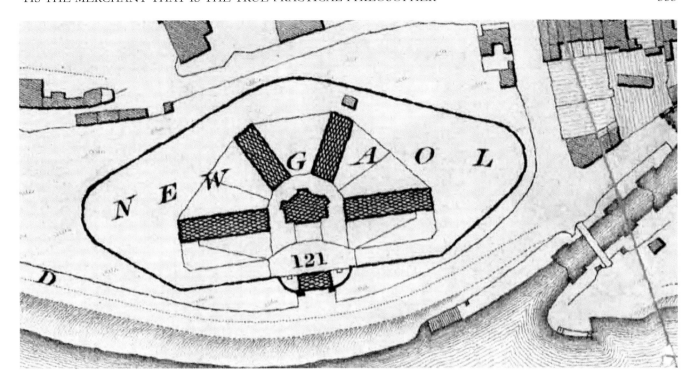

pipes from the treadmill pump and cisterns (Wood *et al* nd, 4). The gaol finally closed in 1883 and the cell blocks and Governor's House were demolished in 1898, but the entrance gate on Cumberland Road and part of the perimeter wall escaped and are still extant (Lord and Southam 1983, 116–17) (Fig 8.56).

Industry and industrialisation

In the course of the 18th and 19th centuries virtually no area of Bristol was left unaffected by industrialisation (Fig 8.57). For the most part, while some significant industries later came to be sited here (*see* p 354), the old city was less directly affected than its medieval suburbs, in that it was colonised by the public and commercial buildings necessary to service the expanding, industrialising economy, rather than by industry itself. The suburbs, in contrast, offered lower land prices for ever-larger premises, direct access to running water and waterfronts and easier access to transport and raw materials, becoming quite densely industrialised and developing land-use patterns that were often a dense patchwork of the residential, commercial and industrial. Around the early modern periphery, much undeveloped land experienced primary industrialisation, where green-field sites were first built on for industrial uses, frequently transport-related. But even the residential squares built in the 18th century with the intention of providing dwellings for polite Bristolians away from workplaces and their workers could suffer reversals of fortune and become colonised by industry – maritime and commercial interests moving into the once exclusively residential Queen Square for example, or late Victorian footwear manufacturers taking over Portland Square and King Square in St Paul's.

The distinct identities of the old suburbs that emerged in the Middle Ages (Redcliffe as a cloth-working district for example) are also apparent in the industrialisation process, particular areas becoming associated with particular industries for reasons that are sometimes obvious, and sometimes subtle. Sugar refining, the industry that is perhaps the most emblematic of the Atlantic economy, also a labour intensive fire-risk, was concentrated along the Frome in the poorer, artisan-dominated suburbs of Lewins Mead and Broadmead to which it had first been drawn in the 1650s and 1660s; it was also to be found to the south in Old Market, and across the river in Redcliffe. The confectionery industry that developed

Figure 8.55 Extract from Plumley and Ashmead's map of 1828, showing the New Gaol (Bristol Archives 04481)

Figure 8.56 Entrance to New Gaol in the early 20th century (Samuel Loxton, Bristol Reference Library S1106)

later closely reflected the geography of the early sugar houses. Glass manufacture too was boosted by the Atlantic trade, beer, wine and cider being exported to the West Indies, and brandy to Africa, in bottles made in Bristol (Leech 2014, 357). The industry, particularly from the 1740s onwards, was concentrated in Redcliffe and Temple, but glassworks were also to be found in Canon's Marsh, Bedminster, St Philip's and even as far east as Crews Hole, around 3km from the city centre.

Maritime-related industries had of course been present from the earliest centuries of Bristol's existence and, in the course of the later 17th, 18th and 19th centuries, expanded out from their medieval core areas along the banks of the Avon through Temple, Redcliffe, the Marsh south of Baldwin Street, and from St Augustine's Reach at the lower end of the Frome. Docks were established in Canon's Marsh from *c*

1700 and were followed by ropewalks and timber yards. The south bank of the Avon followed a similar trajectory from the 1740s, its maritime-industrial character confirmed and then expanded by the creation of the Floating Harbour at the beginning of the 19th century.

The Old City (Fig 8.58)

In the historic core there were both large- and small-scale factories but the smaller manufacturing sites are almost totally unknown. The larger industrial sites are better recorded and have sometimes seen some archaeological investigation. By the late 19th century the Lindrea Leather works lay between Mary-le-Port Street and Bridge Street and there was a brush and bellows factory on the east side of St Peter's Church. The Castle Sugar Refinery on the west side of Queen Street had closed in May 1870 and been bought by Wills, Young and Co. Using

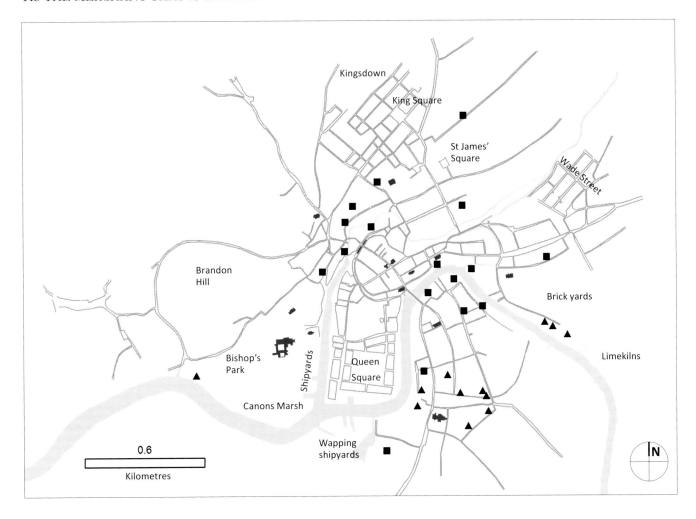

▲   Glasshouses

■   Sugarhouses

●   Potteries

▨   Churches

six boilers to generate the steam for 15 steam engines, the coal supplied by barges to its waterfront on the Avon, the refinery first boiled its raw sugar then filtered it through charcoal, before producing the crystallised sugar by spinning the syrup in large copper wire drums (Anon 1883, 54–61) (Fig 8.59).

On the south side of Castle Green, on the former site of the keep of Bristol Castle, was Bristol's largest brass foundry, owned by Llewellin and James and relocated here in 1846. This was partly excavated during excavation of the Castle Keep in 1989 (BHER 459).

Old Market: sugar refining and food processing (Fig 8.60)

In the mid-1770s the range of trades in the Old Market area was diverse, mainly small craftsmen from butcher and sugar baker to haberdasher and pipe maker, with no particular trade being emphasised, although there was a slight preponderance of food-processing and related trades in Old Market Street. This concentration of food-processing sites in the area was, if anything, more marked by the late 19th century. In the 1830s one of the partners of the Bristol Sugar refinery on

Figure 8.57 Bristol in the late 18th century, showing distribution of sugar houses, glasshouses and potteries

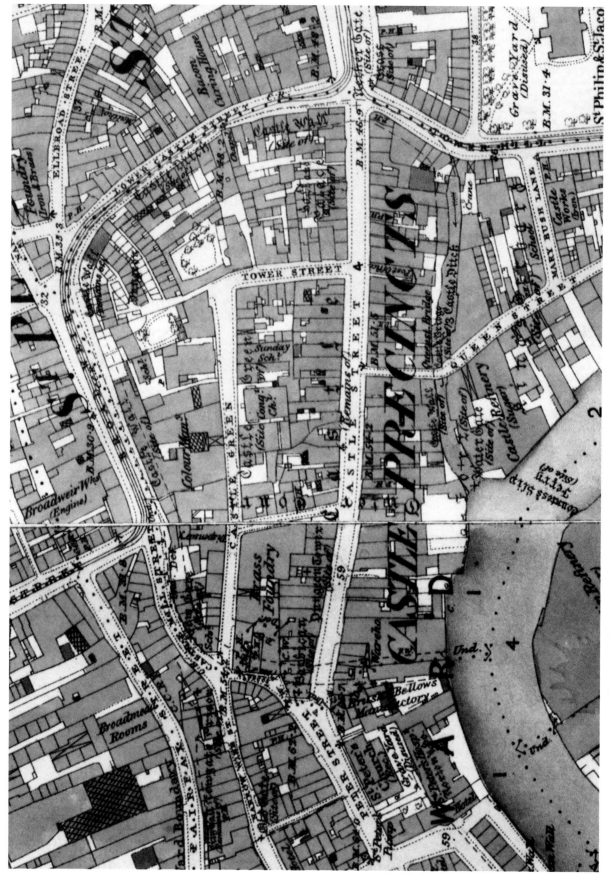

Figure 8.58 Extract from the 1st edition of the Ordnance Survey map of 1884, showing the former Castle Precinct

Figure 8.59 Castle Sugar Refinery in the 1920s (Port of Bristol Authority (PBA) privileges book)

the southern side of Old Market Street was Thomas Guppy, a member of the family which ran the sugar house in Quakers Friars. It was gutted by fire in 1854 and subsequently rebuilt and re-equipped, occupying premises on both sides of Jacob Street and remaining in operation until 1912 (Jones 1996, 22). Beavis Mineral Water Company was on the north side of Jacob Street and Percy's Cocoa and Chocolate factory on the south side, while Rogers' malthouse, founded in 1684, occupied a substantial area on the south side of the junction of Jacob Street and David Street. There was also a large brewery on the south side of Old Market Street. Food animals were processed in West Street. The sanitary survey of 1850 focused its disapprobation on the streets in this part of Old Market; the area north of West Street and east of Bull Paunch Lane (later Butcher Row and now Lawford Street) was 'a street of slaughter houses', while an animal fat refinery in Lamb

Street with its three pigsties and manure depot (still operating in the mid-1880s but out of use by 1896) was considered a health hazard (Clark 1850, 73–4). Almost opposite this in the 1880s were cattle pens, and to the east a large slaughter house which had also closed by 1896. There were sale yards for cattle and pigs on the south side of West Street; the Bristol Hide, Skin and Fat market was sited to the north of the former while James Dole & Co Bacon and Ham curers was next door to the latter.

Old Market had other industrial concerns, sited mainly in the streets behind its main thoroughfares. Baber's Tower on the north side of Unity Street, which, as we have seen earlier (p 293) may have formerly been the premises of William Baber, an unlicensed gunpowder maker in the 17th century, was acquired in the early 18th century by William Champion who built several furnaces on the site, with which he produced some

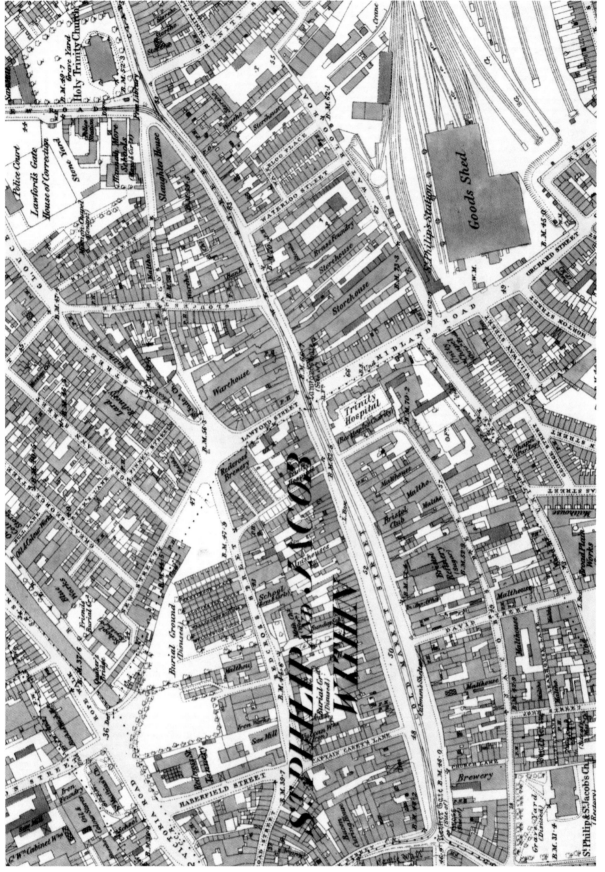

Figure 8.60 Extract from the 1st edition of the Ordnance Survey map of 1884, showing the Old Market area

200 tons of zinc condensed from calamine by a process he had patented (Day 1973, 77). Some of these had been demolished when he applied to the Corporation for the renewal of his lease in July 1743 but it was extended with the condition that he 'erased certain air furnaces' and built a dwelling (Latimer 1893, 244). There were also businesses which exploited the presence of the food industry: leather warehouses on the north side of West Street, shoe factories at No 19 Old Market Street, at the eastern end of Redcross Street and in Braggs Lane, while a large tannery, H Densham & Sons, occupied the whole east side of Haberfield Street. The tannery was laid out so that the hides were passed northwards through the site as they were processed, the lime pits close to Redcross Street and the drying lofts against Victoria Road. There were also cooperages and coach builders and by the late 19th century there were scrap metal warehouses on both sides of Jacob Street.

College Green and Canon's Marsh: shipbuilding, maritime and non-maritime industries (Fig 8.61)

In the 18th century the banks of the Avon and Frome in Canon's Marsh were the site of shipbuilding docks. An earth-cut graving dock, mud dock and 'launching places' were located at the southern end of St Augustine's Reach but the earliest of the more formal docks seems to have been Limekiln Dock, which lay at the foot of Jacob's Wells Road and was in use by 1710 (Bristol Archives DC/E/3/4): a lease of October of that year in the Society of Merchant Venturers' archives refers to a house built by John Evans and also a dock lately made by him (Insole 1998a) (Fig 8.62).

The building of the Floating Harbour at the beginning of the 19th century necessitated the rebuilding of the dock to allow it to continue in use as a dry dock. It served thus through the 19th century, finally being sold to the GWR in the early 20th century who infilled it to construct an extension to the harbour railway. Part of Limekiln Dock was excavated in 1999 (BHER 3398), showing how the west side of a natural pill had been consolidated in the early modern period, the dock built and subsequently developed with a mill and engine house (Cox 1999).

The largest of the docks, Green's Dock (also known as Tomb's Dock), lay on the east side of Canon's Marsh and operated from 1760. An archaeological evaluation inside a now-demolished transit shed, U Shed, in 1995 (BHER 892), found part of the south wall of Tombs dock, 1.6m thick with substantial wooden posts against it; further walls were recorded in a watching-brief in 1997 (BHER 3290: Cox 1998b). Teast's Dock or Albert Dock, further south, was constructed on the site of an 18th-century graving dock owned by the Teast family who ran it from *c* 1790. Plumley and Ashmead's map of 1828 shows that the shipyards associated with it extended south, alongside the Frome.

It was clear to the City Council from the 1870s that more wharfage was needed and it consequently began to buy and infill the docks along St Augustine's Reach, Green's Dock being infilled in 1883 and Teast's dock around the same time (Large 1984, 110–12). New quay walls were built on St Augustine's Reach in the early 1890s followed by transit sheds to service the new facilities: W Shed in 1893 and E Shed in 1894. The infilling of the docks also created new space for other development, the construction of the Rowe Leadworks on Anchor Lane in 1884 over part of the site of Green's Dock being a good example. Relatively little industry was sited outside Canon's Marsh, the most extensive factory being Fuller's Carriage Works in St George's Road, and commercial premises seem to have been the primary non-domestic land use of the rest of the College Green area (Fig 8.63).

With the presence of so many shipbuilders in the marsh, much of the rest of the industry there was maritime-related. South of the ropewalk, timber yards and saw mills were the characteristic businesses, and the sanitary survey of the city in 1850 found that passage along Sea Banks, the lane around the southern edge of the marsh, was impeded by timber lying across it (Clark 1850, 146). Investigations at Canon's Marsh Goods Shed (BHER 456; BHER 3276) recorded part of a building shown on Rocque's 1742 map along with part of the City Saw Mills, and probably also part of Bright, Protheroe, Bonville and Company's ropewalk, built in the early 19th century (Tavener 1997; Cox and Longman 1998).

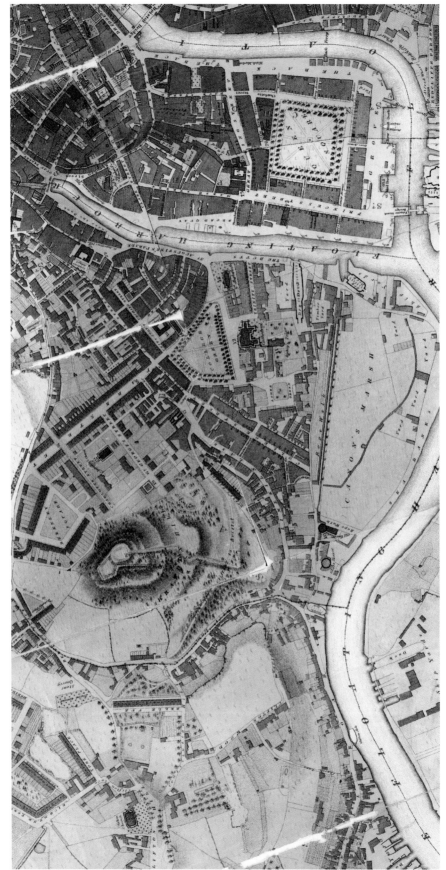

Figure 8.61 Extract from Plumley and Ashmead's map of 1828, showing College Green and Canon's Marsh (Bristol Archives 04481)

There were also other, non maritime-related, industries in the marsh. Child's glassworks to the east of Limekiln Dock operated from the late 17th century and was still producing bottles when it closed in the mid-1830s (Weedon 1983) (Fig 8.64). Analysis of the glass and glass waste carried out during the archaeological investigation of the subsequent gasworks (BHER 4072) revealed that all the glass was of high-lime, low-alkali composition, although the composition changed during the life of the glassworks, perhaps reflecting a move away from the use of terrestrial plant sources during the 18th century and towards other cheaper sources such as soaper's ashes and blast furnace slag (Dungworth 2005).

A large dump of waste ceramics from the Limekiln Lane potteries was found in 1984 during archaeological monitoring of groundworks for Jacob's Court on the north side of St George's Road (BHER 534); samples were collected to provide a typology of the kiln products (Jackson *et al* 1991).

The Bristol and Clifton Oil Gas Company received parliamentary assent to create an oil gas works in the marsh in 1823 and their original works were confined to a small site on the east side of Gasferry Road, the gas holder sited against Anchor Lane (Fig 8.65). With the supply of oil gas too poor to sustain it, the company successfully applied for approval from Parliament to make its gas from coal in 1836. It amalgamated with the Bristol Coal Gas Company in 1853 and the new Bristol United Gas Light Company based its operations there, subsequently expanding, westwards in 1860 taking over the site of the former glassworks and east from the 1840s onwards, a new purifying house being added in 1870 (Nabb 1987, 18–19; Croft 2000). Limited excavation

Figure 8.62 Limekiln Dock, 1826 by T L Rowbotham (Braikenridge Collection, BRSMG M2942)

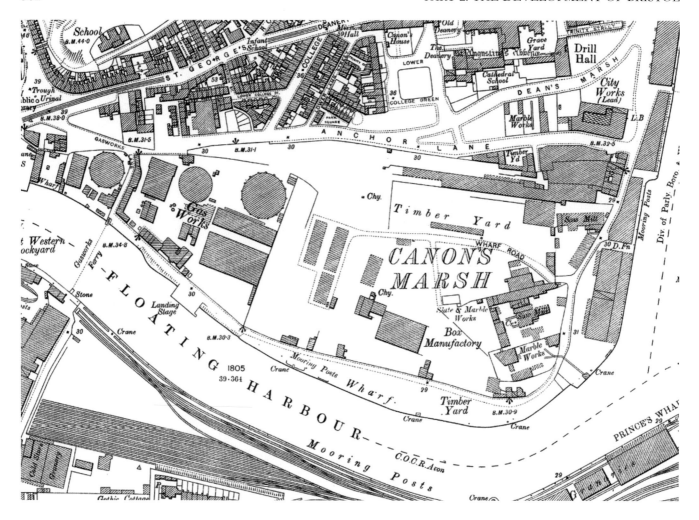

Figure 8.63 Extract from the 2nd edition of the Ordnance Survey map of 1903, showing Canon's Marsh

of the site during remediation was carried out in 2003 and found that the earliest phases of the gasworks were, not unexpectedly, poorly preserved due to later phases of development. However, the buttressed façade of the oil gas retort house and the base of its chimney did survive. The gasholders of the 1840 expansion phase also survived, one being constructed of cast iron (BHER 4072) (Croft *et al* 2005) (Fig 8.66).

Lewins Mead, Broadmead and sugar refining (Fig 8.67)

The concentration of sugar refineries along the River Frome established in the 17th century continued into the 19th century. A sugar house was built in 1728 at Narrow Lewins Mead and still survives, although evidence of process inside the building has been lost. Occupied by a Mr Reed the year after it was built, the sugar refinery was in the possession of Joseph Rigg the younger by 1778 and passed into the

hands of Bamford and Mathews in the early 19th century. Sugar refining ceased on the site in the early 1830s and it subsequently became a dwelling and warehouse for tobacco and snuff manufacturers (Bryant 1994b). Of the other refineries, Daubney's sugar house on the north side of Nelson Street was destroyed by fire in the early 19th century, while the substantial sugar house at Stone Bridge owned by Ames, Wright and Clayfield was another victim of catastrophic fire, this time in 1859. The sugar house established in the 17th century at Whitson Court, to the west of St James's Church, was rebuilt in 1711 by its then owner Michael Pope and was expanded in 1730 by his grandson, coming to comprise a six-pan refinery, warehouse, stable and counting house. When it closed in 1824 the refinery was in the hands of the Dighton family (Hall 1944, 60–1). The grouping of refineries drew confectionery works to the area, including one on the north side of Lewins Mead by the

Figure 8.64 Child's or Limekiln Glasshouse in 1821 by Hugh O'Neill (Braikenridge Collection, BRSMG M3466)

late 19th century and Fry's on the edge of Union Street which expanded into Pithay in the early 20th century. Other large industrial sites included a brewery of Bristol United Brewery, Samuel Rogers & Co, vinegar works and Strachan & Henshaw engineering works by the Unitarian Chapel, while there were a number of footwear factories in the area north of St James's Church, forming a continuum with the western part of St Paul's and the southern fringe of Kingsdown.

In Broadmead, late 18th-century directories (*see* Sketchley for example) show that many craftsmen operating small manufacturing businesses inhabited the streets around Broadmead, while the presence of tanners has been identified in archaeological excavation (*see* p 315). More is known, however, about the larger industrial concerns. A sugar house owned by the Guppy family, for example, operated on the north side of Quakers Friars from 1777 until 1840 (Jones 1996, 17). In the

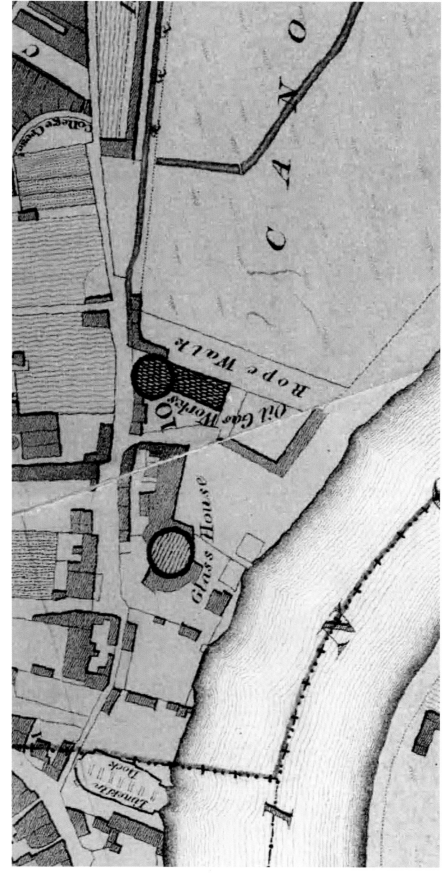

Figure 8.65 Extract from Plumley and Ashmead's map of 1828, showing Bristol and Clifton Oil Gas Works and Child's (Limekiln Lane) glassworks (Bristol Archives 04481)

Figure 8.66 1840s gasholder, Canon's Marsh gasworks, during remediation and investigation in 2003 (photograph R Jones)

same year Joseph Fry moved his chocolate-making business, an offshoot of his trade as an apothecary, to the west side of Union Street (Diaper 1988, 33–8). In the mid-19th century the works were expanded by the construction of a number of large factories in the area between Union Street and Fairfax Street, the last, the No 6 factory, being built on the site of St Bartholomew's Church in 1898 (Leech 1998a).

Redcliffe: the glass industry and other trades (Figs 7.55, 8.29 and 8.57)

The late 17th and early 18th centuries saw the establishment of several glassworks in the suburb, making it the main focus of the Bristol glass industry at that time. To the west of Redcliff Gate a glassworks had been established by the time of Millerd's map of *c* 1715. In 1713 the Venus glassworks was created on the west side of Temple Street while Humphrey Perrott founded a glassworks of his own to the north (Witt *et al* 1984, 45–9).

In 2006 an excavation was carried out of an 18th-century glassworks on the north side of Portwall Lane, east of St Thomas Street, a site which has been largely overlooked in recent works on the glass industry (BHER 4276: Jackson 2007b; Jackson 2010b). The glassworks seems to have been established by 1767, although there is some evidence to suggest an earlier origin. It was owned by Messrs Warren and Co, the company that had previously run a glassworks on the west side of St Thomas Street, excavated in 1999–2000 (Jackson 2004). In 1775 the glassworks passed to Vigor, Stephens and Co who also owned the glassworks on Redcliff Back. Some time after 1785 a second cone was added. This is depicted on a plan of 1797, by which time it is likely that the glassworks were no longer in production (Fig 8.68).

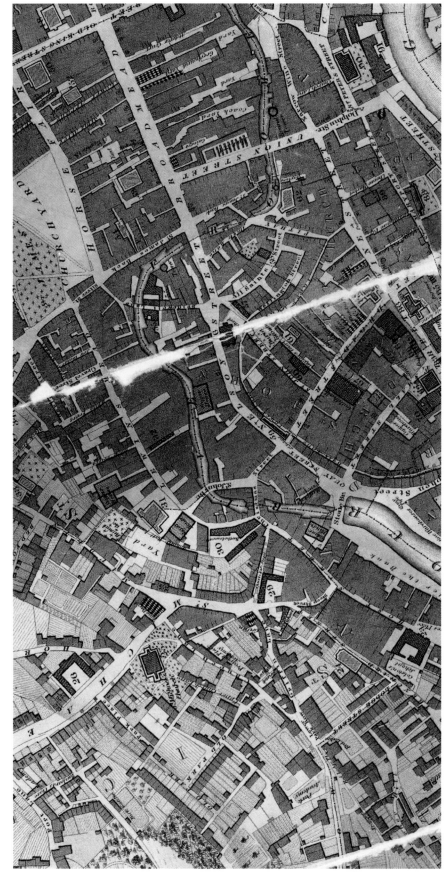

Figure 8.67 Extract from Plumley and Ashmead's map of 1828, showing the Lewins Mead area (Bristol Archives 04481)

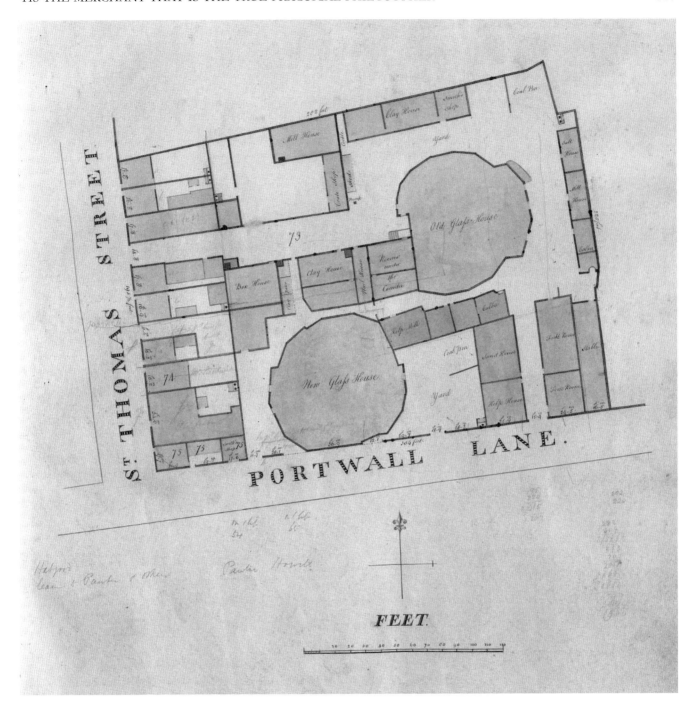

FEET

Figure 8.68 Cooke's plan of 1797 showing the Portwall Lane glasshouse (Bristol Archives P.St MR/E/1/a[f9])

The excavation revealed a remarkably well-preserved series of buildings, including both the original and a second cone, as well as a series of ancillary structures that were used in the working of the glassworks. These buildings included a kelp mill, sand house, salt house, fritting furnace, fritt rooms, clay pens, coal pens and a two-storey counting house. The excavated evidence suggested that the two cones had different designs. The earlier cone had a central furnace served by two Y-shaped flues or passages, subdivided with walls, possibly to control the flow of air to the central furnace. There was a peripheral furnace on the west side of the cone, with a presumed matching furnace on the east. The later cone, constructed after 1785, had a central furnace between sieges which were much larger than those in the 1767 cone. A single straight flue connected to the central furnace from the south, linking through the furnace with a single flue on the north side. There was also what was interpreted as an annealing oven in one of the buildings constructed against the cone wall (Fig 8.69).

Documentary evidence suggested that both window and bottle glass were being made at the glasshouse. Analysis of the glass waste found during the excavation appeared to corroborate this, with a light green glass of mixed-alkali composition, manufactured using kelp, being used for crown window glass production. A much deeper dark green/ brown coloured glass was also produced for bottles. This high-lime, low-alkali glass was also manufactured using kelp, or cullet from mixed alkali glass production with the addition of other industrial waste which would have been responsible for the colour of the glass, but reduced the cost of manufacture. The glass was used to produce dark green bottles, commonly used to bottle wine, the deep colour protecting the contents from sunlight.

Archaeological evaluations at Redcliff Wharf in 2005 and 2007 failed to find evidence for the suspected late 17th-century glassworks there (see Chapter 7), but did find glass manufacturing in the 18th century. A possible glass cone base was discovered in 2005, with contemporary heat-reddened brick surfaces possibly representing annealing oven bases or outlying workshop areas. The 2007 work augmented the information on the glassworks with well-preserved remains of buildings with brick floors and flues, including one which had clearly been subjected to high temperatures (Fig 8.70).

There was also evidence from both investigations for pottery manufacture, with substantial quantities of tin-glazed earthenware kiln waste and vessels, as well as stoneware kiln furniture and waste. The precise location of the pottery kiln remains unknown, although documentary evidence places it on or close to the site of the glassworks (BHER 4261: Cullen 2005; BHER 4397: Collard 2007).

The industrialisation of Redcliffe also saw the construction of the first lead shot tower on Redcliff Hill in the late 18th century by William Watts, the inventor of the process. It involved the addition of a tower to his existing house to achieve a sufficient drop for the molten lead (Fig 8.71). A gasworks was built at Temple Back in 1816 by the Bristol Gas Light Company to light the thoroughfares of central Bristol after the city decided to follow the lead of London. Its metal mains ran along Water Lane, Temple Street and across Bristol Bridge to serve the streets off the Carfax, and the retort house and Aladdin, the first gasholder in the city, a sub-rectangular stone building measuring roughly 19m north–south by 15m wide, were sited there until the works moved to the other side of the Avon in 1824 (Nabb 1987, 5–6) (Fig 8.72).

The suburb retained a very mixed use, industrial, retail and domestic during the later 19th century and was home to large factories. The housing of the area, particularly around St Mary Redcliffe, had a reputation for poverty and squalor by the mid-19th century (Clark 1850, 69–70) (Fig 8.73). W D & H O Wills had a tobacco factory at No 111 Redcliff Street while Edwards Ringer and Co built another at No 60 Redcliff Street. Richard Frank Ring opened a clay pipe factory in Avon Street and had built a clay pipe factory in Temple Back by 1853. The business finally closed in 1888. In 1983 investigation of the site of Ring's clay tobacco pipe factory led to the recovery of parts of a muffle kiln and kiln waste from the factory (Price et al 1984, 264). The Temple Back factory was further investigated in 1995, although the kilns themselves were not located (Burchill 1995c). At the very end of the 19th century, a further clay pipe making firm, Corcoran and Co, was established just off Tower Street, south of Temple Back. This was partly investigated in 2000 (BHER 3566) (Insole and Jackson 2000). The area was scattered with malt houses, oil and colour works, vitriol works, potteries, clothing factories and food manufacturing, like the fish-curing works in Mitchell Lane, Sanders & Son confectionery factory on the east side of Redcliff Street at Nos 41–7, and George's porter brewery in Bath Street. On the west side of Redcliff Backs, Baker and Sons had their flour mills (Fig 8.74).

Acraman's iron works was sited on the east side of Bathurst Basin from at least 1821, with Rankin's Sugar House to the east. When the Bristol General Hospital was rebuilt on the site in the 1850s, it was deliberately designed with warehouse space beneath to gain revenue from its dockside position (Fig 8.75).

The Marsh (Fig 8.76)

South of Baldwin Street, although industry and commerce had been banished from Queen Square at the beginning of the 18th century, throughout the 19th commercial docks on the Grove and Welsh Back remained active. With the social and economic decline of Queen Square and the surrounding streets, maritime-related functions began to re-colonise the interior of the Marsh. The docks office was located at No 19 Queen Square and other buildings serving the maritime community were to be found in Prince Street, now a thoroughfare to Wapping, the Prince Street

Figure 8.69 Aerial view of Portwall Lane excavation in 2006

Figure 8.70 Extract from Jean Rocque's plan of 1750, showing Redcliff Wharf glasshouse with possible spoil heap to the south-west (BRSMG M707)

Figure 8.71 Photograph of William Watts' shot tower in 1965 (Bristol Reference Library, slide 3338, taken 7.8.65. Photograph Geoffrey Langley)

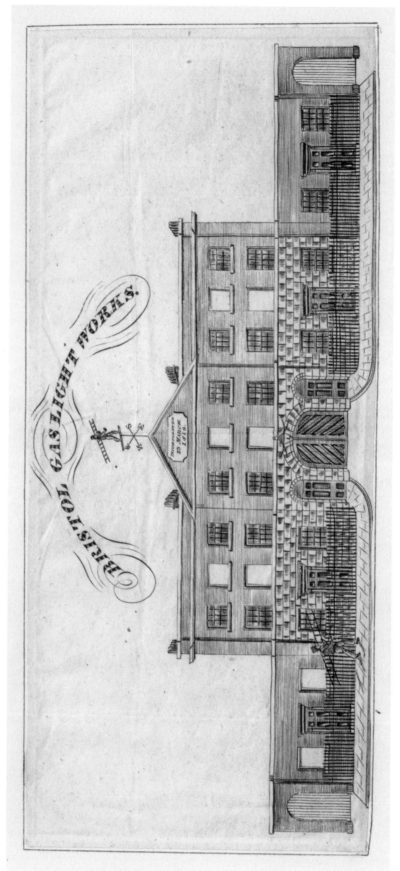

Figure 8.72 Bristol Gas Light Works, 1819 (Bristol Reference Library collections. Ref Braik.XXI.187)

Figure 8.73 Extract from the 1st edition of the Ordnance Survey map of 1884, showing Redcliffe and Temple

Figure 8.74 Spillers and Bakers Mills, Redcliff Backs, in the 1920s (Port of Bristol Authority (PBA) privileges book)

Figure 8.75 Bristol General Hospital, Bathurst Basin 1904. The arches on the dockside served the warehouses beneath the building (Vaughan postcards. Bristol Archives 43207/9/37/46)

Bridge being replaced with a new hydraulic bridge by early 1879.

The Bethel Ark (a floating chapel) was tied up at Mud Dock East in 1828 while the Seamen's Church Institute was at Prince's Hall. From the mid-1850s the Port of Bristol embarked on the building of a series of large transit sheds on the quays in the centre of the city. No 2 Shed at the Grove was built by 1863, part of a process which continued into the 1890s (Large 1984, 58). Welsh Back was one of the foci for the grain trade with Grace Brothers' flour mill on the north side of Mill Avenue and the Granary built in 1869 for Wait and James at the junction with Little King Street (Fig 8.77). The granary served mainly small coastal vessels whose cargoes were unloaded on to Welsh Back and then hoisted into the building (Lord and Southam 1983, 90). Welsh Back also provided one of the remaining large open spaces which the 'leading firms engaged in the Oil, Fruit Petroleum and Grain trades' found so valuable for unloading that they sent a delegation to the Docks Committee in 1883 to object, successfully, to a proposal to build another shed there (Large 1984, 205). Today, the area remains crucial for the understanding of the development of the port and its facilities in 18th and 19th centuries, with transit sheds remaining, notably elements of A and S Sheds on Narrow Quay, and surviving dockside equipment: the hand crane close to Mud Dock for example, or the mooring posts along the east side of The Grove. Evidence for the grain trade in particular survives on Welsh Back.

St Paul's

Industry was starting to become established in the mid-18th century. What appears to have been a ropewalk was sited on the north side of Wilder Street by 1742 and J & F Savage's Sugar House had been constructed at its south-western end by 1772 (Bristol Archives 9685(8)). The refinery was at least five storeys in height, with a tall chimney on its north side (*see* Fig 8.46). Benjamin Donne's 1773 survey indicates two turpentine houses on the west side of Upper York Street.

The first footwear manufacturer, an industry which became increasingly prominent in the area, occupied one of the Portland Square houses at the beginning of the 1870s and by 1875 there were five. Extension to the Young & Melrow Stay and Corset Factory at the rear of 12 Portland Square was built some time after 1877 to a design

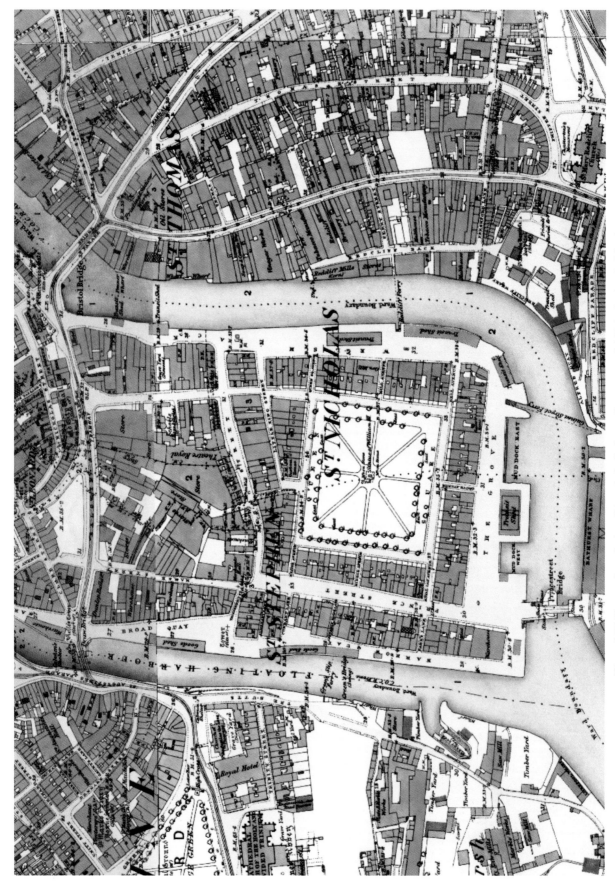

Figure 8.76 Extract from the 1st edition of the Ordnance Survey map of 1884, showing the Marsh area

Figure 8.77 The Granary, Welsh Back (photograph D Martyn)

by the architect Joseph Parker. There was some industry sited in the streets around King Square at the end of the century, the largest of these works being almost exclusively shoe factories, several occupying converted houses. A range of factories was established by the late 1880s, the largest sited around the squares and along Milk Street and Newfoundland Street. These included the Great Western Saw Mills, a vinegar works in Houlton Street and malthouses elsewhere. Timber-related industry was also a major presence, with saw mills at the junction of Wilder Street and Upper York Street and off York Street, Hill's timber yard at Howes Road and Parsloe's timber yard and box factory at the west end of Wilder Street. There were cabinet works at the north-east corner of St James's Square, on the north side of Norfolk Street at Nos 8–10. Where factories were housed within previously domestic buildings considerable internal alteration resulted, often with manufacturing processes separated to different floors and many internal walls removed. By the end of the 19th century the entire area had been developed with dwellings mixed together with industrial works (Fig 8.78).

Spike Island and the north side of the Floating Harbour: shipbuilding and the port (Fig 8.54)

Until the beginning of the 19th century Spike Island and Hotwells were essentially agricultural, enclosed into closes, some owned by the Dean and Chapter of Bristol Cathedral and apparently used for pasture (Bristol Archives AC/M 11/32).

William Champion built a dock on the north side of the Avon near Rownham in 1765, but it did not prosper and was bought at auction in 1770 by the Society of Merchant Venturers (becoming known as Merchant's Dock) and subsequently enlarged (McGrath 1975, 154–6). The creation of the dock was probably the stimulus for the mid-18th-century building recorded at Poole's Wharf, though the relationship between buildings, dock and slipways is not entirely clear (see below). By 1828, however, a dry and a wet dock had been constructed between the Merchants' Dock and Poole's Wharf, the former still extant (Fig 8.79).

An excavation in 1995 (BHER 3265), to the east of Merchant's Dock, found two small slipways and a structural sequence beginning in the mid-18th century with a cobbled yard. A significant assemblage of animal bone was recovered, most of it dated to the 18th century: cow and sheep/goat were the most common species, but beyond an indication that the bones were domestic food refuse, no conclusions could be drawn about patterns of consumption. Some of the bones had been gnawed, and had probably therefore been open to scavenging before disposal by burial. Gorse and insect remains identified during analysis of samples suggested that a building constructed at the end of the 18th century and demolished in the early 19th had been used for stabling (Erskine and Prosser 1997; Erskine 2003) (Fig 8.80).

South of the river Avon, neither the prospect of the city from the south-east published by the Bucks in 1734 (Fig 8.81), nor Rocque's 1742 map, show any buildings west of Wapping, but shipbuilding seems to have been established at Wapping by the end of the 17th century. Rocque's map suggests that the Eastern Wapping dry and floating docks and the Western Wapping dry dock were established by 1742, along, presumably, with their associated shipyards (Fig 8.82). Certainly a survey of Wapping in 1802 records buildings scattered around the docks and a graving dock in the river immediately east of the floating dock and 'building slips' west of the dry dock (Bristol Archives DC/40/44/2).

As in Canon's Marsh, much of the industry which moved in served the maritime interest: a tree-lined ropewalk to the south-west of Western Wapping Dock known as 'Long Rope Walk' operated from the early 18th century until the mid-1870s when the site was taken over for an extension to the harbour railway. However, one of the most extensive industrial sites in the 18th century on the south side of the river was a brickyard at what is now the northern end of Gasferry Road which was working from the 1790s. The internal organisation of the site is not well understood, though there was a large clay pit on the site later to become that of the Great Western Dry Dock and another many metres to the south-east, while the waste products of

Figure 8.78 Extract from the 1st edition of the Ordnance Survey map of 1884, showing the St Pauls area

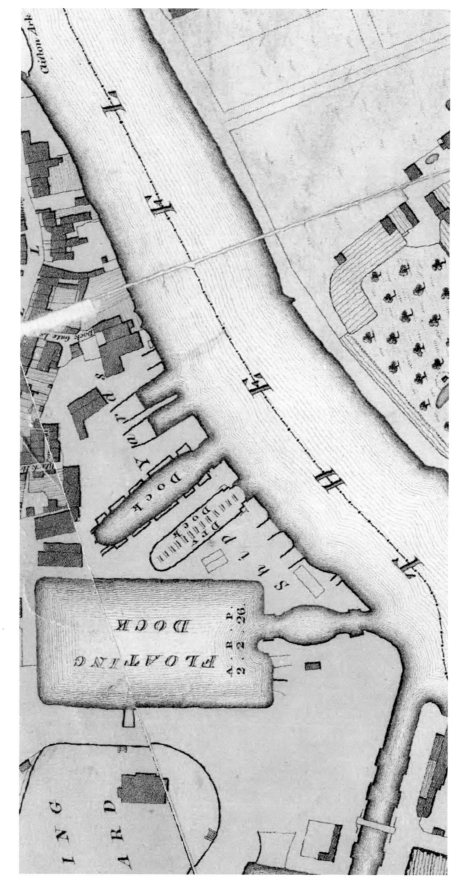

Figure 8.79 Extract from Plumley and Ashmead's map of 1828, showing the Floating Dock, known as Merchants' Dock and adjacent docks and slipways (Bristol Archives 04481)

its kilns were dumped in the Avon; underwater survey outside the walls of the dock in 1998 found vitrified bricks on the bed of the Floating Harbour (BHER 3316; Firth 1998).

A stone-built engine house, possibly used to pump water during the excavation of the New Cut, was located close to the modern junction of Cumberland Road and Hanover Place and survived long enough to be recorded by the Braikenridge artists, while forges were located on what was later to become the site of the New Gaol, apparently to repair tools used in the New Cut excavation (Figs 8.83 and 8.84).

Construction of the floating harbour led to an even greater emphasis on port-related uses in this area. An extensive shipyard was founded on the west side of modern Gasferry Road in 1820 by the Hilhouse family who moved their business from their established yards at Wapping (Fig 8.85). The Albion Dry Dock was the central feature of the new yard and other slips were sited to the west of it. The yards were taken over by Charles Hill & Sons in 1848, who enlarged the dock and built housing on the site for some of their workers, as well as a substantial villa for the manager (Lord and Southam 1983, 82). This and the offices on Cumberland Road still survive.

In the late 1830s The Great Western Steamship Company (GWSC) chose the site of the former brickyard clay pit for the dry dock in which the SS *Great Britain* was to be built. The intention of the GWSC, to construct an integrated yard for the construction of the *Great Britain,* was ambitious and, in the end, financially disastrous, due to problems with the boilers and engine, ultimately requiring their removal and replacement.

The innovative nature of the shipbuilding was reflected in the design of the Engine Works themselves. Excavations on the site of the Engine Works in 2007 (BHER 4433) found evidence for differing uses within the building and a number of important changes made either during construction or after completion. Two large basements appear not to have been finished, and were infilled and then covered with a Pennant sandstone and Portland cement floor, the first ever substantial use (in 1839) of this material in a major building. The insertion of inverted arched foundations and an internal buttress suggested problems caused by the underlying soft alluvium and possibly groundwater issues (Fig 8.86). There was

little archaeological evidence for the location of particular pieces of machinery within the works, partly because the larger southern part of the building probably had a timber floor, which was subsequently removed. However, the possible location of a steam engine and boilers was identified in the southern part of the building and there may have been a smithy in the northern area. The GWSC was liquidated in 1850 and the dockyard was sold to William Patterson, who had been in charge of the building of the *Great Britain*. He sub-let the Engine Works building, which was occupied by the Great Western Tannery from *c* 1855 until at least 1886, the excavated evidence for the tannery closely corroborating what was known of the tannery from contemporary mapping (Ellis and Leivers 2013).

To create more commercial space in the port, a wharf was created at Wapping by the

Figure 8.80 Poole's Wharf: excavation in 1995 showing timbers at the base of a possible stable building

Figure 8.81 Nathaniel Buck's South East Prospect of the City of Bristol 1734 (BRSMG Mb378)

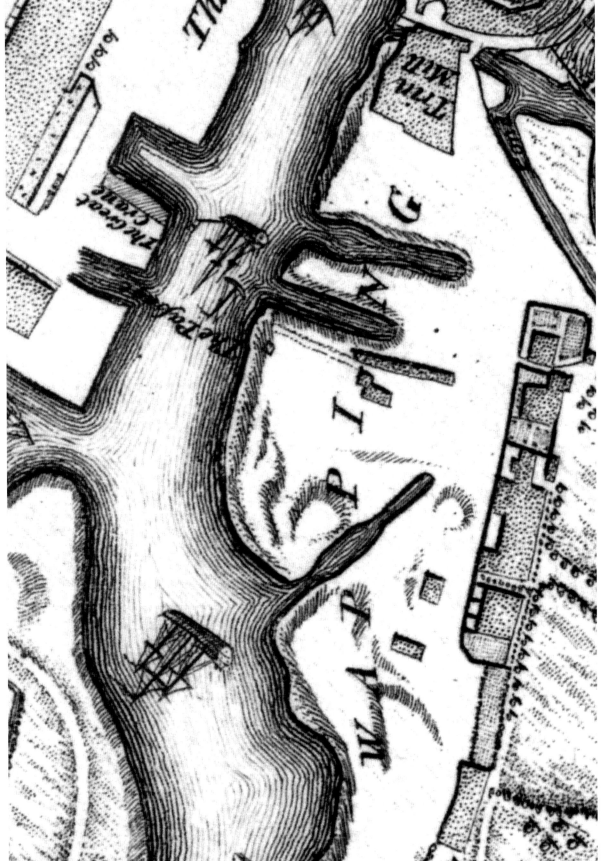

Figure 8.82 Extract from Jean Rocque's plan of 1750, showing the Eastern and Western docks at Wapping (BRSMG M707)

Figure 8.83 Remains of an engine house used during the excavation of the New Cut, early 19th century, by Revd John Eagles (Braikenridge Collection, BRSMG M2958)

Corporation under the 1866 Bristol Harbour Railway Act. It was connected to Temple Meads by a new railway tunnelled beneath St Mary Redcliffe. The success of the new wharf led to the rapid creation of others on either side of the Prince Street Bridge while another, over 1,400ft long, was built further along at Wapping (Vincent 1983, 161–6). In October 1889 the Council approved an extension of the Harbour Railway to Cumberland Basin. Because of shipbuilding, Spike Island was also a major timber storage location, and the timber yards which had been sited at Wapping were moved to the west side of the Albion Dock, forming a continuous line behind the wharves along the southern bank. Some of the yards had ancillary saw mills, the Imperial Saw Mills south of Onega Wharf being a good example. A limited number of non-maritime companies also chose to locate their operations on the island, the Great Western Tannery south of the

Great Western Dry Dock for example, and a malthouse on Gasferry Road which survives, although gutted by fire in the 1930s.

St Philip's: brickworks, glass and soap manufacture (Fig 8.51)

The largest single industrial site in the 18th century was the brickworks on the northern side of Avon Street: the west part of the works was the brickyard while to the east were the brick fields; at the east end was a large pond known as Brick Yard Pool, almost certainly a clay pit.

Sir Abraham Elton built a glasshouse on the south side of Cheese Lane by 1736. However, detailed excavation of the site in 2001 revealed an earlier glasshouse dating to the late 17th century, the earliest glassworks so far examined in Bristol (BHER 3806). Only fragmentary remains of the cone survived but it appeared to be octagonal in shape with a maximum internal width of 12m. The cone is

Figure 8.84 Forges used in the construction of the New Cut, 1806 by Hugh O' Neill (Braikenridge Collection, BRSMG M3378)

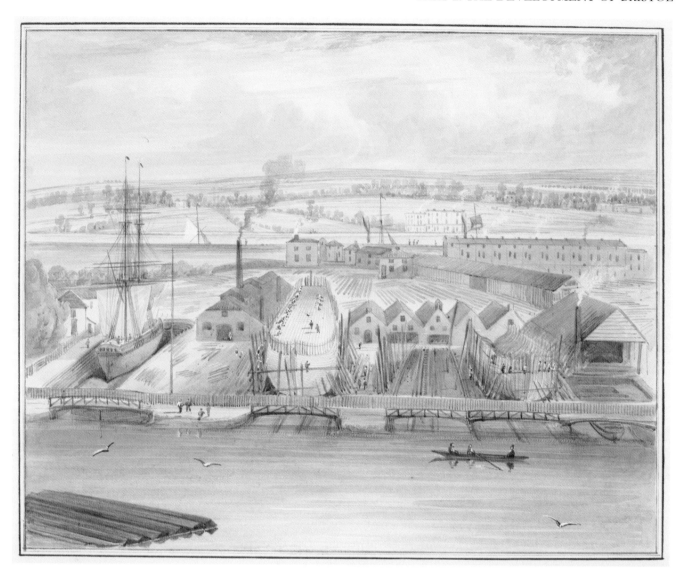

Figure 8.85 Hilhouse's shipyard including what became Albion Dock, with neighbouring docks and dockside buildings in 1826, by T L Rowbotham (Braikenridge Collection, BRSMG M2939)

not depicted on Millerd's map of *c* 1715, but it had perhaps been removed before this prior to the construction of Elton's glass cone by 1736. The later history of the glassworks is unclear but in 1809 the site was sold to Philip George, Charles Murry and Christopher Pope who demolished the glass cone and set up a business manufacturing zinc and copper. When that company was liquidated in 1844 the site was sold and became an ironworks, but quickly passed on to lead sheet and pipe production. The works were bought by Sheldon, Bush and Patent Shot Co in July 1862 and continued to produce sheet lead into the 1990s (Bryant and Brett 1996; Jackson 2005).

On the southern side of Avon Street a group involved in the production of soap built the Soap Boilers glasshouse in 1715,

consisting of two cones, using, it is believed, the large quantities of material left as a residue from soap-making to produce bottles as well as window glass (Powell 1925, 242–3). To the south-east, another cone, known as Hoopers' or Cooksons glasshouse, was built in 1720 by a consortium led by Robert Hiscox, a barber surgeon, also to manufacture glass bottles as well as window glass (Fig 8.87).

In 2007 the site of two of the three glass cones that had formed Powell and Ricketts glassworks, formerly the Hoopers' and the Soapboilers glasshouses, was excavated (BHER 4423) (Fig 8.88).

The site had been partially excavated in 1988 (BHER 343), but the 2007 work was a comprehensive investigation of the glassworks, together with a detailed analysis of the waste

and residues. The glasshouses produced both window and bottle glass and, in the 19th century, adopted the new technology of a Siemens regenerator to preheat incoming air. However, despite the introduction of such technology, it was forced to close in 1923 (Miller 2009; Gregory and Dungworth forthcoming).

Little further development occurred before the early 19th century when the creation of the Floating Harbour reinvigorated the industrialisation process. The Feeder canal was cut through St Philip's Marsh, across the end of Avon Street, to terminate at the new Totterdown Stop Lock and barge basin which connected with the New Cut. The Feeder provided a potential route by which products could be moved via the inland waterways and several major industrial sites were founded there in the years after its construction. In 1821 a new works for the Bristol Gas Light Company at the south end of Avon Street was built to replace the existing plant in Temple

Back; Bristol Vitriol Works was built on the opposite side of the street (Nabb 1987, 12). A soap and candle factory in Broad Plain was developed by Thomas Thomas who, with his son Christopher, established a business there selling soap to Bristolians and in south Wales. After a merger with Samuel Fripp & Co the company diversified to produce soaps for both domestic use and for the textile industry (Diaper 1987, 224–5; Somerville 1991) (Fig 8.89).

Temple Meads and the coming of the railways

Temple Meads – the oldest surviving large railway terminus in the world – was built to Brunel's design between 1839 and 1841 on land between the New Cut and Pipe Lane that had been bought from the Corporation in 1836 when the Railway Act received royal assent (Channon 1985, 25). The station was built of limestone ashlar and Pennant sandstone rubble. The offices faced on to

Figure 8.86 Excavation in 2007 of the Engine Works of the Great Western Steamship Company (photograph Wessex Archaeology)

Figure 8.87 Hoopers' and Soapboilers glasshouses in 1821 by Hugh O'Neill (Braikenridge Collection, BRSMG M2777)

what is now Temple Gate, the engine shed lay behind and the passenger areas behind again. The locomotives were moved from line to line using turntables in the engine shed. The original station had two platforms, one for arrivals and the other for departures; the waiting rooms were located beneath, in a vaulted undercroft, from which the passengers moved up to the platforms. Two goods sheds were built at right-angles to the main line and a dock, Brunel's Dock, was built to the north on the Floating Harbour, making use of an existing pill on the west bank of the Floating Harbour as an entrance (Fig 8.90).

The new terminus was the nucleus for other railway development. The Bristol and Exeter Railway built its passenger station on the opposite side of the line to the GWR Goods Sheds in 1845 having used the GWR Old Station since 1841; the company

also built offices to the south of the Old Station in 1852. From 1868 construction work began on the Bristol Harbour Railway line, linking Temple Meads to a wharf to be built at Wapping. A 282-yard tunnel was cut through the Triassic sandstone beneath St Mary Redcliffe, requiring the demolition of the vicarage and one side of Guinea Street (Vincent 1983, 162). The GWR, Bristol and Exeter, and Midland Railway gained parliamentary permission to build a new passenger terminus, shared between them at Temple Meads, which opened in 1878. The Bristol and Exeter sheds were demolished and the new platforms built as an extension to the old station (Fig 8.91).

In 1871 the route between Temple Meads and Bristol Bridge was made more direct by the creation of Victoria Street, providing a better route to the new Joint Station but destroying much of Temple Street in the process.

Places of worship

The medieval legacy

A number of the old city's medieval parish churches were reconstructed or rebuilt in the course of the 18th and 19th centuries. Rebuilding of the tower of All Saints' Church began in 1712 but was not completed until February 1717 (Gomme *et al* 1979, 121–3). In 1762 St Nicholas' Church was demolished and rebuilt above the crowde, while in the same year the church of St Werburgh was truncated and its east end taken down (Evans 1824, 278) (Fig 8.92). Christ Church was rebuilt to a design by William Paty between 1786 and 1791 (Fig 8.93) and St Ewen demolished in 1823, along with the early 18th-century Council House.

The medieval churches of the inner suburbs underwent similar changes, as did the Cathedral, formerly St Augustine's Abbey. It was finally decided to build a new nave for the cathedral church, a project left unfinished at the dissolution of the abbey in 1539. Accordingly, in 1838 housing which had been built on the site of the demolished medieval nave, together with buildings standing to the west, including Minster House, were removed as part of the preparation for the new building and for a carriage drive to its west front (Bettey 1993, 7–19). The nave itself was completed between 1860 and 1877. The cathedral precincts saw a number of changes in the course of the 19th century, not all planned – the Bishop's Palace was destroyed during the rioting of 1831 (Fig 8.94).

Nearby in College Green, intensive excavation of the site of the parish church of St Augustine-the-Less in 1983 (BHER 1686)

Figure 8.88 Part of the Powell and Ricketts glassworks (furnace C) during excavation by Oxford Archaeology North in 2007, looking south, showing part of the remains of the Siemens regenerative furnace (photograph Oxford Archaeology North)

Figure 8.89 Christopher Thomas Soapworks, now a department store

found that it had been subject to periodic rebuilding in the 18th and 19th centuries. In the 18th century, the aisles and chancel were extended eastwards; in the 19th, a vestry was added and a new window inserted into the chancel. A substantial part of the foundations of the north wall, the north-west corner of the tower and a buttress east of the porch, were all found to have been rebuilt, as a result, the excavator believed, of the density of burial vaults within the church weakening the foundations. Although the majority of the brick burial shafts and vaults had been cleared before the excavation, uncleared vaults were recorded in the chancel. Undisturbed graves were also found beneath the vestry (Boore 1985, 28–31) (Fig 8.95).

Above Broadmead, the church of St James was suffering from overcrowding

as the population of its parish grew. The addition of a gallery to the south aisle in 1753 provided only a temporary solution (Bryant 1993, 23–5), and in 1787 a new parish of St Paul was created out of the eastern half of St James's, Merchant Street marking the boundary between the new parish and the old. The new church of St Paul, in Portland Square, was the subject of an archaeological survey in 1998 (BHER 3713), followed by further investigations in its churchyard in 2000 (BHER 3843, 4205). A subsequent new church, St James-the-Less, was built in 1867 on the south side of Upper Maudlin Street to serve the adjacent penitentiary but was adopted as a chapel-at-ease to the old parish church, possibly in 1873. A gallery, however, seems to have been retained for the exclusive use of the inmates, connecting directly with

Figure 8.90 Great Western Railway Terminus Building in 1841 (Bristol Reference Library Collections ref Braik. XXII.331)

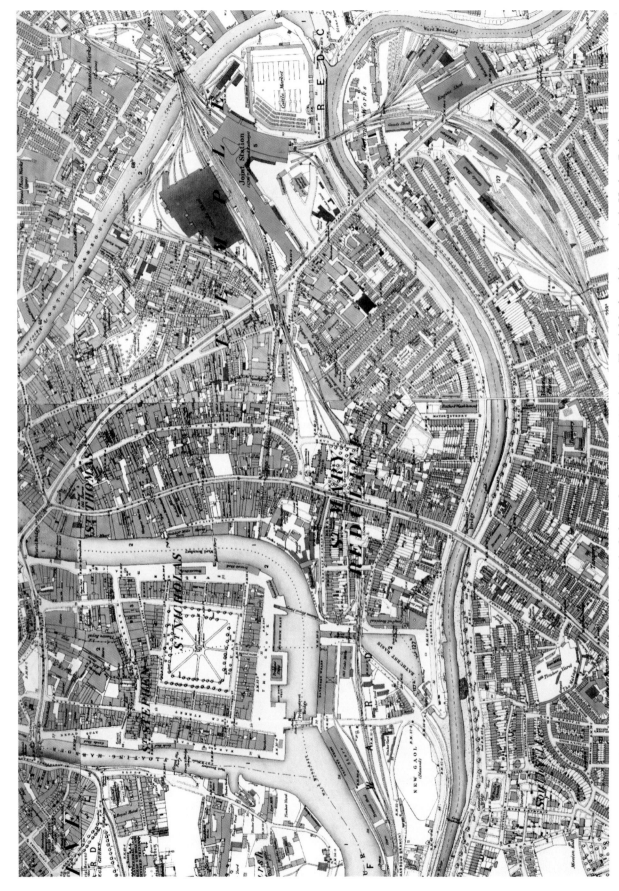

Figure 8.91 Extract from the 1st edition of the Ordnance Survey map of 1884, showing Temple Meads and the route of the Harbour Railway

the penitentiary (Ralph and Cobb 1991, 27; Spear and Arrowsmith 1884, 56).

St Bartholomew's, one of the many Bristol churches created as a result of the ideas of the Oxford movement, was built on the west side of Union Street. Designed by T S Pope and consecrated in 1861, this chapel of ease to St

James was demolished in 1894. The church moved to St Andrew's Park in that year where a new structure was built (Ralph and Cobb 1991, 26).

St Mary Redcliffe was the subject of a considerable amount of work in the 19th century, much of it to designs by

Figure 8.92 North view of St Werburgh's Church, 1821, copied from a drawing by William Halfpenny of 1762, by Hugh O'Neill (Braikenridge Collection, BRSMG M2456)

Figure 8.93 Christ Church in 1824. This painting also shows the site of the Council House before the construction of the present building (the 'Old' Council House) by 1827, by E Cashin (Braikenridge Collection, BRSMG M2341)

Figure 8.94 Ruins of Bishop's Palace, early 20th century (Samuel Loxton, Bristol Reference Library, ref E330)

George Godwin. He was responsible for the restoration of the north and south porches, the re-pewing of the interior with new oak pews, and a new pulpit; a new font was also installed (Fig 8.96).

A reredos designed by Godwin was erected in 1871 (*The Builder*, 30 December 1871, 1024; 1027). The truncated spire (damaged in a storm in 1446) was also restored to its full height (Fig 8.97).

Almost all of the city churchyards and burial grounds were closed by Act of Parliament in the early 1850s and interment shifted to locations out of the centre. Several of these former burial grounds have seen some archaeological work but, in most cases, conditions for the recovery of archaeological data were less than ideal and the human remains were reinterred without study. The exception is the significant assemblage of human remains from St Augustine-the-Less but these have yet to be analysed.

Nonconformism, Catholicism and the Jewish community

Broadmead had seen the foundation of several nonconformist meetings during the Commonwealth, but many more were founded in the 18th century. Evangelicals like John and Charles Wesley and George Whitefield preached at various locations in and around the city from the late 1730s, reviving dissenting religion not only in Bristol but in the country at large. With their congregations outgrowing the available venues, the Methodists built a chapel, the New Room, on the south side of Horsefair and formed the United Society by combining the existing Baldwin Street and St Nicholas Street meetings, but doctrinal disputes within the movement resulted in the Arminians (led by the Wesleys) acquiring control (Morgan 1990, 5). The galleried chapel, which still exists, has rooms above it for the use of the preachers, both these and the chapel being illuminated by a single lantern. To increase its capacity

Figure 8.95 View of St Augustine-the-Less during excavation in 1983–4, showing internal burial vaults and brick-lined shafts (photograph: Bristol Museums, Galleries and Archives)

the building was extended in 1748 (Stell 1986, 68) (Fig 8.98).

In 1747, the Friends rebuilt the Meeting House on the site of the former Dominican Friary, the original Meeting House, built in 1670–2 (*see* Chapter 7) having been demolished. Those elements of the Friary that remained became dwelling houses and tenements, while a sugar house was established by 1777 occupying much of the site of the former friary church. The Friends had acquired much of the land to the north and south of the new Meeting House and a school was established in the former Cutlers Hall in the 1740s, with a men's meeting room to the south of the Meeting House. In 1845 the Friends acquired the rest of the land around the new Meeting House, including the upper floors of the Bakers and Cutlers Halls and the former Lesser Cloister. Excavation and survey during the construction of the Cabot Circus shopping centre have shown that both buildings were heavily restored, with the south wall of Cutlers Hall completely rebuilt and its roof altered. The east window of Bakers Hall was removed and installed in the east wall of Cutlers Hall (Fig 8.99).

Bakers Hall was gutted of the rooms and chambers that had served during its use by the bakers and a new first floor was inserted. A caretaker's cottage was constructed on the eastern end of the hall, perhaps necessitating the removal of the east window. A girls' school was built between 1869 and 1874 to the north of the Meeting House on the site of the east range of the Great Cloister, with the cloister garth becoming the playground. The New Hall was built, firstly in 1847 with a first floor added in 1869, on the site of the former east range of the Lesser Cloister. The traceried windows from the ground-floor arcade of the Bakers Hall were moved to the ground floor of the New Hall (Fig 8.100). The former monastic burial ground, while not initially used for interments, the burial markers having been cleared in 1670, resumed its function as the Friends' burial ground in 1701 and continued in use into the 19th century. Its southern boundary wall, adjacent to the north bank of the Frome, was maintained well into the 19th century (BHER 3849/4279/4281; Jackson and Stevens 2002, 12; Davenport 2013g, 393–5).

Immediately west of Llewellin's Court and adjacent to the newly established Penn Street,

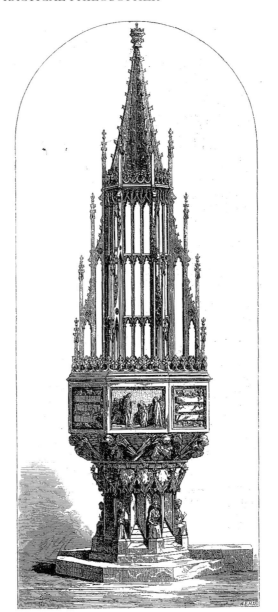

*Figure 8.96 St Mary Redcliffe new font and cover (*The Builder, *9-2-1856, 74)*

laid out in 1743, was the Methodist Tabernacle, built from 1753 to house the Methodist congregation of George Whitefield, whose meetings had been held in Cutlers Hall from 1739 (Stell 1986, 63). Excavation revealed the lower walls and floors of the crypt, which had housed burials until the 1820s. Most burials had been removed during the demolition of the building in the 1960s but 15 graves were identified in the excavation. The Tabernacle had been closely associated with the Wills tobacco family and the building had housed the burial vault of W D Wills who was in fact buried at Arnos Vale cemetery (Davenport 2013g, 397) (Fig 8.101).

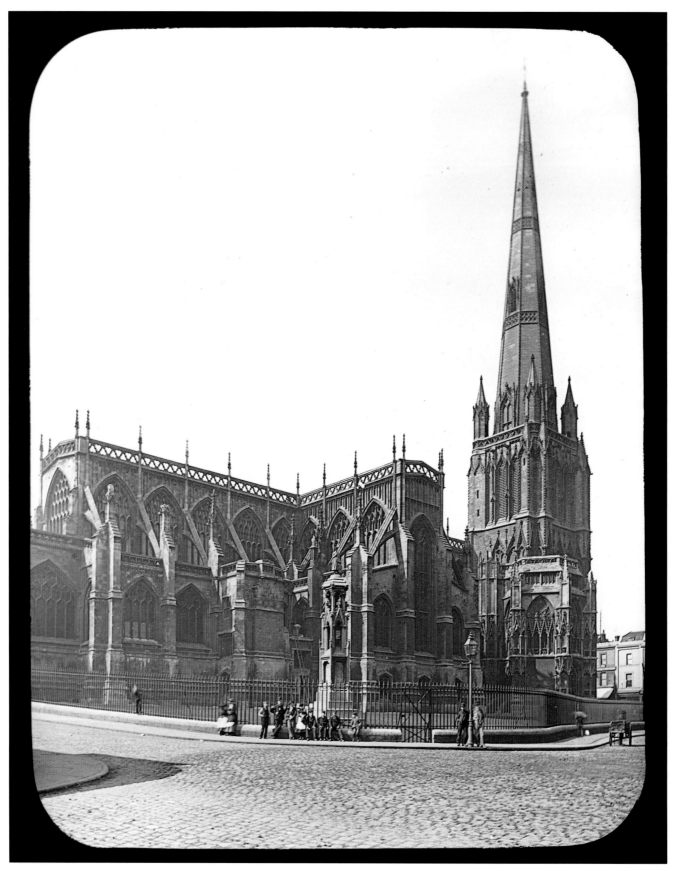

Figure 8.97 St Mary Redcliffe church c *1900 (Bristol Reference Library collections ref LS.8)*

Figure 8.98 John Wesley's New Room, from the south (photograph R Jones)

Lewins Mead, similarly, was home to several nonconformist chapels. The Countess of Huntingdon's Connexion took over a former theatre at St Augustine's Back for its Salem Chapel but this was replaced in 1830 by a purpose-built chapel at the foot of Lodge Street (*see* Fig 6.66).

The Lewins Mead Unitarian Chapel, built between 1787 and 1791, replaced an earlier meeting house built in 1693–4 and was expanded in 1818 when a lecture theatre was added above the coach house and stables, along with a committee room, two schoolrooms and a dwelling for the teachers (Stell 1986, 72) (Fig 8.102).

The Catholic Apostolic Church of Edward Irving built a chapel at Under the Bank between 1839 and 1843 to a design by R S Pope, but the financial problems of the congregation forced its sale to the Roman Catholics soon after its

completion and it was renamed St Mary-on-the-Quay (Hankins 1993, 14–15).

Two groups seeking religious asylum founded their churches in this part of the city. Having lost the exclusive use of the Lord Mayor's Chapel, in 1720 Bristol's Huguenot congregation built its own chapel in Orchard Street (Mayo 1985, 13). Seeking to establish communities outside the restrictions imposed in Saxony, the Moravians initially settled in Bristol at Avon Street, Great Gardens, in 1746 (Dresser 1994, 115). The group was formally established as a congregation in 1755, with members largely drawn from the local community, and it acquired a site on Lower Maudlin Street. There seems, as was usual with Moravian communities, to have been a carefully formulated plan for its development. In August the following year they met for the first time in the newly

built chapel and, following the practice of segregation of the sexes which had emerged at Herrnhut, construction of the Brethren's house began on the 28 August 1756 (Dresser 1994, 117; Dresser 1996b, 309). The central square and its cemetery was an important feature in Moravian planning, around which were arranged the Brethren and Sisters' houses, the school and stables (Murtagh 1998, 9–10). The chapel was brick built, like contemporary American buildings, rather than the rubble and ashlar construction more

Figure 8.100 West front of New Hall (photograph R Jones)

usual in Bristol non-conformist chapels (Stell 1986, 70) (Fig 8.103).

Part of the foundations of the west end of the church were recorded in excavations on Upper Maudlin Street in 1976 (BHER 432); an area enclosed by Pennant flagstones was interpreted as a small garden, and a large cess pit yielded a pottery assemblage of 18th-century date. A watching brief on an adjacent site in 1993 (BHER 471) found that the Moravians' cemetery had not, as had been reported, been cleared, and was substantially undisturbed. The remains of more than 200 individuals were recovered, many from brick burial shafts or vaults, together with an assemblage of coffin furniture. The fieldwork confirmed much of the account of burial practice presented to the sanitary survey of 1850 (Clark 1850, 214), but resources were not available either for the study of the human remains or of the coffin furniture, and the skeletal material was reinterred. A further watching brief (BHER 3586) was carried out in 1999 and 2000 when disarticulated human remains were found together with coffin furniture (Pilkington 2000).

A campaign of investigation of the site of St James's Priory from the late 1980s, particularly excavation in 1995 of the NFU Mutual Insurance site, recorded the foundations of the Scottish Presbyterian Church which had been built there in the 1850s, together with the remains of boundary walls and drains of the dwellings on St James Parade which it replaced. The entire ground plan of the Scottish Presbyterian Church was recorded, including pits dug to secure the scaffolding uprights during its construction (Jones 1989, 5; BHER 413, BHER 3155; Bryant 1993; J Bryant pers comm; Jackson 2006b).

It was, of course, not just in the Frome floodplain that the population was growing and for which new places of worship had to be established. A number of nonconformist chapels were built in the Old Market area in the 19th century, including a Methodist chapel founded on the south side of Redcross Street in 1817. The Baptist cemetery in Redcross Street was investigated archaeologically in 1982 (BHER 3037), many burials remaining *in situ* despite the supposed clearance of the

Figure 8.101 Penn Street Tabernacle, early 20th century (Samuel Loxton, Bristol Reference Library ref E406)

site in 1926 (Iles 1983, 52). For its part, the established church built St Jude's, designed by S B Gabriel, in 1849 in the south-east corner of Poyntz pool, a large part of the funding derived from the Special Fund created by Bishop Monk to encourage godliness (Ralph and Cobb 1991, 28).

In the Stokes Croft area, new places of worship were being built throughout the first half of the 19th century. The Gideon Chapel had been established on the north side of Newfoundland Street with its burial ground to the west and on the south side there were blocks of development to the north bank of the Frome. Brunswick Chapel, on the north side of Brunswick Square, a Congregational chapel designed by William Armstrong, was constructed in 1834–5 for seceding members of the Castle Green congregation (Fig 8.104). St Barnabas Church in Ashley Road was established in 1843 by private subscription (Ralph and Cobb 1991, 26). The United Methodist Free Church chapel on the north side of Milk Street was opened in February 1854.

Although the Jewish community was re-admitted to England in 1656, it does not appear to have re-established itself in Bristol immediately – a synagogue was only established in 1756 (Rubinstein 1996, 65). This was sited in an existing building on the east side of Temple Street (No 146) before being moved in 1786 to the Weaver's Hall by Temple Church (Samuel 1997, 63–7). The Jewish cemetery, in Brook's Court off Rose Street within the former Rack Close, was bought by the community in 1830 having been established in 1811. In 1850 the cemetery was described as 'very small and narrow: house windows overlook it. The soil is marshy, and the whole in a very dirty and neglected state, being used as the back premises of the dwelling house through which it is entered' (Clark 1850). The burial ground had been closed by the 1880s and the human remains and memorials removed to a new burial ground in Fishponds in the early 1920s (Samuel 1997). Another cemetery for the Jewish community had been established on the site of the brickyard in Barton Road in St Philip's Marsh by March 1759 when the yard together with a house and garden were advertised for sale (FFBJ 31 March 1759). This burial ground still exists. A purpose-built synagogue was built in Park Row in 1874 (*see* p 319).

Almshouses and charitable bodies

There were a number of charitable institutions in the Lewins Mead quarter in the 18th century. Foster's Almshouse was rebuilt in stone 'from the ground' in 1702. The building was of two storeys with an eight-window main range parallel with Christmas Steps, abutting the chapel of the Three Kings of Cologne. The fourteen apartments, seven on the ground floor and seven above, each formed of an individual bedroom with fireplace (Manchee 1831, vol 1, 89) (Fig 8.105).

Three schools were among the charities administered by the Corporation, and later Bristol Municipal Charities. Bristol Grammar School had occupied the buildings of St Bartholomew's Hospital since the 16th century and these were refurbished by the Corporation between 1757 and 1762 at a cost of over £2,000 (Hill 1951, 41). A new east range was added in 1818 and this, consisting of an open arcade, a kitchen on the ground floor, a first-floor dining room and bedrooms above, was surveyed during archaeological investigation of the site in 1977 (BHER 3286) (Fig 8.106).

The north range was converted to Poor Law housing in 1856 when the Queen Elizabeth's Hospital School, which had moved there in 1767, moved to Jacob's Wells Road. Subsequently, the buildings were let for industry and the first occupiers, Brightman Brothers' footwear factory, converted them for their purposes in 1881 (Price with Ponsford 1998, 134).

Private charitable interest led to the foundation of the Bristol Royal Infirmary, which opened in December 1737 supported by individual subscriptions of two guineas per annum. The building was sited at the junction of Upper and Lower Maudlin Streets and the original hospital seems, from early illustrations, to have consisted of a three-storey structure with two ranges (Fissell 1991, 74–93). It was replaced in 1784–6 by a larger building, again with

two wings projecting from the main range (Fig 8.107). The burial ground for the infirmary was sited on the southern side of Johnny Ball Lane. This was partially excavated in 2002 and the human remains were passed to the University of Bristol for further study, although no report has been completed (BHER 3928; Samuel 2003).

The charitable impulse also found expression in Broadmead, several almshouses being founded in the 18th century. In 1701, according to a datestone on the building, the Merchant Taylors' Almshouse was rebuilt on the west side of Merchant Street, while in 1722 Elizabeth Blanchard willed that an almshouse be established in her home, apparently at the east end of Milk Street, to 'be enjoyed by three poor old maids, whose labour was done'. The rents of six other

Figure 8.102 Lewins Mead Unitarian Chapel (photograph D Martyn)

houses in Milk Street, including the Bunch of Grapes public house, were used to maintain it (Manchee 1831, vol 1, 199–202). Between 1738 and 1740 Ridley's Almshouses were built at the corner of Milk Street and Old King Street, as the result of a bequest in the will of Sarah Ridley, drawn up in 1716 and not altered before her death in 1726 to provide for five men and five women (Manchee 1831, vol 1, 192–5). The two-storey almshouse had ten individual rooms, as well as a committee room. Surveyed in the early 1950s, the location of the kitchens, if any, could not be established. An extension against the back wall of the building housed water closets but the original sanitary arrangements appeared to have consisted of a dry closet in the cupboards in each room (BHER 920) (St John O'Neil 1951, 62–3) (Fig 8.108).

In Stokes Croft, by the late 1820s the Unitarian Almshouse appears to have been re-fronted, though its financial resources were

coming under strain (Manchee 1831, vol 1, 203–4) (Fig 8.109). Bachelors' Almshouse had been built on the southern side of Grosvenor Road by 1828.

The institutional buildings in Old Market were mainly founded before the 18th century. Some, like Trinity Almshouse in Old Market Street, were rebuilt between the mid-1850s and the early 1880s to designs in a Tudor Revival style by Foster and Wood and extended in 1881 (Gomme *et al* 1979, 314–15).

Dr White's Almshouse in Bear Lane, Redcliffe, was re-fronted in 1824–5 with a two-storey, three-bay building in a Tudor style with a crenellated parapet and castellated miniature turrets at the ends (Fig 8.110). The rear part of the building was rebuilt in the early 1880s to a design by J H Hirst. The overall linear arrangement with the almshouses against the northern edge of the site was retained but the almshouses were rebuilt in Cattybrook brick with limestone ashlar dressings, each having 'a combined living and sleeping room, 15ft

Figure 8.104 Brunswick Chapel, Brunswick Square (photograph D Martyn)

by 12ft and 10ft high, with a separate scullery for each, and open yards with waterclosets at the back' (*The Builder*, 9 December 1882, 759) (Fig 8.111).

Housing

Earlier chapters have traced the gradual eclipse and disappearance of the medieval open hall, and its final manifestation as a mainly symbolic space demonstrating the status and lineage of the wealthiest Bristolians. However, well before the end of the Middle Ages, the city streets – particularly those of the old centre – were characterised by another, simpler form of structure whose design owed more to its congested, urban setting. This was the 'shop-house', a building without a single-storey hall open to the roof, a building which, at its simplest, took the form of a series of vertically stacked rooms: the shop on the ground floor with a living room or parlour (the equivalent of the hall) above, and a chamber above that (*see* Chapter 6).

The middle of the 17th century was a key period in the development of the city – economically, with the rapid growth of the Atlantic economy, geographically, with the laying out of King Street and the redevelopment of the castle, but also architecturally, in that amongst the large number of new houses built, not only were halls absent but, in many instances, so too were shops. Between *c* 1650 and *c* 1800 an ever-increasing proportion of the built-up area consisted of dwellings, pure and simple, without shops. The basic form of the shop-house gave rise to a successor, the 'residential house', which came to dominate the city streets; the gradual separation of workplace from dwelling apparent in the occupational geography of the city being echoed at the level of the individual house and house-plot. As before, this section on the development of housing in Bristol is merely a very brief summary of some of the conclusions arising from the research of Dr Roger Leech, to whom the reader is referred for the definitive account.

Figure 8.105 Foster's Almshouse and the chapel of the Three Kings of Cologne, probably early 1820s, by G Hill (Braikenridge Collection, BRSMG M2557)

The 'residential house', as built in Bristol from the middle of the 17th century, was socially diverse and, with variations in plan-form, materials and detailing, could accommodate the needs and aspirations of all but the very wealthiest citizens. The simplest form was the single-room plan, with stairs giving access to the upper floors set in a corner; dwellings of this type frequently belonged to artisans, or their widows. Examples include Nos 23–9 St Michael's Hill, a row of four three-storeyed buildings built before 1637 (Leech 2014, fig 8.2a) (*see* Fig 7.11), No 8 Pipe Lane, built with the stairs in the back corner in the late 17th century (Leech 2014, fig 8.2b), and Nos 68–70 Colston Street, two of a row of ten houses first occupied in the 1690s (Leech 2014, fig 8.2c) (*see* Fig 7.5).

Houses with one-room footprints continued to be built into the 18th century, as at No 17 Wade Street, built by Nathaniel Wade between *c* 1700 and 1710, with three storeys and a staircase tucked between the chimney on the side wall and the rear corner (Leech 2014, figs 8.2e, 8.3) (*see* Fig 8.10).

This very basic form of dwelling was highly suitable to the most congested urban conditions and could be found in courtyards and alleyways behind main street frontages, forming the most common expression of 'urban infill', the process by which rents were maximised from lower-value inner-city spaces. Examples are known from Tailors Court in the old centre, where two houses survive from *c* 1677 (Leech 2014, figs 8.21, 8.22) and Warry's Court, off Redcliff Street, where eight one-room houses were built *c* 1755 (Leech

Figure 8.106 Interior of St Bartholomew's Hospital in 1820 when in use as Bristol Grammar School, by John Sanders (Braikenridge Collection, BRSMG M2584)

Figure 8.107 The Bristol Royal Infirmary as rebuilt in 1784–6 (Bristol Reference Library Collections Braik. XI.i.282)

2014, fig 8.29). It is no accident that one-room houses were common in areas where labour-intensive industries such as sugar refining, glass and pottery manufacture predominated, and were sometimes built specifically for their workforces, as at the Great House on Welsh Back, a sugar house from *c* 1653 where 13 worker's houses were built around a court in 1661. Later, particularly after the 1740s, artisan housing was mostly of small two-room plan houses (Leech 2014, 190).

The housing of the poorest sections of society is always the least likely to survive, or the most likely to get altered, and intact examples of one-room plan houses in Bristol are inevitably thin on the ground. They have, however, begun to be investigated by excavation. During investigations (BHER 4279/4281) to the east of the former Dominican Friary, an area of contrasting mid-18th-century housing was uncovered. Housing on the main streets, Penn Street and Philadelphia Street, was reasonably substantial; so too was that on Cross Street, a principal side street. The houses there were two or three rooms deep and three storeys high, with stone-paved cellars; sanitation took the form of external cess pits. However, behind Cross Street lay cul-de-sacs, Llewellin's Court and Island Court: here the houses were simpler, cheaper, three-storey single-room plan dwellings, with a tiny external scullery and no sanitation at all, except access at the rear to the increasingly unsavoury River Frome. These houses were constructed from the 1750s and survived until the slum clearance programmes of the 1930s (Figs 8.112, 8.113 and 8.114) (Phillpotts 2013, 29).

The two-room plan was characteristic of houses built for a wealthier clientele from the 1650s, and for artisans a century later; a contemporary referred to the two-room plan as 'the common form of all late built houses' in the 1680s. Nos 33–4 King Street, the oldest house in the street, built in 1658 has a front room whose elaborate, original, fireplace shows that it was never a shop (Leech 2014, figs 7.35, 8.45) (*see* Fig 7.17). Nos 3–5 King Street, built sometime after 1663, departed in form from a shop-house one step further in that the front room was not accessed directly

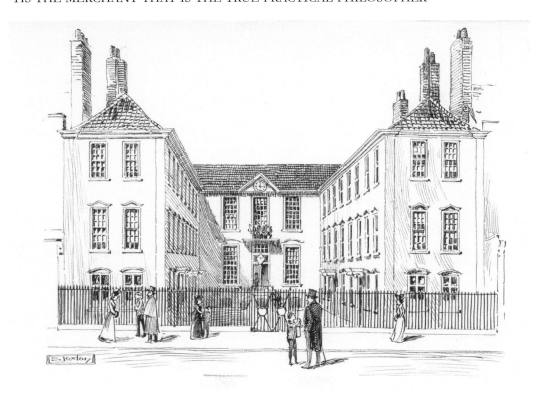

Figure 8.109 Stokes Croft School and Almshouse, early 20th century (Samuel Loxton, Bristol Reference Library V1247)

from the street but from a side passage (Leech 2014, figs 8.46, 8.47a).

A number of other variations on this basic form were possible. The ground-floor rooms were usually a parlour at the front and a kitchen at the back, or, if (as in earlier shop-houses) there was a detached kitchen behind, both ground-floor rooms could be used as parlours – a front, or best, parlour and a back parlour. Staircases were often placed centrally, between the two rooms, a practice that continued through the 18th century. Roger Leech (2014, 201–2) gives as examples the Guinea Street houses built by ships' captains in the 1720s and 1730s, like Nos 10–12 Guinea Street, a row of three such houses built for Edmund Saunders, captain of a slave ship (*see* Fig 8.31).

The same plan form was popular in more expensive houses, as at Nos 4–5 Charles Street (Leech 2014, figs 8.47c, 8.55) their quality advertised by good external brickwork and good staircases within. A central staircase had the additional advantage that (like the cross-passage in earlier centuries) it made houses easier to sub-divide internally if multiple occupancy was desired.

Another variation of the two-room plan saw the staircase installed at the rear, offering the advantages of allowing a fine staircase to be seen from the front door and the stairs to be illuminated via a window in the back wall. Early examples are known: Langton's shop-house at No 12 Welsh Back was built thus in *c* 1623, and No 74 Old Market was rebuilt this way in *c* 1699 (Leech 2014, figs 8.60a, 8.61). By the end of the 18th century most two-room plan houses were built with staircases at the rear, and it was this type that predominated in the mid- and late 18th-century developments in St Augustine's parish, on St Michael's Hill, in Portland Square, Kingsdown and Clifton (Leech 2014, chapter 8).

A continuous thread that runs through the story of the development of Bristol's housing after the mid-17th century is that of the impact and influence of the Atlantic economy, and the slave trade. It was felt indirectly, in the boost that it gave to the city economy, particularly in the building booms of the 18th century, but was also manifest much more directly. Speculative building by ships' captains on the significantly-named Guinea Street has already been mentioned and Roger

Leech's research has identified other, similar, very personal connections. For example, the activities of Llewellin Davies (d 1688), a Bristol clay-pipe maker whose products have been found on Nevis Island, a sugar plantation island in the Caribbean. Davies was also a speculative builder, responsible for Nos 38–41 Old Market Street – two pairs of jettied timber-framed houses. Nos 33–4 King Street, already discussed, were built by the carpenter Thomas Wickham, who was also active in the Caribbean. 18th-century developments on St Michael's Hill frequently had a similar background. Of the ten houses built on Old Park Hill between 1714 and 1722, only two lacked a maritime connection, the other residents being ships' captains, a ship owner and slaver, and a captain's widow. Leech comments that Old Park Hill 'could well have been called slavers' row'. Developments on Kingsdown, at Berkeley Square and Portland Square and in Clifton all had similar association, through their financing, their early residents, or both (Leech 2014, chapter 12).

It is also true to say that architectural form, as well as finance, had, by the end of the 18th century, developed a transatlantic dimension in Bristol with similarities in seaport housing being evident on both sides of the ocean. This was manifest in a number of ways, with, for example, central-stack plans common on the American eastern seaboard, shop-houses in Charleston with unheated front parlours and kitchens to the rear. And even the very distinctively Bristol phenomenon of families owning town-houses as well as second residences on the urban fringe, in the form of the lodges or garden houses built in the 17th century on the hillsides overlooking the city and its port, had parallels in America. William Penn, founder of Pennsylvania, had a residence on St Michael's Hill, probably a garden house on Upper Maudlin Street, in the 1690s; his son Thomas had a country house at Springettsbury, Philadelphia, as his rural retreat. Again, Roger Leech has identified garden houses fringing Charleston on the island of Nevis (Leech 2014, 364).

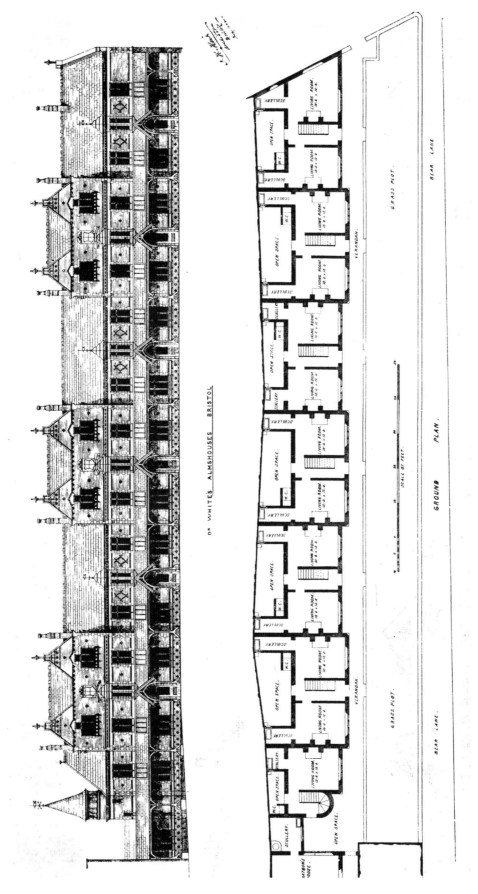

Figure 8.111 Plan and elevation of Dr White's Almshouse in 1882 (The Builder, 9 December 1882)

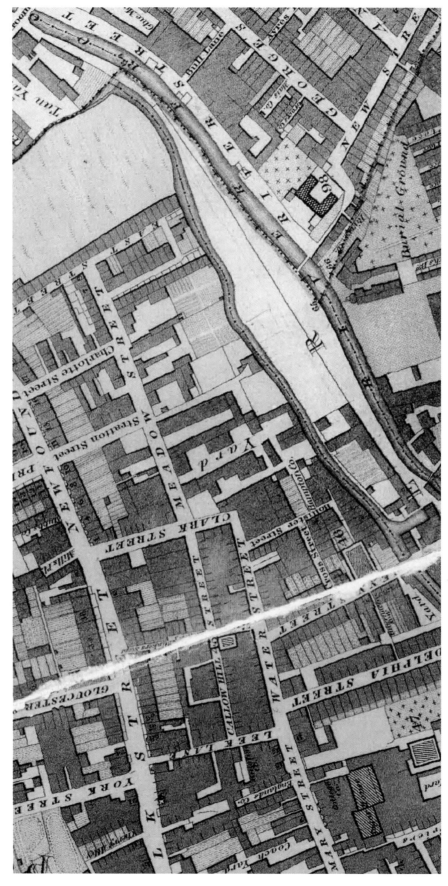

Figure 8.112 Extract from Plumley and Ashmead's map of 1828, showing the area north of the river Frome, developed from the 1720s onwards (Bristol Archives 04481)

In terms of trade, finance, personalities, architecture, Bristol by the end of the 18th century was a truly international city. While it had lost its pre-eminent position in the Atlantic trade by the end of the following century, it was still a city of considerable importance with a newly established port at the mouth of the Avon and a rapidly expanding population, drawn by its new industrial concerns, principally chocolate, tobacco and heavy engineering, but also the still important sugar refining and shipbuilding industries. As Lavars 1887 panorama of the city, produced in the 50th year of Queen Victoria's reign, makes clear (Fig 8.115), the city had been transformed, especially from the end of the 18th century, into something approaching the modern 21st-century city.

Figure 8.113 Overhead view of Cabot Circus excavation showing the Llewellin's Court area (reproduced from Ridgeway and Watts 2013, fig 3.65)

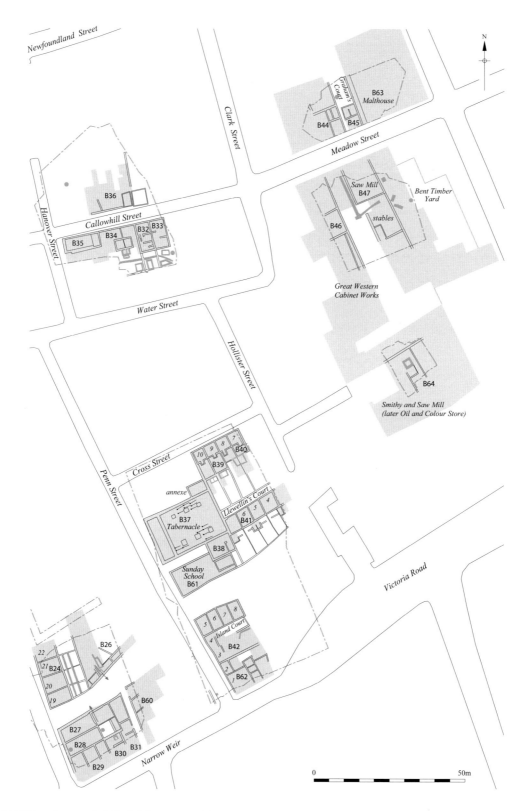

Figure 8.114 Water Street and Callowhill Street area in the 19th century, as revealed in excavation (reproduced from Ridgeway and Watts 2013, fig 6.5)

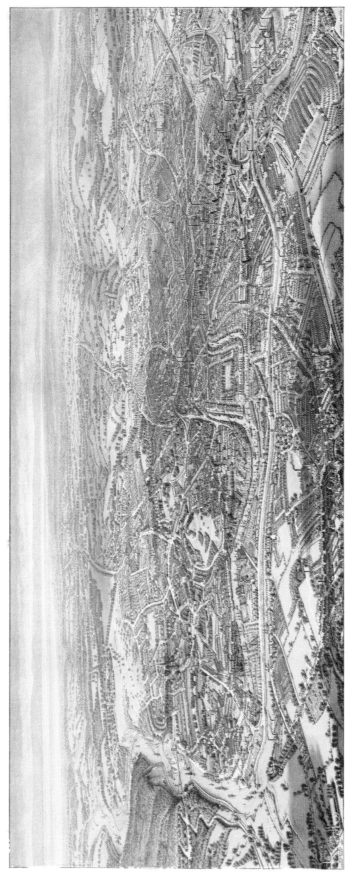

Figure 8.115 Lavars' Panorama of Bristol of 1887 (BRSMG M3336)

PART 3: THE ARCHAEOLOGY OF BRISTOL: AN ASSESSMENT

General

The preceding chapters have considered the range of sources available to the archaeologist and historian and have put forward our understanding of the development of the city and the occupation of its site that preceded its foundation as far as can be suggested from the archaeological and historical evidence currently available. This section summarises some of the ideas put forward in earlier chapters and suggests some broad themes that might be explored in future programmes of research. Such research might arise through the development process although it may well be that some is the result of private research or under the auspices of the two major universities in the city or other educational establishments. Nor is the research agenda intended to be exhaustive and there will inevitably be directions for new research that will become apparent in future.

The sample of the historic built-up area (the study area for this project) that has been investigated by archaeological methods is vanishingly small – probably well under one per cent and in these circumstances any discussion of the evolution and character of the city must be hedged by uncertainty; only the continuation of archaeological research in the long term will extend the sample. It is also the case that the 'archaeological resource' – buried archaeological deposits and standing historic buildings – is finite, and much smaller than the city itself, substantial areas having been subjected to redevelopment that has resulted in the destruction of the buried archaeology. But the recent publication of an initial Bristol archaeological deposit model (Wilkinson *et al* 2013b) has usefully extended past work to identify where the best-preserved buried archaeological deposits might survive.

Unpublished excavations

The existing excavated sample of historic Bristol is, however, further diminished by the 'backlog problem' – a large number of site investigations, particularly from the 1970s but also later, whose material, because of resourcing problems, was never fully analysed or published, inhibiting further research and resulting in the constant recycling of insufficiently tested assumptions. The publication of all sites excavated in the city would be desirable, recognised as an issue at regional level (Rippon and Croft 2008, 201). The previously less accessible 'grey literature', the corpus of unpublished client reports often produced during the planning process is now being made publicly accessible via Bristol City Council's Know Your Place website. Nevertheless, a number of key sites can be recognised as being of particular importance on the basis of their potential to answer some of the research questions posed in this volume (*see* Table 2).

The two sites at Peter Street lie adjacent to the conjectured but unproven eastern limit of the early medieval town and both were within the area of the medieval Jewry. Tower Lane and the nearby site at Newmarket Avenue, the latter excavation conducted in less than ideal conditions, both contained important evidence for Late Saxon occupation in the form of a series of rubbish pits, presumably associated with occupation against the unexcavated street frontage of Broad Street. Both sites also contained evidence for Norman first-floor halls, indicative of the conspicuous wealth of early medieval Bristol. At Small Street, another relatively limited site but in the heart of the medieval town, an earthen bank might represent the precursor to the later stone defences. The various sites within the castle precinct will be important in allowing a more complete

Table 2 List of priority unpublished sites

Site name	Date excavated	Present state of post-excavation analysis
Bristol Castle (various sites)	From 1948	Major synthesis in unpublished MLitt thesis; further analysis required
St Peter's Church, Peter Street (BHER 409)	1970	Short note published; further post-excavation analysis awaited
Greyfriars (BHER 317)	1973	Popular booklet published; further post-excavation analysis awaited
Peter Street (BHER 319)	1975	Interim report published; further post-excavation analysis awaited
Tower Lane (BHER 320)	1979	Popular booklet published; further post-excavation analysis awaited
Redcliff Street (85–7) & Redcliff Backs	1980 & 1999	Post-excavation assessment and grey literature report. Specialist analyses completed
Redcliff Street – Bristol Bridge (BHER 341)	1981	Interim report published; further post-excavation analysis awaited
Redcliff Street – Dundas Wharf (BHER 344)	1982–3	Interim report published; some specialist analyses published; comprehensive post-excavation analysis awaited
Redcliff Street – Canynges House (BHER 447)	1983–5	Interim report published; further post-excavation analysis awaited
Small Street (BHER 313)	1990	Short note published; further post-excavation analysis awaited
Minster House (BHER 1685)	1992	Publication draft produced
Portwall/Tower Harratz (BHER 463, 554, 3158, 3643)	1994 onwards	Grey literature reports
5–7 Welsh Back (BHER 1579)	1995	Publication draft completed. Some additional work required to incorporate results of subsequent watching brief (BHER 3581)
Poole's Wharf (BHER 3265)	1996	Publication draft produced
Redcliff Street (98–103) (BHER 3629)	2000	Post-excavation assessment and grey literature report. Specialist analyses completed
College Square (BHER 3772)	2001	Publication draft produced. Some work required to incorporate results of subsequent watching brief (BHER 4390) and building survey (BHER 4438)
Portwall Lane (BHER 4371)	2006	Publication draft produced

understanding of the form of Bristol Castle itself, a monument of national importance, as well as providing information about a large area of the Saxon town. All these sites will contain evidence for the earliest settlement of the town, its defences and the artefactual and structural data necessary to augment the currently meagre evidence for its form and function, as well as evidence for the subsequent development of the area into the later medieval period.

The Redcliffe sites, where the waterlogged conditions allowed for excellent survival of organic materials, benefited from detailed environmental sampling programmes, especially Dundas Wharf, Canynges House, 98–103 Redcliff Street and Redcliff Backs. These are the most comprehensively excavated sites on the waterfront with rigorous environmental sampling programmes in place from the start. An interim published account of the data derived from partial examination of the diatoms, plant macrofossils and animal bone from the Dundas Wharf site gives an insight into the wealth of evidence awaiting more detailed studies of the excavated material (Jones and Watson 1987). On the other hand, comprehensive analyses of palaeoenvironmental samples have been completed for the sites at 98–103 Redcliff Street and at Redcliff Backs, the latter being an extension of earlier work on Redcliff Street in 1980. Both the latter sites are at an advanced stage in the post-excavation process and could be published without too much further work.

On the opposite bank of the Avon, at Welsh Back, major excavation in 1995 revealed evidence for occupation of the site from the 12th to 19th century, complementing the work by Kenneth Barton to the rear in 1958 (Barton 1960). Good palaeoenvironmental data was recovered. This has been analysed and assessed and a detailed draft publication report has been produced (Blockley 1996).

Important information about the activities associated with the post-medieval expansion of the harbour came from the excavation at Poole's Wharf, south of Hotwell Road, where a slipway and other buildings were recorded, including a possible stable. This was a part of the harbour which lay well to the west of the main harbour area and included Champion's, later Merchants Dock, from 1762.

The excavation at Greyfriars is one of three large-scale investigations of a major monastic complex so far carried out in Bristol (the others being those of St James's Priory and the Dominican Friary, both now published). The future analysis of this excavation is likely to produce important evidence for religious practices as well as for the local economy of this important religious house.

St. Augustine-the-Less and St Mary-le-Port remain the only church sites so far excavated in Bristol. The clues they hold regarding the development of burial practices and changing religious beliefs, together with the information on the health, diet and diseases of the occupants of the burial ground make them two of the most important sites excavated in the last 50 years.

The excavation of the site of Minster House to the west of the present Cathedral provides important detailed information about the early history of St Augustine's Abbey from its foundation in 1140 through its surrender in 1539 at the Dissolution and subsequently when it became a cathedral. Additional information regarding the outer court of the Abbey was recovered during excavation at College Square

where the remains of the possible abbey barn were recorded.

The various works on the Portwall and its associated structures, especially Tower Harratz, remain as grey literature reports and would benefit from an overall summary of the various excavation campaigns carried out from 1994 onwards.

The excavation of the Portwall Lane glassworks remains unpublished despite the fact that it was one of the most remarkable survivals of an 18th-century glassworks complex ever found in the city and has produced important evidence for the technology of the glass industry at this time. A draft report has been produced and could be published with little further work required.

It is also the case that the excavated (fully analysed and published) sample is further compromised by its highly uneven geographical distribution, largely a consequence of the uneven distribution of development, as well as redevelopment without detailed excavation or even observation. Some areas of the city therefore remain virtually untouched by archaeological excavation – the castle is a prime example – with consequences for every historical period, as we will see.

Palaeoenvironmental evidence

A number of important published sites have benefited from programmes of detailed palaeoenvironmental analyses. Notable among these has been the work at Cabot Circus where analyses of animal and fish bone, plant macrofossils and insects have shed considerable light on the local environment, diet and economy relating to the site especially in the medieval period (Warman; Giorgi; Armitage; and Allison in Ridgeway and Watts 2013). To a lesser extent, the work at Union Street, like Cabot Circus alongside the upper reaches of the River Frome, has also provided a detailed view of the local environment, with plant macrofossils and insect remains providing evidence of domestic waste within the site, although the fish bone and animal assemblages did provide some evidence for high status occupancy of the site, at least in the later medieval and early modern periods (Jones; Smith and Tetlow; Higbee; and Nicholson in Jackson 2010a). Other published sites of a reasonable size, St Bartholomew's Hospital and St James's Priory, while providing important information about the development of two religious houses and, in the case of St James's Priory, changing burial practices, nevertheless suffered from the lack of palaeoenvironmental sampling programmes, with consequent biases in the data.

A multi-disciplinary palaeoenvironmental programme at the site at the former Courage Brewery, now known as Finzels Reach, has produced evidence for the local environment, industrial activity and diet. This site produced the largest assemblages of animal and fish bone so far recovered from any Bristol site. It provides vital information about changes in dietary preferences especially through the medieval period and about the changing sources for the fish consumed in the medieval period, with an interesting conclusion that the majority of fish consumed on the site were being caught locally with the fish from more distant fisheries traded through the port before being moved inland (Nicholson 2017). The plant macrofossils, too, provided important information about diet and industry, including some of the earliest evidence for cloth working so far recovered from the city (Jones 2017).

Other sites (98–103 Redcliff Street, Redcliff Backs and Welsh Back) have also produced important evidence for industrial working, particularly cloth working, the exploitation of local resources, such as cereal cultivation, changes in diet and the local environment. Together with the partially analysed material from Dundas Wharf, this material promises to yield further important information to complement that from the already published sites. However, while it is important that these and other individual sites are published, a city-wide, inter-site assessment and synthesis is needed of both published and unpublished bioarchaeological data, allied to the physical evidence and documentary sources, in order to provide answers to some outstanding research questions and to develop future research directions. These may include, for example, the exploitation of the city's hinterland for food and industrial processes; the changing environment of the city over time, particularly at the level of the individual tenement plot; any trends relating to diet, including any discernible differences relating to class or social status; and the changing economy of the city, as it developed into an international trading centre.

A specific project that was commenced in 2010 but never completed, was to use stable isotope and DNA techniques to detect the origin of the cod that was being imported into Bristol and found on archaeological sites of the medieval and early modern periods. It would be desirable to resurrect this project which would augment the documentary sources for the trade with the north Atlantic, especially Iceland, from at least the early 15th century.

The development of the deposit model

The deposit model summarised above in Chapter 2 is the result of work principally by Dr Keith Wilkinson, drawing upon his extensive previous geoarchaeological work in Bristol, as well as available geotechnical records and the results of programmes of archaeological investigation. However, the model is necessarily limited by the variable nature of the records, especially commercial borehole records, and the uneven distribution of such records. A number of recommendations for future work have therefore been made on the basis of the findings of the current study (see Wilkinson *et al* 2013b, 48–51).

1. Archaeological investigations within the floodplain should penetrate beyond the base of the archaeological stratigraphy, ideally to the pre-Quaternary substrate. Archaeological and pre-archaeological deposits should be classified in a consistent manner in accordance with the descriptors set out (*see* Table 1 (p 28) and Wilkinson *et al* 2013b, appendix B).
2. A qualified archaeologist should study all geotechnical logs where subsequent archaeological investigation is to take place. Strata recorded in the logs should be assigned to the categories set out in the appendix as above.
3. Future recording of waterlogged archaeological strata should be undertaken in a uniform and consistent manner, using standard morphological descriptions and observations by specialists for the presence of anthropogenic indicators.

4. The underlying Wentlooge Formation deposits are of importance in assisting in the interpretation of pre-medieval periods. As suggested above, for example, the depth of the Wentlooge Formation deposits might be an indicator of earlier river channel courses, while organic strata may provide proxy indicators of human activity. In some cases it has been possible to date these deposits and it must be a future priority to date these stratigraphic units, either by AMS ^{14}C dating or by other techniques such as Optically Stimulated Luminescence (OSL). The genesis of these strata should be identified (whether alluvial or intertidal, by diatom and/or foraminiferal analysis) and the palynology of organic strata examined.

5. In addition to the above, in view of the uneven coverage of the data so far examined, it will be important to concentrate on filling the gaps in the data in the following areas

   i. Area between the inner town wall and the outer north wall – Nelson Street/ Quay Street/Rupert Street.
   ii. Area between the inner town wall and the Marsh Wall – between Baldwin Street, Marsh Street, King Street and Welsh Back.
   iii. Area to the west of the historic core in the heart of the historic port – Broad Quay, Colston Avenue.

6. Only limited time was spent in examining archaeological records and no time was spent in examining the archive of unpublished excavations. The records of unpublished excavations should be further examined in an attempt to identify the locations and levels of waterlogged archaeological deposits.

7. Examination of further boreholes, including privately held boreholes. While commercial borehole data has been shown to be of less value, they may augment data from more reliable sources. In addition a programme of targeted boreholes, especially in areas highlighted in 5 above, would augment the presently meagre archaeological evidence.

8. With the acquisition of new data from a variety of sources, the model should be updated on a regular basis to refine existing hypotheses and to identify new research questions.

The prehistoric period

Bristol is situated in a region that is rich with sites of all prehistoric periods, from the Palaeolithic gravel terraces at Shirehampton, the Neolithic chambered tomb at Stoke Bishop and the stone and timber circles at Stanton Drew and Priddy, Bronze Age barrows at Kingsweston, a potential Late Bronze Age and Iron Age landscape in the wetlands adjacent to the Severn and major Iron Age hillforts at Clifton, Stokeleigh and Kingsweston. With such a multiplicity of sites in the Bristol hinterland, it is perhaps surprising that so little has so far been found in the inner Bristol area, despite the clear disruption that has taken place over the last 1,000 years. To date, finds of prehistoric material have been limited to stray finds, sometimes without detailed provenance, and now often lost to further study. They have generally been deeply buried: the bronze axe found at Cumberland Basin was 'about 20 feet below the river bank', while the bronze artefacts found to the south of Bristol Bridge were also presumably found at some depth close to the river bank by the bridge. However on the higher ground it is possible that evidence for prehistoric settlement might be found nearer to the present ground surface, within reach of archaeological investigation. The discovery of three undated flint flakes at around 2.5m below the present ground surface at Southwell Street on the south-facing slopes near St Michael's Hill might offer some potential for the discovery in future of evidence for intact prehistoric settlement sites on the higher ground overlooking the Frome and Avon valleys in the city centre. For the more deeply buried sites within the floodplain, while the recovery of artefacts from deep alluvial deposits has been shown to be possible during the observation of deep construction works (*see* Chapter 4), such opportunities are likely to be rare. It is thus probable that we should look to geoarchaeological prospection for the retrieval of evidence for prehistoric occupation and for human impact on the wider landscape as indicated by Wilkinson *et al* (2013b). Such evidence, if found, will be of the greatest significance in reconstructing the past environment of the lower Avon and Frome floodplains. Evidence for the disturbance of lowland woodland areas from the early Neolithic has come from various sites around the Severn, including the evidence from central Bristol (Wilkinson 2006). Pollen analysis from the site at Deanery Road has suggested that prior to 3550–3050 cal BC (Wk-10946) the uplands above the site supported lime woodland with evidence for burning and the influx of ash, perhaps indicating localised forest clearance (Tinsley 2002). Clearly direct evidence for prehistoric settlement both within the valley and on the valley sides will be of major importance in putting into context the various artefacts recovered in earlier works as well as with the prehistoric sites in the wider area.

Research agenda
Dating and analysis of Wentlooge deposits
The tentative deposit model that has been put forward in Chapter 2 has suggested a possible chronology for the onset and development of the Holocene sequence. However, the numbers of reliably dated and sufficiently analysed sequences, using microbiological techniques, are few. As proposed above, samples for dating need to be more widely distributed for a more accurate interpretation of the city's changing topography from the last Ice Age. Further diatom and foraminiferal study of intertidal or alluvial strata, together with the palynology of organic strata will allow a greater understanding of the formation processes and of the manipulation by man of the wider landscape. Such programmes fit well with previously identified research aims such as Research Aim 16 in Webster (ed) 2008, 281–2.

Synthesis of current data for Late Bronze Age settlement in the Avonmouth Levels and production of a deposit model
Fieldwork on the Avonmouth Levels, particularly from 1998 onwards, has produced significant evidence for Late Bronze Age settlement sites, occupied probably only on a seasonal basis, and identified as surviving soil horizons within a gradually accumulating alluvial sequence. Some of this evidence has been brought together by Locock (2001). However, since this publication, further work has been carried out, including the excavation, in severe weather conditions, of a settlement site consisting of one and possibly two dwellings, defined by an outer ditch and with probable internal structures marked by a posthole and stakeholes surrounded by a scatter of stone, pottery and bone (Tuck 2006). The site lay close to a palaeochannel, which appears to be a defining feature of such sites. There is evidence for similar sites and an overall synthesis, together with the full publication of the 2006 work, will bring together the evidence to date, while a deposit model of the Avonmouth Levels will assist in the prediction of the foci of likely Late Bronze Age/Early Iron Age sites, given their apparent location adjacent to former palaeochannels. More recent work, at Smoke Lane, close to the Severn foreshore, and at Hallen, have suggested the possibility of even earlier stabilisation horizons of the early Mesolithic (6410–6250 cal BC (SUERC-48403) or even late Glacial at Hallen (Vanessa Straker, pers comm) (Wessex Archaeology 2013; Wilkinson *et al* 2013a).

Identification of further sites with prehistoric potential
The identification of possible intact prehistoric settlement on the higher ground to the north of the city centre means that sites in a similar topographic location should be targeted for evidence of further settlements, while the hills surrounding the city centre, Clifton and Kingsdown to the north and Totterdown to the south, known as 'Aldebury' in a charter of 1188, could be sites of hitherto undefined prehistoric settlement. Targeted borehole prospection, especially within the valley bottoms, could produce evidence for prehistoric settlement, now obscured by a deep overburden of urban settlement. The location of long established urban forms, such as historic parish boundaries, could also be indicators of prehistoric routes and boundaries.

The Roman period

As has been seen above in Chapter 4, there is an increasing corpus of information about the hinterland of Bristol in the Late Iron Age and Roman period. Bristol lay within a prosperous and settled landscape, characterised by farm settlements, villas at Brislington and Kings Weston and a small town at Sea Mills (Abonae). These were linked by a network of roads, some of which have received archaeological attention. Not surprisingly, given that there has been 1,500 years since the end of Roman rule and 1,000 years of continuous development and renewal, evidence for Roman settlement within the centre of Bristol is slight and discontinuous. As with discoveries of prehistoric material, much of the evidence comes from antiquarian discoveries, often without context. The excavations at Upper Maudlin Street provide the exception where, in the 1970s, evidence was found for what was probably a Roman farm with indications of industrial activity. The discovery in the 19th century of two lead ingots in the channel of the river Frome, close to Wade Street, might indicate a river crossing at this point, although this has not been proved. The route of the Roman road to the north-west of the city, where it crosses the Downs, was demonstrated in excavations at the end of the 19th century and more recently in archaeological evaluation in 2001 (Parry 2001b). To the east of the city, the discovery in 1894 of burials in Redfield, followed in 2002 by the chance discovery of further burials in close proximity and dated to the Late Roman period, or possibly sub-Roman period, has suggested the possibility of a Late Roman cemetery and by implication of a contemporary settlement in the area. So far there has been little evidence for this apart from the discovery of some Roman pottery during evaluation of a site at Pile Marsh in 2003 (Heaton 2004). It is unknown where the associated road system was located. The road from Bath probably entered the Bristol area at around Summerhill Road, south-east of St George's Park, but thereafter its route is unclear, with traces masked or obliterated by the imposition of later road systems, before it emerges as the route previously referred to on Durdham Down. A north–south road system is suspected through Bishopsworth to the south of the city, reaching Bedminster Down, close to a possible villa, while part of the road from Sea Mills to Gloucester was excavated in 2007 (Young 2011). Important work has been carried out at Sea Mills, not least by a local community group undertaking surveys in private gardens and carrying out detailed excavation within the local allotment. Added to the work carried out by professional units in the area, our picture of the layout and function of the small town is evolving, although there remain questions about the detail of its internal geography and the longevity of the settlement.

Research agenda

Encourage further study into pre-medieval road systems
While there is reasonable certainty regarding the points at which the Roman road system from Bath entered the present urban area on the east and left it on the north-west on its way to Sea Mills, there is far less information about its route through the modern city centre. Russell and Williams (1984) have suggested a route to the north of the centre along Redland Road after which there are few clues, although the possible crossing of the Frome around Wade Street might suggest that a route may have existed through St Paul's connecting Arley Hill and Redland Road with a crossing near Wade Street. The relationship to this putative road system of the Roman building excavated in the 1970s adjacent to Upper Maudlin Street is unclear although the site could simply have been selected on the basis of its suitability as a well-drained site on a south-east facing terrace.

Further study of Roman artefact collections in museum-held archives
The various artefacts that have been recovered both from formal programmes of excavation as well as from chance discoveries deserve further study to see if there are any common themes running through the collections, in terms of chronology and materials.

Roman rural settlement
There is increasing evidence for Roman rural settlement in the Bristol hinterland, especially to the north-west around the Lawrence Weston area, where there has been evidence for Roman farming settlement continuing from the Late Iron Age, but also in south Bristol around Inns Court (Jackson, 2007a) in Bedminster and in east Bristol. Study of such sites should look at their economic and environmental evidence in an attempt to place such sites in their wider context and to see if there is any relationship between the development of villa sites such as Kings Weston and rural settlements such as those identified in the Avonmouth Levels. The study of rural land divisions together with known or suspected settlement patterns

might shed some light on the level of impact of Roman settlement in the wider Bristol area.

Abonae

While there has been important work carried out in recent years, there are still major uncertainties regarding the plan form and chronology of the town. Can the fortunes of the town be directly linked to events in the region, such as the transfer of the 2nd legion from Caerleon and the final abandonment of the fortress in the late 3rd century? Do the artefacts recovered from Sea Mills give any clues regarding trading links with the port? Scientific techniques, such as isotope analysis of human and animal bone might also provide some clues to the extent of trade links as well as the origins of the people who lived there. Further opportunities should be sought for the conduct of fieldwork to answer these questions while the continuing involvement of the public is to be promoted. The public should be encouraged to bring chance finds to the attention of the regional Finds Liaison Officer, while archaeological professionals may conduct informal identification sessions in Sea Mills.

The post-Roman period, and the origins of Saxon Bristol

Knowledge of the local, rural, background out of which Bristol emerged towards the end of the pre-Conquest period is extremely scanty. As Chapter 4 noted, there are indications of an early estate centre at Bedminster [and presumably an early minster], while there was also a centre at Westbury-on-Trym by 804 and possibly in the 790s (Orme and Cannon 2010) where an early minster may be postulated (it is referred to as *Westminster* in 804). However these are historical sources – the physical evidence is extremely thin. Physical, excavated, evidence is available from less than a handful of sites within the area of what is now outer Bristol for the post-Roman/Middle Saxon centuries. The recording in 1966 of at least ten inhumations on Kingsweston Hill, thought to date between AD 400 and 700 may point to the continuing occupation of a site that had been in use from the Late Bronze Age and which, due to its elevated position, continued to be a place of great significance to the local population well into the Early Saxon period (Godman, 1972). Excavation in 2005 immediately north of Bristol, at Filton in South

Gloucestershire, produced further evidence for a post-Roman burial site, dating to between the 5th and 7th century AD, probably of British rather than Anglo-Saxon origin (Cullen *et al* 2006). Excavations at Westbury-on-Trym, north-west of the church, produced evidence for timber structures and burials, which could suggest the site of an earlier church, possibly the site of an early minster or a successor to it.

As Chapters 4 and 5 noted, Bristol itself appears quite suddenly in the archaeological record in the early 11th century and the processes and events leading to that point can only be inferred, never demonstrated. Some key sites can however be identified whose further investigation may be able to answer many questions relating to this issue. St Peter's church has many of the characteristics of a pre-Conquest minster church, and was certainly regarded later on as Bristol's senior church – but neither it nor its immediate surroundings have ever been investigated. For coinage to have been minted at Bristol in the early 11th century, it must by law have been a defended place. While it is highly likely that contemporary defences did exist and followed the familiar circular line of the first town wall, this has never been satisfactorily demonstrated by excavation. The question also arises of the antiquity of the defences by the time the first coins were struck: it has been suggested that Bristol could have been a defended place as early as the reign of Offa (757–96) but, however attractive this hypothesis is, it will remain just that in default of excavated dating evidence from the defences themselves. Another fundamental feature of Bristol's identity and function, from which its place-name derives, is the bridge. From the place name there is no doubt of its existence before the Norman Conquest – but how long before is quite unknown; its early form or forms are similarly unknown, and even its exact site has been questioned.

Research agenda
Hinterland settlement

Very little is known of the rural settlement pattern out of which Bristol emerged, or its central places (estate centres, monastic sites). Both Westbury and Henbury have origins that go back probably at least as early as the 8th century, while Bedminster is likely to be the site of a pre-Conquest minster. However, none of these sites has received sufficient archaeological attention, although further analysis and publication of the 1968 excavation of Westbury College may well shed new light on the origins of the early settlement of Westbury. The study of Late Saxon estate patterns as exemplified by the discussion of the AD 883 boundary survey of Stoke Bishop is a good example of how a detailed study of documentary, including cartographic sources, allied to detailed observation of surviving topographic landmarks, may help to identify now hidden rural estates within the hinterland around the emerging settlement of Bristol (Taylor 1910; Russell 1999; Higgins 2002). The degree to which such early landholdings constrained and influenced the form of the early town is one which would benefit from further study.

St Peter's church

Never excavated, this church has some of the hallmarks of an Anglo-Saxon minster church. Its origins, development and landscape context are unknown, but likely to be critical in the early development of Bristol as a central place.

Archaeology under the castle

Excavations have already demonstrated the presence of pre-Conquest activity on the site of Bristol Castle. Investigations in other towns have found preceding high status sites underlying Norman urban castles, and this possibility may also be entertained for Bristol. The presence of a suspected pre-Conquest minster (St Peter's) immediately to the west, adds some weight to this possibility.

Bristol's earliest defences

Implicitly present by the early 11th century, but suggested to have been present as early as the 8th, hard archaeological evidence is singularly lacking. Opportunities for investigating Bristol's early defences will be few but information on the form and date of Bristol's defences is vital to enable the chronology and layout of the early settlement to be better understood.

Late Saxon Bristol

The earliest years of Bristol's urban growth remain, in many ways, a mystery. Its sudden appearance in the archaeological record, and later in the documentary record, may suggest that its growth was extremely rapid – though this impression is doubtless influenced by the

seemingly explosive growth displayed in the foundation of all its principal suburbs in the 12th century. How it grew – in terms of what occupations were followed there – is unknown. It has also often been suggested that the main streets of the Old City – High Street, Broad Street, Wine Street and Corn Street, together with Small Street, form a planned cruciform grid plan that is characteristic of Late Saxon town planning, particularly evident in the Alfredian *burhs* of southern and south-western England. However, once again this remains a hypothesis, in that, apart from Mary-le-Port Street, none of the streets has been dated by archaeology, either directly (as, for example, from coins excavated between layers of metalling, as in Winchester), or indirectly, by dating other features that were clearly associated with them. The underlying problem is the scarcity of archaeological deposits of this period in the Old City, and the extraordinarily limited excavated sample of them. To date, only one complete secular non-military building of pre-Conquest date has been excavated in the Old City (on the Mary-le-Port site), and so the character of the built environment – the range of building types that were present, how they were used, and how they were organised spatially, all remain out of reach.

The same is true of the parish churches. As Chapter 5 noted, the Old City is recognisable as the core of the pre-Conquest town from the concentration of parish churches there; while all can be shown to have been standing by the 12th century, when documentary evidence generally becomes available, only one, St Mary-le-Port, has been comprehensively excavated. While the remainder, particularly the 'gate churches' on the defences, are strongly suspected to be pre-Conquest foundations, none can actually be demonstrated to be so. It therefore goes without saying that their early form (timber-built, or stone-built from the beginning?) and development are unknown.

Pre-Conquest occupation has now been demonstrated in parts of the Old City and spread widely across the ridge to the east that became the site of the Norman castle. This has itself sparked a controversy: which came first, the occupation of the headland/Old City, or occupation on the more constrained but equally or more defensible ridge? As reiterated above, it is more plausibly argued that the headland was primary, if only on account of the concentration of churches there – but perhaps only in terms of a concentration of population. This leaves open the question of the possible role of the castle site as a centre of pre-Norman authority.

The current lack of knowledge of the defences has already, briefly, been noted. But not only is their date of origin unknown, so too is their form in this period, and their structural development. Did they, for example, in this period, follow the trend of many western English *burhs* in having a secondary phase of stone wall inserted into an earth-and-timber original? There is also the complex question of eastward-facing defences. While the circular course around the south, west, north and north-east sides of the headland is fairly self-evident, the same cannot be said of the ridge extending to the east, with three known cross-peninsula defensive features: a double ditch on the Defence/Dolphin Street line, established by excavation; the western castle moat; and the eastern castle moat. All could well have originated in this period but whether as part of the town's public defences, or features associated with, for example, a minster enclosure around St Peter's church and/or a separate high-status enclosure of some kind on the site of the later castle, cannot be said.

The character and form of the castle site presents a host of intractable problems from this period all the way into the mid-17th century: all are a product of the very limited excavated sample available from the area of what is now Castle Park, an inevitability given the lack of development in this area since it was cleared following the bombing of the Second World War. There are both general and particular problems there for this period. In general, it is unclear whether there was any significant difference in character, or date, or status, between the occupation found on the ridge and on the headland. In particular, what are the implications of the gatehouse excavated by Mike Ponsford in the north-eastern quadrant? Did it belong to pre-Conquest public defences or was it part of the first castle? And, in either case, how did it relate to the eastern defences and the approach roads from the east?

The western margin of early medieval Bristol presents what is perhaps one of the more surprising of the unresolved problems of this period: where was the River Frome? It is surprising, in the sense that the diversion of the Frome to its current channel (St Augustine's Reach) is one of the better-known events in the life of the 13th-century town. But where was it before it was diverted? The traditional belief that it followed the curving escarpment below Baldwin Street may possibly still be relevant, but Roger Leech has noted the presence of long plots, possibly of early medieval date, extending south-west from Baldwin Street as far as the later defences, and these seem to have parallels in the watered plot systems that extend out from the margins of many western English towns. Some tentative support for this theory may be forthcoming from the recent deposit model (Wilkinson *et al* 2013b) which tends to suggest, through a greater thickness of Wentlooge Formation deposits near the present junction of the Frome and Avon south of Canon's Marsh and between Baldwin Street and King Street, that the Baldwin Street–King Street area was generally low-lying and may have contained a broad body of water, perhaps later formed into a definable channel. However, the model is hampered by the lack of reliable data in this area and further work is needed. Establishing the course of the Frome in the late pre-Conquest period therefore not only has implications for the form and defensibility of the town at this date, but also for the variety of land uses that may have pertained in the area south of the early line of the defences and the exact nature of the changes wrought by the burgesses in the 1240s.

The outer margins of the late pre-Conquest town cannot, as recent work has shown, be ignored. One of the more dramatic developments in recent research, combining archaeological and historical sources to great effect, has been the identification of a possible fortified bridgehead on the left bank of the Avon, in what was later to become the Redcliffe suburb. This, an area known later as Arthur's Acre or Stakepenny, is a positive indication that, as has been suspected, Bristol Bridge functioned as a defensive barrier as well as a crossing, with fortifications at both ends, as was probably the case at Southwark at the outer end of London Bridge (Schofield 2011, 6), and across the Ouse at Bedford (Haslam 1983), in both cases by *c* 915.

Research agenda

Planning in the Old City

The cruciform street-plan with parallel elements may well represent an episode of Late Saxon town planning, but this has not been established archaeologically. It has also been suggested (Leech 2014, chapter 2) that property boundaries in the northern half of the Old City, between Broad Street and Tower Lane, were reused, urbanised, agricultural boundaries, suggesting perhaps a lesser degree of centralised design; these would be susceptible to archaeological investigation.

Housing and occupation

With the exception of a single building on the Mary-le-Port site, pre-Conquest house types are not yet known from Bristol. Other towns (eg Oxford) offer examples of building types and forms of tenement planning that might be expected, but the excavated sample from the Old City is still extraordinarily small, and this question cannot yet be addressed.

The extent of the Late Saxon Town and urban growth

While the archaeological evidence currently available tends to support the suggestion of a planned Late Saxon settlement focused upon the cruciform plan of streets at the western end of the promontory, corroborative dating evidence is required to conclusively date the laying out of the streets themselves, to complement the so far sparse evidence from the tenement plots adjacent to them. In addition there is the question of the extent of the Late Saxon town – did it extend only as far as the north–south ditch later followed by Dolphin Street in its initial phase or did the settlement extend over the whole of the headland from the start? Can separate phases be detected, with possibly an eastwards expansion as far as the line later reused as the eastern defence of the Castle?

The location and nature of early port facilities

Bristol during the course of the 11th century was becoming a port and trading centre of considerable significance, evidenced by references to Bristol as the point of embarkation for voyages to Ireland and Wales, as well as trading further afield. However, the location of the early port is far from clear. While placenames such as Rackhay (*Rakhyth*) may give a clue as to the location and nature of the early port, perhaps close to the confluence of the early Frome and the Avon, there is no archaeological evidence to support this. Further archaeological work, supplemented by geoarchaeological prospection, in the area south of Baldwin Street, could provide valuable data in assessing both the possible course of the pre-diversion Frome as well as helping to establish whether this area was indeed the location of Bristol's early port.

The origins of the parish churches

Most of Bristol's central churches are likely to have been founded in this period, but only St Mary-le-Port has been investigated. The origin and early form of all the remainder are unknown. The lack of understanding of Bristol's churches in this and subsequent periods was recognised in the South West Archaeological Research Framework as a major gap in knowledge (Rippon and Croft 2008, 201). The excavation of St Mary-le-Port took place over 50 years ago and it could be opportune to revisit and re-assess the archive in the light of more recent research, especially into the ceramic evidence.

The defences, and the castle site

The major uncertainties of Bristol's urban defences in this period are much the same as in earlier periods, their form and development unknown. The problems multiply on the east side of the city and become entangled with the question of the nature of the Late Saxon occupation found on the site of the later castle. Any investigation of the defences in this period is likely to yield results of the highest significance.

The pre-Conquest south bank

Recent excavations and re-assessment of the documentary evidence have combined to show the presence of a pre-Conquest enclosure around the Redcliffe end of the Bristol Bridge. The character of this enclosure is however not yet understood, nor are its origins (primarily defensive? Or a transpontine suburb later defended?).

Norman Bristol

The paucity of information from what is now Castle Park, despite the pioneering excavations there by Mike Ponsford in the 1970s, has already been highlighted, and becomes critical for this episode of the city's history. The years immediately following the Norman Conquest saw the foundation of Bristol Castle as the key instrument for securing and suppressing what was by now a major town. But the earliest form of the castle is not certain. Ponsford has suggested that the castle began as a ringwork, strengthened in a second phase by the addition of a motte. But there is still uncertainty over this sequence and the form of the earliest bailey; moreover, as noted above, it is difficult to distinguish pre-castle from early castle-period features and occupation.

An unusual feature of Bristol at this time is the suspected presence of a masonry town wall. While many shire towns received new defensive circuits towards the end of the 12th century, these were most commonly built as earthwork and timber structures, replaced in stone in the course of the 13th and even 14th centuries. Bristol appears to have had a stone wall encircling the headland and the Old City well before the end of the 12th century, but its date has yet to be accurately established and its architectural character is known only from a few quite limited exposures.

Within the defences, knowledge of the development of domestic houses and their planning is almost nil until the evidence of a handful of excavated sites, and some buildings recorded prior to demolition, becomes available towards the end of the 12th century. Even then, the evidence is selective. The excavated domestic tenements of this date on Redcliff Street are of the first importance but, as is so often the case, the original street frontage lay outside the excavated area. Knowledge is therefore confined to the ranges immediately behind the frontage and those further back down the plot. As a consequence, the development of architectural forms in response to the demands of commerce – fundamentally, the evolution of the shop – is unknown to us. Documentary evidence (mostly plans and photographs) of buildings that survived into the later 19th and 20th centuries is, again, of the greatest value. However, buildings built before *c* 1200 that survived that long are invariably the stone buildings, mostly halls and their undercrofts, of the urban elite. A recent study of Shrewsbury comparing surviving 13th-century buildings with contemporary lists of taxpayers came to the conclusion that the

buildings that survive, or had been recorded prior to recent demolition, represented just the top one per cent of the urban population, a kind of figure that might well be applicable to Bristol in this period (Baker 2010, 153).

Towards the end of this period, in the early and middle 12th century, Bristol seems to have undergone one of the most remarkable episodes in its history, expanding from a place that could be mistaken for an 'average' county town to become the largest of all English provincial towns – beating York by a substantial margin – by 1334 (Hoskins 1972, 238). It achieved this through the almost simultaneous creation of a number of suburbs outside its original river-bounded headland site: Old Market, the *Feria*, from the mid-12th; the Marsh; Broadmead, being developed in the third quarter of the century; Redcliffe and Temple, being built up in the 1130s. Exactly how fast and how far the development process occurred in various quarters remains to be established as does, in particular, the social and economic composition of these new suburban Bristolians.

Only on its northern flank, along the foot of St Michael's Hill, did 12th-century Bristol not have a substantial and fast-growing suburb. Here, where the natural topography was less accommodating for commerce, there grew up instead an unusually dense and extensive cluster of monastic foundations, mostly in the course of the 13th century, though the first foundations were made in the 12th. At St Augustine's Abbey, it is the form of the church itself that poses the greatest problem. The nunnery of St Mary Magdalen is one of the least understood monastic sites in the city: its layout is virtually unknown, it is not even certain whether it had a cloister. Over in Redcliffe, at the Preceptory of the Knights Templar, the circular church is well known but the remainder of its precinct, apart, perhaps, from a contemporary hall, is not.

The 12th century is crucial for our knowledge of Bristol's parish churches in that it was mostly then that they were recorded for the first time. However, their physical form in this period remains largely obscure, apart from the two thoroughly excavated churches of St Mary-le-Port and St Augustine-the-Less. As a consequence it is not yet possible to discuss, for example, the impact that the Norman Conquest had on places of worship. While it might be imagined that it was profound, in the sense that no patron, whether lay or ecclesiastical, would wish their church to be seen to lag behind fast-changing architectural styles, this remains an assumption that cannot be tested against excavated or architectural evidence.

Research agenda

The early form of the castle

Whether it was (as has been suggested) a ringwork, or was given a motte as a primary feature, the early form of the castle is little understood, though from Ponsford's excavations the deposits relevant to this question clearly survive well beneath what is now Castle Park.

The Norman walls

Bristol's urban defences appear to have been upgraded in stone at an exceptionally early date. This needs confirmation and refinement, and any exposures of the earliest town wall encircling the headland will be highly significant.

Houses and housing

With only the smallest excavated sample of the Old City it is no surprise that little more is known of the development and form of housing in this period than in the pre-Conquest period. Nevertheless, by the end of this period many of the 'norms' of medieval urban tenement design were fully established, though how and when this came about is unknown. Understanding the form of early urban housing was recognised as a priority issue regionally and nationally. Regionally, this problem in Bristol has been described as a major gap in knowledge (Rippon and Croft 2008, 201) Nationally, the form of early urban housing was recognised by English Heritage as a priority ('UR 3.3 Survival of early form and fabric in historic towns' in English Heritage 2010).

The early growth of the suburbs

Late medieval Bristol was remarkable for its wealth and its sheer size, the latter achieved by the growth of extensive suburbs around the original river-bound nucleus. All of Bristol's later medieval suburbs were established before the end of the 12th century, but their rate of growth, the take-up of plots, and the occupations that followed on them are only now beginning to be apparent.

The Normanisation of the Church

The Norman rebuilding of great churches and urban cathedrals around the country is well understood, and some towns (Lincoln, Winchester for example) have produced evocative sequences for the rebuilding and extension of urban parish churches. This is so for only two of Bristol's churches (St Mary-le-Port and St Augustine-the-Less), the others remaining uninvestigated.

High medieval Bristol

One of the celebrated episodes in the growth of Bristol – physically, and as a self-governing body – was the diversion of the lower end of the River Frome between 1240 and 1247 to provide better wharfage for the port. But, as noted above (p 428), even this action has an element of uncertainty to it as it is not clear where the old Frome channel ran, nor, therefore, the true implications of what was clearly a major piece of civil engineering. Nor was it alone. In 1247 Bristol Bridge was rebuilt – again, the implications are not quite clear as we have no knowledge of the structure or condition of the bridge prior to this. The 13th century also saw major work on the city defences, during which the old Norman and (presumed) Saxon town wall was eclipsed by new outer defences, which had achieved their maximum extent by the middle of the century, enclosing the areas of recent suburban growth.

The castle, as alluded to already, continues to present major uncertainties in this period. Even its major defensive features – the keep, the curtain walls, towers and gates – present questions of interpretation and there are possibilities for alternative theories for the layout and development of the castle's basic form. Not much is known of the internal arrangement of the castle within the curtain wall, nor to what use much of its space was put. Specifically, how was it divided into wards, and did Castle Street, ostensibly a creation of the 1650s, have any kind of medieval precursor leading to an east gate?

Understanding of Bristol's monastic houses, most of which were founded in the course of the 13th century, varies from site to site, in part because some are more extensively excavated than others, in part because, for some, only interim excavation reports are available. Thus the Priory of St James is relatively well understood in terms of its design and evolution, whereas the nearby Nunnery of St Mary Magdalen remains almost completely obscure. Similarly, St Bartholomew's Hospital is well understood, whereas St Mark's is not. The development of the Franciscan Friary in Lewins Mead is broadly understood from excavations in the 1970s, although these are not yet fully published; the Carmelite Friary is known only from fragments of buildings and from excavated burials; the Dominican Friary in Broadmead is known from surviving buildings and from recent excavations. Understanding of the many lesser religious institutions, hospitals and almshouses, is similarly variable.

Domestic buildings present similar difficulties in this period to that preceding. Understanding of their structure and design is heavily reliant upon documentary evidence and on records made of higher-status dwellings prior to their demolition in recent times. As a consequence, it is the housing of non-elite groups that is most significantly under-represented. To an extent, archaeology can and does fill the gap by excavation, although the number of completely excavated tenements of this date remains very small, and the crucial street frontages are invariably missing, usually as a consequence of the later widening of streets.

Industry and craft production are more amenable to archaeological research in that many processes left physical evidence in the ground (pits, vat furnace-bases and so on) and were located in back-plot areas. Nevertheless the evidential base is heavily skewed towards the Redcliffe suburb, though this has to some extent been corrected by recent excavations north of the Frome.

Our knowledge of the urban population itself, its health or otherwise, rates of mortality and causes of death, is still very limited, with the only fully studied and published assemblage of human remains of this period being from the cemetery of St James's Priory. The opportunities to recover evidence from the city's urban churchyards may be rare, many having been built over or now preserved as protected open spaces.

Research agenda
The growth of the suburbs
Established in the 12th century, the rapid expansion of the suburbs through the 13th and

14th centuries is one of the most remarkable aspects of medieval Bristol. The rate at which areas were built up is susceptible to archaeological investigation, particularly where waterlogged deposits are likely to yield scientific dates.

The internal geography and character of the castle
As before, the castle remains one of the great unknowns of medieval Bristol, in particular in respect of its interior and the functions accommodated there. The question of a medieval predecessor to Castle Street is also perhaps still open; observation in the culvert containing the eastern moat suggests a medieval bridge on the line of Castle Street, supporting the theory of an east gate in this location (*see* Fig 6.26). However, this has not been conclusively dated and was observed in less than ideal conditions. There are rival theories regarding the position of the east gate into the castle (*see* Chapter 6, p 151), some of which are more radical than have been considered to date. The internal arrangement of the castle and even its basic form, which may have been far more complex than previously thought, are not fully understood. Not only could further fieldwork yield significant results, but also a comprehensive re-examination of documentary and cartographic sources, set alongside the important earlier work by Mike Ponsford, could well enable a radical re-interpretation of the development of one of the most important castles in England.

Domestic building
With very limited survival of buildings of medieval date in Bristol, documentary evidence and excavation have an unusually important contribution to make to this area. If they can be found, sites with intact, uncellared street frontages may be of the most crucial importance as the lack of excavated frontages is a problem throughout the country. Many of the areas within the inner Late Saxon town will have been disrupted by cellars of medieval and later date, themselves a subject for fruitful research (*see below*). However, there may well be areas where the potential for the survival of evidence for pre- and post-Conquest housing may be greater, for example to the south of the Exchange on Corn Street, in the area of St Nicholas Market. Outside the early walled town, there

could be surviving evidence in the area of Baldwin Street, Marsh Street and the whole area between the Frome and Avon. North of the walled area, along Gropecuntelane Lane/ Halliers Lane (now Nelson Street), there has been little archaeological work and yet this could be a fruitful area for the survival of evidence for early housing. The documentary record also presents a challenge to future archaeological research in that it suggests that, at least by the 15th century, the smallest hall-houses of the kind found in some other towns (eg Spon Street, Coventry; Tewkesbury) may be absent in Bristol, the inventories recording substantial 'hall-houses' on the one hand and 'shop-houses' on the other.

The study of cellars within the medieval town, especially within the early medieval walled area, can provide important evidence for the commercial arrangements in the medieval and later town, as has been demonstrated by Leech (2014, chapter 7). A distinction may be made between cellars used entirely for storage and those serving a dual function of retail and storage. The latter might be more elaborately furnished and used as a shop or to entertain and impress potential customers, such as at No 35 Corn Street, where an elaborate 15th-century vault leads directly from the street.

One of the most interesting developments susceptible to study from the documentary evidence, particularly from probate inventories, has been the decline of, or changing uses of, the medieval open hall. Investigation of Canynge's House in Redcliff Street has shown that archaeological sources have a great deal to contribute to this subject area, but the excavated sample remains at present too small to progress it.

The late medieval period: suburban contraction?

There are hints that, particularly in the 16th century, when Bristol's economy is known to have been less dynamic than the centuries before and after, some outer suburban areas may have contracted. Documenting this process by future excavation would be likely to make a major contribution to the debate on the varying fortunes of towns in the late medieval and early modern period and enable contrasts to be made with towns such as Gloucester, where whole suburbs were abandoned, tenements becoming gardens.

The study of the urban population

The study of excavated human remains from medieval churchyards will help to answer questions of the prevalence of disease, rates of mortality and the possible differences between social groups. Opportunities are likely to be rare but work in the churchyards of churches currently out of use, such as St Michael-on-the-Mount on St Michael's Hill may offer some opportunities for the recovery and examination of medieval human remains in the event of associated development. The analysis of the already excavated remains from St Augustine-the-Less, while largely of post-medieval date, must also be a priority.

Victualling and food supply

With the exception of a few major sites, such as Cabot Circus and Finzels Reach, few large animal bone assemblages studied from this period have so far been studied or published but there is clearly a very large body of potential evidence here for the study of at least the provision of meat, its sources, and processing within the city. The recognition by Roger Leech through documentary sources of cookshops where Bristol citizens could purchase hot food could be supplemented by archaeological evidence for other purveyors of cooked and uncooked food such as butchers and fishmongers.

Fish formed a staple of the urban diet. Freshwater, estuarine and marine species have all been recovered from excavated deposits, some caught in local waters but with evidence, both documentary and from the excavated assemblages, for the import of fish from more distant fishing grounds, from Iceland and the North Atlantic. An inter-site synthesis, as suggested above (p 422), of fish bone assemblages will help to clarify the type of fishing grounds that were being exploited, especially in the medieval and early modern period, of the fish stocks being imported into the city and the range of fish that comprised the urban diet.

Botanical assemblages too will afford a view of cereal production and consumption from the city hinterland, a priority recognised in the South West Archaeological Research Framework (Straker 2008). The effect of the expansion of the port from the mid-13th century on the range and in particular on the quantities of exotic foodstuffs entering the town has yet to be studied in any detail.

We still understand little of the detail of the interactions between the town, the monastic houses and rural communities in the local area. For example, how did the townspeople interact with the monastic communities? Did they have any access to some of the woodland resources and fishing rights that the monasteries may have controlled? Is there any evidence that the wealth of Bristol is reflected in contemporary rural settlements in the hinterland? Further work on documentary and bioarchaeological evidence could address these questions and identify more precisely the location and character of natural and semi-natural habitats (eg woodland, heathland, pasture, managed hay meadows) close to the town at different times in the historic period.

Early modern Bristol

When Bristol formally achieved city status in 1542, it did so not because it had grown physically or in population but as a consequence of the Dissolution, the former St Augustine's Abbey becoming its cathedral. In fact the physical attributes of a city had been acquired long before and the 16th century was, in contrast, marked by economic and demographic stagnation. Domestically, the trappings of the Middle Ages were discarded only gradually, though, with the coming of the Reformation, the religious life of the city changed suddenly and fundamentally. Economic and demographic growth returned in the 17th century, in the course of which the population doubled. This was the century that moulded the identity of modern Bristol: the Atlantic trade was established, new industries grew up, and public buildings and infrastructure were renewed and expanded to cope. The physical face of the city underwent increasingly rapid change with both outward expansion and inward redevelopment; its complexion changed too, as timber-framing was gradually replaced and superseded by brick and stone.

Research agenda
Urban expansion and contraction
As already noted, the historical evidence for a lack of buoyancy in the city economy in the period c 1520–60 is beginning to be complemented by archaeological evidence from the suburbs, notably Redcliffe, for plots that had been built up in the medieval period falling vacant and not being rebuilt until the 17th century. From the third quarter of the 16th century stages in the expansion of the suburbs can be charted with some precision from historic maps – beginning with William Smith's rather schematic bird's-eye-view of 1568, and with confidence from 1670 when Jacob Millerd's first map was published. But in the decades prior to the surviving cartography, it is primarily archaeological evidence that will allow the waxing and waning of the built-up area to be studied.

One detailed aspect of the mid-17th-century renewal of the city that is often referred to but remains virtually unknown archaeologically is the redevelopment of Bristol Castle in the 1650s. Some details of the housing built there are accessible from documentary sources, and drawings and photographs made before the Second World War, and have been studied by Leech (2014). However, the degree of dislocation between the geography of the later 17th century and the medieval period remains unknown – for exactly the same reasons (lack of work in the area) that so many aspects of the medieval castle itself remain enigmatic.

The growth of the Atlantic economy and its implications
As we have seen there is virtually no aspect of the life or the fabric of Bristol that remained unaffected by the rise of the Atlantic economy, particularly from the 1630s on.

Port facilities
Archaeology has begun to explore the developing infrastructure of the port, particularly in the Marsh where observations and, more recently, excavations, have begun to document the replacement of earth-cut docks by stone-built docks in the 17th century. Sequences similar to those discovered on the site of the St Clement's and Aldworth's docks remain to be explored.

While the development of privately owned moorings and industrial facilities at the back of the Redcliff Street plots are relatively well known (though old excavations – critically – remain unprocessed and unpublished), the uses to which other waterfront areas were put – for example the Frome channel above Broad Quay – have only recently begun to be explored, for example by the Broadmead excavations.

Understanding ports and their infrastructure has been recognised as a national priority by English Heritage (UR 3.6 'Coastal towns and historic ports' in English Heritage 2010). Lack of knowledge of Bristol's port facilities was also recognised as a priority issue in the South West Archaeological Research Framework (Rippon and Croft 2008, 201) and as a regional Research Aim (Research Aim 47c) (Webster (ed) 2008, 291).

New industries

The study of new industries directly or indirectly related to the transatlantic trade is another recent archaeological growth area with great potential. The sugar houses or refineries that appeared in the city from *c* 1607 have not yet received any substantial attention and the questions of their scale and organisation are currently only accessible from the documentary evidence. Glass manufactories are better known archaeologically, but mainly from the 18th century, their late 17th-century predecessors are almost unexplored; Redcliff Wharf has been identified as the most promising area for undisturbed early furnaces. Clay pipe manufactories, similarly, are known from the 18th century but not yet from the 17th.

Artefact assemblages

The changing sources of Bristol's imports can be followed in the pottery and other artefact assemblages, for example in the arrival of Venetian glass. The opposite is also true: Bristol's exports, whether manufactured within the city or its hinterland, may be identified at their destinations (clay pipes and bottles for example), whether the Caribbean or the eastern seaboard of the United States. Ultimately, the successful study of historical international trading patterns will itself require an international approach.

Houses and housing

More complete documentation and more buildings surviving either to the present day or at least long enough to have been recorded, means that understanding of changes in houses and housing is more comprehensive for the 16th and later centuries than for the medieval period. Developments detected by Roger Leech include the acceleration of the abandonment of the multi-functional open hall towards more rooms, and more specialised rooms. Some of the new uses found for old open halls identified by Dr Leech can be and have been demonstrated archaeologically: generally those of an industrial character; others (school rooms and taverns for example) are harder to identify unless through the lucky discovery of diagnostic artefacts in association. This subject area – the transition from medieval to modern urban forms – has been recognised nationally as a priority for investigation (UR 3.3 'Survival of early form and fabric in historic towns' in English Heritage 2010).

Leech's study often links identifiable social groups and occupations, ships' captains for example with particular house types and housing developments; excavation offers the potential to unearth and compare the material culture that may survive below ground in association with them.

The housing stock too was deeply influenced by the character of Bristol's developing international economy, not only in terms of the investment that it allowed but quite specifically in the forms that were built, not only in Bristol itself but in its trading partners across the Atlantic. Leech refers to house types that are characteristic of port towns on both sides of the Atlantic, and also to the replication of the Bristol lodges or garden houses in the Caribbean. As in the case of traded artefacts, there is clearly the potential for an international dimension in the further study of Bristol's housing stock. The lodges themselves are a singular aspect of the development of Bristol's suburbs, particularly on the gradients north of the Frome. Parallels are known, but do not survive, around the fringes of London, but may well be identifiable in other comparable English cities, possibly Norwich.

The Church and religion

The cataclysmic changes of the Reformation have been discussed at length and the general outline of events between the 1530s and 1560s is fairly well known. Much detail remains however to be added to the histories of individual sites, whether parish churches losing altars and chapels, or monastic houses being suppressed and redeveloped, whether for housing (generally high status) or industry. In general, it is still (as in the medieval centuries) the archaeology of the parish churches and non-parochial chapels that is least well developed, despite the total excavation of St Augustine-the-Less and St Mary-le-Port. The archaeology of non-conformism is a recent growth area.

Defence

The removal, or the renewal and replacement, of medieval infrastructure is an issue that is equally germane to the city defences. While the 16th century saw the castle in terminal decline, the city walls, particularly the gates, appear to have been maintained and the ditches (the Portwall ditch at least) recut. This is not to say that they were capable of withstanding gunpowder-propelled artillery and the first Civil War saw a new defensive perimeter established with forts on the tactically dominant heights. Contemporary descriptions have recently begun to be supplemented by direct archaeological evidence as a result of which the character of the Windmill Hill Fort, later the Royal Fort, is becoming clearer. Nevertheless there are areas where the course of the 17th-century perimeter is uncertain (south of Old Market for example) or ambiguous (south of the Portwall in Redcliffe) and further work is required.

Elsewhere the survival or demise of the medieval defences depended largely on their proximity to the built-up area. The inner (Norman) wall was of course long gone; the Marsh Wall was next, surviving intact until the development of King Street immediately outside it in the 1650s began a long process of domestic colonisation and gradual demolition. Similar processes probably affected the outer wall plot-by-plot along the east bank of the Frome, but this process has been little studied.

Victualling and food supply

As with earlier periods, there has been little inter-site analysis of the range of foodstuffs for this period when a greater range of imported exotic foods might be anticipated. This may be because the major sites (eg Cabot Circus, Finzels Reach) produced relatively little for these later periods, possibly because of truncation. It is also the case that relatively few sites of this period have been investigated where deposits of this period can be expected to survive to any degree. One such site which might provide a good example of the type of site that should be targeted in future is that of Nos 42–4 Welsh Back, situated south of the medieval port in an area which became important following the reclamation of the Marsh from the late 17th century. Here the investigation of substantial waterlogged deposits on the west bank of the river Avon produced a large quantity of grapes from a single late 17th-century context, suggesting the dumping of a spoiled cargo on to the quay. Other possibly imported food remains included melon and walnut (Jones 2008–9). Giorgi (1997) has summarised the evidence for diet in late medieval and early modern London with a wide range of plant foods available, increasing as more exotic plant foods became available. However, the evidence has not yet been found in Bristol for the range of exotic imports that might be expected in a city that had growing international aspirations with the rise of the Atlantic trade from the 17th century.

The rise of the modern city

The period from 1700 to 1900 saw the transformation of Bristol from the essentially medieval town depicted by Millerd on his plan of 1673 to one that would be recognisable by today's inhabitants. Inward migration and the successive enlargement of its boundaries in the 19th century meant that its population grew from a modest 20,000 in 1700 to over a third of a million by 1900. New housing was being built in the 18th and 19th centuries, both to house the new working population but also as expressions of the new wealth of the city in the 18th century.

Nonconformism, which had its origins in the early modern period, now took hold, especially in the poorer areas of the city, in Lewins Mead, Broadmead, Redcliffe and St Philips. In these areas of the city, crowded by the courts and alleyways of the lower classes, were located the premises of the new, or expanding industries, many of which had their origins in the 17th century as a direct result of the newly established Atlantic trade. Industries such as sugar refining, glass manufacturing, pottery and clay pipe manufacturing were established in large purpose-built premises which came to dominate the 18th and 19th century urban landscape.

However, even as late as the early 19th century, Plumley and Ashmead's 1828 plan depicts withy beds in the St Philips area, later drained to become the route of the 1835 tramway between Avon Wharf, adjacent to Avon Street, and Coalpit Heath. Even at this date, the city was still close to its rural hinterland and presumably still received much of its produce, both in terms of its foodstuffs and raw materials, from these areas. Stone quarries were opened to the north and west of the city to extract the building stone for the new buildings being constructed in the city, clay pits were dug for the brick and tile works, while coalmines were exploiting the rich coal seams in east and south Bristol, to power the new industrial enterprises as well as for domestic use.

The port was expanding as new docks were built on the western side of the Frome and also to the south of the Avon in the area known as Wapping, as shipbuilding and ship repair shifted to these areas. Buildings were constructed to serve these newly established industries, together with yards for the storage of timber and ropewalks, readily apparent on contemporary maps as long tree-lined avenues.

The gentrification of the city from the late 17th century found expression in the construction of new squares such as Queen Square and St James Square. Alongside these was the construction of the housing for the working population, such as the estate built by Nathaniel Wade in the early 18th century or the slightly later construction by the Penn family to the east of the former Dominican Friary. While the latter has received detailed archaeological attention as part of the Cabot Circus development, for the most part our knowledge of the lowest classes of houses is derived almost entirely from cartographic or pictorial evidence with the consequent lack of information relating to the uses of the various rooms and the quality of life of their inhabitants.

Research agenda
Houses and housing
Dr Leech's recent study of Bristol town houses up to *c* 1800 (Leech 2014) is a welcome innovation in that it investigates houses as working three-dimensional structures containing particular uses and conveying particular messages and aspirations: it is a substantial advance on older, traditional studies that have been almost exclusively concerned with the frontage as an architectural composition. However the study of the houses of the poor and outcast groups is one that has only recently begun to be addressed. Surviving less often, photographed less often, houses built for industrial workers have recently been excavated in the network of streets and courts laid out to the east of the former Dominican Friary, such as Llewellin's Court, together with their associated artefactual assemblages. Such housing is documented throughout the city's manufacturing areas and must have accommodated a large proportion of the rural immigrants that swelled the city population in the 18th and 19th centuries. Some of this housing will have been constructed by the owners of industrial premises to house their workforce, or in some cases as speculative developments. The analysis and publication of the Llewellin's Court buildings is a welcome step forward in the study of this lowest class of urban housing but far more needs to be done to fully understand the nature of housing and living conditions of their inhabitants in this relatively recent period by augmenting Roger Leech's documentary study of workers' and industrial housing (Leech 2014, chapter 8) with archaeological study of some key sites.

Industry and industrialisation
Glass industry
While there have been important studies of individual glassworks of the 18th and 19th centuries, such as Elton's glasshouse on Cheese Lane, the remarkably well-preserved glasshouse on Portwall Lane and the extensive glassworks of the Powell and Ricketts glassworks, formerly the Hoopers' and Soapboilers glassworks on Avon Street, there has been no overall study of Bristol glassworks since the work by Witt *et al* in 1984 or the earlier study by Powell in 1925.

Pottery industry
Bristol had an important pottery industry throughout the post-medieval period with connections with the New World as well as with Europe. Considerable research has been carried out in this area by Reg Jackson and others over a considerable period and further work is desirable, particularly in examining individual production sites as opportunities arise, such as the recently-published work at the Barton Hill pottery, established in the late 19th century (Mason 2017).

Coal extraction
Coal mining was certainly established in the forest of Kingswood by the 14th century, and seems to have gradually increased in volume.

By January 1634 the roads in the parish of Brislington were reported to be in disrepair because of 'the greate resorte of colliers with their horses to certaine cole pitts there of late yeares …' (Bates-Harbin 1908, 203–4). Coalfields were also developed in Somerset and by the late 19th century there were 15 pits in Bedminster alone, some of considerable size. Dean Lane colliery, for example, comprised several shafts, two engine houses and ancillary buildings when it closed in 1906 (La Trobe-Bateman 1997a). However, there has been little archaeological study of individual sites, although there have been important overall studies of the Bristol coalfields (Anstie 1873; Cornwell 2003; Taylor and Shapland 2012).

Quarrying

Many quarries can be identified from cartographic sources, some possibly dating from the medieval period. However, the working practices of quarrying and distribution of raw materials from the quarries for use in the building work of this period (and earlier) have yet to receive archaeological attention.

Shipbuilding

The establishment of new docks in Wapping, south of the river Avon and alongside the western side of the Frome in Canon's Marsh, is well documented in cartography and early paintings, but so far little studied archaeologically, apart from the limited work at Poole's Wharf, yet to be fully published. The associated buildings, the stores and workshops, have received little attention with the major exception of the archaeological work in 2007 at the Great Western Steamship Company's Engine Works.

New technology

The study of technological experimentation has been explored only sporadically and remains a wide field for original research. One obvious impact of the rapid increase in the use of coal as a fuel in the 17th century was the distinctive glass cone which had appeared in Bristol within half a dozen years of its first documented occurrence in 1694 (Crossley 1991). The introduction of the Siemens regenerative furnace at the Powell and Ricketts glassworks in the 19th century has been archaeologically studied and the publication of the results of this work is eagerly awaited

(Gregory and Dungworth forthcoming). In the 18th century there were strong connections between the potteries at Temple Back and Worcester (Owen 2003) and influence also came from further afield. Magnus Lundberg, a painter trained at the Rorstrand factory in Sweden, settled in the city during the late 1740s and probably introduced techniques used there to the Bristol industry (Thomas and Wilson 1980, 5). For the brass industry, John and Thomas Coster, two of the founders of the brass works established at Baptist Mills at the beginning of the 18th century had experience of Dutch brass-making, and workers were brought in from Germany and Holland to overcome a local skills shortage (Buchanan and Cossons 1969, 117). There are several known examples of technical experimentation in the early modern and post-medieval city. For example, a lead smelting works which experimented with coal rather than charcoal as a fuel was founded by London-based partners at Nightingale Valley in March 1679 (King 1996). That Abraham Darby began working in Bristol with funding from the Goldney family in the early 18th century is well known (Raistrick 1970, 19–26), and Day (1973) has explored the local developments in copper smelting a few years later.

Industrial buildings

There has yet to be a comprehensive survey of the development of the construction techniques used in Bristol's industrial buildings to match studies undertaken in Manchester and the effects of the introduction of new materials in the city is not clear (Williams with Farnie 1992, 58–65, 80–5, 101–10). Developments in metals technology had a significant effect on the form of industrial buildings enabling larger structures to be built. In the larger early factories an internal wooden structure was supported on stone or brick walls but cast iron was introduced for its load-bearing and fireproofing properties from the late 18th century and is known to have been used in a number of Bristol buildings, for example the Avonside Ironworks (Cattell 1996). Steel frame construction was introduced from the mid-1880s (Jackson 1998) and reinforced concrete technology at the end of the century and an early example of the two in conjunction was at the WCA Warehouse on Redcliff Backs, designed by the Leeds architect W H Brown (Cocks 1974).

The study of the urban population
Excavation of urban burial grounds
A number of private burial grounds were opened in the 18th and 19th centuries, to relieve pressure on the by now overcrowded parish churchyards. These burial grounds were generally sited within the poorer areas of the city, being particularly evident in the Old Market area. Together with the nonconformist burial grounds and the extensions to the established parochial churchyards, such as those for St Nicholas parish in Crow Lane and Rackhay, they are always liable to development and are thus potentially rich sources of information about the post-medieval urban population. Particularly in the case of post-medieval burial grounds where associated documentary sources may be more available, multi-disciplinary studies may be possible, including the use of DNA analysis which has the potential to assist in the diagnosis of infectious diseases (Mays 1998b), while the pathology of skeletal populations can help in the identification of dietary malnutrition. Conversely, excessive food consumption has been associated with gout or diffuse idiopathic skeletal hyperostosis (DISH) – the laying down of extra bone – which are both detectable from skeletal material. Greater consumption of refined and sweetened food is also associated with increasing wealth and this impacted on oral health, most obviously through the development of caries which increased markedly in the 19th century (Mays 1999, 335). The only major excavation of a post-medieval burial ground, that of St Augustine-the-Less, remains to be fully published and its publication remains a high priority.

Appendix 1: Gazetteer of selected archaeological events in Bristol

Entries have been included where the fieldwork gives a direct record of archaeological material. Negative observations have been omitted, as have documentary and pictorial material.

References are given for the location of the main published descriptions of archaeological excavation and evaluation in parenthesis. Monographs are indicated by the name of the main author and articles by the name of the author or journal, part number and page reference. Full references can be found in the Bibliography. The accompanying maps at the end of the appendix indicate the most precise location for each event currently available, and where possible records the areal extent of excavations and evaluations. Most of the unpublished 'grey literature' can be accessed via Bristol City Council's Know Your Place website (www.bristol.gov.uk/knowyourplace).

Abbreviations:

AGBA	Action Group for Bristol Archaeology
AR	Archaeological Review
BaRAS	Bristol and Region Archaeological Services
BARG Bull	BARG Bulletin
BIAS	Bristol Industrial Archaeological Society
JBAA	Journal of the British Archaeological Association
MSRG Ann Rep	Medieval Settlement Research Group Annual Report

HER No	Location	Field worker	Date	Grid ref

Archaeological excavations

32 — 34 Broad Street — Ponsford, M W — 1970 — ST 58795 73183

Salvage excavation recorded a stone-lined cess pit which produced 18th-century ceramics. A section across Tower Lane exposed road surfaces from the Norman period onward (AR **6**, 39; 47).

88 — 76–96, Victoria Street — Ennis, Trevor — 1995 — ST 59312 72665

Excavation following evaluation (BUAD 894) recorded 12 phases of occupation on the site of medieval tenements (Ennis *et al* 1997).

146 — Headmaster's House, College Square — Godman, Colin — 1959 — ST 58315 72625

Excavation recorded stone buildings possibly associated with the kitchens of St Augustine's Abbey (Wilson and Hurst 1961, 312–13).

159 — Whitson Street — Marochan, Keith — 1956 — ST 58856 73490

A clay tobacco pipe kiln, apparently belonging to Robert Tippett II (*c* 1660–*c* 1722), was excavated on the site of the bus station (Jackson and Price 1974, 129).

218 — Grand Hotel, Broad Street — Price, Roger H — 1973 — ST 58870 73100

A medieval well 50ft deep was excavated and 19th-century wooden winding gear recovered.

283   45 Kingsdown Parade   Jackson, R G   1994   ST 58660 73850
Excavation revealed the wall of No 51 Kingsdown Parade and a pit containing 19th-century pottery (Jackson 1994b).

309   Temple Back   Bryant, John   1983   ST 59556 72583
A 70-metre length of the Portwall with a semi-circular tower at the south end was recorded (Iles 1984, 59).

310   Myrtle Road, Kingsdown   Bryant, John   1992   ST 58463 73670
A section was cut across a ditch used to mark the boundary of the County of Bristol in 1373; 18th-century garden features were also excavated (Williams 1992, 54).

312   Portwall Lane   Bryant, John   1982   ST 59110 72424
A section was excavated across the Portwall ditch. Part of an 18th- to 19th-century building (Iles 1983, 52).

313   Crown Court, Small Street   Bryant, John   1990   ST 58750 73040
Excavation recorded 11th- and 12th-century linear features and wall close to Small Street. Part of a medieval tenement on Leonard Lane was excavated. Tipped deposits beneath this building were interpreted as part of a possible defensive bank (Williams 1992, 54).

314   Water Lane, Temple Street   Good, G L   1971   ST 59320 72750
Part of a building associated with the 12th-century Knights' Templar Church was recorded. This was succeeded by buildings erected by the Knights Hospitaller. A post-medieval limekiln was also excavated (Good 1987a, 66–9; Good 1992, 2–41).

316   Moravian Chapel, Upper Maudlin Street   Ponsford, M W   1973   ST 58720 73420
Part of a 2nd-century AD building, and medieval material, were recorded (Jackson 2000a, 29–110).

317   Greyfriars, Lewins Mead   Ponsford, M W   1973   ST 58748 73359
The northern part of the church, the chapter house and other parts of the eastern claustral range of the Franciscan Friary were excavated as were 13th-century inhumations in wooden coffins. The waterlogging also led to recovery of more wooden finds (Webster and Cherry 1974, 189–90; Cherry 1974, 123).

318   Rackhay, Queen Charlotte Street   Ponsford, M W   1973   ST 58810 72810
14th- or 15th-century buildings were excavated, as well as slots interpreted as the bases for timber structures (possibly cloth-drying racks) and post-medieval buildings. Organic remains were recovered from several features (*BARG Bull* **5(1)**, 9–10; Webster and Cherry 1974 199–200).

319   Castle Park   Boore, Eric J   1975   ST 59110 73130
Excavation in the area of the line of Peter Street recorded the structures and occupation ranging in date from the Late Saxon period to the 20th century, including a possible part of the defences associated with the Burgesses' Revolt and evidence for Jewish settlement in the area (Boore 1982, 7–11).

320   Fitzhardinge House, Tower Lane   Boore, Eric J   1979   ST 58860 73170
The remains of a major Norman building underlain by Late Saxon features was excavated. Occupation deposits associated with the building and dating between the 12th and the 19th century were also recorded (Boore 1984; Boore 1980, 18–26).

322   Temple Back   Pountney, W J   1915   ST59410 72850
A small excavation was carried out 'on the river bank, near the Temple Pottery' (Pountney 1920, xxxii).

341   143–7, Redcliff Street   Williams, Bruce   1981   ST 59015 72862
Part of the 12th-century waterfront was excavated. Structures interpreted as docks were then built, and survived into the 14th century before infilling with organic material. A new stone quay was then built. Dyeing was among the industries recorded (Williams 1981, 12–15; Youngs and Clark 1982, 168–70).

342   Freshford House, Redcliff Street   Williams, Bruce   1980   ST 59085 72475
Excavation recorded 13th-century dye-works which continued with rebuilding into the 18th century, a 15th- to 16th-century bakehouse and a slipway. Part of the Portwall was also identified (Williams 1981a; Williams 1981b, 35–46).

343   Avon Street   Williams, Bruce   1988   ST 59710 72760
The remains of 19th-century glassworks were excavated. Flues from the furnaces and annealing arches were recorded (Egan 1989, 61).

344   Dundas Wharf, Redcliff Street   Good, G L   1982   ST 59009 72747
Excavation traced successive phases of waterfront construction, beginning in the mid-12th century, the construction of medieval tenements, evidence for baking and possibly tanning. An arched slipway, the 'Common Slype', was also excavated (Good 1991, 29–42).

358   St Mary-le-Port, Castle Park   Rahtz, Philip   1962–3   ST 58990 73025
Excavation recorded evidence for Saxon domestic and industrial activity as well as for the development of the fabric of St Mary-le-Port (Watts and Rahtz 1985).

404   Southwell House, Southwell Street   Brett, Jonathan R   1994   ST 58389 73394
Mounded features, probably for cultivation and containing abraded ceramics dating between the 12th and 15th centuries were excavated. Late 18th-century garden features were also recorded (Williams 1994/5, 71; *MSRG Ann Rep* **9** 1994, 32).

408   Portwall Lane   Hebditch, Max G   1965   ST 59180 72412
Excavation of a trench across the Portwall ditch ascertained that the ditch was approximately 7.7m wide during the 17th century. Organic material was noted in this recutting of the medieval ditch. The upper fills were of early 18th-century date (Hebditch 1968, 131–43).

409   St Peter's Church, Castle Park   Ponsford, M W   1970   ST 59091 73121
Medieval and post-medieval buildings were recorded, including part of Simon Oliver's House, and associated features (Wilson and Moorhouse 1971, 146–7).

414   Castle Park   Gettins, G L   1948   ST 59226 73157
Part of the keep of Bristol Castle was excavated in 1948. The underlying motte ditch was also recorded (Marshall 1951, 13–21).

415   Castle Park   Nelson, B A M   1949   ST 59374 73118
14th- and 15th-century cess pits were found in small evaluation trenches in Castle Street (Marshall 1951, 21–3).

416   Castle Street, Castle Park   Marshall, Kenneth   1951   ST 59290 73082
A series of small trenches roughly parallel with the Castle ditch apparently recorded part of the south curtain wall of Bristol Castle. Other features, including a stone cistern, were also recorded (Marshall 1951, 23–30).

417   Wine Street   Gettins, G L   1948   ST 58994 73123
Excavation exposed the face of the town wall (Marshall 1951, 30–2).

418   Narrow Wine Street   Boon, George C   1950   ST 59078 73155
Stretches of the town wall, the biggest *c* 12m long, were recorded during excavation. The wall survived to a height of nearly 1.4m in one place (Marshall 1951, 32–5).

419   Mary-le-Port Street, Castle Park   Boon, George C   1950   ST 59021 73057
Excavation in Mary-le-Port Street identified medieval stratification and a rubbish pit. Live services prevented further excavation (Marshall 1951, 35–7).

420   The Grove   Dawson, David P   1974   ST 58699 72457
The remains of post-medieval buildings at No 4 The Grove and Nos 41–3 Queen Square were excavated (*BARG Bull* **5(3)**, 67).

432   Upper Maudlin Street   Parker, A J   1976   ST 58694 73418
Excavation on the south side of Upper Maudlin Street recorded a late 4th-century Romano-British building, pits containing 18th-century ceramics and the remains of a Moravian Church (*BARG Bull* **5(8)**, 211; Frere 1977, 410).

437   Bush House, Narrow Quay   Price, Roger H   1973   ST 58580 72423
Excavation inside the warehouse recorded floor surfaces and nearly 2m of made ground. No finds dating earlier than 1730 were recovered.

441   St Nicholas Almshouses, King Street   Barton, Kenneth J   1960   ST 58829 72738
A semi-circular tower on the Marsh Wall was excavated to the rear of the almshouses. The tower was founded directly on the alluvial clay (Barton 1964, 184–212).

442   Broad Quay House, Narrow Quay   Good, G L   1978   ST 58609 72689
The remains of two post-medieval docks, interpreted as St Clement's Dock and Aldworth's Dock were recorded. Assemblages of leather, animal remains recovered as well as ribs of a carvel-construction boat from Aldworth's Dock of 17th-century date (Good 1987b, 25–126).

443   Temple Street   Williams, Bruce   1975   ST 59337 72457
Four phases of medieval building were recorded, including dwellings and the possible remains of John Spicer's almshouses (Williams 1988, 107–68).

444   The Abbot's House, Blackfriars   Boore, Eric J   1989   ST 58704 73382
The remains of a medieval ground floor hall were recorded. The building, interpreted as belonging to the Franciscan Friary in Lewins Mead, was removed in the 17th century and the extant house built. Post-medieval garden features were also recorded (Ponsford *et al* 1989b, 42–4).

447   95–7 Redcliff Street   Jones, Robert H   1983   ST 59050 72534
Excavation on part of the site of Canynge's House recorded the construction of successive river walls and waterfront installations, and possible evidence of tanning and baking. Environmental evidence was obtained by sampling of organic deposits (Jones 1986).

448   Castle Park   Ponsford, M W   1968   ST 59395 73165
Fragments of medieval walls and other structures, together with a cobbled surface were excavated. These features were interpreted as the curtain wall and the east gate of Bristol Castle (Wilson and Hurst 1969, 256–8).

451   St Thomas Street   Good, G L   1989   ST 59198 72440
Excavation recorded a series of shallow 14th-century pits over which a building was erected in the 15th century. The site reverted to horticultural use in the 16th century. A building erected in the 17th century was replaced by housing in the 18th (Good 1989 20–9).

452   Cock and Bottle Lane, Castle Park   Ponsford, M W   1968   ST 59243 73149
Part of the motte ditch of Bristol Castle was identified. A floor surface and post-holes built in the 12th century were interpreted as part of a building. Post-medieval pits were also excavated. (Wilson and Hurst 1969, 255)

458   Castle Park   Ponsford, M W   1970   ST 59201 73089
Sections of substantial stone walls, possibly part of the curtain wall of Bristol Castle, were exposed by groundworks and excavated (Wilson and Moorhouse 1971, 146).

459   Castle Park   Williams, Bruce   1989   ST 59224 73157
The surviving parts of the keep of Bristol Castle were excavated as was the motte ditch on which the keep was built. Part of the 19th-century Llewellin and James brassworks built over the keep was recorded (Good 1996, 17–45).

461   Castle Park   Good, G L   1993   ST 59215 73160
Excavation on the site of a new toilet block adjacent to the keep of Bristol Castle recorded no significant archaeological features.

463   Temple Back   Jackson, R G   1994   ST 59590 72683
Excavation exposed the surviving extent of Tower Harratz and the Portwall to the north and south. Evidence of a small gate on the north side of the tower and associated surfaces was also recorded (Williams 1994/5, 74).

464   U Shed, Canon's Marsh   Tavener, Nick   1996   ST 58504 72566
Excavation inside U Shed recorded a length of possible medieval wall and abutting post-medieval features (Tavener 1996a).

465   Rupert Street   Good, G L   1969   ST 58749 73229
The walls, services and associated yard surfaces of buildings ranging in date from the 13th or 14th century to the 17th century were excavated (Wilson and Hurst 1970, 181).

467   70 Redcliff Street   Jones, Robert H   1982   ST 59113 72453
Evidence of industrial use (including possible ironworking) of a 13th-century building was recorded. A replacement building was erected in the 14th century and was itself replaced in the 15th by the building which became 'The Old Fox' public house (R Jones 1983, 37–9).

472   Newmarket Avenue   Good, G L   1990   ST 58854 73135
Excavation recorded a cess pit of Late Saxon or early Norman date, the foundations of a Norman building, later medieval cellars and evidence of post-medieval ironworking (Williams 1992, 53).

475   Castle Park   Ponsford, M W   1970   ST 59214 73106
Excavation recorded post-medieval structures. In the cellar of a 17th-century building a rock-cut tunnel, interpreted as a postern tunnel, 2m high and 18m long was excavated. The roof of the tunnel had been reinforced with stone and it had been backfilled in the 17th century (Wilson and Moorhouse 1971, 146).

476   Castle Park   Ponsford, M W   1970   ST 59213 73173
A short section of wall, interpreted as part of a ringwork, the precursor of the motte and bailey castle, was recorded, as were sections of the motte ditch, north curtain wall and keep of Bristol Castle.

485   Temple Church   Saunders, Andrew   1960   ST 59330 72733
Excavation within the nave recorded remains of walls interpreted as part of the 12th-century circular church of the Knights Templar (Brown 2008, 113–29).

488   Castle Park   Ponsford, M W   1969   ST 59351 73218
Excavation at No 2 Middle Terrace in Castle Green recorded an early land surface and a ditch cutting through it, together with a small forge of Saxon date. Three phases of timber buildings were also found. Subsequently the east curtain wall of the Castle was erected *c* 1070 and this was rebuilt later in the medieval period with the addition of a tower. Evidence for re-fortification in the 17th century was also noted (Wilson and Hurst 1970, 156).

517   Temple Back   Burchill, Rod   1995   ST 59530 72750
Excavation recorded part of the 19th-century Ring's clay tobacco pipe factory (Williams 1996, 86).

523   65 Baldwin Street   Price, Roger H   1974   ST 58902 72924
Part of the town wall, together with medieval features to the south of it, and post-medieval structures built against it were recorded during excavation (Price 1979b).

540   110–12 Redcliff Street   Nicholson, Andrew   1985   ST 59050 72640
Excavation recorded a 12th-century building which was replaced in the 13th century with a new building. This survived, with some post-medieval remodelling, to the mid-19th century when a tobacco warehouse was built on the site (Burchill *et al* 1987, 17–30).

713   Tiffany Court, Redcliff Mead Lane   Coxah, M   1985   ST 59450 72250
Excavation in advance of redevelopment of the Caxton printing works revealed that the site had been in agricultural use until the construction of housing in the 19th century (Burchill *et al 19*87, 11–17).

928   Quakers Friars   Unknown   1933   ST 59227 73343
Excavation of a single trench, probably within the nave of the church of the Dominican Friary, failed to find any evidence of the fabric of the church (Leighton 1933, 164–6).

1503   41–3 Baldwin Street   Rahtz, Philip   1957   ST 58828 72903
Excavation recorded the town wall and 13th- to 16th-century features outside it. A post-medieval building was then erected on the site (Rahtz 1960, 221–50).

1579   Brygstow House, 5 Welsh Back   Blockley, Kevin   1995   ST 58920 72845
Excavation following evaluation (BHER 1065) on the site of the Back Hall complex recorded seven phases of occupation, ranging from 12th-century pre-Back Hall structures to the 19th century (Blockley 1996).

1685   Minster House, Bristol Cathedral   Boore, Eric J   1992   ST 58296 72679
Excavation recorded part of a 12th-century building at the east end of the Cathedral, a medieval bell-founding pit, part of the west claustral range of St Augustine's Abbey and the remains of the 15th-century Minster House (Boore 1992, 42–50; Bryant 2015).

1686   St Augustine-the-Less, College Green   Boore, Eric J   1983   ST 58487 72733
Excavation recorded Saxon inhumations and part of a wall pre-dating the medieval church. A large group of medieval and post-medieval inhumations were recovered from graves and burial shafts within the church (Boore 1985, 21–33; Boore 1986, 211–14).

1688   Victoria Street   Good, G L   1974   ST 59367 72577
The rear plots of properties formerly fronting the east side of Temple Street were investigated. A wall presumed to be part of the Weavers' Hall was found, as well as the eastern end of a house. There was also evidence for pin-making and wool-card-making in the 16th century. Tenement boundaries could be identified and in the gardens were parallel trenches thought to be cultivation trenches (*BARG Bull* **5(2)**, 48–9; Webster and Cherry 1975, 242–3).

1689   Cart Lane, Temple Street   Good, G L   1974   ST 59380 72630
Excavation recorded gullies, interpreted as possible bases for medieval cloth-drying racks, with associated hard standing. Later garden features were also excavated (*BARG Bull* **5(2)**, 48–9); Webster and Cherry 1975, 242–3.

1690   90–1 Redcliff Street   Jones, Robert H   1985   ST 59050 72510
Two clay-lined features, c 1.5m in diameter with a surrounding gully, were recorded. The features were interpreted as possible medieval vat bases which were enclosed within timber superstructures (Youngs *et al* 1986, 119).

2456   Olivetti House, Marsh Street   Burchill, Rod   1995   ST 58680 72715
A section of the Marsh Wall was recorded in advance of the construction of new offices. A section cut through the wall noted that the wall was founded directly on alluvial clay (Williams 1996, 86; Burchill 1995b).

3051   Queen Charlotte Street   Barton, Kenneth J   1958   ST 58890 72870
Excavation recorded parts of the medieval Back Hall complex dating from the 13th century onwards. 17th-century buildings subsequently erected on the site were also recorded (Barton 1960, 251–86).

3078   Haymarket   Mason, Edward   1954   ST 58981 73403
Salvage excavation during groundworks for construction of the John Lewis building recorded 40 inhumations from St James's Churchyard. Some had been disturbed by post-medieval features, including a culvert (Mason 1957, 164–71).

3096   Castle Park   Lucas, H   1982/1983   ST 59372 73137
The foundation trenches for a northern extension to the Castle Park Restaurant at the Vaulted Chambers (472M) in Castle Street, and the new north wall, were excavated by a small archaeological team rather than by the builders. It is unknown what, if anything, was found.

3098   St James's Court, St James's Parade   Arthur, B V   1962   ST 58920 73460
Excavation recorded two undated inhumations. Post-medieval features and a Second World War air raid shelter had disturbed the earlier stratification (*BARG Bull* **1(3)**, 36–7).

3155   St James's Court, St James's Parade   Jackson, R G   1995   ST 58932 73488
Excavation following evaluation (BHER 893) recorded probable evidence of the monastic burial ground of St James's Priory and the east end of the priory church. Elements of 18th-century houses on Cannon Street and a 19th-century Scottish Presbyterian church were also recorded (Jackson 2006b).

3156   Walsingham House, Whitson Street   Bryant, John   1994   ST 58876 73445
Excavation at the west front of St James's Church following evaluation (BHER 413) recorded medieval inhumations over which late medieval/early post-medieval buildings were constructed. Associated occupation deposits were also excavated (Jackson 2006b).

3158   Temple Back   Cox, Simon   1997   ST 59606 72690
Excavation recorded a structure of unknown function outside the line of the Portwall and adjacent to Tower Harratz. A medieval wall had been incorporated into the structure which was of 16th- to 17th-century date (Cox 1997).

3173   Dolphin Street, Castle Park   Rahtz, Philip   1962   ST 59040 73067
Excavation recorded the edge of a ditch interpreted as part of a defensive ditch for the Saxon town (Wilson 1965, 265, Watts and Rahtz 1985, 65).

3234   1–2 Broad Quay   Jackson, R G   1972   ST 58614 72868
Excavation in the cellar of the building exposed a wall 'at least 4.25m thick' which was tentatively interpreted as an element of the town wall. It was also noted that a window of 14th-century date 'had been reused in the W[est] wall' (Fowler 1973a, 53).

3265   Poole's Wharf   Erskine, Jonathan G P   1996   ST 57366 72411
Excavation following evaluation (BHER 3654) recorded the remains of buildings of 18th- to early 20th-century date and parts of two 18th-century slipways (Erskine and Prosser 1997).

3272   St James's Court, St James's Parade   Jones, Robert H   1989   ST 58947 73492
Seven phases of activity were identified. Inhumations from the burial ground of St James's Priory were found beneath subsequent features, including garden deposits from 18th-century houses. Also recorded was part of a 19th-century Scottish Presbyterian church (Jones 1989, 2–7; Jackson 2006b).

3276   New World Square, Canon's Marsh   Cox, Simon   1997   ST 58380 72487
Excavation following evaluation (BHER 456) recorded parts of Bright, Protheroe, Bonville & Company's ropewalk and of the City Saw Mills (Williams 1997, 82; Ponsford and Jackson 1998, 156).

3286   St Bartholomew's Hospital, Host Street   Price, R H   1977   ST 58656 73211
Excavation recorded possible parts of the bank of the pre-1240s course of the river Frome and a postulated creek in the area of Narrow Lewins Mead. A Norman aisled hall was subsequently built and elements were incorporated into St Bartholomew's Hospital founded by the de la Warre family in the 13th century. Evidence for use of the buildings in charitable and industrial roles following the Dissolution was recorded (Price with Ponsford 1998).

3287   Castle Park   Ponsford, M W   1969   ST 59399 73179
Excavation recorded part of a possible Late Saxon land surface with a shallow posthole cut into it. The ditch of Bristol Castle was subsequently dug through it. Evidence of re-cutting and the construction of stone structures in the period of the English Civil War was also recorded (Wilson and Hurst 1970,156).

3367   Bridge Parade   Cox, Simon   1998   ST 59052 72895
The top of the archaeological stratification was exposed across the site, revealing the river wall and walls of medieval buildings. Limited excavation of late post-medieval features was undertaken (Cox 1998d, 1–26).

3398   Graham's Timber Yard, Hotwells Road   Cox, Simon   1999   ST 57810 72541
Excavation following evaluation (BHER 3386) recorded part of Limekiln Dock and associated 18th- and 19th-century buildings, including a boiler house (Cox 1999, 17–34).

3399   Upper Maudlin Street   Jackson, R G   1999   ST 58678 73377
Excavation within the precinct of the Franciscan Friary recorded quantities of residual prehistoric and Roman material, including iron slag, a late 12th- or early 13th-century ditch and cultivation soils associated with the medieval friary. Part of a 17th-century formal garden, a 19th-century Welsh Baptist chapel and other 19th-century industrial buildings were also excavated (Jackson 2000, 29–110; Bradley and Gaimster 2000, 248; Wills 2000, 218).

3404   Redcliff Caves, Redcliff Wharf   Thomas, C Rayner   1939   ST 58940 72306
Excavation was undertaken between 1939 and 1943 inside Redcliff Caves and 'much valuable data was collected' (Jones 1946, 140n).

3472   Choir, Bristol Cathedral   Unknown   1894   ST 58365 72694
A single trench dug in the centre of the choir exposed two foundations, the western thought to be a pier of the Norman church and the eastern of unknown date but suggested to have 'supported a screen which divided the Lady Chapel from the choir' (*JBAA* **51**, 90–1).

3501   Redcliff Backs   Cox, Simon   1999   ST 59035 72464
Excavation on the east side of Redcliff Backs exposed the rear parts of mid-14th-century tenements on Redcliff Street and encountered medieval waste deposits containing dye plants (Bradley and Gaimster 2000, 246; Wills 2000, 217; Williams and Cox 2000).

| 3537 | Canons Way | Parry, Adrian | 2000 | ST 58444 72530 |

Excavation following evaluation (BHER 3333) recorded elements of an early modern formal garden and 18th-century buildings, including the George Hotel. These were rebuilt in the 19th century to create industrial buildings. A timber yard was developed on the site of the garden (Ponsford 2001, 129; Wills 2001, 188–9).

| 3553 | 30–8 St Thomas Street | Jackson, R G | 2000 | ST 59183 72532 |

Excavation following evaluation (BHER 3376) recorded a sequence of development from the later 14th century. The rear wall of a medieval house of some status was recorded. This was demolished in the 16th century and a lodge constructed within the site, garden soils associated with this building being sampled. The site remained a garden until the early 18th century when a glasshouse was constructed and ancillary buildings to the glasshouse were excavated. The site was cleared in 1899 for the construction of a tobacco factory (Jackson 2004).

| 3590 | Union Street | Jackson, R G | 2000 | ST 59009 73204 |

Excavation following evaluation (BHER 3480 and BHER 3641) recorded a river wall constructed to claim land from the river Frome in the 12th century. The former channel was infilled with red sand and industrial buildings, including a circular furnace and at least four metalworking heaths, were constructed on the reclaimed land. These were removed in the late 13th century or early 14th century for the construction of a substantial house. This survived until the 17th century but was apparently destroyed during the English Civil Wars and new housing built. In the 19th century Fry's chocolate factory was developed on the site (Jackson 2010a).

| 3591 | King David Hotel, St Michael's Hill | Longman, Tim | 2000 | ST 58572 73312 |

Medieval inhumations associated with the Priory of St Mary Magdalen were recorded during fieldwork on the site. Part of a probable 16th-century mansion was also recorded (Longman 2001).

| 3617 | King David Hotel, St Michael's Hill | Longman, Tim | 2000 | ST 58584 73314 |

Four medieval walls associated with the Priory of St Mary Magdalen were recorded. This work was part of the excavation BHER 3591 (Longman 2001).

| 3629 | 98–103 Redcliff Street | Insole, Peter | 2000 | ST 59068 72569 |

Excavation following evaluation (BHER 3502) recorded a 12th-century wicker revetment on the east bank of the river Avon and the plan of the medieval tenements which occupied the site (Williams 2000, 141; Bradley and Gaimster 2001, 258; Insole 1999a).

| 3643 | Temple Quay, Temple Way | Cox, Simon | 2000 | ST 59572 72619 |

Excavation on the line of the Portwall recorded a substantial gate at the northern end of the wall close to Tower Harratz giving access to the associated ditch. Evidence for several phases of alteration was found (Bradley and Gaimster 2001, 259–60; Wills 2001 190; Cox 2000).

| 3697 | 1–2 King Street/30 Welsh Back | Parry, Adrian | 2001 | ST 58899 72705 |

There was limited evidence for settlement by the river in the 13th century. However, evidence for 15th-century hardstanding adjacent to the river was found. Rapid deposition of rubbish, including domestic fuel waste, from the 17th century raised the level by about 2m (Parry 2005).

| 3736 | Royal Fort House | Horton, Mark | 2001 | ST 58273 73390 |

An archaeological excavation was carried out at Royal Fort House under the direction of Mark Horton of the University of Bristol.

| 3770 | Courage's Brewery | Jackson, R G | 2000–1 | ST 59088 72920 |

Excavation recorded 12th-century development close to the River Avon, a stone quay, hearths for possible dye vats and a ditch dating to the 13th century. Post-medieval houses and industrial premises, probably including a 17th-century dye house and parts of the 19th-century brewery were also excavated (Jackson 2006a).

| 3772 | College Square | Insole, Peter | 2001 | ST 58220 72610 |

Excavation recorded the remains of a fishpond dating to the 12th century. This was drained and partly filled with stable manure before the construction of a large building of late 13th- or early 14th-century date, constructed of Brandon Hill Grit, interpreted as a barn for St Augustine's Abbey. In the 18th century a terrace of houses had been built over the demolished remains of this building (Insole 2003).

3781   Royal Fort House   Horton, Mark   2001   ST 58273 73390

Two trenches were excavated in advance of landscaping works by Bristol University. What may have been the original road into the Royal Fort Gardens was found. This was first shown on Repton's plan of 1798. The possible north wall of the original Royal Fort House, demolished *c* 1760, was also found. In the second trench two walls may have been of 17th-century date, possibly internal walls within the Royal Fort (Horton 2001).

3806   Cheese Lane   Jackson, R G   2001   ST 59428 72908

Excavation showed that the site had been reclaimed with the construction of a river wall in the mid-17th century. Documentary evidence showed that this was the site of Sir Abraham Elton's glassworks during the 18th century. This phase of glassworks had been extensively disturbed by later development, but the excavation found the cone and other buildings of a hitherto unsuspected late 17th- or early 18th-century glassworks. Subsequently a complex of industrial buildings was erected for the manufacture of glass, copper, spelter, zinc and lead (Jackson 2005).

3822   Deanery Road   Barber, Alastair   2000   ST 58109 72634

During excavation following evaluation (BHER 3592) the foundations of a circular stone structure, thought to be of likely medieval date were recorded (Cox *et al* 2006).

3858   18–20 West Street   Parry, Adrian   2002   ST 59910 73173

The excavation revealed evidence for medieval building adjacent to West Street. Buried soils suggested cultivation of the tenement contemporary with the frontage buildings, with some evidence for smithing at the West Street end of the site. The site continued to be settled during the 16th and 17th centuries with some evidence for metalworking during the 16th century. Structures of the 18th and 19th centuries were found throughout the site, with evidence for light industrial activity confirming the impression from documentary sources (King and Parry 2004).

3906   26–8 St Thomas Street   Cox, Simon   2002   ST 59167 72567

The earliest evidence for settlement consisted of pits and ditches and the remains of a midden deposit, dating from the 11th to 13th centuries. The earliest built structures dated from the late medieval period. These spanned later plot divisions and thus either pre-dated such divisions or were in common ownership. To the rear were substantial soil layers with a few pits and gullies. In the post-medieval period were remains of buildings on the St Thomas Street frontage, to the rear of which were tanks, soakaways, drains and wells (Watts 2011).

3923   30 Gloucester Lane   King, Andrew   2002   ST 59893 73308

The excavation revealed evidence for a defensive bastion or outwork, part of the Civil War defensive circuit, lying beyond Lawford's Gate and overlooking the eastern approaches to the city from London (King 2010).

3928   Johnny Ball Lane   Samuel, Jens   2002   ST 58656 73336

Bristol and Region Archaeological Services were contracted to remove burials from the former Infirmary burial ground, which had been in use from 1757 to 1857. A large assemblage of human skeletal material was removed and submitted to Bristol University for subsequent analysis (Samuel 2003).

3930   42 and 43 Welsh Back   Stevens, David   2002   ST 58875 72492

Excavation demonstrated that this part of the riverbank had not been occupied before the late 17th century although there was evidence for undated wheel ruts in the underlying alluvium. Overlying the alluvium were deep deposits of dumped landfill including domestic and industrial waste dating from 1678 until no later than 1709. The close dating of the deposits allowed an important insight into household industrial activity in the late 17th century. The well-preserved plant remains, which included a deposit consisting almost entirely of grape pips, stalks and the flesh of the fruit, provided detailed evidence for the diet of the city's inhabitants in this period (Jackson 2008–9).

3977   42 Montague Street   King, Andrew   2003   ST 58877 73647

The remains of five cellars fronting Montague Street were found, of three main phases of construction dating from the early to late 18th century. Three wells, the bases of four rainwater collection tanks, the truncated remains of a drain and the footings of a garden wall were also found (King 2004).

3979   3 Redcliff Street   Cox, Simon   2003   ST 59075 72725

The earliest activity, dating to the 11th to 13th century comprised a sandstone wall, pits and postholes, together with a reused wooden board possibly from a well or pit lining. Between the 13th and 15th centuries there was intense development with stone-founded buildings, possible ovens or dye vats and cistern tanks constructed over dumped clay. About six sub-circular tanks or vats were constructed together with an associated cobbled yard in the late 16th or early 17th century. From the 18th century the site was redeveloped with new stone-founded buildings and cellars and the conversion of the sub-circular tanks into a cellar (Cox *et al* 2004; Alexander 2015).

4071   Canon's Marsh   Rodwell, K, and   2003   ST 57989 72494
                                                    Chapman M
Excavation revealed the remains of the earliest oil gasworks, including the plan of the buttressed retort house. The associated gasholder was very fragmentary but sections of distinctive early gas pipe were recovered. Later gasworks structures, especially of three gasholders, were recovered. There was also evidence for the preceding late 17th-century glassworks (Croft *et al* 2005).

4080   Temple Back   Godden, David   2004   ST 59393 72843
Excavation examined the fills of a small inlet on Temple Back which had become choked with silt and debris until it was cleared in the 17th century and replaced by a formal channel and slipway. The channel became filled with domestic and industrial debris so that by the early 18th century no sign of it remained. The area was then reclaimed and built over (Dinwiddy with Chandler 2011).

4087   Canons Way   Cullen, Kate   2004   ST 58200 72414
A small excavation was carried out on the south side of Canons Way (Ponsford 2005, 341).

4088   118–22 Jacob Street   King, Andy   2004   ST 59753 73137
A single cell stone building was recorded dating to the late 17th century and probably forming a garden house or lodge. The land between Jacob Street and No 53 Old Market was used as gardens from the 12th century to the 17th century. The site was gradually developed through the 19th century (Wills 2005, 154).

4120   Drill Hall, 57 Old Market Street   Havard, Tim   2004   ST 59687 73136
A small excavation was sited within the garden of one of the houses of Old Market Street. A number of pits of medieval date cut into the underlying rock (Gaimster and O'Conor 2005, 354).

4146   22–30 West Street, Old Market   King, Andy   2004   ST 59909 73195
Buildings of medieval date were found on the street frontage. Rubbish pits were found to the rear, many dating to the 16th to 18th centuries. There was evidence for an ornamental garden, later built over by a large workshop and low quality dwellings (King 2007b).

4149   Albion Terrace, Johnny Ball Lane   Davis, Elizabeth   2004   ST 58649 73326
A small excavation recorded the remains of cellars associated with Nos 1 and 2 Albion Terrace along with evidence for the earlier 'Soldiers Infirmary' (Ponsford 2005, 341).

4164   Templar House, Temple Way   Colls, Kevin   2004   ST 59420 72570
The excavation found evidence for human settlement on the Avon floodplain from the 14th century onwards. There was evidence for the development of Spring Gardens in the late 17th to early 18th century and the Great Gardens Estate from 1725 (Colls 2010).

4168   Bristol Bus Station, Lower Maudlin Street Stevens, David   2004   ST 58895 73510
The excavation identified foundations of the original claustral range, situated on the north side of the church, and extensive post-medieval development. A total of 25 burials, possibly positioned beneath the cloister walk, were removed.

4231   Former FPS Factory site, Waterloo Road   Davis, Elizabeth   2005   ST 59870 73175
Medieval and early post-medieval pits and gullies and a possible medieval wall were recorded. A 17th-century boundary wall crossed the site and later 17th-century walls were probably parts of buildings behind the Globe Inn on West Street. By the middle of the 19th century the land had been developed with single-storey workshops, sheds and other buildings down either side of alleyways or haulingways (Jackson 2007d).

4244   The Old Council House, Corn Street   Jackson, R G   2005   ST 58844 73055
Continuous occupation from at least the late 12th century to the present was recorded although it was clear that earlier occupation deposits remained unexcavated. The wealth of finds, including a gold ring and rare imported pottery, hinted at the high status of the inhabitants (Jackson 2007c).

4273   55–60 St Thomas Street   Rowe, Michael   2006   ST 59225 72572
Excavation showed that development did not commence until the mid- to late 13th century with property
boundaries laid out. By the 15th century, and possibly before, the site was largely open. Redevelopment of
the site took place in the late 17th century, being fully developed by the early 18th century (Davenport *et al*
2011, 1–72).

4277   51A West Street   King, Andy   2005   ST 59923 73317
An excavation was carried out at land between No 51A West Street and Braggs Lane. A second phase of
excavation was carried out by Stuart Whatley in September 2006.

4279   25 Broadweir   Pickard, Chris   2006   ST 59315 73263
Excavation, carried out as part of the redevelopment of the eastern part of Broadmead for the Cabot Circus
development revealed medieval and later buildings and structures (Ridgeway and Watts 2013).

4280   33–9 Broadweir   Matthews, Bryan   2006   ST 59343 73281
Excavation, carried out as part of the redevelopment of the eastern part of Broadmead for the Cabot Circus
development revealed medieval and later buildings and structures (Ridgeway and Watts 2013).

4281   Penn Street   Webster, Jonathan   2006   ST 59392 73400
Excavation, carried out as part of the redevelopment of the eastern part of Broadmead for the Cabot Circus
development revealed medieval and later buildings and structures (Ridgeway and Watts 2013).

4302   8 Braggs Lane   Young, Andrew   2006   ST 59914 73354
Excavation revealed traces of post-medieval buildings.

4305   55 Victoria Street   Lankstead, Darren   2006   ST 59200 72700
A series of medieval walls and floor surfaces were found fronting on to St Thomas Street. A sequence of
medieval garden soils and cut features were identified (Williams 2006b, 113).

4342   Marsh Street/Broad Quay   Adam, Neil   2006   ST 58632 72816
A possible early (pre-*c* 1240) channel of the river Frome was found. Widespread dumping of clay had taken
place after the mid-13th century to reclaim the marsh. Medieval structures and deposits were recorded
overlying this clay. A possible slipway leading to the Frome was found, associated with the extant remains of
a medieval wall (forming the north wall of No 16 Marsh Street) standing more than 7.5m high. Most of the
south wall of this property was probably built in the 1620s. Remains of the Marsh Wall were found close
to Broad Quay, surviving for a length of 5.7m and at least 1.8m wide. Angled buttresses were found at the
north and south ends (Adam 2008a).

4369   Colston Street/2 Trenchard Street   Heaton, Rachel   2007   ST 58498 73005
A small section of medieval wall, together with a small number of burials, associated with the Carmelite
Friary, were excavated. Pits filled with demolition material are associated with the destruction of the Friary
in the 16th century (Heaton 2008).

4371   Portwall Lane   Jackson, Reg   2006   ST 59140 72515
Excavation revealed a nearly complete complex of an 18th-century glassworks, with two glass cones and
ancillary buildings. The excavation also recorded medieval structures along St Thomas Street (Jackson 2007b;
2010b).

4389   32–6 Victoria Street   King, Andy   2007   ST 59235 72795
The partial remains of five tenement plots fronting Temple Street were recorded dating from the 12th to the
16th century. Part of the Law Ditch was exposed. This had been re-cut at least once (Williams 2007, 151).

4423   Avon Street, St Philips   Robinson, Christina 2007   ST 59780 72701
The remains of a series of glassworks, dating from the 18th to the 20th century were recorded. This work
included the recording of the remains of a Siemens regenerative furnace that had been introduced in the
19th century (Miller 2009).

4433   Gasferry Road   Ellis, Chris   2007   ST 57868 72360
The remains of Brunel's Engine House of the Great Western Steamship Company were recorded. The
remains of the later tannery which occupied the site after *c* 1852 were also recorded (Ellis and Leivers 2013).

| 4435 | Former Purimachos site, West Street | Stevens, Dave | 2007 | ST 60040 73260 |

Excavation revealed evidence for medieval and post-medieval cultivation, the boundary of an 18th- to 19th-century burial ground, the remains of 18th-/19th-century cottages and 19th-/20th-century industrial premises (Longman 2009).

| 4450 | 10–22 Victoria Street | Roper, Simon | 2008 | ST 59151 72844 |

A large drainage ditch was found running west–east across the site, possibly forming one of the boundary ditches defining Arthur's Fee. Short sections of medieval stone walls were found, dating between the 13th and 15th centuries (Roper 2008–9).

| 4455 | Harbourside (buildings 5 and 6) | Cudlip, Dave | 2007 | ST 58262 72562 |

Evidence was recovered for occupation of the site from the period of the foundation of St Augustine's Abbey *c* 1140. A series of medieval watercourses was found together with a small bridge and associated roads. The outer precinct wall of the Abbey was also found. There was evidence for the laying out of a ropewalk, possibly from the 15th or 16th century (Alexander and Harward 2011).

| 4456 | 1–2 Redcliff Street | Pickard, Chris | 2007–8 | ST 59065 72757 |

Remains of timber buildings, some with surviving timbers *in situ*, were excavated. These were succeeded by stone-founded buildings of the 13th and 14th centuries. There was clear evidence for industrial activity, with dyeing and copper manufacturing being carried out. Copper furnaces of the 16th to 17th century were constructed (Alexander 2015).

| 24756 | Hill House, Lewins Mead | Longman, Tim | 2009 | ST 58840 73390 |

The earliest remains, comprising a number of stone walls dating to the 13th to 14th centuries, formed a structure within which were two clay-lined pits, possibly for an industrial use. Post-medieval pits truncated these early features. These were in turn overlain by a post-medieval tenement block and a 19th-century confectionary works (Roper 2012).

| 24786 | Royal Fort, Tyndall Avenue | King, Andy | 2009 | ST 58299 73466 |

The excavation revealed an appreciable part of the Civil War Royal Fort, including a probable barrack block, a possible gunpowder store and part of the ditch (King 2014).

| 24787 | 26–8 Gloucester Lane | O'Neill, Hazel | 2009 | ST 59894 73327 |

A series of north–south and east–west walls were recorded, probably dating to the 18th century. These were sealed by 19th-century and later deposits (O'Neill and Barber 2009).

| 24838 | Finzels Reach (Courage Brewery). | Ford, Ben | 2007–8 | ST 59202 72928 |

A major excavation revealed evidence for a substantial boundary ditch, tentatively dated to the Late Saxon period and possibly forming part of the boundary of the defended bridgehead later known as Arthur's Fee. Evidence for settlement alongside Temple Street, dating from the 12th century was found, as well as the street itself and adjacent drainage ditches. There was considerable evidence for a number of industrial processes, including dyeing and tanning. Important assemblages of palaeoenvironmental material were found, including fish and animal bone, plant and insect remains (Ford *et al* 2017).

| 25013 | Cabot House, Deanery Road | Pickard, Chris | 2008 | ST 58151 72710 |

Excavation revealed evidence for the housing that was constructed on the site of the former Bishop's Park from the 18th century onwards (Holt and Leech 2011).

| 25018 | 9 Pipe Lane | Mason, Cai | 2011 | ST 58470 72990 |

The earliest structure recorded on the site was an early 17th-century stone building with later extensions and alterations. Prior to this was a large quarry pit containing 11th- to early 16th-century finds, dating to the period of the Dissolution (Mason 2012).

| 25111 | Wapping Wharf | Longman, Tim | 2012 | ST 58468 72175 |

Excavation identified the sandstone former cliff of Palaeolithic date close to the southern edge of the excavation area. It also revealed several 18th-/19th-century buildings associated with the former Western Wapping Dock and areas of cobbled surface, including that of a former ropewalk known to have been in existence by 1730 (Longman 2014b).

25157   1 Victoria Street   Williams, Bruce   2012   ST 59026 72844
A wall and construction debris of the 13th-/14th-century cut through 12th-/13th-century dump deposits overlying the river foreshore (Williams 2013).

25238   66 Queen Square   Smith, Tracey   2013   ST 58728 72663
The earliest features on the site possibly dated to the 17th century. There was evidence for reconstruction following the riots of 1831 and for later 19th- and 20th-century development (Smith 2014).

25247   Former Magistrates Court, Nelson Street   Longman, Tim   2013–4   ST 58739 73211
A layer of possible demolition rubble associated with the demolition of the Wheatsheaf in the 1970s was recorded. Part of a late 19th-century alley or haulingway was also recorded. Part of a possible 18th-century boundary was found. However, most of the archaeology on the site had been destroyed when the basement to the court building was constructed in the 1970s (Longman 2014a).

25256   10 Anchor Road   Longman, Tim   2013   ST 57958 72584
25272   Former Bristol General Hospital   Barber, Alistair   2013   ST 58854 72175
The structural remains of two 18th-century buildings fronting on to the southern side of Guinea Street were recorded. Landscaping of the site appears to have occurred from the late 17th or 18th century onwards. Structural remains of a building shown on Plumley and Ashmead's 1828 plan were revealed although its function remains uncertain (Barber 2014a).

25336   Wade Street/Little Ann Street   Potter, Kevin   2014   ST 59824 73498
The excavation identified the initial, early 18th-century activity, and thereafter, into the later 18th and 19th centuries, the clear archaeological narrative was one of progressive subdivision of both houses and their associated plots, and an increasing density of occupation (Avon Archaeology 2014; Corcos 2017).

Archaeological evaluations

278   St Nicholas Church, St Nicholas Street   Bryant, John   1983   ST 58930 72930
A shaft driven from the west wall of the north aisle recorded part of the town wall, remains of steps leading to the upper part of the church and post-medieval burial vaults and inhumations (Iles 1984, 59).

345   Bristol Cathedral   Boore, Eric J and   1988   ST 58407 72690
                                             Williams, Bruce
The foundations of the Lady Chapel of Bristol Cathedral were exposed by an evaluation trench (Ponsford *et al* 1989a, 246).

406   Canon's Marsh   Burchill, Rod   1995   ST 58234 72556
Part of a possible ditch or watercourse as well as 19th-century features were identified (Williams 1996, 84).

413   Walsingham House, Whitson Street   Bryant, John   1993   ST 58872 73442
Evaluation at the west front of St James's Church recorded the remains of medieval and post-medieval structures and associated occupation deposits (Williams 1993, 48).

423   Redcliff Backs   Brett, Jonathan R   1995   ST 59039 72476
Evaluation recorded post-medieval features and deposits at a depth of *c* 2.5m behind Freshford House. On the opposite side of Redcliff Backs late post-medieval made ground to a depth of *c* 3.5m was found (Williams 1996, 83).

425   Bristol Cathedral, College Green   Boore, Eric J   1991   ST 58310 72663
A small evaluation trench on the site of Minster House recorded medieval and post-medieval walls belonging to the building (Boore 1991, 43–8).

446   Redcliff Wharf   Williams, Bruce   1989   ST 58991 72365
Evaluation recorded structures, perhaps the furnace, associated with the 18th- to 19th-century Vigor and Stevens glassworks (Ponsford *et al* 1989b, 44).

449   Courage's Brewery, Counterslip   Jackson, R G   1994   ST 59090 72927
The survival of a deep sequence of well-preserved archaeological deposits on the waterfront was confirmed (Williams 1994/5, 74–5).

456   Canon's Marsh   Tavener, Nick   1997   ST 58391 72475
Industrial structures of 18th- and 19th-century date were identified during evaluation. These had been buried
by material deposited to raise the ground surface. The underlying alluvial clay was sampled (Tavener 1997).

462   Temple Back   Jackson, R G   1994   ST 59577 72684
Evaluation at various locations located the Portwall, Tower Harratz, a post-medieval slipway and part of the
19th-century Rings clay tobacco pipe factory. Although the evaluation was targeted to locate it, no trace of
Duffett's redware pottery was found (Jackson 1994a)

468   Castle Park   Sims, Ken   1993   ST 59202 73081
A trench excavated westward from the section of the south curtain wall of Bristol Castle exposed in 1992
recorded a further 10m length of the wall (Williams 1993, 46).

470   Houlton Street   Bryant, John   1994   ST 59713 73589
Elements of 18th-century buildings were excavated in Houlton Street. These buildings were noted to have
been founded on alluvial clay (Williams 1994/5, 72).

473   30 Welsh Back   Williams, Bruce   1990   ST 58900 72705
Alluvium containing medieval pottery was recorded at a depth of c 2.5m within a warehouse on Welsh Back.
A trench to the rear of the building exposed a post-medieval cobbled surface.

474   St George's Road   Williams, Bruce   1992   ST 58229 72884
Evaluation recorded an undated ditch, as well as evidence of terracing of the hillside (Williams 1992, 53).

509   Portwall Lane   Good, G L   1993   ST 59262 72415
Sections of the Portwall and elements of 18th- and 19th-century structures were recorded (Williams 1993, 46)

553   10–22, Victoria Street   Longman, Tim   1994   ST 59140 72840
Evaluation found that much of the site had been disturbed by cellars. Medieval and post-medieval walls were
identified in trenches within the buildings (Longman 1994)

554   Temple Back   Tavener, Nick   1995   ST 59585 72631
Excavation of a single trench across the Portwall Ditch recorded both sides of the ditch and part of the
Portwall (Williams 1996, 86).

892   U Shed, Canon's Marsh   Tavener, Nick   1995   ST 58510 72596
Evaluation identified a possible medieval wall, post-medieval features and part of a dry dock which went out
of use c 1883 (Williams 1996, 84).

893   St James's Court, St James's Parade   Boore, Eric J   1994   ST 58929 73493
Evaluation on the site of the NFU Mutual Insurance Offices recorded medieval inhumations and post-
medieval features (Williams 1994/5, 72).

894   76–96 Victoria Street   Tavener, Nick   1995   ST 59339 72649
Medieval and post-medieval structures and deposits were identified (Williams 1996, 86–7).

1019   Temple Quay   Cox, Simon   1998   ST 59577 72646
Evaluation on the site of a demolished electricity sub-station exposed a stretch of the Portwall (Rawes and
Wills 1999, 172).

1065   Brygstow House, 5 Welsh Back   Barber, Alistair   1994   ST 58908 72871
Evaluation recorded medieval and post-medieval structures. The presence of deposits rich in organic remains
was also noted (Barber 1994).

1128   Montague Street   Burchill, Rod   1994   ST 58900 73640
Evaluation recorded the remains of post-medieval buildings (Williams 1994/5, 73).

1129   Engineering Building, Park Row   Bryant, John   1994   ST 58190 73140
Evaluation identified part of a large 17th-century ditch, possibly belonging to Essex Work, part of the Civil
War defences (Williams 1994/5, 72).

1132   St Michael on the Mount Primary School   Bryant, John   1992   ST 58516 73260
Evaluation recorded the remains of Llan House and Rupert House. Walls within Llan House were found to be of 15th-century date (Williams 1992, 54).

1578   South side of Avon Street   Brett, Jonathan R   1995   ST59850 72650
Probable early 18th-century industrial structures and a 19th-century dock on the site of Cuckold's Pill were recorded (Williams 1996, 86).

1728   St Thomas Churchyard   Burchill, Rod   1994   ST 59106 72788
Evaluation identified post-medieval burial shafts and vaults containing articulated inhumations. No human remains were removed for study (Burchill 1994b).

2521   Old Leadworks, Canon's Way   Cox, Simon   1996   ST 58445 72590
Evaluation recorded a wall interpreted as the boundary wall of the garden of the Bishop's Palace and other features (Williams 1996, 84).

3062   42–3 Welsh Back   Burchill, Rod   1994   ST 58800 72491
Evaluation recorded 17th-century deposits overlying alluvial clay. The marsh clay was sampled for palaeoenvironmental analysis (Williams 1994/5, 71).

3157   Upper Maudlin Street   Tavener, Nick   1996–7   ST 58617 73368
The evaluation was carried out in three stages. The excavator identified a buried land surface containing animal remains overlying the sandstone brash. This was sealed by a deposit of red clayey silt which contained general domestic refuse, including pottery of 12th-century date. Above this was a mixed black ash and grey-white mortar layer of 18th-century date, itself lying beneath a red-brown silt. All of these deposits were cut by a stone drain which curved from the south-western to the south-eastern trench edges. The drain was sealed by a mortar surface which was associated with a brick wall found along the eastern section of the trench. This was thought to be the party wall between the Nos 27 and 29 Upper Maudlin Street.

3159   Temple Back   Cox, Simon   1996   ST 59538 72605
Evaluation located several sections of the Portwall between Tower Harratz and Pipe Lane. A possible gate was identified close to Tower Harratz (Williams 1996, 87).

3160   Bristol Bridge/Victoria Street   Tavener, Nick   1996   ST 59050 72895
Evaluation identified medieval and post-medieval buildings to the north of Bristol Bridge. Undisturbed medieval stratification was found across the site (Tavener 1996b).

3179   Goods Shed, Canon's Marsh   Tavener, Nick   1997   ST 58374 72576
Evaluation trenches recorded post-medieval wall and a brick culvert. 13th- to 14th-century pottery was found within the alluvial clay. Excavation of engineer's trial pits was also observed.

3180   Grosvenor Hotel, Temple Gate   Cox, Simon   1997   ST 59418 72397
Evaluation recorded part of the Portwall as well as elements of 18th- to 19th-century structures (Williams 1996, 87; Cox 1996).

3271   St James's Court, St James's Parade   Jones, R H   1988   ST 58949 73480
Evaluation recorded a late medieval deposit overlying rock into which a ditch, backfilled in the 17th century, had been cut. Services for 18th-century buildings on St James's Parade and elements of the Scottish Presbyterian Church were also recorded (Anon 1988, 33).

3284   Temple Way   Cox, Simon   1997   ST 59450 72680
Medieval pits and postholes, some associated with a cobbled surface, were recorded by evaluation excavation. The features were interpreted as possible remains of a tenter rack. Post-medieval pits and one wall of the Temple Church Mission Hall were also recorded (Williams 1997, 83).

3297   Castle Park   Insole, Peter   1998   ST 59268 73128
Evaluation of the site of a tethered balloon recorded part of a stone rubble wall dating to the late medieval or early post-medieval period (Rawes and Wills 1999, 169–70; Insole 1998b).

3298   Seahorse Public House, Upper Maudlin St   Longman, Tim   1998   ST 58594 73328
Two small trenches were excavated inside the public house and in its garden, the latter recording stratified deposits. The earliest of these, overlying rock, produced ceramics of 15th- and 16th-century date (Williams 1998, 79; Longman 1998).

3300   Harbourside Centre, Canon's Marsh   Cox, Simon   1997   ST 58465 72433
Two evaluation trenches were excavated, in one of which part of Albert Dock was found (Cox 1998a).

3333   Proposed South Building, Canon's Marsh   Parry, Adrian   1998   ST 58461 72521
Trenching recorded possible indications of industrial activity in the 18th century, an 18th-century culvert and a later 19th-century cobbled area with parallel timbers set at its western end. A rubble wall lying on the north side of this area may have been contemporary with it (Parry 1998)

3334   Entertainment Centre, Frogmore Street   Insole, Peter   1998   ST 58355 72963
A single evaluation trench on the frontage of the site with Frogmore Street recorded a post-medieval stone wall and archaeological stratification beneath approximately 1.3 metres of made ground (Rawes and Wills 1999, 171; Williams 1998, 78; Insole 1998c).

3366   Sheldon, Bush Shot Works, Cheese Lane   Jackson, R G   1998   ST 59428 72902
Evaluation trenches inside the former lead works identified stuctures associated with the early 18th-century glass furnace belonging to Sir Abraham Elton (Jackson 2005; Cox and Jackson 1998).

3369   Queen Square   Insole, Peter   1998   ST 58728 72537
Evaluation to inform the renovation of the square identified dumping of over 2.5 metres of material in the late 17th century to raise the surface of the marsh. A gravel path from the 18th-century laying out of the square as well as a Second World War air raid shelter were also recorded (Rawes and Wills 1999, 171–2; Williams 1998, 80; Insole 1999b).

3375   Sugar House, Lewins Mead   Williams, Bruce   1998   ST 58656 73255
Excavation of a single trench and observation of excavation of a geotechnical trial pit inside the building recorded evidence for two phases of medieval construction on the site, the earliest dating to the late 12th century (Jackson 1998).

3376   60 Redcliff Street   Jackson, R G   1998   ST 59167 72521
Evaluation within the building recorded medieval features, 17th-century garden soils and 18th-century structures, probably including part of the cone of the St Thomas Street Glassworks (Bradley and Gaimster 2000, 247; Wills 2000, 217; Williams 1999, 103; Jackson 1999b).

3386   Graham's Timber Yard, Hotwells Road   Cox, Simon   1999   ST 57812 72539
A single 'L-shaped' trench recorded the wall of Limekiln Dock and part of an ancillary building (Cox 1999, 17–34).

3397   Upper Maudlin Street   Insole, Peter   1999   ST 58675 73379
Two small trenches were excavated to inform the project design for an intended excavation of the site.

3480   Sterling House, All Saints' Street   Leah, Mark   1999   ST 58992 73204
Evaluation of the western half of the site recorded medieval and later features and stratification close to the bank of the river Frome (Williams 1999, 101; Bradley and Gaimster 2000, 247–8; Wills 2000, 216; Barber 1999).

3502   98–103 Redcliff Street   Insole, Peter   1999   ST 59064 72560
Trenches inside and to the south of the building recorded elements of medieval tenements on Redcliff Street, including a section of standing medieval wall, a probable slipway and part of Hort's sugar refinery (Williams 1999, 103; Bradley and Gaimster 2000, 247; Wills 2000, 217).

3516   Central Electric Lighting Station, Temple Back   Parry, Adrian   1999   ST 59393 72838
Two trenches recorded the edge of a post-medieval slip and part of an 18th-century cellared building (Williams 1999, 105–6; Wills 2000, 218–19; Parry 1999b).

3519   Plot 5, Temple Quay   Insole, Peter   1999   ST 59490 72509
Part of the town wall was exposed and recorded, the upper parts surviving within 0.5 metres of the present ground surface (Williams 1999, 105; Wills 2000, 219; Insole 2000c).

3528   Wilson Street   Parry, Adrian   1999   ST 59580 73696
Howell's burial ground was investigated and found to be largely undisturbed. Part of a small early industrial dwelling was also excavated (Williams 1999, 104; Wills 2000, 219; Parry 1999a).

3532   30 Welsh Back   Samuels, Jens   2000   ST 58900 72705
Evaluation recorded elements of Nos 1 and 2 King Street and associated occupation deposits (Williams 2000, 144–5; Ponsford 2001, 131; Wills 2001, 190; Samuel 2000).

3555   Bristol Royal Infirmary, Upper Maudlin Street   Tavener, Nick   1996   ST 58579 73322
Trenches dug on the proposed site for a new childrens' hospital found that the site had been extensively cellared. Some evidence for late 18th- and early 19th-century structures was also recorded (Williams 1996, 84–5).

3589   Johnny Ball Lane   Samuel, Jens   2000   ST 58648 73310
Two trenches on the northern side of the lane recorded the foundations of 18th-century tenements and associated deposits (Williams 2000, 144; Ponsford 2001, 129).

3592   Bryan Brothers, Deanery Road   Barber, Alastair   2000   ST 58103 72633
Elements of 18th-century housing on College Street and part of the surface of College Street itself were recorded (Bradley and Gaimster 2001, 257; Wills 2001, 188; Williams 2000, 142; Barber 2000).

3597   Anchor Road   Insole, Peter   2000   ST 58218 72610
Evaluation recorded a substantial medieval wall which had been reused as the rear wall of 18th-century houses (Williams 2000, 142; Bradley and Gaimster 2001, 257; Wills 2001, 188; Insole 2000a).

3609   Wade Street   Young, Andrew   2000   ST 59850 73472
Housing developed on the site at the beginning of the 18th century was found to be well preserved (Williams 2000, 145; Wills 2001, 191; Young 2000).

3641   Union Street   Jackson, R G   2000   ST 59014 73214
Evaluation of the eastern part of the site recorded a sequence of stratification extending from at least the 16th century (Jackson 2000b).

3654   Pooles Wharf   Erskine, Jonathan   1996   ST 57366 72411
The excavation of the two evaluation trenches at Poole's Wharf confirmed the existence of archaeological evidence for large-scale industrial activity associated with the shipbuilding and repair work known from other sources to have been carried out on this site. It preceded larger excavation work on the site (BHER 3265) (Prosser *et al* 1996).

3672   Georgian House Museum, Great George St   Parry, Adrian   2000   ST 58186 72925
A single trench to the rear of the house recorded elements of the original garden layout dating to the late 18th century. This was overlain by a Victorian garden (Williams 2000, 143; Wills 2001, 189).

3681   118–22 Jacob Street   Hume, Lynn   2001   ST 59757 73139
Evaluation revealed a complex sequence of structural features, largely dating to the 18th and 19th centuries. There was limited evidence for medieval activity on the site (Young 2001).

3707   47 Jacob's Wells Road/Gorse Lane   Erskine, Jonathan   2001   ST 57684 72939
Part of a Cold Bath with Bath stone lining was investigated. The bath building had been converted in the 19th century into a row of cottages, with the bath serving as a coal cellar (Erskine 2001).

3723   30 Gloucester Lane, Old Market   Insole, Peter   2001   ST 59893 73305
Evidence was recovered of an east–west ditch with a possible north–south return, likely to be of Civil War date (Insole 2001b).

3724   Land south of Gorse Lane   Barber, Alistair   2001   ST 57656 72965
A series of 18th-century dump deposits were encountered against a deliberate terracing cut and a brick-built revetment wall-footing. These deposits and features may represent landscaping activity and spoil dumps associated with the construction of the Bellevue properties immediately upslope of the site *c* 1792 (Barber 2001a; Williams 2001, 113; Wills 2002, 241).

3730   6–22 Marsh Street/7–11 Broad Quay   Barber, Alistair   2001   ST 58638 72815
Nine evaluation trenches and seven test pits were excavated. The evaluation established a sequence of
occupation from the late 13th to the 20th century. A possible former channel of the Frome, with waterlogged
deposits including preserved leather and wooden artefacts was recorded. A stone-built structure interpreted
as the remains of a slipway leading to the Frome was recorded, associated with the complex remains of
medieval structures standing to more than 7.5m high in the north wall of 16 Marsh Street; the greater part
of the south wall of the property was probably constructed in the 1620s, after the slipway had gone out of
use (Barber 2001b; Williams 2001, 120; Wills 2002, 239)

3764   College Square   Jackson, R G   2001   ST 58275 72620
The evaluation uncovered archaeological features and deposits of medieval date consisting of a paved stone
surface, pits and occupation layers. Post-medieval path surfaces and layers of dumped material were recorded
(Jackson 2001; Williams 2001, 114; Wills 2002, 236)

3777   Redcross Lane, Old Market   King, Andy   2001   ST 59725 73225
The cut for a 19th-century sewer pipe revealed, in section, stratified deposits dating back to the mid-16th
century and the remains of an unidentified structure of the early 17th century. The construction date for the
standing building was confirmed as early 19th century with the Redcross Lane frontage built directly on top
of an 18th-century wall (King 2001; Williams 2001, 118; Wills 2002, 238).

3798   26–8 St Thomas Street   Townsend, Andrew   2001   ST 59180 72565
Four trenches were excavated revealing features and deposits including buried garden-cultivation soils, masonry
structures, cut-features and construction make-up deposits of medieval and post-medieval date (Townsend
2002a; Bradley and Gaimster 2002, 152; Williams 2001, 116).

3804   18–20 West Street, Old Market   Parry, Adrian   2001   ST 59900 73187
An extensive post-medieval soil horizon, containing 16th-/17th-century pottery was identified, as well as
several features dating ceramically from the period 1680–1750. The remains of a possible 17th-century wall
were also preserved *in situ* beneath a later alleyway, although its character and function were not determined.
Two adjoining 18th-century buildings, one of which was cellared, were sampled by a trench located adjacent
to Waterloo Road. The remains of another 18th-century building were identified behind the West Street
frontage. Wall footings and brick floors belonging to two of the terraced houses in Clarkes Court represented
domestic occupation of the site in the 19th century (Parry 2001c; Bradley and Gaimster 2002, 152; Williams
2001, 119; Wills 2002, 238–9).

3831   George Railway, Temple Gate   Townsend, Andrew   2002   ST 59425 72397
Four trenches were excavated. These contained intact features and deposits that were successfully characterised
as either medieval or post-medieval. No evidence for human occupation of the area prior to the medieval
period was encountered. The features and deposits exposed include a portion of the 13th-century Portwall,
walls and features associated with the 18th-century George Inn and possibly earlier buildings, and soil features
of possibly late medieval date (Townsend and Pilkington 2002; Williams 2004, 110; Wills 2003, 270–1).

3838   18–20 St Thomas Street   Jackson, R G   2002   ST 59158 72670
The archaeological evaluation revealed a substantial area of modern disturbance, possibly a bomb crater,
extending back at least 21 metres from the street frontage. The edges of this disturbance were not defined
except towards the west end of the workshop where it was seen to cut through archaeological deposits. A small
area of undisturbed archaeology was partly excavated revealing an 18th-century stone and brick-built drain
cutting through late 16th- to 18th-century garden soils (Jackson 2002a; Williams 2004, 109; Wills 2003, 269).

3839   22–4 St Thomas Street   Townsend, Andrew   2002   ST 59175 72607
A single evaluation trench was excavated in the front portion of No 24 St Thomas Street revealing intact
archaeological deposits of both medieval and post-medieval date. The features and deposits include buried
soils and masonry structures. One of the masonry structures exposed probably belonged to the original St
Thomas Street frontage (Townsend 2002b; Williams 2004, 104; Wills 2003, 270).

3844   Former Dick Lovett site, Portwall Lane   Townsend, Andrew   2002   ST 59245 72450
Five evaluation trenches were excavated. Features and deposits characterised as post-medieval in date were
exposed including the remnants of the original St Thomas Street frontage and two glass cones and associated
structures of an 18th-century glassworks (Townsend 2002c; Williams 2004, 104).

3849   Quakers Friars   Jackson, R G   2002   ST 59287 73312
A number of structures, features and deposits were revealed which were almost certainly associated with the Dominican Friary, including part of the east range of the Great Cloister and part of the precinct or river wall on the north bank of the Frome. A number of walls dating to the post-Dissolution period were found, perhaps associated with the conversion and sub-division of the friary buildings. The evaluation also found a number of intact burials associated with the Society of Friends and dating from 1670 onwards (Jackson and Stevens 2002; Williams 2004, 107–8; Wills 2003, 271).

3852   Land to rear of Avon Street   Dawkes, Giles   2002   ST 59760 72708
Seven trenches of various sizes were located to identify particular structures of a glassworks dating from the early 18th century. Remains of a late 19th-/early 20th-century glass factory were found in three out of five trenches and appear to survive across the majority of the site, although in an often heavily truncated form. No earlier factory structures were found and it appears that the later rebuilding removed the majority of the earlier phases (Dawkes 2002; Williams 2004, 109).

3855   Marlborough Street   Stevens, David   2002   ST 58908 73514
The evaluation revealed structures possibly associated with the outer buildings constructed following the Dissolution of St James's Priory, or possibly dating to the period of the Priory itself. Later structures probably formed part of houses and commercial buildings that occupied the site in the post-medieval period (Stevens 2002; Williams 2004, 106; Wills 2003, 271–2; Bradley and Gaimster 2003, 220).

3861   Former Courage Brewery site, Counterslip   Jackson, R G   2002   ST 59197 72969
Fourteen trenches were excavated across the site. Ten of the trenches contained late medieval structures or deposits. The other four trenches showed more recent features associated with 18th- and 19th-century activity undoubtedly connected with the sugar refining and brewing industries known to have existed here (Jackson 2002b; Williams 2004, 109; Wills 2003, 270).

3883   25 Redcliff Street   Samuel, Jens   2002   ST 59112 72703
Several medieval deposits and a small amount of structural evidence of the 12th to 15th centuries were unearthed. Early to mid-14th-century kiln waste from the as yet unlocated Bristol/Redcliffe Pottery was also recovered. Numerous post-medieval layers and building remains were also recorded (Samuel 2002a; Williams 2004, 105; Wills 2003, 270; Bradley and Gaimster 2003, 220).

3891   Mitchell Lane, Redcliffe   Townsend, Andrew   2002   ST 59225 72570
A total of six evaluation trenches were excavated revealing intact medieval and post-medieval features and deposits. Vestiges of buildings associated with the medieval street frontages of St Thomas Street and Mitchell Lane were exposed. What appeared to be the remains of medieval buildings were also encountered in areas set back from the street frontages. Possible garden-cultivation soils of the post-medieval, and possibly medieval, periods were exposed (Townsend 2002d; Williams 2004, 104–5; Wills 2003, 270).

3899   18 St Thomas Street   Samuel, Jens   2002   ST 59130 72659
The evaluation consisted of a small sondage which produced definite evidence for the course and approximate extent of the Law Ditch. This was represented by two post-medieval load-bearing building walls which corresponded to property boundaries and the St Thomas/St Mary Redcliffe parish boundary. The culvert constructed between the walls post-dated them and was the latest manifestation of the course of the Law Ditch in the area of the trench (Samuel 2002b; Williams 2004, 110; Wills 2003, 269; Bradley and Gaimster 2003, 220).

3900   Old Bread Street   King, Andy   2002   ST 59636 72868
Six trenches were excavated which revealed structural features and deposits dating from the late 17th century onwards (King 2002; Williams 2004, 108; Wills 2003, 271).

3926   25 Redcliff Street/14 St Thomas Street   Longman, Tim   2002   ST 59108 72717
Two intact lengths of roof of the culverted Law Ditch were located beneath the floor of the former warehouse. One area of probable post-medieval roof was constructed of stone blocks, while the other comprised a 19th-century brick vaulted roof and inspection pit/manhole. A small section of medieval wall was also partially uncovered, as well as several other post-medieval walls and deposits. Survey work at No 14 St Thomas Street involved removing render from the face of a wall and then recording the exposed masonry

and mortar beneath. The middle section of wall proved to be built of stone, probably dating from the 18th or early 19th century, while the eastern and western ends are of late 19th-century brick construction (Longman 2002; Williams 2004, 105; Wills 2003, 270).

3929   Bristol Cathedral   Hollinrake, Nancy   2002   ST 58312 72671
One evaluation trench was positioned within the north-west corner of the Cloisters. The fragmentary remains of the foundations of the inner wall of the West Cloister Walk were recorded along with extensive post-medieval and modern disturbances, services and other features. Two evaluation trenches were positioned within the Undercroft, immediately south-east of the Cloisters, resulting in the recording of a substantial Norman wall foundation oriented east–west within the south part of the room and deep post-medieval deposits in the north-east corner. Those results required two further trenches to be cut within the Undercroft and they confirmed the full width of the Norman foundation and also contained Norman or medieval floor levels and two other early wall foundations (Hollinrake and Hollinrake 2002).

3936   3 Redcliff Street   Colls, Kevin   2002   ST 59061 72715
The evaluation identified a stone-built cellar which had truncated archaeological deposits over much of the evaluation area, with alluvial deposits beneath at 6.50m AOD. A small number of archaeological deposits survived at the northern end of the trench. The foundations of a possible medieval wall were revealed set directly on alluvium at 7.29m AOD. This wall was sealed by a sequence of possible occupation horizons, which in turn were cut by a second possible medieval wall that lay parallel with Redcliff Street (Colls 2002).

3944   Former FPS site, Waterloo Road   King Andy   2003   ST 59873 73177
See 4231 above

3980   Templar House, Temple Way   Colls, Kevin   2003   ST 59443 72622
In the four trenches to the rear (west) of Templar House natural alluvium lay between 6.26 and 6.35m AOD, sealed by two successive clay deposits containing pottery dating to between the 13th and 15th centuries, possibly associated with reclamation of the flood plains from the mid-13th to 14th centuries. Two discrete features cut the uppermost clay deposit and may be associated with the drainage and use of this area for drying cloth. A garden soil dated to the early 18th-century creation of the Spring Garden sealed all these deposits, and in turn was overlain by up to 1.7m of material dumped to raise ground level prior to the development of the Great Gardens Estate in the 1730s. Foundations cutting this deposit, and associated with the creation of the Great Gardens Estate, also survived to the rear of Templar House (Colls 2003).

3983   59–61 Victoria Street   Potter, Kevin   2003   ST 59211 72712
The investigation revealed medieval deposits and archaeology as well as late post-medieval archaeology (Potter 2003; Williams 2005, 136).

3985   22–30 West Street, Old Market   Jackson R G   2003   ST 59920 73190
The evaluation found only limited evidence for medieval occupation on the West Street frontage of Nos 28 and 30 West Street. The remainder of the property seems to have been used as gardens or agricultural land during the medieval period. An 18th-century circular structure with a square central plinth may have had an industrial use or been part of a garden feature. The land at the rear of the premises seems to have been used as gardens during the post-medieval and early modern periods. Fragments of 19th-century walls found on the rear portion of the property formed parts of the buildings shown on contemporary maps (Jackson and Leech 2003).

3990   47 Jacob's Wells Road/Gorse Lane   Erskine, Jonathan   2003   ST 57680 72943
Two earlier stages of evaluation had confirmed that the majority of the footprint of the Bathhouse building had survived from approximately the original ground level. During this final phase of evaluation, unexcavated areas along the east and south of the structure were located and examined to determine the total extent of preservation of the bath structures and associated features in these areas. Further remains of the bathhouse and the attached changing room were recorded in both of these areas, whilst the western wall of the structure was fully exposed and recorded (Erskine 2005; Ducker and Erskine 2004).

4015   100 Temple Street   Barber, Alistair   2003   ST 59300 72463
Three trenches were excavated. Natural estuarine alluvium was encountered between 6.48 and 6.98m AOD and was sealed by a clay deposit suggesting medieval reclamation of the floodplain from the 13th century

onwards. The Law Ditch was identified cutting through this consolidation deposit within trenches 1 and 2. A possible medieval wall footing, associated stone surface, and culvert were recorded on the eastern side of the Law Ditch, within trench 1, within a back plot associated with the Temple Street frontage. Medieval structural remains also appear to survive on the western side of the Law Ditch, within trenches 1 to 3, within tenement plots associated with properties on St Thomas Street. Revetment walls and adjacent areas of hard standing were constructed either side of the Law Ditch during the post-medieval period (Barber 2003; Williams 2005, 136; Wills 2004, 176).

4017   Land to north of Avon Street   Appleby, Stephen   2003   ST 59865 72700
A substantial wall, thought to be associated with land reclamation in the 18th century, was recorded. Several 18th-century basements were recorded. However, there was little evidence for industrial working in the area (Appleby 2003).

4027   Tyndall Avenue   King, Andy   2003   ST 58298 73518
In Trench 1 only bedrock was exposed, part of a cut feature was located in evaluation Trench 2 and deposits containing finds dating from the late 17th century were recovered from trenches 2 and 3. Garden soil and wall footings of the 20th-century housing were also present in trenches 2 and 3 (King 2003; Wills 2004, 176).

4028   32 and 36 Victoria Street   Davis, Liz   2003   ST 59236 72800
Two trenches were excavated at the rear of No 36, and a small test pit at the rear of No 32. The remains of houses fronting on to the pre-war alignment of Temple Street were found, along with deposits underlying the houses. Evidence for the survival of organic remains in the marsh deposits below the houses was also encountered (Davis 2003; Williams 2005, 136; Wills 2004, 176).).

4081   Temple Back   Godden, David   2004   ST 59309 72904
A trench measuring 5m × 5m was excavated to a total depth of *c* 2.7m, which identified an area of ground largely disturbed by 19th- and 20th-century workings, including a number of recent geotechnical test pits and boreholes. Some fragments of glass waste were recovered which are likely to have derived from a glassworks known to have once stood adjacent to the site. No evidence for any structure was revealed, and it is likely that such evidence has either been totally removed by later disturbance, or remains lie to the south-east of the evaluation trench (Godden 2004).

4083   Albion Terrace, Johnny Ball Lane   Davis, Liz   2004   ST 58652 73327
The evaluation trenches uncovered the remains of Nos 2 and 3 Albion Terrace, below which were earlier walls. One of the walls was identifiable as part of the 'Soldiers' Infirmary', and was built against the other, which appeared to be late medieval in date (Davis 2004a; Ponsford 2005, 341; Wills 2005, 152).

4125   Former Courage Brewery, Counterslip   Wragg, Elliot   2004   ST 59195 72978
A large, possibly defensive, medieval ditch with a narrower re-cut was recorded in the west of the site. This was sealed by redeposited alluvium containing 12th-/13th-century pottery, dumped to reclaim this marshy land. The ditch was then replaced by a stone culvert, the Law Ditch, while a series of stone and/or timber structures was constructed within a typical medieval framework of long narrow burgage plots fronting onto the medieval St Thomas Street and Temple Street. Further medieval structural evidence was found further to the east in a plot possibly fronting onto the medieval Counterslip. There was some evidence of a possible decline in activity in the 14th century or change of land use in the western plots, while to the east, more intensive activity appears to have continued. During the 17th/18th centuries further stone structures were constructed across the site, while there was evidence of further land reclamation. During the 18th/19th centuries a new sequence of stone and brick structures was constructed, some of which related to either the brewery or sugar refineries known to have existed on the site (Wragg 2004; Gaimster and O'Conor 2005, 353; Ponsford 2005, 341).

4144   Canon's Marsh   Young, Richard   2003   ST 58240 72555
Undisturbed natural alluvium was encountered between 6.9m and 7.65m AOD. Directly overlying this alluvium were several medieval sandstone walls and an associated surface. These walls are likely to have formed parts of several buildings and gardens that ranged around the southern side of the Outer Court of St Augustine's Abbey and along the lane that linked the Outer Court to Canon's Marsh. The walls were sealed by substantial make-up deposits, principally ash, gravel and rubble, dated to the 17th to 19th centuries. Industrial structures were subsequently constructed in the 19th and 20th centuries (Young 2004; Williams 2005, 133; Wills 2005, 151)

4154   Castle Park   Barber, Alistair   2004   ST 59172 73161
Two medieval cess pits and a north-east/south-west aligned ditch within trench 1 yielded pottery of mid-12th- to 15th-century date, and were sealed by a clay-sand consolidation deposit containing mid-12th- to mid-13th-century pottery. Two robber trenches which cut through this deposit yielded pottery of 19th- to 20th-century date, together with residual medieval sherds, and identify former footings of medieval or post-medieval buildings. Modern drainage structures were also noted, associated with former properties on the northern side of Little Peter Street. Trench 2 revealed the partially-surviving surface of Little Peter Street, together with structural remains associated with a property on its southern side. Within trench 3 the natural sandstone bedrock was directly overlain by modern dump deposits associated with park landscaping (Barber 2004; Gaimster and O'Conor 2005, 353–4; Williams 2005, 134–5; Wills 2005, 152).

4160   Redcliff Backs   Barber, Alistair   2004   ST 59020 72562
Two trenches were excavated across the development area. The evaluation also included observation of four geotechnical trial pits and the logging and assessment of the lithostratigraphic sequence within four geotechnical boreholes. Organic deposits at the base of borehole 1 are potentially of relatively early Holocene date. Further thin organic-rich beds from around 4.5m below present ground level may be contemporary with medieval occupation identified in the evaluation trenches. From the borehole assessment it appeared that medieval deposits extend to a depth of some 6.5m below the existing ground level. Initially, food and other domestic waste were discarded on the foreshore in the vicinity of boreholes 2–4. It was then covered up by further alluvial/intertidal deposition. Subsequently, a revetment was built on a north–south axis through the site separating the area of borehole 1 from areas behind the revetment to the east. Well-preserved waterlogged timbers, of which one was possibly a tieback for a late medieval revetment structure, were revealed in trench 2. Silt and clay layers containing mid-13th- to 15th-century pottery were dumped behind the structure to raise the ground level, thus facilitating the rearward extension of tenement plots extending back from Redcliff Street. Evidence for a medieval building was revealed, together with an adjacent undated wall surviving to present ground level, which may identify a second medieval structure. Evaluation trench 1 revealed an undated stone-built structure that may represent a narrow dock, slipway or similar quayside facility, which had rapidly filled with river silts following its disuse. Walls, cellarage and an associated vaulted structure, constructed over the quayside feature, identify one of a series of post-medieval tenement properties that formerly extended from Redcliff Street to Redcliff Backs (Barber and Cox 2004; Williams 2005, 131–2; Wills 2005, 151–2).

4166   Hannah More School, New Kingsley Road   Davis, Liz   2004   ST 59907 72896
Three trenches were excavated in the car park and playing field. The remains of 19th-century houses and part of an earlier boundary wall were found (Davis 2004b; Wills 2005, 154).

4177   57 West Street, Old Market   Davis, Liz   2004   ST 59916 73330
Two trenches were excavated at the rear of properties on Braggs Lane. Part of a substantial post-medieval wall was found in one trench. This wall may be of 17th-century date, forming the back wall of properties fronting on to West Street. Both trenches revealed remains of rubbish deposits relating to occupation on the site and included some slag and other materials associated with industrial processes. Residual medieval pottery kiln waste was also found (Davis 2004c; Ponsford 2005, 342; Wills 2005, 154)

4197   Wapping Wharf   Havard, Tim   2004   ST 58535 72188
The evaluation identified a former sandstone cliff of Late Pleistocene date running centrally across the site, defining an earlier edge of the River Avon against which alluvial/intertidal silts accumulated. Structural archaeological remains of 18th- to 20th-century date were present across the northern part of the site at varying depths. The earliest deposits represent buildings and surfaces of 18th-/19th-century date associated with a former road known as 'Wapping', a ropewalk, and associated dwellings, yards and workshops. A later (19th-century) dockside building, associated with the early 18th-century West Wapping dry dock, was also recorded in the north-eastern part of the site (Havard and Cox 2004; Ponsford 2005, 342; Williams 2005, 128–9; Wills 2005, 151).

4202   Old Council House, Corn Street   Mordue, Jeremy   2005   ST 58856 73057
See 4244 above (Jackson 2007c).

4221   Marsh House, Marsh Street   Davis, Liz   2005   ST 58694 72802
The northern part of the area was removed by basements in the early 20th century, and here a drainage ditch was found which predated occupation on the site. Samples taken from the drainage ditch and the alluvial

deposits through which it was dug were assessed for geoarchaeological data and the presence of diatoms and pollen. The assessment showed that the alluvial deposits represented a truncated intertidal sequence, but that in the truncated area the preservation of diatoms and pollen was poor (Davis 2005; Wills and Catchpole 2006, 217).

4223   Broadmead (east) and Bond Street   Bingham, Annie   2005   ST 59450 73355
The borehole data identified former watercourses and the extent of made ground across the proposed development area. The 12 trenches and test pits revealed 17th-century to 19th-century deposits, the remains of cellars, and varying amounts of levelling deposits associated with the 19th-century development of the city (Anon 2005; Williams 2006b, 118; Wills and Catchpole 2006, 215).

4230   Former Drill Hall, Old Market Street   Havard, Tim   2005   ST 59670 73120
The evaluation identified 19th-century structural remains of the Old Market Sugar Refinery. These included several walls, a probable cellar, a stone-built base of a chimneystack and a granite sett surface of a haulage way (Havard 2005; Williams 2006a, 100; Wills and Catchpole 2006, 216).

4235   Purimachos site, Waterloo Road, Old Market   Lankstead, Darren   2005   ST 60050 73282
The evaluation revealed the *in situ* remains of the Williams Burial Ground boundary wall, human skeletal material as well as evidence for the post-medieval occupation of the area in the presence of garden soils and industrial structures and deposits (Lankstead 2005a; Wills and Catchpole 2006, 217).

4236   Bristol Royal Infirmary, Upper Maudlin Street   Lankstead, Darren   2005   ST 58616 73562
The archaeological evaluation did not reveal the presence of any archaeology pre-dating the late 18th century. A study of geotechnical data reinforced the evidence obtained from the evaluation concerning the existence of made ground throughout the study area which suggests that considerable dumping of material took place to alter the gradient of the hill-slope before development began in the late 18th century (Lankstead and Jackson 2005).

4241   Great Western Dockyard, Gasferry Road   Ellis, Chris   2005   ST 57843 72378
Archaeological remains relating to the Great Western Steamship Company period include buried walls or wall foundations, drainage and services, a potential machine pit, and floors. These were encountered in Test Pits 1, 2, 3, 4, 7 and 8. Since 1852, the site remained mostly in industrial and commercial use (for example, a shipyard, tannery, granary, bonded warehouse and timber yard). These activities are represented in alterations and additions to the buildings visible in the standing fabric, and archaeologically as tanning pits (in Test Pits 2 and 6), potential pillar or machine bases (in Test Pits 1 and 2) and a railway (in Test Pit 2) (Ellis 2005).

4242   Quakers Friars   Ford, Ben   2005   ST 59270 73343
The evaluation trenches revealed that walls belonging to the Friary buildings survive in places below ground level, as did related deposits such as floor layers and levelling episodes. Evidence was uncovered indicating that the Friary buildings were re-modelled and that they were also reused after the Dissolution. The locations of an 18th-century sugar factory and a 19th-century school on this site were also confirmed (Thacker and Brady 2006).

4246   Gloucester Lane, Old Market   Coleman, Laurence   2005   ST 59888 73270
The evaluation revealed a small area of medieval cultivation soils in the south-west of the site, within which were two medieval pottery wasters, cut through by a cellar of probable Victorian date. The remainder of the deposits encountered related to the deliberate backfilling of the cellar and construction of the car park that presently occupies the site (Cudlip 2005).

4256   Former Cabot House, Deanery Road   Lankstead, Darren   2005   ST 58152 72698
The evaluation revealed the remains of the original 18th- and 19th-century housing and the frontage and basement of a property which lay on the original course of Brandon Street. A substantial depression, filled primarily by 18th-century industrial debris, may also represent the filling of a fishpond immediately prior to the documented development of the area in the 18th century (Lankstead 2005b; Wills and Catchpole 2006, 216).

4258   Tollgate House, Houlton Street   Hiller, Jon   2005   ST 59640 73560
The evaluation revealed layers of probable alluvial clay formed in the medieval period, overlain by deposits of either occupation material or imported soil/rubble used to raise the ground levels above the medieval

levels. The remains of structures of probable 18th-century date, including a sandstone wall and a well were discovered at the south end of Dale Street. Further north, a sandstone and brick wall of probable late 18th-century date was revealed. Here a closely dated group of clay pipes suggests that activity on this part of the site dates at least from the middle of the 18th century. The remains of Victorian brick walls were found in all three trenches towards the top of the sequence, following substantial raising and consolidation of ground levels. These structures represent the remains of outhouses and ancillary structures at the rear of the terraced properties (Hiller 2005).

4261   Redcliff Wharf   Cullen, Kate   2005   ST 58993 72372
No evidence for structures relating to the known earlier 17th-century glasshouse was found. Substantial glass waste deposits dating to the late 17th/early 18th century found throughout all the evaluation trenches do, however, indicate that it lay within the proposed development area. A later drainage system along with flagstone floors and walls all appear to be contemporary with a glass cone base uncovered centrally on the site, and may reflect a large-scale redevelopment with the introduction of the glass cone in the 18th century. Heat-reddened brick surfaces also broadly contemporary with the glass cone may represent annealing oven bases or outlying workshop areas where smithing of glass-making tools may have occurred (Cullen 2005; Williams 2006a, 96; Wills and Catchpole 2006, 217).

4276   Former Drill Hall, Old Market Street   Hart, Jonathan   2006   ST 59677 73102
The evaluation identified structural remains likely to have belonged to the original late 17th-century build of the Old Market (Rodgers) Sugar Refinery and to its 19th-century rebuild. The evaluation also demonstrated that the internal floors of the Drill Hall are likely to be part of the original construction (Hart 2006; Williams 2006b, 118; Wills and Hoyle 2007, 345).

4299   Backfields, Upper York Street   Potter, Kevin   2006   ST 59219 73838
Remains of the 18th-century circular stables were found including two sections of the outer wall (Potter 2006; Williams 2006b, 117; Wills and Hoyle 2007, 347).

4310   Broad Quay   Adam, Neil   2006   ST 58636 72788
See 4342 above

4318   Castle Park   King, Andy   2006   ST 59048 73078
Twenty-four trenches were excavated around the former route of Mary-le-Port Street in the area bounded by High Street, Wine Street and Bridge Street. The fieldwork revealed that extensive cellaring had taken place across the site up to the 1930s. The utilisation of blitzed cellars as a car park in the 1950s, followed by the creation of a park in the early 1970s, has resulted in made ground to depths of over 2m in places and yet medieval archaeology also survives less than half a metre below present ground level in other areas (King 2006a; Williams 2006b, 108; Wills and Hoyle 2007, 344).

4329   Colston House, Colston Street   Heaton, Rachel   2006   ST 58490 73000
See 4369 above

4350   Land adjacent to 90 West Street, Old Market   King, Andy   2006   ST 60040 73323
A cellar was found, the eastern wall of which was at least late 17th century in date. A well was dug in the late 17th century. By the late 18th century outbuildings were being constructed to the rear of the street frontage (King 2006b; Williams 2006b, 119; Wills and Hoyle 2007, 345).

4359   Portwall Lane   Evans, Derek &   2006   ST 59200 72420
                                                                   Saunders, Kelly
Neither the Portwall nor evidence for its removal were recorded during the evaluation. A late 13th- to 14th-century clay deposit present in Trenches 1 and 2 displayed a distinct slope down to the south and probably represents part of the berm indicating that the Portwall itself lies to the north of the evaluation trenches, under the present alignment of Portwall Lane itself (Evans and Saunders 2006; Williams 2007, 145; Wills and Hoyle 2008, 177).

4360   Lewins Mead   Heaton, Rachel   2007   ST 58847 73398
Three trenches were excavated at the Hill House site in Lewins Mead. Remains of a confectionery factory were recorded in all three trenches. Features of medieval date were recorded in Trenches 1 and 3. In Trench

1, the remains of a possible medieval wall, drains and thin deposits containing sherds of 12th- to 14th-century pottery were recorded. In Trench 3, foundations for a possible wall with associated deposits and a 'pit' were recorded, pottery retrieved was dated between the 12th and 15th centuries (Heaton 2007; Williams 2007, 147–8; Wills and Hoyle 2008, 176–7).

| 4388 | Stokes Croft | Ducker, Ray | 2007 | ST 59173 74068 |

The earliest archaeological features located in the evaluation trenches were represented by a series of soil cut features, with primary fills dating from the early 18th century onwards. In Trench 1, the best-preserved section of ditch was shallowly buried and approximately 1.8m deep. Undated soil layers possibly from a flattened or slighted bank were also recorded to the south of the ditch. Extensive evidence of subsequent 18th- and 19th-century residential and commercial buildings was also located (Ducker 2007; Williams 2007, 149).

| 4394 | Welsh Back | Havard, Tim | 2007 | ST 58923 72481 |

The evaluation has identified two phases of riverside reclamation, dating to the 19th and 18th century respectively. Structural features that probably relate to an open-sided late 19th-century precursor of the current M Shed were also encountered (Havard 2007a).

| 4397 | Redcliff Wharf | Havard, Tim | 2007 | ST 58982 72382 |

Evidence for land reclamation was recorded along the waterfront, taking place at least from the 18th century. Wharf walls, pre-dating the existing 19th-century waterfront, were recorded. Further evidence for the structures of an extensive 18th-century glassworks was recorded within the northern and eastern areas of the site, including brick floors and flues, supplementing evidence from a previous phase of evaluation in 2005. A fragment of a high temperature flue with vitrified surfaces from glassworking, previously recorded in a 1989 investigation was re-exposed. This may have formed part of a large glass cone depicted on 18th-century maps, but no other structural remains of this were encountered in the evaluation. Deposits containing considerable quantities of glassworking waste were recovered, often in association with deposits of primary waste, including kiln furniture, from the manufacture of tin-glazed earthenware and stoneware; these derived from a 18th-century pottery manufactory, which must have been in close proximity to the site. The plan form and some floor surfaces of a 19th-century warehouse and Counting House, and part of a residential dwelling were recorded (Collard 2007; Williams 2007, 146; Wills and Hoyle 2008, 178).

| 4398 | Favell House, Crow Lane | Stevens, David | 2007 | ST 58888 72791 |

The results of the evaluation confirmed that human burials are still present within the burial ground. Although the northern end of the trench was disturbed it must be considered possible, and indeed likely, that the remaining area of the site also contains numerous burials (Stevens 2007; Williams 2007, 149; Wills and Hoyle 2008, 179).

| 4404 | 16 Redcross Street, Old Market | Young, Andrew | 2007 | ST 59652 73237 |

Seven archaeological evaluation trenches, including an additional trench (Trench 7), were opened at agreed locations within the footprint of the site. The trenches identified subterranean deposits and structures of probable medieval and post-medieval date alongside features of later post-medieval and modern origin (Young 2007; Williams 2007, 150).

| 4413 | Quakers Friars | Havard, Tim and Barber, Alistair | 2007 | ST 59265 73314 |

The investigations identified evidence for dump deposits and a raising of ground levels, from the medieval period onwards. Evidence was recorded for structures relating to the original construction and later alterations to the east end of Cutlers Hall, which formed part of the Greater Cloister of the 13th-century Dominican Friary, a covered claustral walk or passage around the east side of the Lesser Cloister and possible evidence of a former building or buildings relating to the former east range of the Lesser Cloister, one of which, it was suggested, was partly incorporated into the later Quaker Meeting House. Within the Meeting House further evidence was revealed for the raising of floor levels and construction of supporting sleeper-walls, interpreted as dating from the 1747 rebuilding of the 17th-century Meeting House. Within the Bakers Hall and the Cottage medieval walls were exposed together with evidence for later floor surfaces (Havard 2007b).

| 4414 | Castle Park | Whatley, Stuart | 2007 | ST 58980 73002 |

Four trenches were excavated: Trench 44 within the basement of the Norwich Union building, Trench 45 (divided into areas A and B) located along Bridge Street and part of Castle Park, Trench 47 along Mary-le-Port

Street and finally Trench 48 within the raised ground of the Norwich Union building. The fieldwork revealed that extensive cellaring had taken place across the site up to the 1930s. The excavation of Trench 44 revealed a 19th-century Pennant sandstone floor surface cut into the natural clay. Within Trenches 45A and 45B, the remains of cellars from the former Nos 30–5 Bridge Street were located. The majority of these cellars and walls dated from the late 18th century but there were a few wall foundations, deposits and pits dating from the medieval period. Within Trench 48 the remnants of a medieval barrel vaulted cellar was uncovered containing later post-medieval and early modern walls (Whatley 2007; Williams 2007, 144; Wills and Hoyle 2008, 175–6).

| 4415 | St Pauls Park | Etheridge, David | 2007 | ST 59550 73760 |

A single archaeological trial trench was opened. Within the trench were six recumbent grave ledger slabs, apparently *in situ*, together with two soil cut features interpreted as earth cut graves. Surviving inscriptions on the grave ledger slabs indicate they originated from the first half of the 19th century (1808–50) (Etheridge 2007).

| 4422 | Tyndall Avenue | King, Andy | 2007/8 | ST 58338 73496 |

Four evaluation trenches were excavated on Bristol University land at Tyndall Avenue, Clifton, Bristol; this area was the site of an English Civil War citadel known as the Royal Fort. In December 2007 two additional trenches were excavated revealing a stony-clay deposit, believed to be levelled rampart material, as well as the footings of an 18th-century greenhouse and 19th-century structures. In January 2008 two trenches were excavated inside the former nurses accommodation block exposing one lip of a large cut feature and fill deposits extending over 2.7m below ground level. The nature of the fill and dating evidence indicate that the feature is part of a ditch associated with the Royal Fort (King 2008; Williams 2008–9a, 137; Wills and Hoyle 2009, 308).

| 4426 | Jacob Street, Old Market | Cullen, Kate | 2007 | ST 59729 73118 |

Two trenches were excavated within the development area. A similar sequence was identified in both trenches, primarily the natural red sand overlain by garden soils which had been subsequently disturbed by the construction of the existing building which originated as an 18th-/19th-century malthouse and/or brewery (Cullen 2007; Williams 2007, 150; Wills and Hoyle 2008, 177).

| 4440 | Temple Way | Young, Andrew | 2008 | ST 59490 72910 |

Two trenches were excavated. In trench 1 the alluvium was encountered at *c* 6m above OD. Over the alluvium a series of dumped deposits, dated by stratified pottery to the 17th and early 18th centuries, were thought to represent consolidation of the marsh and included domestic rubbish and quantities of industrial waste. A wall foundation and an indeterminate shallow soil feature may be broadly contemporary as was an adjacent small posthole. Later deposits and structures in the southern part of the trench included part of a masonry and brick-built structure of possibly industrial function, perhaps part of a kiln or furnace, and provisionally dated to the 18th to 19th century. A later structure at the northern end of trench 1 may represent remnants of residential premises (Anon 2008; Williams 2008–9a, 138).

| 4442 | Redcliffe Village | Unknown | 2007 | ST 59160 72660 |

Thirteen trenches were excavated across the development area. Evidence for activity from the 12th/13th centuries onwards was identified behind the Redcliff Street frontage in the western half of the development area, including possible medieval hearth, drains, pits, walls and floor surfaces. The evaluation also identified the post-medieval line of the Law Ditch (Cullen and Barber 2008; Williams 2008–9a, 135; Wills and Hoyle 2009, 306–7).

| 4445 | Cabot Circus (east) | Webster, Jon | 2008 | ST 59627 73584 |

The evaluation revealed evidence for the substantial dumping of deposits in the 19th century. These deposits were sealed by demolition debris dated to the 1950s, relating to post-war redevelopment of the area (Webster 2008; Wills and Hoyle 2009, 306–7).

| 4474 | Wine Street/Union Street | Adam, Neil | 2008 | ST 59009 73152 |

The evaluation uncovered a sequence of re-deposited soil and clay layers. These layers were excavated up to 3.86m below current ground level from where a single sherd of pottery dating from the 12th century was recovered (Adam 2008b; Wills and Hoyle 2009, 307).

| 22333 | Clifton Hill House | Wood, Jennifer | 2004 | ST 57554 72925 |

An evaluation was carried out in the garden of Clifton Hill House by the University of Bristol.

24642   St James's Priory   Longman, Tim   2008   ST 58895 73470
Small areas of walls were stripped of plaster, within the church, and of render, externally. Most of the walls exposed were found to be of late 18th- or 19th-century date, or later. However, a few sections of late medieval and early post-medieval walling were exposed (Longman and Bryant 2008).

24643   St Michael's Church   Roper, Simon   2008   ST 58520 73300
Six small investigative trenches were excavated below the floor of the crypt or undercroft at St Michael-on-the-Mount Church. Beneath the ledgers and floor slabs were found capping stones for burial shafts or vaults, and in one instance the top of a brick vault, mostly within about 150–250mm of the modern floor level. One vault was opened up, to reveal a number of coffins, the uppermost of which lay at about 980mm from the present floor surface (Bryant 2008).

24691   Merchants Almshouses, King Street   Adam, Neil   2008   ST 58700 72710
Two trenches were excavated. The evaluation established the presence of wall foundations associated with the former west wing of the Merchants Almshouses, constructed in the late 17th century. These foundations were themselves established upon what appeared to be the foundations of an earlier building. The former Marsh Wall was not exposed, although a combination of auger survey and observations of subsidence affecting neighbouring standing buildings suggests the route predicted in an earlier desk-based assessment is reasonably accurate (Adam 2008c; Williams 2008–9a, 139; Wills and Hoyle 2009, 306).

24712   26–8 Tyndall Avenue   King, Andy   2009   ST 58315 73487
See 24786 above

24757   Full Moon Hotel, North Street   Hume, Lynn   2009   ST 59083 73641
Late post-medieval and modern activity was represented by a series of intercutting drains and other services. Evidence for earlier activity was represented by two possible postholes, complete with *in situ* post packing, and a highly truncated cut soil feature, possibly the base of a pit. All three features were cut into a deep subsoil deposit that yielded a small assemblage of residual medieval pottery and were themselves dated by pottery to the late 17th and 18th centuries (Hume 2009; Williams 2008–9b, 151–2).

24769   38 Victoria Street   Hughes, Justin   2009   ST 59230 72780
Two trenches, 8m and 2.3m long were excavated in a car park to the rear of the existing building known as Canningford House. The investigation confirmed the location of the western edge of the former route of Temple Street. The remains of a cellar, constructed with rubble stone walling of probable 17th- to 18th-century date was recorded. A section of a possible late medieval wall was also recorded (Hughes 2009; Wills and Hoyle 2010, 234).

24813   College Square   Hogg, Ian   2010   ST 58204 72644
Natural clay was overlain by a sequence of alluvial deposits. A large wall ran north–south across the site, this probably dated to the 17th century. The ground levels were significantly raised during the 18th century so that the first floor of the 17th-century building was level with the basement of buildings from the 18th-century phase (Hogg 2010).

24827   Westmoreland House, Stokes Croft   Brett, Mark   2009   ST 59161 74064
Two trenches were excavated. The evaluation encountered a number of walls and surfaces, as well as cut features, such as pits and features most likely associated with cultivation. The results of the evaluation indicate that the site is not likely to have been developed until the earlier part of the 18th century (Brett 2009).

24865   15 Marlborough Hill   Potter, Kevin   2010   ST 58579 73695
The archaeological evaluation revealed partial remains of a 19th-century brick building that fronted Kingsdown Parade, within the grounds of No 5 and a deeper sequence of modern deposits sealing a red brick wall and possible mortar surface, of unclear provenance, within the grounds of No 6 Kingsdown Parade. Three phases of construction of No 15 Marlborough Hill were identified, comprising late 18th-century remnants within a largely 19th-century building plus later 20th-century and modern alterations (Potter 2010; Williams 2010–11, 52).

24943   Royal Fort   Israel, Richard   2010   ST 58236 73343
In October 2010, Richard Israel of the University of Bristol carried out an archaeological evaluation on the site of the Royal Fort.

25047   Brandon Hill   King, Andy   2011   ST 57891 72976
Two archaeological trial trenches were excavated across the line of features assumed to be part of English
Civil War-era fortifications at the top of Brandon Hill Park. The upper bastion defensive ditch was found
to be steep-sided with a flat base and contained approximately 100 years of silting but no dating evidence.
It had been deeply recut in the late 1890s. Contrary to established belief, the standing masonry walls and
earth bank of the upper bastion were in fact a 'folly' dating from the later 18th century (King 2011; Wills
and Hoyle 2012, 309).

25077   Unity Street, Old Market   Hume, Lynn   2012   ST 59687 73041
A total of six evaluation trenches were opened across the site. The natural weathered sandstone substrate was
reached in two of the six trenches where it was overlain at around 13m OD by soil deposits that produced
pottery sherds dating from the 12th to 13th centuries. Associated medieval features at this level were restricted
to a truncated cut soil feature, possibly part of a gully or beam slot. Later structures and deposits of post-
medieval origin, some reflecting industrial activity, were exposed. These latter structures correspond broadly
with the layout of former buildings and structures shown on mid-19th-century and 20th-century maps of
the site. The deep masonry foundations of a substantial stone building were also revealed. The form and
fabric of the structure, in combination with a suite of ceramics recovered from the backfill of the wall cut,
suggested an early 18th- or possibly late 17th-century date for its construction although the fabric could be
earlier (Hume 2012).

25120   Bristol General Hospital, Redcliffe   Brett, Mark   2012   ST 58846 72169
Four trenches were excavated across the eastern part of the development site. The trenches uncovered evidence
for deposits pre-dating the early development of the site during the 18th century, including a small quantity
of medieval pottery. The remains of 18th-century houses fronting on to Guinea Street were uncovered, as
well as boundary walls and features within the back garden areas of the properties. Structures relating to
18th-century and later industrial development use of the site, and mid-19th-century terraced housing were
recorded within the site, away from the main street frontages. Deep dumped deposits dating to the early to
mid-18th century contained large quantities of waste from industrial glass production (Brett 2012).

25162   Oncology Centre, Horfield Road   Ducker, Ray   2012   ST 58590 73454
The evaluation involved the excavation of a trench across the line of Terrell Street, which revealed extensive,
deep, made-ground deposits that sealed a layer of topsoil, indicating that Terrell Street did not lie in this
location (Ducker 2013).

25199   Wesley Chapel, Horsefair   Mason, Cai   2013   ST 59083 73403
The evaluation uncovered substantial structural remains of two 18th- or early 19th-century cellared buildings,
which formed part of a group of tenements known as Pim's Court. Beyond the cellared area there was a
sequence of dump layers containing mid-17th- to early 18th-century finds (Mason 2013a; Wills 2014, 255).

25282   New Bridewell, Rupert Street   Jackson, David &   2014   ST 58863 73301
                                                                          O'Meara, Don
Two trenches were excavated in the north-east corner of the site at the junction of Bridewell Street and Rupert
Street Six geoarchaeological boreholes were also carried out revealing a deep sequence of palaeoecological
layers to a thickness of c 9m under the present building (O'Meara 2014).

25283   Wade Street/Little Ann Street   Mason, Cai   2013   ST 59829 73501
Early 18th-century cut features and well-preserved structural remains of 18th- and early 19th-century tenements
were recorded. The earliest buildings (along the Wade Street frontage) were constructed between c 1710 and
1720. During the later 18th- and early 19th-century infill development (Swan Court and Pratten's Court)
resulting in a densely built up area of low quality housing that was demolished as part of a slum clearance
project initiated in the 1930s (Mason 2013b; Williams 2012–13, 53; Wills 2014, 259).

25334   Guildhall, Small Street   Barber, Alistair   2014   ST 58804 73101
Cotswold Archaeology carried out an archaeological evaluation at the Guildhall. (Barber 2015; Williams
2014–15a, 98)

25342   Plot 3, Temple Quay   Mason, Cai   2014   ST 59704 72587
An archaeological evaluation at Plot 3, Temple Quay, Bristol, uncovered structural remains of Isambard
Kingdom Brunel's early 1840s Dock and Goods Shed and associated dockside structures, together with

structural remains of a late 1870s rebuilding (Greig and Mason 2014; Williams 2014–15a, 98; Wills 2015, 245).

25346	St Mary Redcliffe	Roper, Simon	2014	ST 59146 72344

A substantial structure located in Trench 1 is probably a retaining wall suggesting a significant difference in height between the churchyard and the buildings which originally fronted on to Pile Street, confirmed by the great depth of dump deposits found in most of the trenches. With the exception of the probable retaining wall, all the other structural remains encountered were close to the surface and probably of 19th-century date (Roper 2014; Williams 2014–15a, 97; Wills 2015, 245).

25773	Queens Building, Woodland Road	Unknown	2014	ST 58204 73267

An archaeological evaluation was carried out at the University of Bristol, Queens Building, Woodland Road (Wills 2015, 247).

25407	Central Fire Station, Temple Back	Barber, Alistair	2014	ST 59291 72818

A disturbed silt-clay alluvial deposit, possibly a trampled or re-deposited layer overlying undisturbed riverine alluvium, contained 12th- to 13th-century pottery within its upper levels. Soil horizons overlying this deposit contained 12th- to 15th-century pottery, suggesting an initially undeveloped area, perhaps utilised as garden, within tenement plots to the rear of medieval properties fronting Water Lane. A stone wall footing and subsequent wall rebuild, of the 14th to 15th centuries was also found (Barber 2014b; Williams 2014–15b, 102).

25410	Albert House, Temple Street	Barber, Alistair	2014	ST 59297 72550

An east–west-aligned medieval ditch, cut through consolidation deposits, was noted within Trench 1. Its primary fill contained 12th- to 13th-century pottery and 12th- to 15th-century pottery was recovered from its tertiary fill. Successive silt deposits, associated with 12th- to 15th-century pottery, encountered within Trenches 2 and 3 appear from their form, location and extent to represent fills of a north–south-aligned section of medieval Law Ditch within the south-western part of the site (Barber 2014c).

25438	Wesley Chapel, Horsefair	Roper, Simon	2014	ST 59080 73399

The evaluation of the courtyard of the New Room Chapel identified mostly 19th-century remains, with one trench providing evidence of 17th- to 18th-century activity. Trench 2 provided the most interesting results with the back wall of the outbuildings of The Horsefair identified. The Horsefair properties were 17th century, however the rear wall was 19th century and built on top of a probable garden soil of 17th-century date. Beneath this was possibly a make-up layer, the base of which was not found, at 1.8m below the existing ground surface. Whilst the evaluation provided evidence of earlier post-medieval activity on the site, no medieval deposits or features were encountered (Roper 2015).

25445	Bristol General Hospital, Guinea Street	Barber, Alistair	2014	ST 58851 72171

Trenching revealed estuarine alluvial silts overlain by consolidation layers in Trenches 1 and 2a/2b, and probable hillside terracing in Trench 3a, associated with preparation of the site for post-medieval and later development. Sandstone wall footings and brick-built drainage structures were encountered within the area of a former 19th-century iron foundry and Rankin's Sugar House depicted on Ashmead's 1828 map of Bristol (Barber 2014d).

25557	Former Ambulance Station, Marybush Lane	Williams, Bruce	2015	ST 59384 73067

Seven trenches totalling in length 84 linear metres were excavated at agreed locations; however, neither the castle wall or gateway to the King's Orchard were found, although it is thought the wall may lie closer to the subterranean culvert that traverses the site from west to east, more or less following the course of the former castle moat. A substantial rock-cut feature, probably a ditch, was revealed in one trench lying surprisingly close to the modern-day land surface. Pottery from the ditch suggests it may have been filled between the middle of the 11th and middle of the 12th centuries. Its location at the eastern edge of a plateau of higher ground, together with its size suggests it was intended for a defensive purpose, possibly as part of the town's Saxo-Norman fortification. As such the filling of the ditch may coincide with the construction of the ward and keep castle (Williams 2015; Williams 2014–15b, 102).

Landscape surveys

192	Civil War defences, Brandon Hill	Ponsford, M W	c 1988	ST 57926 72868
481	Redcliff Caves, Redcliff Wharf	Ponsford, M W	c 1988	ST 58943 72309

| 3336 | Civil War defences, Brandon Hill | Russell, J R | 1993 | ST 57926 72868 |
| 3377 | Bristol Castle | RCHME | 1990 | ST 59283 73144 |

Geophysical surveys

3479	Royal Fort	University of Southampton	1999	ST 58260 73340
4085	Portwall Lane (N side)	Stratascan	2004	ST 59242 72440
4156	Portwall Lane	Geophysical Surveys of Bradford	2004	ST 59202 72422
4205	St Paul's Churchyard, Portland Square	Barker, P and Tomkinson, K	2000	ST 59475 73746
4306	Castle Park	Stratascan	2006	ST 59017 73048
4391	St Pauls Park	Arrow Geophysics	2006	ST 59548 73767
4432	Royal Fort	University of Bristol	2007	ST 58293 73356
24648	St Michael's Church	Stratascan	2008	ST 58519 73300
25389	Backfields, Stokes Croft	AGC	2007	ST 59221 73827
25477	Royal Fort	University of Bristol	2015	ST 58295 73342
25478	Clifton Hill House	University of Bristol	2015	ST 57552 72921

Watching briefs

| 3 | Temple Quay | Pilkington, Jayne | 1998 | ST 59523 72578 |

Observation of geotechnical trial pits at Temple Quay recorded 18th- to 19th-century features, including a culvert, and timbers of unknown function.

| 22 | Avon House, St James Barton | Jackson, R G | 1970 | ST 58980 73520 |

Observation of groundworks for the construction of Avon House, St James Barton recorded no archaeological features.

| 37 | Swallow Royal Hotel, College Green | Dawson, David P | 1970 | ST 584807 2710 |

19th-century coffin furniture and 18th- and 19th-century ceramics were recovered during clearance of St Augustine-the-Less churchyard.

| 46 | Colston House, Colston Street | Pritchard, John E | 1904 | ST 58520 72990 |

Observation of construction on the site of the Carmelite Friary recorded medieval walls and inhumations.

| 58 | Telephone House, Queen Charlotte Street | Dawson, David P | 1969 | ST 58896 72788 |

Observation of groundworks during construction of the office block failed to record any evidence of St John's Chapel.

| 60 | Bristol Cathedral School | Boore, Eric | 1985 | ST 58350 72620 |

A contractor's trial trench at Bristol Cathedral School immediately to the west of the Palliser Martin Hall and 7.5 metres south of the north arcade was observed. The trench was located on the site of the lesser cloister of St Augustine's Abbey. Measuring approximately 1 metre by 0.8 metres, the trench exposed a concrete slab forming the foundations of the hall.

| 63 | St Peter's Churchyard, Castle Park | Price, Roger H | 1972 | ST 59110 73060 |

Parts of Norton's House/St Peter's Hospital and other medieval buildings were recorded.

| 83 | St Nicholas Church, St Nicholas Street | Bryant, John | 1984 | ST 58930 72930 |

Observation of works to the west end of the nave of St Nicholas Church recorded the town wall, evidence for an earlier wall as well as a 5th bay for the church, and post-medieval inhumations.

| 123 | Temple Back | Bryant, John | 1982 | ST 59600 72600 |

Observation of the excavation of engineer's trial holes located sections of the Portwall and Brunel's Dock between Tower Harratz and Temple Meads station.

| 124 | 131–7 Redcliff Street | Williams, Bruce | 1982 | ST 59000 72800 |

Part of a medieval slipway and dock wall were recorded.

126 Castle Park Ponsford, M W 1970 ST 59230 73170
Part of a medieval timber building, possibly a stable, was recorded.

127 Castle Park Ponsford, M W 1971 ST 59210 73180
Foundations of a section of the wall of Bristol Castle, and possibly part of New Gate, were recorded.

128 Castle Park Ponsford, M W 1971 ST 59232 73177
The line of the west curtain wall of Bristol Castle was traced.

131 Castle Park Ponsford, M W 1971 ST 59240 73100
M W Ponsford of the Department of Archaeology, City of Bristol Museums and Art Gallery observed the stub of a buff-mortared wall which lay below the 17th-century levels. This was interpreted as a possible ward division.

132 Castle Park Ponsford, M W 1971 ST 59210 73080
A structure abutting the curtain wall of Bristol Castle was recorded. It was interpreted as the south-west gate of the castle.

134 Castle Park Ponsford, M W 1971 ST 59220 73170
The north-west corner of the keep of Bristol Castle was recorded, together with a wall containing an arch to the north.

135 Castle Park Ponsford, M W 1971 ST 59180 73110
Observation of the castle ditch in front of the west curtain wall of Bristol Castle.

204 St Peter's Hospital, Castle Park Pritchard, John E 1900 ST 59120 73050
Alterations to the fabric of St Peter's Hospital were observed.

225 St James's Church Dawson, David P 1974 ST 58886 73467
Observation of late medieval rubble and post-medieval burial vaults at St James's Church

233 Colston Street Pritchard, John E 1913–14 ST 58510 73000
During excavations associated with the new Bristol Gas Company Offices in Colston Street in October 1913 and early 1914 John Pritchard found human remains and several tiles.

234 Northcliffe House, Colston Avenue Pritchard, John E 1913 ST 58620 73090
Observation of construction of government offices at Northcliffe House, Colston Avenue, recorded post-medieval cellars and finds.

240 Welsh Back Squash and Health Centre Price, Roger H 1974 ST 58930 72650
Observation of groundworks during construction noted 19th-century dumped material against the quay wall and 17th-century material. No significant archaeological features were recorded.

279 94–8 Redcliff Street Jones, Robert H 1989 ST 59060 72530
Observation recorded medieval structural elements, including a blind arch. A 13th-century wall founded on elm piles was also noted.

290 Horsefair Bryant, John 1991 ST59057 73392
Observation of construction of an extension to the Mark's and Spencer store, Horsefair noted no archaeological features.

291 11–12 Lower Park Row Bryant, John 1987 ST 58520 73140
Observation of geotechnical trial holes recorded cellar walls and an earlier boundary between Nos 12 and 13.

295 Spectrum House, Bond Street Bryant, John 1982 ST 59354 73589
Observation of construction recorded no features of archaeological significance.

298 48 Queen Square Bryant, John 1985 ST 58670 72514
Only the cellar was examined. Finds were made below the cellar floor, mainly 17th/18th century in date.

299 Trinity Street, College Green Bryant, John 1989 ST 58470 72670
Observation of reduction of the ground level at Trinity Street recorded a stone drain to serve the houses which formerly stood on the south side of the street.

301   Merchant's Quay   Beckey, Ian   1984   ST 58715 72275
Observation during construction at Merchant's Quay noted a large brick culvert and 19th-century ceramic waste.

308   26–31 St Augustine's Parade   Bryant, John   1983   ST 58534 72943
Redevelopment at St Augustine's Parade was observed.

311   Myrtle Road, Kingsdown   Bryant, John   1992   ST 58460 73658
Observation during construction of the University of Bristol Veterinary School recorded remains of Nos 30–2 Southwell Street.

315   Greyfriars, Lewins Mead   Ponsford, M W   1973   ST 58711 73335
Observation of groundworks identified walls of the church and claustral buildings of the Franciscan Friary.

345   Bristol Cathedral   Boore, Eric   1982   ST 58407 72690
A trial archaeological trench was excavated along the external east face of the eastern Lady Chapel of Bristol Cathedral and along the north face of the buttress. The chapel and buttress foundations were of roughly dressed blocks of Brandon Hill Grit with some Pennant sandstone. Both foundations were bonded in a reddish-orange mortar and were of a single-phase construction, contemporary with the early 14th-century eastern Lady Chapel.

347   Castle Park   Burchill, Rod   1995   ST 59198 73103
Conservation work on the west curtain wall of Bristol Castle was observed and the wall recorded.

348   35 Corn Street   Bryant, John   1995   ST 58761 72975
Construction of a beer-drop was observed.

350   New Gate and Union Street   Jones, Robert H   1986   ST 59086 73128
Part of a town wall, possibly associated with the Burgesses' Revolt of 1312–15 was observed.

352   Nelson Street and Tower Lane   Ponsford, M W   1970   ST 58820 73200
Development of the office buildings was observed.

354   Castle Park   Boore, Eric J   1977   ST 59102 73085
Medieval and post-medieval walls were observed in trenches dug for tree planting in front of the west end of St Peter's Church.

366   43 Broad Street   Bryant, John   1992   ST 58815 73128
Some features were noted in the party wall with No 44 after it was stripped of render. Related work, to demolish the single-storey extension in Tailors Court at the rear of No 43, took place in April–May 1993, and was observed in part. Evidence of a possible medieval building was revealed.

381   46–9 Old Market   Bryant, John   1986   ST 59766 73236
Post-medieval features were recorded. Indications were also noted of the possible line of the Great Ditch.

410   Castle Park   Williams, Bruce   1995   ST 59237 73083
Conservation work on the south and west curtain walls of Bristol Castle, exposed during landscaping work in 1992, noted no new medieval features, though the remains of a post-medieval wall were found immediately in front of the south curtain wall.

421   Phoenix House, Redcliff Hill   Dawson, David P   1970   ST 59013 72300
Observation during construction work noted pits containing ceramic waste from medieval kilns. These were excavated, and the waste recovered.

427   St John's Steep   Pritchard, John E   1911   ST 58860 73200
Observation of the demolition of St John's Gate, St John's Steep.

434   Bristol Grammar School, Tyndall's Park   Burchill, Rod   1993   ST 58010 73393
A large pit, interpreted as a stone quarry, was observed during construction of the Technology Centre.

438   Temple Quay   Pilkington, Jayne   1998   ST 59573 72587
Circular vats or furnaces of a 19th-century alum factory were recorded during observation of groundworks.

453 Broad Quay House, Narrow Quay Webb, F G 1956 ST 58622 72633
Sections of the hulls and structural timbers from at least five post-medieval ships were observed in the remains of Aldworth's Dock during construction of an extension to the CWS building.

469 Castle Park Williams, Bruce 1992 ST 59300 73100
Sections of the south and west curtain walls of Bristol Castle were recorded during landscaping work in Castle Park. The position of St Peter's Pump was also noted.

471 Dental Hospital, Upper Maudlin Street Cross, Lesley 1993 ST 58717 73420
Observation of groundworks on the site of the Moravian burial ground recorded *c* 200 post-medieval inhumations within brick shafts, burial vaults and earth-cut graves. Coffin furniture was recovered. Part of All Saints' conduit was also recorded.

477 St James's Churchyard Insole, Peter 1996 ST 58895 73424
Observation of groundworks in St James's Churchyard recorded disarticulated human remains and a modern structure. No archaeologically significant features were recorded.

490 St James's Parade Little, Bryan 1962 ST 58933 73460
Demolition of Nos 9–12 St James's Parade was observed.

491 11–12, Broad Quay Webb, F G 1961 ST 58627 72805
Observation of groundworks during redevelopment recorded no significant archaeological features.

534 St George's Road Jackson, R G 1984 ST 58020 72645
Large quantities of 18th-century ceramic waste from the Limekiln Lane potteries was recovered during observation of construction.

536 7–8 King Street Jenner, Michael 1967 ST 58841 72709
Alterations to the fabric of the buildings were observed.

539 St Michael's Church, Kingsdown Burchill, Rod 1996 ST 58520 73720
Observation of rebuilding of a boundary wall to the churchyard noted post-medieval burial vaults. 13th- or 14th-century ceramics were recovered from possible colluvium beneath the churchyard.

544 Lord Mayor's Chapel, College Green Barker, W R 1892 ST 58393 72836
Observation of restoration work noted evidence for seven phases of building and some evidence for the plan of the Hospital of St Mark.

574 Gravel Street, Lewins Mead Kent, Oliver and 1973 ST 58760 73400
             Maggs, P
A large quantity of clay tobacco pipe waste was observed in Gravel Street during groundworks for construction of offices in Lewins Mead.

578 Engineering Building, Park Row Bryant, John 1994 ST 58210 73150
Observation of groundworks for the construction of the Engineering building recorded a length of a large mid-17th-century ditch previously identified by evaluation. The ditch possibly belonged to Essex Work, part of the Civil War defences.

606 Courage's Brewery, Counterslip Bryant, John 1985 ST 59220 72930
Medieval features, including walls and an oven, and post-medieval features were recorded during observation of the construction of a keg store.

655 12 Lower Park Row Bryant, John 1987 ST 58510 73151
Work inside the building was observed and features of the medieval building recorded.

671 94 Redcliff Street Jones, Robert H 1989 ST 59080 72530
During observation of demolition and building works part of an arch was recorded in the north wall of the building.

696 62–6, Victoria Street Ponsford, M W 1981 ST 59295 72705
Renovation of the buildings was observed.

714   Houlton Street   Bryant, John   1995   ST 59720 73630
             Observation of development recorded part of No 46 Wellington Road and noted substantial dumps of
             18th- and 19th-century material.

1687   Walsingham House, St James's Church   Jackson, R G   1995   ST 58876 73445
             Observation following archaeological excavation recorded medieval inhumations at the south end of the site.

1730   44–50, Jacob's Wells Road   Burchill, Rod   1996   ST 57724 72913
             Observation of groundworks recovered a small quantity of 12th-century pottery. A well and drain of 18th-
             or 19th-century date were also recorded.

2520   Central Register Office, Quakers Friars   Evans, David R   1995   ST 59272 73318
             Minor internal works to the remains of the Dominican Friary, Quakers Friars were observed.

2831   St Nicholas Church   Bryant, John   1986   ST 58937 72939
             Observation of a partial reflooring of the Lower Church of St Nicholas Church recorded six brick-lined
             burial shafts of 18th- or 19th-century date and parts of gravestones.

2832   Welsh Back   Williams, Bruce   1989   ST 58925 72575
             Observation during redevelopment on the site of C and D transit sheds recorded the medieval bank of the
             River Avon 16 metres back from the existing quay wall. Three stages of post-medieval reclamation were also
             identified.

3017   Wine Street   Pritchard, John E   1914   ST 58940 73092
             Observation of demolition of 'Southey House' noted cellar walls c 2m thick. At the rear was a moulded plinth
             and fragments of tracery believed to be of medieval date. A small quantity of medieval pottery was recovered.

3026   Swallow Hotel, College Green   Boore, Eric J   1989   ST 58490 72730
             An intact, decorated, lead coffin with a breastplate carrying the legend 'T.T. 1818' was recovered during
             groundworks and recorded prior to reinterment elsewhere. The lead coffin contained an internal one of
             wood (possibly of elm).

3027   Trinity Street   Boore, Eric J   1988   ST 58415 72670
             Observation of groundworks recorded 18th- to 19th-century walls.

3031   82 Castle Street   Pritchard, John E   1927   ST 59180 73080
             Demolition of the building was observed.

3033   St Nicholas Church   Bryant, John   1983   ST 58939 72933
             The stripping of plaster from the south wall of the lower church or crowde of St Nicholas Church was
             observed.

3035   5–8 High Street   Pritchard, John E   1914   ST 58920 73033
             Demolition of Nos 5–8 High Street was observed. A semi-base from a transitional Norman column was noted.

3036   Fitzhardinge House, Tower Lane   Boore, Eric J   1980   ST 58862 73165
             Development of the site excavated in 1980 was observed. Further elements of the Norman building were
             recorded.

3037   Baptist burial ground, Old Market Street Bryant, John   1982   ST 59570 73190
             Inhumations were observed along the east edge of the site and a post-medieval cellar and wells in other areas.

3040   25–6, Small Street   Read, W F   1922   ST 58815 73045
             During observation of demolition evidence was found that the building had been a timber structure, probably
             of 15th-century date when a great hall occupied the space of the two rooms of the later building.

3053   Clare Street   Pritchard, John E   1910   ST 58632 72930
             Observation of groundworks during construction of an extension to the Sun Assurance Co. building.

3076   Haymarket   Mason, Edward   1954   ST 59020 73440
             Commercial excavation for the construction of the John Lewis building, on the east side of the street known
             as St James's Churchyard, was observed to identify any burials or inhumations. None were recorded.

3079   Burton's Almshouses, St Thomas Street   Marochan, Keith   1958   ST 59185 72743
Observation of demolition of the almshouses noted that the structure was mainly of 13th-century date and the structure may have originally been more extensive than the elements which survived into the 20th century.

3125   Pithay   Pritchard, John E   1906   ST 58955 73145
During observation of development in 'the Pithay district' a bone pin, pottery and animal remains were found at depths of between *c* 6m and *c* 13m from the ground surface.

3141   Vintry House, Wine Street   Larcombe, S   1957   ST 58983 73121
Part of the town wall was recorded during observation of development.

3143   Temple Church   Longman, Tim   1995   ST 59333 72720
Eight post-medieval burial vaults were recorded during observation of groundworks for the laying of a path on the south side of the church.

3153   Fry's Chocolate factory, Pithay   Pritchard, John E   1900   ST 58965 73140
Observation of groundworks recovered medieval ceramics and possible prehistoric material, which was located at a depth of *c* 4m beneath the floor of a cellar.

3154   St Peter's Church   Boore, Eric J   1980s   ST 59097 73087
An archaeological watching brief undertaken during tree planting by the west front of St Peter's Church revealed brick burial shafts of 18th- or 19th-century date which had apparently been cleared of human remains and backfilled with demolition rubble.

3161   Vaulted Chambers, Castle Park   Insole, Peter   1996   ST 59372 73132
Conservation work inside the building was observed.

3209   1 and 2, Christmas Street   Pritchard, John E   1910–11   ST 58726 73164
Observation of construction of a building for Fry's factory in Quay Street recovered medieval and post-medieval finds. Alluvium was removed to Mercia mudstone beneath.

3243   Walker Street   Burchill, Rod   1996   ST 58451 73716
Observation of groundworks recorded 19th-century walls and cisterns. Evidence of earlier quarrying was also noted.

3255   Elbridge House   Unknown   1990   ST 59743 73414
Parts of 19th-century structures were recorded during observation of groundworks. Finds of mid-19th-century date were also recovered.

3259   St Michael on the Mount Primary School   Erskine, Jonathan G P   1997   ST 58486 73230
Observation of groundworks recorded 17th-century walls terracing the hillside. An 18th-century cesspit and associated finds and 19th-century walls were also recorded.

3264   1 Wine Street   Jackson, R G   1997   ST 58894 73061
Works in the cellar of the building were observed. It was noted that the wall of Christ Church had been used as the northern wall of the cellar.

3266   Bristol Cathedral School, College Green   Boore, Eric J   1979   ST 58402 72636
Observation of construction recorded a medieval dovecote and post-medieval walls.

3267   Bristol Royal Infirmary, Upper Maudlin Street   Burchill, Rod   1997   ST 58616 73376
Observation of groundworks recorded an undated well and a 19th-century drain gout.

3275   Broad Quay   Burchill, Rod   1997   ST 58625 72716
An archaeological watching brief was carried out during the construction of a new flood relief sewer. The works consisted of the excavation of three deep trenches, each approximately 4 metres square, and located immediately north of Broad Quay House, in the centre of the southern carriageway of Broad Quay and in the centre of Broad Quay opposite the end of Marsh Street. The brick arch of Mylne's Culvert was exposed. The remains of wood shuttering was found *in situ*. The second square trench, in the centre of the southern carriageway of Broad Quay (centred on ST 58629 72720), a backfilled cellar was exposed immediately beneath

the road surface, and its walls (constructed of Pennant sandstone rubble) were observed. Beneath the cellar was a deposit of made ground which sealed a brown clay layer roughly 1 metre thick. Under this was a spread of medium to very large stones, gravel and clay. It was aligned north-east to south-west but did not appear to form a cohesive or recognisable structure. The stone was mainly Brandon Hill Grit, and it was noted that the spread was similar to the material that formed the base for the Marsh Wall to the east.

3276   Canon's Marsh   Cox, Simon   1997   ST 58493 72567
Observation of excavation for services noted the continuation of a possible medieval wall previously recorded at U Shed, the line of Tomb's Dock and other 18th- and 19th-century features.

3277   Horsefair   Burchill, Rod   1997   ST 58949 73379
Six inhumations from St James's Churchyard were recorded during re-landscaping work.

3275   Broad Quay   Burchill, Rod   1997   ST 58625 72716
Observation of three deep excavations recorded an area of stonework, of similar construction to the base of the Marsh Wall at Venturers' House, outside the line of the wall. The top of a brick arch forming an extension to Mylne's Culvert was also recorded.

3290   Canon's Road   Cox, Simon   1997   ST 58382 72728
Observation of service diversions recorded part of a late 13th- or early 14th-century rubble wall, probably associated with St Augustine's Abbey, as well as later post-medieval walls, including parts of the northern and southern walls of Tomb's Dock. A stone culvert was also recorded.

3291   College Green   Boore, Eric J   1992   ST 58382 72728
Near the north porch of Bristol Cathedral a small area of cobbling and crushed oolitic limestone, believed to be associated with the rebuilding of the nave of the cathedral in the 19th century, was found. The area was found to have been disturbed by works associated with the lowering of the level of College Green in the 1950s.

3292   Bristol Cathedral School   Boore, Eric J   1987   ST 58336 72615
Observation of groundworks for the construction of a new 6th form block recorded part of the wall of the lower cloister of St Augustine's Abbey and a medieval arched stone culvert.

3293   Swallow Royal Hotel, College Green   Boore, Eric J   1989   ST 58490 72730
Observation of groundworks for construction of the hotel recorded 18th- to 19th-century burial shafts from the churchyard of St Augustine-the-Less, walls, and a stone retaining wall in the south-east corner of the site

3294   Bristol Cathedral, College Green   Boore, Eric J   1992   ST 58298 72663
Groundworks for a proposed visitor centre at the west end of the nave were observed.

3309   Governor House, Canon's Marsh Gas Works   Erskine,   1998   ST 57990 72523
                                                     Jonathan G P
Groundworks on the site were observed although excavation was not ultimately deep enough to disturb archaeological stratification. The surviving elements of the Governor House were also photographed. A borehole excavated close to Gasferry Road was noted to produce medieval ceramics and butchered animal remains.

3326   Castle Park   Boore, Eric J   1995   ST 59170 73150
In 1975 or 1976, during work to landscape the Castle Park, a large hole was dug by contractors using a mechanical excavator a little to the south-east of the lower part of (the street) New Gate. This revealed one or more features (possibly a medieval wall), which were recorded by the team then excavating the site at Peter Street.

3332   45 Kingsdown Parade   Pilkington, Jayne   1998   ST 58648 73837
Monitoring of groundworks for construction of flats recorded no archaeological features.

3335   St Matthias Park/River Street   Cox, Simon   1998   ST 59580 73380
Observation of the excavation of a new section of sewer in a children's play area at the junction of the two streets recorded the remains of the rear part of post-medieval properties fronting on New Street and, at a depth of *c* approx. 5 metres from the ground surface a ditch, cut into alluvium, and probably on the line of the boundary of the medieval county of Bristol.

| 3337 | U Shed, Canon's Road | Longman, Tim | 1998 | ST 58510 72560 |

Observation of groundworks for redevelopment recorded no features of archaeological significance.

| 3338 | Greyfriars, Lewins Mead | Price, Roger H | 1973 | ST 58756 73356 |

Observation of development recorded features associated with the Franciscan Friary, notably a large arched conduit.

| 3365 | Temple Quay, Temple Back | Parry, Adrian | 1998 | ST 59621 72676 |

Monitoring of the insertion of a new sewer recorded several 19th-century features including the walls of Brunel's Dock.

| 3368 | St John's Church, Broad Street | Pilkington, Jayne | 1997 | ST 58758 73169 |

Conservation works to the crypt of the church were monitored and elevations of the walls made when these had been stripped of plaster.

| 3371 | New World Square, Canon's Marsh | Longman, Tim | 1997 | ST 58384 72477 |

Construction of the new public square and associated underground car park was monitored.

| 3372 | Explore at Bristol, Canon's Marsh | Longman, Tim | 1997 | ST 58399 72558 |

Groundworks for the construction of the new science exploratory were observed.

| 3373 | Quakers Friars | Cox, Simon | 1998 | ST 59254 73311 |

Enhancement work to the streetscape at Quakers Friars was monitored. A fragment of wall likely to be of medieval date was found to the east of the former meeting house. The wall on the east side of a covered walk leading from Rosemary Street to the meeting house.

| 3383 | Fiennes Court, Fairfax Street | Burchill, Rod | 1998 | ST 59014 73204 |

Observation of geotechnical works recorded no archaeological material of significance.

| 3384 | Sugar House, Lewins Mead | Burchill, Rod | 1998 | ST 58642 73252 |

Observation of geotechnical works noted a stone wall.

| 3464 | 2 Trenchard Street | Beachus, Kevin | 1999 | ST 58494 73006 |

In March 1999 during refurbishment works inside No 2 Trenchard Street a trench, measuring 2.4 metres long by 1.1 metres wide, was excavated by workmen. The trench was located in the south-east corner of the building and disturbed a quantity of human remains. These were disarticulated having been disturbed in antiquity (associated finds indicating that this had probably been in the 17th century) and reburied. In the northern section of the trench a cellar wall was observed. This wall was 0.9 metres wide, was bonded in a grey-white mortar, and survived to a height of up to twelve courses. It had apparently been reused as the foundation for a wall of an adjoining property. Excavation of a second trench, roughly 2 metres long by 1 metre wide identified a cellar with a brick-vaulted roof which had been infilled in the 19th century.

| 3478 | Bridge Parade | Pilkington, Jayne | 1999 | ST 59051 72899 |

Observation of piling work noted that the depth of made ground increased from the east part of the site to the west. Little archaeological information was gathered during the work, however.

| 3497 | Castle Park | Burchill, Rod | 1999 | ST 59278 73128 |

Observation of groundworks associated with the installation of a tethered balloon failed to record any archaeological finds or features.

| 3500 | Haymarket | Longman, Tim | 1999 | ST 58992 73458 |

Excavation of pits for four lighting columns in the central reservation was monitored but no archaeological features or finds were recorded.

| 3508 | Temple Quay, Temple Back | Pilkington, Jayne | 1999 | ST 59608 72574 |

Monitoring of groundworks recorded the remains of 18th- and 19th-century structures, some associated with buildings on the east side of Portwall Lane and with the 1840s railway goods shed north of Temple Meads station.

| 3515 | Queen Square | Etheridge, David | 1999 | ST 58770 72560 |

Groundworks associated with the restoration of Queen Square were observed.

3517   Centre   Burchill, Rod   1999   ST 58577 72842
Monitoring of works associated with redesign of the Centre recorded elements of the quay walls infilled in the
late 1930s and socketed granite blocks which probably formed the bases for the columns of Transit Shed A.

3521   2–3 Redcliff Street   Brett, Alex   1999   ST 59089 72728
Observation of the excavation of geotechnical trial pits found evidence of surviving archaeological stratification
across the site, particularly east of the Redcliff Street frontage. It was also noted that there was high potential
for the survival of organic material below 6.75 metres OD.

3522   Rackhay   Parry, Adrian   1999   ST 58839 72782
Laying of a gas main through the extension cemetery for St Nicholas Church at Rackhay was observed and
a quantity of human remains recovered for analyis.

3523   St George's Road   Bryant, John   1999   ST 58035 72595
The terracing of the garage buildings into the hillside was found to have removed all archaeological material.

3530   60 Redcliff Street   Pilkington, Jayne   1999   ST 59152 72522
Monitoring of the excavation of geotechnical trial pits recorded no archaeological features.

3533   Wapping Wharf   Pilkington, Jayne   1999   ST 58143 72215
Groundworks for housing development were monitored. Structures associated with the use of the site as a
rail yard in the 19th century were observed.

3536   Former Blind Workshops, St George's Road Burchill, Rod   2000   ST 58225 72883
Monitoring of the excavation of groundworks recorded no archaeological features.

3550   The Red Lodge, Park Row   Bryant, John   2000   ST 58432 73119
Two trenches to investigate the foundation of a wall of the Red Lodge were observed.

3554   Bristol Brewery, Counterslip   Insole, Peter   2000   ST 59169 72988
Drilling of boreholes across the site was monitored and samples recovered for analysis.

3566   Temple Quay, Temple Way   Insole, Peter   2000   ST 59528 72643
Monitoring of groundworks recorded the base of a clay tobacco pipe kiln dating to the early 20th century.

3577   48–54 West Street   Insole, Peter   2000   ST 59957 73264
During monitoring of groundworks a large medieval ditch was recorded on the street front. Evidence for
later structures on the site was also found.

3581   Brygstow House, 5 Welsh Back   Townshend, Andrew 2000   ST 58916 72862
Monitoring of groundworks revealed medieval structures and well-preserved associated organic finds.

3582   60 Redcliff Street   Pilkington, Jayne   1999   ST59192 72535
Observation of geotechnical trial pits recorded no archaeological features.

3583   98–103 Redcliff Street   Insole, Peter   2000   ST 59060 72541
Observation of geotechnical trial pits recorded the foundations of standing historic structures within the site.

3586   Upper Maudlin Street   Pilkington, Jayne   1999   ST 58695 73404
Disarticulated human remains from the Moravian burial ground were found at the north-eastern end of the
site. These finds included three incomplete skulls and a number of other bones. Parts of a lead coffin and
coffin furniture, including a coffin plate, were also recovered.

3595   Central Electric Lighting Station, Temple Back   Pontin, Lawrence   2000   ST 59317 72896
Observation of geotechnical pits recorded no archaeological features.

3628   Wilson Street   Parry, Adrian   2000   ST 59588 73700
Observation of groundworks recorded a small 18th-century house as well as the cellars and ancillary structures
of Nos 7–11 Wilson Street.

3642   1–13 St Paul's Street   Samuel, Jens   2000   ST 59515 73665
Groundworks during redevelopment of the site behind the retained façade of Nos 1–13 were monitored and
archaeological material associated with the late 18th-century buildings recorded.

3644   2–5 Montague Place   Pilkington, Jayne   2000   ST 58534 73743
Monitoring of groundworks recorded elements of the Kingsdown Brewery.

3691   Redcliff Backs   Cox, Simon   1999   ST 59035 72473
The watching brief followed archaeological excavation of the site (see 3501 above).

3706   100 Temple Street   Hume, Lynn   2001   ST 59335 72517
No significant archaeological finds or features were observed during the work.

3728   40 Corn Street   Cox, Andrea   2001   ST 58810 72980
Monitoring of refurbishment works revealed 19th- and 20th-century features and two deposits of earlier date. A 1m high thick wall running north-west/south-east across the site was of medieval date. The construction of 18th- and 19th-century cellars had removed much of the evidence for earlier activity.

3762   Prewett Street   King, Andy   2001   ST 59250 72245
The main features were a well with an adjacent brick-vaulted water tank associated with the malthouse and another well and water tank beneath one of the two Georgian houses to the south-west. 20th-century underground brick and concrete encasements for fuel tanks had also been constructed on the site. Waste material from the workings of a nearby glass cone had been freely used to raise ground level, possibly as infill for a basement beneath the malthouse.

3765   Tyndall Avenue   Longman, Tim   2001   ST 58220 73525
Reduction of the ground level across the site exposed the backfilled cellars of a late Victorian terrace on Tyndall Avenue.

3771   Former Courage Brewery, Bath Street   Unknown   2001   ST 59095 72923
See 3770 above

3779   13–17 Broadmead   King, Andy   2001   ST 59280 73375
Walls of late 18th-century construction were identified together with a small section of late medieval wall, probably part of the Dominican Friary. The stratigraphy exposed showed disturbance from demolition deposits up to 2m below the level of modern ground surface.

3796   22–4 Queen Square   Townsend, Andrew   2001   ST 58864 72498
The excavation of the test pits exposed a layer of very dark ashy soil from which artefacts dating to the late 17th and early 18th centuries were recovered (pottery sherds and fragments of clay tobacco pipe).

3821   2 Leonard Lane   Bryant, John   2002   ST 58710 73053
Parts of the subterranean structure appear to be medieval in origin, although much has either been rebuilt or repointed. Above ground the building may previously have seen use as a stable and/or warehouse; the basement floors were until recently connected with cellars both beneath the lane and beyond in what is now St Stephen's Street.

3823   Deanery Road   Unknown   2000   ST 58134 72624
Groundworks associated with redevelopment of the site were monitored.

3827   98–103 Redcliff Street   Insole, Peter   2000   ST 59063 72569
During groundworks evidence for the ground plans of several medieval tenements and a stone slipway on the line of Ferry Street was recorded.

3952   Marlborough House, Marlborough Street   Price, Roger   *c* 1980   ST 58950 73615
Groundworks for the construction of the Marlborough House office building were monitored.

3954   17 Wade Street   Longman, Tim   2003   ST 59772 73510
An archaeological watching brief was maintained during groundworks associated with the construction of an extension to No 17 Wade Street

3959   Castle Park   King, Andy   2003   ST 59187 73080
An archaeological watching brief was maintained during the excavation of cable runs and column bases for the insertion of Closed-Circuit Television columns in Castle Park.

3965   University Walk, Tyndall's Park   Longman, Tim   2003   ST 58274 73272
An archaeological watching brief was maintained during groundworks associated with the construction of two new buildings for the Faculty of Engineering, University of Bristol on the southern side of University Walk. No archaeological features or finds were recorded during the work.

3967   30 Gloucester Lane, Old Market   King, Andy   2003   ST 59896 73305
An archaeological watching brief was maintained during groundworks associated with redevelopment of No 30 Gloucester Lane, Old Market. A possible medieval wall was found beneath the pavement in Gloucester Lane and a further 4–8m of the Civil War ditch was found, previously identified in excavation.

3968   20 St Thomas Street   Longman, Tim   2003   ST 59176 72665
An archaeological watching brief was maintained during the excavation of a trench in the footway outside No 20 St Thomas Street. No archaeological features were recorded during the work.

3974   11–12 Portland Square   Kenyon, David   2001   ST 59460 73657
An archaeological watching brief was maintained during groundworks associated with development at 11–12 Portland Square.

3976   Montague Street   Davis, Elizabeth   2003   ST 58895 73645
The monitoring of groundworks carried out before and after the main excavation recorded evidence of further garden walls and cellar features (see also 3977 above).

3978   Water gate, Temple Quay   Townsend, Andrew   2003   ST 59569 72620
An archaeological watching brief was carried out during groundworks associated with the creation of a presentation scheme for the Water gate (1418M) at the northern end of the Portwall.

3991   Gorse Lane, Jacob's Wells Road   Unknown   2003   ST 57679 72942
An archaeological watching brief was maintained during groundworks associated with development at Gorse Lane, Clifton (see also 3707 above).

3995   St Mary Redcliffe   Burchill, Rod   2003   ST 59095 72276
The excavation of a small trench for a memorial stone in the churchyard of St Mary Redcliffe was monitored.

4009   Cherry Lane and Charles Street   Heaton, Rachel   2003   ST 58988 73682
An archaeological watching brief was maintained during groundworks associated with redevelopment of a site between Cherry Lane and Charles Street.

4011   Wapping Wharf   Bryant, John   2003   ST 58540 72185
An archaeological watching brief was maintained during geotechnical works and contamination survey works at Wapping. The remains of the old dry dock, where Brunel's first great ship the *Great Western* was built, were located. A possible structure associated with a nearby timber yard was also found. Substantial depths of made ground were noted in the centre of the site and towards its western end. Iron-working slag and glass cullet were found in several pits, also a few objects, dating back as far as the 17th century.

4014   Penn Street and Wellington Road   Mordue, Jeremy   2003   ST 59450 73322
An archaeological watching brief was maintained during geotechnical works on the two culverts of the River Frome between Penn Street and Wellington Road. The crown of the Frome culvert as well as both north and south edges were identified.

4016   Avonside Ironworks   Stephenson, A and   2004   ST 59864 72699
                                                      Alexander, M
The excavation of a new sewer on the former site of the Avonside Ironworks between Barton Road and Avon Street and on the southern side of Avon Street was monitored in a watching brief at Temple Quay North, Bristol.

4072   Canon's Marsh   Chapman, Mike   2003   ST 57990 72500
An archaeological watching brief was maintained during remediation works to deal with contamination on the site of the Canon's Marsh Gasworks.

4073   Little George Street   Longman, Tim   2002/3   ST 59778 73547
Development groundworks were monitored during the extension of the Salvation Army hostel in Little George Street. This work failed to record any archaeological features or deposits of any significance.

4074   Narrow Quay   King, Andy   2004   ST 58589 72429
A watching brief was carried out during groundworks at the Arnolfini Gallery, Narrow Quay. Three 19th-century wall footings representing parts of the original layout of the 1832 Bush warehouse were exposed. A mixed layer of Pennant sandstone demolition rubble was present across the excavation up to 900rnrn in depth. A slab of worked timber was recovered from beneath the 19th-century foundations. The timber would originally have formed part of a 'knee' brace within the hull of a boat or ship.

4075   18–20 West Street   King, Andy   2004   ST 59898 73190
A watching brief during groundworks was carried out associated with redevelopment of Nos 18–20 West Street, Old Market (see 3858).

4086   157–9 Kingsland Road   Townsend, Andrew   2004   ST 60219 72658
An archaeological watching brief was maintained during groundworks associated with the construction of an extension to Nos 157–9 Kingsland Road. The vestiges of what appeared to be 19th-century working-class housing were observed.

4091   10–14 Cheese Lane   Mordue, Jeremy   2004   ST 59425 72908
In March 2004 an archaeological watching brief was maintained during groundworks associated with development at Nos 10–14 Cheese Lane (see 3806).

4126   Courage's Brewery, Counterslip   Wragg, Elliott   2004   ST 59195 72979
In May 2004 archaeological monitoring of the excavation of geotechnical trial pits within the site of Courage's Brewery was carried out (see also 24838).

4128   3–6 Wilson Street   Lankstead, Darren   2004   ST 59552 73687
An archaeological watching brief was maintained during groundworks associated with redevelopment at Nos 3–6 Wilson Street, St Paul's. The reduced level dig revealed an extensive deposit comprising the debris derived from the demolition of the previous buildings. Further trenching revealed *in situ* deposits which may have been derived from the backfilling of the original basements as well as a small portion of the original street frontage.

4129   Cumberland Road   Bryant, John   2004   ST 57008 72157
The excavation of trenches forming part of the preparatory works for refurbishment of the railway overbridge at Cumberland Road was observed. Excavation removed the trackbed, comprising approximately 0.3 metres of stone ballast, which covered a layer of redeposited red sandstone (probably Redcliffe Sandstone) approximately 0.3 metres thick. Beneath was estuarine alluvium which did not appear to have been disturbed.

4133   Plot 1b Temple Quay   Longman, Tim   2004   ST 59528 72738
An archaeological watching brief was maintained during groundworks associated with development at Plot 1b Temple Quay. The foundation of the west wall of the Alum Works was located during the watching brief, but no other structures were recorded associated with it. The foundations of several walls were recorded on the site of the former clay tobacco pipe works and several pipe stems (kiln waste) were recovered, but no floors, kilns or deposits of unfired pipe clay were recorded.

4134   118–22 Jacob Street   Potter, Kevin   2004   ST 59750 73138
An archaeological watching brief was maintained during groundworks associated with development at Nos 118–22 Jacob Street (see also 4088).

4148   22–30 West Street   King, Andy   2004   ST 59909 73196
An archaeological watching brief was carried out at Nos 22–30 West Street (see also 4146).

4150   Albion Terrace, Johnny Ball Lane   Davis, Elizabeth   2004   ST 58650 73326
An archaeological watching brief was carried during groundworks at Albion Terrace, Johnny Ball Lane (see also 4149).

4153   Old Bread Street   Townsend, Andrew   2004   ST 59716 72880
An archaeological watching brief was maintained during the groundworks associated with construction of new loading bays at Gardiner's Builders Merchants, Old Bread Street. Features of 18th- 19th- and 20th-century date were encountered.

4159   Redcliff Backs   Unknown   2004   ST 59019 72562
In August 2004 geotechnical investigations to the rear of Huller House, on the west side of Redcliff Backs were monitored.

4162   134–50 Hotwell Road   Ducker, Raymond   2004   ST 57438 72485
An archaeological watching brief was maintained during groundworks associated with the development of housing at Nos 134–50 Hotwell Road. Deposits recorded during the watching brief comprised modern made-up ground material overlying archaeologically sterile pennant sandstone and clays of geological origin. No significant archaeological deposits or finds were located during the course of the development work.

4174   22 Tyndall Avenue   Longman, Tim   2004   ST 58304 73522
An archaeological watching brief was carried out during ground works associated for development of a car park between the H H Wills Physics Building and No 22 Tyndall Avenue. No archaeological features or deposits were observed other than the remains of a brick and sandstone wall associated with an Edwardian terraced house that formerly stood on the site.

4214   Merchant Street   Hirons, Heather   2005   ST 59147 73387
An archaeological watching brief was carried out during groundworks for the insertion of a kiosk on the western side of Merchant Street in Broadmead.

4220   St Peter's Church   Longman, Tim   2005   ST 59107 73092
The excavation of a pit for a baseplate for a new lightning conductor on St Peter's Church was monitored.

4224   Broadmead (east)   Palmer, Samantha   2005   ST 59450 73357
The drilling of a series of boreholes in the eastern part of Broadmead and the area to the east of Bond Street was monitored (see also 4280, 4281)

4229   53 Old Market Street   Bryant, John   2005   ST 59742 73164
An archaeological watching brief was maintained during groundworks associated with construction of an extension at the rear of the Mason's Arms, No 53 Old Market Street.

4245   22–4 Queen Square   Whatley, Stuart   2005   ST 58875 72491
A watching brief was carried out during groundworks associated with construction at the site of Nos 22–4 Queen Square. Revealed in the watching brief were the remains of two houses and the former Bell public house fronting Bell Avenue and No 25 Queen Square.

4247   24a Orchard Street   Potter, Kevin   2005   ST 58456 72936
An archaeological watching brief was carried out during works to No 24a Orchard Street. The watching brief revealed the presence of back-filled deposits in the yard area behind the building.

4249   New Kingsley Road   Longman, Tim   2005   ST 59865 72945
An archaeological watching brief was maintained during groundworks associated with the construction of a new sports hall for Hannah More Infants School, New Kingsley Road.

4250   8–22 Hotwell Road   Cudlip, David   2005   ST 57778 72568
An archaeological watching brief was maintained during groundworks associated with the construction of an extension to Mardyke House, Nos 8–22 Hotwell Road. No features or deposits of archaeological interest were observed during groundworks and no material pre-dating the modern period was recovered.

4252   Broad Quay   Unknown   2005   ST 58610 72858
An archaeological watching brief was maintained during groundworks for a new pumping main in Broad Quay. A section of 17th-century wall sited on the former dockside was recorded.

4257   Broadmead   Sims, Mike   2005   ST 59550 73450
An archaeological watching brief was carried out during the diversion of telecommunications cabling at Broadmead (see also 4280, 4281).

4262   Marsh Street   Whatley, Stuart   2006   ST 58693 72805
A watching brief was maintained during development at Marsh House, on the eastern side of Marsh Street. No features or deposits of archaeological significance were observed during the intrusive groundworks.

4268   160–2 Hotwell Road   Heaton, Rachel   2006   ST 57418 72498
An archaeological watching brief was maintained during groundworks associated with the development of housing at Nos 160–2 Hotwell Road. No features or deposits of archaeological significance were observed during the intrusive groundworks.

4274 Queen's Parade Potter, Kevin 2006 ST 57979 72675

The excavation of a trench for the insertion of an electricity cable at Queen's Parade, Brandon Hill was monitored. Underlying the turf was a deposit of dark brown garden soil containing late 19th-century material including plastic. At *c* 500mm below the modern ground surface was a deposit of sandy grey mortar. At the north-east end of the trench was a deposit of mixed 19th-century building rubble and 17th-century kiln wasters overlying an electricity cable installed in the 1980s. The kiln waste comprised kiln furniture including shelves, girders, saggars and also fragments of tin-glazed earthenware vessels. It is suggested that the tin-glazed earthenware waste can be attributed to the Limekiln Lane pottery.

4282 Wade Street Young, Andrew 2006 ST 59815 73530

An archaeological watching brief was maintained during groundworks associated with development at Wade Street.

4283 Westmoreland House, Stokes Croft Longman, Tim 2006 ST 59178 74050

The excavation of geotechnical trial pits at Westmoreland House, Stokes Croft was monitored. No features or significant deposits were observed.

4293 9–10 Charles Street Potter, Kevin 2006 ST 58956 73680

An archaeological watching brief was carried out at Nos 9–10 Charles Street. An old Lias limestone wall, possibly a former field or garden wall, was recorded. The remains of the former St James's Parish Hall, built at Nos 9–10 in 1899 but later blitzed, had been reconstructed as a two-storey warehouse after the war. Parts of the old No 8 also survived. The watching brief revealed two earlier walls and a drain, and one wall that represented the foundations of an internal wall of the Hall.

4294 The Crescent Centre, Temple Back Price, Roger H 1979 ST 59403 72749

A group of pits containing pottery waste from the Temple Back pottery was exposed during groundworks associated with the construction of The Crescent Centre, Temple Back.

4295 Frogmore Street MacIntyre, H and 2006 ST 58402 72982
    Slator, J

An archaeological watching brief was maintained during the excavation of a new sewer between Frogmore Street and St Augustine's Parade. An assemblage of 37 artefacts was recovered from the test pits. This consisted predominantly of post-medieval pottery sherds and animal bone fragments with a small number of tile fragments, slate fragments, clay tobacco pipe fragments and an oyster shell piece. Datable artefacts such as pottery, tile and tobacco clay pipe indicate that the assemblage is dominated by post-medieval and modern finds.

4297 King Street Unknown 2006 ST 58808 72714

An archaeological watching brief was carried out during the construction of two underground chambers and associated storage pits in King Street.

4298 26–8 Gloucester Lane Unknown 2006 ST 59903 73329

An archaeological watching brief was maintained during the groundworks associated with development at the rear of Nos 26–8 Gloucester Lane, Old Market (see 24787)

4303 Terrell Street Heaton, Rachel 2006 ST 58620 73550

An archaeological watching brief was maintained during groundworks associated with the development of a new cardiothoracic unit at Terrell Street within the Bristol Royal Infirmary precinct.

4304 55 Victoria Street Lankstead, Darren 2006 ST 59210 72710

An archaeological watching brief was maintained during groundworks associated with the redevelopment of the former Hartwells garage at No 55 Victoria Street, Redcliffe.

4311 23–35 St George's Road Unknown 2007 ST 58139 72769

An archaeological watching brief was maintained during groundworks associated with development at Nos 23–35 St George's Road.

4314 Phoenix House, Redcliff Hill Heaton, Rachel 2006 ST 59015 72248

An archaeological watching brief was carried out at Phoenix House, Redcliff Hill. The groundworks revealed that the ground had been heavily disturbed by modern service trenches and through the original construction of Phoenix House. However, the remains of early 19th-century structures (cellar wall and cistern) were recorded on the western side of the development.

4315   St James's, The Horsefair   Lankstead, Darren   2006   ST 58956 73383
An archaeological watching brief was carried out during groundworks associated with the construction of two kiosks at St James's, The Horsefair. No features or deposits of archaeological significance were observed during the intrusive groundworks.

4323   Backfields Industrial Estate   Potter, Kevin   2006   ST 59225 73825
The excavation of trial pits to assess the presence of asbestos at Backfields Industrial Estate, Backfields was monitored. The depth of the excavations was insufficient to encounter the underlying archaeology and, with the exception of trench 8, no deposits pre-dating the modern period were encountered. Trench 8 uncovered a south-east to north-west oriented wall running along its east section. The wall was constructed from evenly sized sandstone blocks bonded with dark grey ash mortar. It is likely that this wall is a part of a south-east to north-west wall recorded on the OS.

4328   11–16 King Square Avenue   Cullen, Kate   2003   ST 58980 73715
An archaeological watching brief was maintained during groundworks associated with redevelopment of Nos 11–16 King Square Avenue. In the north-east portion of the site a substantial stone-built wall was uncovered. The wall could not be dated, however. The appearance and type of mortar suggested a possible late medieval date. It is possible that this may have been a structure contemporary with St James's Priory, perhaps an ancillary building within the estate. The other walls identified in the test pits were indicative of 18th-century cellar walls, and it is clear that no trace of the buildings above these cellars survived. In addition, the excavation of the basement car park, all drainage works and pile cap excavations were monitored. In several instances the excavated depths exceeded 3m, removing all archaeological features and deposits. The natural substrate was identified in several locations between approximately 1m and 1.8m below the existing ground surface. This was consistently overlain by sandy clay and modern rubble demolition deposits. No further archaeological features or deposits were identified, and no artefactual material pre-dating the modern period was recovered.

4341   Drill Hall, Old Market Street   Sheldon, Steve and   2007   ST 59673 73101
                                                      Cullen, Kate
An archaeological watching brief was carried by Cotswold Archaeology on groundworks associated with the development of the site of the former Drill Hall, Old Market Street. The earliest deposits appeared to comprise post-medieval cultivation soils, possibly associated with a garden of former tenement plots fronting on to Old Market Street. All the structures identified during the watching brief appeared to be later than these deposits and were founded on post-medieval levelling layers. It is likely that the structures relate to the late 19th-century sugar refinery, rebuilt due to a fire which destroyed the original 17th-century refinery.

4343   College Green   Harris, Jane   2006   ST 58338 72750
An archaeological watching brief was carried out during the excavation of a series of narrow pits on the south side of College Green. No archaeological features or deposits were found during the digging process.

4346   Back of Bridge Street   King, Andy   2006   ST 59020 72963
The excavation of geotechnical trial pits in Back of Bridge Street was monitored No archaeological deposits or features were present.

4352   Waterloo Road   Heaton, Rachel   2006   ST 59870 73173
Groundworks associated with the redevelopment of the former FPS factory in Waterloo Road were monitored (see also 4231).

4354   Anvil Street and Avon Street   Unknown   2006   ST 59860 72720
Groundworks associated with the redevelopment of the area between Anvil Street and Avon Street in St Philip's were monitored.

4358   Queen Street   Sheldon, Steven   2005   ST 59306 73028
Groundworks associated with the development of an extension to the King's Orchard office building on the west side of Queen Street were monitored. No features or deposits of archaeological interest were observed during groundworks.

4362   5–11 Midland Road, Old Market   Potter, Kevin   2006   ST 59833 73190
An archaeological watching brief to monitor groundworks associated with the redevelopment of Nos 5–11
Midland Road, Old Market, was carried out. The site was observed after demolition of the existing buildings
and nothing of archaeological interest was noted (note: this observation was based on a swift and informal
look at the site and should not be viewed as definitive).

4364   13 Redcross Street, Old Market   Ponsford, M W   2006   ST 59591 73217
A watching brief on groundworks and a building survey associated with the redevelopment of No 13 Redcross
Street, Old Market was carried out. Eight trial pits and a garden trench were recorded and several elevations
drawn. Results showed that the main structure, built in 1909, incorporated elements of earlier buildings dating
to back to the 16th to 17th centuries.

4365   53–5 Stokes Croft   Ponsford, M W   2006   ST 59074 73853
Monitoring of groundworks associated with the redevelopment of Nos 53–5 Stokes Croft was carried out.

4367   Wapping Road   Whatley, Stuart   2006   ST 58558 72222
The excavation of geotechnical pits on land at the rear of the Bristol Industrial Museum, L and M Sheds,
on the west side of Wapping Road was monitored. The groundworks revealed the remains of the former
cobbled dock surface in Test pits 1, 2, 4 and 5, the brick pile foundations of the 1888 granary building in
Test Pits 4 and 5, and the former wall of the Wapping Wharf dry dock in Trench 1. Borehole 3 revealed the
stratigraphy of the Wapping Wharf dry dock.

4372   Bond Street   Sheldon, S and   2007   ST 59555 73405
                                                        Cudlip, D
The excavation of four geotechnical pits on the site of a proposed new hotel on the western side of Bond
Street, part of the redevelopment of the Broadmead Shopping centre, was monitored. The only archaeological
feature observed during the watching brief was a concrete surface encountered at a depth of 2m below
the present ground level. The depth at which this surface was encountered would suggest that it represents
the floor of a cellar. The remaining deposits encountered during the watching brief represent the modern
backfilling of cellars or modern dumping and ground make-up in areas that had been truncated during the
development of the area in the 19th to 20th century.

4390   College Square   Bryant, John   2007   ST 58219 72609
An archaeological watching brief was maintained during groundworks associated with the development of
a new building for Bristol Cathedral School on the west side of College Square (see also 3772).

4393   Church Lane, Clifton Wood   Rowe, Mike and   2007   ST 57515 72525
                                                        Rowe, Emily
Cotswold Archaeology carried out an archaeological watching brief at the former printworks site, Church
Lane, Clifton Wood. No features or deposits of archaeological interest were observed during groundworks.

4400   Fosters Almshouses, Colston Street   Potter, Kevin   2007   ST 58594 73161
Bristol and Region Archaeological Services carried out an archaeological watching brief at Fosters Almshouses,
Colston Street, Bristol.

4405   Jubilee Place   Potter, Kevin   2007   ST 58939 72269
An archaeological watching brief was carried out on two engineering test pits at Jubilee House, Jubilee Place,
Redcliffe. Both trenches contained (below the modern overburden) similar stratigraphic sequences of mixed
red-brown sandy clay deposits, containing mortar flecks and charcoal, overlying degraded sandstone natural.
There was limited artefactual evidence comprising a clay pipe stem and glass bottle bottom retrieved from
the upper deposits of trench 2. There were also a small number of re-deposited sandstone blocks bonded
with possible medieval red sandy mortar attached which were excavated from within a 20th-century rubble
deposit below the concrete floor surface of trench.

4411   Royal Fort House   Newland, Cassie   2007   ST 58278 73385
The University of Bristol, Dept of Archaeology carried out a watching brief on groundworks associated with
the resurfacing of the drive in front of Royal Fort House.

4412   Temple Back   Armstrong, Andrew   2007   ST 59357 72872
Wessex Archaeology carried out a watching brief on land at Temple Back, during development groundworks, on the site of the former Central Electric Lighting Station. A number of archaeological features at the south-east end of the site were noted. These included a possible 17th-century cobbled surface or slipway running south-west to north-east across the south of the site. Also noted were a waterfront retaining wall, a drain associated with the 18th-century cellar structure, and a post-medieval or modern culvert. The watching brief was able to establish that the number and spacing of timber piles corresponded closely to the original existing plans of the former Station. A sample of wood taken was identified as fir, a tree species which does not appear in Britain until the 18th century.

4417   47–9 Barton Vale   Longman, Tim   2007   ST 59985 72844
Bristol and Region Archaeological Services carried out an archaeological watching brief at Nos 47–9 Barton Vale, St Philips. No features or deposits of archaeological significance were observed during the programme of intrusive groundworks.

4418   Tyndall Avenue   Potter, Kevin   2007   ST 58338 73496
Bristol and Region Archaeological Services carried out a watching brief during the excavation of geotechnical trial pits at Tyndall Avenue. A total of 13 trenches were excavated. Little of archaeological interest was encountered. Trenches 5 to 8 contained backfilled rubble deposits with traces of white lime mortar and sandstone blocks which could be demolition remains from the Royal Fort. Trench 3 revealed a red Pennant sandstone wall bonded with light grey lime and ash mortar.

4424   2–3 Charles Street and 11–16 Dighton Street   Stevens, Dave   2007   ST 58915 73666
Bristol and Region Archaeological Services carried out an archaeological watching brief at Nos 2–3 Charles Street and at Nos 11–16 Dighton Street. No archaeological features or deposits were encountered.

4425   Hotwell Road   Mason, Cai   2006   ST 57835 72564
Context One Archaeological Services carried out an archaeological watching brief during groundworks associated with a new sewage scheme at Beany Block Kerb, Hotwell Road. Groundwork excavations throughout the pipeline revealed a vertical sequence of modern road and pavement surfaces, overlying 18th- and 19th-century made ground and levelling layers. The remains of several walls, wells and floor surfaces were revealed during groundworks, almost exclusively relating to modifications made to the docks and surrounding areas, throughout the 18th and 19th centuries. In total 12 walls, 2 wells, 2 floor surfaces, 1 culvert and 1 sewer pipe were observed. It is likely that at least three of the walls revealed during pipeline excavations relate to the building and/or extension of the Limekiln Dock.

4431   Backfields   Saunders, Kelly   2007   ST 59220 73833
Cotswold Archaeology carried out an archaeological watching brief on land at Backfields, St Pauls. The fieldwork involved monitoring the mechanical excavation of five geotechnical test pits. A number of stone wall footings relating to a 18th-century circular stable block were identified together with a stone wall footing pre-dating the construction of the circular stable block. Brick-built structures, probably relating to 19th-century housing, modern concrete foundations and services were also identified.

4434   Gasferry Road   Ellis, Chris   2008   ST 57823 72368
Wessex Archaeology carried out an archaeological watching brief on development groundworks associated with phase development of the former Great Western Steamship Company shipyard (see also 4433).

4437   Former Purimachos site, West Street   Stevens, Dave   2007   ST 60040 73260
Bristol and Region Archaeological Services carried out an archaeological watching brief at the site of the former Purimachos building (see also 4435).

4439   Tyndall Avenue   King, Andy   2008   ST 58198 73467
Bristol and Region Archaeological Services carried out an archaeological watching brief at the University of Bristol Physics Building, Tyndall Avenue.

459   Backfields   Unknown   2008   ST 59222 73840
Cotswold Archaeology carried out an archaeological watching brief on construction works at Backfields. Stone wall footings and drains comprising the remains of the 18th-century circular stable block were identified and

have been correlated with the cartographic evidence. The identified remains primarily comprised the external wall of the Circular Stables, individual stables within the structure and an internal corridor.

| 4443 | 4 Christmas Steps | Robinson, Fay | 2008 | ST 58631 73178 |

Context One Archaeological Services carried out a watching brief on behalf of Wessex Water for a repaired drain at No 4 Christmas Steps. No archaeological remains/features were observed during the course of the watching brief.

| 4444 | Houlton Street | Unknown | 2008 | ST 59630 73580 |

Cotswold Archaeology carried out an archaeological watching brief on groundworks for new offices at the junction of Newfoundland Street and Houlton Street.

| 4446 | 117–33 Wilder Street | Potter, Kevin | 2008 | ST 59418 73914 |

Bristol and Region Archaeological Services carried out an archaeological watching brief on groundworks at Nos 117–33 Wilder Street. The watching brief recorded the foundations of early 19th-century terraced cottages which stood on the site until the 1950s. A culvert, probably contemporary with the cottages, was found running across the back of the site. The archaeological deposits encountered were broadly contemporary with the cottages, the earliest, through which the terrace foundations were cut, contained 17th-century pottery and clay tobacco pipes.

| 4451 | 10–22 Victoria Street | Roper, Simon | 2008 | ST 59152 72844 |

Bristol and Region Archaeological Services carried an archaeological watching brief on groundworks for the construction of an extension of Nos 10–22 Victoria Street (see also 4450).

| 4452 | Wapping Wharf | Longman, Tim | 2008 | ST 58574 72254 |

Bristol and Region Archaeological Services carried out an archaeological watching brief at Wapping Wharf. The groundworks revealed a length of the west wall of the Western Wapping Dock, which was in use as a shipbuilding facility from the early 18th century until the mid-1860s. The dock, where I K Brunel's ship the SS *Great Western* was built in 1836–7, was filled in by the early 1870s prior to the construction of the Bristol Harbour Railway and associated quayside infrastructure. The site was later occupied by the Corporation Granary. Some of the substantial foundations of this large building, which stood on the site from the late 1880s until its destruction during the Blitz in 1941, were exposed during the latest excavations on the site. That building was, in turn, replaced by L and M sheds in the early 1950s.

| 4454 | St Nicholas of Tolentino, Lawfords Gate | Bryant, John | 2008 | ST 59936 73507 |

Bristol and Region Archaeological Services carried out an archaeological watching brief on the site of a new presbytery for St Nicholas of Tolentino RC parish church. Remains of the previous building, formerly a Roman Catholic school, had been removed in 2008 and the site excavated down 0.6m or more and then backfilled. Trenching for the new building cut into the natural red-brown sand below and revealed a short length of foundations from the earlier, 1850s, school, and two possible minor features that may have been of recent origin.

| 4457 | St Paul's Park, St Pauls | Ducker, Ray | 2008 | ST 59544 73766 |

Avon Archaeological Unit carried out an archaeological monitoring project at St Paul's Park, St Pauls. The various groundwork excavations revealed a simple sequence of deposits comprising modern imported made ground overlying a buried topsoil and archaeologically sterile natural clay. A number of grave ledger slabs were also located, buried between 0.1m and 0.6m below the modern ground surface.

| 4460 | Tankards Close | Whatley, Stuart | 2008 | ST 58365 73347 |

Bristol and Region Archaeological Services carried out an archaeological watching brief at the University of Bristol Mathematics Department, Tankards Close.

| 4466 | Old Bread Street | Corcos, Nick | 2008 | ST 59687 72859 |

Bristol and Region Archaeological Services carried out an archaeological watching brief at Old Bread Street. The work identified a limited number of features associated both with the building's former industrial use starting in the late 19th century, and structures (chiefly walls) on alignments that appear to represent earlier phases of built occupation and activity.

4473   53–5 Stokes Croft   Ponsford, Mike   2008   ST 59083 73861
Cardiff Archaeological Consultants carried out a watching brief at Nos 53–5 Stokes Croft.

22021   Cliftonwood House   Leech, Roger H   2004   ST 57528 72725
An archaeological watching brief was maintained during groundworks associated with development at
Cliftonwood House by Dr Roger Leech for Cultural Heritage Services.

24666   Theatre Royal, King Street   Longman, Tim   2008   ST 58800 72750
Bristol and Region Archaeological Services carried out an archaeological watching brief at the Theatre
Royal, King Street. No archaeological deposits of any significance were recorded in either BHI or BH2. The
boreholes merely recorded undated fill deposits to depths of about 1.8m below ground level. The underlying
geological deposits then comprised approximately 11.5- to 12-metre thick layers of alluvial clays and gravels
of the Pleistocene period overlying Mercia Mudstone of the Triassic period (British Geological Survey 1962).
However, significant archaeological deposits in the form of layers of 'organic material' were recorded in both
boreholes (BH3 and BH4) drilled beneath the building. Both deposits (contexts 304 and 406) were sandwiched
beneath soft yellowish brown clays and sealed stiff, dark grey clays.

24668   114 Jacob Street   Cullen, Kate   2007   ST 59726 73124
Cotswold Archaeology carried out an archaeological watching brief at No 114 Jacob Street. The trial pits
indicate that the natural substrate lies close to the current ground level in the eastern part of the site, and is
generally overlain by possible cultivation soils, and post-medieval demolition/construction debris. No evidence
for medieval pits was uncovered. The presence of a well indicated that some post-medieval activity beyond
agricultural use may survive within the site, as well as former phases of the existing building represented by
walls and former floor surfaces, possibly belonging to the malthouse/brewery that stood on the site in the
18th/19th century.

24694   Plots 15 and 16, Broadmead   Aston, K and   2007   ST 59550 73400
                                                       Loader, A
An archaeological watching brief was undertaken by Cotswold Archaeology during groundworks associated
with the construction of a Future Inns Hotel on plots 15 and 16, Broadmead Redevelopment. The roof of the
River Frome culvert and one supporting buttress were encountered between 0.54m and 2.0m below present
ground level. The culvert is on a north-east/south-west alignment, with a revetment wall for the earlier open
river channel running parallel approximately 1.0m to the north.

24698   St Mary Redcliffe & Temple School, Redcliffe   Clarke, Chris   2009   ST 59280 72083
AOC Archaeology carried out an archaeological watching brief at St Mary Redcliffe and Temple School,
Redcliffe. The watching brief revealed a series of features associated with the remains of 19th-century
residential properties and a 20th-century swimming pool. No early features were identified.

24707   Temple Quay   Edwards, Kate   2000   ST 59511 72528
Bristol and Region Archaeological Services carried out an archaeological watching brief at Plot 5 Temple
Quay. Structural remains to the north and west of the Portwall seen during the watching brief were largely of
18th- and 19th-century construction and were associated with both domestic and industrial processes taking
place across the site from the 13th century to the present day.

24710   Beckett Hall, Little Thomas Lane   Hirons, Heather   2009   ST 59088 72773
Bristol and Region Archaeological Services carried out an archaeological watching brief on four test pits at
Beckett Hall, Little Thomas Lane. The test pits revealed possible stone vaulting, previous lane surfaces and
the medieval footings of the tower of the Church of St Thomas the Martyr, the footings for Beckett Hall,
and a brick-built drain associated with Beckett Hall.

24711   Church of St Thomas, Thomas Lane   Hirons, Heather   2009   ST 59115 72766
Bristol and Region Archaeological Services carried out an archaeological watching brief at the Church of St
Thomas, Thomas Lane. The watching brief revealed an empty burial chamber and a possible crypt entrance
associated with the current 18th-century church as well as a wall, possibly part of the earlier medieval church.

24746   Plot 2B, Temple Quay   Edwards, Kate   2000   ST 59515 72575
Bristol and Region Archaeological Services carried out an archaeological watching brief at Plot 2B, Temple
Quay. The stratigraphy of the site was generally very disturbed, and characterised by poorly consolidated

made-up ground, demolition rubble and deposits of an industrial origin; there were also frequent deposits of ceramic waste from the 18th and 19th centuries. Undisturbed, greyish brown alluvial clay was visible beneath the slab of the basement.

24747   Plot 4D, Temple Quay   Edwards, Kate   2001   ST 59569 72516
Bristol and Region Archaeological Services carried out an archaeological watching brief at Plot 4D, Temple Quay. Unstratified deposits of ceramics and kiln furniture and lenses of ash and clinker were regularly observed amongst otherwise homogenous made ground, loose silts and demolition rubble. Isolated dumps of re-deposited clean, orange/brown clay were occasionally observed within otherwise mixed soils. The collection of clay pipes found amongst a spread of material from a demolished kiln date from the mid-19th century, although the production of pipes by the Ring family continued until *c* 1884.

24748   Plot 4B, Temple Quay   Edwards, Kate   2000   ST 59625 72529
Bristol and Region Archaeological Services carried out an archaeological watching brief at Plot 4B, Temple Quay. The archaeological watching brief found that no development appears to have taken place on the site of the study area prior to the 19th century until the development of the Great Western Railway Goods Shed. The construction and subsequent demolition of the Goods Shed had resulted in substantial disturbance of the ground.

24759   St Mary Redcliffe   Bryant, John   2009   ST 59142 72323
Bristol and Region Archaeological Services carried out an archaeological watching brief at St Mary Redcliffe during investigations associated with the possible replacement of air ducts between the external blowing chamber. The watching brief was restricted to a small area of floor in the area known as 'Canynges Kitchen', on the south side of the lower (western) portion of the room. Removal of the floor slabs revealed ceramic drainage pipes (used to channel the air flow to the organ) encased in concrete. No remains pre-dating the 1930s were revealed.

24772   46 Wade Street   Etheridge, David   2009   ST 59850 73472
Avon Archaeological Unit carried out an archaeological watching brief on land adjacent to No 46 Wade Street. The monitoring of ground works for foundations to a depth of 1 metre below the ground surface recorded several sandstone walls, remnant cellar roofs and associated finds that related to the former 18th-century tenements.

24774   Cumberland Basin   Coe, Richard   2009   ST 56761 72416
Bristol and Region Archaeological Services monitored geotechnical works on the island adjacent to the outer lock at Cumberland Basin. The groundworks revealed part of the back wall to the north lock and also the concrete footing for a mooring post.

24776   Hill House, Lewins Mead   Longman, Tim   2009   ST 58849 73394
Bristol and Region Archaeological Services carried out an archaeological watching brief at Hill House, Lewins Mead (see also 24756).

24784   Tyndall Avenue   King, Andy   2009   ST 58284 73484
Bristol and Region Archaeological Services carried out an archaeological watching brief during infrastructure works at the University of Bristol.

24790   Royal Fort Gardens, Tyndall Avenue   Pollard, Joshua   2009   ST 58221 73368
University of Bristol Archaeology Department carried out an archaeological watching brief at the Royal Fort Gardens, Tyndall Avenue, in advance of the erection of a sculpture. A former flower bed, drains and post-War concrete culvert were revealed; the flower bed perhaps, but by no means certainly, relating to the early 19th-century Repton remodelling of Royal Fort grounds. A small assemblage of post-medieval ceramics and other material was recovered.

24793   Bristol Maternity Hospital, St Michael's Hill   Ducker, Ray   2009   ST 58489 73495
Bristol and Region Archaeological Services carried out an archaeological watching brief at Bristol Maternity Hospital, St Michael's Hill. During the development groundworks deposits recorded largely comprised modern surfaces of concrete and asphalt sealing garden soils and/or made-ground deposits, natural clays

and mudstone. A length of post-medieval wall was recorded in section in a service trench and a large diesel fuel storage tank was removed from between three of the pile-caps.

| 24803 | Redcliffe Village | Barber, Alistair | 2008 | ST 59160 72660 |

Cotswold Archaeology carried out an archaeological watching brief on geotechnical site investigations. Sixteen trial pits, three test trenches and five inspection pits were excavated within the proposed development area, together with five boreholes, in order to investigate ground conditions. The geotechnical works identified natural sandstone bedrock, overlain by estuarine alluvium, throughout the site. Evidence was identified behind the Redcliff Street frontage for activity from the 12th/13th centuries onwards, including possible medieval floor surfaces, a dye-vat base and medieval and later garden soils. The post-medieval line of the Law Ditch, an originally medieval feature that runs north–south through the centre of the development area, was also noted. A probable medieval wall-footing, together with garden soils of both medieval and post-medieval date, were noted east of the Law Ditch, in areas that would have been to the rear of plots fronting St Thomas Street.

| 24808 | Vaulted Chambers, Castle Park | Hirons, Heather | 2009 | ST 59377 73139 |

Bristol and Region Archaeological Services carried out an archaeological watching brief during electric cable laying at the Vaulted Chambers, Castle Park. The only deposit predating the 20th century was visible in one corner and no finds were recovered.

| 24810 | Cumberland Basin | Bryant, John | 2009 | ST 56950 72350 |

Bristol and Region Archaeological Services carried out an archaeological watching brief during modernisation of the Entrance and Junction Locks at Cumberland Basin. Alluvium was exposed in a number of excavations, usually with about 0.7–0.8m of made ground above it. The main south-west wall of Entrance Lock was noted as becoming thicker with depth on its landward side. Rams used to swing Junction Lock Bridge were recorded prior to their removal. Little else of interest was seen, although part of the deep base of a mooring post was photographed.

| 24814 | Cattle Market Road | Waterfall, Dan | 2009 | ST 59941 72378 |

Museum of London Archaeology Service carried out an archaeological watching brief on the site of the Former Sorting Office, Cattle Market Road. Groundworks were monitored in October 2009 during removal of five fuel tanks previously used to store fuel for the Post Office vehicle fleet. Removal of the fuel tanks created a single trench measuring 20.40m by 20.10m. No evidence of the 1832 cholera burial ground or any other feature of archaeological interest was observed. Natural ground was observed at 7.28m OD.

| 24820 | St James's Church | Cai Mason | 2010 | ST 58895 73470 |

Bristol and Region Archaeological Services carried out an archaeological watching brief and building recording works during internal and external refurbishment of St James's Church. The archaeological work revealed a number of post-medieval structures in and around the Church of St James. Monumental inscriptions and a number of post-medieval brick-lined graves were also recorded. Medieval floor tiles and fragments of worked stone were recovered as residual finds in later contexts, the most significant of which is a part of a medieval sundial.

| 24841 | Brandon Hill | Hirons, Heather | 2010 | ST 57946 72744 |

Bristol and Region Archaeological Services carried out an archaeological watching brief at Brandon Hill during groundworks associated with an extension to an existing play area, including new items of play equipment. No features or deposits of archaeological significance were observed.

| 24843 | Brunswick Square Cemetery Gardens | Hirons, Heather | 2010 | ST 59278 73725 |

Bristol and Region Archaeological Services carried out an archaeological watching brief at Brunswick Cemetery, during groundworks associated with the re-landscaping of Brunswick Square Cemetery Gardens, St Pauls. The groundworks revealed a total of 88 monuments and graves, including headstones, ledger stones, entrance slabs, low monuments, the bases of chest tombs, graves marked with plain stone kerbs as well as ornate moulded ceramic edging and brick vaults and stone capped tombs.

| 24890 | Red Lodge | Hirons, Heather | 2010 | ST 58431 73110 |

Bristol and Region Archaeological Services carried out an archaeological watching brief at the Red Lodge.

| 24898 | Bristol Cathedral | Blockley, Kevin | 2010 | ST 58334 72659 |

Cambrian Archaeological Projects carried out an archaeological watching brief within the cloister of Bristol Cathedral. Significant remains of the Conduit House were recorded as well as two phases of post-Reformation additions to the structure, and demolition levels when the structure was levelled in 1853/4.

| 24917 | College Square | Mason, Cai | 2010 | ST 58272 72630 |

Bristol and Region Archaeological Services carried out an archaeological watching brief at College Square during groundworks associated with the remodelling of College Square. The groundworks revealed an undated, but probably post-medieval, stone wall foundation. A sequence of 18th-century dump layers and surfaces were also uncovered in the southern half of the Square.

| 24923 | 44 Jacob's Wells Road | Israel, Richard | 2010 | ST 57724 72902 |

An archaeological watching brief was carried out on land at No 44 Jacob's Wells Road.

| 24937 | 61 Old Market Street | Longman, Tim and Ducker, Ray | 2010 | ST 59712 73103 |

Bristol and Region Archaeological Services carried out an archaeological watching brief to the rear of No 61 Old Market Street. Initially, monitoring comprised a watching brief during the excavation of three small test pits. The natural, weathered red sandstone was recorded at a depth of 0.8m in Test Pit 3, but was not encountered in the other two. Sealing the geology in Test Pit 3, and recorded also in Test Pits 1 and 2, was a layer of reddish brown sandy silt (a so-called 'garden soil'). No finds were recovered from the context, which in turn was sealed beneath a layer of made-ground, comprising dark greyish-brown sandy silty soil with abundant small stone inclusions and mortar flecks plus occasional brick fragments. Later monitoring of removal of the concrete yard surface revealed deposits comprising a post-medieval, brick yard surface which had been cut for the insertion of a variety of concrete pads, stanchion bases, beam slots and walls prior to the laying of a modern concrete floor above it. Below the brick surface were made-ground deposits of post-medieval date the full extent of which was not tested. No features or deposits of archaeological significance were observed during the intrusive groundworks.

| 24954 | St Nicholas of Tolentino, Lawfords Gate | Ducker, Ray | 2010 | ST 59933 73510 |

Bristol and Region Archaeological Services carried out an archaeological watching brief at St Nicholas of Tolentino RC Church, Pennywell Road. The groundworks revealed deposits of made ground, including mortar lenses, sealing either buried topsoil and subsoil or directly overlaying archaeologically sterile deposits of sandy clay and sandstone. A few sections of wall of 19th-century date, probably the remains of demolished school buildings, were also recorded.

| 24957 | John Wesley's Chapel, Broadmead | Powlesland, Ian | 2010 | ST 59106 73362 |

An archaeological watching brief was carried out during landscape works to the courtyard area of John Wesley's Chapel, Broadmead.

| 24967 | Brunel Lock, Cumberland Basin | Hume, Lynn | 2011 | ST 56796 72330 |

Avon Archaeological Unit carried out an archaeological watching brief during construction of cycle path link and associated landscaping and planting at Brunel Lock. The development revealed an extensive area of re-deposited demolition rubble, probably associated with Cumberland Buildings, and several cast iron bollards, at least one of which may be *in situ*. The remains of an intertidal timber structure, probably the footings for a 19th-century pier, were also revealed.

| 24981 | Wine Street, Castle Park | Mason, Cai | 2011 | ST 59070 73112 |

Bristol and Region Archaeological Services carried out an archaeological watching brief on land at Wine Street, Castle Park. A north–south aligned stone wall was uncovered beneath the concrete surface of the former Dolphin Street. Possible interpretations include the possibility that this wall defines the edge of a cellar associated with a building situated along the west side of Dolphin Street. Conversely it may form one side of a stone-lined culvert. The wall is probably early post-medieval in date, and is likely to overlie earlier archaeological deposits.

| 24983 | Nelson Street | King, Andy and Longman, Tim | 2011 | ST 58721 73221 |

Bristol and Region Archaeological Services carried out an archaeological watching brief during geotechnical works at the former Magistrates Court, Nelson Street. This involved an archaeological watching brief during the mechanical excavation of four trial pits and the drilling/coring of two boreholes and three window samples at specific locations across the site. These mostly revealed varying depths of construction related disturbance. However, in three locations (TP4, BH1 and BH2) it appears that layers of stratified archaeological deposits, in the form of buried garden soils and a single layer of peaty clay, are present.

| 24990 | Theatre Royal, King Street | Mason, Cai | 2011 | ST 58804 72756 |

Bristol and Region Archaeological Services carried out an archaeological watching brief at the Theatre Royal, King Street. The archaeological work uncovered a number of features pre-dating the construction of the theatre in 1764–6, including pits, postholes and a beam slot, the earliest of which were medieval. Numerous structural details of the theatre were also recorded, including the foundations of the original stage front and musicians' area, extensive areas of the flagstone flooring, wall foundations and numerous blocked openings. Work outside the theatre revealed foundations of an 18th- or early 19th-century cellared building and three post-medieval inhumation burials.

| 24991 | Bristol City Museum and Art Gallery | Unknown | 2011 | ST 58074 73225 |

Bristol and Region Archaeological Services carried out an archaeological watching brief at Bristol City Museum and Art Gallery.

| 25000 | 51 Barton Road | Baddeley, Gary | 2011 | ST 59990 72807 |

Bristol and Region Archaeological Services carried out an archaeological watching brief at No 51 Barton Road, St Philips. The groundworks revealed that the site had probably been truncated by industrial extraction of the alluvial clays in the 19th century and so natural bedrock lay immediately below up to 3m of mixed, made ground/demolition deposits. Stone structures survived under and within the made ground layers. The earliest of these dated to around the 1840s and represented a boundary wall and a building fronting Barton Road. The building went through various stages of extensions and redevelopment before it became a Beer House by the 1940s. It was demolished in the 1960s or early 1970s. A cobbled surface and brick surface were found to the east of the site. They potentially date back to at least 1874. The cobbled surface still survives as a lane outside the site to the south-east.

| 25011 | Quay Street-Nelson Street | Wilkinson, Alexandra | 2011 | ST 58742 73158 |

An archaeological watching brief was undertaken by Cotswold Archaeology during groundworks associated with the replacement of a gas main at Quay Street, Nelson Street and through the arch of St John's Church. Six trenches were excavated in the area disturbed by the existing service trench and through modern road make-up deposits. No features or deposits of archaeological interest were observed during groundworks, and no artefactual material pre-dating the modern period was recovered.

| 25022 | 1–2 Wilson Street | | 2011 | ST 59543 73688 |

Cotswold Archaeology carried out an archaeological watching brief at Nos 1–2 Wilson Street, St Pauls.

| 25032 | St Mary Redcliffe | Mason, Cai | 2011 | ST 59084 72273 |

Bristol and Region Archaeological Services carried out an archaeological watching brief at the churchyard of St Mary Redcliffe. Stone foundations of an early 19th-century gate were uncovered next to the present south-eastern churchyard gateway. A small number of disarticulated human bones were also recovered; the bones were re-buried in the churchyard.

| 25055 | Temple Gate | Mason, Cai | 2011 | ST 59425 72403 |

Bristol and Region Archaeological Services carried out a watching brief during the demolition of a railway viaduct and adjoining buildings to the rear of the George and Railway Hotel, Temple Gate. The watching brief observed a number of structural elements of a late 19th-century railway viaduct and an adjoining stable block.

| 25060 | Terrell Street | Ducker, Ray | 2011 | ST 58605 73486 |

Bristol and West Archaeology carried out an archaeological watching brief on the site of the former nurses accommodation at Terrell Street to the rear of the Bristol Royal Infirmary. During the monitoring, no significant archaeological deposits, features or structures were revealed. Deposits exposed comprised made-ground (some of very recent deposition) overlying natural clays and sandstone and, at the west side of the site, possible buried topsoil. Structural remains recorded were all of post-medieval date, almost certainly elements of the recently demolished Beaufort House and Bedford Row buildings.

25061 Tyndall Avenue King, Andy 2011 ST 58345 73510
Bristol and Region Archaeological Services carried out an archaeological watching brief at the University of Bristol Life Sciences, Tyndall Avenue and St Michael's Hill. Two phases of watching brief were carried out, one in 2011–12 prior to construction of the Life Sciences building, the other in 2012–14 during subsidiary building and landscaping works to the west. The first phase uncovered little of archaeological interest, mainly due to the heavy truncation of the site from previous development. The second phase, in a much less disturbed area, revealed numerous features including probable Civil War ditches, the foundations of the 17th-century Garway's House and later structures associated with 18th- and 19th-century occupation of the hill.

25064 Cumberland Road Mason, Cai 2011 ST 58433 72098
Bristol and Region Archaeological Services carried out an archaeological watching brief at the former stables at the Old Gaol, Cumberland Road. The groundwork uncovered part of the perimeter wall of the New Gaol and structural remains of the Old Gaol Stables, comprising two internal partition-walls, a brick-lined drain, and a possible water trough or drainage gully.

25087 1 Victoria Street Longman, Tim 2012 ST 59030 72845
Bristol and Region Archaeological Services carried out an archaeological watching brief during the excavation of geotechnical pits at No 1 Victoria Street.

25098 St Mary Redcliffe Mason, Cai 2012 ST 59132 72264
Bristol and Region Archaeological Services carried out an archaeological watching brief at St Mary Redcliffe Churchyard. A small number of disarticulated human bones were uncovered during the course of the work; the bones were re-buried in the churchyard.

25107 Plot 3, Temple Quay Mason, Cai 2012 ST 59699 72599
Bristol and Region Archaeological Services carried out an archaeological watching brief at Plot 3, Temple Quay. The groundworks revealed only layers of modern make-up and concrete floor slabs or footings, overlaying probable 19th-century made ground.

25115 Wapping Wharf Longman, Tim 2012 ST 58423 72124
Bristol and Region Archaeological Services carried out an archaeological watching brief at Plots A and C, Wapping Wharf.

25153 5 Kingsdown Parade Krakowicz, Lee Roy 2012 ST 58552 73662
Bristol and Region Archaeological Services carried out an archaeological watching brief at land to the rear of No 5 Kingsdown Parade.

25155 19 Jacob's Wells Road Etheridge, David 2012 ST 57703 72808
Bristol and West Archaeology carried out an archaeological watching brief at No 19 Jacob's Wells Road. A series of geotechnical test pits through the solid concrete floor of the building were monitored, but nothing of archaeological significance was found.

25158 1 Victoria Street Unknown 2012 ST 59024 72843
Bristol and West Archaeology carried out an archaeological watching brief at No 1 Victoria Street.

25166 Christmas Steps Brace, Daniel 2012 ST 58628 73185
Context One carried out an archaeological watching brief at Rice Box, Christmas Steps.

25174 New Street Longman, Tim 2012 ST 59682 73326
Bristol and Region Archaeological Services carried out an archaeological watching brief at the site of the former Seven Ways Public House, Old Market. The earliest archaeological remains recorded on site were the substantial foundations of a boundary wall alongside St Matthias Park (road) that appears to date from the 17th century. Structural remains belonging to both the 'Old Swan' pub built in the 18th century (including an extensive network of contemporary subterranean cellar passages or 'tunnels'), its replacement the 'New Swan' built in 1891 and substantial alterations carried out in the early/mid-1970s were also recorded. Of

particular interest were the deposits of ash, kiln waste and fragments of clay tobacco pipe stems and bowls, which had been used to infill the cellar passages in the early 1890s when the old inn was being demolished. This waste material is thought likely to have originated from the site of a clay tobacco pipe factory located, at that time, across the road at No 22 New Street.

25178   Tyndall's Park Road   Wright, J and   2012   ST 57872 73578
                                                            Haines, C
Cotswold Archaeology carried out an archaeological watching brief at Tyndall's Park Road. Three residential property boundary walls of late 19th- and early 20th-century date were observed. One of the walls corresponds to the boundary between Westbury-on-Trym and St Michael's parishes which is first depicted on Ashmead's 1828 map of Bristol. The parish boundary appears to have been 'fossilised' as this property boundary. A further wall identified is believed to relate to terracing in the formal garden of neighbouring Samber House which was built between 1840 and 1855.

25182   66 Queen Square   Smith, Tracey   2013   ST 58729 72660
Bristol and Region Archaeological Services carried out an archaeological watching brief at No 66 Queen Square and Nos 22–3A King Street. The work showed that structural remains of buildings survive beneath the modern offices but these could not be investigated due to the limited size of the test pits. Evidence for extensive post-medieval dumping across the whole site was recorded.

25191   Ashton Avenue   Mason, Cai   2012   ST 58271 72161
Bristol and Region Archaeological Services carried out an archaeological watching brief during the excavation of three trial pits for the proposed Bristol Rapid Transit project between Ashton Avenue Bridge and Prince's Wharf. The test pits at Wapping Railway Wharf uncovered post-medieval dump layers overlain by late 19th- and 20th-century railway track bedding layers. Test pits above the Underfall uncovered the top of the 19th-century sluice.

25235   Wilder Street   Ducker, Ray   2013   ST 59267 73772
Bristol and West Archaeology carried out an archaeological watching brief at Wilder Street car park. This revealed a simple sequence of modern surfaces sealing made-ground deposits and a former topsoil/subsoil horizon overlying archaeologically sterile deposits of sandy clay. The modern surfaces sealed several 19th-century walls, brick and sandstone paving and a well that represented the remains of terrace houses (Brunswick Terrace) that stood on the site until it was destroyed during a bombing raid in 1940.

25237   66 Queen Square   Smith, Tracey   2013   ST 58731 72663
Bristol and Region Archaeological Services carried out an archaeological watching brief at No 66 Queen Square (see above 25238).

25248   51A and 57 West Street   Unknown   2013   ST 59925 73324
Bristol and West Archaeology carried out an archaeological watching brief on land to the rear of Nos 51A and 57 West Street, Old Market.

25255   Theatre Royal, King Street   Unknown   2013   ST 58806 72727
Bristol and Region Archaeological Services carried out an archaeological watching brief during works at the Front of House, Theatre Royal, King Street.

25258   Marsh Street   Unknown   2013   ST 58660 72760
Cotswold Archaeology carried out work at Marsh Street.

25262   30–2 Tyndall's Park Road   Smith, Tracey   2013   ST 58049 73673
Bristol and Region Archaeological Services carried out an archaeological watching brief at Nos 30–2 Tyndall's Park Road. No traces of the City Boundary were found during the groundworks, which included ground reduction to 1.1m below the existing surface. A concrete footing was uncovered relating to Second World War activity on site and a small segment of a possible refuse pit or tree throw, likely dating to the 18th century, was uncovered in the eastern baulk.

25264   47–9 Barton Rd   Corcos, Nick   2013   ST 59973 72823
Avon Archaeology carried out an archaeological watching brief at Nos 47–9 Barton Rd.

25279   City Road   Logan, Will   2013   ST 59266 73958
Border Archaeology undertook a programme of archaeological observation on a water mains renewal scheme
in two specific areas along City Road, St Pauls. Within the trenching excavated at the junction of Stokes Croft
and City Road, a deep soil deposit was identified which could represent either a landscaping deposit relating
to formal gardens associated with a detached property of late 18th-century date which occupied a large
corner plot to the east of the Stokes Croft street frontage, or a levelling layer associated with the demolition
of the house and the subsequent construction of City Road in the early 1860s. During the course of the
groundworks between Brunswick Street and Brigstocke Road, a compact lime mortar surface was revealed,
at a depth of 0.75m below the current ground level (18.08m AOD), which was interpreted as a trackway or
yard surface of possible post-medieval date.

25281   New Bridewell, Rupert Street   MacIntyre, Helen J   2013   ST 58864 73302
Wardell Armstrong Archaeology (South) carried out an archaeological watching brief at New Bridewell,
Rupert Street. Significant archaeological features were uncovered so that a formal evaluation subsequently
was carried out (see above 25282).

25338   Castle Park   Cook, J and   2013   ST 59061 73099
                                                       Priestley, S
Border Archaeology carried out a programme of archaeological observation during works in Castle Park
associated with water mains replacement schemes. Observation identified a section of extant Pennant sandstone
masonry walling at the junction of High Street and Back Bridge Street. This section of wall survived in a
fragmentary condition and had been heavily truncated by late 19th- to 20th-century construction activity
and service trenching. On the line of Back Bridge Street, a void was encountered at the base of a pit which
appears to have been associated with a late 18th- to 19th-century chamber or cellar leading to the waterfront.

25339   Victoria Street – Old Market   Cook, J and   2013   ST 59852 73130
                                                       Logan ,W
Border Archaeology carried out an archaeological watching brief during water mains replacement along a route
from Victoria Street to New Trinity, Old Market. Significant remains were found along the route including
the footings of masonry walls close to the junction of Temple Street and Counterslip, a wall of late medieval
or early post-medieval date, situated to the rear of a former tenement on the west side of Temple Street,
two sandstone masonry walls on the south side of Passage Street, three substantial Pennant sandstone walls
probably associated with No 8 Narrow Plain, the remains of a deep, rough-hewn masonry culvert at the
crossroads of Old Market Street, Midland Road, West Street and Lawford's Gate and possible evidence of
industrial activity at Pennywell Road, represented by several well-stratified deposits containing vitrified fuel
waste, charcoal and clinker, representing evidence for glass production or working and possibly copper smelting.

25340   Jacob's Wells Road   McGlenn, Claire   2014   ST 57757 72793
Border Archaeology carried out an archaeological watching brief during water mains replacement in the area
of Jacob's Wells Road. The remains of three north–south wall foundations were recorded in the northern
extent of Trench 1 on John Carr's Terrace, near its junction with Jacob's Wells Road. Trench 2 on Jacob's
Wells Road revealed a north-west/south-east aligned, post-medieval stone-built culvert running along the
southern extent of the trench and two wall foundations aligned east–west and north–south.

25341   Victoria Street   McGlenn, Claire   2014   ST 59284 72669
Border Archaeology carried out an archaeological watching brief during water mains replacement works on
Victoria Street. No significant archaeology was present in any of the trenches.

25347   Cumberland Basin   Unknown   2014   ST 57128 72246
Bristol and Region Archaeological Services carried out an archaeological watching brief at South Junction
Lock, Cumberland Basin.

25350   Bishop Street/Dean Street   2014   ST 59446 73814
Bristol and West Archaeology carried out an archaeological watching brief at The Willows, Bishop Street/
Dean Street, St Pauls.

25369   78 Horfield Road   Byford-Bates, Alistair 2014   ST 58532 73618
Bristol and Region Archaeological Services carried out an archaeological watching brief on land at No 78
Horfield Road, Kingsdown. No significant archaeological features or finds were identified.

25372   Horton Street and Midland Road   Dias, Susana and   2014   ST 59889 73003
                                                              Newns, Sarah
Avon Archaeology carried out an archaeological watching brief at a site on the corner of Horton Street and
Midland Road, Old Market. Only the northern edge of the site, immediately adjacent to Horton Street and
Midland Road, revealed the presence of archaeological features, from which historical information could be
drawn. All the monitored areas comprised modern rubble deposits, which filled the entire site and covered
all archaeological structures.

25401   Wapping Wharf   Unknown   2014   ST 58569 72172
Bristol and Region Archaeological Services carried out an archaeological watching brief during the excavation
of geotechnical test pits at Wapping Wharf, Wapping Road.

25409   Cattle Market Road   Unknown   2014   ST 59945 72416
Bristol and West Archaeology carried out an archaeological watching brief on the site of the former Post
Office Sorting Office, Cattle Market Road.

25412   Wade Street   Unknown   2014   ST 59828 73496
Avon Archaeology carried out an archaeological watching brief at the corner of Wade Street and Little Ann
Street, St Jude's.

25414   Redcliff Backs   Unknown   2014   ST 59002 72554
Bristol and Region Archaeological Services carried out an archaeological watching brief at Huller House and
the adjoining Cheese Warehouse, Redcliff Backs.

25418   Queen Charlotte Street   McGlenn, Claire   2014   ST 58861 72798
Border Archaeology carried out an archaeological watching brief at Queen Charlotte Street. Excavation revealed
seven well-preserved, though partial inhumations, all of which were associated with the former Crow Lane
cemetery. Trenching in Rackhay to the west of Queen Charlotte Street on the site of the second extension
to the former St Nicholas Churchyard (closed for burials in 1854) failed to reveal further evidence of the
disturbed human remains previously encountered during gas main excavations in 1999.

25419   Victoria Street to Knowle   Unknown   2013   ST 60976 70731
Border Archaeology carried out an archaeological watching brief during ground works associated with a water
mains renewal scheme between Victoria Street and the Knowle Reservoir.

25427   Wilder Street   Unknown   2014   ST 59305 73834
Bristol and West Archaeology carried out an archaeological watching brief at a site on the corner of Wilder
Street and Brunswick Street, St Pauls.

25436   Jacob's Wells Road   Unknown   2014   ST 57797 72967
Wessex Archaeology carried out an archaeological watching brief at Queen Elizabeth's Hospital School,
Jacob's Wells Road.

25447   Temple Back   Brannlund, Luke   2014   ST 59289 72829
Cotswold Archaeology carried out an archaeological watching brief on the site of the Avon Fire Station,
Temple Back. No features or deposits of archaeological interest were observed during groundworks.

25456   Cattlemarket Road   Unknown   2015   ST 59951 72326
Bristol and Region Archaeological Services carried out a watching brief at Totterdown Lock, Cattlemarket Road.

Observations

2   Brandon Hill   Bennett, Julian   1972   ST 58000 72680
Early 18th-century pottery waste was found during re-seeding work on Brandon Hill.

4   Lower Castle Street   Bennett, Julian   1972   ST 59390 73220
18th-century ceramics were found in commercial excavations in Lower Castle Street.

5   Lower Castle Street   Bennett, Julian   1972   ST 59390 73230
The work revealed a pit containing early 19th-century clay tobacco pipe waste and kiln debris.

| 7 | Petticoat Lane, Temple | Jackson, R G | 1972 | ST 59350 72780 |

Late 18th-century pottery waste and other ceramics were found in commercial excavations in Petticoat Lane, Temple.

| 9 | Tyndall's Park | Jackson, R G | 1972 | ST 58280 73230 |

Elements of the Royal Fort in Tyndall's Park, Kingsdown were noted.

| 10 | North Street | Jackson, R G | 1972 | ST 59050 73600 |

Observation of a 16th-century stone wall in North Street.

| 11 | Temple Way | Jackson, R G | 1972 | ST 59450 72740 |

Late 18th-century pottery waste was found during road-widening.

| 12 | Temple Back | Jackson, R G | 1972 | ST 59290 72900 |

Late 18th-century pottery waste was found.

| 15 | Lower Castle Street | Jackson, R G | 1971 | ST 59380 73220 |

The backfill was observed of a retaining wall at the corner of Lower Castle Street and Broad Weir which consisted of a heap of clay tobacco pipe kiln waste of 1782–92. This contained examples of approximately forty types of tobacco pipes including those of several previously unknown makers.

| 16 | Temple Street | Bennett, Julian | 1970 | ST 59258 72808 |

Observation of a possible medieval building in a commercial excavation.

| 18 | Temple Church | Price, Roger | 1970 | ST 59330 72850 |

Observation of commercial excavation north of Temple Church

| 20 | Castle Park | Jackson, R G | 1970 | ST 59220 73170 |

Early 18th-century ceramics found in a commercial excavation.

| 21 | Upper Maudlin Street | Miles, D | 1970 | ST 58608 73440 |

During the laying of a water pipe in Upper Maudlin Street, the remains of a medieval conduit (traditionally attributed to the Franciscans who had a friary in Lewins Mead) were recorded. The conduit was almost 2 metres high and in three branches with slightly pointed vaults. A complete 13th-century freestone doorway was also recorded. The conduit was reported to have been retained below the new carriageway.

| 23 | Lewins Mead | Ponsford, M W | 1970 | ST 58720 73330 |

Observation of five medieval inhumations in a commercial excavation.

| 24 | Castle Park | Jackson, R G | 1970 | ST 59180 73180 |

Observation and recording of a medieval road surface at New Gate.

| 26 | Redcliff Caves | Unknown | 1970 | ST 59270 72850 |

17th- and 18th-century pottery waste found in Redcliff Caves.

| 28 | Castle Park | Unknown | 1970 | ST 59110 73060 |

Observation of deep trenching in Castle Park.

| 30 | Temple Back | Escritt, Janet M | 1970 | ST 59200 72800 |

Dutch delft tiles were recovered from a 19th-century building.

| 31 | Temple Way | Unknown | 1970 | ST 58610 72860 |

Observation of a medieval cistern and post-medieval ceramics during construction of the *Evening Post* building.

| 33 | Hilton National Hotel, Redcliffe Way | Unknown | 1970 | ST 59270 72850 |

Observation of construction of the hotel in the area Prewett Street glassworks noted that the site had been heavily disturbed in the 19th century.

| 34 | Prince Street | Unknown | 1970 | ST 58800 72450 |

During construction of Pearl Assurance House 18th-century ceramics were recovered from material dumped to raise the level of Queen Square.

| 36 | St Mary-on-the-Quay | Dawson, David P | 1970 | ST 58600 73040 |

18th-century pottery was recovered from the backfill of a foundation trench of St Mary-on-the-Quay

| 40 | St Nicholas Church | Unknown | 1971 | ST 58930 72930 |

Probable observation of part of the town wall in the crypt of St Nicholas Church.

| 41 | Castle Park | Ponsford, M W | 1968 | ST 59420 73120 |

Observation of two wells, possibly of medieval date.

| 42 | Castle Park | Hebditch, Max G | 1965 | ST 59310 73080 |

Observation of a possible gate of Bristol Castle in Castle Street.

| 43 | Queen Charlotte Street | Ponsford, M W | 1968 | ST 58880 72670 |

Observation of two stone-lined wells during construction at Telephone House.

| 44 | Queen Charlotte Street | Ponsford, M W | 1968 | ST 59810 72750 |

Observation of medieval occupation deposits during construction at Telephone House.

| 47 | Temple Street | Pritchard, John E | 1903 | ST 59390 72410 |

Wooden water pipes were discovered in Temple Street.

| 49 | Tyndall's Avenue | Pritchard, John E | 1903 | ST 58250 73510 |

During observation of the construction of Tyndall's Avenue, Kingsdown 17th- and 18th-century ceramics were recovered. No archaeological features were reported.

| 50 | Bath Street | Unknown | 1874 | ST 59060 72870 |

Bronze Age axes and part of a sword blade were found during road-widening at Bristol Bridge.

| 51 | St Mary Redcliffe | Rice, William | 1870 | ST 59100 72330 |

Observation of the foundations of the tower of St Mary Redcliffe Church.

| 52 | Castle Park | Leaker, R H | 1878 | ST 59230 73150 |

Observation of the remains of the keep of Bristol Castle.

| 53 | Castle Park | Nicholls, J F | 1878 | ST 59231 73150 |

A 'dungeon' was observed on the site of the keep of Bristol Castle.

| 54 | Tyndall's Park | Price, Roger H | 1974 | ST 58330 73410 |

Observation of the foundations of the gatehouse of the Royal Fort.

| 55 | Horsefair | Bryant, John | 1991 | ST 59015 73883 |

Observation of a probable 15th-century wall in Horsefair.

| 56 | Castle Park | Dawson, David P | 1970 | ST 59130 73080 |

Observation of a wall painting in the south aisle of St Peter's Church.

| 57 | Castle Park | Jackson, R G | 1970 | ST 59100 73090 |

Observation of trial pits against the tower of St Peter's Church recorded its foundations and noted former graves.

| 59 | SS Philip and Jacob | Unknown | 1868 | ST 59487 73000 |

The bases of the piers supporting the arches which divide the aisles from the nave were found at about 18 inches below the floor surface.

| 61 | Castle Park | Jackson, R G | 1970 | ST 59240 73100 |

Observation of the wall of a 17th-century building in Castle Park.

| 64 | St Nicholas Church | Ponsford, M W | 1972 | ST 58920 72940 |

Observation of the town wall during building work below the tower of St Nicholas Church.

| 65 | St Stephen's Street | Dawson, David P | 1973 | ST 58710 73070 |

Observation of the town wall in the cellar of the White Lion public house.

| 66 | Corn Street | Unknown | 1824 | ST 58860 73055 |

Possible Norman architectural fragments and a skeleton were found during construction of the Old Council House on the site of St Ewen's Church.

| 68 | Colston Avenue | Bryant, John | 1981 | ST 58580 73041 |

Observation of a medieval wall to the rear of St Mary-on-the-Quay.

| 72 | King Street | Dawson, David P | 1979 | ST 58776 72718 |

Observation of alterations to No 35 King Street.

| 74 | Portland Square | Leech, Roger H | 1974 | ST 59410 73760 |

Observation of the buildings and groundworks at Nos 1–4 Portland Square before demolition.

| 75 | Trenchard Street | Bryant, John | 1981 | ST 58520 73110 |

Inhumations found during redevelopment of the site of the Roman Catholic chapel.

| 76 | 4 Lodge Street | Bryant, John | 1981 | ST 58500 73080 |

A well was discovered during building work. The feature was located 8 metres from the rear wall of No 4 Lodge Street.

| 79 | St Stephen Street | Ponsford, M W | 1971 | ST 58700 72994 |

Observation of No 12 St Stephen Street during renovation.

| 80 | St Thomas Street | Ponsford, M W | 1975 | ST 59182 72700 |

Observation of an undated stone wall and conduit in St Thomas Street.

| 81 | The Grove | Unknown | *c* 1974 | ST 58780 72430 |

Observation of work at Nos 4–7 The Grove.

| 82 | Queen Square | Jackson, R G | 1973 | ST 58910 72620 |

Observation of renovation of No 10 Queen Square noted that 17th-century deposits were undisturbed beneath the cellar floor.

| 85 | Small Street | Anon | 1887 | ST 58800 73100 |

Observation of 'clustered piers with cushioned capitals' surviving parts of a possible Norman building in the Law Library.

| 86 | Corn Street | Taylor, John | 1887 | ST 58880 73025 |

Observation of four 'stunted circular piers with plain cushion capitals' of ?12th-century date at the west end of the nave of All Saints' Church.

| 90 | Colston Avenue | Hudd, Alfred E | 1892 | ST 58670 73113 |

Roman coins were recovered from the River Frome at Stone bridge.

| 91 | Lamb Street | Bryant, John | 1986 | ST 59800 73350 |

Observation of post-medieval and possible late medieval walls at Lamb Street.

| 93 | Lewins Mead | Dawson, David P | 1972 | ST 58720 73330 |

Possible medieval walls observed at Greyfriars.

| 97 | Queen Square | Jones, Robert H | *c* 1996 | ST 58829 72461 |

Observation of the interior of No 29 Queen Square.

| 98 | Temple Street | Boore, Eric J | 1972 | ST 59360 72800 |

Observation of walls at Temple Street, probably associated with the Templar and Holy Cross churches.

| 99 | Baldwin Street | Price, Roger H | 1973 | ST 58750 72870 |

Observation of commercial excavation noted a possible medieval stone wall.

| 100 | Baldwin Street | Price, Roger H | 1973 | ST 58756 72869 |

Observation of a possible medieval stone wall in commercial excavation.

101   Queen Charlotte Street   Price, Roger H   1973   ST 58850 72850
      Observation of commercial excavation at Queen Charlotte Street.

103   Castle Street   Beddoe, Dr John   1888   ST 59380 73120
      Observation of medieval vaults in Castle Street.

104   Bridewell Street   Unknown   1894   ST 58900 73328
      Discovery of a medieval tile pavement at Silver Street.

105   College Green   Hughes, W W   1901   ST 58250 72668
      Recording and recovery of wall paintings at the Old Deanery.

106   College Green   Pryce, George   1850   ST 58250 72668
      Recording of additional wall paintings [see above] at the Old Deanery, College Green.

110   Narrow Wine Street   Marochan, Keith   1956   ST 59100 73170
      Observation of a 14th-century refuse pit at Narrow Wine Street.

111   Union Street   Marochan, Keith   1956   ST 59120 73180
      Observation of the town wall at Union Street.

115   Horsefair   Marochan, Keith   1955   ST 59070 73422
      A 14th-century jewellery mould and 17th-century pottery found at Horsefair.

116   Whitson Street   Marochan, Keith   1957   ST 59250 73410
      Clay tobacco pipe waste found at Whitson Street.

121   Merchant Street   Marochan, Keith   1956   ST 59215 73300
      18th-century glass waste and bottles found at Nos 18–30 Merchant Street.

125   Rupert Street   Ponsford, M W   1970   ST 58670 73180
      Observation and recording of Frome Bridge during road widening in Rupert Street.

129   Christmas Street   Unknown   c 1875   ST 58720 73163
      A medieval roof was recorded at the rear of No 2 Christmas Street.

138   St Michael's Hill   Burchill, Rod   1993   ST 58330 73430
      Observation of an 18th-century stone drain during construction of an extension to the Childrens' Hospital,
      Kingsdown.

139   Bridewell Street   Reed, W H B   1926   ST 58900 73328
      Part of the town wall was reported to have been observed at Bridewell.

140   Bridewell Street   Reed, W H B   1926   ST 58943 73264
      Observation of part of Needless Bridge at Bridewell.

141   Castle Park   Pritchard, John E   1898   ST 59370 73190
      Observation of part of a massive stone wall at Castle Green, interpreted as part of the north curtain wall
      of Bristol Castle.

148   Penn Street   Marochan, Keith   1958   ST 59396 73414
      Observation of the clay tobacco pipe kiln of John Oakley III (d 1799) at Penn Street.

151   Quakers' Friars   Marochan, Keith   1956   ST 59246 73340
      Medieval floor tiles were found at Quakers Friars.

153   Lewins Mead   Weare, G E   1894   ST 58700 73316
      Inhumations in oak coffins were disturbed by a service trench. The inhumations were believed to be from
      the burial ground of the Franciscan Friary.

156   Park Row   Unknown   1894   ST 58370 73110
      Two inhumations of unknown date were found beneath the pavement at Park Row.

| 165 | Castle Park | Rahtz, Philip | 1963 | ST 59270 73090 |

Observation of a *c* 30m stretch of the south curtain wall of Bristol Castle.

| 166 | Whitson Street | Unknown | 1898 | ST 58900 73510 |

A carved stone head, probably from the Priory of St James, was found during extension of the tramline on the north side of St James's Church.

| 181 | Clare Street | Pritchard, John E | 1902 | ST 58630 72920 |

Medieval pottery recovered during deep excavation for the construction of offices on the site of No 2 Colston Street.

| 182 | Bridewell Street | Unknown | 1902 | ST 58900 73270 |

Observation of the construction of a new magistrates' court did not record any archaeological evidence.

| 188 | Fairfax Street | Pritchard, John E | 1903 | ST 59150 73198 |

Bone needles and other finds from Fairfax Street. The finds were 'over 20 feet below the sloping bank of the Frome, in the blue alluvial deposit'.

| 193 | Cotham Road | Pritchard, John E | 1905 | ST 58180 73920 |

Stone walls, apparently of 17th-century date, were recorded during construction work at Cotham Road.

| 194 | Cotham Road | Tyson, William | 1829 | ST 58210 73870 |

Observation of the remains of Bewell's Cross, at Cotham Parish Church.

| 195 | College Green | Hayward, Mr. | 1905 | ST 58380 72670 |

Observation of a Norman column base within Bristol Cathedral.

| 196 | Bridewell Street | Pritchard, John E | 1926 | ST 58900 73300 |

Foundations of a watermill, the arch of the 1850 section of the culvert of the River Frome and several wells were observed during construction of the Police and Fire Brigade HQ at Bridewell. Several finds were made.

| 197 | Bath Street | Unknown | 1911 | ST 59120 72900 |

Observation of a two-light gothic headed window at Bath Street.

| 199 | St Thomas Street | Pritchard, John E | 1900 | ST 59111 72741 |

Observation of the demolition of a pair of gabled houses adjacent to the Seven Stars public house, St Thomas Lane.

| 206 | Castle Park | Pritchard, John E | 1930 | ST 59270 73160 |

An underground vault found in Castle Green.

| 207 | St Stephen's Avenue | Unknown | 1901 | ST 58720 72960 |

Medieval pottery was found during construction work at St Stephen's Avenue. Deeper excavation recovered a bone needle.

| 209 | Castle Park | Unknown | 1902 | ST 59160 73170 |

Drainage works near the 'Cat and Wheel', Castle Green, exposed part of the town wall which was reported to be *c* 5m thick.

| 211 | Castle Park | Pritchard, John E | 1929 | ST 59338 73155 |

Observation of the demolition of a polygonal tower in Castle Street, interpreted as probably a surviving part of Bristol Castle.

| 212 | Corn Street | Pritchard, John E | 1926 | ST 58740 72950 |

Observation of massive foundations at the junction of Corn Street and Clare Street, possibly the foundations of St Leonard's Gate.

| 213 | St John's Church, Broad Street | Unknown | ? | ST 58760 73173 |

A wall painting was recorded inside the church.

| 215 | College Green | Boore, Eric J | 1988 | ST 58460 72740 |

Observation of two disarticulated human skeletons in Deanery Road.

216   King David Residences, Upper Maudlin Street   Nicholls, J F   1883   ST 58577 73300
Observation of the historic fabric of St Mary Magdalen Nunnery at the King David Inn, Upper Maudlin Street. It was reported that the font of the nunnery was 'standing on the horse-block in the yard'.

217   Small Street   Beddoe, Dr John   1878   ST 58800 73010
Observation and recovery of human remains from St Werburgh's Church during clearance of the churchyard.

220   St Augustine's Parade   Selley, Alfred   1910   ST 58490 72855
Observation of a 'pebble track' or 'cobbled causeway', associated with Roman finds, during construction work at the Hippodrome, St Augustine's Parade.

221   College Green   Holmes, James G   1897   ST 58353 72683
Fragments of a medieval tracery were found to have been reused as part of the fabric of Bristol Cathedral.

226   St Thomas Street   Gough, W V   1916   ST 59100 72760
Observation of the base of a respond and a medieval floor surface during construction work in St Thomas's Church.

227   Lewins Mead   Pritchard, John E   1915   ST 58800 73368
Fragments of a medieval stone building, apparently a surviving element of the Franciscan Friary were removed to Bristol Museum when the building was demolished.

228   Royal Fort, Kingsdown   Unknown   1915   ST 58140 73430
Observation of the construction of University Walk, Kingsdown recorded no archaeological features.

230   Broad Street   Unknown   1913   ST 58850 73070
Floor tiles found during construction of the City Rates Office. The tiles may have come from St Ewen's Church.

232   Nelson Street   Pope, T S   1888   ST 58820 73230
Observation of two, possibly reused, Norman pillars in a property in Nelson Street.

237   Host Street   Bryant, John   1981   ST 58640 73170
Observation of a 19th-century stone-lined well in Host Street warehouse.

238   Baldwin Street   Ponsford, M W   1974   ST 58730 72870
Observation of an undated well in Baldwin Street.

242   Christmas Street   Unknown   1914   ST 58690 73220
Coins and tokens found at St John's Bridge.

244   Temple Back   Seyer, Samuel   1823   ST 59590 72690
Observation of surviving part of Tower Harratz, Temple Back. It was used as 'a warehouse, or part of a manufactory'. Also the Portwall 'continued from it a little way into the river'.

245   Temple Back   Seyer, Samuel   1823   ST 59603 72692
Observation of the Portwall ditch, which was in use as a drain, open in places and culverted in others.

246   Clare Street   Seyer, Samuel   1823   ST 58620 72900
Samuel Seyer noted in 1823 that part of the town wall known as the Marsh Wall had been found below ground during construction of Clare Street c 1771. It had a thickness of 5½ feet

247   King Street   Unknown   1818   ST 58820 72740
Observation of part of the Marsh Wall at Coopers' Hall. The wall was noted to be c 2m thick.

248   Queen Charlotte Street   Seyer, Samuel   1819   ST 58860 72740
Observation of a surviving part of the springing of Back Street Gate.

253   Temple Back   Seyer, Samuel   1823   ST 59040 72440
Observation of the Portwall, 'most of which remains'.

259   Baldwin Street   Seyer, Samuel   1785   ST 58860 72880
Observation of the 'thoroughs' of a Baldwin's-cross water mill at the junction of Baldwin Street and Queen Charlotte Street.

260   Broad Weir   Seyer, Samuel   1821   ST 59400 73180
        Observation of the 'cold bath' at Castle Ditch.

261   Merchant Street   Seyer, Samuel   1821   ST 59210 73220
        Observation of the remains of a mill, reported to be the Castle mill, at the junction of Castle Mill Street
        and Merchant Street.

263   Castle Park   Seyer, Samuel   1821   ST 59400 73160
        Observation of a square tower 'at the back part of Mr. H's house near the Castle-wall'.

266   Fairfax Street   Seyer, Samuel   1821   ST 59080 73180
        Observation of a bastion of the town wall between Fairfax Street and New Gate. It was reported to be 'still
        about perfect'.

267   Tower Lane   Seyer, Samuel   1821   ST 58880 73160
        Observation of a tower on the town wall in Tower Lane. The tower had been incorporated into a house.

268   Pithay   Seyer, Samuel   1821   ST 59030 73140
        Observation of parts of the town wall within buildings at Pithay.

269   Pithay   Seyer, Samuel   1821   ST 59000 73170
        Observation of a tower on the town wall near Pithay. The tower was c 4m square and had been converted
        into a (?public) house known as 'The Compasses'.

270   St John's Steep   Seyer, Samuel   1821   ST 58860 73200
        Observation of Blind Gate at St John's Steep. It was reported that the 'original facing of the gateway at the
        top of the steps is still visible'.

274   Rupert Street   Seyer, Samuel   1821   ST 58850 73297
        Observation of part of the town wall in Rupert Street or New Bridewell. The wall was reported to be c 3m
        thick and 'in the last state of dilapidation'.

282   Jacob's Wells Road   Bryant, John   1987   ST 57690 72870
        A medieval Jewish ritual bath ('Mikveh') was recorded at No 33 Jacob's Wells Road.

284   Frogmore Street   Pryce, George   1850   ST 58466 73000
        Observation of a niche, presumed to be for a statue, in the northern corner of No 9 Pipe Lane.

286   Cotham Road South   Seyer, Samuel   1823   ST 58520 73770
        Observation of the remains of Colston's Mount, Kingsdown. The mound was reported to have been cut
        away for a road.

287   Broad Street   Bryant, John c 1991   ST 58761 73136
        Observation of the medieval wall of the cellar of No 29 Broad Street.

289   Frogmore Street   Good, G L c 1988   ST 58388 72953
        Observation of construction of an electricity sub-station next to The Hatchet public house noted no
        archaeological features.

292   Colston Street   Bryant, John c 1991   ST 58585 73090
        Observation of redevelopment at Nos 22–8 Colston Street recorded no significant archaeological features.

293   Crow Lane   Bryant, John   1985   ST 58890 72798
        Observation of service trenches excavated in Crow Lane, Welsh Back recorded inhumations and a brick burial
        vault associated with the extension burial ground for St Nicholas Church.

294   Pritchard Street   Bryant, John   1988   ST 59420 73585
        Observation of redevelopment at Nos 12–20 Pritchard Street noted no archaeological features.

296   Wilder Street   Bryant, John   1990   ST 59105 73690
        Observation of redevelopment at the Moon Street/Wilder Street junction recorded no features of
        archaeological significance.

297   Jacob Street   Bryant, John   1982   ST 59820 73125
Observation of a site at Jacob Street/Midland Road recorded the remains of a possible tannery at Unity Street, a 17th-century wall on the line of the medieval defences.

300   Upper Maudlin Street   Bryant, John   1989   ST 58670 73370
Post-medieval walls were recorded at Nos 34–8 Upper Maudlin Street.

302   St Nicholas Street   Price, Roger H   1977   ST 58855 72923
A medieval wall was recorded in the pavement in front of No 17 St Nicholas Street.

303   Corn Street   Price, Roger H   1977   ST 58755 72939
The face of part of the town wall was observed on the east side of the cellar of No 30 Corn Street.

304   King Square   Bryant, John   1992   ST 58880 73828
Post-medieval walls were recorded at Nos 10–11 King Square.

307   Newmarket Avenue   Bryant, John   1993   ST 58863 73137
Observation of construction of a car park in Newmarket Avenue noted stone arches in a rubble wall against Fitzhardinge House and the remains of stone walls against Tower Lane.

321   Portwall Lane   Pountney, W J   1915   ST 59241 72405
Observation of the Portwall Ditch in which was exposed by commercial excavation noted that the ditch had been filled with early 18th-century industrial waste, including ceramic waste.

325   Queen Square   Unknown   ?   ST 58780 72462
The 'cranium of a man' was 'found in digging a foundation at the Marine School, Queen Square' according to an accession card in Bristol Museum and Art Gallery.

349   Castle Park   Unknown   1970   ST 59080 73090
Observation of the excavation of large service trenches revealed what was interpreted as a defensive ditch running under Dolphin Street. Only 18th-century deposits were exposed.

355   Temple Way   Bryant, John   1987   ST 59469 72670
A pit containing clay tobacco pipe waste was observed during road widening on the west side of Temple Way.

356   College Green   Unknown   1927   ST 58470 72690
Inhumations, apparently belonging to the burial ground of St Augustine-the-Less, were found during construction of an extension to the Royal Hotel in Trinity Street.

357   Temple Back   Ponsford, M W   1970   ST 59300 72840
Observation of construction of the Fire Brigade HQ, Temple Back, noted the destruction of medieval deposits.

379   West Street   Bryant, John   1987   ST 59915 73214
Post-medieval inhumations and a stone rubble wall observed during illegal disturbance to the former burial ground, near West Street, Old Market.

380   West Street   Bryant, John   1988   ST 59904 73245
Two stone rubble walls of probable 15th-century date observed at Nos 32–6 West Street, Old Market.

389   Brunswick Square   Bryant, John   1986   ST 59268 73694
A brick burial vault associated with the Brunswick Square burial ground was observed in a foundation trench north of Surrey Lodge.

397   Brandon Hill   Seyer, Samuel   ?   ST 57934 72957
Observation of a mound surrounded by ditch, to the rear of Brandon Hill Fort.

405   Broad Quay   Morris, Horace   1970   ST 58620 72775
Observation of part of the town wall at Broad Quay. The wall was not recorded.

407   Broad Quay   Price, Roger H   1979   ST 58625 72745
Development work at the Bristol and West Building, Broad Quay exposed part of the town wall and a water gate. The features were rapidly recorded before destruction.

411   Quay Street   Unknown   1848   ST 58719 73135
A logboat was discovered in Quay Street 'at a considerable depth from the surface' during excavation for a sewer. The find, 'fourteen feet long, and four feet wide, shaped from a single trunk of timber', was sawn through, part being left *in situ*.

426   Bridewell Street   Seyer, Samuel 1821   ST 58920 73300
Observation of a circular building upstream of Bridewell, *c* 4m in diameter which had been converted into an oven during the post-medieval period. Its function was not clear.

428   Bridewell Street   Seyer, Samuel 1821   ST 58920 73290
Observation of a semi-circular three-storey tower on the town wall near Bridewell. The tower had been 'lately taken down'.

429   Unknown   1902   ST 58945 73258
Artefacts, believed to be of Iron Age date, were found 'on the sloping bank of the [River] Froom, from deep excavations'. The finds included bone needles and stone and pottery spindle whorls.

431   Bristol Bridge   Jackson, R G   1975   ST 58980 72926
A deep service trench at the junction of Bristol Bridge and Baldwin Street revealed medieval stonework interpreted as one of the piers of the medieval Bristol Bridge.

433   Passage Street   Williams, Bruce 1987   ST 59326 72985
A medieval stone wall, interpreted as the quay wall, or possibly a boundary wall of the King's Orchard associated with Bristol Castle, was observed during groundworks on the site of a former cold store.

439   Baltic Wharf   Good, G L   1977   ST 57248 72144
Observation of machine excavation of a new slipway at Baltic Wharf noted upright timbers and a stone pier close to the dock wall.

445   Lower Maudlin Street   Boore, Eric J 1989   ST 58849 73424
Observation of a medieval wall, in a service trench on the west side of Lower Maudlin Street, interpreted as possibly the boundary wall between St James's Priory and the Franciscan Friary.

450   College Green   Brett, Jonathan R 1996   ST 58360 72811
Observation of pits dug for tree planting on the northern side of College Green noted no archaeological evidence.

454   Colston Street   Fox, Francis F 1889   ST 58714 73147
Observation of 'an ancient arch of peculiar construction' on the River Frome beneath Fry's factory (now the site of Westgate House)'.

455   Broad Quay   Webb, F G   1962   ST 58627 72824
Observation of groundworks at No 8 Broad Quay recorded no archaeological features.

489   Temple Street   Unknown   1872   ST 59331 72734
Lowering of the floor in Temple Church exposed the foundations of a circular building measuring 43ft by 23ft. This was believed to be the original Knights Templar Church.

497   Corn Street   Brett, Jonathan R 1996   ST 58883 73049
An undated wall or possible paved surface was observed in a small commercial excavation at the eastern end of Corn Street.

508   St Nicholas Street   Bindon, John   1850   ST 58812 72950
Observation of the remains of a medieval building during construction of the Athenaeum, St Nicholas Street.

532   St George's Road   Jones, Robert H 1993   ST 58100 72700
Observation of groundworks for new student accommodation on the northern side of St George's Road noted that any archaeological deposits on the site had been destroyed by later cellars.

533   Temple Back   Price, Roger H 1972   ST 59408 72847
Observation of a possible slipway of medieval date in a commercial excavation on the site of the former Central Electric Lighting Station on Temple Back.

545	College Green	Unknown	1824	ST 58365 72841

Wall paintings associated with St Mark's Hospital found during redecoration in the adjoining house in College Green.

546	Unity Street	Archdeacon Norris	1883	ST 58377 72856

A fragment of masonry, interpreted as part of the cloister of the Hospital of St Mark, was observed during groundworks for construction of the Merchant Venturers' College.

567	John Street	Unknown	?	ST 58854 73292

An inhumation was found beneath the pavement in John Street, just outside St John's Churchyard.

607	Counterslip	Bryant, John	1985	ST 59194 72857

The boundary wall of No 6 Temple Street was recorded before demolition during redevelopment of Courage's Brewery, Counterslip, in 1985.

638	Broad Weir	Pritchard, John E	1906	ST 59325 73268

'Portions of a carved chimney-piece' were found 'in pulling down the principal room' of the 'Old Crown' tavern, Broad Weir.

646	Denmark Street	Bryant, John	1989	ST 58503 72836

It was concluded as a result of internal inspection that Nos 22–3 Denmark Street were partly of 18th-century origin.

659	Castle Park	Pritchard, John E	1905	ST 58996 73035

Renovation of Nos 38 and 40 Mary-le-Port Street was observed.

660	Merchant Street	Pritchard, John E	1905	ST 59145 73375

Demolition of Nos 3 and 5 Old King Street was observed.

661	Merchant Street	Pritchard, John E	1908	ST 59137 73389

Demolition of Nos 11 and 13 Old King Street was observed.

663	Castle Park	Pritchard, John E	1904	ST 59099 73111

Demolition of Nos 4 and 5 Peter Street was observed.

666	Host Street	Pritchard, John E	1902	ST 58617 73090

Demolition of properties between Host Street and Christmas Street after structural collapse was observed. The buildings were thought to date between the 17th and 19th centuries.

675	Castle Park	Pritchard, John E	1901	ST 59125 73097

Repair work to St Peter's Church was observed and several features observed, including a pointed doorway on the north side of the chancel, and a piscina.

678	St Thomas Street	Pritchard, John E	1914	ST 59160 72709

Demolition of the 'Court Sampson' was observed.

679	St Thomas Street	Pritchard, John E	1911	ST 59176 72727

Demolition of the 'Three Kings Inn' was observed.

680	Small Street	Pritchard, John E	1903	ST 58739 73066

The interior of No 7 Small Street was visited before demolition.

685	SS Philip and Jacob	Pritchard, John E	1907	ST 59490 73005

Alterations to the interior of the church were observed.

698	Welsh Back	Pritchard, John E	1903	ST 58930 72888

Observation of the demolition of No 3 Welsh Back.

909	Bridge Street	Pritchard, John E	1913	ST 59014 73007

Demolition of Bridge Street Chapel was observed.

916	King Street	Pritchard, John E	1904	ST 58786 72725

Demolition of Nos 35 and 36 King Street was observed.

931   Redcliffe Way   Bryant, John   1983   ST 59217 72391
Internal works to Chatterton House, Redcliffe Way were observed.

961   Corn Street   Unknown   1977   ST 58785 72962
Observation of conversion work at Nos 32 and 36, Corn Street recorded medieval walls were in three places on the south-western side of No 36. A cess pit of possible 13th-century date was noted to the rear of the building.

1501   Perry Road   Unknown   1868   ST 58589 73288
Observation of an 'octangular tower'.

1502   Bristol Cathedral, College Green   Unknown   1923   ST 58355 72664
When the floor of the vestibule of the Chapter House was lowered to its original level a coffin slab of 13th-century date was found.

1648   College Square   Williams, Bruce   ?   ST 58295 72626
Observation at the Registrar's House.

2457   Brandon Hill   Ellis, Frederick   1897   ST 57933 72958
Human remains of unknown date were found during excavation of the foundations of Cabot Tower. Post-medieval features, possibly associated with the Civil War defences, were also observed.

2469   High Street   Pryce, George   1850   ST 58910 73003
Observation of an inscribed oak beam interpreted as possibly from All Saints' Almshouse, High Street.

2518   Wade Street   Reynolds, John   1865   ST 59798 73500
During commercial excavation in Wade Street two Roman lead ingots were found. Both carried the inscription 'IMP' CAES' A[NTON]INI' AUG' PII P' P'.

2525   Quakers' Friars   Unknown   1814   ST 59300 73300
Three stone coffins containing 'the entire skeletons of two men and one woman' were discovered during excavations between Rosemary Street and Merchant Street.

2590   Bristol Bridge   Barrett, William   1767   ST 59000 72910
Wooden ?piles were observed in the stone piers of Bristol Bridge during its reconstruction.

2868   Small Street   Pritchard, John E   1909   ST 58750 73040
Observation of excavation for the extension of the Post Office in Small Street noted a number of finds at depths between *c* 4 and 5m. The finds included animal and human remains, medieval and post-medieval pottery and a stone mortar.

2869   Colston Avenue   Pritchard,John E   1910   ST 58640 73100
The excavation of piles for the construction of government offices at a site at the junction where Zed Alley meets Colston Avenue was observed.

3020   Elton Road   Unknown   1910   ST 58065 73510
During commercial excavation at 'the green plot of ground in front of the Grammar School entrance' (possibly at Nos 10–11 Elton Road) workmen found walling interpreted as the remains of 18th-century farm buildings destroyed in the 19th century.

3023   Broad Street   Unknown   1911   ST 58839 73080
Demolition of Nos 8–11 Broad Street was observed. A gravestone from St Ewen's Churchyard was recovered.

3028   Denmark Street   Pritchard, John E   1911   ST 58480 72855
Demolition of early 18th-century buildings in Denmark Street and Hanover Street was observed.

3029   Castle Park   Pritchard, John E   1907   ST 59020 73020
Observation of groundworks between Bridge Street and Mary-le-Port Street noted that the site had previously been excavated.

3030   Castle Park   Pritchard, John E   1910   ST 59310 73097
Observation of demolition at No 63 Castle Street noted that the 17th-century building stood on massive stone foundations, believed to be of medieval date.

3034   Tyndall's Park   Unknown   1750   ST 58280 73350
Several Roman coins were found at the Royal Fort in Tyndall's Park when Thomas Tyndall 'reformed and walled in a large garden there'. The finds included coins of Constantine, Constantius, Gordian and Tetricus.

3038   Temple Street   Gough, W V   1910   ST 59332 72732
Works to the interior of Temple Church were observed.

3039   Temple Street   Pritchard, John E   1910   ST 59332 72732
Works in Temple Churchyard were observed.

3044   High Street   Pryce, George   1850   ST 58900 73002
During rebuilding work at No 41 High Street in October 1850 a wooden roof was observed at the rear of the property. The roof was an arch brace truss with plain wind braces and was divided into two main bays.

3047   Marsh Street   Pritchard, John E   1907   ST 58675 72700
Observation of the insertion of a girder beneath the reception room of the Merchant Venturers' Hall in Marsh Street noted the lower portion of a four-light window was noted, assumed to be set in the west wall of St Clement's Chapel.

3057   High Street   Pritchard, John E   1927   ST 58960 72973
Cellars of late medieval date below Nos 23, 24 and 25 High Street were observed before demolition.

3058   Lewins Mead   Unknown   1892   ST 5873 7339
A medieval building in Lewins Mead, believed to be part of the Franciscan Friary, was observed, together with some 13th-century arches, 'one of which is situated underground'.

3059   Lewins Mead   Unknown   ?   ST 5875 7335
'Commercial excavation to the rear of a warehouse in Lewins Mead found an 'underground passage', apparently of medieval date. Large quantities of human bones were also found'.

3060   Lewins Mead   Unknown   1851   ST 5875 7335
Excavation to connect a warehouse in Lewins Mead to the main sewer disturbed inhumations and 'the remains of oak coffins' were found.

3061   Culver Street   Reed, Keith   1959   ST 58323 72935
A stencilled wall painting, possibly of 18th-century date, was found beneath wallpaper in an upper storey room of a house in Culver Street.

3082   Corn Street   Unknown   1906   ST 58885 73050
Service trenches dug by the former Council House, Corn Street 'cut into the arches of some cellars, and into some massive stonework which appeared to have been a sustaining arch'.

3097   Bristol Cathedral, College Green   Unknown   1831   ST 58358 72669
Work on the floor of the Chapter House, Bristol Cathedral revealed a Saxon carved stone, 'the Harrowing of Hell stone', and medieval stone coffins.

3139   Small Street   Unknown   1887   ST 58787 73034
During demolition of buildings in Small Street to make way for the construction of the new post office 'two tiers of ancient cellars, one below the other' were observed. These were believed to be part of the medieval Creswicke mansion.

3142   Whitson Street   Russett, V R   1992   ST 58848 73450
An undated stone culvert was exposed by excavation of a service trench close to the White Hart public house.

3166   St Augustine's Parade   Bryant, John   1997   ST 58535 72852
The remains of the front wall foundation of the former No 12 St Augustine's Parade were observed in a commercial excavation in the pavement by the Hippodrome theatre, St Augustine's Parade.

3174   Tyndall's Park   Gullidge, Phillip   1985   ST 58263 73372
During pipe-laying work close to the north-west corner of Royal Fort House, Royal Fort Road two walls were observed. These have been interpreted as part of a structure depicted by Rocque's 1742 map which may be associated with the Civil War fort.

| 3176 | Wellington Road | Brett, Jonathan and Bryant, John | 1997 | ST 59567 73440 |

Observation of a section of a 19th-century culvert of the River Frome behind houses on Wellington Road. The culvert was apparently enclosing the leat which served the castle mill.

| 3182 | Colston Street | Burchill, Rod | 1997 | ST 58670 73114 |

The dock gates controlling the water level in the Floating Harbour and the remains of the mid-18th-century Stone Bridge were observed at the junction of Colston Avenue and Rupert Street.

| 3183 | Broad Weir | Burchill, Rod | 1997 | ST 59225 73191 |

The Fosse Gate river control gates beneath Broad Weir were observed. These were noted to be contained within a modern brick chamber.

| 3197 | Temple Gate | Jones, Robert H | 1997 | ST 59393 72405 |

Part of the disturbed remains of the Portwall was observed in a service trench at Temple Gate.

| 3205 | Pithay | Pritchard, John E | 1899 | ST 58957 73123 |

Demolition of the 'Prince of Wales' public house at Pithay was observed.

| 3206 | St John's Steep | Pritchard, John E | 1910 | ST 58875 73206 |

Medieval and post-medieval ceramics and other finds were recovered from the site of St John's Almshouse, St John's Steep after its demolition. Also noted 'at a depth of 40 feet were several oak trunks', apparently in a palaeochannel of the Frome.

| 3207 | Christmas Street | Pritchard, John E | 1910 | ST 58720 73163 |

A 17th-century chimney-piece was observed in a first-floor room of No 2 Christmas Street during its demolition.

| 3208 | Christmas Street | Pritchard, John E | 1910 | ST 58730 73162 |

During demolition of the 'Ship' public house, Christmas Street a medieval roof was observed.

| 3235 | Narrow Quay | Unknown | 1932 | ST 58625 72656 |

An axe and a spearhead of Bronze Age date were found during excavation for the construction of an extension to the Co-operative Wholesale Building.

| 3244 | Corn Street | Unknown | 1833 | ST 58740 72959 |

Excavation of a sewer at the west end of Corn Street exposed part of the town wall.

| 3253 | King Street | Jones, Robert H | 1996 | ST 58841 72737 |

The interior of St Nicholas's Almshouse was observed during renovation.

| 3273 | St Thomas Street | Taylor, C J | 1881 | ST 59125 72761 |

Architectural fragments of the medieval church were found in the walls of the post-medieval St Thomas Church when these were stripped for replastering in 1881.

| 3274 | Marsh Street | Jones, Robert H | 1997 | ST 58653 72803 |

Inspection of the interior of No 22 Marsh Street noted that the building had a modern roof. No features earlier than the 19th century were observed but the side walls of the property were obscured by render.

| 3279 | Marsh Street | Jones, R H | 1997 | ST 58648 72818 |

Inspection of the interior of No 16 Marsh Street noted medieval and later features in the side walls of the building.

| 3280 | Baldwin Street | Unknown | c 1932 | ST 58816 72883 |

A part of a bone object, believed to be a comb of 'Early Iron Age Type' 4½" long was found in the area of Baldwin Street.

| 3282 | Cumberland Basin | Unknown | 1870 | ST 56768 72436 |

A Bronze Age socketed axe was found during construction of a new lock.

| 3283 | All Saints' Street | Pritchard, John E | 1900 | ST 58904 73187 |

A Roman coin of the emperor Maximianus was found 'at a depth of 11 feet below the roadway, at the corner of All Saints' Avenue, in the blue clay deposit'.

3296   Lamb Street, Old Market   Reed, Keith   1957   ST 59810 73360
Waste material from a clay tobacco pipe kiln and an infilled post-medieval well were observed.

3313   Temple Back   Jackson, R G   1983   ST 59540 72750
Part of a working floor and brick arched coal cellars of Ring's clay tobacco pipe factory were recorded in a
service trench at Temple Back. Part of a muffle kiln and ceramic kiln waste were recovered.

3316   Great Western Dry Dock, Gasferry Road   Firth, Antony   1998   ST 57760 72448
Underwater survey of the dock walls by Great Western Dry Dock identified timber piles and stakes set in
the bed of the Floating Harbour.

3325   7 Frog Lane (Frogmore Street)   Bryant, John   1998   ST 58334 72909
John Bryant observed a gable in the rear of No 7 Frog Lane. The visible elements of the building were of
Brandon Hill Grit rubble construction and there was a Pennant sandstone rubble stack on the west side,
probably serving the rear room. It was also noted that a door had been inserted in the gable at attic level in
the position which would have been occupied by the attic window. The two-window three-storey front is of
brick, probably dating to the 18th or 19th centuries, suggesting that the building has been refronted. There
was an entrance on the east end of the south side. The roof was hipped at the front. It was believed that the
building was of 17th-century date, and that the plan suggested there may have been a detached kitchen block.

3378   Bristol and West House, Broad Quay   Unknown   1936   ST 58630 72797
Construction of a depot for Bristol Waterworks Company at No 13 Broad Quay is reported to have revealed
part of a medieval tower on the Marsh Wall.

3402   Castle Park   Unknown   1937   ST 59370 73137
During demolition of No 20 Tower Street elements of historic fabric thought to be surviving parts of Bristol
Castle, including an arched doorway, were exposed.

3407   Quakers' Friars   Unknown   1933   ST 59228 73342
A large medieval traceried window was uncovered during work to a wall of City Motors Ltd Garage, north
of Cutlers' Hall.

3424   Quakers' Friars   Woolley, W H   1936   ST 59235 73344
Remnants of a large medieval traceried window, adjacent to a similar, earlier find, were uncovered during
work to a wall of City Motors Ltd Garage, north of Cutlers' Hall.

3494   98–103 Redcliff Street   Brett, Jonathan R   1999   ST 59052 72568
Historic standing walls were observed within and at the rear of No 101 Redcliff Street, including part of the
south wall of a medieval tenement, the rear walls of Nos 102 and 103 Redcliff Street and the west walls of
two small houses which stood on Golden Lion Passage.

3534   Redcliff Hill   Brett, Jonathan R   2000   ST 59057 72292
Investigative highway works in the carriageway on Redcliff Hill exposed the cellars of houses which stood
on the west side of the hill until the road was widened in the late 1960s.

3584   Victoria Street   Brett, Jonathan R   2000   ST 59072 72856
Excavation in the middle of Victoria Street for water main renewal exposed part of a post-medieval stone
culvert orientated south-west to north-east.

3587   St Michael's Church   Brett, Jonathan R   2000   ST 58520 73297
Lifting of slabs covering burial vaults in the crypt of the church was monitored.

3665   St Nicholas Church   Unknown   1763   ST 58940 72940
Inhumations were discovered in the walls of St Nicholas Church during demolition.

3666   Pipe Lane   Unknown   1788   ST 58477 73005
'A great quantity of human bones and some entire skeletons' were found during excavation 'at the corner
of Pipe Lane'.

3668   College Green   Unknown   1850   ST 58428 72757
Excavation of the foundation of the replica High Cross exposed human remains 'at a considerable depth'.

| 3669 | Kingsdown Parade | Unknown | 1835 | ST 58850 74040 |

Excavation 'at the brow of the hill in Dame Pugsley's Field' exposed a pit containing lead musket balls and clay tobacco pipes.

| 3670 | Victoria Street | Nicholls, J F | 1869 | ST 59340 72600 |

The floor of the Weaver's Hall and an adjoining building were observed during demolition to allow construction of Victoria Street.

| 3715 | Redcliff Caves, Redcliff Wharf | Scarth, H M | 1868 | ST 58844 73015 |

Redcliff Caves were explored by members of Bath Natural History and Antiquarian Field Club when excavation for a railway cutting broke into the southern end of the caves.

| 3719 | Anchor Road | Unknown | 1896 | ST 58370 72610 |

Part of a wall was discovered thought most likely to be part of the Bishop's Palace.

| 3788 | Redcliff Caves, Redcliff Wharf | Roberts, J H F | 1868 | ST 58926 72240 |

Redcliff Caves were explored when excavation for a railway cutting broke into the southern end of the caves.

| 3791 | Bristol Cathedral | Street, G E | 1869 | ST 58330 72685 |

Groundworks for the foundations of the new nave of the cathedral exposed the foundations of an earlier nave, interpreted as that of the Norman abbey church.

| 3794 | St Mary Redcliffe Church | Pryce, George | 1852 | ST 59113 72306 |

Work to the south aisle of the church exposed two medieval tombs.

| 3851 | 151 Hotwell Road | Brett, Jonathan R | 2002 | ST 57406 72457 |

The building was a house of two storeys and attic. The building was constructed of Brandon Hill Grit in a random rubble construction bonded in a white lime mortar.

| 3868 | 29–31 West Street, Old Market | Brett, Jonathan R | 2002 | ST 59889 73264 |

A wall at the rear of Nos 29–31 West Street was bonded in an orange-red mortar of likely 17th-century date.

| 3918 | Temple Back | Beckey, Ian | 1988 | ST 59405 72805 |

Material was recovered from a layer of clay tobacco pipe kiln waste at Temple Back. The material originated at the nearby factory of Richard Frank Ring.

| 3919 | Monk Street | Beckey, Ian | 1992 | ST 59892 73869 |

A dump of clay tobacco pipe waste was observed on the former site of Nos 37–9 Monk Street.

| 3920 | Wellington Road | Beckey, Ian | ? | ST 59590 73420 |

A small service trench in Wellington Road was observed and a layer of clay tobacco pipe waste was observed in the section.

| 4232 | Quakers Friars | Unknown | ? | ST 59210 73362 |

In the late 1920s or early 1930s six inhumations were discovered on either side of Quakers Friars.

| 4233 | Quakers Friars | Hunt, Marshall | ? | ST 59196 73351 |

In the late 1920s or early 1930s 'paving', probably of medieval date and associated with the Dominican Friary was discovered in a garage on the southern side of Rosemary Street.

| 4317 | Tyndall's Park Road | Brett, Jonathan R | 2006 | ST 58198 73829 |

A parish boundary marker stone was observed at the back of the footway, against the boundary wall of former Homeopathic Hospital, on the northern side of the junction of Tyndall's Park Road with St Michael's Hill.

| 24685 | St Stephen's Church | Insole, Peter | 2008 | ST 58671 72986 |

A small excavation at the west end of St Stephen's Church revealed a stone slab immediately beneath the Victorian encaustic tiles.

Building surveys

| 38 | Wheatsheaf public house | ? | 1970 | ST 58730 73180 |
| 70 | National Westminster Bank, Corn Street | University of Bath | 1979 | ST 58780 72960 |

84	SS Philip and Jacob, Tower Hill	Godwin, E W	1862	ST 59497 72998
97	29 Queen Square	Jones, Robert	?	ST 58829 72461
109	117–20 Redcliff Street	?	1973	ST 59030 72691
271	Tower Street	Seyer, Samuel	1821	ST 59370 73130
360	13–17 Bath Street	Bryant, John	1985	ST 59147 72880
361	The Abbot's House, Blackfriars	Bryant, John	1989	ST 58711 73389
362	Greyhound Hotel, Broadmead	Bryant, John	1988	ST 59112 73295
363	24 Broad Street	Bryant, John	1988	ST 58776 73112
364	25 Broad Street	Bryant, John	1988	ST 58766 73112
365	43 Broad Street	Bryant, John	1979	ST 58815 73128
366	43 Broad Street	Bryant, John	1992	ST 58815 73128
367	Buildings at Cyder House Passage	Bryant, John	1989	ST 58860 73140
368	Standing walls at Cyder House Passage	Bryant, John	1991	ST 58847 73138
369	17–19 Christmas Street	Bryant, John	1983	ST 58657 73187
370	1 and 1a Christmas Street	Kear, D	1977	ST 58649 73171
371	Cellar, 35 Corn Street	Bryant, John & Dawson, David	1984	ST 58757 72978
372	35 Corn Street	Bryant, John	1995	ST 58750 72990
373	31–3 Corn Street	Bryant, John	1988	ST 58738 72982
374	33 King Street	Bryant, John	1980	ST 58761 72715
375	34 King Street	Bryant, John	1986	ST 58769 72713
376	Old Rectory, Lower Church Lane	Bryant, John	1980	ST 58533 73265
377	10 Lower Park Row	Bryant, John	1978	ST 58500 73145
385	Stag and Hound, 74 Old Market Street	Bryant, John	1986	ST 59596 73110
386	40 and 41 Old Market Street	Bryant, John	1982	ST 59722 73200
387	42 Old Market Street	Bryant, John	1980	ST 59725 73210
388	71 Old Market Street	Bryant, John	1986	ST 59619 73116
392	38–9 Old Market Street	Unknown	1981	ST 59715 73200
393	22 Old Market Street	Bryant, John	1988	ST 59600 73182
457	Avonside Ironworks, Avon Street	Cattell, John	1996	ST 59870 72821
479	Sheldon, Bush Shot Works, Cheese Lane	Bryant, John	1996	ST 59421 72892
480	The Dominican Friary, Quakers' Friars	Godwin, E W	1853	ST 59259 73309
484	Town wall, 41–3 Baldwin Street	Rahtz, Philip	1957	ST 58827 72911
486	Room above Newton Chapel, Bristol Cathedral	Warren, Robert Hall	1906	ST 58369 72675
487	Elevation at St Bartholomew's Hospital	Gough, W V	1901	ST 58639 73202
495	Cellar, 22 High Street	Pope, T S	1887	ST 58953 72980
498	Registrar's House, College Square	Pritchard, John E	1896	ST 58295 72623
503	St Mary Redcliffe Church	Britton, John	1813	ST 59126 72315
504	West front of St James's Church	Maclean, John	1888	ST 58879 73461
505	Crypt of St Nicholas Church	Nicholls, J F	1878	ST 58941 72940
506	St Lawrence's Church, Broad Street	Bindon, John	1850	ST 58738 73143
511	Ye Ould Friendship, Castle Green	Pritchard, John E	1901	ST 59350 73161
512	Vaulted Chambers, Castle Park	Ponsford, M W	1970	ST 59373 73129
515	Lady Chapel, Bristol Cathedral	Warren, Robert Hall	1908	ST 58391 72681
516	Cellars, Bishop's Palace, Bristol Cathedral	Lynam, Charles	1905	ST 58367 72631
524	Vaulted Chambers, Castle Park	Nicholls, J F	1878	ST 59372 73129
527	St Mary Redcliffe Church	Norris, J P	1879	ST 59125 72313
528	St Mary Redcliffe Church	Brakspear, Harold	1922	ST 59154 72314
529	51–67 Union Street/1–3 Silver Street	Jones, Robert	1982	ST 58933 73353
530	95–6 Redcliff Street	Winstone, John	1982	ST 59084 72538
531	St Peter's Hospital, Castle Park	Simpson, J J	1926	ST 59117 73063
535	The Dominican Priory, Quakers Friars	Leighton, Wilfrid	1934	ST 59265 73313
541	114 St Michael's Hill	Price, Roger H	1974	ST 58344 73620
542	Bristol Cathedral	Godwin, E W	1863	ST 58365 72689

543	Bristol Cathedral	Paul, Roland W	1912	ST 58335 72658
547	Bristol Cathedral	Britton, John	1830	ST 58348 72689
551	St Mary Redcliffe	Harvey, Alfred	1909	ST 59130 72315
602	St Michael's Manor, St Michael's Hill	Bryant, John	1983	ST 58450 73306
608	117–23 Redcliff Street	Bryant, John	1983–9	ST 59020 72690
609	119 Redcliff Street	Price, Roger H	1972	ST 59020 72690
610	144–5 Redcliff Street	Price, Roger H	1972	ST 59022 72845
611	144–5 Redcliff Street	Bryant, John	1981	ST 59015 72840
612	138–40 Redcliff Street	Bryant, John	1981	ST 59010 72805
613	141–2 Redcliff Street	Bryant, John	1981	ST 59010 72825
614	128 Redcliff Street	Bryant, John	1982	ST 59026 72742
616	26–31 St Augustine's Parade	Bryant, John	1979	ST 58544 72924
622	2 Trenchard Street	Bryant, John	1989	ST 58483 73010
623	St James's Church	Bryant, John	1993	ST 58895 73470
624	Church House, Whitson Street	Bryant, John	1993	ST 58878 73479
625	St John the Baptist, Broad Street	Bryant, John	1987	ST 58758 73171
626	53 St Michael's Hill	Bryant, John	1986	ST 58450 73392
627	Colston Almshouse, St Michael's Hill	Unknown	1984	ST 58510 73380
628	St Nicholas Church	Bryant, John and Bell I	1979–80	ST 58937 72939
629	St Nicholas Church	Bryant, John	1980	ST 58945 72951
630	St Nicholas Church	Bryant, John	1987	ST 58943 72943
631	St Stephen's Church	Bryant, John	1992	ST 58697 72978
632	10–11 Small Street	Bryant, John	1981	ST 58715 73080
633	1 Tailor's Court	Bryant, John	1991	ST 58829 73154
636	Guildhall Chambers, Broad Street	Unknown	1992	ST 58784 73116
640	Dorter passage, Bristol Cathedral	Bryant, John	1992	ST 58355 72664
641	62 Colston Street	Unknown	1974	ST 58586 73216
642	66 Colston Street	Unknown	1974	ST 58588 73224
643	56 Colston Street	Bryant, John	1987	ST 58587 73206
647	Rising Sun, Lower Castle Street	Pritchard, John E	1906	ST 59392 73245
649	5–8 High Street	Pritchard, John E	1914	ST 58919 73034
650	21 High Street	Pritchard, John E	1914	ST 58955 72985
654	13–15 King Street	Bryant, John	1981	ST 58798 72698
656	20–1 Lower Park Row	Oultram, J	1991	ST 58547 73170
658	35, Mary-le-Port Street	Pritchard, John E	1904	ST 59021 73048
662	Full Moon, North Street	Dawson, David P	?	ST 59080 73668
664	Pithay Chapel, Pithay	Pritchard, John E	1907	ST 58992 73162
665	Red Lodge, Park Row	Bryant, John	?	ST 58438 73110
667	93–5 Redcliff Street	Price, Roger H	1972	ST 59028 72535
668	93–5 Redcliff Street	Jones, Robert H	1985	ST 59028 72535
670	90–1 Redcliff Street	Jones, Robert H	1984	ST 59085 72507
674	44–5 Mary-le-Port Street	Pritchard, John E	1920	ST 58961 73012
676	St Peter's Church	Rome, A M	1972	ST 59125 73097
677	St Peter's Church	Boucher, C E	1909	ST 59125 73097
683	Former Post Office, Small Street	Bryant, John	1989	ST 58750 73045
686	45–9 Stokes Croft	Bryant, John	1981	ST 59074 73842
687	1 and 2 Tower Lane	Bryant, John	1979	ST 58863 73166
688	Stotesbury Tiles, Water Lane	BIAS Survey Unit	1975	ST 59440 72794
690	Temple Church	Field, B V	1974	ST 59332 72732
692	Museum Lecture Theatre, University Road	Mason, R	1983	ST 58030 73255
694	Bristol Old Station, Temple Gate	Unknown	1991	ST 59575 72400
695	58–66 Victoria Street	Unknown	1975	ST 59294 72709
697	115 and the Crabb's Well, Victoria Street	Pritchard, John E	1907	ST 59331 72552

901	Back Hall, Welsh Back	O'Neill, B H St John	1941	ST 58920 72861
902	The Granary, Welsh Back	Falconer, Keith	1988	ST 58886 72671
903	Lamb Inn, West Street	Pritchard, John E	1905	ST 59839 73239
904	The Old School House, Wilson Street	Bryant, John	1992	ST 59614 73793
905	Buildings in Bath Street	Bryant, John	1985	ST 59140 72843
906	10–22 Victoria Street	Bryant, John	1987	ST 59150 72835
907	Bakehouse, 17 Alfred Place	Bryant, John	1986	ST 58481 73714
908	2 Victoria Street	Bryant, John	1985	ST 59098 72866
910	St George's Church, Brandon Hill	Unknown	1978	ST 58140 72985
911	4–7 College Green	Bryant, John	1989	ST 58423 72721
912	Hole in the Wall, The Grove	Unknown	1971	ST 58856 72443
913	Warehouse, Host Street	Unknown	1978	ST 58630 73152
914	19 Jacob's Wells Road	Simeon Zell	1990	ST 57705 72808
915	19 and 20, King Street	Bryant, John	1991	ST 58765 72679
919	Theatre Royal, King Street	Edwards, J Ralph	1943	ST 58795 72763
920	Ridley's Almshouse, Milk Street	O'Neill, B H St John	?	ST 59143 73444
921	St James House, Moon Street	Bryant, John	1989	ST 59103 73694
922	16 Narrow Quay	Bryant, John	1981	ST 58588 72470
923	1 New Street	Unknown	?	ST 59630 73357
924	Assembly Rooms, Prince Street	Pritchard, John E	1912	ST 58622 72610
925	Prince's Hall, Prince Street	Bryant, John	1981	ST 58650 72506
929	83 Redcliff Street	Bryant, John	1980	ST 59050 72460
930	Chatterton House, Redcliffe Way	Unknown	1980	ST 59217 72391
932	Former warehouse, Redcliff Wharf	Maggs, Peter	1975	ST 58935 72330
933	St Augustine's Hall	Bryant, John	1982	ST 58498 72907
934	Red Brick House, Orchard Place	Unknown	1988	ST 58515 72906
935	Orchard Place	Bryant, John	1988	ST 58498 72907
936	63 and 65 St George's Road	Bryant, John	1981	ST 58090 72675
937	85 and 87 St George's Road	Bryant, John	1981	ST 58029 72646
939	The Red Lodge, Lower Park Row	Unknown	?	ST 58438 73110
940	43 Broad Street	Leech, Roger H	1979	ST 58815 73128
941	3, 4 and 5 King Street	Unknown	1955	ST 58879 72713
942	Cellars, 21–5 High Street	Unknown	?	ST 58957 72980
943	Glebe House, All Saints' Church	Unknown	?	ST58874 73014
944	All Saints' Church	O'Connor, P and Bryant, John	1988	ST 58889 73027
945	Cellars, 49–50 Broad Street	Unknown	?	ST 58835 73135
946	49–50 Broad Street	Unknown	1989	ST 58835 73135
947	Cellars, 35, 36, 37 and 38 Broad Street	Unknown	?	ST 57880 73152
948	Langton's House, Welsh Back	Street, Philip E W	1931	ST 58917 72834
956	New Room, Horsefair	Stell, Christopher	?	ST 59090 73388
957	Portland Chapel, Portland Street	Stell, Christopher	?	ST 58515 73820
960	Unitarian Chapel, Lewins Mead	Stell, Christopher	?	ST 58670 73295
2017	Glebe House, All Saints' Court	Leech, Roger H	1981	ST 58874 73014
2018	The Abbot's House, Blackfriars	Leech, Roger H	1993	ST 58710 73389
2019	25A–25B Broad Street	Leech, Roger H	?	ST 58733 73124
2020	35 Broad Street	Leech, Roger H	1980	ST 58770 73152
2021	36 Broad Street	Leech, Roger H	?	ST 59776 73148
2022	4 Charles Street	Leech, Roger H	1993	ST 58936 73658
2023	5 Charles Street	Leech, Roger H	1993	ST 58739 73658
2024	1 and 1A Christmas Steps	Leech, Roger H	?	ST 58649 73171
2025	5 Christmas Steps	Leech, Roger H	?	ST 58627 73179
2026	6 Christmas Steps	Leech, Roger H	1983	ST 58623 73179
2027	7 Christmas Steps	Leech, Roger H	1984	ST 58619 73181

2028	8 Christmas Steps	Leech, Roger H	?	ST 58616 73182
2029	16 Christmas Steps	Leech, Roger H	1983	ST 58617 73190
2030	18 Christmas Steps	Leech, Roger H	?	ST 58628 73188
2031	20 Christmas Steps	Leech, Roger H	?	ST 58644 73186
2032	17 Christmas Street	Leech, Roger H	1983	ST 58657 73182
2033	18 Christmas Street	Leech, Roger H	1983	ST 58658 73186
2034	19 Christmas Street	Leech, Roger H	1983	ST 58662 73189
2035	54 Colston Street	Leech, Roger H	1983	ST 58587 73202
2036	56 Colston Street	Leech, Roger H	1983	ST 58586 73206
2037	66 Colston Street	Leech, Roger H	1983	ST 58587 73229
2038	68 Colston Street	Leech, Roger H	1983	ST 58587 73231
2039	70 Colston Street	Leech, Roger H	1983	ST 58587 73233
2040	35 Corn Street	Leech, Roger H	2012	ST 58750 72990
2041	Hatchet Inn, Frogmore Street	Leech, Roger H	?	ST 58378 72949
2042	Llandoger Trow, King Street	Leech, Roger H	?	ST 58874 72713
2043	6 King Street	Leech, Roger H	1993	ST 58850 72712
2044	33 King Street	Leech, Roger H	1997	ST 58761 72715
2045	34 King Street	Leech, Roger H	1997	ST 58767 72717
2046	12 Little Anne Street	Leech, Roger H	1996	ST 59848 73504
2047	The Red Lodge, Park Row	Leech, Roger H	1997	ST 58438 73110
2048	The Crown, All Saints Lane	Leech, Roger H	1981	ST 58900 72980
2049	37–8 Broad Street	Leech, Roger H	1981	ST 58779 73147
2050	41–2 Broad Street	Leech, Roger H	1981	ST 58804 73132
2051	43 Broad Street	Leech, Roger H	1981	ST 58814 73125
2052	1 Tailor's Court	Leech, Roger H	1981	ST 58829 73154
2053	44 Broad Street	Leech, Roger H	1981	ST 58818 73123
2054	49–50 Broad Street	Leech, Roger H	1981	ST 58824 73120
2055	51 Broad Street	Leech, Roger H	1981	ST 58829 73120
2056	42 High Street	Leech, Roger H	1981	ST 58908 73017
2057	43 High Street	Leech, Roger H	1981	ST 58907 73019
2058	44 High Street	Leech, Roger H	1981	ST 58906 73023
2059	45 High Street	Leech, Roger H	1981	ST 58902 73026
2060	47 High Street	Leech, Roger H	?	ST 58895 73036
2061	35 Old Market Street	Leech, Roger H	1996	ST 59699 73195
2062	36 Old Market Street	Leech, Roger H	1996	ST 59705 73197
2063	37 Old Market Street	Leech, Roger H	1996	ST 59710 73197
2064	38–9 Old Market Street	Leech, Roger H	1979	ST 59715 73198
2065	40 Old Market Street	Leech, Roger H	1979	ST 59721 73199
2066	41 Old Market Street	Leech, Roger H	1979	ST 59724 73201
2067	52 Old Market Street	Leech, Roger H	?	ST 59745 73171
2068	53 Old Market Street	Leech, Roger H	1997	ST 59739 73168
2069	59 Old Market Street	Leech, Roger H	1997	ST 59702 73150
2070	60 Old Market Street	Leech, Roger H	?	ST 59695 73148
2071	61 Old Market Street	Leech, Roger H	?	ST 59690 73147
2072	62 Old Market Street	Leech, Roger H	1982	ST 59684 73145
2073	70 Old Market Street	Leech, Roger H	1997	ST 59624 73118
2074	71 Old Market Street	Leech, Roger H	1993	ST 59619 73116
2075	Stag and Hounds, Old Market Street	Leech, Roger H	1993	ST 59596 73110
2076	5 Pipe Lane	Leech, Roger H	1993	ST 58490 72979
2077	6 Pipe Lane	Leech, Roger H	1993	ST 58485 72982
2078	7 Pipe Lane	Leech, Roger H	1993	ST 58479 72984
2079	8 Pipe Lane	Leech, Roger H	1993	ST 58475 72987
2080	69 Old Market Street	Leech, Roger H	1993	ST 59629 73121
2081	68 Prince Street	Leech, Roger H	2009	ST 58605 72459

2082	70 Prince Street	Leech, Roger H	1993	ST 58603 72450
2083	Church House, Whitson Street	Leech, Roger H	1984	ST 58877 73479
2084	Manor House, Park Place	Leech, Roger H	1979	ST 58449 73305
2085	Oldbury House, St Michael's Hill	Leech, Roger H	1998	ST 58305 73628
2086	10 Small Street	Leech, Roger H	1981	ST 58720 73080
2087	11 Small Street	Leech, Roger H	?	ST 58708 73085
2088	13 Small Street	Leech, Roger H	1981	ST58735 73093
2089	14 Small Street	Leech, Roger H	1981	ST 58739 73085
2090	15 Small Street	Leech, Roger H	1981	ST 58746 73082
2091	16–17 Small Street	Leech, Roger H	1981	ST 58739 73074
2092	The Shakespeare, Victoria Street	Leech, Roger H	?	ST 59302 72677
2093	15 Orchard Street	Leech, Roger H	1994	ST 58431 72942
2094	16 Orchard Street	Leech, Roger H	1994	ST 58436 72946
2095	36–8 Queen Square	Leech, Roger H	?	ST 58741 72479
2096	29 Queen Square	Leech, Roger H	1994/2003	ST 58829 72460
2097	25 Victoria Street	Leech, Roger H	?	ST 59120 72800
2098	27 Victoria Street	Leech, Roger H	?	ST 59121 72794
2099	29 Victoria Street	Leech, Roger H	?	ST 59123 72789
2100	31 Victoria Street	Leech, Roger H	?	ST 59125 72785
2101	82 Hotwell Road	Leech, Roger H	1978	ST 57612 72506
2102	17 Wade Street	Leech, Roger H	1975	ST 59772 73510
2871	15 Queen Square	Pritchard, John E	1912	ST 58870 72575
3046	The Dutch House, High Street	Pritchard, John E	1907	ST 58906 73049
3178	Vaulted Chambers, Castle Park	Rome, Alan	1972	ST 59373 73128
3181	Vaulted Chambers, Castle Park	Winstone, John	1994	ST 59373 73128
3256	Naval Volunteer, 17–18 King Street	Jackson, R G	1997	ST 58778 72689
3278	Temple Church	Keystone	c 1995	ST 59332 72732
3281	23–9 St Michael's Hill	Leech, Roger H	1997	ST 58504 73330
3285	Governor House, Canon's Marsh	Thorp, John	1997	ST 58067 72536
3288	St John's Church, Broad Street	Barry, P H	1942	ST 58755 73168
3289	Tower, St Mary-le-Port Church, Castle Park	Dawson, David P	1982	ST 58979 73017
3310	Vicarage, Temple Church	Smith, J T	1969	ST 59304 72739
3314	Protheroe's Warehouse, Denmark Street	Insole, Peter	1998	ST 58450 72892
3324	Rowe's Leadworks, Anchor Lane	Thorp, John	1998	ST 58453 72582
3330	Watts Shot Tower, Redcliff Hill	Mosse, John	1998	ST 59035 72313
3339	Canons Marsh Gas Works, Anchor Road	RemedX	1998	ST 57987 72497
3362	27 Horfield Road	Leech, Roger	1998	ST 58500 73475
3363	St Michael's Church, St Michael's Hill	RCHME	1998	ST 58521 73301
3374	Exchange, Corn Street	Leech, Roger	1998	ST 58859 72992
3405	Crown Inn, All Saints' Lane	Leech, Roger	1999	ST 58903 72972
3406	Bakers' Hall andCutlers' Hall, Quakers' Friars	Henderson, J C de. C	1934	ST 59257 73312
3408	Full Moon, North Street	Leech, Roger	1997	ST 59079 73668
3409	30 College Green	Leech, Roger	1998	ST 58397 72823
3410	31–31a College Green	Leech, Roger	1998	ST 58402 72814
3411	22 St Michael's Hill	Leech, Roger	1998	ST 58501 73333
3412	Naval Volunteer, 17–18 King Street	Leech, Roger	1998	ST 58778 72688
3413	41 High Street	Leech, Roger	1998	ST 58905 73010
3414	7–8 King Street	Leech, Roger	1998	ST 58841 72708
3415	Eye Hospital, Lower Maudlin Street	Leech, Roger	1998	ST 58781 73448
3416	Market Tavern, All Saints' Lane	Leech, Roger	1998	ST 58810 72988
3417	9 Redcliff Parade West	Leech, Roger	1998	ST 58874 72297
3418	68 Old Market Street	Leech, Roger	1998	ST 59635 73123
3419	10 Guinea Street	Leech, Roger	1998	ST 58947 72187
3420	11 Guinea Street	Leech, Roger	1998	ST 58942 72190

3421	12 Guinea Street	Leech, Roger	1998	ST 58936 72193
3422	Court House, Tailor's Court	Leech, Roger	1998	ST 58854 73152
3423	St Mary Redcliffe Church	Lyons, John	1717	ST 59129 72313
3498	William III statue, Queen Square	English Heritage	1999	ST 58773 72560
3518	Former Mess/Toilet Block, Exchange Avenue	Leech, Roger H	1999	ST 58850 72958
3529	Wall at 60 Redcliff Street	Bryant, John	1999	ST 59113 72532
3549	Old Station, Temple Meads	Mosse, John	1971	ST 59605 72421
3552	101 Redcliff Street	Upson, Anne	2000	ST 59063 72563
3557	Medieval building in Lewins Mead	Godwin, E W	c 1858	ST 58700 73290
3559	Medieval building in Blackfriars	Pope, T S	1892	ST 58730 73387
3576	WCA Warehouse, Redcliff Backs	Cocks, David	1973	ST 59000 72515
3580	St James Church	Godwin, E W	?	ST 58897 73460
3588	H D Pochin Alum works, Temple Back	Temple Local History Group	1987	ST 59555 72734
3606	Old Council House, Corn Street	Leech, Roger H	2000	ST 58863 73053
3607	93 Stokes Croft	Pilkington, Jayne	2000	ST59104 73979
3616	Bristol Bridge	Leech, Roger H	2000	ST 59013 72900
3627	Sailors Home, The Grove	Pilkington, Jayne	2000	ST 58828 72442
3631	Sacristy door, Bristol Cathedral	Harrison, Hugh	1999	ST 58355 72672
3645	11–12 Portland Square	Oakey, Niall	2000	ST 59458 73660
3656	41 Broad Street	Leech, Roger H	2000	ST 58805 73133
3664	Custom House, Queen Square	Ministry of Works	1970	ST 58780 72660
3671	Central Electric Lighting Station, Temple Back	Upson, Anne	2000	ST 59350 72858
3678	Old Bread Street	Pilkington, Jayne	2000	ST 59685 72872
3690	43 Broad Street	AGBA	1974	ST 58814 73127
3710	St George's Church, Brandon Hill	Selwood, R W	1984	ST 58138 72987
3711	St Michael's Church, St Michael's Hill	Selwood, R W	1984	ST 58521 73380
3712	St James Church House, Whitson Street	Selwood, R W	1988	ST 58799 73480
3713	St Paul's Church, Portland Square	Selwood, R W	1998	ST 59477 73745
3716	Nails, Corn Street	Lepard, Samuel	1858	ST 58916 72238
3720	George Railway, Temple Gate	Jenner, Michael	2001	ST 59440 72390
3725	Gorse Lane	Barber, Alistair	2001	ST 57651 72968
3731	6–22 Marsh Street	Cotswold Archaeology	2001	ST 58630 72815
3733	St Mary-le-Port	Leech, Roger H	2001	ST 58980 73015
3761	Store building, west side Exchange Avenue	Pilkington, Jayne	2001	ST 58848 72958
3763	Sheldon, Bush Works Cheese Lane	Pilkington, Jayne	2001	ST 59420 72910
3769	Stag and Hounds, Old Market	Davenport, Peter	2001	ST 59595 73115
3775	Temple Church	Taylor, John	1999	ST 59332 72732
3778	17 Queen Square	Pilkington, Jayne	2001	ST 58882 72540
3784	The Exchange	Leech, Roger H	2001	ST 58890 72978
3786	Courage Brewery	George, Jeffrey	2001	ST 59190 72975
3792	St Mary Redcliffe Church	Godwin, E W and Hines, James	?	ST 59117 72315
3793	Temple Church	Burder, W C	?	ST 59330 72732
3811	Prior House, Robin Hood Lane	Leech, Roger H	2001	ST 58472 73467
3812	16 King Street	Leech, Roger H	2001	ST 58786 72694
3813	22–4 Orchard Street	Pilkington, Jayne	2001	ST 58472 72950
3814	Young and Neilson Corset Factory, St Pauls	Kenyon, David	2001	ST 59464 73645
3816	22–4 Queen Square and 42–4 Welsh Back	Jenner, Michael	2001	ST 58875 72492
3832	6 Christmas Steps	Erskine, Jonathan	2002	ST 58623 73178
3837	George Railway Hotel, Temple Gate	Pilkington, Jayne	2002	ST 59455 72390
3843	St Paul's Church	Hughes, Philip	2000	ST 59482 73733
3846	Malthouse, Braggs Lane	Fielding, Susan	2001	ST 59918 73355

3893	TR Warehouse, St Thomas Street	Townsend, Andrew	2002	ST 59117 72724
3896	43 Welsh Back	Bryant, John	2002	ST 58888 72485
3901	Broad Plain Soap and Candle Works	Bryant, John	2002	ST 59715 72879
3913	Bristol Sailors Home, The Grove	Leech, Roger H	2001	ST 58828 72440
3914	29 Queen Square	Joyce, N and Hughes, P	1996	ST 58830 72461
3915	St Paul's Church	Pilkington, Jayne & Bryant, John	2002	ST 59472 73745
3927	14 St Thomas Street	Longman, Tim	2002	ST 59147 72732
3945	FPS Factory site, West Street, Old Market	Bryant, John	2003	ST 59874 73177
3947	Courage Brewery, Counterslip	Bryant, John	2000	ST 59104 72946
3948	10–11 Denmark Street	Bryant, John	2000	ST 58471 72832
3952	Custom House, Queen Square	Bryant, John	2000	ST 58780 72560
3956	1–13 St Paul Street	Samuel, Jens	2000	ST 59514 73663
3984	22–30 West Street, Old Market	Leech, Roger H	2003	ST 59884 73228
3986	Old Tramshed, 25 Lower Park Row	Heaton, Rachel	2003	ST 58545 73194
3992	Cherry Lane	Bryant, John	2003	ST 58989 73670
3994	Bristol Sailors Home, The Grove	Leech, Roger H	2003	ST 58829 72441
4013	Tropic Club, 84 Stokes Croft	Leech, Roger H	2003	ST 59150 73958
4067	Purimachos site, Waterloo Road	Heaton, Rachel	2003	ST 60050 73270
4082	Central Electric Lighting Station, Temple Back	Rous, Matthew *et al*	2004	ST 59352 72857
4096	St Peter's Church	Dening, C F W	?	ST 59134 73100
4097	St Mary-le-Port Church	Dening, C F W	?	ST 58999 73027
4098	St Nicholas Church	Dening, C F W	?	ST 58950 72945
4099	St Thomas Church	Dening, C F W	?	ST 59132 72775
4100	Temple Church	Dening, C F W	?	ST 59346 72738
4101	Christ Church	Dening, C F W	?	ST 58905 73082
4102	1 Trinity Street	Dening, C F W and Clemes, F	?	ST 58425 72684
4103	St Michael's Hill House, St Michael's Hill	Dening, C F W	?	ST 58413 73516
4104	46 St Michael's Hill	Dening, C F W	?	ST 58459 73435
4105	35 Prince Street	Dening, C F W	?	ST 58619 72552
4112	Theatre Royal, King Street	Unknown	1969	ST 58793 72761
4113	St Mary Redcliffe	Monckton, Linda	?	ST 59120 72315
4115	Canynge's House, Redcliff Street	Dollman, Francis T	?	ST 59081 72542
4116	Spicer's Hall, Welsh Back	Dollman, Francis T	?	ST 58920 72863
4117	Colston's House, Small Street	Dollman, Francis T	?	ST 58794 73059
4118	17 Orchard Street	Bryant, John	2003	ST 58453 72967
4124	Llandoger Trow, 3–5 King Street	Driscoll, Paul	2004	ST 58880 72712
4131	16 Cherry Lane	Leech, R H and Herman, B L	1996	ST 59007 73671
4137	Gatehouse, Bristol Cathedral	Arnold, A J	2003	ST 58277 72686
4147	22–30 West Street	King, Andy	2004	ST 59910 73195
4151	Gatehouse, Bristol Cathedral	Rodwell, Warwick	2003	ST 58279 72686
4152	George Railway Hotel, Temple Gate	Bryant, John	2004	ST 59432 72389
4165	251 Hotwell Road	Bryant, John and Longman, Tim	2004	ST 57103 72539
4178	Redcliff Wharf	Stevens, Dave	2004	ST 59037 72384
4189	Abbey House, Bristol Cathedral School	Paul, Roland W	1899	ST 58303 72631
4195	Courage's Brewery, Counterslip	Dixon, James	2004	ST 59196 72992
4198	16 King Street	Bryant, John	2004	ST 58787 72694
4199	35 Corn Street	Leech, R H	2005	ST 58755 72980
4209	22–9 St Michael's Hill	Leech, R H	2005	ST 58500 73335
4222	Bristol Cathedral sacristy	Paul, Roland W	1885	ST 58384 72677

4228	Mason's Arms, 53 Old Market Street	Bryant, John	2005	ST 59738 73170
4237	Gloucester House and Kelston View	Jackson, Reg	2005	ST 58550 73530
4238	Huller House and Cheese Warehouse	Jenner, Michael	2005	ST 59000 72555
4248	Hannah More Infants School	Longman, Tim	2005	ST 59860 72938
4259	69–73 Queen Square	Leech, R H	2005	ST 58730 72653
4266	28 Portland Square and 2–6 Cave Street	George and Toni Demidowicz	1995	ST 59367 73762
4292	9–10 Charles Street	Bryant, John	2006	ST 58960 73688
4300	Drill Hall, Old Market	Morriss, Richard K	2006	ST 59676 73100
4301	135 St Michael's Hill (rear of)	Morriss, Richard K	2006	ST 58293 73681
4345	The Guildhall, Broad Street	Leech, R H	2004	ST 58794 73090
4349	Prince's Wharf, Wapping	Leech, R H	2005	ST 58540 72257
4361	2–4 West Street, Old Market	Bryant, John	2006	ST 59825 73205
4363	St Paul's Churchyard (N & E boundary walls)	Etheridge, David	2006	ST 59553 73814
4368	2 Trenchard Street	King, Andy	2006	ST 58485 73008
4374	118–22 Jacob Street, Old Market	Bryant, John	2004	ST 59758 73128
4385	Lord Mayor's Chapel	Severn, Joseph	2007	ST 58390 72835
4399	County Tyres building, Gasferry Road	Longman, Tim	2007	ST 57912 72228
4409	The Swan public house, 39 Midland Road	Unknown	2006	ST 59872 73122
4410	Former FPS Site, Waterloo Road	Bryant, John	2005	ST 59880 73165
4428	Vestry Hall, Pennywell Road	Etheridge, David	2007	ST 59945 73592
4436	Purimachos, West Street, Old Market	Potter, Kevin	2007	ST 60040 73260
4438	Anchor Road (Cathedral School car park)	Bryant, John	2007	ST 58226 72617
4447	Cumberland Road, Wapping Wharf	Roper, Simon	2008	ST 58524 72127
4453	St Nicholas House and Tolentino House	BaRAS	2008	ST 59936 73507
4458	McArthurs Warehouse, Gasferry Road	Wessex Archaeology	2008	ST 57832 72296
4467	Soapworks, Old Bread Street	Bryant, John	2008	ST 59687 72859
4471	Rear of St Michael's Children's Hospital	Roper, Simon	2008	ST 58318 73483
21074	Richmond House, Lower Clifton Hill	Pilkington, Jayne	2002	ST 57480 72940
21213	Churchyard of St John's Church	AGBA	1974	ST 58525 71408
21342	Hope Chapel, Hotwells	Stell, Christopher	?	ST 56905 72665
24584	Taurus House, St Philips	Bruce, Jo	2007	ST 60022 72885
24662	114 Jacob Street	GCP Chartered Architects	2007	ST 59726 73124
24755	Dove Lane	Morriss, Richard	2009	ST 59650 73830
24771	6 King Street	Etheridge, David	2009	ST 58856 72711
24783	Cathedral School Fortune Theatre	Capon, Les	2009	ST 58199 72639
24809	Cumberland Basin	BaRAS	2009	ST 56950 72350
24830	16 Redcross St and 32 Old Market St	Etheridge, David	2009	ST 59660 73200
24835	24 St Michael's Hill	Townsend, Andrew	2010	ST 58516 73359
24869	73–7 St Michael's Hill/22–4 Tyndall Ave	Bryant, John	2010	ST 58362 73483
24870	Beaufort House and 7–10 Bedford Row	Townsend, Andrew *et al*	2010	ST 58612 73492
24893	7 Broad Quay	Wotton, Andrew	2010	ST 58622 72834
24960	Naval Volunteer, 17–18 King Street	King, Andy	2010	ST 58777 72692
24962	Depts of Biological Sciences and Geography	Bryant, John	2010	ST 58129 73325
24990	Theatre Royal, King Street	Mason, Cai	2011	ST 58804 72751
25014	Pate's Building, Bristol Cathedral School	Clarke, Chris	2011	ST 58336 72639
25066	Old Fire Station, Silver Street	Mason, Cai	2011	ST 58901 73329
25069	19 Jacob's Wells Road	Longman, Tim	2011	ST 57706 72813
25139	Merchant Seaman's Almshouses, King Street	Mason, Cai	2012	ST 58714 72707
25154	19 Jacob's Wells Road	Etheridge, David	2012	ST 57701 72807
25181	69–73 Queen Square	BaRAS	2012	ST 58730 72652
25190	GWR Staff Club, Temple Meads Station	Bryant, John	2013	ST 59590 72386

25201	93 Stokes Croft	Bryant, John	2013	ST 59106 73978
25227	Magistrates Courts, Nelson Street	Wardell Armstrong Archaeology	2013	ST 58733 73205
25231	Former Gaol at Wapping Wharf	Bryant, John	2013	ST 58456 72096
25249	31 and 31a, College Green	BaRAS	2013	ST 58404 72815
25254	Theatre Royal, King Street	BaRAS	2013	ST 58809 72728
25271	Bristol General Hospital	Davenport, Peter	2013	ST 58856 72167
25355	Candle Building, Ashley Road	Etheridge, David	2014	ST 59225 74101
25359	31 College Green	BaRAS	2014	ST 58404 72813
25404	Former Magistrates Court, Bridewell Street	Bryant, John	2014	ST 58893 73279
25406	Fry Building, Woodland Road	BaRAS	2014	ST 58137 73285
25413	Huller House and Cheese Warehouse	BaRAS	2014	ST 59000 72551
25425	151 Hotwell Road	Unknown	2014	ST 57407 72455
25430	1 College Lane	BaRAS	2014	ST 58412 72823
25433	Colston's Almshouse	BaRAS	2014	ST 58514 73362
25439	New Room, Broadmead	BaRAS	2014	ST 59078 73396
25451	Bristol Ambulance Station, Marybush Lane	Avon Archaeology	2015	ST 59390 73021
25452	City Hall, College Green	BaRAS	2015	ST 58265 72794
25470	41 Stokes Croft	AC Archaeology	2015	ST 59063 73818
25472	Harris Warehouse, Farrs Lane	Heaton, Rachel	2015	ST 58588 72493

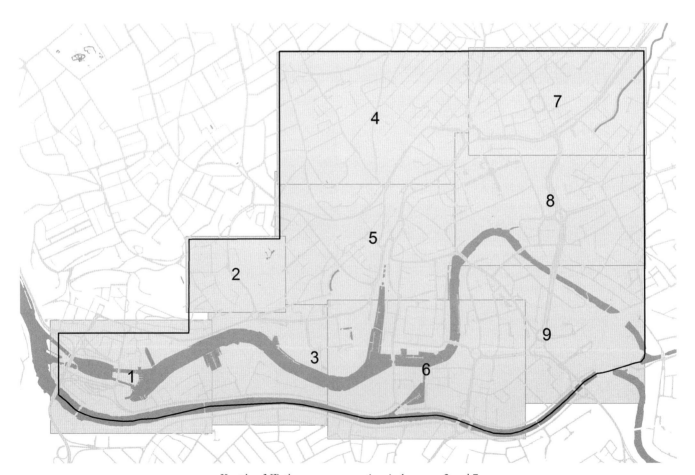

Key plan. NB there are no excavations in key areas 2 and 7

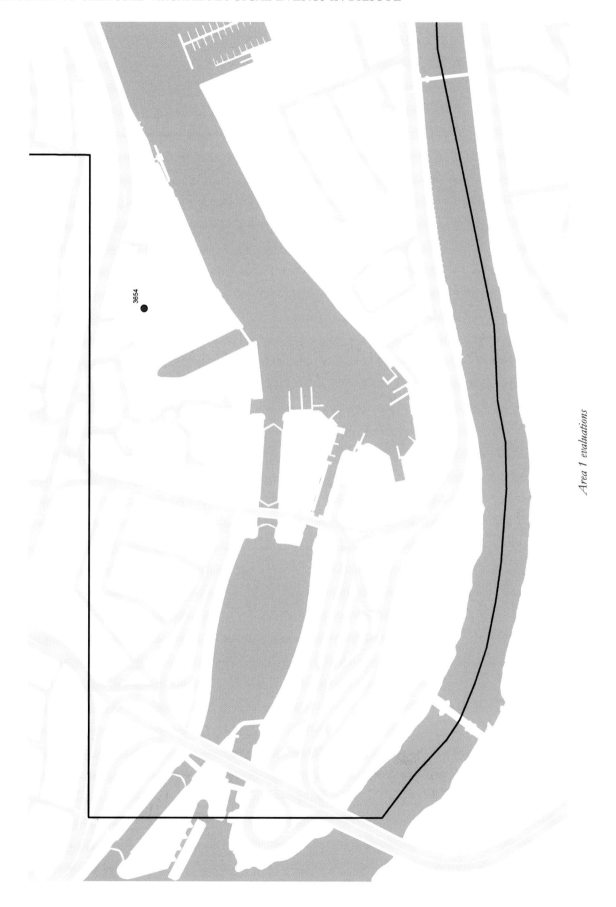

Area 1 evaluations

Area 2 evaluations

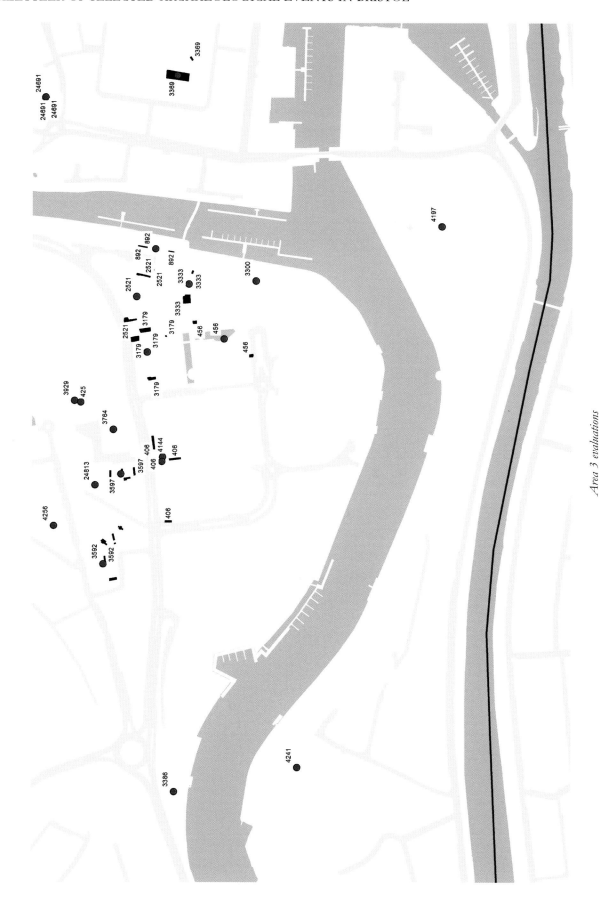

Area 3 evaluations

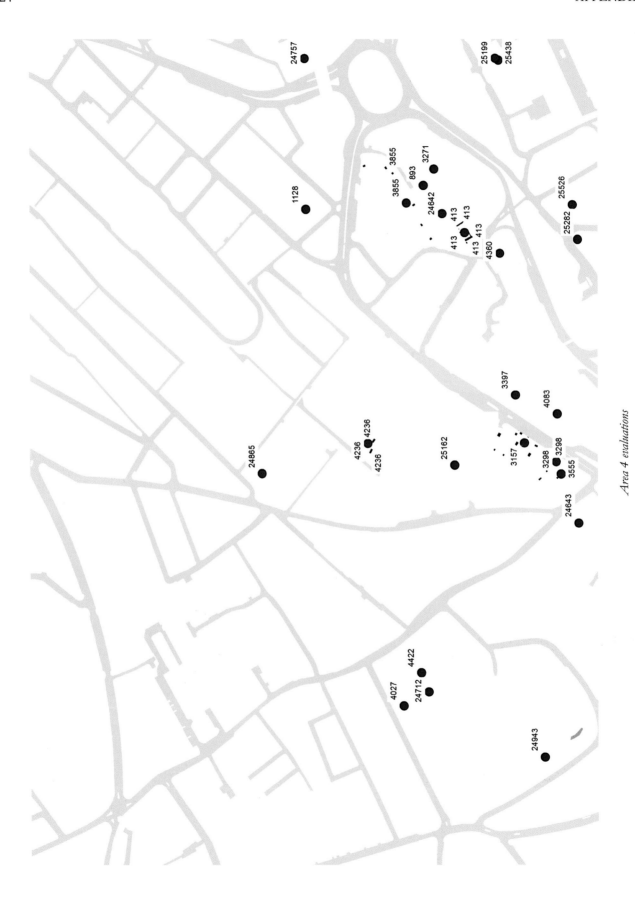

Area 4 evaluations

Area 5 evaluations

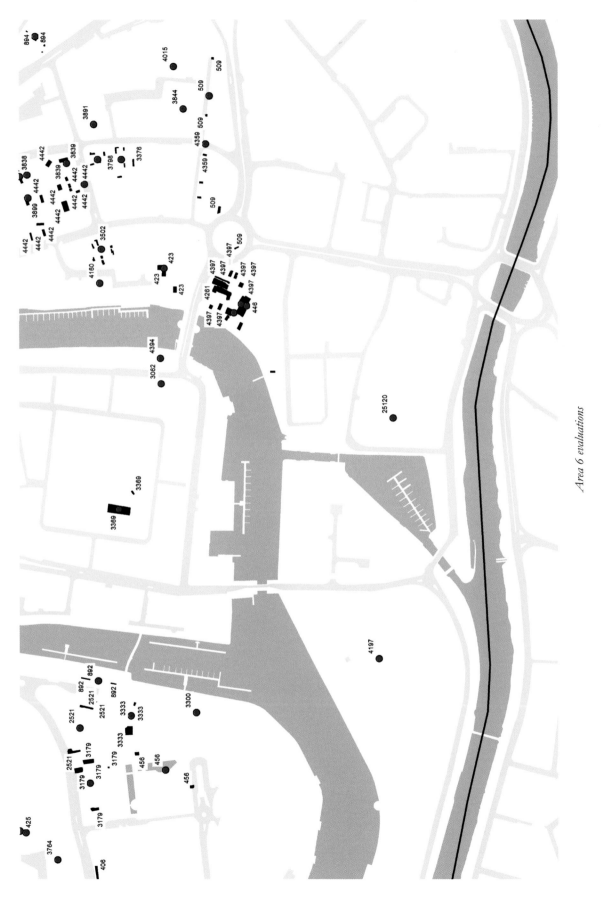

Area 6 evaluations

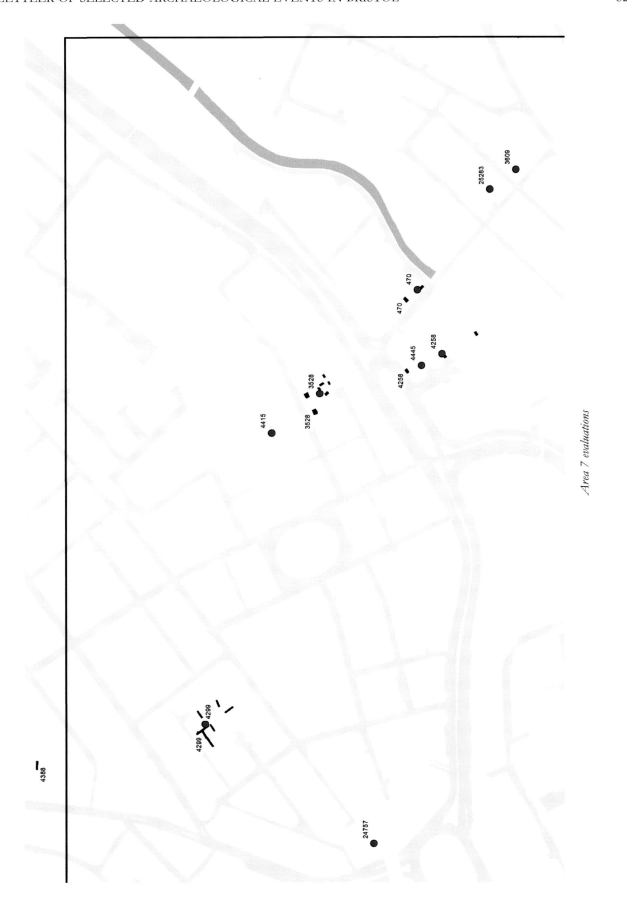

Area 7 evaluations

Area 8 evaluations

Area 9 evaluations

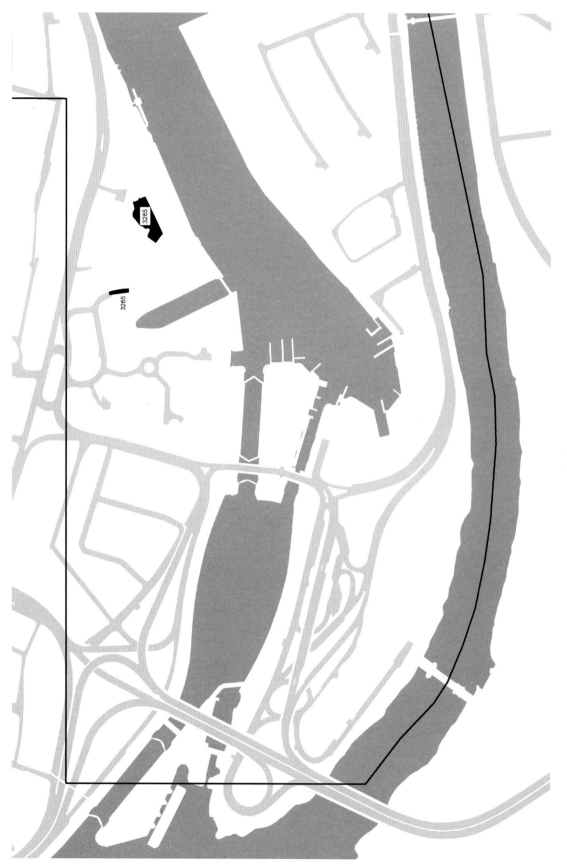

Area 1 excavations

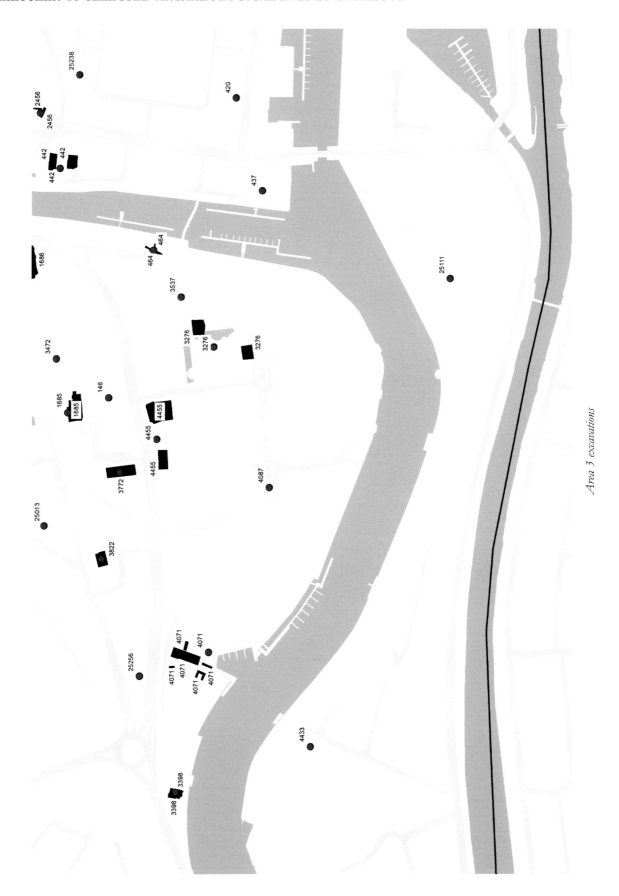

Area 3 excavations

Area 4 excavations

Area 5 excavations

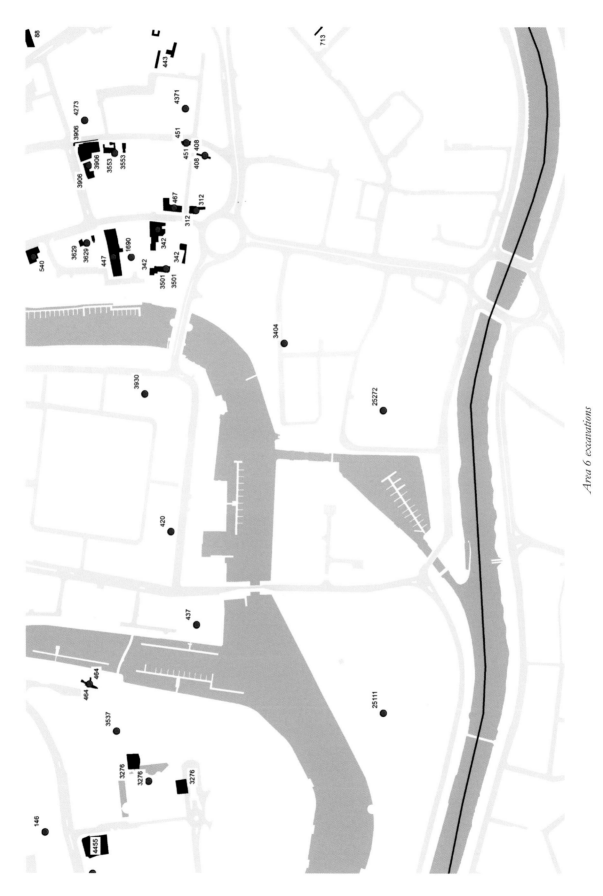

Area 6 excavations

Area 8 excavations

Area 9 excavations

Bibliography

Abbreviations

BEP   *Bristol Evening Post*
BM   British Museum
BMC   Bristol Municipal Charities
BRSMG   Bristol Museum and Art Gallery
BTM   *Bristol Times and Mirror*
FFBJ   Felix Farley's Bristol Journal
L & P   *Letters and Papers, Foreign and Domestic*
NMR   National Monuments Record
ODNB   *Oxford Dictionary of National Biography*

Published and unpublished sources

Adam, N J 2008a '7–11 Broad Quay/Marsh Street, Bristol. Post-excavation assessment and updated project design'. Cotswold Archaeology, unpublished report no 07147

Adam, N J 2008b 'Land at the corner of Wine Street and Union Street, Bristol. Archaeological evaluation'. Cotswold Archaeology, unpublished report no 08112

Adam, N J 2008c 'Merchants Almshouses, King Street, Bristol. Archaeological evaluation'. Cotswold Archaeology, unpublished report no 08250

Addyman P V, 1966, 'Excavations at Lydford, Devon: Third interim report'. Archaeology Dept, Queen's University, Belfast

Adler, M 1928 'The Jews of Bristol in pre-expulsion days'. *Jewish Historical Studies – Transactions of the Jewish Historical Society* **12** (1928–31), 117–86

Airs, M 1995 *The Tudor and Jacobean Country House: A Building History*. Thrupp: Alan Sutton Publishing Ltd

Alcock, L 1995 *Cadbury Castle, Somerset: The Early Medieval Archaeology*. Cardiff: University of Wales Press

Alexander, M (ed) 2015, *Medieval and Post-Medieval Occupation and Industry in the Redcliffe Suburb of Bristol. Excavations at 1–2 and 3 Redcliff Street, 2003–10*. Cotswold Archaeology Monograph **8**

Alexander, M and Harward, C, 2011, 'Harbourside, Bristol: Investigations from 2003–8', *in* Watts, M (ed) *Medieval and Post-medieval Development within Bristol's Inner Suburbs*. Bristol and Gloucestershire Archaeological Report **7** (Cotswold Archaeology), 79–119

Alford, B W E 1976 'The economic development of Bristol in the 19th century: an enigma?', *in* McGrath, P and Cannon, J (eds) *Essays in Bristol and Gloucestershire History*. Bristol: Bristol and Gloucestershire Archaeological Society, 252–83

Allen, J R L and Rae, J 1987 'Late Flandrian shoreline oscillations in the Severn Estuary: a geomorphological and stratigraphical reconnaissance'. *Philosophical Transactions of the Royal Society of London Series B – Biological Sciences* **315**, 185–230

Allen, S J 2017 'Woodworking technology', *in* Ford, Ben M, Brady, Kate and Teague, Steven *From Bridgehead to Brewery. The Medieval and Post-medieval archaeological remains from Finzel's Reach, Bristol*. Oxford Archaeology Monograph **27**, 242–57

Allison, E 2013 '5.6 Insects' *in* Ridgeway, V and Watts, M (eds), *Friars, Quakers, Industry and Urbanisation. The Archaeology of the Broadmead Expansion Project, Cabot Circus, Bristol, 2005–8*. Cotswold Archaeology/Pre-Construct Archaeology, 311–7

Ambers, J, Matthews, K, and Bowman, S 1991 'British Museum natural radiocarbon measurements XXII'. *Radiocarbon* **33**, 51–68.

Andrews, K (ed) 1959 *English Privateering Voyages to the West Indies, 1588–95*. Cambridge: Cambridge University Press

Anon 1852 'Discovery at St. Mary's Redcliff, Bristol'. *The Builder* **10** (1852), 585

Anon 1859 'Proceedings of the Association: January 12'. *Journal of the British Archaeological Association*, 265–82

Anon 1866 'Notices of Roman pigs of lead found at Bristol'. *Archaeol J* **23**, 277–9

Anon 1875 'The tumulus of Westbury'. *Transactions of the Clifton College Scientific Society* **2**, 80–2

Anon 1876 'The inaugural meeting'. *Trans Bristol Gloucestershire Archaeol Soc* **1**, 7–30

Anon 1877 *A schedule of the lands, houses, grounds and fee-farm rents and other property belonging to the Trustees of the Municipal Charities of the City of Bristol…*. Bristol: H Hill

Anon 1883 *Work in Bristol: A Series of Sketches of the Chief Manufactures in the City*. Bristol: Bristol Times and Mirror

Anon 1897–9 'Proceedings of the Society of Antiquaries. Thursday, February 16th, 1899'. *Proc Soc Antiq London* 2 Ser **17**, 330–44

Anon 1906 'Proceedings at the annual summer meeting at Bristol, Tuesday, Wednesday and Thursday, July 17th, 18th and 19th, 1906'. *Trans Bristol Gloucestershire Archaeol Soc* **29**, 17–60

Anon 1937 'Ancient Bristol'. *Trans Bristol Gloucestershire Archaeol Soc* **59**, 309–20

Anon 1942 'The Council for the Preservation of Ancient Bristol: observations submitted to the Bristol Replanning Advisory Committee, January 1942'. *Trans Bristol Gloucestershire Archaeol Soc* **63**, 244–7

Anon 1975 'King size in Bristol'. *Architectural Review* **158**, 197–223

Anon 1988 'Archaeology in Bristol 1988–9 [short summaries of excavations and watching briefs]'. *Bristol Avon Archaeol* **7**, 33–6

Anon 2005 'Main Scheme and Quakers Friars, Broadmead Expansion, Bristol. Archaeological Evaluation Report'. Unpublished report, Oxford Archaeology

Anon, 2008 'Temple Way House, Narrow Plain, Bristol. Archaeological Evaluation Project'. Unpublished report, Avon Archaeological Unit

Anstie, J 1873 *The Coal Fields of Gloucestershire and Somersetshire 1873*. Bath

Appleby, S C 2003 'Land to the north-west of Avon Street, Bristol. Archaeological evaluation and follow-on works. Final report'. Unpublished report, AOC Archaeology

Armitage, P, 2013, '5.3 Fish bone' *in* Ridgeway, V and Watts, M (eds), *Friars, Quakers, Industry and Urbanisation. The Archaeology of the Broadmead Expansion Project, Cabot Circus, Bristol, 2005–8*. Cotswold Archaeology/Pre-Construct Archaeology, 283–8

Armitage, P, 2015, '5.2 Fish bones' *in* Alexander, M (ed), *Medieval and Post-Medieval Occupation and Industry in the Redcliffe Suburb of Bristol. Excavations at 1–2 and 3 Redcliff Street, 2003–10*. Cotswold Archaeology Monograph **8**, 101–4

Astill, G G 1993 *A Medieval Industrial Complex and Its Landscape: The Medieval Watermills and Workshops of Bordesley Abbey*. London: Council for British Archaeology

Aston, M 1982 'The medieval pattern, 1000–1500', *in* Aston, M, and Burrow, I (eds) *The Archaeology of Somerset: A Review to 1500AD*. Taunton: Somerset County Council, 123–33

Atkinson, B J 1987 'An early example of the decline of the industrial spirit? Bristol enterprise in the first half of the 19th century'. *Southern History* **9** (1987), 79–81

Avon Archaeology 2014 'Land at the corner of Wade Street and Little Ann Street, St Jude's, Bristol: Archaeological excavation 2014. Assessment report and updated project design'. Unpublished report, Avon Archaeology Ltd

Ayers, B S 1991 'From cloth to creel – riverside industries in Norwich', *in* Good, G, Jones, R H, and Ponsford, M (eds) *Waterfront Archaeology; Proceedings of the Third International Conference, Bristol, 1988*. London: CBA Research Report **74**, 1–8

Bailey, M 1998 'The commercialisation of the English economy, 1086–500'. *J Medieval Hist* **24**, 297–311

Baker, N J, 2010, *Shrewsbury. An Archaeological Assessment of an English Border Town*. Oxbow

Baker, N J, Lawson, J B, Maxwell, R and Smith, J T, 1993. 'Further work on Pride Hill, Shrewsbury'. *Trans Shropshire Archaeol Hist Soc* **68**, 3–64

Baker, N J and Holt R A, 2004, *Urban Growth and the Medieval Church: Gloucester and Worcester*. Aldershot: Ashgate

Banks, J (ed) 1898 'Journal of an excursion to Eastbury and Bristol etc., in May and June 1767'. *Proc Bristol Naturalists Soc* 2 Ser **9** (1898–900), 6–37

Bantock, A and Members of the Malago Society 1997 *Bedminster*. Stroud: Chalford Publishing

Barber, A 1994 'Welsh Back, Bristol: archaeological evaluation'. Unpublished report, Cotswold Archaeological Trust

Barber, A 1999 'Sterling House/Fiennes Court, off Union Street and Fairfax Street, Bristol. Archaeological evaluation'. Unpublished report, Cotswold Archaeological Trust

Barber, A 2000 'Land to the north of Anchor Road, Bristol: archaeological evaluation'. Unpublished report, Cotswold Archaeological Trust

Barber, A 2001a 'Land South of Gorse Lane, Clifton, Bristol. Archaeological evaluation'. Unpublished report, Cotswold Archaeological Trust

Barber, A 2001b '6–22 Marsh Street & 7–11 Broad Quay, Bristol: Archaeological evaluation. Vol 1: Stratigraphic account and assessment of historic buildings'. Unpublished report, Cotswold Archaeological Trust

Barber, A 2003 'Land to the rear of 100 Temple Street, Bristol. Archaeological evaluation'. Cotswold Archaeology, unpublished report no 03151

Barber, A 2004 'Land at Castle Park, Bristol. Archaeological evaluation'. Cotswold Archaeology, unpublished report no 04140

Barber, A 2014a 'Bristol General Hospital, Guinea Street, Bristol. Archaeological excavation'. Cotswold Archaeology, unpublished report no 14165

Barber, A 2014b 'Avon Fire Station, Temple Back, Bristol. Archaeological evaluation'. Cotswold Archaeology, unpublished report no 14403

Barber, A, 2014c 'Land at Albert House, 103 Temple Street to 111 Victoria Street, Bristol. Archaeological evaluation'. Cotswold Archaeology, unpublished report no 14531

Barber, A 2014d 'Bristol General Hospital, Guinea Street, Bristol. Archaeological evaluation phase 2'. Cotswold Archaeology, unpublished report no 14158

Barber, A 2015 'Guildhall Chambers, Broad Street, Bristol. Archaeological evaluation and historic building recording'. Cotswold Archaeology, unpublished report no 14106

Barber, A and Cox, S 2004 'Land east of Huller House/South Warehouse, Redcliff Backs, Bristol. Archaeological evaluation'. Cotswold Archaeology, unpublished report no 04176

Barber, G nd 'Minster House, Bristol Cathedral 17/92, the animal bone'. Unpublished draft report

Barber, M 1994 *The New Knighthood: A History of the Order of the Temple*. Cambridge: Cambridge University Press

Barker, K 1973 *Entertainment in the Nineties*. Bristol: Bristol Branch of the Historical Association

Barker, K 1974 *The Theatre Royal, 1766–966: Two Centuries of Stage History*. London: The Society for Theatre Research

Barker, W R 1892 *St. Mark's or the Mayor's Chapel, Bristol (formerly called the Church of the Gaunts)*. Bristol: W C Hemmons

Barlow, F, Biddle, M, von Feilitzen, O and Keene, D J 1976 *Winchester in the Early Middle Ages: An Edition and Discussion of the Winton Domesday* (Winchester Studies I). Oxford: Clarendon Press

Barrett, J C, Freeman, P W M, and Woodward, A 2000 *Cadbury Castle Somerset: The Later Prehistoric and Early Historic Archaeology*. London: English Heritage

Barrett, W 1789 *The history and antiquities of the City of Bristol*. Bristol: William Pine

Barrow, J 1995 'Urban cemetery location in the high middle ages', *in* Bassett, S (ed) *Death in Towns: Urban Responses to the Dying and the Dead, 100–1600*. London: Leicester University Press, 78–100

Barry, J 1985 'The cultural life of Bristol, 1640–775'. Unpublished DPhil thesis, University of Oxford

Barry, J 1993 'Cultural patronage and the Anglican crisis: Bristol, *c*. 1689–775', *in* Walsh, J, Haydon, C, and Taylor, S (eds) *The Church of England c.1689–c.1833: From Toleration to Tractarianism*. Cambridge: Cambridge University Press, 191–208

Barry, J 1996 'The history and antiquities of the City of Bristol: Chatterton in Bristol'. *Angelaki* **2**, 55–81

Barry, J 1998 'Bristol as a 'Reformation city' *c*. 1640–780', *in* Tyacke, N, (ed) *England's Long Reformation, 1500–800*. London: UCL Press Ltd, 261–84

Barry, T 1992 *The Archaeology of Medieval Ireland*. London: University Press

Bartlett, A 1994 'Spatial order and psychiatric disorder', *in* Parker Pearson, M and Richards, C (eds) *Architecture and Order: Approaches to Social Space*. London: Routledge, 178–95

Barton, C M, Strange, P J, Royse, K R and Farrant, A R 2002 *Geology of the Bristol District*. Nottingham. British Geological Survey

Barton, K J 1960 'Excavations at Back Hall, Bristol, 1958'. *Trans Bristol Gloucestershire Archaeol Soc* **79**, 251–86

Barton, K J 1964 'The excavation of a medieval bastion at St. Nicholas Almshouses, King Street, Bristol'. *Medieval Archaeol* **8**, 184–212

Barton, K J 1983 'A medieval pottery kiln at Ham Green, Bristol'. *Trans Bristol Gloucestershire Archaeol Soc* **82**, 95–126

Batchelor, R, Giorgi, J, Warman, S and Watts, M 2013, 6.6. 'Economy, diet and health', *in* Ridgeway, V and Watts, M (eds), *Friars, Quakers, Industry and Urbanisation. The Archaeology of the Broadmead Expansion Project, Cabot Circus, Bristol, 2005–8*. Cotswold Archaeology/Pre-Construct Archaeology, 381–7

Bateman, D 1988 'The growth of the printing and packaging industry in Bristol, 1800–914', *in* Harvey, C E, and Press, J (eds) *Studies in the Business History of Bristol*. Bristol: Bristol Academic Press, 83–107

Bates, M R and Wenban-Smith, F 2005 'Palaeolithic research framework for the Bristol Avon basin'. Unpublished report

Bates-Harbin, E (ed) 1908 *Quarter Sessions Records for the County of Somerset Vol. 2. Charles I, 1625–39*. London: Somerset Record Series **24**.

Bates-Harbin, E (ed) 1912 *Quarter Sessions Records for the County of Somerset. Vol. 3 Commonwealth, 1646–60*. London: Somerset Record Series **28**

Baynton, D 1993 '"Savages and Deaf-mutes": evolutionary theory and the campaign against sign language in the 19th century', *in* Van Cleve, J (ed) *Deaf History Unveiled: Interpretations from the New Scholarship*. Washington DC: Gallaudet University Press, 92–112

Beachcroft, G and Sabin, A 1938 *Two Compotus Rolls of Saint Augustine's Abbey, Bristol*. Bristol: Bristol Record Series **9**

Beaton, M, Chapman, M, Crutchley, A, and Root, J 1999 *Bath Historical Streetscape Survey*. Bath: Bath and North-East Somerset Council

Beckey, I and Jackson, R G 1986a '19th century kiln waste from Bristol'. *Soc Clay Pipe Res Newsletter* **9**, 24–9

Beckey, I and Jackson, R G 1986b '19th-century pipes by Jonathan Moul of Bristol'. *Bristol Avon Archaeol* **5**, 45–50

Beckles, H McD 1998 'The "Hub of Empire": the Caribbean and Britain in the 17th century', *in* Canny, N (ed) *The Oxford History of the British Empire. Vol.1 The Origins of Empire: British Overseas to the Close of the 17th Century*. Oxford: Oxford University Press, 218–240

Beddoe, J 1878–9 'On certain crania disinterred at St Werburgh's, Bristol'. *Trans Bristol Gloucestershire Archaeol Soc* **3**, 79–82

Beddoe, J 1904–6 'Report on two skulls found at great depths at Bristol Dockgate and at Avonmouth Dock'. *Proc Bristol Naturalists Soc* 2 Ser **1**, 61–5

Beddoe, J 1906 'Notes on crania found on the site of the Carmelite friary. Appendix to Mr. Pritchard's paper'. *Trans Bristol Gloucestershire Archaeol Soc* **29**, 142–6

Behagg, C 1990 *Politics and Production in the Early 19th Century*. London: Routledge

Bell, M Caseldine, A and Neumann, H 1999 *Prehistoric Intertidal Archaeology in the Welsh Severn Estuary*. York: CBA Res Rep **120**

Belsey, J 1996 *A Small Light in the Far West: Victorian Photographers in Bristol*. Bristol: James Belsey and Cartwrights Solicitors

Bennett, J 1985 *The Roman town of Abonae: Excavations at Nazareth House, Sea Mills, Bristol, 1972*. Bristol: City of Bristol Museum and Art Gallery

Berg, M 1994 *The Age of Manufactures, 1700–820: Industry, Innovation and Work in Bristol*. London: Routledge

Berg, M and Hudson, P 1992 'Rehabilitating the industrial revolution'. *Economic Hist Rev* **45**, 24–50

Bettey, J H 1979 *Bristol Parish Churches During the Reformation c. 1530–60*. Bristol: Bristol Branch of the Historical Association

Bettey J H 1983 *Church and Community in Bristol During the 16th Century*. Bristol: Bristol Record Society

Bettey, J H 1985 'Two Tudor visits to Bristol', *in* McGrath, P (ed) *A Bristol Miscellany*. Bristol: Bristol Record Series **37**, 1–15

Bettey, J H 1986 *Bristol Observed: Visitors' Impressions of the City from Domesday to the Blitz*. Bristol: Redcliffe Press

Bettey, J H 1990 *The Suppression of the Religious Houses in Bristol*. Bristol: Bristol Branch of the Historical Association

Bettey, J H 1992 *St. Augustine's Abbey, Bristol*. Bristol: Bristol Branch of the Historical Association

Bettey, J H 1993 *Bristol Cathedral: The Rebuilding of the Nave*. Bristol: Bristol Branch of the Historical Association

Bettey, J H 1996 *St. Augustine's Abbey, Bristol*. Bristol: Bristol Branch of the Historical Association

Bettey, J H 1997 *The Royal Fort and Tyndall's Park: The Development of a Bristol Landscape*. Bristol: Bristol Branch of the Historical Association

Bettey, J 1998 'Late-medieval Bristol: from town to city'. *Local Historian* (February 1998), 3–15

Bettey, J H 2003 *The First Historians of Bristol: William Barrett and Samuel Seyer*. Bristol: Bristol Branch of the Historical Association

Bettey, J H 2004 'Feuding gentry and an affray on College Green, Bristol, in 1579'. *Trans Bristol Gloucestershire Archaeol Soc* **122**, 153–9

Bettey, J H and Harrison, H 2004 'A 12th-century door in Bristol Cathedral'. *Trans Bristol Gloucestershire Archaeol Soc* **122**, 169–71

Bickley, F (ed) 1900 *The Little Red Book of Bristol*, 2 vols. Bristol: W C Hemmons

Biddle, M and Hill, D 1971, 'Late Saxon planned towns'. *Antiq J* **51**, 70–85

Biddle, M, and Hudson D M, with Heighway, C 1973 *The Future of London's Past: A Survey of the Archaeological Implications of Planning and Development in the Nation's Capital*. Worcester: Worcester Rescue

Bindon, J 1853 'On the desecrated and destroyed churches of Bristol'. *Memoirs Illustrative of the History and Antiquities of Bristol*. London: The Archaeological Institute, 118–41

Bingham, F nd *Horfield Miscellanea: An Account of Horfield from Early Times to 1900*. Portsmouth: W H Barrell

Birch, W de Gray 1875 'Original documents relating to Bristol and the neighbourhood'. *J Brit Archaeol Assoc* **31**, 289–385

Bird, P J 1960 'Bristol Cathedral: The bells in the central tower'. *Ringing World* (13 May 1960), 321

Blackburn, R 1997 *The Making of New World Slavery*. London: Verso

Blair, I, Hillaby, J, Howell, I, Sermon, R and Watson, B 2001–2 'The discovery of two medieval *mikva'ot* in London and a reinterpretation of the Bristol '*mikveh*'. *Jewish Historical Studies – Trans Jewish Hist Soc England* **37**, 1–26

Blockley, K 1996 'Spicer's Hall, Bristol: excavation of a medieval merchant's house, 1995'. Unpublished report, Bristol and Region Archaeological Services

Blockley, K, 2010, 'Bristol Cathedral Cloister, 2010. Archaeological Evaluation & Watching Brief'. Unpublished report, Cambrian Archaeological Projects

Bolton, J L 2000 'Irish migration to England in the late middle ages: the evidence of 1394 and 1440'. *Irish Hist Stud* **32**, 1–21

Boon, G C 1945 'The Roman site at Sea Mills, 1945–6'. *Trans Bristol Gloucestershire Archaeol Soc* **66**, 258–95

Boon, G C 1978 'Excavations on the site of a Roman quay at Caerleon, and its significance', *in* Boon, G C (ed) *Monographs & Collections Relating to Excavations Financed by H M Department of the Environment in Wales: I Roman sites*. Cardiff: Cambrian Archaeological Association, 1–24

Boore, E J 1979 'Bristol Cathedral School classroom extension'. *BARG Bulletin* **6(8)**, 198–200

Boore, E J 1980 'A summary report of excavations at Tower Lane, Bristol, 1979–80'. *BARG Review* **1** (1980), 18–26

Boore, E J 1982 'Excavations at Peter Street, 1975–6'. *Bristol Avon Archaeol* **1**, 7–11

Boore, E J 1984 *Excavations at Tower Lane, Bristol*. Bristol: City of Bristol Museum and Art Gallery

Boore, E J 1985 'Excavations at St. Augustine the Less, Bristol, 1983–4'. *Bristol Avon Archaeol* **4**, 21–33

Boore, E J 1986 'The church of St Augustine the Less, Bristol: an interim statement'. *Trans Bristol Gloucestershire Archaeol Soc* **104**, 211–4

Boore, E J 1989 'The lesser cloister and a medieval drain at St. Augustine's Abbey, Bristol'. *Trans Bristol Gloucestershire Archaeol Soc* **107**, 217–22

Boore, E J 1991 'The Minster House – Bristol Cathedral', *Bristol Avon Archaeol* **9**, 43–8

Boore, E J 1992 'The Minster House at Bristol Cathedral – excavations in 1992'. *Bristol Avon Archaeol* **10**, 42–50

Boore, E J, 1995a 'Archaeological desktop study of Southmead Manor gardens and gazebo'. Unpublished report, Bristol and Region Archaeological Services

Boore, E J 1995b 'A Romano-British quarry site at Lawrence Weston, Bristol: excavations at Lawrence Weston Road-Long Cross, Lawrence Weston, Bristol, 1995'. Unpublished report, Bristol and Region Archaeological Services

Boore, E J 1998 'Burial vaults and coffin furniture in the West Country', *in* Cox, M (ed) *Grave Concerns: Death and Burial in England 1700–800*. York: CBA Research Report **113**, 67–84

Borsay, P 1989 *The English Urban Renaissance: Culture and Society in the Provincial Town, 1660–770*. Oxford: Clarendon Press

Boswell, J 1980 *Life of Johnson*. Oxford: Oxford University Press

Boucher, C E 1909 'St. Peter's Church, Bristol'. *Trans Bristol Gloucestershire Archaeol Soc* **32**, 260–300

Boucher, C E 1938 'The Black Death in Bristol'. *Trans Bristol Gloucestershire Archaeol Soc* **60**, 31–46

Boucher, C E 1939 'St. Edith's Well and St. Peter's Cross'. *Trans Bristol Gloucestershire Archaeol Soc* **61**, 95–106

Boyer, P 2013 '6.5 Broadmead industries', in Ridgeway, V and Watts, M (eds), *Friars, Quakers, Industry and Urbanisation. The Archaeology of the Broadmead Expansion Project, Cabot Circus, Bristol, 2005–8*. Cotswold Archaeology/Pre-Construct Archaeology, 376–81

Bradley, J and Gaimster, M 2000 'Medieval Britain and Ireland in 1999', *Medieval Archaeol* **44**, 235–354

Bradley, J and Gaimster, M 2001 'Medieval Britain and Ireland in 2000', *Medieval Archaeology* **45**, 233–379

Bradley, J and Gaimster, M 2002 'Medieval Britain and Ireland in 2001', *Medieval Archaeology* **46**, 125–264

Bradley, J and Gaimster, M 2003 'Medieval Britain and Ireland in 2002', *Medieval Archaeology* **47**, 199–339

Bradley, R 1990 *The Passage of Arms: An Archaeological Analysis of Prehistoric Hoards and Votive Deposits*. Cambridge: Cambridge University Press

Brady, K 2017 'The established medieval suburb', *in* Ford, Ben M, Brady, Kate and Teague, Steven, *From Bridgehead to Brewery. The Medieval and Post-medieval archaeological remains from Finzel's Reach, Bristol*. Oxford: Oxford Archaeology Monograph **27**, 126–39

Brady, K and Teague, S 2017, 'Chapter 3. The high medieval period (*c* AD 1225–550)', *in* Ford, Ben M, Brady Kate and Teague, Steven *From Bridgehead to Brewery. The Medieval and Post-medieval Archaeological Remains from Finzel's Reach, Bristol*. Oxford: Oxford Archaeology Monograph **27**, 57–93

Brakspear, H 1922 'St. Mary Redcliffe, Bristol'. *Trans Bristol Gloucestershire Archaeol Soc* **44**, 271–92

Brett, J R 1994 'Archaeological excavation to the rear of Nos 78–100 St. Michael's Hill, Kingsdown, Bristol'. Unpublished report, Bristol and Region Archaeological Services

Brett, J R 1995 'Archaeological evaluation of land at Avon Street, Bristol'. Unpublished report, Bristol and Region Archaeological Services

Brett, J R 1996 'Archaeology and the construction of Royal Edward Dock, Avonmouth, 1902–8'. *Archaeology in the Severn Estuary* **7**, 115–20

Brett, J R and Bryant, J 1997 'Bristol Urban Archaeology Database. Final report for English Heritage and Bristol City Council'. Unpublished report, Bristol City Council

Brett, J R *et al*, 2002, 'Bristol: Urban Archaeological Assessment. First Draft'. Unpublished typescript. Bristol City Council

Brett, J R *et al*, 2005, 'Bristol: Urban Archaeological Assessment. Second Draft'. Unpublished typescript. Bristol City Council

Brett, M 2009 'Westmoreland House, Stokes Croft, Bristol. Archaeological Evaluation'. Cotswold Archaeology, unpublished report no 09214

Brett, M 2012 'Bristol General Hospital, Guinea Street, Bristol. Archaeological Evaluation'. Cotswold Archaeology, unpublished report no 12141

Britnell, R H 1986 *Growth and Decline in Colchester, 1300–525*. Cambridge: Cambridge University Press

Britnell, R H 1993 *The Commercialisation of English Society 1000–300*. Cambridge: Cambridge University Press

Britnell, R H and Campbell, B M S (eds) 1993 *A Commercialising Economy: England 1086 to c.1300*. Cambridge: Cambridge University Press

Britton, J 1813 *An Historical and Architectural Essay Relating to Redcliffe Church, Bristol*. London: Longman, Hurst, Rees, Orme and Brown

Britton, J 1830 *The History and Antiquities of the Abbey and Cathedral Church of Bristol*. London: Longman, Rees, Orme, Brown & Green

Brodie, A, Winter, G, and Porter, S nd 'The Law Court 1800–2000: development in form and function'. Unpublished report for English Heritage, The Court Service & The Lord Chancellor's Department

Bronk Ramsey, C 1995 'Radiocarbon calibration and analysis of stratigraphy: The OxCal Program'. *Radiocarbon* **37**, 425–30

Brown, A 1996 'Parish church building: the fabric', *in* Blair, J and Pyrah, C (eds) *Church Archaeology: Research Directions for the Future*. York: CBA Research Report **104**, 63–8

Brown, R A, Colvin, H, and Taylor, A 1963 *The History of the King's Works: Vol.2 The Middle Ages*. London: HMSO

Brown, S 1997 'The stained glass of the Lady Chapel of Bristol Cathedral; Charles Winston (1814–64) and stained glass restoration in the 19th century', *in* Keen, L (ed) *'Almost the richest city': Bristol in the Middle ages*. London: British Archaeological Association, 107–17

Brown, S, 2008 'Excavations at Temple Church, Bristol: a report on the excavations by Andrew Saunders, 1960'. *Trans Bristol Gloucestershire Archaeol Soc* **126**, 113–29

Bryant, J 1992 'Archaeological evaluation for County of Avon Property Services Department. St. Michael's Primary School, Bristol'. Unpublished report, Bristol and Region Archaeological Services

Bryant, J 1993 'Architectural recording at St. James' Priory, Bristol'. *Bristol Avon Archaeol* **11**, 18–34

Bryant, J 1994a 'Archaeological desktop study of Courage's Brewery, Bristol'. Unpublished report, Bristol and Region Archaeological Services

Bryant, J 1994b 'Archaeological desktop study of The Sugar House Lewin's Mead, Bristol, Avon'. Unpublished report, Bristol and Region Archaeological Services

Bryant, J 1994c 'Archaeological evaluation of Park Row and Woodland Road, Clifton, Bristol'. Unpublished report, Bristol and Region Archaeological Services

Bryant, J 1994d 'Archaeological excavation at 19–35 Houlton Street, St. Paul's, Bristol, Avon'. Unpublished report, Bristol and Region Archaeological Services

Bryant, J 1995a 'Archaeological watching brief and survey of 35 Corn Street, Bristol'. Unpublished report, Bristol and Region Archaeological Services

Bryant, J 1995b 'Archaeological watching brief at Houlton Street, Bristol'. Unpublished report, Bristol and Region Archaeological Services

Bryant J 1999a 'Archaeological desktop evaluation of the Broadmead redevelopment site, Bristol'. Unpublished report, Bristol and Region Archaeological Services

Bryant, J 1999b 'Archaeological desktop study of Ashley Court, Montpelier, Bristol'. Unpublished report, Bristol and Region Archaeological Services

Bryant, J 1999c 'Archaeological desktop study of land at Wilson Street, St Paul's, Bristol'. Unpublished report, Bristol and Region Archaeological Services

Bryant, J 2008 'Archaeological evaluation in the crypt of St Michaels Church, St Michaels Hill, Bristol'. Unpublished report, Bristol and Region Archaeological Services

Bryant, J 2015 'Excavations at Minster House, Bristol, 1992'. Unpublished report, Bristol and Region Archaeological Services

Bryant, J and Brett, J 1996 'Archaeological desktop study and survey of the former lead works, Cheese Lane, Bristol'. Unpublished report, Bristol and Region Archaeological Services.

Bryant, J and Kear, D 1982 'An 18th century bakery at Christmas Steps, Bristol'. *Bristol Avon Archaeol* **1**, 45–9

Bryant, J and Leech, R H 2000 'Archaeological desk-based evaluation of the Broadmead redevelopment site, Bristol'. Unpublished report, Bristol and Region Archaeological Services

Bryant, J and Root, J 1999 'Archaeological and historical study of College Square, Bristol'. Bristol and Region Archaeological Services

Bryant, J and Winstone, J 1983 'A 17th century house at 10 Lower Park Row, Bristol'. *Bristol Avon Archaeol* **2**, 45–7

Buchanan, B 1995–6 'The technology of gunpowder making in the 18th century: evidence from the Bristol region'. *Trans Newcomen Soc* **67**, 125–59

Buchanan, R A 1969 'The construction of the Floating Harbour in Bristol: 1804–9'. *Trans Bristol Gloucestershire Archaeol Soc* **88**, 184–204

Buchanan, R A and Cossons, N 1969 *Industrial Archaeology of the Bristol Region*. Newton Abbot: David & Charles

Burchill, R 1993 'Desktop study & fieldwork, Bristol Grammar School, Tyndall's Park, Clifton, Bristol'. Unpublished report, Bristol and Region Archaeological Services

Burchill, R 1994a 'Archaeological evaluation of 42–43 Welsh Back, Bristol, Avon'. Unpublished report, Bristol and Region Archaeological Services

Burchill, R 1994b 'Archaeological excavation of St. Thomas burial ground, St. Thomas Street, Bristol, Avon'. Unpublished report, Bristol and Region Archaeological Services

Burchill, R 1995a 'Archaeological evaluation of land at Canon's Marsh, Bristol (Bristol Harbourside Development)'. Unpublished report, Bristol and Region Archaeological Services

Burchill, R 1995b 'Archaeological excavation at Olivetti House, King Street/Marsh Street, Bristol, Avon'. Unpublished report, Bristol and Region Archaeological Services

Burchill, R 1995c 'Archaeological excavation of the site of Ring's Clay tobacco pipe works, Temple Back, Bristol'. Unpublished report, Bristol and Region Archaeological Services

Burchill, R 1996a 'Archaeological watching brief at 44–50 Jacobs Wells Road, Clifton, Bristol'. Unpublished Bristol and Region Archaeological Services Report

Burchill, R 1996b 'Archaeological watching brief at St. Michael's Church graveyard, St Michael's Hill, Bristol'. Unpublished report, Bristol and Region Archaeological Services

Burchill, R 1996c 'Archaeological watching brief at Walker Street, Kingsdown, Bristol'. Unpublished report, Bristol and Region Archaeological Services

Burchill, R 1997 'The Horsefair burial ground revisited'. *Bristol Avon Archaeol* **14**, 49–54

Burchill, R 1998 'Watching brief at Broad Quay, Bristol'. Unpublished report, Bristol and Region Archaeological Services

Burchill, R 1999a 'Archaeological desktop study of Steevens House, 34 Old Market Street, Bristol'. Unpublished report, Bristol and Region Archaeological Services

Burchill, R 1999b 'Archaeological monitoring at 2, Trenchard Street'. Unpublished report, Bristol and Region Archaeological Services

Burchill, R, Coxah, M, Nicholson, A, and Ponsford, M W 1987 'Excavations in Bristol in 1985–6'. *Bristol Avon Archaeol* **6**, 11–30

Burder, W C, Hine, J and Godwin, E W 1851 *The Architectural Antiquities of Bristol and its Neighbourhood*. Bristol: W C Burder, James Hine & E W Godwin

Burgess, C 1985 '"For the increase of Divine Service": chantries in the late medieval Bristol'. *J Ecclesiastical Hist* **36**, 46–65

Burgess, C 1987 '"By quick and by dead": wills and pious provision in late medieval Bristol', *English Historical Review* **102**, 837–58

Burgess, C 2002 'Educated parishioners in London and Bristol on the eve of the Reformation', *in* Barron, C M and Stratford, J (eds) *The Church and Learning in Later Medieval Society: Essays in Honour of R B Dobson*, Donington: Harlaxton Medieval Studies **XI**, 286–304

Burgess, C (ed) 1995 *The Pre-reformation Records of All Saints', Bristol. Part 1*. Bristol: Bristol Record Series **46**

Burnett, J 1986 *A Social History of Housing, 1815–985*. London: Methuen

Butcher, E E (ed) 1932 *Bristol Corporation of the Poor: Selected Records 1696–834*. Bristol: Bristol Record Series **3**

Butler, K M 1995 *The Economics of Emancipation: Jamaica and Barbados 1823–843*. London: University of North Carolina Press

Butler, L A S 1986 'Church dedications and the cults of saints in England', *in* Butler, L A S and Morris, R K (eds) *The Anglo-Saxon Church: Papers on History, Architecture, and Archaeology in Honour of Dr. H M Taylor*. London: CBA Research Report **60**, 44–50

Campbell, B, Galloway, J, Keene, J, Keene, D and Murphy, M 1993 *A Medieval Capital and its Grain Supply: Agrarian Production and Distribution in the London Region c.1300* London: Historical Geography Research Group

Cannadine, D 1980 *Lords and Landlords: The Aristocracy and the Towns, 1774–967*. Leicester: Leicester University Press

Cannadine, D 1984 'The present and the past in the English industrial revolution'. *Past & Present* **103**, 131–72

Cannon, J 2004a 'The absent figure: on authorship and meaning in the 14th-century eastern arm of St Augustine's, Bristol'. *Trans Ancient Monuments Soc* **48**, 21–48

Cannon, J 2004b 'Gothic remodelling itself? Restoration and intention at the outer north porch of St. Mary Redcliffe, Bristol'. Unpublished paper presented to the British Archaeological Association

Capp, B 1989 *Cromwell's Navy: The Fleet and the English Revolution, 1648–60*. Oxford: Clarendon Press

Carlin, M 1998 'Fast food and urban living standards', *in* Carlin, M and Rosenthal, J (eds) *Food and Eating in Medieval Europe*. London: Hambledon Press, 27–51

Carlin, M and Rosenthal, J (eds) 1998 *Food and Eating in Medieval Europe*. London: Hambledon Press

Carus-Wilson, E M 1928 'The merchant adventurers of Bristol in the 15th century'. *Trans Royal Hist Soc* 4 Ser **11**, 61-82

Carus-Wilson, E M 1967 *Medieval Merchant Venturers: Collected Studies*. London: Methuen and Co. Ltd.

Carus-Wilson, E M (ed) 1937 *The Overseas Trade of Bristol in the Later Middle Ages*. Bristol: Bristol Record Society **7**

Cattell, J 1996 'Former Avonside Ironworks, Avon Street, Bristol'. Unpublished report, RCHME

Chadwyck Healey, C E H (ed) 1897 *Somersetshire Pleas (Civil and Criminal), from the Rolls of the Itinerant Justices (Close of the 12th Century – 41 Henry III)*. London: Somerset Record Society **11**

Chalklin, C W 1989 'Estate development in Bristol, Birmingham and Liverpool, 1660–720', *in* Chalklin, C and Wordie, J (eds) *Town and Countryside: The English Landowner in the National Economy, 1660–800*. London: Unwin Hyman, 102–15

Channon, G 1985 *Bristol and the Promotion of the Great Western Railway*. Bristol: Bristol Branch of the Historical Association

Chard, J *et al* 1995 *Brislington*. Stroud: Chalford

Chase, S M 1995 'Rural adaptations of suburban bungalows, Sussex county, Delaware', *in* Collins Cromley, E and C L Hudgins, C L (eds) *Perspectives in Vernacular Architecture V* Knoxville: University of Tennessee Press, 1995, 179–89

Cherry, J 1974 'Post-medieval Britain in 1973'. *Post-medieval Archaeology* **8**, 120–36

Cherry, J 1975 'Post-medieval Britain in 1974'. *Post-medieval Archaeology* **9**, 240–60

Children's Employment Commission 1864 *Second Report of the Commissioners with Appendix*. London: HMSO

Children's Employment Commission 1866 *Fifth Report of the Commissioners with Appendix*. London: HMSO

Childs, W 1981 'England's iron trade in the 15th century'. *Economic Hist Rev* 2 Ser **34**, 25–47

Childs, W 1996 'The English export trade in cloth in the 14th century', *in* Britnell, R and Hatcher, J (eds) *Progress and Problems in Medieval England: Essays in Honour of Edward Miller*. Cambridge: Cambridge University Press, 121–47

Christie, N, Creighton, O, Edgeworth, M and Hamerow, H, 2013, *Transforming Townscapes. From Burh to Borough: The Archaeology of Wallingford, AD 800–1400*. Soc Medieval Archaeol Monograph **35**

Christie, O F 1935 *A History of Clifton College, 1860–934*. Bristol: J W Arrowsmith

Church, R 2000 'Advertising consumer goods in 19th-century Britain: reinterpretations'. *Economic Hist Rev* 2 Ser **53**, 621–45

Clark, D 2000 'The shop within? An analysis of the architectural evidence for medieval shops'. *Architect Hist* **43**, 57–87

Clark, G 1850 *Report to the General Board of Health on a Preliminary Inquiry into the Sewerage, Drainage, and Supply of Water, and the Sanitary Condition of the Inhabitants of the City and County of Bristol*. London: HMSO

Clark, P 2000 *British Clubs and Societies 1580–800: The Origins of an Associational World*. Oxford: Oxford University Press.

Clarke, C, 2010 'St Bede's Catholic School, Long Cross, Bristol. An archaeological post-excavation assessment report'. Unpublished report, AOC Archaeology

Clay, R M 1941 *Samuel Hieronymus Grimm of Burgdorf in Switzerland*. London: Faber

Clifton, R 1984 *The Last Popular Rebellion: The Western Rising of 1685*. London: Maurice Temple Smith

Cobain, S, 2015 '5.3 Plant macrofossil and charcoal remains', *in* Alexander, M (ed), *Medieval and Post-Medieval Occupation and Industry in the Redcliffe Suburb of Bristol. Excavations at 1–2 and 3 Redcliff Street, 2003–10*. Cotswold Archaeology Monograph **8**, 104–21

Cobb, P 1988 *The Oxford Movement in 19th Century Bristol*. Bristol: Bristol Branch of the Historical Association

Cocks, D 1974 'The WCA Warehouse'. *BIAS Journal* **7**, 4–8

Cohen, N 1996 'Thames archaeological survey 1996'. *Rescue News* **70**, 3

Collard, M, 2007 'Redcliff Wharf, Bristol. Archaeological Evaluation, phase 2'. Cotswold Archaeology, unpublished report no 07080

Colley, L 1992 *Britons: Forging the Nation, 1707–837*. New Haven: Yale University Press

Collinson, J 1791 *The History and Antiquities of the County of Somerset* (3 vols.). Bath: R Cruttwell.

Collinson, P and Craig, J (eds) 1998 *The Reformation in English Towns, 1500–640*. Basingstoke: Macmillan Press Ltd.

Colls, K 2002 '3 Redcliff Street. Archaeological evaluation'. Cotswold Archaeology, unpublished report no 02112

Colls, K 2003 'Templar House, Temple Way, Bristol. Archaeological evaluation'. Cotswold Archaeology, unpublished report no 03044

Colls, K 2010, 'The Avon floodplain at Bristol: excavations at Templar House, Temple Way, in Bristol 2004 and 2005'. *Trans. Bristol Gloucestershire Archaeological Society* **128**, 73–120

Colvin, H 1963 *The History of the King's Works Volume II The Middle Ages* London: HMSO

Connolly, P and Martin, G (eds) 1992 *The Dublin Guild Merchant Roll c.1190–265*. Dublin: Dublin Corporation

Conway, H 1991 *People's Parks: The Design and Development of Victorian Parks in Britain*. Cambridge: Cambridge University Press

Cooper, D and Donald, M 1995 'Households and "hidden" kin in early 19th-century England: four case studies in suburban Exeter, 1821–61'. *Continuity and Change* **10**, 257–78

Corcos, N *et al* 2017 'Excavations in 2014 at Wade Street, Bristol - a documentary and archaeological analysis'. *Internet Archaeology* 45. https://doi.org/10.11141/ia.45.3

Cornwell, J 2003 *The Bristol Coalfield*. Landmark Publishing

Costello, K and Burley, R 1997 *Charity on Camera in Edwardian Bristol: A Photographic Survey of the Bristol Municipal Charities, 1906*. Derby: Breedon Books Publishing Company

Costen, M 1992 *The Origins of Somerset*. Manchester: Manchester University Press

Coulson, C 1995 'Battlements and the bourgeoisie: municipal status and the apparatus of urban defence in later-medieval England', *in* Church, S and Harvey, R (ed) *Medieval Knighthood V: Papers from the Sixth Strawberry Hill Conference 1994*. Woodbridge: The Boydell Press, 119–95

Cox, S 1996 'Archaeological evaluation at Portwall Lane East, Temple Gate, Bristol'. Unpublished report, Bristol and Region Archaeological Services

Cox, S 1997 'Archaeological excavation at the redoubt, Temple Quay, Bristol'. Unpublished report, Bristol and Region Archaeological Services

Cox, S 1998a 'Archaeological evaluation at the proposed site of The Harbourside Centre, Canon's Marsh, Bristol'. Unpublished report, Bristol and Region Archaeological Services

Cox, S 1998b 'Archaeological watching brief at Canon's Road, Canon's Marsh, Bristol. Unpublished report, Bristol and Region Archaeological Services

Cox, S 1998c 'Archaeological watching brief at Quaker's Friars, Bristol'. Unpublished report, Bristol and Region Archaeological Services

Cox, S 1998d 'Excavations on the medieval waterfront at Bridge Parade, Bristol, 1999' [*sic*]. *Bristol Avon Archaeol* **15**, 1–26

Cox, S 1999 'Excavations at the site of the former Limekiln Dock, Hotwells Road, Harbourside, Bristol'. *BIAS Journal* **32**, 17–34

Cox, S 2000 'Archaeological excavation of a medieval water gate at Temple Quay, Bristol, 2000'. Unpublished report, Bristol and Region Archaeological Services

Cox, S and Jackson, R G 1998 'Archaeological evaluation at the former lead works, Cheese Lane, Bristol'. Unpublished report, Bristol and Region Archaeological Services

Cox, S and Longman, T 1998 'Excavations at New World Square, Canon's Marsh, Bristol'. Unpublished report, Bristol and Region Archaeological Services

Cox, S, McSloy, E and Watts, M, 2004, 3 Redcliff Street, Bristol. Post-Excavation Assessment and Updated Project Design. Unpublished report, Cotswold Archaeology

Cox, S, Barber, A and Collard, M, 2006, 'The archaeology and history of the former Bryan Brothers' Garage site, Deanery Road, Bristol: the evolution of an urban landscape'. *Trans Bristol Gloucestershire Archaeological Soc* **124**, 55–71

Crafts, N F R 1985 *British Economic Growth During the Industrial Revolution*. Oxford: Clarendon Press

Creighton O and Higham R A, 2005, *Medieval Town Walls: An Archaeology and Social History of Urban Defence*, Tempus, 2005

Croft, R 2000 'Canon's Marsh Gas Works, Bristol: development, recording and archaeological assessment'. *BIAS Journal* **33** (2000), 37–48

Croft, R, Rodwell, K and Chapman, M, 2005 'Canon's Marsh Gasworks, Bristol. Archaeological watching brief; excavation report: final report'. RemedX Ltd, Privately circulated

Cronne, H A 1946 *Bristol Charters, 1378–499*. Bristol: Bristol Record Series **11**

Cronne, H A and Davis, R H C (eds) 1968 *Regesta Regum Anglo-Normannorum, 1066–154* vol 3 Oxford: Clarendon Press

Cross, L H 1993 'Durnford Quarry, Long Ashton: archaeological evaluation in advance of proposed development'. Unpublished report, Avon Archaeological Unit

Crossley, D 1991 'Current research on English glass furnaces', *in* Mendera, M (ed) *Archeologia e storia della produzione del vetro preindustriale*. Firenze: All'insegna del Giglio, 411–22

Crossley, D 1998 'The archaeologist and evidence from field sampling for medieval and post-medieval technological innovation', *in* Bayley, J (ed) *Science in Archaeology: An Agenda for the Future*. London: English Heritage, 219–23

Crouch, D 2000 *The Reign of King Stephen, 1135–154*. Harlow: Pearson Education Ltd

Cruikshank, D and Burton, N 1990 *Life in the Georgian City*. London: Viking

Cudlip, D 2005 'Land between 46 Gloucester Lane and 29–37 West Street, Old Market, Bristol. Archaeological Evaluation'. Cotswold Archaeology, unpublished report no 05151

Cullen, K, 2005 'Redcliff Wharf, Bristol. Archaeological evaluation'. Cotswold Archaeology, unpublished report no 05143

Cullen, K 2007 '114 Jacob Street, Old Market, Bristol. Archaeological evaluation'. Cotswold Archaeology, unpublished report no 07108

Cullen, K and Barber, A 2008 'Redcliffe Village, Bristol. Archaeological evaluation'. Cotswold Archaeology, unpublished report no 07095

Cullen, K, Holbrook, N, Watts, M, Caffell, A and Holst, M 2006 'A post-Roman cemetery at Hewlett Packard, Filton, South Gloucestershire: Excavations in 2005', in Watts (ed) *Two Cemeteries From Bristol's Northern Suburbs*. Bristol and Gloucestershire Archaeological Reports No **4**

Cunliffe, B 1984 'Gloucestershire and the Iron Age of southern Britain'. *Trans Bristol Gloucestershire Archaeol Soc* **102**, 5–15

Cutting, R and Cummings, I 1999 'Water meadows: their form, operation and plant ecology', *in* Cook, H and T Williamson, T (eds) *Water Management in the English Landscape: Field, Marsh and Meadow*. Edinburgh: Edinburgh University Press, 157–78

Cuttler, R, Hunt, J and Ratkai, S, 2009 'Saxon *burh* and royal castle: re-thinking early urban space in Stafford'. *Staffordshire Archaeol Hist Soc Trans* **43**, 39–85

DCLG 2012, *National Planning Policy Framework*. Department for Communities and Local Government, 2012

Dallaway, J 1834 *Antiquities of Bristow in the Middle Centuries Including The Topography by William Wyrcestre and The Life of William Canynges*. Bristol: Mirror Office

Daniell, C 1997 *Death and Burial in Medieval England*. London: Routledge

Daniels, S 1993 'Re-visioning Britain: mapping and landscape painting, 1750–820', *in* Baetjer, K (ed) *Glorious Nature: British Landscape Painting, 1750–850*. New York: Hudson Hills, 61–72

Daniels, S 1999 *Humphry Repton: Landscape Gardening and the Geography of Georgian England*. London: Yale University Press

Darby, H C 1954 'Gloucestershire', *in* Darby, H C and Terrett, I (ed) *The Domesday Geography of Midland England*. Cambridge: Cambridge University Press, 1–56

Darlington, R (ed) 1928 *The Vita Wulfstani of William of Malmesbury…* Camden Society 3 Ser **40**. London: Royal Historical Society

Darvill, T 1989 'The circulation of Neolithic stone and flint axes: a case study from Wales and the mid-west of England'. *Proc Prehist Soc* **55**, 27–43

Darvill, T and Gerrard, C 1994 *Cirencester: Town and Landscape*. Cirencester: Cotswold Archaeological Trust Ltd.

Davenport, P, 2013a 'Period 3: 16th to 17th centuries (post-medieval)', *in* Ridgeway, V and Watts, M (eds), *Friars, Quakers, Industry and Urbanisation. The Archaeology of the Broadmead Expansion Project, Cabot Circus, Bristol, 2005–8*. Cotswold Archaeology/Pre-Construct Archaeology, 341–4

Davenport, P, 2013b 'Period 4: 18th century', *in* Ridgeway, V and Watts, M (eds), *Friars, Quakers, Industry and Urbanisation. The Archaeology of the Broadmead Expansion Project, Cabot Circus, Bristol, 2005–8*. Cotswold Archaeology/Pre-Construct Archaeology, p 344-8

Davenport, P, 2013c 'Period 5: 19th century', *in* Ridgeway, V and Watts, M (eds), *Friars, Quakers, Industry and Urbanisation. The Archaeology of the Broadmead Expansion Project, Cabot Circus, Bristol, 2005–8*. Cotswold Archaeology/Pre-Construct Archaeology, 348–352

Davenport, P, 2013d '6.3 The medieval suburb', *in* Ridgeway, V and Watts, M (eds), *Friars, Quakers, Industry and Urbanisation. The Archaeology of the Broadmead Expansion Project, Cabot Circus, Bristol, 2005–8*. Cotswold Archaeology/Pre-Construct Archaeology, 365–70

Davenport, P, 2013e '6.4 The post-medieval suburb', *in* Ridgeway, V and Watts, M (eds), *Friars, Quakers, Industry and Urbanisation. The Archaeology of the Broadmead Expansion Project, Cabot Circus, Bristol, 2005–8*. Cotswold Archaeology/Pre-Construct Archaeology, 371–6

Davenport, P, 2013f '6.7 18th- and 19th-century urban expansion', *in* Ridgeway, V and Watts, M (eds), *Friars, Quakers, Industry and Urbanisation. The Archaeology of the Broadmead Expansion Project, Cabot Circus, Bristol, 2005–8*. Cotswold Archaeology/Pre-Construct Archaeology, 387–93

Davenport, P, 2013g '6.8 The Non-Conformist community', *in* Ridgeway, V and Watts, M 2013, *Friars, Quakers, Industry and Urbanisation. The Archaeology of the Broadmead Expansion Project, Cabot Circus, Bristol, 2005–8*. Cotswold Archaeology/Pre-Construct Archaeology, 393–8

Davenport, P, Leech, R H and Rowe, M, 2011 '55–60 St Thomas Street, Redcliffe, Bristol: Excavations in 2006', *in* Watts, M (ed) *Medieval and Post-medieval Development within Bristol's Inner Suburbs*. Cotswold Archaeology: Bristol and Gloucestershire Archaeological Report **7**

Davey, P 1987 'The post-medieval period', *in* Schofield, J and Leech, R H (eds) *Urban Archaeology in Britain*. London: CBA Research Report **61**, 69–80

Davies, C S L 1994 'The alleged 'Sack of Bristol': international ramifications of Breton privateering, 1484–5'. *Historical Research* **67**, 230–9

Davies, J A 1927 *Early Life in the West*. Bristol: Baker

Davies, J 1991 *Gentlemen and Tarpaulins: The Officers and Men of the Restoration Navy*. Oxford: Clarendon Press

Davies, N (ed) 1971–6 *Paston Letters and Papers of the 15th Century*, 2 vols (vol.1 1971; vol.2 1976). Oxford: Clarendon Press

Davis, E 2003 'Archaeological evaluation of land at Nos 32 & 36 Victoria Street, Bristol'. Unpublished report, Bristol and Region Archaeological Services

Davis, E 2004a 'Archaeological evaluation on the site of Albion Terrace, Johnny Ball Lane, Bristol'. Unpublished report, Bristol and Region Archaeological Services

Davis, E 2004b 'Archaeological evaluation at Hannah More School, New Kingsley Road, St Philips, Bristol'. Unpublished report, Bristol and Region Archaeological Services

Davis, E 2004c 'Archaeological evaluation at Nos 51A & 57 West Street, Old Market, Bristol'. Unpublished report, Bristol and Region Archaeological Services

Davis, E 2005 'Analysis of environmental samples from the archaeological evaluation at Marsh House, No 11 Marsh Street, Bristol'. Unpublished report, Bristol and Region Archaeological Services

Davis, P, Harvey, C and Press, J 1988 'Locomotive building in Bristol in the age of steam, 1837-1958', *in* Harvey, C and Press, J (eds) *Studies in the Business History of Bristol*. Bristol: Bristol Academic Press, 109–36

Davis, R 1994 *The War of the Fists: Popular Culture and Public Violence in Late Renaissance Venice*. Oxford: Oxford University Press

Dawkes, G 2002 'Land to the rear of Avon Street, Bristol. Report on an archaeological evaluation'. Unpublished report, AOC Archaeology

Dawson, D 1981 'Archaeology and the medieval churches of Bristol, Abbots Leigh and Whitchurch'. *BARG Review* **2**, 9–24

Dawson, D 1982 'Archaeology and the churches of Bristol, Abbots Leigh and Whitchurch, 1540-1850'. *Bristol Avon Archaeol* **1**, 28–44

Dawson, D *et al* 1972 'Medieval kiln wasters from St Peter's Church, Bristol'. *Trans Bristol Gloucestershire Archaeol Soc* **91**, 159–67

Dawson, K 1995 'Town defences in early modern England'. Unpublished PhD Thesis, University of Exeter

Day, J 1973 *Bristol Brass: A History of the Industry*. Newton Abbot: David & Charles

De La Beche, H 1845 *Health of Towns Commission. Report on the State of Bristol and Other Large Towns*. London: HMSO

Dening, C F W 1923 *The 18th Century Architecture of Bristol*. Bristol: J W Arrowsmith

Dennis, R 1986 *English Industrial Cities of the 19th Century: A Social Geography*. Cambridge: Cambridge University Press

Department of Culture Media and Sport; Department of Transport, Local Government and the Regions 2001 *The Historic Environment: A Force for our Future*. London

Department of the Environment 1990 *Archaeology and Planning*. Planning Policy Guidance Note 16. London: HMSO

Department of the Environment 1994 *Planning and the Historic Environment*. Planning Policy Guidance Note 15. London: HMSO

Diaper, S J 1987 'Christopher Thomas & Brothers Ltd.: the last Bristol soapmakers. An aspect of Bristol's economic development in the 19th century'. *Trans Bristol Gloucestershire Archaeol Soc* **105**, 223–32

Diaper, S J 1988 'J S Fry & Sons: growth and decline in the chocolate industry', *in* Harvey, C and Press, J (eds) *Studies in the Business History of Bristol*. Bristol: Bristol Academic Press, 34–54

Dickinson, J C 1976 'The origins of St. Augustine's, Bristol', *in* McGrath, P and Cannon, J (eds) *Essays in Bristol and Gloucestershire History*. Bristol: Bristol and Gloucestershire Archaeological Society, 109–26

Dinwiddy, K E with Chandler, J, 2011, 'Temple Back: Excavating Bristol's industrial history', *Trans Bristol Gloucestershire Archaeol Soc* **129**, 79–116

Dollman, F T and Jobbins, J R 1863 *An Analysis of Ancient Domestic Architecture, Exhibiting Examples in Great Britain*. London: J R Jobbins

Donaldson, A, Jones, A and Rackham, D 1980 'Barnard Castle, County Durham. A dinner in the Great Hall: report on the contents of a 15th century drain', *in* Austin D 'Barnard Castle. Inner Ward, 1976–8'. *J British Archaeol Assoc* **133**, 74–96

Dorrell, P 1989 *Photography in Archaeology and Conservation*. Cambridge: Cambridge University Press

Douet, J 1998 *British Barracks, 1600–914*. London: The Stationery Office

Drage, C, 1987 'Urban castles', *in* Schofield J and Leech, R (eds) *Urban Archaeology in Britain*. London: Council for British Archaeology Research Report **61**, 117–32

Dresser, M 1994 'The Moravians in Bristol', *in* Barry, J and Morgan, J (eds) *Reformation and Revival in 18th-Century Bristol*. Bristol: Bristol Record Society **45**, 105–48

Dresser, M 1996a 'Protestants, Catholics and Jews: religious differences and political status in Bristol, 1750--1850', *in* Dresser, M and Ollerenshaw, P (eds) *The Making of Modern Bristol*. Tiverton: Redcliffe Press, 96–123

Dresser, M 1996b 'Sisters and brethren: power, propriety and gender among the Bristol Moravians, 1746-1833'. *Social History* **21**, 304–29

Dresser, M 2001 *Slavery Obscured: The Social History of the Slave Trade in an English Provincial Port*. London: Continuum

Druce, D 1997 'Palaeoenvironmental constraints on Mesolithic to Romano-British communities of the Severn Estuary'. *Archaeology in the Severn Estuary* **8**, 99–102

Druce, D 2000 'Mesolithic to Romano-British archaeology and environmental change of the Severn Estuary, England'. Unpublished PhD thesis, University of Bristol

Ducker, R K 2007 'Archaeological evaluation at Westmoreland House, Ashley Road, Stokes Croft, Bristol'. Unpublished report, Avon Archaeological Unit

Ducker, R K 2013 'BRI Haematology and Oncology Centre, Horfield Road, Bristol. Archaeological evaluation and watching brief report'. Unpublished report, Bristol and West Archaeology

Ducker, R K and Erskine, J G P 2004 'Land adjacent to 47 Jacobs Wells Road/Gorse Lane, Clifton, Bristol. Archaeological evaluation and watching brief'. Unpublished report, Avon Archaeological Unit

Dunn, R 1986 'Penny wise and pound foolish: Penn as a businessman', *in* Dunn, R & Dunn, M (eds) *The World of William Penn*. Philadelphia: University of Pennsylvania Press, 37–54

Duffus Hardy, T (ed) 1835 *Rotuli patentium in Turri Londinensi*. [London]: Commissioners on the Public Records of the Kingdom

Duffy, E 1992 *The Stripping of the Altars: Traditional Religion in England, 1400–580*. New Haven: Yale University Press

Dungworth, D, 2005, 'Investigation of 18th century glass and glassworking waste from Limekiln Lane, Bristol'. English Heritage Centre for Archaeology, report 7/2005

Dyer, A 2000 'Ranking lists of English medieval towns', *in* Palliser, D M (ed) *The Cambridge Urban History of Britain: Volume I, 650–1540*. Cambridge: Cambridge University Press, 747–70

Dyer, C 1983 'English diet in the later Middle Ages', *in* Aston, T, Cox, P, Dyer, C and Thirsk, J (eds) *Social Relations and Ideas: Essays in Honour of R H Hilton*. Cambridge: Cambridge University Press, 191–216

Dyer, C 1988 'Changes in diet in the later middle ages: the case of harvest workers'. *Agricultural Hist Rev* **36**, 21–37

Dyer, C 1989 *Standards of Living in the Later Middle Ages: Social Change in England c. 1200–520*. Cambridge: Cambridge University Press

Dyer, C 1994 *Everyday Life in Medieval England*. London: Hambledon Press

Eaglen, R 1992 'The evolution of coinage in 13th-century England' *in* Coss, P R and Lloyd S D (eds) *13th Century England IV: Proceedings of the Newcastle Upon Tyne Conference 1991*. Woodbridge: The Boydell Press, 15–24

Earle, P 1989 *The Making of the English Middle Class: Business, Society and Family Life in London, 1660–730*. London: Methuen

Eason, H 1982 *Bristol's Historic Inns*. Bristol: Redcliffe Press

Edwards, J 1942 'The Theatre Royal, Bristol'. *Archaeol J* **99**, 123–26

Egan, G 1989 'Post-medieval Britain and Ireland in 1988'. *Post-medieval Archaeol* **23**, 25–67

Egan, G 1991 'Industry and economics on the medieval and later London waterfront', *in* Good, G L, Jones, R H and Ponsford, M W (eds) *Waterfront Archaeology: Proceedings of the Third International Conference, Bristol 1988*. London: CBA Research Report **74**, 9–18

Ekirch, A 1987 *Bound for America: The Transportation of British Convicts to the Colonies, 1718–75*. Oxford: Clarendon Press

Elkin, P W 1991 'Aspects of the recent development of the port of Bristol', *in* Good, G L, Jones, R H and Ponsford, M W (eds) *Waterfront Archaeology: Proceedings of the Third International Conference, Bristol 1988*. London: CBA Research Report **74**, 27–35

Elkin, P W 1995 *Images of Maritime Bristol*. Derby: Breedon Books

Elkington, H D A 1976 'The Mendip lead mines', *in* Branigan, K and Fowler, P (eds) *The Roman West Country: Classical Culture and Celtic Society*. Newton Abbot: David and Charles, 183–97

Ellis, C 2005 'Great Western Dockyard, Bristol. Phase II Development, Archaeological Evaluation Report'. Unpublished report, Wessex Archaeology

Ellis, C and Leivers, M, 2013, 'Excavations on the site of the Great Western Steamship Company's Engine Works, Bristol'. *Post-Medieval Archaeol* **47(1)**, 195–221

Ellis, F 1893–6 'Roman remains near Bristol – II. At Sea Mills, Gloucestershire III – At Whitchurch, Somerset'. *Proc Clifton Antiquarian Club* **3**, 16–21

Ellis, M J 1987 *The Early Years of the Telephone Service in Bristol, 1879–931*. London: British Telecommunications

Ellis, P 1987 'Sea Mills, Bristol: the 1965–8 excavations in the Roman town of Abonae'. *Trans Bristol Gloucestershire Archaeol Soc* **105**, 15–108

Emanuel, R R 2000 'The Society of Antiquaries' Sabbath lamp'. *Antiq J* **80**, 308–15

Emanuel, R R and Ponsford, M W 1994 'Jacob's Well, Bristol, Britain's only known medieval Jewish ritual bath (*Mikveh*)'. *Trans Bristol Gloucestershire Archaeol Soc* **112**, 73–86

English Heritage 1992 *Managing the Urban Archaeological Resource*. London: English Heritage, 1992.

English Heritage 2010 *A Thematic Research Strategy for the Urban Historic Environment*. English Heritage

Ennis, T, Rackham, D J and Richmond, A 1997 'An archaeological excavation at Victoria Street, Bristol in connection with permission for town development. 76–96 Victoria Street, Bristol: archaeological assessment report'. Unpublished report

Erskine, J G P 1994–5 'Excavation of a Bronze Age settlement at Savages Wood, Bradley Stoke'. *Bristol Avon Archaeol* **12**, 18–23

Erskine, J G P 1997 'St. Michael's on the Mount Without Church of England primary school, Bristol, additional classroom'. Unpublished report, Avon Archaeological Unit

Erskine, J G P 2001 'Land adjacent to: 47 Jacobs Wells Road/Gorse Lane, Clifton, Bristol. Archaeological Evaluation and Supplementary Excavation'. Avon Archaeological Unit

Erskine, J G P 2003 'Poole's Wharf 1996: archaeological sample excavation programme'. *BIAS Journal* **36**, 13–25

Erskine, J G P 2005 'The excavation and preservation of a Georgian cold bath at Gorse Lane, Clifton, Bristol'. *Bristol Avon Archaeol* **20**, 7–15

Erskine, J G P and Prosser, L 1997 'Poole's Wharf, Hotwells, Bristol. Archaeological excavation prior to redevelopment'. Unpublished report, Avon Archaeological Unit

Estabrook, C B 1998 *Urbane and Rustic England: Cultural Ties and Social Spheres in the Provinces 1660–780*. Manchester: Manchester University Press

Etheridge, D 2007 'St Pauls Park, St Pauls, Bristol. Archaeological evaluation'. Unpublished report, Avon Archaeological Unit

Eustace, K 1982 *Michael Rysbrack: Sculptor 1694–770*. Bristol: Friends of Bristol Art Gallery

Evans, D, Holbrook, N and McSloy, E R, 2006, 'A Later Iron Age cemetery and Roman settlement at Henbury School, Bristol: Excavations in 2004', *in* Watts, M (ed), *Two Cemeteries From Bristol's Northern Suburbs*. Cirencester: Bristol and Gloucestershire Archaeological Reports No **4**, 1–50

Evans, D and Saunders, K 2006 'Land to the south of Portwall Lane, Bristol. Archaeological evaluation'. Cotswold Archaeology, unpublished report no 07036

Evans, J 1824 *A Chronological Outline of the History of Bristol*. Bristol: J Evans

Evans, R 1982 *The Fabrication of Virtue: English Prison Architecture, 1750–840*. Cambridge: Cambridge University Press

Eveleigh, D 1996 *Bristol, 1850–919*. Stroud: Sutton Publishing Limited

Eveleigh, D 1998 *Bristol, 1920–69*. Stroud: Sutton Publishing Limited

Exwood, M and Lehmann, H (eds) 1993 *Journal of William Schellink's Travels in England, 1661–3*. London: Camden Society 5 Ser **1**

Eyles, A 2002 *Odeon Cinemas. 1: Oscar Deutsch Entertains our Nation*. London: Cinema Theatre Association

Falconer, K 1991 *Surveys of the Development Corporation Areas: Bristol*. London: RCHME

Fawcett, E 1938 'Coffin slab, Bristol Cathedral'. *Trans Bristol Gloucestershire Archaeol Soc* **60**, 342–3

Fenwick, V H (ed) 1978 *The Graveney Boat: A 10th-Century Find from Kent*. Oxford: British Archaeol Rep, **3**

Firth, A 1998 'SS Great Britain project. Great Western Dry Dock and quayside: archaeological appraisal'. Unpublished report, Wessex Archaeology

Firth, C H (ed) 1925 'The siege and capture of Bristol by the Royalist forces in 1643'. *J Soc Army Historical Research* **4**, 180–203

Firth, C H (ed) 1992 *The Clarke Papers: Selections from the Papers of William Clarke*. London: Royal Historical Society

Fissel, M C 1994 *The Bishops' Wars: Charles I's Campaigns against Scotland, 1638–40*. Cambridge: Cambridge University Press

Fissell, M E 1991 *Patients, Power and the Poor in 18th-Century Bristol*. Cambridge: Cambridge University Press

Flanagan, M 1989 *Irish Society, Anglo-Norman Settlers, Angevin Kingship: Interactions in Ireland in the Late 12th Century*. Oxford: Clarendon Press

Fleming, P 2000 'Conflict and urban government in later medieval England: St. Augustine's Abbey, Bristol'. *Urban History* **27**, 325–43

Fleming, P 2001 'Sanctuary and authority in pre-reformation Bristol, *in* Bettey, J (ed) *Historic Churches and Church Life in Bristol: Essays in Memory of Elizabeth Ralph 1911–2000*. Bristol: Bristol & Gloucestershire Archaeological Society, 73–84

Fleming, P 2004 *Bristol Castle: A Political History*. Bristol: Bristol Branch of the Historical Association

Fleming, P, 2013, 'Time, space and power in later medieval Bristol'. Working paper. University of the West of England.

Ford, Ben M, Brady, Kate and Teague, Steven, 2017, *From Bridgehead to Brewery. The Medieval and Post-Medieval Archaeological Remains from Finzel's Reach, Bristol*. Oxford Archaeology Monograph **27**

Foundations Archaeology, 2010, 'Hadrian Close, Sea Mills, Bristol. Archaeological evaluation phase 2'. Unpublished report, Foundations Archaeology 2010

Fowler, P J 1972a 'Medieval'. *Archaeological Review* **6**, 50–60

Fowler, P J 1972b 'Post-medieval'. *Archaeological Review* **6**, 60–5

Fowler, P J 1973a 'Medieval'. *Archaeological Review* **7**, 53

Fowler, P J 1973b 'Post-medieval period'. *Archaeological Review* **7**, 60–5

Fox, F F 1880 *Some Account of the Ancient Fraternity of Merchant Taylors of Bristol, with Transcripts of Ordinances and Other Documents*. Bristol: J Wright & Co.

Fox, F F (ed) 1910 *Adams's Chronicle of Bristol*. Bristol: J W Arrowsmith

Fox, F 1998 'Hired men-of-war, 1664–7: Part I'. *The Mariner's Mirror* **84**, 13–23

Fox, F and Fox, C 1834 *History and Present State of Brislington House near Bristol. An asylum for the cure & reception of insane persons established by Edward Long Fox M D, A. D. 1804 and now conducted by Francis and Charles Fox*. Bristol: Light and Rider

Fox, F and Taylor, J (eds) 1889 *Some Account of the Guild of Weavers in Bristol: Chiefly from Mss*. Bristol: William George's Sons

Franklin, A 1989 'Privatism, the home and working class culture: a life history approach'. Unpublished PhD thesis, University of Bristol

Fraser, J 1935 *Spain and the West Country*. London: Burn Oates & Washbourne Ltd.

Frere, S S 1977 'Roman Britain in 1976. I Sites explored'. *Britannia, Society for the Promotion of Roman Studies* **8**, 356–425

Fryer, A C 1895 'Recent discoveries in Bristol'. *J Brit Archaeol Assoc* **51**, 90–1

Fryer, A C 1897 'Discoveries on Brandon Hill'. *J Brit Archaeol Assoc* 2 Ser **3**, 219–20

Fryer, A C 1908 'Head of an early 14th-century effigy in St. Philip's Church, Bristol'. *Trans Bristol Gloucestershire Archaeol Soc* **31**, 282–3

Fryer, A C 1924 'Monumental effigies made by Bristol craftsmen (1240–550)'. *Archaeologia* **74**, 1–72

Fuller, E 1894–5 'The tallage of 6 Edward II (Dec. 16, 1312) and the Bristol rebellion'. *Trans Bristol Gloucestershire Archaeol Soc* **19**, 171–278

Gaimster, M and O'Conor, K (eds) 'Medieval Britain and Ireland in 2004'. *Medieval Archaeol* **49**, 323–473

Gardiner, J, Allen, M J, Hamilton-Dyer, S, Laidlaw, M and Scaife, R G 2002 'Making the most of it: late prehistoric pastoralism in the Avon Levels, Severn Estuary'. *Proc Prehist Soc* **68**, 1–39

Gardner, K 1998 'Wansdyke Diktat? A discussion paper'. *Bristol Avon Archaeol* **15**, 57–65

Gardner, P 1984 *The Lost Elementary Schools of Victorian England*. London: Croom Helm

Gairdner, J and Brodie, R H (eds) 1903 *Letters and Papers, Foreign and Domestic, of the Reign of Henry VIII* (Vol **19** Part 1). London: HMSO

Gelling, M 1993 *Place-names in the Landscape*. London: J M Dent

Gentles, I 1992 *The New Model Army in England, Ireland and Scotland, 1645–53*. Oxford: Blackwell

Gilchrist, R 1995 *Contemplation and Action: The Other Monasticism*. London: Routledge

Gilchrist, R 1997 *Gender and Material Culture: The Archaeology of Religious Women*. London: Routledge

Gill, M and Howard, H 1997 'Glimpses of glory: paintings from St. Mark's Hospital, Bristol, *in* Keen, L (ed) *'Almost the richest city': Bristol in the Middle Ages*. London: British Archaeological Association, 97–106

Giorgi, J 1997 'Diet in late medieval and early modern London: the archaeobotanical evidence', *in* Gaimster, D and Stamper, P (eds.) *The Age of Transition: The Archaeology of English Culture, 1400–600*. London: Society for Medieval Archaeology, 197–213

Giorgi, J 2013 '5.4 Plant macro remains' *in* Ridgeway, V and Watts, M (eds), *Friars, Quakers, Industry and Urbanisation. The Archaeology of the Broadmead Expansion Project, Cabot Circus, Bristol, 2005–8*. Cotswold Archaeology/Pre-Construct Archaeology, 288–301

Girouard, M 1975 *Victorian Pubs*. London: Studio Vista

Gittos, B and Gittos, M 1997 'Alfred Fryer's 'Monumental effigies by Bristol craftsmen': a reassessment', *in* Keen, L (ed) *'Almost the richest city': Bristol in the Middle Ages*. London: British Archaeological Association, 88–96

Glassie, H 1975 *Folk Housing in Middle Virginia: A Structural Analysis of Historic Artifacts*. Knoxville: University of Tennessee Press

Godden, D 2004 'Temple Back (area adjacent to St Philips Bridge, Bristol). Archaeological evaluation report'. Unpublished report, Wessex Archaeology

Godman, C 1972 'Kings Weston Hill, Bristol: its prehistoric camps and inhumation cemetery'. *Proc University of Bristol Spelaeological Soc* **13**, 41–8

Godwin, E W 1853 'Notes, historical and architectural, of the priory of Dominicans, Bristol', *in* Archaeological Institute of Great Britain and Ireland. *Memoirs Illustrative of the History and Antiquities of Bristol, and the Western Counties of Great Britain*. London: George Bell, 142–9

Godwin, E W 1863 'Bristol Cathedral'. *Archaeol J* **20**, 38–63

Godwin, E W 1867 'On ancient Bristol'. *Somersetshire Archaeol Natur Hist Soc Proc* **14**, 23–42

Gomme, A, Jenner, M and Little, B nd 'Street index of buildings of architectural or historic interest'. Unpublished typescript

Gomme, A, Jenner, M and Little, B 1979 *Bristol: An Architectural History*. London: Lund Humphries

Good, G L 1987a 'An 18th–19th century limekiln at Water Lane, Bristol'. *Bristol Avon Archaeol* **6**, 66–9

Good, G L 1987b 'The excavation of two docks at Narrow Quay, Bristol, 1978-9'. *Post-medieval Archaeol* **21**, 25–126

Good, G L 1989 'An excavation at the corner of St. Thomas Street and Portwall Lane, Bristol, 1989'. *Bristol Avon Archaeol* **8**, 20–9

Good, G L 1991 'Some aspects of the development of the Redcliffe waterfront in the light of excavation at Dundas Wharf'. *Bristol Avon Archaeol* **9** (1990/91), 29–42

Good, G L 1992 'Excavation at Water Lane, by Temple Church, Bristol, 1971'. *Bristol Avon Archaeol* **10**, 2–41

Good, G L 1993 'Archaeological evaluation of Redcliffe Way, Bristol'. Unpublished report, Bristol and Region Archaeological Services

Good, G L 1996 'Bristol Castle keep – a reappraisal of the evidence and report on the excavations in 1989'. *Bristol Avon Archaeol* **13**, 17–45

Good, G L, Jones, R H and Ponsford, M W (eds) 1991 *Waterfront Archaeology: Proceedings of the Third International Conference, Bristol, 1988*. London: CBA Research Report **74**

Goodburn, D M 1991 'New light on early ship and boatbuilding in the London area', *in* Good, G L, Jones, R H and Ponsford, M W (eds) *Waterfront Archaeology: Proceedings of the Third International Conference, Bristol, 1988*. London: CBA Research Report **74**, 105–15

Goodburn, D M 1998 'The death of the wildwood and the birth of woodmanship in southeast England', *in* Bernick, K (ed) *Hidden Dimensions: The Cultural Significance of Wetland Archaeology*. Vancouver: UBC Press, 130–8

Goodburn, D M 2013 '4.13 Historic woodwork', *in* Ridgeway, V and Watts, M (eds), *Friars, Quakers, Industry and Urbanisation. The Archaeology of the Broadmead Expansion Project, Cabot Circus, Bristol, 2005–8*. Cotswold Archaeology/Pre-Construct Archaeology, 247–57

Gough, J W 1930 *The Mines of Mendip*. Newton Abbot: David & Charles

Gould, S 1999 'Planning, development and social archaeology', *in* Tarlow, S and West, S (eds) *The familiar Past? Archaeologies of Later Historical Britain*. London: Routledge, 140–54

Gourvish, T R and Wilson, R G 1998 *The British Brewing Industry, 1830–980*. Cambridge: Cambridge University Press

Graham, R 1907 'The religious houses', *in* Page, W (ed) *The Victoria History of the County of Gloucester*. Vol 2. London: Archibald Constable & Co. Ltd., 52–126

Grant, A 1988a 'Animal resources', *in* Astill, G & Grant, A (eds), *The Countryside of Medieval England*. Oxford: Blackwell, 149–87

Grant, A 1988b 'Food, status and religion in England in the middle ages: an archaeozoological perspective', *Anthropozoologica* **2**, 139–46

Graves, C P 1989 'Social space in the English medieval parish church'. *Economy and Society* **18**, 297–322

Gray, I 1981 *Antiquaries of Gloucestershire and Bristol*. Bristol: Bristol and Gloucestershire Archaeological Society

Green, C 1995 'Trows and the Severn coastal trade'. *Archaeology in the Severn Estuary* **6**, 97–113

Green, C 1996 'The forest ports of the Severn estuary'. *Archaeology in the Severn Estuary* **7**, 107–13

Green, E (ed) 1888 *The Survey and Rental of the Chantries, Colleges and Free Chapels, Guilds, Fraternities, Lamps, Lights and Obits in the County of Somerset as returned in the 2nd year of King Edward VI A.D. 1548*. Taunton: Somerset Record Series **2**

Green, J 1848 *Account of the Recent Improvements in the Drainage and Sewerage of Bristol*. London: W Clowes & Sons

Greenacre, F 1973 *The Bristol School of Artists: Francis Danby and Painting, 1810–40*. Bristol: City of Bristol Museum and Art Gallery

Greenacre, F 1982 *Marine Artists of Bristol, Nicholas Pocock and Joseph Walter*. Bristol: City of Bristol Museum and Art Gallery

Greenacre, F 1988 *Francis Danby, 1793–861*. London: Tate Gallery

Greenacre, F 2005 *From Bristol to the Sea. Artists, the Avon Gorge and Bristol Harbour*. Redcliffe Press, in association with Bristol Museums and Art Gallery

Greenacre, F and Stoddard, S 1986 *The Bristol Landscape: The Watercolours of Samuel Jackson, 1794–869*. Bristol: City of Bristol Museum and Art Gallery

Greenacre, F and Stoddard, S 1991 *W J Müller, 1812–45*. Bristol: Friends of Bristol Art Gallery

Gregory, R and Dungworth, D, forthcoming 'Exploring Bristol's historic glass industry: archaeological investigation at the Soap Boilers' and Hoopers' Glasshouses, and the Powell & Ricketts Bottle Works, Avon Street, Glass Wharf, Bristol'. *Post-Medieval Archaeol*

Greig, I and Mason, C 2014 'Plot 3, Temple Quay, Bristol. Archaeological evaluation'. Unpublished report, Bristol and Region Archaeological Services

Greig, J 1988 'Plant resources', *in* Astill, G & Grant, A (eds) *The Countryside of Medieval England*. Oxford: Blackwell, 108–27

Grenville, J 1997 *Medieval Housing*. London: Leicester University Press

Griffiths, O 1959 'The chapels of St. Werburgha and St. Blaise'. *Trans Bristol Gloucestershire Archaeol Soc* **78**, 167–9

Griffiths, R A 1991 *King and Country: England and Wales in the 15th Century*. London: Hambledon Press

Grinsell, L V (ed) 1964, *A Survey and Policy Concerning the Archaeology of the Bristol Region. Part 1: To the Norman Conquest*. Bristol: Bristol Archaeological Research Group

Grinsell, L V (ed) 1965 *A Survey and Policy Concerning the Archaeology of the Bristol Region. Part 2: From the Norman Conquest*. Bristol: Bristol Archaeological Research Group

Grinsell, L V 1979 'The Druid Stoke megalithic monument'. *Trans Bristol Gloucestershire Archaeol Soc* **97**, 119–21

Grinsell, L V nd 'The mints of Bath and Bristol', *in* Iles, R and Aston, M (eds) *The Archaeology of Avon*. Bristol: Avon County Council, 173–5

Grinsell, L V and Dawson, D P 1970 'Recent archaeological accessions in the City Museum, Bristol'. *BARG Bulletin* **3(9)**, 240–1

Grössinger, C 1997a 'The Bristol misericords and their sources', *in* Keen, L (ed) *'Almost the richest city': Bristol in the Middle Ages*. London: British Archaeological Association, 80–7

Grössinger, C 1997b *The World Upside-Down: English Misericords*. London: Harvey Miller

Grove, J and Croft, B (eds) 2012 *The Archaeology of South West England. South West Archaeological Research Framework. Research Strategy 2012–7*

Guttridge, G H (ed) 1934 *The American Correspondence of a Bristol Merchant, 1766–76: Letters of Richard Champion*. Berkeley, California: University of California Press

Haldane, J W 1975 'The excavations at Stokeleigh Camp, Avon'. *Proc University of Bristol Spelaeological Soc* **14**, 29–74

Hall, I V 1925 'A history of the sugar industry in England: with specific attention to the sugar trade of Bristol'. Unpublished MA thesis, University of Bristol

Hall, I V 1944 'Whitson Court sugar house, Bristol, 1665–1824'. *Trans Bristol Gloucestershire Archaeol Soc* **65**, 1–97

Hall, I V 1949 'John Knight, junior, sugar refiner at the Great House on St. Augustine's Back (1654–79). Bristol's second sugar house'. *Trans Bristol Gloucestershire Archaeol Soc* **68**, 110–64

Hall, I V 1957 'Temple St. sugar house under the first partnership of Richard Lane and John Hine (1662–78)'. *Trans Bristol Gloucestershire Archaeol Soc* **76**, 118–40

Hall, I V 1965 'The Daubneys: one of the most energetic sugar bakers families in 18th century Bristol at the Temple St. and Halliers lane refineries'. *Trans Bristol Gloucestershire Archaeol Soc* **84**, 113–40

Hankins, K 1993 *In My Father's House: St. Mary-on-the-Quay, Bristol's Oldest Catholic Church*. Bristol: St Mary-on-the-Quay

Hardesty, D L 1998 'Power and the industrial mining community in the American West', *in* Knapp, A B, Piggott, V C and Herbert, E W (eds) *Social Approaches to an Industrial Past: The Archaeology and Anthropology of Mining*. London: Routledge, 81–96

Harding, N 1930 *Bristol Charters, 1155–373*. Bristol: Bristol Record Series **1**

Harding, S and Lambert, D 1994 (eds) *Parks and Gardens of Avon*. Bristol: Avon Gardens Trust

Hargreaves-Mawdsley, R (ed) 1954 *Bristol and America: A Record of the First Settlers in the Colonies of North America, 1654–85*. London: R Sydney Glover

Harley, J B 1980 'The mature topographical survey', *in* Seymour, W A (ed) *A History of the Ordnance Survey*. Folkestone: Dawson, 168–77

Harley, J B 1988 'Maps, knowledge, and power', *in* Cosgrave, D and Daniels, S (eds) *The Iconography of Landscape: Essays on the Symbolic Representation, Design and Use of Past Environments*. Cambridge: Cambridge University Press, 277–312

Harris, R B 1994 'The origins and development of English medieval townhouses operating commercially on two storeys'. Unpublished DPhil thesis, University of Oxford

Harrison, H 2000 'Report on the Sacristy door at Bristol Cathedral'. Unpublished report

Harrison, M 1988 'Symbolism, 'ritualism' and the location of crowds in early 19th-century English towns', *in* Cosgrave, D and Daniels, S (eds) *The Iconography of Landscape. Essays on the Symbolic Representation, Design and Use of Past Environments*. Cambridge: Cambridge University Press, 194–213

Harriss, G 2005 *Shaping the Nation: England, 1340–461*. Oxford: Clarendon Press

Hart, J, 2006 'The Former Drill Hall, Old Market Street, Bristol. Additional archaeological evaluation'. Cotswold Archaeology, unpublished report no 06044

Hart, W H (ed) 1863 *Historia et cartularium monasterii Sancti Petri Gloucestriae*. Vol. 1. London: Longman, Green, Longman, Roberts & Green

Harvey, A 1909 'The vaulting of the Church of St. Mary, Redcliff'. *Proc Clifton Antiquarian Club* **7** (1909–19), 51–64

Harvey, C and Press, J 1988a 'Industrial change and the economic life of Bristol since 1800', *in* Harvey, C and Press, J *Studies in the Business History of Bristol*. Bristol: Bristol Academic Press, 1–32

Harvey, C and Press, J 1988b 'Sir George White and the urban transport revolution in Bristol, 1875-1916', *in* Harvey, C and Press, J (eds) *Studies in the Business History of Bristol*. Bristol: Bristol Academic Press, 137–63

Harvey, J H 1969 *William Worcestre: Itineraries*. Oxford: Oxford University Press

Hasegawa, J 1992 *Replanning the Blitzed City Centre: A Comparative Study of Bristol, Coventry and Southampton 1941–50*. Buckingham: Open University Press

Hasegawa, J 1999 'The rise and fall of radical reconstruction in 1940s Britain'. *20th Century British History* **10**, 137–61

Haslam, J, 1983, 'The origin and plan of Bedford'. *Bedfordshire Archaeol* **16**, 29–36

Haslam, J, 2011, 'Daws Castle, Somerset, and civil defence measures in southern and midland England in the 9th to 11th centuries'. *Archaeol J* **168**, 195–226

Haslett, S K, Davies, P and Strawbridge, F 1997 'Reconstructing Holocene sea-level change in the Severn estuary and Somerset Levels: the foraminifera connection'. *Archaeology in the Severn Estuary* **8**, 29–40

Hatcher, J 1993 *The History of the British Coal Industry. Vol. 1 Before 1700: Towards the Age of Coal*. Oxford: Clarendon Press

Hatcher J 1996 'The great slump of the mid-15th century', *in* Britnell, R and Hatcher, J (eds) *Progress and Problems in Medieval England*. Cambridge: Cambridge University Press, 237–72

Havard, T 2005 'The Former Drill Hall, Old Market, Bristol. Archaeological evaluation'. Cotswold Archaeology, unpublished report no 05071

Havard, T 2007a 'M Shed, Welsh Back, Bristol. Archaeological evaluation'. Cotswold Archaeology, unpublished report no 07044

Havard, T 2007b 'Broadmead Expansion Bristol: Quakers Friars archaeological evaluation and building recording; The Cotswold Archaeology & Pre-Construct Archaeology (CAPCA) Consortium'. Cotswold Archaeology, unpublished report 07052

Havard, T and Cox, S 2004 'Land at Wapping Wharf, Bristol. Archaeological evaluation'. Cotswold Archaeology, unpublished report no 04183

Haworth-Booth, M 1997 *Photography: An Independent Art. Photographs from the Victoria and Albert Museum*. London: V & A Publications

Hayden, R (ed) 1974 *The Records of a Church of Christ in Bristol, 1640–87*. Bristol: Bristol Record Series **27**

Heaton, R 2004 'Archaeological evaluation of land at nos 25–43 Pilemarsh, St George, Bristol'. Unpublished report, Bristol and Region Archaeological Services

Heaton, R 2007 'Archaeological evaluation of land at Hill House, Lewins Mead, Bristol'. Unpublished report, Bristol and Region Archaeological Services

Heaton, R, 2008, 'A post-excavation assessment report on the archaeological excavation at Colston House, Bristol'. Unpublished report, Bristol and Region Archaeological Services

Hebditch, M 1968 'Excavations on the medieval defences, Portwall Lane, Bristol, 1965'. *Trans Bristol Gloucestershire Archaeol Soc* **87**, 131–43

Hembry, P 1990 *The English Spa, 1560–1815: A Social History*. London: The Athlone Press

Hershon, D 1991 *A History of 150 Years of Deaf Education in Bristol, 1841–991*. Bristol: Deaf Studies Trust

Heuman, G 1999 'The British West Indies', *in* Porter, A (ed) *The Oxford History of the British Empire. Vol. 3 The 19th Century*. Oxford: Oxford University Press, 470–93

Higbee, L 2010 'Faunal remains', in Jackson, R G, 2010a, *The Archaeology of the Medieval Suburb of Broadmead, Bristol. Excavations in Union Street, 2000*. Bristol's Museums, Galleries & Archives, 105–23

Higgins, D, 2017 'Clay tobacco pipes', in Ford, Ben M, Brady, Kate and Teague, Steven *From Bridgehead to Brewery. The Medieval and Post-medieval Archaeological Remains from Finzel's Reach, Bristol*. Oxford: Oxford Archaeology Monograph **27**, 194–203

Higgins, D H 2002, 'The Anglo-Saxon charters of Stoke Bishop: a study of the boundaries of *Bisceopes stoc*'. *Trans Bristol Gloucestershire Archaeol Soc* **120**, 107–31

Hill, C, Reay, B and Lamont, W 1983 *The World of the Muggletonians*. London: Temple Smith Ltd.

Hill, C P 1951 *The History of Bristol Grammar School*. London: Sir Isaac Pitman & Sons, Ltd.

Hill, R A 1944 'A letter-book of St. Augustine's, Bristol'. *Trans Bristol Gloucestershire Archaeol Soc* **65**, 141–56

Hillaby, J 2003 'Jewish colonisation in the 12th century', in Skinner, P (ed) *The Jews in Medieval Britain: Historical, Literary and Archaeological Perspectives*. Woodbridge: The Boydell Press, 15–40

Hillaby, J and Sermon, R 2004 'Jacob's Well, Bristol: Mikveh or Bet Tohorah? *Trans Bristol Gloucestershire Archaeol Soc* **122**, 127–51

Hiller, J 2005 'Broadmead Expansion, Bristol. Archaeological evaluation report, Tollgate House, Main Scheme'. Unpublished report, Oxford Archaeology

Hills, H 1996 'Mapping the early modern city'. *Urban History* **23**, 145–70

Hirst, H C M 1924 'Redcliffe conduit, Bristol, and Robert de Berkeley'. *Trans Bristol Gloucestershire Archaeol Soc* **46**, 353–62

Hobhouse, E (ed) 1887 *Calendar of the Register of John de Drokensford, Bishop of Bath and Wells (A.D. 1309–29)*. Taunton: Somerset Record Series **1**

Hobhouse, E (ed) 1890 *Church-wardens' Accounts of Croscombe, Pilton, Yatton, Tintinhull, Morebath, and St. Michael, Bath, ranging from A.D. 1349 to 1560*. Taunton: Somerset Record Series **4**

Hogg, I 2010 'The Fortune Building, Bristol Cathedral School, Bristol; an archaeological investigation report'. Unpublished report, AOC Archaeology Group

Holbrook, N 1994 'Corinium Dobunnorum: Roman civitas capital and provincial capital', *in* Darvill, T and Gerrard, C *Cirencester: Town and Landscape*. Cirencester: Cotswold Archaeological Trust, 57–86

Hollinrake, C and Hollinrake, N 2002 'An archaeological evaluation in the cloisters and undercroft of Bristol Cathedral'. Unpublished report

Hollis, D (ed) 1949 *Calendar of the Bristol Apprentice Book, 1532–65. Part 1, 1532–42*. Bristol: Bristol Record Series **14**

Hollis, D and Ralph, E (ed) 1952 *Marriage Bonds for the Diocese of Bristol. Vol. 1 1637–700*. Gloucester: Records Section of the Bristol and Gloucestershire Archaeological Society

Holmes, J G 1897–9 'A lost architectural fragment of Bristol Cathedral'. *Proc Clifton Antiquarian Club* **4**, 217–9

Holt R A and Baker N J, 2001 'Towards a geography of sexual encounter: prostitution in English medieval towns', *in* Bevan, L (ed), *Indecent Exposure: Sexuality, Society and the Archaeological Record*. Cruithne Press, 201–5

Holt, R and Leech, R 2011 'Cabot House, Deanery Road, Bristol: investigations in 2008', *in* Watts, M (ed) *Medieval and Post-medieval Development within Bristol's Inner Suburbs*. Bristol and Gloucestershire Archaeological Report **7** (Cotswold Archaeology), 121–44

Horton, M, 2001, 'Archaeological evaluation and method statement. Royal Fort Gardens, University of Bristol'. Unpublished report, University of Bristol.

Hoskins, WG, 1972, *Local History in England. 2nd ed*. London: Longman.

Houlbrooke, R 1998 *Death, Religion and the Family in England, 1480–750*. Oxford: Clarendon Press

Howard, H 2003 *Pigments of English Medieval Wall Painting*. London: Archetype Publications

Hudd, A E 1887–8 'Proceedings of the Club 1887–8'. *Proc Clifton Antiquarian Club* **1**, 277–96

Hudd, A E 1892–3 'Proceedings of the Club 1892–93'. *Proc Clifton Antiquarian Club* **2**, 259–72

Hudd, A E 1894–5 'Two Bristol calendars'. *Trans Bristol Gloucestershire Archaeol Soc* **19**, 105–41

Hudd, A E 1904–8 'Some of old glass from Temple Church, Bristol representing St Katherine … and other saints'. *Proc Clifton Antiquarian Club* **6**, 62–96

Hudson, A 1988 *The Premature Revolution: Wycliffite Texts and Lollard History*. Oxford: Clarendon Press

Hudson, B 1994 'William the Conqueror and Ireland'. *Irish Historical Studies* **29**, 145–58

Hudson, B 1999 'The changing economy of the Irish Sea province: AD 900–1300, *in* Smith, B (ed) *Britain and Ireland 900–1300: Insular Responses to Medieval European Change*. Cambridge: Cambridge University Press, 39–66

Hughes, J 2009 'Archaeological evaluation at Canningford House, 38 Victoria Street, Bristol'. Unpublished report, Historic Environment and Archaeology Service, Worcestershire County Council

Hughes, P 1997 'Documentary sources for the 'Mikveh' site at Jacob's Well, Bristol'. Unpublished report

Hughes, P, Root, J and Heath, C 1996 'The history and development of Queen Square'. Unpublished report, Bristol City Council

Hughes, W W 1900–3 'Mural decorations in a dormitory of the Old Deanery, College Green, Bristol'. *Proc Clifton Antiquarian Club* **5**, 147–53

Hulton, P H (ed) 1959, *Drawings of England in the 17th century by Willem Schellinks, Jacob Esselens and Lambert Doomer*. London: The Walpole Society **35**

Hume, L 2009 'Full Moon Hotel and Attic Bar, No 1, North Street, Stokes Croft, Bristol. Archaeological evaluation project'. Unpublished Report, Avon Archaeological Unit

Hume, L 2012 'Backlands site at Unity Street, Hawkins Street and Jacob Street, Old Market, Bristol. Archaeological Evaluation Report'. Unpublished report, Avon Archaeological Unit

Hurley, M F and Scully, O M B with McCutcheon, S W J 1996 *Late Viking and Medieval Waterford: Excavations 1986–92*. Waterford: Waterford Corporation

Hurst, D G (ed) 1961 'Medieval Britain in 1960'. *Medieval Archaeology* **5**, 322

Hurst, J G 1977 'Spanish pottery imported into medieval Britain'. *Medieval Archaeology* **21**, 68–105

Hussey, D 2000 *Coastal and River Trade in Pre-industrial England: Bristol and its Region, 1680–730*. Exeter: University of Exeter Press

Hutchins, E and Steadman, S 1999 'Evidence for 17th and 18th century cattle improvements in Bedford'. *Environmental Archaeol* **4**, 87–92

Hutton, R 1991 *Charles II: King of England, Scotland and Ireland*. Oxford: Oxford University Press

Hutton, R 1993 *The Restoration: A Political and Religious History of England and Wales, 1658–67*. Oxford: Clarendon Press

Iles, R 1983 'Avon archaeology 1982'. *Bristol Avon Archaeol* **2**, 48–57

Iles, R 1984 'Avon Archaeology 1983'. *Bristol Avon Archaeol* **3**, 54–65

Iles, R and Aston, M (eds) nd *The Archaeology of Avon: A Review from the Neolithic to the Middle Ages*. Bristol: Avon County Council

Iles, R & Kidd, A 1987 'Avon archaeology, 1986 & 1987'. *Bristol Avon Archaeol* **6**, 44–56

Insole, P 1998a 'Archaeological desktop study of Site A1 (Graham's Timber Yard), Harbourside/Gas Ferry Lane, Bristol'. Unpublished report, Bristol and Region Archaeological Services

Insole, P 1998b 'Archaeological evaluation trenches at Castle Park Arena, Bristol'. Unpublished report, Bristol and Region Archaeological Services

Insole, P 1998c 'Archaeological evaluation at the former Entertainments Centre, Frogmore Street, Bristol'. Unpublished report, Bristol and Region Archaeological Services

Insole, P 1999a 'Archaeological evaluation at 98–103 Redcliff Street, Redcliffe, Bristol'. Unpublished report, Bristol and Region Archaeological Services

Insole, P 1999b 'Archaeological investigation of Queen Square'. Unpublished report, Bristol and Region Archaeological Services

Insole, P 2000a 'Archaeological evaluation of land adjacent to College Square, Bristol'. Unpublished report, Bristol and Region Archaeological Services

Insole, P 2000b 'Archaeological watching brief at 48–54 West Street, Bristol''. Unpublished report, Bristol and Region Archaeological Services

Insole, P, 2000(c), 'Archaeological excavation at Plot 5, Temple Quay, Bristol'. Unpublished report, Bristol and Region Archaeological Services

Insole, P 2001a 'Archaeological excavation of land at 98–103 Redcliff Street, Bristol, 2000'. Unpublished draft report, Bristol and Region Archaeological Services

Insole, P 2001b 'Archaeological evaluation of 30 Gloucester Lane, Old Market, Bristol'. Unpublished report, Bristol and Region Archaeological Services

Insole P, 2003 Archaeological excavation of land at College Square, Bristol. Unpublished report, Bristol and Region Archaeological Services

Insole, P and Jackson, R G, 2000 'Excavation of a clay tobacco pipe kiln at Temple Quay, Bristol'. *Bristol Avon Archaeol* **17**, 129–38

Insole, P and Leech, R H 1998 'Archaeological desktop study of Upper/Lower Church Lane, Bristol'. Unpublished report, Bristol and Region Archaeological Services

Ison, W 1952 *The Georgian Buildings of Bristol*. London: Faber

Jackson, A A 1998 'The development of steel framed buildings in Britain 1880–905'. *Construction History* **14**, 21–40

Jackson, R G 1994a 'Archaeological evaluation and excavation at Quay Point, Temple Meads, Bristol'. Unpublished report, Bristol and Region Archaeological Services

Jackson, R G 1994b 'Archaeological excavation at 45 Kingsdown Parade, Kingsdown, Bristol'. Unpublished report, Bristol and Region Archaeological Services

Jackson, R G 1995 'Archaeological evaluation of Courage's Brewery, Bath Street, Bristol, Avon'. Unpublished report, Bristol and Region Archaeological Services

Jackson, R G 1998 'Archaeological evaluation at the Sugar House, Lewins Mead, Bristol'. Unpublished report, Bristol and Region Archaeological Services

Jackson, R G 1999a 'An interim report on the excavations at Inns Court, Bristol, 1997–9'. *Bristol Avon Archaeol* **16**, 51–60

Jackson, R G 1999b 'Archaeological evaluation of 60 Redcliff Street, Bristol'. Unpublished report, Bristol and Region Archaeological Services

Jackson, R G 2000a 'Archaeological excavations at Upper Maudlin Street, Bristol, in 1973, 1976 & 1999'. *Bristol Avon Archaeol* **17**, 29–110

Jackson, R G 2000b 'Archaeological evaluation at 15–29 Union Street, Bristol'. Unpublished report, Bristol and Region Archaeological Services

Jackson, R G 2001 'Archaeological evaluation of land at College Square, Bristol'. Unpublished report, Bristol and Region Archaeological Services

Jackson, R G 2002a 'Archaeological evaluation at 18–20 St Thomas Street, Bristol'. Unpublished report, Bristol and Region Archaeological Services

Jackson, R G 2002b 'Archaeological evaluation at the former Courage Brewery site, Counterslip, Bristol'. Unpublished report, Bristol and Region Archaeological Services

Jackson, R G 2004 'Archaeological excavations at Nos 30–8 St. Thomas Street and No 60 Redcliff Street, Bristol, 2000'. *Bristol Avon Archaeol* **19**, 1–63

Jackson, R G 2005 'Excavations on the site of Sir Abraham Elton's glassworks, Cheese Lane, Bristol'. *Post-Medieval Archaeology* **39/1**, 92–132

Jackson, R G 2006a 'Archaeological excavations at the former Courage Brewery, Bath Street, Bristol, 2000–1'. *Bristol Avon Archaeol* **21**, 1–59

Jackson, R G 2006b *Excavations at St James's Priory, Bristol*. Oxbow

Jackson, R G 2007a *A Roman Settlement and Medieval Manor House in South Bristol. Excavations at Inns Court*. Bristol and Region Archaeological Services. Bristol's Museums Galleries & Archives

Jackson, R G 2007b 'Portwall Lane Glassworks: rescuing industrial archaeology'. *Current Archaeology* **207**, 32–7

Jackson, R G 2007c 'Excavations at the old Council House, Corn Street, Bristol, 2005'. *Bristol Avon Archaeol* **22**, 47–78

Jackson, R G 2007d 'Archaeological excavation of land at the former FPS site, Waterloo Road, Bristol'. Unpublished report, Bristol and Region Archaeological Services

Jackson, R G 2008–9 'Archaeological work at 22–5 Queen Square and 42–44 Welsh Back, Bristol, 2002–6'. *Bristol Avon Archaeol*, **23**, 1–66

Jackson, R G 2010a *The Archaeology of the Medieval Suburb of Broadmead, Bristol. Excavations in Union Street, 2000*. Bristol's Museums, Galleries & Archives.

Jackson, R G 2010b, Portwall Lane Glassworks. Unpublished report, Bristol and Region Archaeological Services

Jackson, R G and Price, R H 1974 *Bristol Clay Pipes: A Study of Makers and Their Marks*. Bristol: City of Bristol Museum and Art Gallery

Jackson, R G, Jackson, P and Price, R 1982 *Bristol Potters and Potteries, 1600–800*. Stoke-on-Trent: Stoke-on-Trent City Museums

Jackson, R G, Jackson, P and Beckey, I 1991 'Tin-glazed earthenware kiln waste from the Limekiln Lane potteries, Bristol'. *Post-medieval Archaeol* **25**, 89–114

Jackson, R G and Stevens, D 2002 'Archaeological evaluation at Quakers Friars, Broadmead, Bristol'. Unpublished report, Bristol and Region Archaeological Services

Jackson, R G and Leech, R H 2003 'Archaeological evaluation & photographic survey of 22–30 West Street, Old Market, Bristol'. Unpublished report, Bristol and Region Archaeological Services

Jancar, J 1972 'Fifty years of Brentry Hospital (1922–72)'. *Bristol Medico-Chirugical Journal* **87**, 23–30

Jeayes, I H 1889–90 'Abbot Newland's roll of the Abbots of St. Augustine's Abbey by Bristol'. *Trans Bristol Gloucestershire Archaeol Soc* **14**, 117–30

Jenkinson, H (ed) 1929 *Calendar of the Plea Rolls of the Exchequer of the Jews Preserved in the Public Record Office. Vol. III Edward I, 1275–7*. London: Jewish Historical Society of England

Johnson, C and Cronne, H (eds) 1956 *Regesta regum Anglo-Normannorum, 1066–154*. Vol 2 Oxford: Clarendon Press

Johnson, M 1993 *Housing Culture: Traditional Architecture in an English Landscape*. London: UCL Press

Johnson, M 1996 *An Archaeology of Capitalism*. Oxford: Blackwell

Johnston, A and MacLean, S 1997 'Reformation and resistance in Thames/Severnside parishes: the dramatic witness', *in* French, K, Gibbs, G and Kümin, B (eds) *The Parish in English Life, 1400–600*. Manchester: Manchester University Press, 35–55

Jones, D 1991 *Bristol: A Pictorial History*. Chichester: Phillimore and Co.

Jones, D 1996 *Bristol's Sugar Trade and Refining Industry*. Bristol: Bristol Branch of the Historical Association

Jones, F 1946 *The Glory that was Bristol*. Bristol: St Stephen's Bristol Press

Jones, J 1995 'Welsh Back, Bristol. An assessment of the potential of the biological remains'. Unpublished report.

Jones, J 1996 'The plant macrofossils', *in* Blockley, K *Spicer's Hall, Bristol: Excavation of a Medieval Merchant's House, 1995*. Unpublished report, Bristol and Region Archaeological Services

Jones, J 1998 'Plant and insect remains', *in* Price, R H with Ponsford, M W *St. Bartholomew's Hospital, Bristol. The Excavation of a Medieval Hospital: 1976–8*. York: CBA Res Rep **110**, 193–7.

Jones, J 2008–9 'Plant macrofossil remains', in Jackson, R G 'Archaeological work at 22–5 Queen Square and 42–4 Welsh Back, Bristol, 2002–6'. *Bristol Avon Archaeol* **23**, 47–53

Jones, J 2010 'Plant macrofossil remains', in Jackson, R G, 2010a *The Archaeology of the Medieval Suburb of Broadmead, Bristol. Excavations in Union Street, 2000*. Bristol's Museums, Galleries & Archives, 77–95

Jones, J, 2017 'Plant macrofossil remains', in Ford, Ben M, Brady, Kate and Teague, Steven *From Bridgehead to Brewery. The Medieval and Post-medieval archaeological remains from Finzel's Reach, Bristol*. Oxford: Oxford Archaeology Monograph **27**, 269–73

Jones, J and Watson, N 1987 'The early medieval waterfront at Redcliffe, Bristol', *in* Balaam, N D, Levitan, B and Straker, V (eds) *Studies in Palaeoeconomy and Environment in South West England*. Oxford: Brit Archaeol Rep, Brit Ser **181**, 135–62.

Jones, O 1983 'The contribution of the Rickett's mold to the manufacture of the English "wine" bottle, 1820–50'. *J Glass Stud* **25**, 167–77

Jones, P M E 1988 'An early theatre in Bristol'. *Trans Bristol Gloucestershire Archaeol Soc* **106**, 207–8

Jones, R H 1983 'Excavations at 68–72 Redcliff Street, 1982'. *Bristol Avon Archaeol* **2**, 37–9

Jones, R H 1986 *Excavations in Redcliffe 1983–5: Survey and Excavation at 95–97 Redcliff Street*. Bristol: City of Bristol Museum and Art Gallery

Jones, R H 1989 'Excavations at St. James' Priory, Bristol, 1988–89'. *Bristol Avon Archaeol* **8**, 2–7

Jones, R H 1996 'Lost sites: a tale of woe at Bradley Stoke'. *Rescue News* **68**, 1

Jones, W (ed) 1883 *The Register of St. Osmund*. Vol 1 London: Longman & Co

Jordan, S, Wardley, P and Woollard, M 1999 'Emerging modernity in an urban setting: 19th-century Bristol revealed in property surveys'. *Urban History* **26**, 190–210

Karras, R M 1996 *Common Women: Prostitution and Sexuality in Medieval England*. Oxford: Oxford University Press

Keene, D 1985 *Winchester Studies 2. Survey of Medieval Winchester. Parts 1 & 2*. Oxford: Clarendon Press

Keene, D and Harding, V 1987 *Historical Gazetteer of London Before the Great Fire: Part 1, Cheapside*. Cambridge: Chadwyck Healey

Kelsall, A F 1974 'The London house plan in the later 17th century'. *Post-medieval Archaeol* **8**, 80–91.

Kent, O 1996 'Roots of industry: the Brislington pottery in context'. Unpublished MA thesis, Staffordshire University

Keyser, C F 1892 'On some mural paintings recently discovered in the churches of Little Horwood and Padbury, Buckinghamshire'. *Archaeol J* **49**, 333–44

Keystone Historic Building Consultants 1995 'Temple Church: the church of Holy Cross, Bristol'. Unpublished report, Keystone Historic Building Consultants

King, A 2001 'Archaeological evaluation at Redcross Lane, Old Market, Bristol'. Unpublished report, Bristol and Region Archaeological Services

King, A, 2002 'Archaeological evaluation of land at Avon Street/Old Bread Street, St Philips, Bristol'. Unpublished report, Bristol and Region Archaeological Services

King, A 2003 'Archaeological evaluation of land at the HH Wills Physics Laboratory Car Park, Tyndall Avenue, Bristol'. Unpublished report, Bristol and Region Archaeological Services

King, A, 2004 'Archaeological excavation at No 42 Montague Street, St James, Bristol'. Unpublished report, Bristol and Region Archaeological Services

King, A 2006a 'Archaeological evaluation at High Street, Wine Street, Mary-le-Port Street & Bridge Street, Bristol'. Unpublished report, Bristol and Region Archaeological Services

King, A 2006b 'Archaeological evaluation of land adjoining No 90 West Street, Old Market, Bristol'. Unpublished report, Bristol and Region Archaeological Services

King, A, 2007a 'Archaeological building recording at No 2 Trenchard Street, Bristol'. Unpublished report, Bristol and Region Archaeological Services

King, A, 2007b 'Archaeological excavation, building survey & watching brief at 22–30 West Street, Old Market, Bristol, 2004'. *Bristol Avon Archaeol* **22**, 1–46

King, A 2008 'Archaeological evaluation of land off St Michaels Hill & Tyndall Avenue, Clifton, Bristol'. Unpublished report, Bristol and Region Archaeological Services

King, A, 2010 'A Royalist bastion? Evidence from 30 Gloucester Lane, Old Market, Bristol'. *Trans Bristol Gloucestershire Archaeol Soc* **128**, 121–45

King, A, 2011 'Archaeological evaluation at Brandon Hill, Bristol'. Unpublished report, Bristol and Region Archaeological Services

King, A, 2014 'Not fullye so loftye': excavations at the Royal Fort, St Michael's Hill, Bristol'. *Post-Medieval Archaeol* **48(1)**, 1–44

King, A & Parry, A 2004 'Archaeological excavation & watching brief at Nos 18–20 West Street, Old Market, Bristol'. Unpublished report, Bristol and Region Archaeological Services.

King, P W 1996 'The cupola near Bristol: smelting lead with pitcoal'. *Somerset Archaeol Natur Hist* **140**, 37–51

Krausman Ben-Amos, I 1991 'Women apprentices in the trades and crafts of early modern Bristol'. *Continuity and Change* **6**, 227–52

Krausman Ben-Amos, I 1994 *Adolescence and Youth in Early-modern England*. New Haven: Yale University Press

La Trobe-Bateman, E 1997 'Avon Extensive Area Survey: Bedminster'. Unpublished report

La Trobe-Bateman, E 1997 'Avon Extensive Area Survey: Clevedon'. Unpublished report

La Trobe-Bateman, E 1997 'Avon Extensive Area Survey: Keynsham'. Unpublished report

Lacaille, A D 1954 'Palaeoliths from the lower reaches of the Bristol Avon'. *Antiq J* **34**, 1–27

Laird, M and Harvey, J 1997 'The garden plan for 13 Upper Gower Street, London: a conjectural review of the planting, upkeep and long-term maintenance of a late 18th-century town garden'. *Garden History* **25**, 189–211

Lambert, D 1997 'Bristol's urban parks, a historical survey: priority urban parks, other urban parks and city squares'. Unpublished report

Lambert, D 2000 *Historic Public Parks: Bristol*. Bristol: Avon Gardens Trust

Lambert, D 2002 'The prospect of trade: the merchant gardeners of Bristol in the second half of the 18th century', *in* Conan, M (ed) *Bourgeois and Aristocratic Cultural Encounters in Garden Art, 1550–850*. Washington DC: Dumbarton Oaks Colloquium on the History of Landscape Architecture **23**, 123–45

Langford, P 1994 *Public Life and the Propertied Englishman, 1689–798*. Oxford: Oxford University Press

Lankstead, D 2005a 'Archaeological evaluation of land at the former Purimachos factory site, Waterloo Road, Bristol'. Unpublished report, Bristol and Region Archaeological Services

Lankstead, D 2005b 'Archaeological evaluation of land at Cabot House, Deanery Road, Bristol'. Unpublished report, Bristol and Region Archaeological Services

Lankstead, D and Jackson, R G 2005 'Historic landscape analysis, building survey & archaeological evaluation at Bristol Royal Infirmary, Upper Maudlin Street, Bristol'. Unpublished report, Bristol and Region Archaeological Services

Large, D (ed) 1984 *The Port of Bristol, 1848–84*. Bristol: Bristol Record Series **36**

Large, D (ed) 1985 'Records of the Bristol Local Board of Health, 1851–72', *in* McGrath, P (ed) *A Bristol Miscellany*. Bristol: Bristol Record Series **37**, 123–99

Large, D 1995 *Bristol and the New Poor Law*. Bristol: Bristol Branch of the Historical Association

Large, D 1999 *The Municipal Government of Bristol 1851–901*. Bristol: Bristol Record Series **50**

Larking, L B (ed) 1857 *The Knights Hospitallers in England; being the report of prior Philip de Thame to the Grand Master Elyan de Villanova for A.D. 1338*. London: Camden Society

Latham, R C (ed) 1947 *Bristol Charters, 1509–899*. Bristol: Bristol Record Series **12**

Latham, R and Matthews W (eds) 1995 *The Diary of Samuel Pepys. Vol. 9, 1668–9*. London: HarperCollins Publishers

Latimer, J 1887 *Annals of Bristol in the 19th Century*. Bristol: W & F Morgan

Latimer, J 1893 *Annals of Bristol in the 18th Century*. Bristol: John Latimer

Latimer, J 1897–9 'A deed relating to the partition of the property of St. James's Priory, Bristol'. *Proceed Clifton Antiquarian Club* **4**, 109–38

Latimer, J 1900 *Annals of Bristol in the 17th Century*. Bristol: William George's Sons

Latimer, J 1901 'The hospital of St. John, Bristol'. *Trans Bristol Gloucestershire Archaeol Soc* **24**, 172–8

Latimer, J 1902 *Annals of Bristol in the 19th Century (Concluded), 1887–900*. Bristol: William George's Sons

Lawrence, S 1999 'Towards a feminist archaeology of households: gender and household structure on the Australian goldfields', *in* Allison, P M (ed) *The Archaeology of Household Activities*. London: Routledge, 121–41

Lea-Jones, J 1984 *St. John the Baptist Church – Medieval Conduit at Bristol, England: A Report and Survey of Features Surviving in August 1984*. Bristol: Temple Local History Group

Leech, R H 1981 *Early Industrial Housing; the Trinity area of Frome*. London: HMSO

Leech, R H 1989 'Aspects of the medieval defences of Bristol: the town wall, the castle barbican and the Jewry', *in* Bowden, M, Mackay, D and Topping, P (eds) *From Cornwall to Caithness: Some Aspects of British Field Archaeology. Papers Presented to Norman V Quinnell*. Oxford: Briti Archaeol Rep, Brit Ser **209**, 235–50

Leech, R H 1996 'The prospect from Rugman's Row: the row house in late sixteenth- and early 17th-century London'. *Archaeol J* **153**, 201–42

Leech, R H 1997a 'King Street, No 33, Ristorante La Taverna Dell' Artista'. Unpublished report

Leech, R H 1997b 'The medieval defences of Bristol revisited', *in* Keen, L (ed) *'Almost the Richest City': Bristol in the Middle Ages*. London: British Archaeological Association, 18–30

Leech, R H 1997c *The Topography of Medieval and Early Modern Bristol. Part 1: Property Holdings in the Early Walled Town and Marsh Suburb North of the Avon*. Bristol: Bristol Record Series **48**

Leech, R H 1998a 'An archaeological desk top evaluation of Nos 15–33 Union Street, Bristol and adjacent properties'. Unpublished report, Cultural Heritage Services

Leech, R H 1998b 'A desk top evaluation of the area bounded by High Street, Wine Street, Dolphin Street and the River Avon, Bristol'. Unpublished report, Cultural Heritage Services

Leech, R H 1999a 'An historical and architectural survey and analysis of The Exchange, Corn Street, Bristol'. Unpublished report, Cultural Heritage Services

Leech, R H 1999b 'An historical and architectural survey and analysis of No 41 High Street, Bristol'. Unpublished report, Cultural Heritage Services

Leech, R H 1999c 'The processional city: some issues for historical archaeology', *in* Tarlow, S and West, S (eds) *The Familiar Past? Archaeologies of Later Historical Britain*. London: Routledge, 19–34

Leech, R H 2000a 'A desk top evaluation of the Countership Brewery Site, Bristol'. Unpublished report, Cultural Heritage Services

Leech, R H 2000b 'An archaeological and documentary study of Bristol Bridge, Bristol'. Unpublished report, Cultural Heritage Services

Leech, R H 2000c 'An historical and architectural survey and analysis of No 41 Broad Street, Bristol'. Unpublished report, Cultural Heritage Services

Leech, R H 2000d 'An historical and architectural survey and analysis of the Old Council House, Corn Street, Bristol'. Unpublished report, Cultural Heritage Services

Leech, R H 2000e *The St. Michael's Hill precinct of the University of Bristol: Medieval and Early Modern Topography*. Bristol: Bristol Record Series **52**

Leech, R H 2000f 'The symbolic hall: historical context and merchant culture in the early modern city'. *Vernacular Architecture* **31**, 1–10

Leech, R H 2001 'An archaeological and historical study of the Redcliff Way area'. Unpublished report, Cultural Heritage Services

Leech, R H 2003 'The garden house: merchant culture and identity in the early modern city', *in* Lawrence, S (ed) *Archaeologies of the British: Explorations of Identity in Great Britain and its Colonies 1600–945*. London: Routledge, 76–86

Leech, R H 2004 'The Atlantic world and industrialization: contexts for the structures of everyday life in early modern Bristol', *in* Barker, D and Cranstone, D (eds) *The Archaeology of Industrialization*. Leeds: Maney Publishing, 155–64

Leech, R H 2009 'Arthur's Acre: a Saxon bridgehead at Bristol'. *Trans Bristol Gloucestershire Archaeol Soc* **127**, 11–20

Leech, R H 2014 *The Town House in Medieval and Early Modern Bristol*. English Heritage

Leech, R H and Bryant, J 2000 'Archaeological desktop evaluation of the Broadmead Redevelopment Site, Bristol'. Unpublished report, Bristol and Region Archaeological Services

Lees, B (ed) 1935 *Records of the Templars in England in the 12th Century*, London: Oxford University Press

Lehmberg, S 1996 *Cathedrals under Siege: Cathedrals in English Society, 1600–700*. Exeter: University of Exeter Press

Leighton, W 1913 'Trinity Hospital, Bristol'. *Trans Bristol Gloucestershire Archaeol Soc* **36**, 251–87

Leighton, W 1933 'The Black Friars, now Quaker's Friars, Bristol'. *Trans Bristol Gloucestershire Archaeol Soc* **55**, 151–90

Letters and Papers, Foreign and Domestic, Henry VIII (21 vols and addenda, London, 1864–932

Levitan, B 1983 'Dundas Wharf: Sieving sampling programme'. Unpublished report

Levitan, B, Bell, M, Shackleton, J and Watson N nd 'Waterfront archaeology in Bristol: the environmental evidence'. Unpublished report

Levitt, S 1990 *Pountneys: The Bristol Pottery at Fishponds, 1905–69*. Bristol: Redcliffe Press Ltd

Lewis, M E 2000 'The impact of industrialisation: an assessment of the morbidity and mortality of non-adult skeletons from medieval and post-medieval England (AD 850–1859)'. Paper presented at the Association for Environmental Archaeology conference on The Environmental Archaeology of Industry, 14–16 April 2000

Liddy, C D 2005 *Bristol, York and the Crown, 1350–400*. London: Royal Historical Society Studies in History New Series **45**

Litten, J 1991 *The English Way of Death: The Common Funeral since 1450*. London: Robert Hale

Little, B 1979 *Church Treasures in Bristol*. Bristol: Redcliffe Press Ltd.

Liversidge, M 1978 *The Bristol High Cross*. Bristol: Bristol Branch of the Historical Association

Liversidge, M and Farrington, J (eds) 1993 *Canaletto and England*. London: M Holberton

Livock, D M (ed) 1966 *City Chamberlains' Accounts in the 16th and 17th Centuries*. Bristol: Bristol Record Series **24**

Llewellyn, N 1996 'Honour in life, death and in the memory: funeral monuments in early modern England'. *Trans Royal Historical Soc* 6 Ser **6**, 179–200

Llewellyn, N 2000 *Funeral Monuments in Post-reformation England*. Cambridge: Cambridge University Press

Lobel, M D 1968 'The value of early maps as evidence for the topography of English towns'. *Imago Mundi* **22**, 50–61

Lobel, M D and Carus-Wilson, E M 1975 *Atlas of Historic towns: Bristol*. London: The Scolar Press Ltd.

Locker, A 1999 'The fish bones recovered from excavations of medieval tenements at 76–96 Victoria Street, Bristol'. Unpublished report

Locock, M, Robinson, S and Yates, A 1998 'Cabot Park phase 2: Poplar, Packgate and Moorend, Avonmouth, Bristol. Archaeological evaluation'. Unpublished report, Glamorgan-Gwent Archaeological Trust

Locock, M 1999 'Buried soils of the Wentlooge formation'. *Archaeology in the Severn Estuary* **10**, 1–10

Locock, M 2001 'A later Bronze Age landscape on the Avon Levels: settlement, shelters and saltmarsh at Cabot Park', *in* Brück, J (ed) *Bronze Age Landscapes: Traditions and Transformations*. Oxford: Oxbow Books, 121–8

Locock, M, Robinson, S and Yates, A 1998 'Late Bronze Age sites at Cabot Park, Avonmouth'. *Archaeology in the Severn Estuary* **9**, 31–5

Longman, T 1994 'Archaeological evaluation of 10–22 Victoria Street, Bristol'. Unpublished report, Bristol and Region Archaeological Services

Longman, T 1998 'Archaeological evaluation at the former Seahorse public house, Upper Maudlin Street, Kingsdown, Bristol'. Unpublished report, Bristol and Region Archaeological Services

Longman, T 2001 'Excavations on the site of the Priory of St Mary Magdalen, Upper Maudlin Street, Bristol, 2000'. *Bristol Avon Archaeol* **18**, 3–29

Longman, T 2002 'Archaeological evaluation at 25 Redcliff Street/14 St Thomas Street, Redcliffe, Bristol'. Unpublished report, Bristol and Region Archaeological Services

Longman, T, 2008–9, 'Archaeological monitoring on the site of Broomwell House, Brislington, Bristol, 2003–4'. *Bristol Avon Archaeol* **23**, 83–90

Longman, T, 2009 'Building survey, excavation & watching brief on the site of the former Purimachos Fire Cement Works, Waterloo Road, St Philips, Bristol. Unpublished report, Bristol and Region Archaeological Services

Longman, T 2014a 'Archaeological excavation & watching brief at the former Magistrates Court, Nelson Street, Bristol'. Unpublished report. Bristol and Region Archaeological Services

Longman, T 2014b 'Post-excavation assessment report on the archaeological excavation & watching brief at Wapping Wharf, (Plots A, C & L), Wapping Road, Bristol'. Unpublished report. Bristol and Region Archaeological Services

Longman, T and Bryant, J 2008 'Exploratory works at St James Priory, Bristol'. Unpublished report, Bristol and Region Archaeological Services

Lord, J and Southam, J 1983 *The Floating Harbour: A Landscape History of Bristol City docks*. Bristol: The Redcliffe Press

Lowe, B J 2003 *Decorated Floor Tiles of Somerset*. Taunton: Somerset Archaeological and Natural History Society and Somerset County Museums Service

Lowe, J 2001 'Description and analysis: Listed and non-listed walls at 98–103 Redcliff Street, Bristol'. Unpublished report, CgMs Consulting

Loxton, S 1992 *Loxton's Bristol: The City's Edwardian Years in Black and White*. Bristol: Redcliffe Press Ltd.

Luck, M, Wood, G, Shaw, S and Rawlinson, M 2001 *Bristol Legible City: From Here to There*. Bristol: Bristol City Council

Lydon, J 1999 'Pidgin English: historical archaeology, cultural exchange and the Chinese in the Rocks, 1890–1930', *in* Funari, P P A, Hall, M and Jones, S (eds) *Historical Archaeology: Back from the Edge*. London: Routledge, 255–83

Lynam, C 1904–8 'Some Norman remains of St. Augustine's Abbey, Bristol'. *Proc Clifton Antiquarian Club* **6**, 59–61

Lynch, J 1998 'Bristol shipping and Royalist naval power during the English civil war'. *Mariners Mirror* **84**, 260–7

MacInnes, C 1939 *Bristol: A Gateway of Empire*. Bristol: J W Arrowsmith

Maclean, J 1878–9 'Trans Bristol Gloucestershire Archaeol Soc'. *Trans Bristol Gloucestershire Archaeol Soc* **3**, 1–47

Maclean, J (ed) 1883 *The Lives of the Berkeleys, Lords of the Honour, Castle and Manor of Berkeley*. Vol 1. Gloucester: John Bellows

Maclean, J (ed) 1883–4 'Chantry certificates, Gloucestershire (Roll 22)'. *Trans Bristol Gloucestershire Archaeol Soc* **8**, 229–308

MacPhail, R 2000 'Industrial activities – some suggested microstratigraphic signature'. Paper presented at the Association for Environmental Archaeology conference on The Environmental Archaeology of Industry, 14–16 April 2000.

Maggs, C 1992 *The Bristol and Gloucester Railway and the Avon and Gloucestershire Railway*. Headington: The Oakwood Press

Malaws, B A 1997 'Process recording at industrial sites'. *Industrial Archaeol Rev* **19**, 75–98

Malpass, P and King, A 2009 *Bristol's Floating Harbour: The First 200 Years*. Bristol: Redcliffe Press

Manchee, T J (ed) 1831 *The Bristol Charities, being the report of the Commissioners for inquiring concerning charities in England and Wales so far as relates to the charitable institutions in Bristol* 2 volumes. Bristol: Thomas John Manchee

Manchester, K 1992 'The palaeopathology of urban infections', *in* S Bassett, S (ed) *Death in Towns: Urban Responses to the Dying and the Dead, 100–1600*. Leicester: Leicester University Press, 8–14

Manco, J 2009 'The Saxon origins of Bristol'. *http://www.buildinghistory.org/bristol/origins.shtml*

Manson, M 1997 *Riot!: The Bristol Bridge Massacre of 1793*. Bristol: Past & Present

Marcy, P 1968 'Bristol's roads and communications on the eve of the Industrial Revolution, 1740–80'. *Trans Bristol Gloucestershire Archaeol Soc* **87**, 149–72

Marochan, K 1962 'The Crew's Hole pottery, St. George, Bristol'. *Trans Bristol Gloucestershire Archaeol Soc* **81**, 189–93

Marochan, K and Reed, K W 1959 'Burton's Almshouse, Long Row, Bristol'. *Trans Bristol Gloucestershire Archaeol Soc* **78**, 119–28

Marsh, C 2001 '"Common prayer" in England 1560–640: the view from the pew'. *Past & Present* **171**, 66–94

Marshall, K 1951 'Excavations in the city of Bristol, 1948–51'. *Trans Bristol Gloucestershire Archaeol Soc* **70**, 5–50

Martin, A T and Ashby, T 1901 'Excavations at Caerwent, Monmouthshire, on the site of the Roman city Venta Silurum, 1899 and 1900'. *Archaeologia* **57(2)**, 295–316

Mason, C, 2012, *Archaeological Work at No 9 Pipe Lane & No 42 Frogmore Street, Bristol, 2011–12*. Bristol and Region Archaeological Services. http://www.baras.org.uk/learning-resources/baras-reports

Mason, C 2013a 'Archaeological evaluation at New Room Chapel, No 36 The Horsefair, Bristol'. Unpublished report, Bristol and Region Archaeological Services

Mason, C 2013b 'Archaeological evaluation at Wade Street/Little Ann Street, St Judes, Bristol'. Unpublished report, Bristol and Region Archaeological Services

Mason, C 2017 'Barton Hill Pottery and the post-medieval redware industry in Bristol'. *Post-Medieval Archaeol* **51(1)**, 108-131

Mason, E W 1957 'The Horsefair cemetery, Bristol'. *Trans Bristol Gloucestershire Archaeol Soc* **76**, 164–71

Masschaele, J 2002 'The public space of the marketplace in medieval England'. *Speculum* **77**, 383–421

Masters, B and Ralph, E (eds) 1967 *The Church Book of St. Ewen*. Bristol: Bristol and Gloucestershire Archaeological Society

Matson, C 1998 *Merchants and Empire: Trading in Colonial New York*. Baltimore: Johns Hopkins University Press

Matsumura, T 1983 *The Labour Aristocracy Revisited: The Victorian Flint Glass Makers, 1850–80*. Manchester: Manchester University Press

Mayo, R 1985 *The Huguenots in Bristol*. Bristol: Bristol Branch of the Historical Association

Mays, S 1998a *The Archaeology of Human Bones*. London: Routledge

Mays, S 1998b 'The archaeological study of medieval English human populations, AD1066-1540', *in* Bayley, J (ed) *Science and Archaeology: an agenda for the future*. London: English Heritage, 195-210

Mays, S 1999 'The study of human skeletal remains from English post medieval sites', *in* Egan, G and Michael, R (eds) *Old and New Worlds: Historical/post medieval Archaeology Papers from the Societies' Joint Conferences at Williamsburg and London 1997 to Mark Thirty Years of Work and Achievement*. Oxford: Oxbow Books, 331–41

McDonald, R A 1997 *The Kingdom of the Isles: Scotland's Western Seaboard, c. 1000–336* (Scottish Historical Review Monograph no **4**). Phantassie: Tuckwell Press

McFarlane, K B 1957 'William Worcestre: a preliminary survey', *in* Conway Davies, J (ed) *Studies Presented to Sir Hilary Jenkinson, C.B.E., LL.D., F.S.A.* London: Oxford University Press, 196–221

McGrail, S 1978 *Logboats of England and Wales. Parts I & II*. Oxford: Brit Archaeol Rep, Brit Ser **51**

McGrail, S 1981 'Medieval boats, ships and landing places', *in* Milne, G and Hobley, B (eds) *Waterfront Archaeology in Britain and Northern Europe* London: CBA Res Rep **74**, 17–23

McGrail, S and Switsur, R 1979 'Medieval logboats of the river Mersey – a classification study', *in* McGrail, S (ed) *The Archaeology of Medieval Ships and Harbours in Northern Europe*. Oxford: Brit Archaeol Rep, Int Ser **66**, 93–115

McGrath, P V 1950 'The Merchant Venturers and Bristol shipping in the early 17th century'. *The Mariners Mirror* **36**, 69–80

McGrath, P V 1953 'The Society of Merchant Venturers and the Port of Bristol in the 17th century'. *Trans Bristol Gloucestershire Archaeol Soc* **72**, 105–28

McGrath, P V 1975 *The Merchant Venturers of Bristol: A History of the Society of Merchant Venturers of the City of Bristol from its Origin to the Present Day*. Bristol: The Society of Merchant Venturers of Bristol

McGrath, P V 1981 *Bristol and the Civil War*. Bristol: Bristol Branch of the Historical Association

McGrath, P V (ed) 1952 *Records Relating to the Society of Merchant Venturers of the City of Bristol in the 17th-Century*. Bristol: Bristol Record Series **17**

McGrath, P V (ed) 1955 *Merchants and Merchandise in 17th-century Bristol*. Bristol: Bristol Record Series **19**

McGrath, P V (ed) 1979 *Bristol's Inns and Alehouses in the Mid-18th Century*. Bristol: Bristol City Council

McGuire, R H 1991 'Building power in the cultural landscape of Broome County, New York 1880 to 1940', *in* McGuire, R H and Paynter, R (eds) *The Archaeology of Inequality*. Oxford: Basil Blackwell, 102–24

McGurk, J 1997 *The Elizabethan Conquest of Ireland: the 1590s Crisis*. Manchester: Manchester University Press

McKenny Hughes, T 1892 'On the recent discovery of two ancient ditches and objects of medieval date between Hobson Street and Sidney Street, Cambridge'. *Proc Cambridge Antiq Soc* **8**, 32–55

McKisack, M 1959 *The 14th Century, 1307–99*. Oxford: Oxford University Press

McSheffrey, S 2005 'Heresy, orthodoxy and English vernacular religion 1480–1525'. *Past & Present* **186**, 47–80

McSloy, E R 2015, '4.5 Clay mould debris', *in* Alexander, M (ed), *Medieval and Post-Medieval Occupation and Industry in the Redcliffe Suburb of Bristol. Excavations at 1–2 and 3 Redcliff Street, 2003–10*. Cotswold Archaeology Monograph **8**, 60–4

Medieval Settlement Research Group 1994 'Fieldwork and excavation in 1994'. *Annual Report* **9**, 30–50

Meller, H E 1976 *Leisure and the Changing City, 1870–914*. London: Routledge & Kegan Paul

Millea, N 2003 *Street Mapping: An A to Z of Urban Cartography*. Oxford: Bodleian Library

Miller, I (ed) 2009 'Temple Quay North, Bristol, Avon. Post-excavation assessment'. Unpublished report, Oxford Archaeology North

Miller, N F and Gleason, K L 1994 'Fertilizer in the identification and analysis of cultivated soil', *in* Miller, N F and Gleason, K L (eds) *The Archaeology of Garden and Field*. Philadelphia: University of Pennsylvania Press, 25–43

Minchinton, W 1954 'Bristol – metropolis of the west in the 18th century'. *Trans Royal Hist Soc* 5 Ser **4**, 69–89

Molleson, T and Cox, M with Waldron, H and Whittaker, D 1993 *The Spitalfields Project. Volume 2: The Anthropology. The Middling Sort*. York: CBA Res Rep **86**

Monckton, L 1997 'The myth of William Canynges and the late medieval rebuilding of St. Mary Redcliffe', *in* Keen, L (ed) *'Almost the richest city': Bristol in the Middle Ages*. London: British Archaeological Association, 57–67

Monckton, L 1999 'Late gothic architecture in south-west England: four major centres of building activity at Wells, Bristol, Sherbourne and Bath'. Unpublished PhD Thesis, University of Warwick

Montgomery, D 1987 *The Fall of the House of Labor: The Workplace, the State and American Labor*. Cambridge: Cambridge University Press

Moorcroft, D and Campbell-Sharp, N 1998 *Bristol in Old Photographs from the Fred Little Collection*. Thrupp, Stroud: Budding Books

Moore, J (ed) 1982 *Domesday Book, Gloucestershire*. Chichester: Phillimore

Moorhouse, S 1971 'Medieval Britain in 1970. II Post-conquest'. *Medieval Archaeol* **15**, 137–79

Morgan, K 1990 *John Wesley in Bristol*. Bristol: Bristol Branch of the Historical Association

Morgan, K 1993 *Bristol and the Atlantic Trade in the 18th Century*. Cambridge: Cambridge University Press

Morgan, K 1996 'The economic development of Bristol, 1700–1850', *in* Dresser, M and Ollerenshaw, P (eds) *The Making of Modern Bristol*. Tiverton: Redcliffe Press, 48–75

Morris, C (ed) 1995 *The Illustrated Journeys of Celia Fiennes 1685–c.1712*. Far Thrupp, Stroud: Alan Sutton Publishing

Morris, R K 1989 *Churches in the Landscape*. London

Morris, R K 1997 'European prodigy or regional eccentric? The rebuilding of St. Augustine's Abbey church, Bristol', *in* Keen, L (ed) *'Almost the richest city': Bristol in the Middle Ages*. London: British Archaeological Association, 41–56

Mortimer, R (ed) 1977 *Minute Book of the Men's Meeting of the Society of Friends in Bristol, 1686–1704*. Bristol: Bristol Record Series **30**

Morton, H V 2000 *In Search of England*. London: Methuen

Morton, R and Oakey, N 2000 '11–12 Portland Square, Bristol: archaeological desk-based assessment and architectural survey'. Unpublished report, Cotswold Archaeology

Mosse, J 1969 'Redcliff shot tower'. *BIAS Journal* **2**, 4–5

Mosser, M and Teyssot, G 1991 'Introduction: the architecture of the garden and architecture in the garden', *in* Mosser, M & Teyssot, G (eds) *The History of Garden Design: The Western Tradition from the Renaissance to the Present Day*. London: Thames and Hudson, 11–21.

Mowl, T 1991 *To Build the Second City: Architects and Craftsmen of Georgian Bristol*. Bristol: Redcliffe Press

Mukerji, C 1997 *Territorial Ambition and the Gardens of Versailles*. Cambridge: Cambridge University Press

Muñoz de Migel, M 1997 'The iconography of Christ *Victor* in Anglo-Saxon art: a new approach to the study of the 'Harrowing of Hell' relief in Bristol Cathedral', *in* Keen, L (ed) *'Almost the richest city': Bristol in the Middle Ages*. London: British Archaeological Association, 75–80

Munro, J H 1999 'The 'industrial crisis' of the English textile towns, c.1290–c.1330', *in* Prestwich, M *et al* (eds) *13th-century England: Proceedings of the Durham Conference 1997*. Woodbridge: Boydell Press, 103–42

Munzel, S 1986 'Coding system for bone fragments', *in* Van Wijngaarden-Bakker, L (ed) *Database Management and Zooarchaeology*, PACT **14**, 193–5

Murtagh, W 1998 *Moravian Architecture and Town Planning: Bethlehem, Pennsylvania, and Other 18th-century American Settlements*. Philadelphia: University of Pennsylvania Press

Muthesius, S 1982 *The English Terraced House*. New Haven: Yale University Press

Mytum, H 1999 'Welsh cultural identity in 19th-century Pembrokeshire: the pedimented headstone as a graveyard monument', *in* Tarlow, S and West, S (eds) *The Familiar Past? Archaeologies of Later Historical Britain*. London: Routledge, 215–30

Nabb, H 1987 *The Bristol Gas Industry, 1815–1949*. Bristol: Bristol Branch of the Historical Association

Nasmith, J 1778 *Itineraria Symonis Simeonis et Willelmi de Worcestre*. Cambridge

Nayling, N 1998 *The Magor Pill Medieval Wreck*. York: CBA Res Rep **115**

Nayling, N and McGrail, S 2004 *The Barland's Farm Romano-Celtic Boat*. York: CBA Res Rept **138**

Neale, F 1985 'The Mary-le-Port area, historical and topographical survey', *in* Watts, L and Rahtz, P 1985 *Mary-le-Port, Bristol: Excavations, 1962–1963*. Bristol: City of Bristol Museum and Art Gallery, 27–55

Neale, F (ed) 2000 *William Worcestre: The Topography of Medieval Bristol*. Bristol: Bristol Record Series **51**

Nicholls, J F 1878–9 'Bristol Castle'. *Trans Bristol Gloucestershire Archaeol Soc* **3**, 185–92

Nicholls, J F 1878–9 'The crypt of St Nicholas Church, Bristol'. *Trans Bristol Gloucestershire Archaeol Soc* **3**, 168–81

Nicholls, J F 1882–3 'The old hostelries of Bristol'. *Trans Bristol Gloucestershire Archaeol Soc* **7**, 307–17

Nicholls, J F and Taylor J 1881–2 *Bristol Past and Present*. 3 vols (vol 1 Civil History 1881; vol 2 Ecclesiastical History 1881; vol 3 Civil and Modern History 1882). Bristol: J W Arrowsmith

Nicholson, R 2010 'Fish remains', in Jackson, R G *The Archaeology of the Medieval Suburb of Broadmead, Bristol. Excavations in Union Street, 2000*. Bristol's Museums, Galleries & Archives, 124–7

Nicholson, R 2017 'Fish', in Ford, Ben M, Brady, Kate and Teague, Steven *From Bridgehead to Brewery. The Medieval and Post-medieval Archaeological*

Remains from Finzel's Reach, Bristol. Oxford: Oxford Archaeology Monograph **27**, 264–8

Nicholson, R A and Hillam, J 1987 'A dendrochronological analysis of oak timbers from the early medieval site at Dundas Wharf, Bristol'. *Trans Bristol Gloucestershire Archaeol Soc* **105**, 133–45

Nightingale, P 2000 'Knights and merchants: trade, politics and the gentry in late medieval England'. *Past & Present* **169**, 36–62

Norris, J P 1878–9 'Notes on the church of St Mary Redcliffe'. *Trans Bristol Gloucestershire Archaeol Soc* **3**, 193–210

Norris, J P 1888 *Early History and Architecture of Bristol Cathedral*. Bristol: I E Chillcott

Nott, H E (ed) 1935 *Deposition Books of Bristol. Vol. 1 1643–1647*. Bristol: Bristol Record Series **6**

Oakes, C 2000 'Romanesque architecture and sculpture' *in* Rogan, J (ed) *Bristol Cathedral: History & Architecture*. Stroud: Tempus, 64–87

O'Callaghan, B 1996 'The spire of St. Mary Redcliffe'. Paper presented at the British Archaeological Association Bristol Conference 20–24 July 1996.

O'Connor, T P 1989 *Bones from Anglo-Scandinavian Levels at 16–22 Coppergate*. York: Archaeology of York **15/3**

O'Connor, T P 1991 *Bones from 46–54 Fishergate*. York: Archaeology of York **15/4**

O'Donovan, D 2003 'English patron, English building? The importance of St. Sepulchre's archiepiscopal palace, Dublin'. In Duffy, S (ed) *Medieval Dublin IV: Proceedings of the Friends of Medieval Dublin Symposium 2002'*. Dublin: Four Courts Press, 253–78

O'Meara, D 2014 'Geoarchaeological survey. New Bridewell, Bristol: Environmental and geoarchaeological analysis'. Unpublished report. Wardell Armstrong Archaeology

O'Neill, H and Barber A 2009, '26–28 Gloucester Lane, Old Market, Bristol. Archaeological strip, map and sample'. Unpublished report. Cotswold Archaeology

O'Neill, T 1987 *Merchants and Mariners in Medieval Ireland*. Dublin: Irish Academic Press

Orme, N 1976 *Education in the West of England, 1066–1548: Cornwall, Devon, Dorset, Gloucestershire, Somerset, Wiltshire*. Exeter: University of Exeter

Orme, N 1978 'The Guild of Kalenders, Bristol'. *Trans Bristol Gloucestershire Archaeol Soc* **96**, 32–52

Orme, N 2004 'Education in medieval Bristol and Gloucestershire'. *Trans Bristol Gloucestershire Archaeol Soc* **122**, 9–27

Orme, N and Cannon, J 2010, *Westbury-on-Trym: Monastery, Minster and College*. Bristol: Bristol Record Society **62**

Otway-Ruthven, A 1968 *A History of Medieval Ireland*. London: Ernest Benn Ltd.

Ove Arup & Partners and York University 1991 *York Development and Archaeology Study*. Manchester: Ove Arup & Partners

Owen, J V 2003 'The geochemistry of Worcester porcelain from Dr. Wall to Royal Worcester: 150 years of innovation'. *Historical Archaeol* **37**, 84–96

Pagano de Divitiis, G 1997 *English Merchants in 17th-century Italy*. Cambridge: Cambridge University Press

Page, W, 1907, 'House of Augustinian canonesses: The priory of St Mary Magdalen, Bristol', *A History of the County of Gloucester*: Vol 2, 93

Painter, S 1943 *Studies in the History of the English Feudal Barony* (The Johns Hopkins University Studies in Historical and Political Science Series **61(3)**. Baltimore: Johns Hopkins University Press

Pantin, W A 1962–3 'Medieval English town-house plans'. *Medieval Archaeol* **6–7** (1962–3), 202–39

Pantin, W A 1963 'Some medieval English town houses: a study in adaptation', *in* Foster, I L and Alcock, L (eds) *Culture and Environment: Essays in Honour of Sir Cyril Fox*. London: Routledge & Kegan Paul, 445–78

Parker, A J 1998 'Remains of boats at Purton (East), Gloucestershire'. *Archaeology in the Severn Estuary* **9**, 91–4

Parker, A J 1999 'A maritime cultural landscape: the port of Bristol in the Middle Ages'. *International Journal of Nautical Archaeology* **28**, 323–42

Parker, G 1929 'Tyndall's Park, Bristol, fort royal and the fort house therein'. *Trans Bristol Gloucestershire Archaeol Soc* **51**, 123–41

Parker, G 1996 *The Military Revolution: Military Innovation and the Rise of the West, 1500–1800*. Cambridge: Cambridge University Press

Parry, A, 1998 'Archaeological evaluation of the site of the South Building, Canons Marsh, Bristol'. Unpublished report, Bristol and Region Archaeological Services

Parry, A 1999a 'Archaeological evaluation of land at Wilson Street, St. Paul's, Bristol'. Unpublished report, Bristol and Region Archaeological Services

Parry, A 1999b 'Archaeological evaluation at the Central Electric Lighting Station, Temple Back, Bristol'. Unpublished report, Bristol and Region Archaeological Services

Parry, A 2000a 'Archaeological evaluation at The Georgian House, 7 Great George Street, Bristol'. Unpublished report, Bristol and Region Archaeological Services

Parry, A 2000b Archaeological watching brief at Wilson Street, St. Pauls, Bristol'. Unpublished report, Bristol and Region Archaeological Services

Parry, A 2001a 'Archaeological excavation on the site of the South Building, Canons Marsh'. Unpublished report, Bristol and Region Archaeological Services

Parry, A, 2001b 'Archaeological evaluation of land adjacent to Stoke Road, Durdham Down, Clifton, Bristo'l. Unpublished report, Bristol and Region Archaeological Services

Parry, A 2001c 'Archaeological Evaluation at 18–20 West Street, Old Market, Bristol'. Unpublished report, Bristol and Region Archaeological Services

Parry, A, 2005 'Archaeological fieldwork at 1–2 King Street, Bristol, 1990, 2000 & 2001'. *Bristol Avon Archaeol* **20**, 25–57.

Patterson, R (ed) 1973 *Earldom of Gloucester Charters: The Charters and Scribes of the Earls and Countesses of Gloucester to AD 1217*. Oxford: Clarendon Press

Paul, R W 1885 'The Sacristy, Bristol Cathedral'. *The Builder* (8 August 1885)

Paul, R W 1899 'Bristol Cathedral'. *The Builder* (27 May 1899)

Paul, R W 1912 'The plan of the church and monastery of St. Augustine, Bristol'. *Archaeologia* 2nd Ser **63** (1911–12), 231–50

Peacey, A 1996 *The Development of the Clay Tobacco Pipe in the British Isles*. Oxford: Brit Archaeol Rep, Brit Ser **246**

Pelteret, D 1981 'Slave raiding and slave trading in early England', *in* Clemoes, P (ed) *Anglo-Saxon England* **9**. Cambridge: Cambridge University Press, 99–104

Penn, S A C 1989 'Social and economic aspects of 14th century Bristol'. Unpublished PhD Thesis, University of Birmingham

Petit, S and Watkins, C 2003 'Pollarding trees: changing attitudes to a traditional land management practice in Britain 1600-1900'. *Rural History* **14** (2003), 157-176

Phillpotts, C 2013 '2.1 Historical background', in Ridgeway, V and Watts, M (eds), *Friars, Quakers, Industry and Urbanisation. The Archaeology of the Broadmead Expansion Project, Cabot Circus, Bristol, 2005–2008*. Cotswold Archaeology/Pre-Construct Archaeology, 13–29

Pilkington, J 1998 'Archaeological watching brief on the excavation of trial pits at Temple Quay, Bristol'. Unpublished report, Bristol and Region Archaeological Services

Pilkington, J 1999 'Archaeological recording during conservation work at St John the Baptist Church crypt, Bristol, 1998'. *Bristol Avon Archaeol* **16**, 61–71

Pilkington, J 2000 'Archaeological watching brief at the former Moravian Chapel, Upper Maudlin Street, Bristol'. Unpublished report, Bristol and Region Archaeological Services

Pilkington, J 2001 'Archaeological watching brief at 93 & 95 Stokes Croft, Bristol'. Unpublished report, Bristol and Region Archaeological Services

Pilkinton, M C 1983 'The playhouse in Wine Street, Bristol'. *Theatre Notebook* **37**, 14

Pilkinton, M C 1988 'New information on the playhouse in Wine Street, Bristol'. *Theatre Notebook* **42**, 73–5

Pilkinton, M C (ed) 1997 *Records of Early English Drama: Bristol.* Toronto: University of Toronto Press

Ponsford, M W nd(a) 'Bristol', *in* Iles, R and Aston, M (eds) *The Archaeology of Avon: A Review from the Neolithic to the Middle Ages.* Bristol: Avon County Council, 145–59

Ponsford, M W nd(b) *Excavations at Greyfriars, Bristol.* Bristol: City of Bristol Museum and Art Gallery

Ponsford, M W 1974 'Excavations at Victoria Street, Bristol'. *BARG Bulletin* **5(2)**, 48–9

Ponsford, M W 1979 'Bristol Castle: archaeology and the history of a royal fortress'. Unpublished MLitt thesis, University of Bristol

Ponsford, M W 1981 'Excavations at Westbury College, Bristol'. *BARG Review* **2**, 24–6

Ponsford, M W 1985 'Bristol's medieval waterfront: "the Redcliffe Project"', *in* Herteig, A (ed) *Conference on Waterfront Archaeology in North European Towns No 2.* Bergen: Historisk Museum Bergen, 112–21

Ponsford, M W 2001 'Post-medieval Britain and Ireland in 2000'. *Soc Post-Medieval Archaeol* **35**, 122–289

Ponsford, M W (ed) 2005, 'Post-medieval fieldwork in Britain and Northern Ireland in 2004'. *Soc Post-medieval Archaeol* **39**, 335–428

Ponsford, M W *et al* 1989a 'Archaeology in Bristol 1986–89'. *Trans Bristol Gloucestershire Archaeol Soc* **107**, 243–51

Ponsford, M W *et al* 1989b 'Archaeology in Bristol 1989'. *Bristol Avon Archaeol* **8**, 41–5

Ponsford, M W and Burchill, R 1995 'Iberian pottery imported into Bristol 1200–1600', *in* Gerrard, C M, Gutierrez, A and Vince, A G (eds) *Spanish Medieval Ceramics in Spain and the British Isles.* Oxford: Brit Archaeol Rep, Int Ser **610**, 315–18

Ponsford, M W and Jackson, R G 1998 'Post-medieval fieldwork in Britain and Ireland in 1997'. *Society Post-Medieval Archaeol* **32**, 145–206

Poole, S 1996 'To be a Bristolian: civic identity and social order, 1750–1850', *in* Dresser, M and Ollerenshaw P (eds) *The Making of Modern Bristol.* Tiverton: Redcliffe Press, 76–95

Pope, P E 1997 *The Many Landfalls of John Cabot.* Toronto: University of Toronto Press

Porter, S 1994 *Destruction in the English Civil Wars.* Far Thrupp, Stroud: Alan Sutton Publishing Ltd.

Portway-Dobson, D 1939 'Excavations at Sea Mills, near Bristol, 1938'. *Trans Bristol Gloucestershire Archaeol Soc* **61**, 202–23

Potter, K R (ed) 1955 *The Historia Novella.* London: T Nelson

Potter, K R (ed) 1955 *Gesta Stephani.* Oxford: Oxford University Press

Potter, K 2003 'Archaeological evaluation of land at Nos 55–61 Victoria Street, Bristol'. Unpublished report, Bristol and Region Archaeological Services

Potter, K 2006 'Archaeological evaluation of land at Nos 1 & 2 Backfields Industrial Estate, Upper York Street, Bristol'. Unpublished report, Bristol and Region Archaeological Services

Potter, K 2010 'Nos 5 & 6 Kingsdown Parade & 15 Marlborough Hill, Kingsdown, Bristol. Archaeological Evaluation & Recording Project'. Unpublished report, Avon Archaeological Unit

Potto Hicks, F W 1932 'Medieval history of St. James, Bristol'. Unpublished MA thesis, ???

Potto Hicks, F W 1934 'Original documents relating to Bristol'. *Trans Bristol Gloucestershire Archaeol Soc* **56**, 165–77

Pountney, W J 1920 *Old Bristol Potteries.* Bristol: J W Arrowsmith

Powell, A C 1925, 'Glass making in Bristol'. *Trans Bristol Gloucestershire Archaeol Soc* **47**, 211–57

Powell, C 1981 'The scope of industrial housing in Avon'. *BARG Review* **2**, 2–8

Powell, C 1990 '"Widows and others" on Bristol building sites: some women in 19th-century construction'. *Local Historian* **20**, 84–7

Price, R H 1979a 'An excavation at Bristol Bridge, Bristol, 1975', *in* Thomas, N (ed) *Rescue Archaeology in the Bristol Area: 1: Roman, Medieval and Later Research Organised by the City of Bristol Museum and Art Gallery.* Bristol: City of Bristol Museum and Art Gallery, 29–33

Price, R H 1979b 'Excavation at the town wall, Bristol, 1974', *in* Thomas, N (ed) *Rescue Archaeology in the Bristol Area: 1: Roman, Medieval and Later Research Organised by the City of Bristol Museum and Art Gallery.* Bristol: City of Bristol Museum and Art Gallery, 15–27

Price, R H 1979c 'Survey and excavation near St. Peter's Churchyard, Bristol, 1972', *in* Thomas, N (ed) *Rescue Archaeology in the Bristol Area: 1: Roman, Medieval and Later Research Organised by the City of Bristol Museum and Art Gallery.* Bristol: City of Bristol Museum and Art Gallery, 35–48

Price, R H 1991 'An excavation at Broad Quay (Water gate), Bristol, 1979'. *Bristol Avon Archaeol* **9** (1990/91), 24–8

Price, R H, Jackson, R G and Jackson, P 1984 'The Ring family of clay tobacco pipe manufacturers'. *Post-medieval Archaeol* **18**, 263–300

Price, R H with Ponsford, M W 1998 *St. Bartholomew's Hospital, Bristol. The Excavation of a Medieval Hospital: 1976–8.* York: CBA Research Report **110**

Priest, G 1980 'Building the Exchange and markets of the City of Bristol'. Unpublished PhD Thesis, University of Bristol

Priest, G 2003 *The Paty Family: Makers of 18th-century Bristol.* Bristol: Redcliffe Press.

Priest, G and Cobb, P 1980 *The Fight for Bristol: Planning and the Growth of Public Protest.* Bristol: Bristol Civic Society

Priestley, U and Corfield, P J 1982 'Rooms and room use in Norwich housing, 1580–730'. *Post-medieval Archaeol* **16**, 93–123

Pritchard, J E 1893–6 'The Registrar's House, Lower College Green, Bristol'. *Proc Clifton Antiquarian Club* **3**, 204–9

Pritchard, J E 1895 'Archaeological notes'. *Proc Clifton Antiquarian Club* **3** (1893–6), 175–6

Pritchard, J E 1896 'Archaeological notes. 1894'. *Proc Clifton Antiquarian Club* **3** (1893–6), 88

Pritchard, J E 1898 'Archaeological notes for 1898'. *Proc Clifton Antiquarian Club* **4** (1897–9), 158–61

Pritchard, J E 1900 'Bristol archaeological notes for 1900'. *Trans Bristol Gloucestershire Archaeol Soc* **23**, 262–75

Pritchard, J E 1901 'Bristol archaeological notes for 1901'. *Trans Bristol Gloucestershire Archaeol Soc* **24**, 274–82

Pritchard, J E 1903 'Bristol archaeological notes for 1902'. *Trans Bristol Gloucestershire Archaeol Soc* **26**, 138–49

Pritchard, J E 1904 'Bristol archaeological notes for 1903'. *Trans Bristol Gloucestershire Archaeol Soc* **27**, 327–39

Pritchard, J E 1906a 'Bristol archaeological notes for 1904'. *Trans Bristol Gloucestershire Archaeol Soc* **29**, 127–45

Pritchard, J E 1906b 'Bristol archaeological notes for 1905'. *Trans Bristol Gloucestershire Archaeol Soc* **29**, 265–83

Pritchard, J E 1907a 'Bristol archaeological notes for 1906'. *Trans Bristol Gloucestershire Archaeol Soc* **30**, 151–66

Pritchard, J E 1907b 'Bristol archaeological notes for 1907'. *Trans Bristol Gloucestershire Archaeol Soc* **30**, 212–32

Pritchard, J E 1908 'Bristol archaeological notes for 1908'. *Trans Bristol Gloucestershire Archaeol Soc* **31**, 288–309

Pritchard, J E 1909 'Bristol archaeological notes for 1909'. *Trans Bristol Gloucestershire Archaeol Soc* **32**, 313–33

Pritchard, J E 1911 'Bristol archaeological notes for 1910'. *Trans Bristol Gloucestershire Archaeol Soc* **34**, 65–89

Pritchard, J E 1912 'Bristol archaeological notes for 1911'. *Trans Bristol Gloucestershire Archaeol Soc* **35**, 96–115

Pritchard, J E 1913 'Bristol archaeological notes for 1912'. *Trans Bristol Gloucestershire Archaeol Soc* **36**, 103–29

Pritchard, J E 1920 'Bristol archaeological notes 1913–9'. *Trans Bristol Gloucestershire Archaeol Soc* **42**, 125–48

Pritchard, J E 1922 'Bristol archaeological notes, 1920–3 including the latest "Chatterton Find"'. *Trans Bristol Gloucestershire Archaeol Soc* **44**, 79–100

Pritchard, J E 1926a 'Old plans and views of Bristol'. *Trans Bristol Gloucestershire Archaeol Soc* **48**, 325–53

Pritchard, J E 1926b 'The Pithay, Bristol'. *Trans Bristol Gloucestershire Archaeol Soc* **48**, 251–73

Pritchard, J E 1929 'Bristol archaeological notes XVI, 1924–9'. *Trans Bristol Gloucestershire Archaeol Soc* **51**, 225–43

Prosser, L, Erskine, J G P and Houghton, G 1996 'Poole's Wharf, Hotwells, Bristol. Archaeological Desktop Study and Site Evaluation'. Unpublished report, Avon Archaeological Unit

Pryce, G 1850 *Notes on the Ecclesiastical and Monumental Architecture and Sculpture of the Middle Ages*. Bristol: W Mack

Pryce, G 1854 'Examination of the church of St. Mary Redcliffe'. *Archaeologia* **35**, 279–97

Pryce, G 1861 *A Popular History of Bristol, Antiquarian, Topographical and Descriptive, from the Earliest Period to the Present Time*. Bristol: W Mack

Rackham, D 1986 'Assessing the relative frequencies of species by the application of a stochastic model to a zooarchaeological database', *in* Van Wijngaarden-Bakker, L (ed) *Database Management and Zooarchaeology*, PACT **14**, 185–92

Rackham, D 1994a *Animal Bones* London: British Museum Publications

Rackham, D 1994b 'Economy and environment in Saxon London', *in* Rackham, D (ed) *Environment and Economy in Anglo-Saxon England*, London: CBA Res Rep **89**, 126–35

Rahtz, P nd 'Post Roman Avon', in Iles, R and Aston, M (eds) *The Archaeology of Avon: A Review from the Neolithic to the Middle Ages*. Bristol: Avon County Council, 73–81

Rahtz, P 1956–7 'Kings Weston Down Camp, Bristol, 1956'. *Proc University of Bristol Spelaeological Soc* **1**, 30–8

Rahtz, P 1958–9 'Blaise Castle Hill, Bristol, 1957'. *Proc University of Bristol Spelaeological Soc* **3**, 141–71

Rahtz, P 1960 'Excavation by the town wall, Baldwin Street, Bristol, 1957'. *Trans Bristol Gloucestershire Archaeol Soc* **79(2)**, 221–50

Raistrick, A 1970 *Dynasty of Iron Founders: The Darbys and Coalbrookdale*. Newton Abbot: David & Charles

Ralph, E 1944 'Grants and leases of lands in King Street, Bristol'. *Trans Bristol Gloucestershire Archaeol Soc* **65**, 160–6

Ralph, E 1973 *Government of Bristol 1373–973* Bristol: Bristol Corporation

Ralph, E 1981 *The Streets of Bristol*. Bristol: Bristol Branch of the Historical Association

Ralph, E (ed) 1979 *The Great White Book of Bristol*. Bristol: Bristol Record Series **32**

Ralph, E (ed) 1985 'Bishop Secker's diocese book', *in* McGrath, P (ed) *A Bristol Miscellany*. Bristol: Bristol Record Series **37**

Ralph, E and Cobb, P 1991 *New Anglican Churches in 19th Century Bristol*. Bristol: Bristol Branch of the Historical Association

Ralph, E and Hardwick N (eds) 1980 *Calendar of the Bristol Apprentice Book. Part 2, 1542–52*. Bristol: Bristol Record Series **33**

Ralph, E and Williams M (eds) 1968 *The Inhabitants of Bristol in 1696*. Bristol: Bristol Record Series **25**

Rawes, J and Wills, J (eds) 1999 'Archaeological review No 23'. *Trans Bristol Gloucestershire Archaeol Soc* **117**, 167–86

Reddaway, T F and Ruddock, A A (eds) 1969 'The accounts of John Balsall, purser of the Trinity of Bristol 1480–1' *in Camden Miscellany XXIII* (Camden 4th Ser **7**). London: Royal Historical Society

Reed, K and Marochan, K 1960 'An 18th century wall decoration from Culver Street, Bristol'. *Trans Bristol Gloucestershire Archaeol Soc* **79(2)**, 308

Reeve, J and Adams, M 1993 *The Spitalfields Project Vol. 1: The Archaeology. Across the Styx*. York: CBA Res Rep **85**

RemedX 1999 'Buildings recording and archaeological assessment of Canon's Marsh Gas Works, Bristol'. Unpublished report, RemedX

Reynish, S, 2008, 'Land at Backfields, St Paul's, Bristol. Archaeological watching brief (Construction)'. Cotswold Archaeology. CA Report 08148

Richards, J and MacKenzie, J M 1986 *The Railway Station: A Social History*. Oxford: Oxford University Press

Richards, M P and Hedges, R E M 1998 'Stable isotope analysis reveals variations in human diet at the Poundbury Camp cemetery site'. *J Archaeol Sci* **25**, 1247–52

Richardson, D 1998 'The British empire and the Atlantic slave trade, 1660–807', *in* Marshall, P J (ed) *The Oxford History of the British Empire. Vol. 2 The 18th Century*. Oxford: Oxford University Press, 440–64

Richardson, H 1960 *The English Jewry under Angevin kings*. London: Methuen & Co. Ltd.

Richardson, H (ed) 1998 *English Hospitals, 1660–948: A Survey of Their Architecture and Design*. Swindon: Royal Commission on the Historical Monuments of England

Richardson, R 1989 *Death, Dissection and the Destitute*. London: Penguin Books

Richmond, C 1996 *The Paston Family in the 15th Century: Falstolf's Will*. Cambridge: Cambridge University Press

Ridgeway, V and Watts, M (eds) 2013, *Friars, Quakers, Industry and Urbanisation. The Archaeology of the Broadmead Expansion Project, Cabot Circus, Bristol, 2005–8*. Cotswold Archaeology/Pre-Construct Archaeology

Ridyard, S 1988 *The Royal Saints of Anglo-Saxon England: A Study of West Saxon and East Anglian Cults*. Cambridge: Cambridge University Press

Rigby, S 1988 'Urban 'oligarchy' in late-medieval England', *in* Thomson, J F F (ed) *Towns and Townspeople in the 15th-century*. Gloucester: Alan Sutton, 62–86

Rippon, S J 1997 *The Severn estuary: landscape evolution and wetland reclamation*. Leicester: Leicester University Press

Rippon, S J and Croft, B (eds) 2008 'Post-Conquest medieval', in Webster, C J (ed), *The Archaeology of South West England. South West Archaeological Research Framework. Resource Assessment and Research Agenda*. Somerset County Council, 195–207

Rodger, N A M 1997 *The Safeguard of the Sea*. London: Harper Collins

Rodwell, W 1997 'Landmarks in church archaeology: a review of the last thirty years'. *Church Archaeology* **1**, 5–16

Rodwell, W J, 2004, 'The architectural history of St Mary's Church: a summary', in Drury, M *St Mary Redcliffe. Conservation Plan. Part 2: The Church*, 24–75

Roe, D 1974 'Palaeolithic artefacts from the River Avon terraces near Bristol'. *Proc University of Bristol Spelaeological Soc* **13**, 319–26

Rogers, P 1999 'Chatterton and the Club', *in* Groom, N (ed) *Thomas Chatterton and Romantic Culture*. Basingstoke: MacMillan Press Ltd, 121–50

Rome, A 2000 'Gothic architecture', *in* Rogan, J (ed) *Bristol Cathedral: History & Architecture*. Stroud: Tempus, 88–112

Roper, S 2008–9 'Excavations at 10–22 Victoria Street, Bristol, 2008'. *Bristol Avon Archaeol* **23**, 99–118

Roper, S 2012 'Excavation assessment report of the former Hill House Hammond site, Lewins Mead, Bristol'. Unpublished report. Bristol and Region Archaeological Services

Roper, S 2014 'Archaeological excavation at St Mary Redcliffe Church, Bristol'. Unpublished report, Bristol and Region Archaeological Services

Roper, S 2015 'Archaeological evaluation at New Room Chapel, No 36 The Horsefair, Broadmead, Bristol'. Unpublished report, Bristol and Region Archaeological Services

Roslyn, H E 1928 *The History of the Antient Society of St. Stephen's Ringers, Bristol*. Bristol: St. Stephen's Press

Ross, C D (ed) 1959 *Cartulary of St. Mark's Hospital, Bristol*. Bristol: Bristol Record Series **21**

Rosser, G 1997 'Crafts, guilds and the negotiation of work in the medieval town'. *Past & Present* **154**, 1–31

Rostow, W 1960 *The Stages of Economic Growth: A Non-communist Manifesto*. Cambridge: Cambridge University Press

Rothschild, N A 1990 *New York City Neighbourhoods. The 18th century*. San Diego: Academic Press

Roy, I (ed) 1975 *The Royalist Ordnance Papers, 1642–6. Part 2*. Wheatley: Oxfordshire Record Society

RCHME 1929 *An Inventory of the Historical Monuments in London. Vol. 4 The City*. London: HMSO

Rubinstein, W 1996 *A History of the Jews in the English-speaking World: Great Britain*. London: Macmillan

Rudder, S 1779 *A New History of Gloucestershire*. Cirencester: Samuel Rudder

Rugg, J 1998 'A new burial form and its meanings: cemetery establishment in the first half of the 19th century', *in* Cox, M (ed) *Grave Concerns: Death and Burial in England, 1700–850*. York: CBA Res Rep **113**, 44–53.

Rushforth, G McN 1927 'The painted glass in the Lord Mayor's Chapel, Bristol'. *Trans Bristol Gloucestershire Archaeol Soc* **49**, 301–31

Russell, J C 1948 *British Medieval Population*. Albuquerque

Russell, J R 1983 'Romano-British burials at Henbury Comprehensive School, Bristol: a preliminary report'. *Bristol Avon Archaeol* **2**, 21–4

Russell, J R 1984 'A new Roman site at Horfield'. *BARG Bulletin* **12**, 7

Russell, J R 1988 'The north almshouse at Westbury-on-Trym, Bristol: excavations 1975–8'. *Bristol Avon Archaeol* **7**, 14–25

Russell, J R 1991 'An 18th century bath house & garden layout at Crew's Hole Road, Bristol'. *Bristol Avon Archaeol* **9** (1990–1), 51–3

Russell, J R 1999 'The archaeology of the parish of Clifton, with a note on the 883 Boundary Survey of Stoke Bishop'. *Bristol Avon Archaeol* **16**, 82–3

Russell, J R 2003, *The Civil War Defences of Bristol: Their Archaeology & Topography*. 2nd edn. Bristol

Russell, J R and Williams, R G J 1984 'Romano-British sites in the City of Bristol – a review & gazetteer'. *Bristol Avon Archaeol* **3**, 18–26

Russett, V 1991 'Hythes and bows: aspects of river transport in Somerset', *in* Good, G, Jones, R H and Ponsford, M W (eds) *Waterfront Archaeology; Proceedings of the Third International Conference, Bristol, 1988*. London: CBA Res Rep **74**), 60–6

Rutherford, S 2004 'Victorian and Edwardian institutional landscapes in England'. *Landscapes* **5**, 25–41

Rutter, J 1829 *Delineations of the North-western Division of the County of Somerset, and of its Antediluvian Bone Caverns, with a Geological Sketch of the District*. London: Longman, Rees, and Co. and J and A Arch, Cornhill

Sabin, A 1957 'The 14th-century heraldic glass in the eastern Lady Chapel of Bristol Cathedral'. *Antiq J* **37**, 54–70

Sacks, D H 1991 *The Widening Gate: Bristol and the Atlantic Trade*. Berkeley: University of California Press

Sacks, D H 1989 'Celebrating authority in Bristol, 1475–640', *in* Zimmerman, S and Weissman, R (eds) *Urban Life in the Renaissance*. Newark: University of Delaware Press, 187–223

St John O'Neill, B H 1951 'Ridley's Almshouses, Bristol'. *Trans Bristol Gloucestershire Archaeol Soc* **70**, 54–63

Sampson, W C 1909 'The almshouses of Bristol'. *Trans Bristol Gloucestershire Archaeol Soc* **32**, 84–108

Samuel, J 1997 *Jews in Bristol: The History of the Jewish Community in Bristol from the Middle Ages to the Present Day*. Bristol: Redcliffe Press

Samuel, J 2000 'Archaeological evaluation of land adjacent to the Llandoger Trow Public House, King Street, Bristol'. Unpublished report, Bristol and Region Archaeological Services

Samuel, J 2001 'Archaeological watching brief at 1–13 St. Paul Street, St. Pauls, Bristol'. Unpublished report, Bristol and Region Archaeological Services

Samuel, J 2002a 'Archaeological evaluation at TR Warehouse, St Thomas Street/Redcliff Street, Bristol'. Unpublished report, Bristol and Region Archaeological Services

Samuel, J 2002b 'Archaeological evaluation at timber yard to the rear of No 18 St Thomas Street, Redcliffe, Bristol'. Unpublished report, Bristol and Region Archaeological Services

Samuel, J, 2003, 'The Infirmary burial ground, Johnny Ball Lane, Bristol'. Unpublished report, Bristol and Region Archaeological Services

Saunders, C J G 1960 *The Bristol Eye Hospital*. Bristol: Board of Governors of the United Bristol Hospital

Saywell, R 1964 *Mary Carpenter of Bristol*. Bristol: Bristol Branch of the Historical Association

Scammell G V 1961 'Shipowning in England, *c*.1450–550'. *Trans Royal Hist Soc* 5 Ser **12**, 105–22

Scammell, G 1986 'The English in the Atlantic islands, *c*.1450–650'. *Mariner's Mirror* **72**, 295–318

Scarth, H M 1874 'On an inscribed stone found at Sea Mills in 1873, on the east side of the river Avon, two miles below Bristol'. *Archaeol J* **31**, 41–6

Schmidt, B 1997 'Mapping an empire: cartographic and colonial rivalry in 17th-century Dutch and English North America'. *William and Mary Quarterly* 3 Ser **54**, 549–78

Schofield, J 1995 *Medieval London Houses*. New Haven: Yale University Press

Schofield, J, 2011, *London 1100–600, the Archaeology of a Capital City*. Sheffield: Equinox Publishing

Schofield, J and Vince, A 1994 *Medieval Towns*. London: Leicester University Press

Schwind, A P 1983 'English glass imports in New York, 1770–90'. *J Glass Stud* **25**, 179–85

Scott Holmes, T (ed) 1914 *The Register of Nicholas Bubwith, Bishop of Bath and Wells, 1407–24. From the Original in the Registry Vol. 1*. Taunton: Somerset Record Series **29**

Semple, J 1993 *Bentham's Prison: A Study of the Panopticon Penitentiary*. Oxford: Clarendon Press

Seyer, S 1812 *The Charters and Letters Patent, Granted by the Kings and Queens of England to the Town and City of Bristol*. Bristol: J M Gutch

Seyer, S 1821–3 *Memoirs Historical and Topographical of Bristol and its Neighbourhood…* 2 vols (vol 1 1821; vol 2 1823). Bristol: J M Gutch

Shackleton, J and Douglass, J 1983 'Environmental sampling in Redcliff Street, 1982–3'. *Bristol Avon Archaeol* **2**, 35–6.

Shammas, C 1993 'Changes in English and Anglo-American consumption from 1550–800', *in* Brewer, J and Porter, R (eds) *Consumption and the World of Goods*. London: Routledge, 177–205

Sharp, M (ed) 1982 *Accounts of the Constables of Bristol Castle in the 13th and Early 14th Centuries*. Bristol: Bristol Record Series **34**

Sharpe, K 1992 *The Personal Rule of Charles I*. New Haven: Yale University Press

Sherbourne, J 1985 *William Canynges 1402–74*. Bristol: Bristol Branch of the Historical Association

Shiercliff, E 1793 *Bristol and Hotwell Guide: Containing an Historical Account of the Ancient and Present State of that Opulent City*. Bristol: E Shiercliff

Shoesmith, R 1991 *Excavations at Chepstow 1973–4*. Bangor: The Cambrian Archaeological Society

Sies, M C 1991 'Toward a performance theory of the suburban ideal, 1877–917', *in* Carter, T and Herman, B L (eds) *Perspectives in Vernacular Architecture IV*. Columbia: University of Missouri Press, 198–9.

Simon, B 1960 *Studies in the History of Education, 1780–1870*. London: Lawrence and Wishart

Simpson, J J 1926 'St. Peter's Hospital'. *Trans Bristol Gloucestershire Archaeol Soc* **48**, 193–226

Simpson, J 1931 'The wool trade and the woolmen of Gloucestershire'. *Trans Bristol Gloucestershire Archaeol Soc* **53**, 65–97

Singleton, T A 1985 *The Archaeology of Slavery and Plantation Life*. Orlando: Academic Press Ltd.

Skeeters, M 1993 *Community and Clergy: Bristol and the Reformation, c.1530–c.1570*. Oxford: Clarendon Press

Slack, P 1990 *The Impact of Plague in Tudor and Stuart England*. Oxford: Clarendon Press

Smith, A H 1964 *The Place-names of Gloucestershire. Part 3*. Cambridge: Cambridge University Press

Smith, B R 1999 *The Acoustic World of Early Modern England: Attending to the O-factor*. Chicago: University of Chicago Press

Smith, D and Tetlow, E 2010 'Insect remains', *in* Jackson, R G, *The Archaeology of the Medieval Suburb of Broadmead, Bristol. Excavations in Union Street, 2000*. Bristol's Museums, Galleries & Archives, 101–5

Smith, G H 1989 'Evaluation work at the Druid Stoke megalithic monument, Stoke Bishop, Bristol, 1983'. *Trans Bristol Gloucestershire Archaeol Soc* **107**, 27–37

Smith, J T 1983 '[The] English town house in the 15th and 16th centuries', in Chastel, A and J Guillaume, J *La Maison de Ville à la Renaissance.* Paris: Picard

Smith, M Q 1976 'The Harrowing of Hell relief in Bristol Cathedral'. *Trans Bristol Gloucestershire Archaeol Soc* **94**, 101–6

Smith, M Q 1979 *The Roof Bosses of Bristol Cathedral.* Bristol: Friends of Bristol Cathedral

Smith, M Q 1983 *Stained Glass of Bristol Cathedral.* Bristol: Redcliffe Press for the Friends of Bristol Cathedral

Smith, M Q 1991 *The Art and Antiquity of St. Augustine's Abbey now Bristol Cathedral.* Bristol: University of Bristol History of Art Department Occasional Paper No **1**

Smith, M Q 1995 *St. Mary Redcliffe: An Architectural History.* Bristol: Redcliffe Press

Smith, T 2014 *Archaeological Work at No 66 Queen Square & Nos 22–23A King Street, Bristol, 2014.* Bristol and Region Archaeological Services. http://www.baras.org.uk/learning-resources/baras-reports

Smollett, T 1984 *The Expedition of Humphrey Clinker.* Oxford: Oxford University Press

Solly, N Neal 1875 *Memoirs of the Life of William James Müller.* London: Chapman and Hall

Somerville, J 1991 *Christopher Thomas Soapmaker of Bristol: The Story of Christr. Thomas & Bros. 1745–954.* Bristol: White Tree Books

Spear, H and Arrowsmith, J 1884 (eds) *Arrowsmith's Dictionary of Bristol.* Bristol: J W Arrowsmith

Spencer-Wood, S M 1987 'Introduction', in Spencer-Wood, S M (ed) *Consumer Choice in Historical Archaeology.* New York: Plenum Press, 1–24

Spink, I 1995 *Restoration Cathedral Music, 1660–714.* Oxford: Clarendon Press.

Sprigge, J 1854 *Anglia Rediviva; England's Recovery: Being the History of the Motivations, Actions, and Successes of the Army Under the Conduct of his Excellency Sir Thomas Fairfax KT….* Oxford: Oxford University Press

Stacey, R C 2003 'The English Jews under Henry III', in Skinner, P (ed) *The Jews in Medieval Britain: Historical, Literary and Archaeological Perspectives.* Woodbridge: The Boydell Press, 41–54

Stalley, R 1990 'The medieval sculpture of Christ Church Cathedral, Dublin', in Clarke, H (ed) *Medieval Dublin: The Making of a Metropolis.* Dublin: Irish Academic Press, 202–26

Starkey, D J, 2000, 'The distant-water fisheries of south west England in the early modern period', in Starkey, D J, Reid, C, and Ashcroft, N (eds), *England's Sea Fisheries. The Commercial Sea Fisheries of England and Wales since 1300.* London: Chatham Publishing, 96–104

Steedman, K, Dyson, T, and Schofield, J 1992 *The Bridgehead and Billingsgate to 1200.* London: London and Middlesex Archaeological Society Special Paper **14**

Stell, C 1986 *An Inventory of Nonconformist Chapels and Meeting-Houses in Central England.* London: HMSO

Stembridge, P 1996 *Thomas Goldney's Garden Grotto: The Creation of an 18th Century Garden.* Bristol: Avon Gardens Trust

Stembridge, P (ed) 1998 *The Goldney Family, a Bristol Merchant Dynasty.* Bristol: Bristol Record Series **49**

Stephenson, C 1933 *Borough and Town: A Study of Urban Origins in England.* Cambridge, MA: The Medieval Academy of America

Stevens, D 2002 'Archaeological evaluation of land at Marlborough Street bus station, Bristol'. Unpublished report, Bristol and Region Archaeological Services

Stevens, D 2007 'Archaeological evaluation at Favell House, Crow Lane, Bristol'. Unpublished report, Bristol and Region Archaeological Services

Stewart, I 1992 'The English and Norman mints, *c.* 600–1158', in Challis, C (ed) *A New History of the Royal Mint.* Cambridge: Cambridge University Press, 1–82

Stiles, R 1969 'The Old Market sugar refinery, 1684–908'. *BIAS Journal* **2**, 10–17

Stock, G 1996 'A survey of Quaker burial grounds in Bristol and Frenchay monthly meeting'. *Bristol Avon Archaeol* **13**, 1–9

Stoddard, S 1981 *Mr. Braikenridge's Brislington.* Bristol: City of Bristol Museum and Art Gallery

Stoddard, S 1983 'George Weare Braikenridge (1775–856): a Bristol antiquarian and his collections'. Unpublished MLitt thesis, University of Bristol

Straker, V 2001 'Section 3.3.9 Archaeological remains', *in* Briggs, D E G and Crowther, P R (eds) *Palaeobiology II.* Oxford: Blackwell, 325–8

Strid, L 2017 'Animal bone', in Ford, Ben M, Brady, Kate and Teague, Steven, *From Bridgehead to Brewery. The Medieval and Post-medieval Archaeological Remains from Finzel's Reach, Bristol.* Oxford: Oxford Archaeology Monograph **27**, 261–4

Stuiver M *et al* 1998 'INTCAL98 Radiocarbon Age Calibration, 24000–0 cal BP'. *Radiocarbon* **40**, 1041–83

Stuiver, M, and Reimer, P J 1986 'A computer program for radiocarbon age calculation'. *Radiocarbon* **28**, 1022–30

Sturmy, S 1669, *The Mariner's Magazine: Or, Sturmy's Mathematical and Practical Arts. Containing, the Description and Use of the Scale of Scales; it Being a Mathematical Ruler, that Resolves Most Mathematical Conclusions: and Likewise the Making and Use of the Crostaff, Quadrant, and the Quadrat, Nocturnals ….* London: Printed by E Cotes for G Hurlock, W Fisher, E Thomas, and D Page [1669]

Suarez, M F 1993–4 'What Thomas knew: Chatterton and the business of getting into print'. *Angelaki* **1**, 83–94

Swayne, S 1879–80 'On the recent discovery of remains of the foundations of the keep of Bristol Castle and of three ancient wells adjacent, with notes on one of the wells'. *Trans Bristol Gloucestershire Archaeol Soc* **4**, 329–32

Sweetman, P D 1984 'Archaeological excavations at Shop Street, Drogheda, Co. Louth'. *Proceedings of the Royal Irish Academy* **84C(5)**, 171–224

Tavener, N 1995a 'Archaeological evaluation of 76–96 Victoria Street, Bristol'. Unpublished report, Bristol and Region Archaeological Services

Tavener, N 1995b 'Archaeological excavation at the Portwall and ditch, Temple Back, Bristol'. Unpublished report, Bristol and Region Archaeological Services

Tavener, N 1996a 'Archaeological excavation of the Bristol exhibition centre – U Shed, Canons Marsh, Bristol'. Unpublished report, Bristol and Region Archaeological Services

Tavener, N 1996b 'Archaeological evaluation at 1–3 Bridge Parade/ Bristol Bridge, Bristol'. Unpublished report, Bristol and Region Archaeological Services

Tavener, N 1997 'Archaeological evaluation at New World Square, Harbourside, Bristol'. Unpublished report, Bristol and Region Archaeological Services

Taylor, C S 1897–9 'The church and monastery of Westbury-on-Trym'. *Proc Clifton Antiquarian Club* **4**, 20–42

Taylor, C S 1904 'The old church of St. Thomas the Martyr, Bristol'. *Trans Bristol Gloucestershire Archaeol Soc* **27**, 340–51

Taylor, C S 1906 'The religious houses of Bristol and their dissolution'. *Trans Bristol Gloucestershire Archaeol Soc* **29**, 81–126

Taylor, C S 1909 'The chronological sequence of the Bristol parish churches'. *Trans Bristol Gloucestershire Archaeol Soc* **32**, 202–18

Taylor, C S 1910 'The parochial boundaries of Bristol'. *Trans Bristol Gloucestershire Archaeol Soc* **33**, 126–39

Taylor, D S (ed) 1971 *The Complete Works of Thomas Chatterton: A Bicentenary Edition.* Oxford: Clarendon Press

Taylor, F W 1967 *The Principles of Scientific Management.* New York: Norton

Taylor, J 2000 'Temple Church, Bristol: building recording archive report' (2 vols). Unpublished report, Wessex Archaeology vol. 1.

Taylor, M & Shapland, M 2012 *Bristol's Forgotten Coalfield Bedminster: A Detailed History of the Coal Mines*

Teague, S and Brady K 2017a 'Chapter 2. The natural landscape and early development (to *c* AD 1225)' *in* Ford, Ben M, Brady, Kate and Teague, Steven *From Bridgehead to Brewery. The Medieval and Post-medieval Archaeological Remains from Finzel's Reach, Bristol*. Oxford: Oxford Archaeology Monograph **27**, 25–56

Teague, S and Brady K 2017b 'Discussion' in Ford, Ben M, Brady, Kate and Teague, Steven *From Bridgehead to Brewery. The Medieval and Post-medieval Archaeological Remains from Finzel's Reach, Bristol*. Oxford: Oxford Archaeology Monograph **27**, 123–43

Thacker, A, 1985 'Kings, saints and monasteries in pre-Viking Mercia'. *Midland History* **10**, 1–25

Thacker, G and Brady, K 2006 'Quakers Friars North, Bristol Broadmead. Archaeological evaluation report'. Unpublished report, Oxford Archaeology

Thirsk, J 1992 'The Crown as projector on its own estates, from Elizabeth I to Charles I', *in* Hoyle, R W (ed) *The Estates of the English Crown, 1558–640*. Cambridge: Cambridge University Press, 297–352

Thomas, H 1997 *The Slave Trade. The History of the Atlantic Slave Trade: 1440–870*. London: Picador

Thomas, N 1986 'J E Pritchard and the archaeology of Bristol'. *Trans Bristol Gloucestershire Archaeol Soc* **104**, 7–25

Thomas, N and Wilson, A 1980 *Bristol Fine Wares, 1670–970* (Ceramics in Bristol, 21 September 1979–31 January 1980, exhibition catalogue). Bristol: City of Bristol Museum and Art Gallery

Thorp, J 1998 'Rowe's Leadworks, Anchor Lane, Bristol'. Unpublished report, Keystone Historic Buildings Consultants Report

Thurlby, M 1997 'The Elder Lady Chapel at St. Augustine's, Bristol, and Wells Cathedral', *in* Keen, L (ed) *'Almost the richest city': Bristol in the Middle Ages*. London: British Archaeological Association, 31–40

Tilly, G 1998 'Engineering methods of minimising damage and preserving archaeological remains in situ', *in* Corfield, M, Hinton, P, Nixon, T and Pollard, M (eds) *Preserving Archaeological Remains In Situ: Proceedings of the Conference of 1st–3rd April 1996*. London: Museum of London Archaeology Service, 1–7

Tinsley, H 2002 '7. Pollen Analysis' in Wilkinson, K 'Land at Anchor Road/Deanery Road, Bristol. Stratigraphy and palaeoenvironment'. Unpublished report, Cotswold Archaeology, 19-28

Toulmin-Smith, L (ed.) 1872 *The Maire of Bristowe is Kalendar*. London: Camden Society 2 ser, **5**

Toulmin-Smith, L (ed) 1906–10 *The Itinerary of John Leland in or about the years 1533–43* (5 vols). London: G Bell and Sons

Townsend, A 2002a 'Archaeological evaluation at 26–28 St Thomas Street, Redcliffe, Bristol'. Unpublished report, Bristol and Region Archaeological Services

Townsend, A 2002b 'Archaeological evaluation at 22–24 St Thomas Street, Redcliffe, Bristol'. Unpublished report, Bristol and Region Archaeological Services

Townsend, A 2002c 'Archaeological evaluation of land at Dick Lovett Site, Portwall Lane, Bristol'. Unpublished report, Bristol and Region Archaeological Services

Townsend, A 2002d 'Archaeological evaluation of land at Mitchell Lane, Redcliffe, Bristol'. Unpublished report, Bristol and Region Archaeological Services

Townsend, A 2003 'Nos 5–7 Welsh Back, Bristol: archaeological recording programme'. Unpublished report, Avon Archaeological Unit

Townsend, A, 2011, 'Archaeological desk-based assessment of land at Brandon Hill, Bristol'. Unpublished report, Bristol and Region Archaeological Services

Townsend, A and Pilkington, J 2002, 'Archaeological building survey and evaluation of the George Railway Hotel and adjoining premises, Temple Gate, Bristol'. Unpublished report, Bristol and Region Archaeological Services

Tracy, C (ed) 1962 *The Poetical Works of Richard Savage*. Cambridge: Cambridge University Press

Tratman, E K 1925 'Second report on King's Weston Hill, Bristol'. *Proc University of Bristol Spelaeological Soc* **2**, 238–43

Tratman, E K 1946 'Prehistoric Bristol'. *Proc University of Bristol Spelaeological Soc* **5(3)** (1944–6), 162–82

Tratman, E K 1961–2 'Some ideas on Roman roads in Bristol and North Somerset'. *Proc University of Bristol Spelaeological Soc* **9(3)**, 159–76

Trice-Martin, A 1900 'The Roman road on Durdham Down'. *Trans Bristol Gloucestershire Archaeol Soc* **23**, 309–11

Trice-Martin, A 1923 'Excavations at Sea Mills, Bristol, 20th–28th August, 1923'. *Trans Bristol Gloucestershire Archaeol Soc* **45**, 193–201

Trinder, B, 2005, *Barges and Bargemen, A Social History of the Upper Severn Navigation 1660–1900*. Chichester: Phillimore

Tuck, M, 2006 'Plot P11, Cabot Park, Avonmouth, Bristol: archaeological watching brief. Interim report'. Glamorgan-Gwent Archaeological Trust. GGAT report no 2006/105

Vanes, J 1977 *The Port of Bristol in the 16th Century*. Bristol: Bristol Branch of the Historical Association

Vanes, J 1984 *'Apparelled in red': The History of the Red Maids School*. Gloucester: Alan Sutton Publishing Limited

Vanes, J (ed) 1974 *The Ledger of John Smythe, 1538–50, from the Transcript by John Angus BA*. London: Bristol Record Series **28**

Vann, R 1986 'Quakerism: made in America?', *in* Dunn, R and Dunn, M (eds) *The world of William Penn*. Philadelphia: University of Pennsylvania Press, 157–70

Vann, R and Eversley, D 1992 *Friends in Life and Death: The British and Irish Quakers in the Demographic Transition, 1650–900*. Cambridge: Cambridge University Press

Varley, J 1948 'John Rocque. Engraver, surveyor, cartographer and map-seller'. *Imago Mundi* **5**, 83–91

Vaughan, A 1997 'Brunel as a creator of environment', *in* Burman, P and Stratton, M (eds) *Conserving the Railway Heritage*. London: E & F N Spon, 75–88

Veale, E W W (ed) 1931 *The Great Red Book of Bristol. Introduction (Part 1). Burgage Tenure in Mediæval Bristol*. Bristol: Bristol Record Series **2**

Veale, E W W (ed) 1933 *The Great Red Book of Bristol. Text (Part 1)*. Bristol: Bristol Record Series **4**

Veale, E W W (ed) 1938 *The Great Red Book of Bristol. Text (Part 2)*. Bristol: Bristol Record Series **8**

Veale, E W W (ed) 1950 *The Great Red Book of Bristol. Text (Part 3)*. Bristol: Bristol Record Series **16**

Veale, E W W (ed) 1953 *The Great Red Book of Bristol. Text (Part 4)*. Bristol: Bristol Record Series **18**

Vigneras, L A 1956 'New light on the 1497 Cabot voyage to America'. *Hispanic American Historical Review* **36**, 503–9

Vince, A 1984 'The medieval ceramic industry of the Severn valley'. Unpublished report, PhD thesis, University of Southampton

Vince, A 1990 *Saxon London: An Archaeological Investigation*. London: Seaby

Vince, A and Bell, R 1992 '16th-century pottery from Acton Court, Avon', *in* Gaimster, D and Redknap, M (eds) *Everyday and Exotic Pottery from Europe c.650–1900: Studies in Honour of John G. Hurst*. Oxford: Oxbow Books, 101–9

Vincent, M 1983 *Reflections on the Portishead Branch*. Poole: Oxford Publishing Co.

Wadley, T (ed) 1886 *Notes or Abstracts of the Wills Contained in the Volume Entitled the Great Orphan Book and Book of Wills*. Bristol: Bristol and Gloucestershire Archaeological Society

Wakelin, A P 1991 'Pre-industrial trade on the river Severn: a computer-aided study of Gloucester Port Books, *c*.1640–770'. PhD thesis, CNAA/Wolverhampton Polytechnic

Walker, D 2000 'The estates of St. Augustine's Abbey, Bristol, *in* Bettey, J (ed) *Historic Churches and Church Life in Bristol: Essays in Memory of Elizabeth Ralph 1911–2000*. Bristol: Bristol & Gloucestershire Archaeological Society, 11–27

Walker, D (ed) 1998 *The Cartulary of St. Augustine's Abbey, Bristol*. Bristol: Gloucestershire Record Series **10**

Walker, J 1714 *An Attempt Towards Recovering an Account of the Numbers and Sufferings of the Clergy of the Church of England, Heads of Colleges, Fellows, Scholars, &c. Who Were Sequester'd, Harras'd, &c. in the Late Times of the Grand Rebellion*. London

Wallace, P 1983 'North European pottery imported into Dublin 1200–500', in Davey, P and Hodges, R (eds) *Ceramics and Trade: The Production and Distribution of Later Medieval Pottery in North-west Europe*. Sheffield: Department of Prehistory and Archaeology, University of Sheffield, 225–30

Walton Rogers, P 1997 *Textile Production at 16–22 Coppergate*. York: Archaeology of York The Small Finds **17/11**

Walters, H B 1918–19 'The Gloucestershire bell founders. II The Bristol foundry'. *Trans Bristol Gloucestershire Archaeol Soc* **30**, 49–86

Walvin, J 1993 *Black Ivory: A History of British Slavery*. London: Fontana

Ward, J 1978 'Speculative building at Bristol and Clifton'. *Business History* **20**, 3–18

Ward, J and Mainland, I L 1999 'Microwear in modern rooting and stall-fed pigs: the potential of dental microwear analysis for exploring pig diet and management in the past'. *Environmental Archaeol* **4**, 25–32

Warman, S, 2013, '5.2 Animal bone', in Ridgeway, V and Watts, M (eds) *Friars, Quakers, Industry and Urbanisation. The Archaeology of the Broadmead Expansion Project, Cabot Circus, Bristol, 2005–8*. Cotswold Archaeology/Pre-Construct Archaeology, 268–83

Warren, R Hall 1893–6 'On some encaustic tiles recently found in Bristol'. *Proc Clifton Antiquarian Club* **3**, 95–8

Warren, R Hall 1900–3 'Tiles of Bristol Cathedral'. *Proc Clifton Antiquarian Club* **5**, 122–7

Warren, R Hall 1904 'Bristol Cathedral: the choir screen'. *Trans Bristol Gloucestershire Archaeol Soc* **27**, 127–30

Warren, R Hall 1904–8a 'St. Augustine's Abbey, Bristol: the east end of Abbat Knowle's Lady Chapel'. *Proc Clifton Antiquarian Club* **6**, 142–52

Warren, R Hall 1904–8b 'The choir screen of Bristol Cathedral'. *Proc Clifton Antiquarian Club* **6**, 6–10

Warren, R Hall 1907 'The medieval chapels of Bristol'. *Trans Bristol Gloucestershire Archaeol Soc* **30**, 181–211

Warren, W 1973 *Henry II*. London: Eyre and Methuen

Watt, J A 1986 'Dublin in the 13th century: the making of a colonial capital city', in Coss, P R and Lloyd, S D (eds) *13th Century England I: Proceedings of the Newcastle Upon Tyne Conference 1985*. Woodbridge: The Boydell Press, 150–7

Watts, L and Leach, P 1996 *Henley Wood, Temples and Cemetery: Excavations 1962–9 by the Late Ernest Greenfield and Others*. York: CBA Res Rep **99**

Watts, L and Rahtz, P 1985 *Mary-le-Port, Bristol: Excavations, 1962–3*. Bristol: City of Bristol Museum and Art Gallery

Watts, M (ed) 2011 *'Medieval and Post-medieval Development within Bristol's Inner Suburbs'*. Bristol and Gloucestershire Archaeological Report **7**. (Cotswold Archaeology)

Watts, M 2011, 26–28 St Thomas Street, Redcliffe, Bristol: Excavations in 2002', in Watts, M (ed) *Medieval and Post-medieval Development within Bristol's Inner Suburbs*. Bristol and Gloucestershire Archaeological Report **7**. (Cotswold Archaeology), 73–78

Watts, M and Davenport, P 2013 '6.2 The medieval friary' in Ridgeway, V and Watts, M (eds), *Friars, Quakers, Industry and Urbanisation. The Archaeology of the Broadmead Expansion Project, Cabot Circus, Bristol, 2005–8*. Cotswold Archaeology/Pre-Construct Archaeology, 352–65

Weare, G E 1893 *A Collectanea Relating to the Bristol Friars Minors (Gray Friars) and their Convent*. Bristol: W Bennett

Weaver, F M (ed) 1901 *Somerset Medieval Wills (1383–500)*. Taunton: Somerset Record Series **16**

Webb, J 1993 'Wills of their own: women tobacco workers in Bedminster, Bristol, 1919–39'. Unpublished MA thesis, University of Warwick

Webster, C J (ed), 2008, *The Archaeology of South West England. South West Archaeological Research Framework. Resource Assessment and Research Agenda* Somerset County Council

Webster, J 2008 'Buildings 12A and 12B, Cabot Circus, Bristol. Archaeological evaluation'. Cotswold Archaeology, unpublished report no 08024

Webster, L and Cherry, J 1974 'Medieval Britain in 1973'. *Medieval Archaeol* **18**, 174–223

Webster, L and Cherry, J 1975 'Medieval Britain in 1974'. *Medieval Archaeol* **19**, 220–60

Weedon, C 1983 'The Bristol glass industry: its rise and decline'. *Glass Technology* **24**, 241–58

Wells-Cole, A 1997 *Art and Decoration in Elizabethan and Jacobean England: The Influence of Continental Prints, 1558–625*. New Haven: Yale University Press

Wessex Archaeology 1994 'The Southern Rivers Palaeolithic Project report no 3: The Sussex raised beaches and the Bristol Avon'. Unpublished report, Wessex Archaeology

Wessex Archaeology 2013 'Smoke Lane Anti-Aircraft Battery, Land at Smoke Lane, Avonmouth, Bristol. Stage 3: Palaeoenvironmental Assessment'. Unpublished report, Wessex Archaeology. Report ref 77892.05

Whatley, S 2007 'Archaeological evaluation of land between High Street & Bridge Street, Castle Park, Bristol'. Unpublished report, Bristol and Region Archaeological Services

Whitelock, D (ed) 1961 *The Anglo-Saxon Chronicle*. London: Eyre and Spottiswode

Whiting, J 1975 *Prison Reform in Gloucestershire, 1776–820: A Study of the Work of Sir George Onesiphorus Paul, Bart*. Chichester: Phillimore & Co. Ltd.

Wilkinson, K 2002 'Land at Anchor Road/Deanery Road, Bristol. Stratigraphy and palaeoenvironment'. Unpublished report, Cotswold Archaeology

Wilkinson, K, 2006 'Period 1: prehistoric to early medieval (to AD 1066)' in Cox, S, Barber, A and Collard, M, 2006 'The archaeology and history of the former Bryan Brothers' Garage site, Deanery Road, Bristol: the evolution of an urban landscape'. *Trans Bristol Gloucestershire Archaeological Soc* **124**, 60–1

Wilkinson, K 2013 '5.10 Radiocarbon Dating' in Ridgeway, V and Watts, M (eds) *Friars, Quakers, Industry and Urbanisation. The Archaeology of the Broadmead Expansion Project, Cabot Circus, Bristol, 2005–8*. Cotswold Archaeology/Pre-Construct Archaeology, 332–3

Wilkinson, K, Cameron, N, Jones, J, Kreiser, A and Tinsley, H 2002 'Stratigraphy and environment of Deanery Road, Bristol'. Unpublished report 02/01, University College, Winchester

Wilkinson, K, Batchelor, R, Athersuch, J, Banerjea, R, Cameron, N and Watson, N, 2013a, 'Willow Farm Hallen: Geoarchaeological and palaeoenvironmental analysis'. Unpublished report. ARCA, Department of Archaeology, University of Winchester. Report no 1213-5

Wilkinson, K, Jones, R and Meara, R, 2013b, *Distribution and Significance of Urban Waterlogged Deposits in Bristol*. Cotswold Archaeology, for English Heritage and Bristol City Council

Williams, A 1995 *The English and the Norman Conquest*. Woodbridge: The Boydell Press

Williams, A F 1962 'Bristol port plans and improvement schemes of the 18th century'. *Trans Bristol Gloucestershire Archaeol Soc* **81**, 138–88

Williams, B 1981a *Excavations in the Medieval Suburb of Redcliffe, Bristol, 1980*. City of Bristol Museum and Art Gallery

Williams, B 1981b Excavations at Redcliffe, 1980. *BARG Review* **2**, 35–46

Williams, B 1982 'Excavations at Bristol Bridge, 1981'. *Bristol Avon Archaeol* **1**, 12–15

Williams, B 1988 'The excavation of medieval and post-medieval tenements at 94–102 Temple Street, Bristol, 1975'. *Trans Bristol Gloucestershire Archaeol Soc* **106**, 107–68

Williams, B 2013 'Number One Victoria Street, Bristol. Post-excavation assessment report'. Unpublished report. Bristol and West Archaeology

Williams, B 2015 'Former Central Ambulance Station, Marybush Lane, Bristol. Archaeological evaluation report'. Unpublished report. Bristol and West Archaeology

Williams, B (ed) 1992 'Archaeology in Bristol 1990–2'. *Bristol Avon Archaeol* **10**, 53–4

Williams, B (ed) 1993 'Archaeology in Bristol 1993'. *Bristol Avon Archaeol* **11**, 45–8

Williams, B (ed) 1994/5 'Bristol and Region Archaeological Services Projects 1994'. *Bristol Avon Archaeol* **12**, 70–5

Williams, B (ed) 1996 'Review of archaeology 1995–6'. *Bristol Avon Archaeol* **13**, 79–91

Williams, B (ed) 1997 'Review of archaeology 1996–7'. *Bristol Avon Archaeol* **14**, 75–89

Williams, B (ed) 1998 'Review of archaeology 1998'. *Bristol Avon Archaeol* **15**, 71–83

Williams, B (ed) 1999 'Review of archaeology 1998–9'. *Bristol Avon Archaeol* **16**, 95–111

Williams, B (ed) 2000 'Review of archaeology, 1999–2000'. *Bristol Avon Archaeol* **17**, 139–51

Williams, B (ed) 2001 'Review of archaeology, 2000–1'. *Bristol Avon Archaeol* **18**, 109–26

Williams, B (ed) 2004 'Review of archaeology, 2001–2'. *Bristol Avon Archaeol* **19**, 99–114

Williams, B (ed) 2005 'Review of archaeology, 2003–4'. *Bristol Avon Archaeol* **20**, 121–40

Williams, B (ed) 2006a 'Review of archaeology, 2005'. *Bristol Avon Archaeol* **21**, 93–104

Williams, B (ed) 2006b 'Review of archaeology, 2006'. *Bristol Avon Archaeol* **21**, 107–24

Williams, B (ed) 2007 'Review of archaeology, 2007'. *Bristol Avon Archaeol* **22**, 141–55

Williams, B (ed) 2008–9a 'Review of archaeology, 2008'. *Bristol Avon Archaeol* **23**, 129–43

Williams, B (ed) 2008–9b 'Review of archaeology, 2009'. *Bristol Avon Archaeol* **23**, 145–56

Williams, B (ed) 2010–1 'Review of archaeology, 2011'. *Bristol Avon Archaeol* **24** (2010–1), 49–55

Williams, B (ed) 2012–13 'Review of archaeology, 2013'. *Bristol Avon Archaeol* **25**, 49–57

Williams, B (ed) 2014–15a 'Review of archaeology, 2014'. *Bristol Avon Archaeol* **26**, 95–100

Williams, B (ed) 2014–15b 'Review of archaeology, 2015'. *Bristol Avon Archaeol* **26**, 101–3

Williams, B and Cox, S 2000, 'Excavations at 82–90 Redcliff Street, Bristol 1980 and 1999: the development of the medieval waterfront'. Unpublished report, Bristol and Region Archaeological Services

Williams, E 1950 *The Chantries of William Canynges in St. Mary Redcliffe, Bristol*. Bristol: William George's Sons Ltd

Williams, J H 1979 *St. Peter's Street, Northampton: excavations 1973–6*. Northampton: Northampton Development Corporation

Williams, M with Farnie, D A 1992 *Cotton Mills in Greater Manchester*. Preston: Carnegie Publishing Ltd.

Williams, N 1992 'Death in its season: class, environment and the mortality of infants in 19th-century Sheffield'. *Social History of Medicine* **5**, 71–94

Williams, R J G 1983 'Romano-British settlement at Filwood Park, Bristol'. *Bristol Avon Archaeol* **2**, 12–20

Williamson, J 1962 *The Cabot Voyages and Bristol Discovery under Henry VII*. Cambridge: Hakluyt Society 2 Ser **120**

Williamson, T 1995 *Polite Landscapes: Gardens and Society in 18th-Century England*. Far Thrupp, Stroud: Alan Sutton Publishing Ltd.

Williamson, T 2004 'Designed landscapes: the regional dimension'. *Landscapes* **5** (2004), 16-25

Wills, J (ed) 2000 'Archaeological review no 24 1999'. *Trans Bristol Gloucestershire Archaeol Soc* **118**, 213–34

Wills, J (ed) 2001 'Archaeological review no 25 2000'. *Trans Bristol Gloucestershire Archaeol Soc* **119**, 185–210

Wills, J (ed) 2002 'Archaeological review no 26 2001'. *Trans Bristol Gloucestershire Archaeol Soc* **120**, 233–56

Wills, J (ed) 2003 'Archaeological review no 27 2002'. *Trans Bristol Gloucestershire Archaeol Soc* **121**, 267–89

Wills, J (ed) 2004 'Archaeological review no 28 2003'. *Trans Bristol Gloucestershire Archaeol Soc* **122**, 173–92

Wills, J (ed) 2005 'Archaeological review no 29 2004'. *Trans Bristol Gloucestershire Archaeol Soc* **123**, 149–85

Wills, J (ed) 2014 'Archaeological review no 38 2013'. *Trans Bristol Gloucestershire Archaeol Soc* **132**, 249–74

Wills, J (ed) 2015 'Archaeological review no 39 2014'. *Trans Bristol Gloucestershire Archaeol Soc* **133**, 241–70

Wills, J and Rawes, J (ed) 1999 'Archaeological review no 23 1998'. *Trans Bristol Gloucestershire Archaeol Soc* **117**, 167–86

Wills, J and Catchpole, T (eds) 2006 'Archaeological review no 30 2005'. *Trans Bristol Gloucestershire Archaeol Soc* **124**, 213–32

Wills, J and Hoyle, J (eds) 2007 'Archaeological review no 31 2006'. *Trans Bristol Gloucestershire Archaeol Soc* **125**, 341–66

Wills, J and Hoyle, J (eds) 2008 'Archaeological review no 32 2007'. *Trans Bristol Gloucestershire Archaeol Soc* **126**, 173–91

Wills, J and Hoyle, J (eds) 2009 'Archaeological review no 33 2008'. *Trans Bristol Gloucestershire Archaeol Soc* **127**, 303–22

Wills, J and Hoyle, J (eds) 2010 'Archaeological review no 34 2009'. *Trans Bristol Gloucestershire Archaeol Soc* **128**, 229–47

Wills, J and Hoyle, J (eds) 2012 'Archaeological review no 36 2011'. *Trans Bristol Gloucestershire Archaeol Soc* **130**, 307–32

Wilson, A 2017 'Mineralised concretions and possible hair samples' in Ford, Ben M, Brady, Kate and Teague, Steven *From Bridgehead to Brewery. The Medieval and Post-medieval archaeological remains from Finzel's Reach, Bristol*. Oxford: Oxford Archaeology Monograph **27**, 276–7

Wilson, C 1973 *Food and Drink in Britain*. London: Constable

Wilson, D 1869 *Chatterton: A Biographical Study*. London: Macmillan and Co.

Wilson, D M 1964 'Medieval Britain in 1962 and 1963'. *Medieval Archaeol* **8**, 231–99

Wilson, D M and Hurst, D G 1961 'Medieval Britain in 1960'. *Medieval Archaeol* **5**, 309–39

Wilson, D M and Hurst, D G 1969 'Medieval Britain in 1968'. *Medieval Archaeol* **13**, 230–87

Wilson, D M and Hurst, D G 1970 'Medieval Britain in 1969'. *Medieval Archaeol* **14**, 155–208

Wilson, D M and Moorhouse, S 1971 'Medieval Britain in 1970'. *Medieval Archaeol* **15**, 124–79

Wilson, E 1885–8 'The bone cave or fissure of Durdham Down'. *Proc Bristol Naturalists Society* 2 Ser **5**, 31–45

Wilton, A 1979 *The Life and Work of J M W Turner*. London: Academy Editions

Wilton, A and Lyles, A 1993 *The Great Age of British Watercolours, 1750–880*. London: Royal Academy

Winchell, F, Rose, J and Moir, R 1995 'Health and hard times: a case study from the middle to late 19th century in eastern Texas', *in* Grauer, A (ed) *Bodies of Evidence: Reconstructing History Through Skeletal Analysis*. New York: Wiley-Liss, Inc., 161–72

Winstone, R 1957 *Bristol as it was, 1939–14*. Bristol: Reece Winstone

Winstone, R 1962 *Bristol in the 1880s*. Bristol: Reece Winstone

Winstone, R 1964 *Bristol as it was, 1950–3*. Bristol: Reece Winstone

Winstone, R 1966 *Bristol as it was, 1874–66*. Bristol: Reece Winstone

Winstone, R 1967 *Bristol as it was, 1866–0*. Bristol: Reece Winstone

Winstone, R 1970 *Bristol's earliest photographs*. Bristol: Reece Winstone

Winstone, R 1972 *Bristol as it was, 1866–0*. Bristol: Reece Winstone

Winstone, R 1979 *Bristol as it was, 1928–33*. Bristol: Reece Winstone

Winstone, R 1983 *Bristol as it was, 1845–1900*. Bristol: Reece Winstone

Winstone, R 1986 *Bristol as it was, 1956–9*. Bristol: Reece Winstone

Winstone, R 1987 *Victorian and Edwardian Bristol from Old Photographs*. London: Portman Books

Witt, C, Weeden, C and Schwind, A P 1984 *Bristol Glass*. Bristol: Redcliffe Press

Wohl, A 1983 *Endangered Lives: Public Health in Victorian Britain*. London: J M Dent & Sons

Wood, J 1969 *A Description of the Exchange of Bristol*. Bath: Kingsmead Reprints

Wood, J, Ricketts, H and Sanders, J nd *Report of the Visiting Justices on the Recent Alterations in, and Introduction of the Separate System into, the Gaol and Bridewell of the City of Bristol. Presented to the Town-Council, October the 27th 1841*. Bristol: William Henry Somerton

Wragg, E 2004 'An archaeological evaluation and watching brief at the Bristol Brewery, Counterslip, City of Bristol'. Unpublished report, Pre-Construct Archaeology

Wymer, J 1999 *The Lower Palaeolithic Occupation of Britain*. Salisbury: Trust for Wessex Archaeology and English Heritage

Yalland, P 1996 *Death in the Victorian Family*. Oxford: Oxford University Press

Yentsch, A E 1994 *A Chesapeake Family and their Slaves: A Study in Historical Archaeology*. Cambridge: Cambridge University Press

Yentsch, A E and Kratzer, J M 1994 'Techniques for excavating buried 18th-century garden landscapes', *in* Miller, N F and Gleason, K L (eds) *The Archaeology of Garden and Field*. Philadelphia: University of Pennsylvania Press, 168–201

Young, A 1994–5 'Summary of Avon Archaeological Unit fieldwork projects 1994–5'. *Bristol Avon Archaeol* **12**, 68–9

Young, A 2000 'Land adjacent to 46 Wade Street, St. Judes, Bristol: archaeological evaluation project'. Unpublished report, Avon Archaeological Unit

Young, A 2001 '118–22 Jacob Street, Old Market, Bristol. Archaeological evaluation project'. Unpublished report, Avon Archaeological Unit

Young, A 2007 'Archaeological trial excavations at no 32 Old Market Street & no 16 Redcross Street, Old Market, Bristol'. Unpublished report, Avon Archaeological Unit

Young, D, 2011 'The M541 from Abonae: Excavation of a Roman road at Henbury, Bristol'. *Trans Bristol Gloucestershire Archaeol Soc* **129**, 53–67

Young, A and Young, D 2014–5 'Excavations at the Former Mail Marketing International Site, Bristol, 2005–8 – Evidence for multi-period occupation in the historic settlement of Bedminster'. *Bristol Avon Archaeol* **26**, 1–60

Young, R 2004 'Land to the south of Anchor Road, Harbourside development area, Canons Marsh, Bristol. Archaeological evaluation'. Cotswold Archaeology, unpublished report no 04086

Youngs, S M and Clark, J 1982 'Medieval Britain in 1981'. *Medieval Archaeol* **26**, 164–227

Youngs, S M, Clark, J and Barry, T 1983 'Medieval Britain and Ireland in 1982'. *Medieval Archaeol* **27**, 161–229

Youngs, S M, Clark, J and Barry, T 1985 'Medieval Britain and Ireland in 1984'. *Medieval Archaeol* **29**, 158–230

Youngs, S M, Clark, J and Barry, T 1986 'Medieval Britain and Ireland in 1985'. *Medieval Archaeol* **30**, 114–98

Zierden, M and Calhoun, J 1984 *An Archaeological Preservation Plan for Charleston, South Carolina*. Charleston: The Charleston Museum

Zierden, M and Calhoun, J 1986 'Urban adaptation in Charleston in Charleston, South Carolina, 1730–820'. *Historical Archaeol* **20**, 29–43.

Zierden, M Buckley, D, Calhoun, J and Hacker, D 1987 *Georgian Opulence: Archaeological Investigations of the Gibbes House*. Charleston: The Charleston Museum

Index

Page numbers in italics are figures; with 't' are tables; with 'n' are notes.